Shanghai

The Complete **Residents'** Guide

Passionately Publishing...

EXPLORER

Shanghai Explorer 1st Edition   ISBN 13 - 978-9948-03-320-2   ISBN 10 - 9948-03-320-5

Front Cover Photograph: Jing'an Temple Door – Pamela Grist

Printed and bound by Emirates Printing Press, Dubai, United Arab Emirates.

Explorer Publishing & Distribution
PO Box 34275, Dubai
United Arab Emirates
Phone   (+971 4) 335 3520
Fax   (+971 4) 335 3529
Email   Info@ExplorerPublishing.com
Web   www.ExplorerPublishing.com

Welcome...

You've just made living in Shanghai a whole lot easier by buying this book. In the following pages you'll find out everything you need to know to get settled into – and then get the most out of – your new life in one of the world's most exciting cities. From hiring a driver to finding an apartment or drinking cocktails on the Bund, we can tell you how and where to do it.

The **General Information** chapter fills you in on Shanghai's history, geography and culture, and provides details of how to get around and where to stay when you first arrive.

The **Residents** chapter takes away all the headaches involved in setting up your new home. With information on visas, residential areas, schools and red tape, this section will tell you how to deal with all the formalities.

After settling in, take a look at **Exploring**. This chapter guides you through Shanghai's different neighbourhoods, telling you all about its museums, architecture and parks, and detailing annual festivals and where to go to see more of China. There's also a checklist of must-dos to work your way through.

If you've still got time on your hands, move on to **Activities**. Here you'll find out where to practise tai chi, how to join a drama group, and where to learn Mandarin. If you'd prefer to indulge, there's also a wealth of well-being options to digest, from acupuncture to yoga, with a bit of spa in between.

Now that you're living in Shanghai, you'll also have full access to all the retail that one of China's best **Shopping** cities has to offer. We've got a whole chapter dedicated to helping you discover the top markets, malls and high streets in which to splash the cash.

Don't spend it all in the shops though – save some for the evening. Our **Going Out** chapter gives you a detailed run-down on Shanghai's premier places for eating, drinking and partying.

Nearly all of the places of interest have references that correspond to the detailed **Maps** in the back of the book – use these for everything from taking the Metro to exploring Shanghai's old lanes.

And if you think we have missed something, please let us know. Go to www.explorerpublishing.com, fill in the Reader Response form, and share the knowledge with your fellow explorers.

The Explorer Team

Explorer online

Life can move pretty fast so make sure you keep up at **www.explorerpublishing.com.** Register for updates on the latest happenings in your city, or let us know if there's anything we've missed out by filling in our reader response form. You can also check out residents' info on various cities around the world, read up on featured articles or post messages on the discussion boards. Details on all our titles, from residents' guides to mini visitors' guides, mini maps to photography books, are available to purchase online so you need never be without us.

There are so many things the Shanghai Explorers love about this buzzing city: the adrenaline rush of entering the metropolis on the world's fastest train (p.44); watching old-timers playing mahjong in the park against a backdrop of 21st century skyscrapers (p.211); getting all nostalgic for a bygone era in the cool French Concession beat den JZ Club (p.392); sitting on the terrace of New Heights at sunset with a cold Tsingtao, seeing Pudong lights come to life (p.370); the sense of relief as you make it safely to the other side when crossing one of the chaotic roads; the feeling of community among the singers, musicians, dancers and badminton players on a Saturday in Lu Xun park (p.213); and the sheer raw urban grittiness of being in one of Asia's largest, most full-on, amazing cities.

Bridget Lee After studying Chinese at a small college in the US, Bridget wanted to find the biggest, most exciting city to practise her language skills. After freelancing for several Shanghai publications and managing a graphic design company, she is now working on her first play. **City must-do:** Spend an afternoon in Lu Xun Park (p.213) **Best view:** Grand Hyatt cafe (p.34)

Camilla Bjorkman Having come for love and language, Swedish-born Camilla has fallen for Shanghai. A freelance fashion journalist, she recently turned her attentions to travel writing. Few cafes in the city can say they haven't served as her temporary office. **City must-do:** Get custom-made clothes from the Fabric Market (p.339) **Best cultural experience:** A Sunday jog with locals in the park (p.211)

Danielle Chu Two years ago Danielle bought a one-way ticket to Shanghai and has never looked back. She manages a China travel guide and is the Shanghai correspondent and editor for an education magazine. Danielle enjoys meeting distant relatives and surviving Chinese banquets. **Favourite daytrip:** Shengsi Island **Best place to meet locals:** Any of the amusement arcades (p.216)

Jarrett Wrisley After a brief time studying Chinese language at university in the US, Jarrett packed his bags and headed for Shanghai. Since then, he's helped to create 8 Days/SH and contributes to Travel + Leisure and Newsweek Select, among others. **Favourite restaurant:** Xinjiang Fengwei (p.362) **Best view:** From the monument on the Bund (p.174)

Jemimah Steinfeld This Brit arrived in Shanghai in 2006 after more than two decades in the UK, with a return ticket for six months later. She quickly became besotted by the city and decided to stay. Since settling here, Jemimah has worked for various lifestyle and business magazines. **Best place for a cocktail:** The terrace of Face Bar (p.390) **City must-do:** Stroll through the French Concession (p.177)

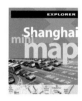

*Having trouble navigating your way around sprawling Shanghai? Look no further than the **Shanghai Mini Map**, an indispensable pocket-sized aid to getting to grips with the roads, areas and attractions of this mega-metropolis.*

*Now that you've moved to Shanghai, it won't be long before you're playing host to wave upon wave of visiting family and friends – and we've got the perfect guide to help them get the most out of their sightseeing. Packed with info on Shanghai's shops, restaurants and tourist spots, you can't go wrong with the **Shanghai Mini Explorer**.*

Juliet Holdsworth Juliet's addiction to China first began in 1999 during a trip to Shanghai with her father. After several return stints and obtaining a degree in Mandarin, she finally moved to the city in 2005 to work as a freelance writer. **City must-do:** A trip to one of the over-the-top bath houses **Best city memory:** Calm, flooded streets after a typhoon **Favourite restaurant:** Yin (p.364)

Peter Ellegard Shanghai is Peter's home away from home. A travel writer for 25 years, Peter recently presented a travel documentary series on exploring China for CCTV9. He has written extensively about China for several publications. **Favourite restaurant:** Jade on 36 (p.391) **Best place to drink with locals:** Velvet Lounge (p.399) **Best city memory:** Letting off fireworks on New Year's Eve

Peter Fong Having lived most of his adult life in the US state of Montana, Peter moved to Shanghai with his family in 2005 and soon settled in to navigating the city by bicycle while living in Jiading and Minhang. Peter has been published in the *San Francisco Chronicle* and the *New York Times*. **Favourite restaurant:** Yang's on Wujiang Lu (p.170) **Best city memory:** Eating pan-fried soup dumplings

Sophie Lloyd Sophie first came to Shanghai on a three-month internship, and nearly three years later she's still here. After a stint as a writer for English-language lifestyle magazine *SH*, she now works as a freelance journalist and copywriter. **Best view:** Looking at the Bund at night from the Yan'an highway **Worst thing about Shanghai:** Stinky tofu in the summer time

Thanks...

As well as our star team of authors, whose expert advice and incredible research have ensured the **Shanghai Explorer** is the most up-to-date and comprehensive guide to expat life for the city, there are a number of other people who have made great contributions towards making this book a success. Massive thanks go to: the Shanghai sales team – Sacha Dunas, Alexandre Grey, Stephan Iscovici, Julien Wagner, Fatima Zahra and Shelly Weng; hard-working India cartographers Asiq Babu and Noufal Madathil; top translators Danielle Chu and Zhou Xin; Amy Thompson, Lilian Zhang and Donna Campbell, for local hospitality and knowledge; and last but by no means least, Hannah Jordan, for support and sandwiches.

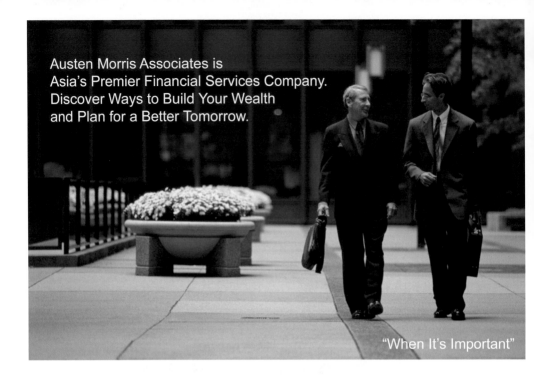

Austen Morris Associates is
Asia's Premier Financial Services Company.
Discover Ways to Build Your Wealth
and Plan for a Better Tomorrow.

"When It's Important"

At Austen Morris Associates we believe that a robust financial future has to be planned for.

Our experienced advisors are in a position to help you achieve these goals in a simple and effective way.

As an independent company we are not restricted in the advice we can give or the products we can introduce you to.

We give you more than the essentials, we give you after care and build a relationship that lasts until your goals are realised.

Our services include free advice on savings, investments, banking, retirement and education planning, mortgages, insurance, and estate planning.

As you look to the future look to Austen Morris Associates.

In Association with
TIMESONLINE

Austen Morris Associates   www.austenmorris.com   info@austenmorris.com
6E, Guangdong Development Bank Tower 555 Xu Jia Hui Road Shanghai 200023
Tel: 86 21 6390 1233 Fax: 86 21 6390 1235
Wholly Foreign Owned Enterprise - Registration No. 34776

Guanxi™

Your Mobile City Guide

Guanxi Mobile Search is a division of *m*Info Inc.

mini storage

No Space ?

Your Space !

Why Mini-Storage ?

- **Convenience** (central locations)
- **Optimal space** (1sqm - 400 sqm)
- **Flexible lease terms** (1 – 12 months)
- **High Security and Access** (24/7)
- **Lowest Price**

Now available in Shanghai !!!

mini storage

Contact us!

www.mini-storage.cn   store@mini-storage.cn

Work Visas p.54
Weekend Breaks p.155

Written by residents, the Hong Kong Explorer is packed with insider info, from arriving in the city to making it your home and everything in between.

Hong Kong Explorer Residents' Guide
We Know Where You Live

WHERE NOT
PERFECT TH

Visit **Malaysia** 2007

Celebrating 50 Years of Nationhood

HING IS THE
ING TO DO

Malaysia has all the right ingredients for a perfect beach holiday. In Langkawi, Penang and all along the coasts of Terengganu and Sabah, you can enjoy picture-postcard beaches where you'll sometimes feel like the only person on earth. Take a dip. Soak up the sun. Enjoy a nap. Read a book. You'll never run out of things to do, including doing nothing at all. If you're looking for the perfect beach holiday, the time is now, the place is Malaysia.

Malaysia
Truly Asia

Residents' Guides

All you need to know about living, working and enjoying life in these
exciting destinations

Abu Dhabi

Amsterdam

Bahrain

Barcelona

Beijing *

Berlin *

Dubai

Dublin

Geneva

Hong Kong

Kuala Lumpur *

Kuwait

London

Los Angeles *

New York

New Zealand

Oman

Paris

Qatar

Shanghai

Singapore

Sydney

Tokyo *

Vancouver *

* Covers not final; titles released second quarter 2008

Mini Guides
The perfect pocket-sized
Visitors' Guides

Mini Maps
Wherever you are,
never get lost again

Contents

Contents

SHANGHAI YELLOW PAGES

ENGLISH EDITION

- The Only Comprehensive English Directory in Shanghai
- The Most Useful English Language Map of Shanghai, with a Street Index
- Living and Business Guides for Foreigners

en.yellowpage.com.cn

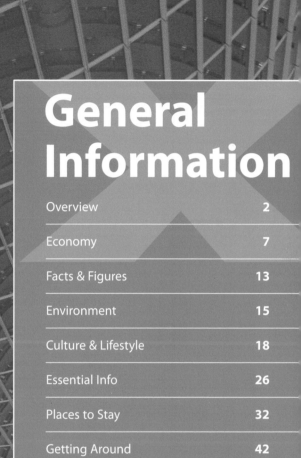

General Information

General Information

Geography

The People's Republic of China is in eastern Asia. It ranks behind Russia and Canada in area and is almost identical in size to the United States. China considers Taiwan as its 23rd province (*sheng*), making it the world's third-largest nation. Mainland China covers about 9.6 million square kilometres, and measures 5,250km from west to east and 5,500km north to south. It shares borders with 14 countries; the longest is with Mongolia, at nearly 4,700km, and the shortest is with Afghanistan, at less than 80km. It has a coastline, measuring 14,500km, with the Yellow Sea, East China Sea and South China Sea, part of the Pacific Ocean. The country is divided into 22 provinces (23 including Taiwan). There are also five autonomous regions, four municipalities (including Shanghai and Beijing) and two special administrative regions – Hong Kong and Macau (see Government & Politics, p.12).

Size Matters
As well as being the third-largest country on the planet, China is also home to the world's third and sixth-largest rivers (Yangtze and Yellow), the highest point (Everest), the second-lowest point (Turpan Depression), and the most people (1.3 billion).

Physical Geography

China encompasses a variety of landscapes by virtue of its size. Its west is mostly mountainous and high plateau terrain, the landscape dropping down in steps, punctuated by several mountain ranges, to the bountiful plains of the east coast. The mighty Himalayas form the borders with four of its neighbours – Nepal, Bhutan, India and Pakistan – and encompass the world's highest peaks. At 8,850m, Everest (*Qomolangma*) towers above all and lies partly in Tibet, while other notable peaks in Chinese territory include K2 (8,611m) and Shishapangma (8,013m). To the north-east of the Himalayas, the Tibetan Plateau extends over a huge area and has an average elevation in excess of 4,500m. Some of Asia's longest rivers begin there, including the east-flowing Yellow (*Huanghe*) and Yangtze (*Changjiang*) rivers, plus the Mekong, which flows south. Great swathes of China's north-west are desert, the most notable being the Taklamakan and Gobi deserts. Also in the north-west is the Turpan Depression, which lies at 154m below sea level and is the lowest place in China and the second lowest on the planet.

China Fact Box

Co-ordinates: China's geographical centre is at 35° 00" north, 105° 00" east

Bordering countries: Afghanistan, Bhutan, Burma, India, Kazakhstan, North Korea, Kyrgyzstan, Laos, Mongolia, Nepal, Pakistan, Russia, Tajikistan and Vietnam

Total land borders: 22,117km

Total land area: 9.6 million sq km

Bordering seas: Yellow Sea, East China Sea, South China Sea

Total coastline: 14,500km

Highest point: Mt Everest (Qomolangma), 8,850m

Lowest point: Turpan Depression, 154m below sea level

Shanghai

Shanghai is on the east coast, bordering the wealthy provinces of Jiangsu and Zhejiang at the mouth of the Yangtze. China's longest river, and the world's third-longest, after the Nile and Amazon, it flows east across the country for more than 6,300km and empties into the East China Sea. Shanghai is China's largest city and has a total population estimated to be approaching 21 million (see p.13). The city is pierced by the Huangpu River, which runs for 113km from Taihu Lake and flows into the mouth of the Yangtze. It divides the older Puxi area on the western side from the brash new Pudong district to the east. The administrative centre, main shopping areas and key sights and attractions are all in Puxi, while Pudong is the financial heart of Shanghai and is where most of its shiny new skyscrapers have sprung up. The old centre is compact, but Shanghai's 19 districts cover an area of almost 5,300 square kilometres and include China's third-largest island, Chongming. The city extends 120km north to south and nearly 100km east to west. It is mostly flat, averaging just four metres above sea level. The highest point is Dajin Hill, in the south-west of the city, with an elevation of just over 103m.

History

Shanghai's history may be just a snapshot in time compared with that of China, yet it has played a pivotal role in helping to shape the country as it is today. The origins of China go back more than 4,000 years, to the Bronze-Age Xia and Shang cultures. They were mostly in the north, whereas the Zhou, who followed them about 3,000 years ago, spread down from present-day Shaanxi province to the Yangtze River after shifting their capital from Xi'an farther east to Luoyang. Little could they have realised how important this mighty waterway would become. The next 500 years were a black period of warring kings and states, brightened by the appearance, in what is now Shandong province, of Confucius, the sage and teacher whose philosophies have stood the test of time. A quarter of a century later, the first Chinese empire was united under emperor Qin Shihuangdi. It was the mighty Qin who left an incredible time capsule of the period with the burial of an entire army of terracotta warriors and their horses. Under the Han Dynasty, the Silk Road was established, bringing China into contact with the outside world for the first time and taking its treasured silk far into central Asia and on to Rome. For more than 1,500 years, the Silk Road caravans would snake their way through deserts, across plains and over mountain passes, taking their

Pudong skyline

precious cargo west and bringing culture, influences and travellers east. Marco Polo was such a traveller, if legend is to be believed. The Venetian explorer is said to have spent 17 years in China in the late 13th century, and in his journal claimed he was governor of Yangzhou, a town near the junction of the Yangtze and the Grand Canal, for three years. This was during the period of the Mongol rule over China; the Southern Song capital, Hangzhou, falling to them in 1276. The Mongols were chased out and Chinese rule re-established with the Ming, whose leader, Zhu Yuanzhang, set up his capital at Nanjing before it was moved to Beijing.

Seeds of History
The seed of a flower changed the history of China – and the world – in the 19th century. British merchants began shipping opium, made from poppy seeds, from the subcontinent into China to counteract a huge trade deficit. China banned its import in 1839. Smuggling continued, tensions escalated, and the British attacked. By 1842 the two countries signed the Treaty of Nanjing, which gave the British low-tariff access to Chinese ports and control of Hong Kong.

Opium for the Masses

In the 1600s, the Ming were vanquished by the Manchus, who set up the Qing Dynasty. Shanghai's beginnings came about as a result of a stand-off between the Qing and the British, who had been restricted to using one Chinese port – Canton, today's Guangzhou – for trade. The British had begun importing opium into China, but when the Chinese seized and destroyed a consignment it sparked the first Opium War. The Chinese were defeated and for payment the British demanded that five new ports should be opened. One was a town at the mouth of the Yangtze, the gateway to Nanjing and eastern China. According to popular mythology, Shanghai was little more than a sleepy little fishing village which was transformed by the new trade. Yet the exquisite Yu Garden (*Yuyuan*), with its ornate 16th century Huxinting Teahouse and labyrinthine walkways, reveals that it had already been a trading town of some substance; in fact, it once boasted a wall to protect it from the threat of pirates. Once it became a treaty port in 1842, Shanghai was used by opium-laden ships and it soon grew into a sizeable town. But the ships also brought misery to the local population. Many became addicted to the drug and opium dens sprang up across the city. In 1909, US president Theodore Roosevelt opened the Shanghai Opium Commission, the world's first collaborative effort to stamp out drug use.

Golden Years

The foundation for Shanghai's cosmopolitan feel was laid well over a century ago. The French followed the British there with the Americans close behind, while the Japanese arrived in numbers in the latter years of the 19th century. Their numbers were swelled by White Russians fleeing the Revolution in 1917. They all brought with them their customs and culture, and the areas where they lived became known as the International Settlement and French Concession. Evocative colonial-style buildings began to grace the skyline, echoing the classical European styles of their homelands many thousands of miles away. The most stylish buildings of all swept gracefully in an arc alongside the Huangpu River, and the area became known as the Bund. These were the headquarters of international banks, shipping and insurance companies as well as foreign consulates – the pre-cursors to today's multinationals and their glass and steel castles. Wealthy Jewish entrepreneur Sir Victor Sassoon built the Cathay Hotel, now the Peace Hotel (p.206). It became the place to stay in town and its jazz band was legendary. Noel Coward finished writing his play *Private Lives* while staying there in 1929. This was the golden age of Shanghai, a time of divine decadence in a city everyone knew as the 'Paris of the east' for its laissez-faire attitude, classical architecture and chic lifestyle. Yet it hid far less savoury goings-on: racketeering, slave labour, drug smuggling, illegal opium dens and prostitution on a vast scale. Much of the crime owed its existence to organised gangs, with the notorious Green Gang the chief culprit. Behind its glamorous facade Shanghai was a shabby den of iniquity.

4

Shanghai Timeline

751	The administrative district of Huating County is set up in what is now the south-west suburbs of modern Shanghai.
991	Shanghai town is established within Huating County.
1260	From 1260 until 1274, Shanghai develops into a key trading port.
1292	The establishment of Shanghai County, regarded as the beginning of Shanghai City.
1553	A city wall, 8m high and 4.5km long, is built around Shanghai to protect it against Japanese pirates plaguing China's east and south coasts. A 6m-deep moat is built outside the wall.
1685	Shanghai sets up its first customs office with the opening of the Shanghai Customs House, after the ban on sea trade is lifted to ease trading along the east coast. The original building is burnt down in the Taiping Rebellion in 1853.
1839	The First Opium War breaks out when China's Qing Dynasty tries to stop the trade in opium by the British. Hong Kong is captured by the British in 1841 and an expeditionary force heads north-east up the coast, attacking successive cities.
1842	Shanghai is occupied by the British after the Chinese are defeated at the mouth of the Yangtze. The Treaty of Nanjing is signed on August 29, ending the Opium War. China cedes Hong Kong to Britain. Shanghai becomes one of five treaty ports, open to foreign trade.
1845	The British Concession is established in Shanghai, making it exempt from local law.
1849	The French Concession is created, and continues to operate with extraterritorial rights until 1946.
1853	Following the Taiping Rebellion of 1850, Shanghai is occupied by a triad from the religious zealot group called the Small Sword Society.
1854	New legislation allows Chinese people to live in the concessions, pushing land prices higher and providing westerners with a new source of income and control.
1863	The British and American Concessions are merged to create the International Settlement after the failure of a proposal the previous year to make Shanghai an independent free city.
1912	Shanghai's wall is demolished after revolution brings China's dynastic period to an end. The first provisional president of the new republic is Sun Yatsen, who lives in Shanghai from 1918 to 1924.
1921	The Chinese Communist Party is founded in Shanghai on July 1, when the first Congress is held in a small French Concession building, with Mao Zedong in attendance.
1927	Shanghai is captured by the Nationalist army under Chiang Kaishek on April 12. Communist leaders are rounded up and executed, starting a lengthy civil war.
1929	The Cathay Hotel, later renamed the Peace Hotel, opens on the Bund. The Bund's European-style architectural elegance is offset by the vice and mob crime of the now-decadent city.
1937	The Japanese invade and capture the city in August for the second time in five years during the Second Sino-Japanese War, finally overcoming resistance in November.
1949	Communists liberate Shanghai on May 25 without bloodshed. Chiang Kaishek escapes to Taiwan. Chen Yi becomes Shanghai's first Communist mayor. People's Republic of China proclaimed by Mao on October 1 in Beijing.
1995	Asia's tallest structure, the Oriental Pearl Tower, opens in Shanghai and symbolises the dynamic, new city. Fortune 500 Global Economic Forum is held in Shanghai.
2002	Shanghai wins the bid to host World Expo 2010 and unveils redevelopment plans for Huangpu River and downtown riverfront.
2003	The Maglev becomes the world's fastest-operating train when it starts running between Pudong International Airport and Shanghai. It can reach speeds of more than 350kph.

5

Storm Clouds

Even while the parties were going on, tensions and unrest were building in Shanghai. The arrival of all the foreign groups had made the locals virtually exiles in their home city, and the low pay and gruelling working conditions only fanned the growing flames. The Communist Party of China was born out of a meeting in the French Concession in 1921, attended by Mao Zedong. In 1927, two years after taking the reins of the Kuomintang Nationalist Party, Chiang Kaishek marched an army of Kuomintang troops in to Shanghai, where they rounded up and executed thousands of Communists. Ten years of feuding ensued between the two factions, during which time the Communists embarked on their perilous Long March to Yan'an in Shaanxi, with Mao at the helm. The Japanese took advantage of the internecine strife and invaded Manchuria, setting up a puppet regime fronted by the last emperor, Puyi, in 1931. Six years later, Japan invaded the rest of China, including Shanghai. The inhabitants of Jiangsu's capital, Nanjing, suffered brutally, and the atrocities are still the cause of deep resentment by many towards the Japanese. During the second world war, several thousand Jewish refugees took safe harbour in Shanghai to escape persecution elsewhere, although they still had to endure poor conditions. After the war's end and defeat for Japan, full-scale civil war erupted between the Communists and Kuomintang. The nationalists suffered heavy defeats in 1948 and early 1949, including the loss of Beijing. By April 1949, the Communists had crossed the Yangtze and the Kuomintang fled to Taiwan. Shanghai was 'liberated' on May 25. Mao Zedong then proclaimed the People's Republic of China in Tiananmen Square on October 1, 1949.

New Beginning

The 1960s brought with it the Cultural Revolution, which led to turbulent times in Shanghai. The Gang of Four, who controlled much of the revolutionary activity, were based in the city, and one of the major ideologies was to get rid of things 'old' – customs, habits, culture and thinking. Much of the city's religious heritage was destroyed, and an estimated one million Shanghainese workers were forced to migrate to rural areas to work in communes.

It wasn't until 1990 that China's future seemed to brighten with president Deng Xiaoping's announcement that Shanghai would become the centre of China's economic reforms. Deng was succeeded in 1994 by former Shanghai mayor Jiang Zemin, who is said to have surrounded himself with the 'Shanghai Clique', a group of officials important to the city at the time. In 1998, Zhu Rongji, a member of the Clique and a former Shanghai mayor himself, became prime minister and was responsible for driving home the economic reforms announced in 1990. The following decade saw unprecedented development of the city, particularly Pudong (see New Developments, p.10). Then, in 2002, Shanghai was announced as the host for Expo 2010. With billions of dollars' worth of developments under way, a skyline which has become the envy of the world and economic growth outpacing that of China, the future is looking very rosy for Shanghai.

The Bund

China Overview

China's economic miracle has awoken the dragon from its slumbers and propelled it to the forefront of the global economy. In just 30 years, the still staunchly communist country has successfully turned from a planned central economy fuelled by inefficient, state-run factories to become the workshop of the world. It has embraced this change in direction with such fervour, dynamism and enterprise that it is now the globe's fourth-largest economy; some believe it could become the world's largest within 30 years. Its gross domestic product grew by 10.7% to reach ¥20.94 trillion ($2.68 trillion) in 2006. Some observers are worried its economy might overheat, leading to a spectacular crash; inflation fears have already triggered a yo-yo effect on the Shanghai stock exchange. The government is trying to keep the economy in check – it set a growth target of 8% for 2007, although the World Bank has raised its forecast to 10.4% growth from its previous prediction of 9.6%.

Industry

The country's economy is underpinned by a powerful manufacturing base, with a fast-growing automotive industry as well as ones for aircraft, railway engines, ships and military equipment. It has turned its attention to the high-tech worlds of IT and telecommunications, and is a major manufacturer of toys, clothes and footwear. China is also the world's fifth-largest oil producer – but the second-highest oil consumer. Key exports are electrical machinery, power generation equipment, clothing, iron and steel, optics and medical equipment, furniture, chemicals, toys, vehicles and plastics. Much of its exports come from the Pearl River delta – including China's first special economic zone, Shenzhen, plus Hong Kong and Macau – and the Yangtze delta, led by Shanghai. Its main export partners, excluding Hong Kong and Macau, are the US, Japan, Korea, Germany, the Netherlands, the UK, Singapore and Italy.

Tourism is also a major earner for China. Foreign visitor numbers reached 22.2 million in 2006, up nearly 10% from 2005, when tourism receipts totalled $29.3 billion. China is forecast by the World Tourism Organisation to become the world's most-visited country by 2015. Its strong economy is stoking growing domestic demand as disposable income levels rise. Yet with much of China still a rural subsistence economy, the disparity between city and countryside is growing. The average annual disposable income per capita of urban households was ¥11,759 (about US$1,500) in 2006, while rural households had an average per capita net annual income of ¥3,587 (about $460). That compared with average household income of £32,342 in the UK and median household incomes of $46,000 in the US. According to the World Bank, China is still home to 18% of the world's poor and about 150 million people live on less than $1 a day. The Chinese government has vowed to tackle urban unemployment and reduce it to below 4.6% by creating at least nine million new jobs while keeping inflation below 3%.

Shanghai Overview

Shanghai is said by many to be the driving force behind China's rampant economy. One look at the skyline of Pudong, its modern financial district with a forest of cranes and shiny new offices thrusting ever-skyward, and it isn't hard to understand why. Shanghai's economy has always been heavily based on manufacturing, with everything from cars and ships to laptops made in the city and the Yangtze delta. The region still produces 20% of China's output, but Shanghai's service sector – notably financial services – is now driving much of its growth. Foreign investment is key to the city's phenomenal rise. In 2006, it approved more than 4,000 foreign-funded projects worth $14.5 billion, two-thirds of which went into the service sector. More than 500 multinationals have set up regional headquarters in Shanghai as the city has wooed the world's corporate investors – 20 were authorised in 2006 in Pudong, along with 11 research and development centres. Meanwhile, joint-venture arrangements between western firms and local counterparts have increased exponentially. Shanghai's GDP almost doubled between 2000 and 2005, when the total reached ¥915 billion, more than 50% of which was attributed to the service sector. The city's per capita GDP stood at ¥67,500 in 2005, double the ¥32,000 level of 1999.

Growth

The pace of Shanghai's economy has been outstripping the national growth rate and reached 12% in 2006, the 15th straight year of double-digit growth, but the city's administration is now aiming to cool the pace to about a 9% rise rate. The booming economy comes at a price though. Shanghai has the highest cost of living in China after Beijing and rose up the global rankings from 30th position in 2005 to 20th in 2006, according to a survey by international consultancy firm Mercer Human Resources Consulting. That put it only marginally behind Paris and ahead of cities including Rome, Helsinki, Dubai and Los Angeles.

Trade

Shanghai is one of China's key export ports, and foreign trade is mirroring its white-hot economy in growth levels. From 2000 to 2005 the value of exports overseas, excluding Hong Kong and Taiwan, more than tripled from $22.5 billion to $80 billion. Its main trading partners are the US and Japan, followed by Germany, the Netherlands, Korea, the UK, Singapore, Malaysia, Canada and Australia. Exports include cars, laptops, petrochemicals, clothing, electronics and telecommunications equipment.

Rural Migration

While most people in China still live in rural communities, the demographics of the country are changing fast as more people leave the impoverished countryside and move to the cities. In 1995, 29% of the population lived in urban areas while 71% lived in rural areas. According to government figures, by 2005 the percentage of people living in cities rose to 43%.

Employment

The city had a workforce of 8.6 million people by the end of 2005. Of those, 10% worked for foreign-funded companies, 17% in state enterprises, 26% in collectively owned companies, 28% in private businesses, and 19% in 'other economic sectors'. Unemployment was marginally lower than in 2004 at 4.4% and in 2006 more than 96% of the city's 129,000

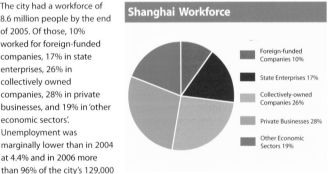

Shanghai Workforce

- Foreign-funded Companies 10%
- State Enterprises 17%
- Collectively-owned Companies 26%
- Private Businesses 28%
- Other Economic Sectors 19%

university graduates found jobs. Just over 95,000 foreign residents lived and worked in Shanghai in 2005, the largest national group being Japanese (28%), followed by citizens from Korea, Malaysia, Singapore, Germany, the UK, Canada, the US, Australia and France. Since 2004, China's government has been issuing green cards to significant investors as well as high-level foreign workers in the economic, scientific and technology sectors. The cards give freedoms such as being able to enter and exit the country without having to renew visas. Salary levels in Shanghai rose faster than in other Chinese cities in 2006, according to Mercer, rising 7.7% from 2005. The Shanghai Statistical Bureau listed the average annual wage in Shanghai in 2005 as ¥27,000 overall and ¥34,000 for companies with foreign investment. The highest-paid sectors were financial, scientific research, and leasing and business services, which paid between ¥107,000 and ¥128,000. Foreign staff earn much higher levels than locally

Dry Cleaners p.74
Divorce Lawyers p.108

Written by residents, these unique guidebooks are packed with insider info, from arriving in a new destination to making it your home and everything in between.

Explorer Residents' Guides
We Know Where You Live

hired staff, particularly if on a remuneration package with benefits and which is paid in euros or US or Hong Kong dollars. Shanghai's minimum wage is ¥750 per month.

Leading Industries

Shanghai is the centre of China's banking industry and home to the Chinese stock market – which quadrupled in value in little more than a year before worries about the economy overheating resulted in wild fluctuations in June 2007. Banking and finance, information technology, electronics, chemicals and petrochemicals are all key industries. Shanghai is China's largest car manufacturing centre. It is expected to be the world's biggest shipbuilding base by 2015 and currently 70% of the world's laptops are produced in the Yangtze delta, a figure predicted to surpass 87% by 2010 according to US-based IT market intelligence firm iSuppli.

Sprawling Metro-polis

In a build up to World Expo 2010, Shanghai's Metro has been growing at an incredible rate. The five current lines (carrying more than two million people per day) are being extended, and the Shanghai Metro Corporation hopes to have 11 lines operating throughout the city by 2025. Line 8 is reportedly the next to open and, by the end of 2007, should run from New Jiangwan City in the north, through People's Square, to Zhongshan Nan Lu in the south.

New Developments

Developments under way or on the drawing board defy belief by their sheer scale. At least ¥30 billion is being invested by Shanghai to stage the World Expo 2010 extravaganza, which is expected to attract 70 million visitors in the six months it will be open (between May 1 and October 31, 2010). A huge area of downtown alongside the Huangpu River is being transformed into a city of pavilions and exhibition halls, most of which will be torn down after the event. Infrastructure due to be finished in time for the event will include ¥20 billion worth of roadworks with a tunnel under the Huangpu lit by solar power (to fit in with the event's eco-theme), the renovation of docks to accommodate 60 new ferries, several new Metro lines and the extension of existing ones, and the redevelopment of the Shanghai South Railway Station with an initial capacity of 12.7 million passengers. The renovated station will connect with the Metro's Line 3 and the Shanghai-Hangzhou railway line, which was set to have a ¥35 billion, high-speed Maglev track ready by 2010 with trains doing the 175km journey in half an hour. However, concerns over radiation affecting nearby residents have halted the scheme. The once suspended World Financial Centre is now nearing completion and already dwarfs the neighbouring Jinmao Tower and Oriental Pearl Tower in Pudong's Lujiazui area. At 498m high, the 101 storey building will be the tallest in mainland China and only marginally shorter than the 508m Taipei 101 in Taiwan when it opens in March 2008. Work is also under way on a new bridge between Pudong and Chongming Island in the mouth of the Yangtze, the site of an important bird reserve. The bridge will serve a massive new eco-friendly city called Dongtan – one of 10 satellite cities being built around Shanghai. Constructed on China's third-largest island, the first phase will have a population of 25,000 and be ready by 2010. After completion in 2040, Dongtan should house 500,000, as will three of the other satellite cities.

World Expo 2010

After winning its 2002 bid to host World Expo 2010, Shanghai has become obsessed with expanding, improving and grooming itself ahead of this showcase. Expo 2010 is slated to be the most attended event of its kind in history, with estimates putting the turnout at over 70 million. 'Better City – Better Life' is the theme, and Shanghai hopes to prove its eagerness to join the green movement by promoting its ever-growing Metro system, and powering the fairgrounds with solar energy. The Expo site lies between the Nanpu and Lupu bridges on both sides of the Huangpu River.

Tourism

Tourism is playing an increasingly important role in Shanghai's economy. Overseas arrivals through Shanghai customs doubled from 890,000 in 1990 to 1.8 million in 2000, and by 2005 that had trebled to 5.7 million. The growth in foreign visitors (not including Hong Kong and Macau Chinese or those from Taiwan) is even more impressive, registering a tenfold increase from 460,000 in 1990 to more than 4.5 million in 2005. Those figures only take into account visitors arriving directly at Shanghai from overseas points and not those entering via other Chinese gateways. According to the Shanghai Municipal Tourism Administrative Commission, the city actually attracted over six million overseas tourists in 2006 – more than Beijing is anticipating during its Olympics year in 2008.

Attractions

Although known as a financial hub, Shanghai is part of China's tourism 'golden triangle' along with Beijing and Xi'an and has many attractions: the futuristic Oriental Pearl Tower, the classical European architecture of the Bund and French Concession, which hark back to its days as the 'Paris of the east,' and a growing reputation as one of the world's most energetic cities.

Shanghai's broad appeal attracts a wide cross-section of visitors, from mature travellers on escorted tours to affluent young couples on weekend breaks. While most of the new hotels are geared towards corporate travellers, there are a growing number of boutique hotels catering to leisure guests. The big business hotels generally have extensive leisure facilities and spas, with discounted weekend rates to attract tourists. Shanghai has big plans in the run-up to hosting the World Expo (see box opposite). It has set a target of 10 million overseas visitors in 2010, and is planning a series of promotions in Europe, the Americas, Asia and Oceania to attract more tourists. The city had 351 star-rated hotels by the end of 2005, 66 of them four star and above, offering a total of nearly 62,000 rooms. An extra 8,000 rooms are due online by 2008.

Yu Garden Bazaar

Government & Politics

The People's Republic of China has been run by the Communist Party of China since its foundation in 1949. The head of state is President Hu Jintao, who holds the three most powerful positions in China: general secretary of the Communist Party, chairman of the Central Military Commission and paramount leader of the country. Hu was elected president in 2003 by the 10th National People's Congress (NPC), which also elected Zeng Qinghong as vice president.

The NPC is the highest political body in China and is a single legislative chamber. It comprises nearly 3,000 deputies who are elected for five-year terms by local people's congresses. Each has a vote for both aforementioned posts, the result being decided by simple majority. The NPC meets for two weeks each year to decide policy issues, laws and the budget. While not in session, power is wielded by the Standing Committee, which can have up to nine members, and is effectively China's cabinet. The military also plays a key role in government as one of the main hierarchies. The State Council is the main administrative body of the government, responsible for the day-to-day running of the country and implementing policy decisions. It is chaired by the prime minister, currently Wen Jiabao, who has up to four deputies. Below state level, there are 22 provinces (Anhui, Fujian, Gansu, Guangdong, Guizhou, Hainan, Hebei, Heilongjiang, Henan, Hubei, Hunan, Jiangsu, Jiangxi, Jilin, Liaoning, Qinghai, Shaanxi, Shandong, Shanxi, Sichuan, Yunnan and Zhejiang), plus Taiwan, which China sees as its 23rd province. There are also five autonomous regions (Guangxi, Inner Mongolia, Ningxia, Xinjiang and Tibet) and four municipalities (Beijing, Shanghai, Tianjin and Chongqing), all of which come under the jurisdiction of the State Council. All ministries, bureaux, administrations and institutions, including news agencies, come under the State Council. The ministry of national defence comes under the State Council but the council does not control the military. Provinces have governors elected by local congresses. Municipalities are large cities with the same status as provinces. Autonomous regions are ethnic province-level areas which have an elected chairman instead of a governor. The special administrative regions of Hong Kong and Macau have a high level of autonomy under China's 'one country, two systems' policy, brought in when they were transferred back to China from Britain and Portugal respectively in the 1990s.

International Relations

The country's economic might gives it plenty of political clout in the global arena. It maintains good relations with the rest of the world in general, despite certain thorny and sensitive issues, largely because everyone wants to be its ally for trading purposes or to win approved destination status to allow Chinese tourists to visit. China and Japan have made recent efforts to improve their relations, which continually fluctuate on issues dealing with the latter's pre-second world war invasion of the former. China is a member of international organisations including the UN, the International Monetary Fund and Unesco, and is one of the five permanent members of the UN Security Council. It is also a member of the G-77 coalition of developing nations, and although not a member, Chinese president Hu Jintao has addressed outreach sessions of G8 several times. China is a member of the Asia-Pacific Economic Cooperation forum, a body comprising Pacific Rim countries, and an observer of the Non-Aligned Movement. It has tended to take a back seat in international affairs, but is beginning to play a more active role, particularly as peace-broker in international wrangles involving the likes of North Korea and Iran. There are nearly 50 foreign consulates in Shanghai. These are mostly located around Nanjing Lu, Yan'an Lu, Huihuai Lu and Fuxing Lu, all in Puxi (see Embassies & Consulates table, p.28).

Shanghai Population – Age Breakdown*

(in million)

Age	
60+	
35-59	
18-34	
0-17	

0M 1M 2M 3M 4M 5M 6M 7M 8M

Source: Shanghai Statistical Bureau
* Residents with permanent registered papers

Foreign Population – Nationality

30,000
25,000
20,000
15,000
10,000
5,000
0

Australia Canada France Germany Japan Malaysia Korea Singapore UK US

Source: Shanghai Municipal Public Security Bureau

Population

According to China's last official census in 2000, the Shanghai metropolitan area is home to 16.74 million residents. Current estimates put it somewhere in the 20-21 million range, placing Shanghai behind only Mexico City, Tokyo, Sao Paulo and New York. The city's booming economy has been acting like a magnet, drawing in migrant workers from other regions of China and from overseas. The previous official census in 1990 reported a population of 13.34 million, which correlates to a 25% increase in 10 years.

China's one-child policy has had a huge impact on Shanghai's birth rate; at just over 6 per 1,000 population, it has more than halved since 1985's 12.74 per 1,000, and is dramatically lower than the 40 per 1,000 level of the 1950s, when the first forms of the policy were enacted. Currently, the national birth rate is closer to 12.4 per 1,000. The average size of family households is the lowest in Shanghai, at 2.7 people per household, compared with the national average of 3.44. Shanghai's resident population comprises of 49.2% men and 50.8% women; the average life expectancy for men is 78 and 82 for women. By the end of 2006, there were registered expats from 133 countries living and working in Shanghai, of which 70% worked in foreign or joint-venture companies.

National Flag

China's national flag, the Five-Starred Red Flag, was the winning design in a country-wide competition held in 1949. It was first erected by Mao Zedong in Tiananmen Square in Beijing on October 1, 1949, the day the People's Republic was founded, and is flown on buildings and parks across China on the same date each year, China's National Day. The flag features a red background symbolising revolution, with one large five-pointed yellow star and a semi-circle of four smaller ones in the top left corner signifying the unity of the Chinese people under the leadership of the Communist Party of China. The flag is raised at sunrise and lowered at sunset every day in a ritual ceremony with People's Liberation Army soldiers in Tiananmen Square. It is flown throughout the year on key public buildings, airports, ports, railway stations and border posts and by schools during term times. It may also be flown elsewhere on occasions, including New Year's Day and the Spring Festival (see p.52).

National flags on Century Avenue

Time Zones	
Athens	-6
Bangkok	-1
Berlin	-7
Canberra	+2
Dallas	-14
Denver	-15
Dubai	-4
Dublin	-8
Hong Kong	0
Johannesburg	-6
London	-8
Los Angeles	-16
Manila	0
Mexico City	-14
Moscow	-5
Mumbai	-2.5
Munich	-7
New York	-13
Paris	-7
Perth	0
Prague	-7
Rio de Janeiro	-11
Rome	-7
Santiago	-12
Sydney	+2
Tokyo	+1
Toronto	-13
Wellington	+4

Local Time

Despite its size, the whole of China observes the same time as Beijing, which is eight hours ahead of UCT (Universal Coordinated Time, the same as Greenwich Mean Time, or GMT). Daylight saving is not operated, so clocks stay the same all year. The table, left, lists time differences between Shanghai and various cities around the world, not incorporating daylight saving time in any country.

Social & Business Hours

The working week in Shanghai is Monday to Friday, although some companies also operate on Saturdays. Offices generally work from 09:00 to 17:00. Government offices and foreign consulates may start at 08:30, closing for an hour for lunch. Some banks and post offices open on Saturdays; main post office branches open as early as 07:00 and stay open until 19:00 or later. Meals in China are generally eaten earlier than in other countries, reflected in the opening times of most Shanghai restaurants. Lunch typically runs from 11:00-14:30 and dinner from 17:00-21:30. Restaurants in popular areas and in major hotels generally stay open later, often until 23:00 and some as late as 01:00. With its fast-paced lifestyle, people in Shanghai work hard and party hard too, particularly on weekends. The many bars and clubs across the city don't get going until late into the evenings. Most close by 02:00, but several keep the action going until 04:00.

Public Holidays

China has four main public holidays, three of which are 'golden weeks'. Although golden weeks are officially three days long, virtually all offices close for the week, and New Year's Day follows the same pattern. The first golden week marks the Spring Festival (Chinese New Year) and starts on the first lunar day of the first lunar month of the Chinese calendar, usually falling somewhere in late January or February. The second starts on Labour Day and the third on China's National Day. Foreign consulates also close on Christmas Day, Boxing Day and at Easter, and some western companies prefer to stay open during some golden weeks. Secondary schools get 10 or 11 weeks of holiday and primary schools 13 weeks. Both are spread over summer, Chinese New Year, March and April. Other traditional Chinese holidays include the Qingming Festival, when family tombs are traditionally visited and swept, the Dragon Boat Festival (*Duan Wu Jie*), and the Mid-Autumn Festival (see p.55).

Public Holidays	
New Year's Day	Jan 1
Spring Festival	Feb 7-9 (2008); Jan 26-28 (2009)
International Women's Day	Mar 8
Qingming Festival	Apr 5
Labour Day	May 1
National Youth Day	May 4
International Children's Day	Jun 1
Dragon Boat Festival	Jun 8 (2008); Jun 27 (2009)
CPC Founding Day	Jul 1
Army Day	Aug 1
Mid-Autumn Festival	Sep 25 (2007); Sep 14 (2008); Oct 3 (2009)
National Day	Oct 1

Photography

Although most Chinese people don't mind having their photo taken, it's always best to ask before clicking. A quick showing of the image in the digital viewer usually makes things easier. Airports are off limits for photography, although snaps from inside the terminal are unlikely to be reprimanded. Photographing military installations is forbidden and can result in a lot of hassle, and cameras are not welcomed at public disturbances. Temples often charge for taking pictures inside and it's customary to refrain from doing so while services are in progress.

Climate

Subtropical Shanghai has four seasons, with grey and cold winters, oppressively humid summers and beautiful springs and autumns. According to the Shanghai Meteorological Bureau, the city's climate is getting warmer – and the winter of 2006-07 was the hottest on record. Thanks to its proximity to the sea, Shanghai rarely sees snow but occasionally experiences sub-zero temperatures. Maximum temperatures in the summer can hit 40°C, although the average high for July and August is 32°C. Most of Shanghai's rain falls between April and September in three periods: spring rain, plum rain, and autumn rain. The plum rain season, a phenomenon of the lower Yangtze region, is named after the fruit that ripens with its arrival in mid-June and early July. Typhoon season lasts from June to October and the storms bring strong winds, heavy rains and storm surges, which sometimes cause flooding in downtown areas.

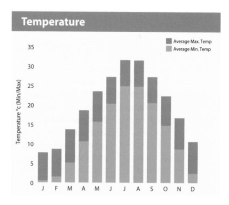

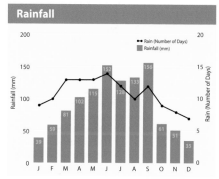

Flora & Fauna

The pockets of greenery dotted in and around Shanghai are perfect for escaping the intense urban chaos. China's second-largest municipal botanical garden, the Shanghai Botanical Garden (p.219), contains greenhouse displays and several gardens and is particularly noted for its collection of miniaturised bonsai plants (*penjing*). Other plants on show include orchids, roses and the spring-flowering white magnolia, Shanghai's official city flower. In Xuhui district lies Guilin Park (p.212), a small, traditional Chinese garden restored in 1957 after it was destroyed by the Japanese 20 years earlier. The park is best visited in autumn when the fragrant scent of its 1,000-plus osmanthus trees fills the air. In the heart of downtown, People's Park provides a welcome sanctuary with floral gardens and a lotus-filled pond (see p.213). North-east of the city centre, bordering the Huangpu River, Gongqing Forest Park (p.212) is Shanghai's second-largest park and only forested environment. Intensive agriculture has resulted in little natural diversity of the lower Yangtze region, although wild plants can be found along water courses, around rural villages and in hilly areas.

Fauna

Shanghai's native wildlife has suffered from the city's rapid development. Species such as the civet cat, which thrived prior to 1949, have disappeared from the city's natural areas. Non-native species, however, are doing well. A recent report from the Shanghai Maritime University highlights the increase in the number of alien species, such as

Mini Explorer

Don't let the size of this little star fool you – it's full of insider info, maps, contacts, tips and facts for visitors. From shops to spas, bars to bargains and everything in between, the Mini Explorer range helps you get the most out of your stay in the city, however long you're there for.

15

styan's squirrels, that have been found in Gongqing and Zhongshan parks after being released by owners who had bought them as pets.

Caged Companions
Despite the persistent threat of a bird flu outbreak in east Asia, the custom of keeping songbirds is still relatively strong among Shanghai locals. The best time for 'songbird watching' is in the early mornings when retirees hang the cages on park trees so their feathered friends can chirp in harmony.

Birds

Although the city centre's parks provide habitat for such distinct birds as huamei songbirds and azure-winged magpies, the real destination of choice for birdwatchers is Chongming Island (see p.192). One of China's most important wetland bird habitats, the world's largest alluvial island is home to the Chongming Dongtan Nature Reserve (p.219). More than 300 species have been spotted at the reserve, including over 30 nationally protected species such as tundra swans, hooded cranes, black-faced spoonbills and both white and black storks. Visiting the reserve requires a permit, and the only way to reach it is by ferry. Like the rest of Shanghai, Chongming Island is undergoing constant renovation; city planners envision it as the home of Dongtan, a vast eco-city connected to the mainland via a bridge.

Shanghai cats

Marine Life

Degradation of water quality has impacted Shanghai's marine life. The Yangtze is home to the endangered Chinese sturgeon, one of 63 species of fish which spawn and feed in the estuarial waters off Chongming Island. More than 100,000 captive-bred sturgeon were released with other rare fish in April 2007 as part of continuing efforts to combat falling numbers in the river, but unfortunately several large sturgeons were found dead in the river soon after. The critically endangered Shanghai soft-shell turtle, also called the Yangtze giant soft-shell turtle, is one of the world's largest freshwater turtles and once inhabited the river. Now just four living specimens are known. Red-eared slider turtles, pets originally from Brazil, have been seen in Yanzhong Park, and a predatory freshwater garfish was caught in a fishing net near Shanghai in May 2007.

Environmental Issues

According to the World Bank, 20 of the 30 most polluted cities on the planet are in China, which is largely due to motor vehicles and high coal usage. In 2005 it overtook the US as the world's largest municipal solid waste generator. China's booming economy caused it to miss its goal of cutting both energy consumption and pollution levels by 2006. As a result, it set up a task force under prime minister Wen Jiabao to ensure its environmental goals are met by 2010. Meanwhile, Shanghai has been underlining its green credentials with plans of its own to improve energy efficiency and environmental protection ahead of the World Expo 2010 (see p.10), which focuses on sustainable development and green cities. The plans include increased dependence on renewable energy and restrictions on private transportation. Among other advancements, public recycling bins now dot city streets and Shanghai has opened its first recycling centre for unwanted electronic items.

Ecosystems

Shanghai's breakneck growth has brought with it huge environmental problems, water pollution chief among them. Falling levels of fish, particularly protected species such as the Chinese sturgeon, are a concern. Suzhou Creek, once home to many fish species, became so polluted by the 1970s that nothing could survive in it. Clean-up work in the creek has begun and, together with improvements to the sewage pumping stations discharging into it, should be finished by the end of 2010. Freshwater Chinese suckers, a native fish, are being reintroduced to test the environment. Shanghai's most important ecosystem is the Chongming Dongtan Nature Reserve on the eastern end of Chongming Island (p.192). With its extensive fresh and saltwater marshes, reedbeds, tidal creeks and mudflats, the island provides refuge for millions of birds and rich, offshore marine life.

Water Usage and Desalination

Despite being virtually surrounded by water, the city is facing a serious water shortage and the Shanghai Water Affair Bureau concedes that demand has almost reached the present supply limit. Some climate change experts have warned that Shanghai will need to use desalinated water within 10 years, as well as import water from south-west China. Excessive pumping of water from underneath the city coupled with overdevelopment of skyscrapers has resulted in Shanghai sinking by an average of 10mm per year. The city has sunk more than two metres since 1921 and the government has limited building heights and begun pumping water back underground in an effort to stop the trend.

Water Green Idea
Shanghai's World Expo 2010 organisers are planning to use as much rainwater as possible to save the city's precious freshwater supplies from being wasted during the event, which coincides with the plum rain season. They plan to design the roofs of the pavilions and exhibition halls to collect rainwater which can then be used for flushing toilets, watering gardens or creating landscapes.

Environmental Organisations

The Shanghai Environmental Protection Bureau, part of the Shanghai Municipality, is the body responsible for formulating the city's environmental protection plans, monitoring pollution and enforcing environmental laws. It also manages natural resources and ecosystems such as the Chongming Island wetlands. Of the thousands of non-governmental organisations proliferating in China now, a number are based in Shanghai and tackle environmental issues. Among them is Roots & Shoots (p.248), part of the international Jane Goodall Institute and the first foreign NGO registered by the government. It encourages young people to enrol in environmental projects and welcomes adult volunteers. Projects include tree planting, organic gardening, and paper and printer ink cartridge recycling, carried out in conjunction with local and international schools.

Greenery in the city

Culture

If Beijing is China's brain and Guangzhou its guts, then Shanghai is most definitely the country's heart. Pulsing away with 24 hour electric energy, the city is a melting pot of different ethnic groups, both domestic and international, the majority with the same main goal: to make some cash. Money has long since taken over from religion or politics as the predominant force shaping the culture of Shanghai, and evidence of this can be found everywhere: from the western businessman flashing his gold card at one of the city's high-end bars to the local girl proudly showing off her new Jimmy Choos, all the way down to the migrant worker embarking on yet another all-nighter in the hope of making a few extra yuan to send back to his family in the countryside. People from every corner of both China and the globe migrate here in the belief that, no matter who you are, enough hard work will lead to a bigger bank balance and a higher social position.

Chinese dancers

This constant influx of people from different backgrounds has created a culturally diverse landscape within the city's 20 million-plus population. Domestically, aside from the born-and-bred Shanghainese, there is a substantial presence of people from regions as widespread as Xinjiang in the far west, Inner Mongolia in the far north and Guizhou in the deep south, while large European, American, Australian and Korean communities give the city a truly international feel.

These local and expat communities live in what could justifiably be called a state of happy mutual exclusivity. Unlike in Beijing, where members of both groups can be found sharing a dancefloor, Shanghai's nightspots tend to cater either for one or the other. Within the domestic community there are further segregations, the Shanghainese being notoriously cliquey. The international population is more cosmopolitan, with different nationalities mixing on a social and residential level.

Occasionally tensions between locals and foreigners can be felt (a taxi driver refusing to take a foreigner is not uncommon). Generally, however, Shanghai remains a harmonious city, with the 'money-making foreigners' who were booted out during the Communist revolution of the 1940s and 50s being increasingly welcomed back. This change in attitude of both authorities and locals can especially be seen in Shanghai where many foreign enterprises have invested large amounts of money into China and have offered locals well-paid jobs, granting them entrance into an ever-expanding middle class. In business particularly, both foreigners and locals are realising the great financial and social benefits that a mutually friendly relationship can bring.

One aspect of traditional Chinese culture that endures is the concept of 'family'. Of higher importance than the individual, the family is considered to be the smallest unit in society, with all members expected to act as part of a larger single whole. Families generally remain close and even after marriage children will often continue to live with their parents; in poorer families especially, three or even four generations can be found living under one roof. Children, having come of age, are traditionally expected to look after parents and grandparents in their old age. The pressures on a young Chinese man are particularly demanding since, once married, he will be expected to provide not only for his own family but also for the parents of his new bride.

Life in the fast lane?

Life can move pretty quickly so make sure you keep in the know with regular updates from **explorerpublishing.com**

Or better still, share your knowledge and advice with others, find answers to your questions, or just make new friends in our community area

explorerpublishing.com — for life in real time

Language

Other options **Language Schools** p.258

Other options **Language Schools** p.258

Street Wise
*There are a variety of
ways of writing
addresses in Shanghai,
but we've opted to use
Pinyin words
throughout this guide.
Common examples
that you'll notice are lu
(road), jie (street) and
dadao (avenue), and
compass points – bei
(north), nan (south),
dong (east) and xi
(west). Think of this as
the first of many
impromptu Mandarin
lessons you'll receive
during your time as a
Shanghai resident.*

Shanghai's official language is Mandarin Chinese (*Putonghua*). A notoriously difficult language to learn, it has no set alphabet and instead uses characters, a type of pictogram, which number at approximately 50,000. Luckily for Mandarin learners, not all are in everyday use and knowledge of about 3,000 should be enough to read a newspaper. Learning spoken Mandarin is made easier through the use of Pinyin, a system that uses the Roman alphabet to represent the pronunciation sounds. Refrain, however, from breathing a sigh of relief, since spoken Chinese is a tonal language and, in itself, tricky to master. Each character is assigned one of five tones in the spoken form: first tone (high and level), second tone (rising from medium to high), third tone (starting low, dipping lower and then rising again), fourth tone (sharply falling from high to low) and the fifth neutral tone.

Characters with the same Pinyin 'spelling' have numerous meanings, each dependent on the particular tone used during pronunciation. A well-known but clear example of this potentially confusing aspect of spoken Chinese uses the word 'ma': pronounced with the first tone (mā) it means 'mother'; with the second tone (má) it means 'hemp'; with the third tone (mǎ) it means 'horse'; with the fourth tone (mà) it means 'to swear or reprimand'; and with the fifth tone (ma) it takes on the grammatical use of a question particle. A slip of the tonal tongue can, therefore, prove embarrassing.

In practice, the word on the city's streets belongs to a far livelier local dialect: Shanghainese or *Shanghaihua. Shanghaihua* is derived from the Northern Wu dialect, one of 11 spoken across China. With no standardised written form, *Shanghaihua* exists only as an everyday spoken lingo and is hugely different in pronunciation to Mandarin. Fortunately, however, Mandarin is the official language of teaching in schools and can be understood and spoken by the great majority of Shanghainese.

There are a few potential pitfalls to be aware of, however. The Mandarin sound 'shi' is pronounced 'si' in *Shanghaihua*, meaning that any conversations relating to the numbers four (*si*) or 10 (*shi*) can be highly confusing if due care is not taken. The pronunciations of many other words are even further removed from their Mandarin counterparts: 'hello, how are you?' or '*ni hao ma?*' in Mandarin becomes '*nong ho ma?*' in Shanghainese, and 'goodbye' changes from '*zaijia*' to an almost unrecognisable '*zewei*'.

For a foreign student of Mandarin this can pose serious comprehension problems. Regardless of whether you can understand or not, Chinese people greatly appreciate foreigners trying to learn the language and take such efforts as a sign of respect. Learning at least a few phrases is therefore a good way of ingratiating yourself with locals, particularly as many do not speak English.

In business or administrative situations, it is, however, advisable to stick to your native tongue. Starting off with the few Mandarin phrases that you have practised may give the impression you understand more than you do.

Pinyin

Pinyin was first approved in China in 1958, and by 1979 had replaced several other Romanised forms of Mandarin, including Wade-Giles and Gwoyeu Romatzyh, as the standard method. Some Pinyin consonants are particularly confusing when compared with their English equivalents: c, for example, should be pronounced like the 'ts' in 'hits'; q should be pronounced like the 'ch' in 'cheeky'; sh as in 'shout' but with the tongue curled back; x as the 'sh' in 'ship'; z as the 'dz' sound in 'buds'; and zh as the 'j' in 'judge' but with the tongue curled back.

Culture & Lifestyle

Fortunately, as well as standard Mandarin, English is broadly accepted as the language of business in Shanghai, with countless firms hiring English teachers to train their Chinese employees. Many local restaurants and bars also cater to an ever-increasing expat population and now have bilingual menus. Venture outside these 'safe-havens', however, and you'll be faced with page-upon-page of Chinese characters.

A lack of use of native English proofreaders means that numerous examples of 'Chinglish' can be found anywhere from shop signs to instruction manuals, many needing code-breakers to decipher. Luckily the majority of street signs avoid this trend and stick to Pinyin, making navigation of the city relatively easy.

Basic Mandarin

General Words

English	Pinyin	Characters
Yes	shìde	是的
No	búshì	不是
Please	qǐng	请
Thank you	xièxiè	谢谢

Greetings

English	Pinyin	Characters
Good morning	zǎo an	早安
Hello	nǐ hǎo	你好
Goodbye	zàijiàn	再见
How are you?	nǐ hǎo ma?	你好吗？
Fine, thank you	hén hǎo, xièxiè nǐ	很好，谢谢 你
Welcome	huānyíng	欢迎

Introduction

English	Pinyin	Characters
My name is (first name)	wǒ jiào...	我叫.
My name is (last name)	wǒ xìng...	我姓.
Where are you from?	nǐ shì nǎlǐ rén?	是哪里人？
I am from (country/city)	wǒ shì (country/city) rén	我是 (country/city)人

Questions

English	Pinyin	Characters
How much?	duōshǎo?	多少？
Where?	nǎr?	哪儿？
When?	shénme shíhou?	什么时候？
How?	zěnme?	怎么？
What?	shénme	什么？
Why?	wèishénme?	为什么？
Who?	shéi?	谁？

Taxi or Car Related

English	Pinyin	Characters
Is this the road to (place)?	zhège lù dào bú dào... ?	这个路到 不到？
I'd like to go to (place)	wǒ yào qù	我要去
Stop	tíng chē	停车
Turn right	wǎng yòu guǎi	往右拐
Turn left	wǎng zuǒ guǎi	往左拐
Straight	yìzhí zǒu	一直走
Ahead	zài qiánmiàn	在前面
North	běi	北
South	nán	南
East	dōng	东
West	xī	西
Turning (street corner)	lùkǒu	路口
First	dì yīge	第一个
Second	dì èrge	第二个
Road	lù	路
Street	jiē	街
Avenue	dàdào	大街
Roundabout	huándào	环岛
Traffic light	hónglǜdēng	红绿灯
Near	jìn	近
Petrol station	jiāyóuzhàn	加油站
Airport	fēijīchǎng	飞机场
Hotel	jiǔdiàn or bīnguǎn	酒店 or 宾馆
Restaurant	fàndiàn or cānguǎn	饭店 or 餐馆
Please slow down	qǐng nǐ kāi màn yìdiǎnr	请你开慢 一点儿

Accidents & Emergencies

English	Pinyin	Characters
Police	jǐngchá	警察
Licence	zhízhào	执照
Accident	shìgù	事故
Papers	wénjiàn	文件
Insurance	bǎoxiǎn	保险
Sorry	duìbuqǐ	对不起
Hospital	yīyuàn	医院
Doctor	yīshēng	医生
Ambulance	jiùhùchē	救护车

Numbers

English	Pinyin	Characters
One	yī	一
Two	èr	二
Three	sān	三
Four	sì	四
Five	wǔ	五
Six	liù	六
Seven	qī	七
Eight	bā	八
Nine	jiǔ	九
Ten	shí	十
One hundred	yì bǎi	一百
One thousand	yì qiān	一千

Religion

Taoist, Buddhist and Confucian temples, places of worship for the three traditional beliefs in China, are dotted throughout the city, but no single religion dominates. Although genuinely faithful communities do exist, when asked about their belief in God, most young locals will answer with 'no, I believe in myself.' The roots of this attitude can be traced back to the Cultural Revolution of the 1960s and 70s, when religious activity was not encouraged, but the 1980s brought a new era of religious semi-tolerance with Deng Xiaoping's open-door policies. Practitioners are free to worship, as long as their places of worship are officially registered with the government's department for religious affairs and not deemed to be threatening the stability of society.

The Catholic community in particular has a growing presence in Shanghai and boasts several impressive churches. Split between the 'official', state-run church and the Vatican-aligned 'clandestine' church, the two forms of Catholicism in China are slowly shrinking the gap, with Pope Benedict XVI quietly agreeing to recognise some bishops ordained by the Chinese Catholic Patriotic Association. Christmas is actively celebrated in Shanghai but, for most locals, it is simply an excuse to hang up decorations and exchange presents.

The Jewish community has a complex and important history in Shanghai, with the Sephardic, Russian and European Jews migrating into the city in three separate waves during the early 1900s, 1920s, and 1940s and 50s respectively. The Sephardic Jews from Baghdad and Bombay were particularly significant in the development of Shanghai, forming powerful business empires that constructed many landmark buildings still seen today; they also housed subsequent Jewish immigrants fleeing persecution in Russia and Europe. The current Jewish population has dwindled to approximately 250 but remains close-knit, with dedicated schools and synagogues. Islam was first introduced into China in the sixth century AD, and current statistics suggest that there are nearly 20 million Chinese Muslims. This demographic is spread across 10 different ethnic minorities: most notably the Hui and Uighur, both of which practice diluted forms of Islam. The Turkic Uighurs, living primarily in Xinjiang province, have been greatly influenced by central Asia. The far more assimilated Hui, on the other hand, subscribe to what has been called 'Islam with Chinese Characteristics'. The Uighurs have not always found favour with the government, but recently there have been signs of a softer approach from the authorities: 2007 is China's Year of the Pig but the government has banned images of the animal being shown on television out of respect for Muslim communities.

Places of Worship		
Abundant Grace Church	Pudong	5899 0380
All Saints' Church	Luwan	6385 0906
Chenxiang Temple	Huangpu	6328 7884
Christ the King Catholic Church	Luwan	6217 8107
Dongjiadu Cathedral	Huangpu	6378 7214
Fuyou Lu Mosque	Huangpu	6328 2135
Holy Trinity Church	Huangpu	na
Hudong Church	Yangpu	6533 7102
Huxi Church	Xuhui	6259 7389
Huxi Mosque	Jing'an	6277 2076
Jade Buddha Temple (Buddhist)	Putuo	6266 7647
Jing'an Temple (Buddhist)	Jing'an	6256 6366
Jingxing Lu Mosque	Yangpu	6541 3199
Longhua Temple (Buddhist)	Xuhui	6456 6085
Mu'en Church	Huangpu	6322 5069
Ohel Rachel Synagogue	Jing'an	5771 4057
Peach Garden Mosque	Huangpu	6377 5442
Pudong Mosque	Pudong	5054 0416
Sacred Heart of Jesus Catholic Church	Pudong	5854 6621
Sanwei Temple (Buddhist)	Huangpu	6377 2722
Shanghai Buddhist Association	na	6266 5943
Shanghai Jewish Centre	Hongkou	6278 0225
Sheshan Cathedral	Songjiang	5765 1521
Songjiang Mosque	Songjiang	5771 4057
St Ignatius Cathedral	Xuhui	6438 2595
St Joseph's Church	Huangpu	6328 0293
Temple of the City God (Taoist)	Huangpu	6386 5700
Wenmiao Confucian Temple	Huangpu	6377 9101
White Cloud Temple (Taoist)	Huangpu	6387 6402
White Cloud Temple (Taoist)	Huangpu	6386 5800
Youag John Allen Memorial Church	Hongkou	6324 3021
Zhabei Catholic Church	Zhabei	5662 9409
Zhenru Temple (Buddhist)	Putuo	6254 6340

Jade Buddha Temple

Shanghai's Muslims are also currently enjoying a renewed sense of freedom as evidenced by the seven active mosques throughout the city and several popular Halal restaurants.

National Dress

The days of the 'Mao suit' (*Zhongshan* suit in Mandarin) are long gone in Shanghai. This simple, greyish military-style jacketed outfit with buttoned-down pockets was the national dress during China's revolution and was worn by both party leaders and the general population to show allegiance to a proletariat unity. Today, it is only rarely seen on members of the older generation, plus on some young overseas Chinese people who consider it a form of retro-chic. A similar situation exists with the *qipao* (or *cheung-sam* in Cantonese). Often regarded as the national dress for Chinese women, these brightly coloured silk brocade dresses with thigh-high splits were popularised by the infamously risque Shanghainese women of the 1920s. Now, however, they are more frequently seen on hotel staff, tourists or expat wives than on local girls.

If there is a rule of dress in 21st century Shanghai, it is simply to 'dress up'. Without a doubt, Shanghai is China's capital of fashion, with Armani, Gucci and Prada shops lining the streets, and high-octane catwalk shows frequently featured on the events calendar. Affordable, albeit illegal, copies of designer brands are readily available, contributing to the overall stylishness of the population. The young Shanghainese in particular are very image conscious, with clothes shopping having become a major pastime. Whether with heels or hemlines, the current motto for young Shanghainese women seems to be 'the higher the better'. For the middle-aged, middle-management man of Shanghai, there appears to be an unofficial uniform of short-sleeved shirt, fake Gucci belt with attached mobile phone, and obligatory under-the-arm washbag that acts as a briefcase.

Food & Drink

Other options **Eating Out** p.350

Doing Lunch
Long business dinners
are the norm for
corporate
entertainment, with
many a deal being
negotiated through a
fog of cigarette smoke
and baijiu fumes. To
'ganbei', literally
meaning to 'dry your
cup', is a form of toast-
making instigated by the
host or other important
guests, in which you are
expected to gulp down
the contents of your
glass in one go.

It is impossible to go hungry in Shanghai. The local culture of socialising over food mixed with a history of foreign influence and an ever-increasing expat population has led to an abundance of restaurants serving a vast array of Chinese and international cuisines at all price levels. Whether you need to entertain a client, romance a date, or simply go solo, there are Japanese sushi bars and German brauhauses, Indian buffets and Italian bistros – all waiting to cater to even the pickiest palate, most restricted wallet or most delicate situation.

Eating out in Shanghai is much cheaper than in other international cities such as London, Tokyo or Paris, but if you crave a home-cooked meal there are many different food-shopping options. If you've got the stomach for it, go to a local 'wet market' (see Shopping, p.344); these markets sell a mind-boggling range of live poultry, fish, mammals and reptiles at the most competitive prices around. Otherwise, Chinese supermarkets sell local ingredients at low prices. If you are homesick for overseas goods such as balsamic vinegar, olive oil, cheeses and wine, then there are large hypermarkets such as Carrefour or smaller supermarkets like City Shop, which sell imported foods at comparatively high prices.

Local Cuisine

Highly regarded Shanghai cuisine is part of the eastern Chinese school of cooking, which makes great use of the abundance of fresh vegetables, fish and seafood found in the lush farmlands and coastal regions south of the Yangtze River. It is less spicy than the chilli pepper-infused dishes of Sichuan in the west of China, more highly seasoned than the delicate Cantonese fare found in southern China, but not as salty as the sauce-rich dishes of Beijing and the rest of northern China. Shanghainese chefs use more sugar and oil than in other regional cuisines and often add locally brewed *shaoxing* rice wine or soy sauce, giving the food a distinctive sweet-and-sour flavour. 'Drunken shrimp' and 'twice-cooked chicken' are two typical local dishes. In the first, live shrimp are placed in a bowl on your table and doused in rice wine until so drunk they passively allow themselves to be eaten. The second is an example of the 'red-cooking' (*hong shao*) method, which first slow boils a whole chicken in sweet soy sauce and then deep fries it to a crispy perfection.

Just like having afternoon tea in London, or smoking shisha in the Middle East, eating street snacks in Shanghai has become an intrinsic part of the city's food culture. Little crab or meat soup-filled dumplings (*xiaolongbao*), skewered shrimp balls (*xiaqiu*) and fried stinky tofu (*choudoufu*) are just a few examples of the large range of cheap snacks sold from street carts all over the city. Alongside these everyday staples, special treats are sold during traditional Chinese occasions such as the Spring Festival, when New Year glutinous rice cakes are particularly popular.

No food is taboo in Shanghai. China's history of famine has led to anything that moves being fair game for consumption, with food markets being filled with live frogs, chicken feet, skewered locusts and spicy duck neck. Dairy products, once considered to be a peculiar taste of foreigners, have become hugely popular among the local Shanghainese population and icecream parlours are springing up across the city.

Drink

Alcohol is liberally consumed in Shanghai. Chinese red wines such as Great Wall and Grace Vineyard, which, until very recently, were completely unpalatable, have improved radically, and at prices as low as ¥30 per bottle are good value alternatives to pricier imported wines. Chinese beers such as Tsingtao and Harbin are sold for as little as ¥4 per 700ml bottle, and the Xinjiang (north-west China) brewed black beer sold in the expat-popular Uighur restaurants is a worthy contender to overpriced, imported Irish stout. For something a little stronger, try *baijiu*.

Literally 'white liquor,' this grain-based spirit, brewed to slightly different recipes throughout China, often reaches 50% (v/v) alcohol and is potent enough to alter both your taste buds and your perception of the world for some time to come. A gentler liquid refreshment is 'pearl milk tea' (*zhenzhu naicha*), a sweet, milky, black tea filled with chewy sago balls and sold either warm or cold in plastic cups from small kiosks everywhere.

For something a little purer, try some of China's health-promoting green tea (*lucha*). Consumed faithfully by the Chinese, who believe that it staves off cancers and prevents premature ageing, green tea comes in different forms from different regions and can be bought from numerous local stores or large tea markets, such as those in Caobao Lu and Datong Lu. And if your clothes are feeling a little tight, drink some oolong tea, which is believed to have metabolism-boosting and fat-burning properties. Sweet-smelling teas such as jasmine (*molihuacha*) and cholesterol-lowering pu'er tea are also popular.

Face Facts
When invited to a meal, never insist on paying your share of the bill as this would imply the host cannot afford it and result in a loss of 'face'. The face games don't end there; China has an intricate system of subtle-but-important social codes that can potentially cause irreparable damage. Other examples: don't publicly yell at someone and never imply that a colleague can't perform his or her job.

Chopsticks

Chopsticks remain the eating tool of choice in Shanghai's Chinese restaurants, although most mid to high-end eateries will provide a knife and fork on request. Table manners are generally not strict and, particularly in the cheaper establishments, slurping, burping and spitting out bones on the table is common. There are, however, some important rules of social etiquette, especially regarding seating arrangements (VIP guests always sit to the right of the host) and payment (never offer to pay your share of the bill – see Face Facts box).

In Emergency

It is possible you may find yourself in an emergency situation during your stay in Shanghai and so with this in mind, it is advisable to register at your country's consulate as soon as you settle in the city. Informing it of your existence is important in the event of any major disturbances or health threats, such as the 2003 Sars outbreak, as the embassy will keep you updated of the genuine situation as it develops and might organise any necessary evacuations. If you are a new resident, make sure to register with your local Public Security Bureau (see table), for should you become involved in a police situation and they discover that you have not done so, you could face hefty fines as well as uncooperative behaviour. You should register in person, taking along a copy of your passport and the address of where you are living so that you can be issued with a pink temporary residents' certificate (see p.62). Hotels automatically process the registration for visitors.

For emergency police assistance, call 110. English-speaking operators are available. For non-urgent matters go to your local police station but be prepared for lengthy questioning as Shanghai police can be suspicious of foreigners.

Emergency Numbers	
Emergency Services	
Ambulance	120
Fire	119
Police (emergency)	110
Police (traffic)	5631 7000
Public Security Bureau Division for Foreigners	6357 6666
International SOS (24 hour service)	6295 0099
Shanghai Call Centre (information hotline in English)	962288
Shanghai Directory Enquiries	114
Utilities	
Electricity Hotline	95598
Gas Hotline	962777
Water Hotline	962626
Medical Services	
Shanghai East International Medical Centre (24 hour care)	5879 9999
Shanghai Huadong Hospital	6248 3180
Shanghai Huashan Worldwide Medical Centre	6248 3986
Shanghai Wu Yao 24 hour pharmacy	6294 1403
World Link International Medical Centre	6445 5999

For ambulance service, call 120 but be aware that it is generally not particularly quick or reliable, and that it is preferable to make your own way to the hospital by taxi or private car. If you need emergency medical assistance you can either visit a local hospital with a dedicated foreigners' clinic, such as Huadong, or you can go to one of the western medical clinics such as Word Link or International SOS which have 24 hour emergency services and western or western-trained staff. These international clinics offer high levels of service but come at a price, so bring along your credit card. Few places allow direct billing to the insurance company so make sure to keep your receipts safe (see Health, p.128, for further options).

Lost or Stolen Property

If you find yourself a victim of theft then you must report the crime at the local Public Security Bureau (PSB) within 24 hours, and be sure to get a police report for future insurance claims. If the incident occurred in a hotel, then first inform the hotel security, or if it happened on the Metro then go to the PSB office at People's Square Metro station. For Pudong International Airport lost property, call 6834 6324; for Honqiao Airport, call 6268 8899. Try to keep your taxi receipts – if you leave something behind you can call the phone number on the receipt and quote the driver number in the hope that he may still have it. For lost passports, consult your country's consulate and register the loss at the large PSB office (1500 Minsheng Lu, Pudong; 2895 1900). If possible, take along a copy of your passport to ease the administration process.

Police

The relatively well-trained Shanghai police come in different forms. Everyday officers wear light and dark blue uniforms and navy blue peaked caps and man the local police stations or patrol the streets in white Volkswagens. Traffic police wear similar uniforms with white metal helmets, ride motorbikes, and bravely try to instil some sort of order on Shanghai's chaotic streets. Detectives usually don black suits and turn up at crime scenes or interrogation rooms. Except for detectives, the police rarely carry guns, making do with handcuffs, batons and pepper-spray. Very few police in Shanghai speak English, which sometimes translates to gruff and aggressive behaviour with foreigners. It's impossible not to notice the marshals at pedestrian crossings. Although not technically policemen, they batter the eardrums of anyone trying to cross the street on a red light. Whistling is not the only punishment on hand; if caught, jaywalkers can be issued on-the-spot fines of up to ¥50.

Hock, Spit, Jump
One thing that's not strictly illegal is the very Chinese habit of spitting – although authorities have been encouraging citizens to be discreet with the green stuff in recent times. Taxi drivers especially seem to have turned the custom into an Olympic sport, but well-to-do middle-aged women and restaurant diners have also been known to have extraordinary aim.

Crime & Safety

In general, Shanghai is a safe city with a relatively low crime rate, although petty crime is on the rise. Often working in groups of two or three, pick-pocketers focus on crowded tourist hotspots, markets, and other expat-popular areas such as Hengshan Lu and Huaihai Lu. Scams are also becoming increasingly common so watch out for attractive strangers with promises of great drink deals at 'authentic' bars or nightclubs; those promises usually result in inflated bills and demanding managers. Scams rarely get violent and, provided you remain streetwise, you are probably safer in Shanghai than in most other big, international cities.

As for the public transport system, crime is rarely a problem compared with the threat of traffic accidents. Every six months sees about a quarter of a million traffic accidents on China's roads, resulting in around 45,000 deaths. Luckily Shanghai's taxi drivers are improving thanks to recently passed laws banning them from smoking or speaking on the phone while driving. Nevertheless, always wear your seatbelt when riding in the front of the car. If a taxi driver has acted incorrectly in any way, call the taxi complaint hotline (6323 2150) and quote the driver ID, the six-digit number second from the top on the taxi receipt.

Traffic Accidents & Violations

If you are involved in an accident where you are the driver, there are certain rules to follow. Firstly, do not move your vehicle until the traffic police show up, which often takes 30 minutes and accounts for the long jams regularly afflicting Shanghai's roads. Secondly, if either party has suffered any injuries then all persons involved should visit the hospital together. And most importantly, do not sign any documents unless you have had them fully translated or can read Chinese.

Despite being seemingly non-existent, traffic laws in Shanghai can result in huge fines if not obeyed. Speeding infractions come in two forms. Moving at speeds up to 50% over the speed limit earns a ¥200 fine, while moving at any speed above that same mark could incur fines of up to ¥2,000. Tickets are sent through the mail, and foreigners must pay the fines in person at one of the hard-to-reach offices listed on the penalty notice. Shanghai uses a points system, and a speeding ticket will cost you three points. Licences are revoked after drivers accumulate 12 points (see Certificates & Licences, p.66).

Driving under the influence of alcohol is illegal in Shanghai, with the legal limit being 20mg of alcohol per 100ml of blood. Drivers caught with blood-alcohol levels higher than that are fined between ¥200 and ¥500 and lose their licence for one to two months. Drivers caught with a blood-alcohol level higher than 80mg per 100ml may be treated as a drunk, fined up to ¥2,000, have their licence suspended for up to six months and be held in prison for up to 15 days. Serious accidents caused by traffic violations can lead to criminal investigations and detention.

Mini Explorer

Don't be fooled by the size of this little star – it's full of insider info, maps, contacts, tips and facts about Hong Kong. From shops to spas, bars to bargains and everything in between, the Mini Explorer helps you get the most out of your stay in the city, however long you're staying.

Getting Arrested in Shanghai

Any foreigner arrested in Shanghai will immediately be taken to their local or district Public Security Bureau. There they will be questioned, probably fined, possibly detained or even deported. According to Chinese law, a person may be detained for up to 15 days without charge and police are legally allowed to hold a foreigner for up to four days without having to contact their consulate or allowing them to make a phone call. During this time, the other party involved in the dispute will often demand large amounts of money from the foreigner in return for them dropping the charges. If no agreement is made, the case may go to trial, and detained foreigners sometimes have to wait up to a year for the trial to begin. What's more, foreigners are not allocated a state lawyer and are rarely granted bail. Any foreigner who finds himself in this situation should contact their consulate in Shanghai as soon as possible to receive information on their rights.

Victims of Crime

If you find yourself a victim of petty crime in Shanghai you should first contact your local Public Security Bureau (see table, p.26). Sometimes you will find that reporting a small crime is more trouble than it is worth – bike thefts, for example, happen so often and so quickly that by the time a report is made the bike may have already been sold.

Embassies & Consulates

Argentina	6278 0300	Mexico	6437 3451
Australia	5292 5500	Netherlands	6209 9076
Austria	6474 0278	New Zealand	5407 5858
Belgium	6437 6579	Norway	6323 9988
Brazil	6437 0110	Peru	5298 5900
Canada	6279 8400	Philippines	6279 8337
Chile	6236 0770	Poland	6433 9288
Cuba	6275 3078	Portugal	6288 6767
Czech Republic	6471 2420	Russia	6324 2682
Denmark	6209 0500	Singapore	6278 5566
Egypt	6433 1020	South Africa	5359 4977
Finland	5292 9900	South Korea	6219 6417
France	6103 2200	Spain	6321 3542
Germany	6217 1520	Sweden	6391 6767
India	6275 8882	Switzerland	6270 0519
Iran	6433 2997	Thailand	6323 4095
Ireland	6279 8729	Turkey	6474 6838
Israel	6209 8008	Ukraine	6433 1108
Italy	5407 5588	United Arab Emirates	10 6532 7650
Japan	6278 0788	United Kingdom	6279 7650
Korea	6295 5000	United States	6433 6880
Malaysia	5292 5424		

For more serious crimes it is best to first call your local consulate in Shanghai. It may not be able to intervene directly on your behalf but can at least advise you on your rights and of any available legal counsel you may require. For crimes involving the theft of your credit card make sure you have the number of your card issuer or bank stored separately and call it immediately.

Women

Compared with many of the world's large cities, Shanghai is very safe for women. It is not uncommon to see women walking or taking public transport alone at night. Local men often stare at women but rarely do anything worse, and women shouldn't feel the need to dress modestly to ensure their safety. That's not to say women shouldn't be vigilant. There have been claims that the use of date-rape drugs is on the rise, especially in Shanghai's high-end bars. More recently, several women have reported being attacked by groups of female beggars while withdrawing money from ATMs late at night. If you feel that you have been seriously threatened, immediately contact the police by dialling 110 and consider writing to the editor of a local expat magazine or website, who may publish your story as a helpful warning to others (see p.50).

Little Emperors
Expect to see a good number of over-fed and over-spoilt children running around. China's one-child policy, and the need for both parents to work, often results in the 'little emperors' receiving all the constant love and attention of not only their parents but also of two sets of grandparents.

Travelling with Children

Shanghai, for the most part, is pretty kid-friendly. Hongqiao's Hongmei Lu pedestrian street holds Moon River Diner (p.356) and Blue Frog (p.388), which both have inside and outside play areas and extensive kids' menus. Mesa (p.370) in the French Concession offers a great family Sunday brunch, complete with highchairs, kids' corner and on-hand nannies. Shanghai also has plenty of attractions aimed at children. Hongqiao's Shanghai Zoo (p.220), Pudong's Natural Wild Insect Kingdom (p.220), and Ocean Aquarium (p.218) are fantastic for animal lovers. Other options

People's Square

include the Science & Technology Museum in Pudong (p.202), the Jinjiang Amusement Park in Hongqiao (p.217), and Dino Beach water park (p.219) in Minhang. To give parents a much-needed break, there are plenty of children's activity groups and classes available, ranging from drama and art to sports clubs (see Activities, p.236). *City Weekend* and *that's Shanghai* list details on parent groups such as Bumps and Babes (6247 2880), which offers support to new and expecting mothers. Established babysitting services are hard to come by in Shanghai, mainly because most expat families hire a maid or *ayi* (see p.117) who looks after their children while cooking and cleaning.

Gay & Lesbian

Shanghai's gay community is the proverbial pink elephant: glaringly present but rarely openly acknowledged. The alternative sexuality movement is built on turbulent foundations. When Mao came to power in 1949, he famously declared that homosexuality contributed to the 'moldering [sic] lifestyle of capitalism'. The Communist regime clamped down on the gay community. Long gone were the days when homosexual British writer WH Auden raved about the excess and debauchery of

1930s Shanghai; instead, same-sex relations, where they did exist, moved underground. The chains started to loosen around the turn of the 21st century, first with the decriminalisation of sodomy in 1997 and then with the removal of homosexuality from the Chinese Classification and Diagnostic Criteria of Mental Disorders in 2001. Nevertheless, homosexuality is still not flaunted. With old values persisting, recent statistics suggest that as many as 90% of China's LGBTs (lesbian, gay, bisexual and transgender) enter heterosexual matrimony.

Homosexuality in both principle and practice remains a sensitive topic. LGBTs might feel uncomfortable being pink in public, while their avenues for private expression are subject to police attention and subsequent closure. In reality, same-sex relations might be coming out of the Chinese closet, but the steps taken are slow and cautious.

There are several useful resources that offer up-to-date information on Shanghai's growing gay community. The Chiheng Foundation provides a lesbian hotline to which calls can be made between 14:00 and 16:00 (800 988 929 or 6380 4448). For more information on China's gay scene, try www.utopia-asia.com/chinshan.htm, or www.gaychina.com.

People with Disabilities

Disabled Access

The Shanghai Museum, Shanghai Urban Planning Exhibition Centre and Shanghai Library all have facilities for disabled people. The modern shopping mall in Xintiandi is fitted with lifts, as are some of the Metro stations on Line 2, including Central Henan Lu, Jing'an Temple and Zhongshan Park, but no guarantee can be made of their working order.

The fact that you rarely see any of the city's half a million disabled people in public is a telling sign that Shanghai is not particularly accommodating. Most Metro stations don't provide lifts, disabled public toilets hardly exist, very few roads have ramp access, only one bus route offers barrier-free facilities (926) and, reportedly, only one taxi in the entire city can remove its seats to make room for a wheelchair. Despite regulations requiring newly constructed buildings to provide adequate facilities, most neglect to do so, claiming that the infrequency of their usage makes them redundant or at least not worthy of good maintenance. Only in the airports and high-end hotels are you sure to find functioning disabled toilets, for example.

The problem lies in many Chinese people's self-confessed attitude towards disabled people, who have traditionally been seen as a burden on society. Shanghai's hosting of the Special Olympics in October 2007 should go some way towards changing this. The Shanghai Disabled Persons' Federation, in conjunction with the Shanghai Urban Transport Management Bureau, has pledged to provide at least 90 taxis and 30 more buses with wheelchair access, and has already added more than 1,000km of special lanes for the blind (*mang dao*) to the city's pavements. Many of the downtown parks have special Braille maps by their entrances, and in April 2007 local authorities announced plans to train guide dogs for the blind. Shanghai law, however, prohibits any dogs from entering public buildings or public transport.

Dress

In terms of fashion, Shanghai is a modern, open-minded city, so visitors should feel free to dress as they do in their home country. Do keep in mind, however, that westerners already stand out from the crowd, so unless you are looking for extra attention it may be better to avoid anything too racy or provocative.

Shanghai is a typically temperate seasonal location. Winters can be very cold and wet, so hats, scarves, a waterproof coat and even rubber boots are useful attire, while summer brings with it stifling heat and drenching humidity, so light, loose clothes and a thin raincoat are essential. If you're out and about in the mild Shanghai spring or autumn, summer clothes with an additional pullover or jacket are adequate. The streets are dirty and often wet, so choose closed-toe sandals over flip-flops. Many cinemas, restaurants and offices crank up the air conditioning during the summer months, so bring an extra layer of clothing just in case.

Dos & Don'ts

In a country where 70% of adult males smoke 30% of the world's cigarettes it is hardly surprising that smoking is allowed in most of Shanghai's bars, restaurants and other public places. Chinese drinking laws are pretty relaxed, but remember that being found drunk and disorderly on the streets could mean a few days in a prison cell. Registering with the local Public Security Bureau is a must as failing to do so will incur large fines when the time comes to extend your visa (see p.63). Don't talk openly about major controversial political issues, or you'll be faced

China Tourism Offices Overseas		
Australia	Sydney	+61 2 9299 4057
France	Paris	+33 1 5659 1010
Germany	Frankfurt	+49 69 520135
Singapore	Singapore	+65 3372220
UK	London	+44 20 7935 9787
USA	New York	+1 888 760 8218

with hushed silences and suspicious stares (Googling these same issues repeatedly will result in your server being shut down). For drivers, try to refrain from incessant horn honking, which could land you a ¥200 fine (see p.163). Don't be offended when smartly dressed men and women spit on the ground in front of you, it's a common practice in China. When invited to dinner, never offer to pay your share of the bill or your host will lose 'face.' And finally, remember to give and receive business cards with two hands as a sign of respect – cards are seen as an extension of the owner so bending or dropping them is a big no-no.

Holiday Hullabaloo

Visitors to China might want to avoid travelling in the first week of October, when the country celebrates National Day. During the 2006 holiday, more than four million people visited Shanghai while its 86 major scenic attractions were enjoyed by 2.2 million people, up 30% from the same period in 2005. Beijing recorded 5.2 million visitors just to Tiananmen Square that week.

Tourist Information

Shanghai has a handful of tourist information offices located around the city. The ones situated inside Hongqiao Airport (6268 8918; www.shairport.com) and Pudong International Airport (9608 1388; www.shairport.com) are useful if you are flying into the city, and the main Shanghai Tourist Information Service Centre, located at 303 Moling Lu near the south exit of Shanghai Railway Station, is good if you are arriving by train.

Apart from the English-speaking Tourist Information hotline on 6252 0000, these will be your best bets for finding staff who can speak English. The Luwan district office is particularly good at catering for foreigners and has its own English language website at www.luwan.sh.cn, which features a good selection of maps and free informative guides.

Most of these information centres can easily be mistaken for domestic travel

Tourist Information	
Information & Service Centres	
Jing'an District	6248 3259
Luwan District	5386 1882
North Huangpu	5353 1117
Pudong New Area	3878 0202
Putuo District	5606 2120
Shanghai	5123 4490
International Services	
Shanghai Information Centre for International Visitors	6384 9366

agencies as they tend to specialise in trying to sell you hotel or travel deals, but they can be useful for finding free maps and up-to-date contact details. For residents wanting to discover what is really happening in and around the city, the best bet is to pick up a copy of one of the free expat magazines found in any western bar or restaurant.

For help before you come to China, the China National Tourist Office has locations around the world; three good websites are for the US (www.cnto.org), UK (www.cnto.org.uk) and Australia (www.cnto.org.au) offices. Also check out www.china-enews.com for news on China's tourism industry.

31

Places to Stay

Shanghai has a vast variety of temporary accommodation options, ranging from opulent five-star hotels to cheap-but-not-so cheerful hostels, many of which have opened since China's economy went into overdrive at the beginning of the 21st century. All the major global brands are here: hotels such as the Park Hyatt, Westin and St Regis are hungrily trying to entice a 20 million strong population and a tourist industry that is booming in the run up to the World Expo 2010. The sky's the limit on prices, with premier suites in top hotels such as the Westin costing up to ¥70,000 per night. The mid-range category, which was once sorely under-represented, now has a growing number of interesting options, particularly in the form of guesthouses and bed and breakfasts. Budget travellers are also becoming better catered for, with motel chains such as Motel 168 providing clean, affordable places to stay. Traditionally focused on the business traveller, Shanghai's accommodation options have recently begun to evolve in a more creative manner, with a rising number of boutique hotels opening around the city, each promising to bring a little bit of style into your life (for a not-so-little cost, of course).

Hotels

Other options **Main Hotels** p.34, **Weekend Break Hotels** p.230

The hotel industry in Shanghai is big business. New establishments, on top of those 500 or so already in existence, are opening almost every day, and big brands such as Park Hyatt are planning their second or even third incarnation. Most still seem to be catering to the business traveller, and therefore fall squarely into the four and five-star categories, both in terms of service and price. These sumptuous hotels generally offer spacious rooms, broadband internet access, indoor pools, 24 hour concierge

Jinmao Tower

services, and club lounges with complimentary drinks (for those willing to pay an extra ¥300 or so for the privilege). They tend to be centred in either Pudong, convenient for business visitors working in Shanghai's financial district around Lujiazui; near the Bund, good for exploring the Old City and People's Square; and the French Concession, great for bon vivants, with its wealth of superb restaurants, bars and clubs. The French Concession also houses some of the more historic, yet still pricey, options such as the Okura Garden Hotel or 88 Xintiandi, the latter being one of a growing number of boutique hotels in the city.

With the established and well-known high-end hotels you can generally trust their four or five-star ratings as being compliant with international standards. There is however another classification system offered by the government's own 'Office of Assessment Commission for Star-leveled Foreign Hotel in Tourism under the Shanghai Tourism Administrative Committee' [sic], which does not always correspond completely with western expectations. This makes it advisable to check out independent websites such as www.tripadvisor.com or www.expedia.com for their own ratings systems. Price is one of the easier ways to categorise

Shanghai's temporary accommodation options. Four and five-star standard hotels range from about ¥1,600 for a double room to more than ¥50,000 for a suite. This is fine on a corporate allowance, but for those without the gold Amex, the lack of decent, western-standard three-star hotels can be frustrating. For this price range (approximately ¥500-¥1,500 per night), you can, however, often find good deals at some of the more historic hotels such as the Ruijin Guesthouse, Hengshan Moller Villa or the Anting Villa Hotel, which make up for their lack of modern facilities with buckets of old-world charm.

Budget Accommodation

Shanghai is full of cheap, older-style, Chinese-run hotels but unless you don't mind only having hot water for four hours a day, a rock-solid mattress and a smell reminiscent of the smokers' room in an airport, then you'd be better off with the few modern options for under ¥500 per night that come with a recommendation. Try the reliable Motel 168 and Jinjiang Inn chains all across the city, and the newly opened Celebrity Service Apartments. There are also some good value hostels including the Captain Hostel, housed in a 1920s block near the Bund and offering dorm beds for ¥60 per night, and the Le Tour Hostel, in Putuo district, which offers cosy private rooms at only ¥75 per person.

Hotels

88 Xintiandi	5383 8833	www.88xintiandi.com
Anting Villa Hotel	6433 1188	www.sinohotel.com
Astor House Hotel	6324 6388	www.pujianghotel.com
Captain Youth Hostel	6328 5053	www.captainhostel.com.cn
Celebrity Service Apartments	5407 8088	www.sinohotel.com
Crowne Plaza Hotel Fudan	5552 9999	www.ichotelsgroup.com
Donghu Hotel	6415 8158	www.donghuhotel.com
Four Seasons	6256 8888	www.fourseasons.com
Grand Hyatt, Pudong	5049 1111	www.shanghai.hyatt.com
Hengshan Moller Villa	6247 8881	www.mollervilla.com
Hilton Hotel	6248 0000	www.hilton.com
Howard Johnson Plaza	3313 4888	www.hojoshanghai.com
JIA Shanghai	na	www.jiahongkong.com
Jianguo Hotel	6439 9299	www.jianguo.com
Jinjiang Inn	6326 0505	www.jj-inn.com
JW Marriott	5359 4969	www.marriotthotels.com
Le Royal Meridien	3318 9999	www.starwoodhotels.com
Le Tour Hostel	5251 0800	www.letourshanghai.com
M Suites	5155 8399	www.msuites.com.cn
Manpo Boutique Hotel	6280 1000	www.manpo.cn
Mansion House Hotel	5403 9888	www.chinamansionhotel.com
Metropole Hotel	6321 3030	www.metropolehotel-sh.com
Okura Garden Hotel	6415 1111	www.gardenhotelshanghai.com
Peace Hotel	6321 6888	www.shanghaipeacehotel.com
Portman Ritz-Carlton	6279 8888	www.ritzcarlton.com
Pudong Shangri-La	6882 8888	www.shangri-la.com
Radisson Hotel Shanghai New World	6359 9999	www.radisson.com
Renaissance Shanghai Pudong	3871 4888	www.marriott.com
Renaissance Yangtze Shanghai	6275 0000	www.renaissancehotels.com
Ruijin Guest House	6472 5222	www.shedi.net.cn/outedi/ruijin/
St Regis Shanghai	5050 4567	www.stregis.com
Westin Hotel	6335 1888	www.westin.com

Main Hotels

Crowne Plaza Shanghai 上海银星皇冠酒店

400 Panyu Lu
Xuhui
番禺路400号
徐汇
Ⓜ Xujiahui
Map p.435 D3 **1**

6280 8888 | www.shanghai.crowneplaza.com

The 506 guestrooms and suites of this 26 storey hotel were renovated in 2005, and are comfortable rather than breathtaking. There are several restaurants offering a range of Italian, Japanese and Chinese cuisines, and if you fancy a dance or a pint over a football match, then you can head up to level one where Charlie's Bar has a live band and a big screen for sports events. There are also extensive sports facilities, including an indoor heated pool.

Donghu Hotel 东湖宾馆

70 Donghu Lu,
French Concession
Luwan
东湖路70号,
法租界
卢湾
Ⓜ Shanxi Nan Lu
Map p.436 A1 **2**

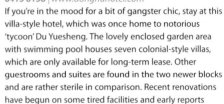

6415 8158 | www.donghuhotel.com

If you're in the mood for a bit of gangster chic, stay at this villa-style hotel, which was once home to notorious 'tycoon' Du Yuesheng. The lovely enclosed garden area with swimming pool houses seven colonial-style villas, which are only available for long-term lease. Other guestrooms and suites are found in the two newer blocks and are rather sterile in comparison. Recent renovations have begun on some tired facilities and early reports suggest a big improvement. The location just off bustling Huaihai Lu is great for exploring the charming back streets of the former French Concession.

Grand Hyatt Shanghai 上海金茂君悦大酒店

88 Shiji Dadao
Pudong
世纪大道88号
浦东
Ⓜ Lujiazui
Map p.432 A3 **3**

5049 1111 | www.shanghai.hyatt.com

Looking up in the atrium of the Grand Hyatt is like staring along an endless vertical tunnel. At 33 dizzying storeys, it forms part of the world's highest hotel, and occupies the 53rd to the 87th floors of the Jinmao Tower. The views from the floor-to-ceiling windows in all 555 guestrooms are breathtaking, and the rooms themselves are huge, finely decorated in Chinese art deco-style and full of addictive gadgets such as sensor-controlled lights and TV internet access. Book early, as this place has an exceptionally high occupancy rate.

Hilton Hotel 上海希尔顿酒店

250 Huashan Lu
Jing'an
华山路250号
静安
Ⓜ Jing'an Temple
Map p.435 E1 **4**

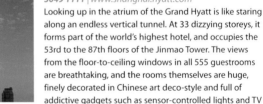

6248 0000 | www.hilton.com

The benefits of this hotel are a good central location, decently sized rooms and very friendly staff who seem like they have worked here for years. They probably have as nothing seems to have changed much since this hotel opened back in the 1990s. Bathrooms are rather small and the old-fashioned TVs simply cannot compete with the 42 inch plasmas now dominating the rooms of other upmarket hotels – this is perhaps one of the few members of the Hilton clan that hasn't had a facelift.

595 Jiujiang Lu
Huangpu
九江路595号
黄埔
People's Square
Map p.431 D3 **5**

Howard Johnson Plaza 古象大酒店

3313 4888 | *www.hojoshanghai.com*

This modern hotel has a fantastic location near People's Square and is only a 10 minute stroll to the Bund. Attractive facilities include a Balinese spa and glass-roofed swimming pool. Foodies will be kept entertained with six bars and restaurants covering a range of cuisines from Mediterranean to Chinese and modern American. Rooms are comfortable and clean, and while it may not be one of the glamourous options it's an excellent value top-end hotel for both business travellers and casual visitors.

Tomorrow Square, 399 Nanjing Xi Lu
Huangpu
明天广场,
南京西路399号
黄埔
People's Square
Map p.430 C3 **6**

JW Marriott 金威万豪酒店

5359 4969 | *www.marriotthotels.com/shajw*

You never need worry about losing your way back to this hotel. Soaring upwards from the Puxi skyline like a heaven-bound arrow, the JW Marriott occupies the top 22 floors of the landmark 60 storey Tomorrow Square building. Right in the centre of downtown Shanghai, you are as close to the bars on the Bund as you are to the museums in People's Square. All 342 guestrooms are fitted out to luxurious five-star standards, with marbled bathrooms, hydraulic massage showers and high-speed internet access. Sipping afternoon tea and admiring the view from the sky-high lobby on the 38th floor is a must.

789 Nanjing Dong Lu
Huangpu
南京东路789号
黄埔
People's Square
Map p.430 C3 **7**

Le Royal Meridien 上海世茂皇家艾美酒店

3318 9999 | *www.starwoodhotels.com*

With wall-to-wall, floor-to-ceiling windows and a glass-partitioned bedroom and bathroom, it's a good thing this hotel rises as high as 66 storeys. This iconic building, which looks like a Transformer complete with flashing antennas, stands by lively Nanjing Lu, just a couple of blocks from the Bund. There are 761 guestrooms and suites decked out with numerous gadgets, 10 restaurants and bars, and a well-equipped gym and indoor pool. Le Meridien is a good choice for business and private travellers and often ranks highly in customer surveys.

Pier One, 88 Yichang Lu
Putuo
1号码头,宜昌路88号
普陀
Zhongtan Lu
Map p.429 E1 **8**

M Suites 一号码头精品酒店

5155 8399 | *www.msuites.com.cn*

Forming part of the new and showy nightclub/restaurant/hotel complex known as Pier One, near Shanghai's Suzhou Creek, this 24 room boutique hotel is a little way out from downtown Shanghai. Nevertheless, for anyone interested in exploring the main art area of Moganshan Lu, it is perfect at just a stone's throw away. Rooms are modern in design, some with round beds and flat-screen TVs, and have the added bonus of being in the same converted Union Brewery complex as the Mimosa Supperclub restaurant (p.370) and Monsoon rooftop bar (5155 8318).

35

Okura Garden Hotel 花园饭店

58 Maoming Nan Lu,
French Concession
Luwan
茂名南路58号,
法租界
卢湾
🚇 *Shanxi Nan Lu*
Map p.436 A1 🟦

6415 1111 | www.gardenhotelshanghai.com

The beautiful seven-acre garden, surrounding what was once the French Club in the 1920s, makes this hotel feel like an oasis in the middle of the French Concession. The magic continues in the baroque-style main building, which houses two sweeping staircases and an opulent ballroom, all favoured haunts of Chairman Mao in 1959. The modern, concrete block which houses the 492 guestrooms and suites is less attractive from the outside. The rooms themselves are comfortable (bar the hard beds) with all the attention to detail (kimono robes, heated loo seats) you would expect from a Japanese chain.

Portman Ritz-Carlton 波特曼丽嘉大酒店

1376 Nanjing Xi Lu
Jing'an
南京西路1376号
卢湾
🚇 *Jing'an Temple*
Map p.429 F4 🔟

6279 8888 | www.ritzcarlton.com

Having opened back in 1998, the Portman Ritz-Carlton (part of the Shanghai Centre) is now in the older generation of the city's big brand hotels. It remains, however, one of the best. In addition to the 598 elegant rooms decorated with Italian marble and expensive woods, there are further features including a good gym and spa and a classy Italian restaurant, Palladio. The waterfall-filled front courtyard houses a fantastic City Shop filled with imported goods, a tasty Element Fresh cafe (p.381), an HSBC bank, a Toni & Guy hair salon and a World Link Medical Centre.

Pudong Shangri-La 浦东香格里拉酒店

33 Fucheng Lu
Pudong
富城路33号
浦东
🚇 *Lujiazui*
Map p.431 F3 🔢

6882 8888 | www.shangri-la.com

With 1,000 rooms, the two-winged Shangri-La in Pudong is one of Shanghai's largest hotels. The second tower, which opened in 2005 at an estimated cost of $138 million, is a striking architectural feat in all glass, and has some of the most generous rooms in Shanghai. All are elegantly decorated and many have stunning views of the Bund. The hotel's Chi, The Spa (p.292) offers a soothing massage with healing stones, and its Jade on 36 (p.391) restaurant and bar is not to be missed. The hotel also has the two largest ballrooms in the city.

Radisson Hotel Shanghai New World 上海新世界丽笙大酒店

88 Nanjing Xi Lu
Huangpu
南京西路88号
黄埔
🚇 *People's Square*
Map p.430 C3 🔢

6359 9999 | www.radisson.com/shanghaicn_newworld

With enough gilding to make a Russian tsar feel at home, this over-the-top hotel nevertheless has 520 comfortable guest rooms with free broadband internet access, a great indoor pool, a revolving restaurant (Epicure on 45) on the 45th floor and a superbly central location above exit seven of People's Square Metro station. Its prices are generally lower than other five-star hotels in the city, making it an all-round good choice.

100 Changliu Lu
Pudong
长柳路100号
浦东
🚇 **Shanghai Science & Technology Museum**
Map p.440 A2 13

Renaissance Shanghai Pudong 淳大万丽大酒店

3871 4888 | www.marriott.com

A cut above the Renaissance Yangtze on the other side of town, this hotel on the edge of Shanghai's financial district is stylish and popular. Its location is good for those requiring peace and quiet but may be a bit far from the Bund or French Concession if you intend to indulge in a lot of shopping, eating or partying. Bonuses include an impressive lobby, great gym, spacious rooms and helpful staff.

118 Ruijin Er Lu, French Concession
Luwan
瑞金二路118号,
法租界
卢湾
🚇 **Shanxi Nan Lu**
Map p.436 B1 14

Ruijin Guest House 瑞金宾馆

6472 5222 | www.shedi.net.cn/OUTEDI/Ruijin/

Ex-presidents including Richard Nixon and Communist VIPs such as Zhou Enlai have all stayed in this historic guesthouse that was once the Morriss Estate, home of a 1920s media magnate. Set in beautiful parkland, and home to the fantastic Face Bar (p.390), the hotel is made up of five villas. The best rooms can be found in Building no.2, which was the original family home. The lack of modern gadgets is made up for by its abundance of historical charm and peaceful gardens in the middle of the leafy French Concession.

889 Dongfang Lu
Pudong
东方路889号
浦东
🚇 **Dongchang Lu**
Map p.433 D4 15

St Regis Shanghai 瑞吉红塔大酒店

5050 4567 | www.stregis.com/shanghai

If only you could pick up this hotel and plonk it in downtown Shanghai, then it could seriously be in the running for the city's best. St Regis butlers ensure impeccable service; the executive lounge offers free nibbles and is open to all guests; the beds are to die for, as are the large marble bathrooms; and, to cap it all off, there is a huge indoor pool. Its location in Pudong is not convenient for the sights and eateries of central Shanghai but may be a good option for stopover or business travellers arriving at Pudong Airport.

Bund Centre, 88 Henan Zhong Lu
Huangpu
外滩中心,
河南中路88号
黄埔
🚇 **Nanjing Dong Lu**
Map p.431 E3 16

Westin Hotel 威斯汀大饭店

6335 1888 | www.westin.com/shanghai

Part of the Bund Centre office complex, with its iconic lotus-flower shaped roof, this is a predominately corporate hotel hosting regular delegations and conferences. Its style is certainly not dry, however, with a large and slightly gaudy lobby reminiscent of a cruise ship. It is here, in the Stage restaurant, that you can over-indulge in the fabulous Sunday Brunch while watching Chinese opera singers belting out Pavarotti. The 570 rooms all have comfortable beds, rainforest showerheads and broadband internet access. For a mere ¥70,000 you could have all this and more in the luxurious China Suite.

Hotel Apartments

It is difficult to negotiate a short-term contract on a lease in Shanghai. Estate agents do not get paid commission on anything under a year so will normally tell you that it is either impossible or that the landlord will not accept it. Expat-popular serviced apartments do exist, either as specialised apartment blocks or as part of a hotel. Fully furnished and more spacious than a hotel room, they often have kitchens and access to extensive facilities. They can be rented out on a daily, weekly, monthly and even yearly basis, with prices ranging from ¥7,500 to more than ¥50,000 per month for a two-bedroom apartment; the longer the stay, the better the price.

Hotel Apartments

41 Hengshan Road	6473 1818	www.41hengshan.com
Changning Equatorial Serviced Apartments	6210 0889	www.equatorial-cesa.com
Hankar Serviced Apartments	5089 0303	www.servicedapartmentschina.com
InnShanghai	5465 7322	www.innshanghai.com
New Harbour Serviced Apartments	6355 1889	www.newharbour.com.cn
Park Avenue International	6876 1988	www.parkavenueintl.com
Park View Apartment	5241 8028	www.parkview-sh.com
Pinnacle Property Management ▶ p.39	2306 3600	www.pinnaclechina.com.cn
Pudong Shangri-La	6882 8888	www.shangri-la.com
Regalia Serviced Apartments ▶ p.41	6227 2311	www.regalia.com.cn
Shama Luxe at Xintiandi ▶ p.IBC	6385 1818	www.shama.com
Shanghai Centre	6279 8502	www.shanghaicentre.com
Shanghai Penthouse	6120 2828	www.shanghaiph.com
Tomorrow Square Marriott Executive Apartments	5359 4969	www.marriott.com
Union Square Marriott Executive Apartments	2899 8888	www.marriott.com

Guesthouses & Bed and Breakfasts

There are several guesthouses and bed-and-breakfast establishments in Shanghai that provide a good-value alternative to hotels of a similar standard. Although some may provide broadband internet access, they are not as geared towards business travellers as the larger hotels and generally do not have a hotel's full range of facilities, such as a well-equipped gym or swimming pool. Some may be a little worn around the edges but a homely atmosphere and plenty of historic charm tends to make up for this. There is no set rating system for B&Bs or guesthouses, so your best bet is to check out websites such as www.tripadvisor.com for independent reviews and listings.

Two particularly good B&Bs are The Old House Inn, a small, independently run place in a traditional lane house in Jing'an, with romantic rooms that are beautifully decorated with Ming Dynasty-style furniture (6428 6118); and No.9, a five-bedroom B&B in a 1920s mansion in Luwan, decked out in a mixture of traditional, art deco and modern styles, and run by a Taiwanese wine-connoisseur/furniture designer/dinner party host called David Huang (6471 9950).

Motels & Rest Houses

Not motels in the sense of a 'motoring hotel', but nevertheless worthy of a proper mention, are the clean, simple and cheap Motel 168 (www.motel168.com) and Motel 268 chains that have swept through Shanghai. Motel 168 rooms were originally priced at ¥168 per night (hence the name) but they have improved their standards and raised their prices, which now average at about ¥348 for a double room. Motel 268 is often found next door to the 168s and offers a slightly more expensive but higher standard of accommodation. Call the reservations hotline on 6316 8168 for further details.

Hostels

There are a growing number of clean, well-run hostels that offer budget travellers the chance to stay in the heart of Shanghai. They're not just for young travellers or backpackers happy to camp down in dorms either; some offer private rooms for lower prices than most of the hotels, making them a good choice for couples on a budget. Most have several computers with internet access (some, such as the UCool hostel, even have Wi-Fi areas) but these are normally shared, making hostels generally unsuitable for business travellers who may need further office facilities or services such as a concierge or dry cleaners. Much emphasis is put on socialising in communal areas, meaning older travellers may find hostels too noisy for their liking. Again, with this stress on communal living, some families with small children may have certain concerns over security.

Hostels		
Beehome Hostel	na	www.beehome-hostel.com
Captain Youth Hostel	6328 5053	www.captainhostel.com.cn
Koala International Youth Hostel	6276 9430	na
Le Tour Hostel	5251 0800	www.letourshanghai.com
Mingtown Etour Hostel	6327 2482	www.hostels.com
Mingtown Hiker International Hostel	6329 7889	www.hostelworld.com
Shanghai City Central International Hostel	5291 6823	www.hostelsweb.com
Summer Hostel	133 9128 3668	www.hostels.com
UCool International Hostel	6330 8800	www.ucoolchina.com
Yes Inn	6282 6070	www.yesinn.com
YMCA Hotel	6326 1040	www.ymcahotel.com

Pudong Shangri-La

Westin Hotel

Grand Hyatt

Getting Around

Other options **Exploring** p.168

Cars have begun to replace bicycles as the favoured mode of transport among Shanghai's growing middle-classes, and after the 'mandatory' Rolex have become the next most popular show of wealth among a group with rising dispensable incomes. In 2006, there were already more than one million car owners, with reports suggesting that numbers are doubling every couple of years. Unsurprisingly, traffic congestion on Shanghai's roads is a huge problem.

Central Shanghai is surrounded by one major ring-road, Zhongshan Lu, which links Puxi to Pudong via the Nanpu Bridge. Bisecting central Shanghai laterally is Yan'an Lu, running westwards to Hongqiao Airport. Splitting the city up and down is Gonghe Xin Lu/Chongqing Nan Lu, running north towards Shanghai Railway Station. Smaller roads of great importance include the shopping strips of Huaihai Lu and Nanjing Lu. Fuxing Lu, which is parallel to these, leads into the Fuxing Tunnel that runs under the Huangpu River into the financial district of Pudong.

Of course, only a relatively small part of this enormous population can afford the luxury of a private car, with the remainder relying on public buses, bikes, scooters, taxis and

Shanghai traffic

the Metro system. Buses are cheap and routes are plentiful, but the daily rush-hour crowding from 07:30 to 10:00 and 17:00 to 19:30, both inside the bus and on the roads, can make journeys long and uncomfortable – a situation not helped by the lack of specified bus lanes. Dodging these buses, often with a hair's width to spare, are the city's huge fleet of taxis: cheap in comparison to any other major international city, and plentiful, except during rain, when finding an empty taxi becomes next to impossible. The Metro is also cheap, between ¥3 and ¥7 for a single ticket, and much faster than

overground transport. It is, however, still afflicted by the daily pre and post-work crush. The government wants to ensure that 30% of all journeys will be made on public transport by World Expo 2010. To aid this, it is planning a total of six new Metro lines and line extensions: Line 2, for example, will be extended all the way out to Hongqiao Airport; another brand new line will run from the northern Yangpu district through the centre of town to the deep south; and Line 4 will eventually run like a ring road all the way around the city through both Puxi and Pudong. The high speed Maglev train, which currently only runs from Pudong Airport to a stop still 30 minutes from the city centre, is being considered for extension all the way into Shanghai Railway Station, potentially cutting travel time from the airport to Puxi to an astonishing 16 minutes.

Air

Shanghai has two major airports: Pudong International (PVG) takes on most of the international flights, and Hongqiao (SHA) services the majority of domestic routes. The city has become an important air travel hub and you can now fly directly from Shanghai to most international destinations. Flights, especially domestic ones, are numerous, meaning that cut-price tickets can easily be found. The English language website www.elong.net is a good place to search. Sometimes flights are even cheaper than trains, and they are certainly faster: a 12-14 hour overnight train trip from Shanghai to Beijing is cut to two and a half hours by plane (¥1,125 one-way). Although now officially part of China, Hong Kong still counts as an international destination, with a high number of direct flights daily. China's flag-carrier is Air China, which operates out of Beijing and Chengdu. The largest airline, in terms of fleet size and number of passengers carried, is China Southern Airlines, operating out of Guangzhou. After that comes China Eastern Airlines, which is based in Shanghai.

Airlines

Aeroflot Russian Airlines	6279 8033	www.china.aeroflot.aero/eng
Air Canada	6375 8899	www.aircanada.ca
Air China	6269 2999	www.airchina.com.cn
Air France	6350 9268	www.airfrance.com.cn
British Airways	800 810 8012	www.ba.com
China Eastern	95808	www.ce-air.com
China Northwest Airlines	6267 4233	www.cnwa.com
China Southern Airlines	20 95539	www.csair.com
Dragon Air	6375 6375	www.dragonair.com
Emirates	3222 9999	www.emirates.com
KLM	6387 8888	www.klm.com
Lufthansa	5352 4999	www.lufthansa.com.cn
Northwest Airlines	6279 8789	www.nwa.com
Qantas	6279 8660	www.qantas.com
Shanghai Airlines	6255 0550	www.shanghai-air.com
Singapore Airlines	6289 1000	www.singaporeair.com
United Airlines	6279 8009	www.united.com
Virgin Atlantic	5353 4600	www.virgin-atlantic.com

Hongqiao Airport

Located in Shanghai's western suburbs, 13km from the city centre, Hongqiao Airport is primarily reserved for domestic flights. The older of the two airports, Hongqiao can be reached by taxi, bus or private car but offers fewer food and retail options than Pudong. There are plans to build another runway at the airport and an additional terminal. Once the construction is completed by 2010, Hongqiao Airport hopes to handle 40 million passengers annually. In good traffic, a taxi ride from downtown should take 30 minutes and cost about ¥45.

Pudong International Airport

Thirty kilometres to the south-east of Shanghai city centre, Pudong International Airport handles the majority of Shanghai's international flights. Queues for customs and immigration can be painfully long, especially if you are arriving into Pudong after lunchtime, so plan accordingly. Also worth noting is the tendency for some airlines, such as Emirates and Qantas, to weigh hand luggage on departure and to reject anything over the limit – so it's best to check restrictions before you pack. There are huge plans to expand the airport, with the aim of handling around 100 million passengers a year by 2020. A cab ride from downtown takes about an hour and shouldn't cost more than ¥160, or you can opt for the Maglev (see p.44).

Airport Transfers

In addition to the special buses put on by many of Shanghai's top hotels, and of course the futuristic Maglev (from 06:30 to 21:30), there are regular bus services linking the city centre to both Hongqiao and Pudong airports. These services are available from outside the arrival halls of both. To and from Hongqiao, the following bus routes are useful: Airport Shuttle Bus (¥4) to the Airport City Terminal (1600 Nanjing Xi Lu); Line 1 (¥30) to Pudong Airport; Line 925 (¥4) to People's Square; Line 941 (¥4) to Shanghai Railway Station. The following services are useful from Pudong International: Line 1 (¥30) to Hongqiao Airport; Line 2 (¥19) to Airport City Terminal (1600 Nanjing Xi Lu); Line 5 (¥18) to Shanghai Railway Station; Line 6 (¥20) to Zhongshan Park.

43

Maglev

Shanghai's 'Magnetic Levitation' high-speed train (2890 7777) whizzes between Pudong International Airport and Longyang Station at the Pudong end of Line 2, at an average speed of 340kph, making the journey time a mere seven minutes. Currently, on arrival at Longyang Station passengers must take a further 30 minute taxi ride to get into Puxi, but by 2010 the Maglev line is due to have been extended to Shanghai Railway Station, cutting travel time from the airport to Puxi to approximately 16 minutes. Tickets can be bought by the entrance gates to the Maglev: singles cost ¥40 provided you can show a same-day plane ticket, otherwise prices are ¥50/¥80 for a standard single/double. Trains run every 20 minutes, from 07:00 until 21:00.

Boat

For a relaxing alternative to trans-Huangpu traffic, there are several ferries departing from different points on the Puxi side of the river; a convenient one leaves from the end of Jinling Dong Lu by the Bund. From 06:00 to 21:00, the ferry departs every 15 minutes. Tickets are 5 jiao/¥1 for a standard single/return, or ¥2/¥4 for a boat with air conditioning. Crossings take 10-15 minutes. For a more leisurely journey you can take a Huangpu River Cruise (8285 0707), which departs from the southern end of the Bund and costs around ¥25 for an hour's journey.

Bus

There are more than 1,000 bus routes in Shanghai, operated by a variety of private companies. Direct journeys are relatively cheap at around ¥2 for a single ticket on an air-conditioned bus, but because of the different parent companies, journeys requiring a transfer could cost more. It is advisable to buy a Shanghai Transportation Card (*jiaotong ka*); these can be purchased at Metro stations for ¥100, including a ¥30 refundable deposit. They can be used on all of Shanghai's buses, Metro lines, ferries and taxis. In some areas unreachable by the current Metro system, such as Hongqiao Airport and the villa complexes in Minhang district, buses are the only available mode of public transport. But a severe lack of English-language bus maps, timetables or bus-stop signs tends to put off both tourists and expats from using them; for non-Chinese readers it is a good idea to ask the driver or conductor to signal you when your stop is approaching. For further information you can contact the Shanghai Urban Transportation Bureau on 6317 6355, although don't expect more than basic English.

Car

Other options **Transportation** p.158

Driving in Shanghai is a chaotic, confusing and often dangerous business. Major east-west roads cross the city; they are divided into east (*dong*), middle (*zhong*) and west (*xi*) sections and are often named after Chinese cities, such as Yan'an Lu, Nanjing Lu and Beijing Lu. Major north-south roads are divided into north (*bei*), middle (*zhong*) and south (*nan*) sections, and some of them are named after Chinese provinces, for example Shanxi Lu and Xizang Lu. Those commuting from the outlying residential areas of Hongqiao will most likely use Yan'an Lu, which runs from Hongqiao Airport all the way to the Bund and through the Yan'an Tunnel into the financial district of Pudong. Major roads like these can be highly congested, especially during rush hours. Cars are supposed to drive on the right-hand side of the road but often weave in and out of lanes trying to gain the best advantage. Speed limits on the city's single-lane roads are 30-40kph, on the major roads they are 70-80kph, and on the city expressways they are 100kph, although the congestion rarely allows for speed

Need Direction?

The *Explorer Mini Maps* pack a whole city into your pocket and, once unfolded, are excellent navigational tools for exploring. Not only are they handy in size, with detailed information on the sights and sounds of the city, but also their fabulously affordable price means they won't make a dent in your holiday fund. Wherever your travels take you, from the Middle East to Europe and beyond, grab a mini map and you'll never have to ask for directions.

demons to get their fix. Road signs are written in Pinyin as well as Chinese characters, but they can be confusing: at a T-junction, for example, the sign will not show the name of the road running left or right but rather the name of the road that you will reach if you take that left or right turning. How far away the said road is anyone's guess.

Shanghai does not have a congestion charge, but the government tries to reduce the number of cars on the roads by limiting the amount of licence plates it issues: approximately 80,000 per year (see p.66). These licences cost upwards of ¥30,000, an affordable sum for members of a growing middle class with rising disposable incomes. Other expenses facing drivers include car insurance, ranging from ¥2,000 to ¥8,000 per year; a monthly 'road maintenance fee' of ¥250; petrol costs of approximately ¥4.90 per litre; and parking fees which average ¥10 an hour in public places. Violation of minor traffic rules will incur fines of up to ¥200, and two points will be put on the licence of somebody caught speeding, ignoring a traffic light or using a mobile phone when driving.

Who's the Fastest?

With a top trial speed of 501kph, Shanghai's Maglev train is undoubtedly speedy, but it's not the fastest. In similar trial runs, Japan's experimental Maglev train hit 581kph and France's TGV reached 574kph.

Hiring a Car

To hire a car in Shanghai you must first acquire a local driving licence (p.66). Once you have your licence you should shop around at several of the city's independent car-hire companies for the best price. You should expect to pay about ¥300 per day for a basic Chinese model or a VW Santana, ¥800 per day for an Audi A6 and around ¥3,000 per day for a Mercedes-Benz S350. These prices usually include a limit of 100-200km per day with additional charges for anything above. For monthly rentals expect to pay about ¥9,000 for a VW Santana, including insurance and petrol. There are several different options in terms of car-hire companies, for both short-term and long-term lease. See the table in Residents (p.160) for more information.

Personal Drivers

With all the red-tape involved in gaining a driving licence, it can be easier to hire a personal driver. Companies often offer them as part of an expat package, but for approximately ¥2,000-¥3,000 per month you can hire yourself one individually. For this price, your driver will be available to you for most of the day and evening, although nothing is set in stone and should be negotiated with the individual on starting a contract. Private drivers often offer their services on the noticeboards of stores and supermarkets such as City Shop. Drivers can also be hired by the day and prices will depend on your negotiating skills, although ¥600-¥700 for about nine hours is considered reasonable.

Cycling
Other options **Bicycles** p.311

Two thirds of private journeys in Shanghai are still made by two-wheeled vehicles, with bicycles and scooters being enormously popular modes of transport, not to mention cheap to buy and run. Bikes constantly battle for space with cars, buses and pedestrians on the city's streets. The limited bicycle lanes that do exist are not cordoned off, making them popular haunts for scooters, overtaking taxis or pedestrians trying to escape the crowded pavements. Central Puxi is very accessible by bike, but cycling further afield, to Pudong for example, is difficult, as major tunnels do not allow cyclists to enter.

You should arm yourself with a decent bike lock as theft is very common, and buying a cheap bike (preferably in an inconspicuous colour) is also advisable. Wearing a helmet is highly recommended too.

45

If you do find yourself in an accident, be aware that there is no defining law on where you stand. Both sides should argue their point to the traffic policeman who will arrive on the scene within 30 minutes. By this time crowds will have inevitably formed, and if the other party is a local, be prepared for the majority to take their side in the matter.

Metro

Shanghai's Metro system is by far the quickest way to travel across the city. Trains are very rarely delayed and, at busy stations such as People's Square, come every three to five minutes. Currently you can reach most areas in central Shanghai using Line 1 and 2: Line 1 runs from Xinzhuang in the south via People's Square to Gongfu Xincun in the north; the eastern end of Line 2 reaches as far as Zhangjiang in Pudong and then runs

Shanghai's favourite mode of transport

under the Bund, through People's Square and westwards to Zhongshan Park. This line will soon be extended out to Hongqiao Airport. The partially elevated Line 3 and Line 4 circumvent the inner city; Line 4 will eventually be extended to include parts of Pudong. Line 5 extends south to Minhang from the end of Line 1. See inside back cover for a detailed Metro map. Line 8, which will run from New Jiangwan City south to Zhongshan Nan Lu, is set to open by the end of 2007. The city's five-year guidelines for urban traffic improvements state that by 2010, 75% of Shanghai residents will have access to the rail network within 600m of their homes. Currently 1.8 million people use the Metro each day, a large proportion of them during the daily rush hours of 07:30-10:00 and 17:00-19:30, when carriages can become unbearably crowded. Tickets are cheap at between ¥3 and ¥7 for a single journey and can be bought at a counter or at the surprisingly helpful self-service machines inside the stations. If you have a Shanghai Transport Card (*jiaotong ka*) you simply need to swipe this over the scanner on the turnstyles as you enter and exit the platforms. Once on board, announcements are made in both English and Chinese. Metro Line 1 operates from 05:20 to 23:30, Line 2 from 06:30 to 23:00, while other lines start between 06:00 and 07:00 and run until 21:30-22:30.

Grab a Cab

Hailing a cab is simple, but during rush hours you must be ruthless or someone else will get in before you. Stand by the side of the road, but not too near a traffic light (where they cannot stop), and stretch out your arm. Stepping slightly off the curb may be a little dangerous but will ensure you are seen.

Taxi

There are approximately 43,000 taxis in Shanghai, belonging to seven privately run companies. The largest and most reliable are the turquoise Da Zhong taxis, the gold Qiangsheng taxis and the light green Bashi taxis. Smaller companies tend to opt for red cars, and some of the darker red taxis tend to be less monitored and trustworthy than the larger firms. All should, however, have meters, which the drivers must start at the beginning of the journey. Pick-up price is ¥11 for the first 3km and then ¥2.1 for any additional kilometres. After 23:00 the pick-up price increases to ¥14 with ¥2.7 charged for additional kilometres.

There are approximately 1,000 taxi ranks dotted around Shanghai, but most cabs are simply hailed on the side of the road. An empty taxi is

Taxi Companies	
Bashi	96840
Da Zhong	96822
Haibo	96933
Haihong	6516 0897
Jinjiang	96961
Qiangsheng	6258 0000

recognised by a green, lit-up sign saying 'kong che' (empty car) on the dashboard. It is generally easy to pick up a taxi, unless it is raining or mid rush-hour when it is practically impossible.

Taxi drivers are primarily born-and-bred Shanghainese and know their city well. They are not, however, used to getting vague instructions, so try and have a definite address to give them, and make sure to have the address written in Chinese characters before you set off (the addresses in this book should help). It is a loss of 'face' for a taxi driver to admit he doesn't know the way, meaning he will often prefer to drive around in circles than to stop and ask for directions; try and keep a map (in Chinese and English) with you, plus a general idea of your route. Try to avoid cabs not from reputable firms. If a driver gives unsatisfactory service then call the complaints hotline on 6323 2150 and quote the driver's number printed on the back of his seat. For all taxis you can either pay in cash or use your Shanghai Transportation Card.

Train

China's trains are punctual, efficient and comfortable as long as you book yourself a soft seat or bed (ruanzuo/ruanwo), rather than the hard versions (yingzuo/yingwo), which can be noisy, crowded and smelly. Although they do not run within Shanghai city itself, the rail networks to other cities and provinces are comprehensive. Most offer overnight services in which you can choose between a hard-sleeper and a soft-sleeper ticket. A hard-sleeper ticket will offer you a bed in a doorless, six-berth compartment with triple bunks on either side. The lowest bunk (xiapu) is the most expensive as it offers the most room, but be warned that your bed may be invaded during the day by others using it as a seat. At half the price of soft-sleeper tickets, hard sleepers are extremely popular so be sure to book them a day or two in advance. The average price of a hard-sleeper ticket from Shanghai to Beijing is ¥250. Soft-sleeper tickets offer a bed in an enclosed, lockable four-berth cabin. The average price from Shanghai to Beijing is ¥500.

Most trains arrive and depart at the main Shanghai Railway Station and the brand new Shanghai South Railway Station. For timetables and further information on rail travel, visit www.rail.sh.cn. To buy tickets, either queue up at Shanghai Railway Station's ticket office (counter 10 has some English-speaking staff) or visit a ticket office in the city, such as the ones at 108 Nanjing Xi Lu, Jing'an (6327 8430); 121 Xizang Nan Lu, Luwan (6374 3856); and 431 Fuzhou Lu, Huangpu (9326 0303).

Shoo, Shoe

There are more hazards than cars and bikes for the Shanghai pedestrian to be wary of. Stand still on a downtown street corner for more than a few seconds and before you know it, you'll be having your footwear polished by an eager shiner – fine if you want your leathers buffing for a few yuan, not so great if they've just squirted white polish over your favourite suedes.

Walking

Central Shanghai is easily accessible by foot. The former French Concession districts of Xuhui and Luwan are particularly good places for walking, with restaurants, shops and housing all situated close to one another. Pavements are generally well maintained and many now have raised lanes for the blind. Dangers occur when cyclists and scooters use the pavements in an attempt to avoid traffic jams, a practice the police are trying to stop. Most major roads have pedestrian overpasses and/or underpasses and minor roads have plenty of pedestrian crossings. If these are without traffic lights then do not expect drivers to stop for you. Be very careful when crossing and make sure to look both ways several times. This advice is also applicable when crossing on a green man at a traffic light because cars often disregard traffic lights when turning, and Chinese drivers never give way to those on foot.

In a bid to try to make crossings safer, many traffic light intersections now have marshals, who viciously blow their whistles at anyone attempting to jaywalk (and occasionally issue fines). Sadly, however, their presence seems to have little effect on drivers.

Exchange Rates

Foreign Currency (FC)	1 Unit FC = ¥x	¥1 = xFC
Australia	6.28	0.15
Bahrain	20.11	0.05
Bangladesh	0.11	9.04
Canada	7.06	0.14
Croatia	1.4	0.71
Cyprus	17.76	0.06
Czech Republic	0.36	2.73
Denmark	1.37	0.72
Euro	10.24	0.10
Hong Kong	0.97	1.03
India	0.18	5.35
Israel	1.77	0.56
Japan	0.06	15.44
Jordan	10.7	0.09
Kuwait	26.87	0.04
Malaysia	2.17	0.46
New Zealand	5.43	0.18
Norway	1.27	0.78
Oman	19.69	0.05
Pakistan	0.12	7.96
Philippines	0.16	6.09
Qatar	2.8	0.47
Russia	0.29	3.38
Saudi Arabia	2.02	0.49
Singapore	4.94	0.20
South Africa	1.02	0.97
South Korea	0.01	122.98
Sri Lanka	0.07	14.76
Sweden	1.09	0.91
Switzerland	6.25	0.15
Taiwan	0.22	4.35
Thailand	0.23	4.19
UK	15.08	0.07
United Arab Emirates	2.06	0.48
USA	7.58	0.13

Rates from August 2007

Money

Cash is still the primary method of payment in Shanghai, although debit cards issued by domestic banks are accepted in most of the larger retailers and restaurants. All high-end hotels, most internationally operating travel agencies and an increasing number of well-established, brand-name shops and even cafes such as Starbucks are now taking both international and domestic cards with Visa and MasterCard logos. Occasionally, luxury hotels will take payment in US dollars, but in general only Chinese currency is accepted in Shanghai.

Local Currency

Taking its name from the People's Bank of China (*Zhongguo Renmin Yinhang*), Chinese currency is known as *renminbi* or 'people's money'. The basic unit of renminbi is the yuan (or *kuai* in the spoken form). One yuan is made up of 10 jiao (*mao* in the spoken form), and one jiao is subsequently broken down into 10 fen. Paper notes are available only for yuan and come in the following denominations: 100, 50, 20, 10, 5 and 1. Although still widely used in Beijing, the ¥1 paper note is gradually being phased out in Shanghai in favour of the ¥1 coin. Other coins available are 5 jiao, 1 jiao and the now rarely used 5 fen, 2 fen and 1 fen.

Until 2005, the yuan was pegged at a fixed exchange rate to the US dollar. Pressure from US and G7 finance ministers then pushed the Chinese government to change its policy and to instead peg the yuan to a number of world currencies. Yuan is a relatively stable currency and is now fully accepted in Hong Kong as well as in parts of some other Asian countries such as Vietnam.

Banks

There are numerous branches of Chinese domestic banks in almost every district of Shanghai. Major names include Bank of China, ICBC, China Merchants' Bank, and China Construction Bank, all of which allow foreigners to open either yuan or US dollar accounts (see Bank Accounts, p.77). These domestic banks all offer debit cards, internet banking and currency exchange services, although the latter may not always be possible at some of the smaller branches. The Bank of China is internationally recognised and will generally accept the transfer of money to and from your home country. For credit card services and easy access to funds back home, it is best to hold an international bank account. Rather confusingly, opening times vary from bank to bank and from branch to branch, but in general they are open from 09:30 to 16:30 Monday to Friday with an hour's lunch break from 12:30 to 13:30, and from 09:30 to 12:30 on Saturdays. Note that some ICBC branches also close on Wednesdays.

ATMs

Domestic banks' ATMs can be found in most of their local branches as well as in many of the city centre's shopping malls and department stores. Conveniently, some ICBC and China Construction Bank ATMs now take Cirrus and MasterCard, and all Bank of China ATMs accept the Visa/Plus card system. International bank ATMs, which only accept foreign cash cards, can now be found in many high-end hotels and luxury shopping malls and are often 24 hour. Try not to visit ATMs alone, late at night; there have been reports of women being harassed and robbed.

Forging a Head
Be aware of counterfeit money as there are many fake ¥100 and ¥50 notes on the market. To identify a real note, feel for a textured surface and look for a distinct watermark of Mao Zedong.

Money Exchanges

Provided you show a copy of your passport, cash and travellers' cheques can easily be exchanged at the currency exchange counters found in most hotels, major banks and at Pudong International Airport. Independent money exchanges do not exist outside of the black market, which is not recommended due to the high number of counterfeit notes. Rates are generally consistent wherever you go, but hotels sometimes charge higher commissions than banks, which generally take between 0.75-1% or sometimes a fixed fee of up to ¥50 per transaction. One particularly easy way to exchange money from funds back home is to use your international credit card at a compatible ATM and pay a 2-3% commission.

Credit Cards

MasterCard, Visa, American Express, Diner's Club and JCB cards are accepted in the majority of Shanghai's hotels, some high-end restaurants and a selection of larger retailers. Shops usually use a combination of chip-and-pin and signature but often restaurants only ask for the latter. Smaller shops, particularly those in markets, rarely accept anything but cash. It is well worth subscribing to a credit card protection policy that will replace your card anywhere in the world in the event of its loss or theft, arrange for cash advances to be sent to you if you are stranded without money or cards, organise temporary travel documents for you if you lose your passport and cover you in the event of credit card fraud. You can apply for these protection plans through your individual international bank or directly with companies such as CCP Direct (www.ccp.co.uk) or Sentinel Card Protection (www.sentinelcardprotection.com).

Tipping

Until very recently tipping was actively discouraged by the local authorities and in most places tips would be fearfully rejected. The growing number of tourists and expats coming to Shanghai over the past few years has led to tipping becoming a more common practice, but it is still not expected. It is entirely up to you who you tip and how much you give them – telling a friendly taxi driver to 'keep the change' or slipping a 5-10% tip to your hairdresser or beautician is perfectly normal if they have done a good job. Luxury hotels and some high-end bars often add a 15% service charge to the bill and, although these do not generally go to the wait staff themselves, further tips are rarely given. In restaurants, if you think your waiter or waitress deserves a little monetary praise, then slip them a ¥10 or ¥20 note, making sure to do it discreetly so that the boss does not claim it as his own. Tips are, almost without exception, given in cash.

Play Your Cards Right

Credit card use is still in its infancy in China; local 'credit cards' are normally just debit cards with Visa and MasterCard logos. Some banks are beginning to offer genuine credit services but as a foreigner they are hard to get. You will need to prove your residency and that you have had a regular income over the past six months. Even this will not guarantee you a successful application, as Chinese banks are worried about foreigners running up huge credit bills and then leaving the country.

49

Newspapers & Magazines

Shanghai's major English-language newspaper is the *Shanghai Daily*, sold for ¥2 at stands across the city. This China-friendly publication covers everything you would expect in a modern daily, with articles on local and international news, restaurant

reviews and mild-mannered lifestyle reports. Similar in both style and content to *Shanghai Daily* is *Shanghai Star*, a weekly English-language newspaper owned by the national *China Daily* newspaper. Both publications employ a number of foreign journalists whose articles are constantly checked for any 'unpatriotic' references and edited accordingly.

For practising your Mandarin reading skills you have the choice of several Chinese-language newspapers including *Shanghai Jie Fang Daily*, *Wen Hui Bao* and *XinMin Evening News*.

All of Shanghai's local papers are limited when it comes to in-depth international news, but you can now buy day-old copies of the *International Herald Tribune* (¥24), *USA Today* (¥20), Hong Kong's *South China Morning Post* (¥17), *Wall Street Journal* (¥25) and *Financial Times* (¥30) from the gift shops at most high-end hotels. For a Shanghai-centric view on the city's business news, try the free of charge English-language *Shanghai Business Review*.

Several English-language entertainment magazines dominate the freebie scene. There are two free monthly mags: *that's Shanghai* and *Shanghai Talk*, both of which contain general interest articles, listings and useful bar and restaurant addresses and reviews. The two major weeklies are *City Weekend*, which likes to tackle controversial cultural issues alongside the usual reviews and listings, and *8 Days/SH*, which focuses more on day-to-day art,

Shanghai Daily

music and bar events, and has a pull-out classified section. Many of the western-style restaurants and bars carry at least one of the free publications.

Books

Often the best way to get a feel for Shanghai is by reading fictional and historical novels set in the city and written by locals. A good book to start with is Nien Cheng's *Life and Death in Shanghai*, a moving and often terrifying autobiography describing her maltreatment at the hands of the Red Guard during China's Cultural Revolution. For an even more controversial read, try the semi-autobiographical *Shanghai Baby*, by Wei Hui, which tells about a young, vain Chinese girl in contemporary China and was both banned and burned upon its publication in 1999. Kazuo Ishiguro also likes to use Shanghai as a backdrop to his novels; *When We Were Orphans* is set in 1920s Shanghai and *The White Countess*, set in the 30s, has recently been made into a high budget film starring Ralph Fiennes. *Shanghai: The Rise and Fall of a Decadent City* by Stella Dong is a fascinating historical account of the hedonistic times of the late 19th and early 20th centuries.

Websites

Supplementing the free entertainment magazines are their corresponding websites, offering up-to-date listings, expat forums, and classified ads covering personals, jobs, things for sale and flats for rent. SmartShanghai.com is a self-styled 'urban webzine' that has recently joined the throng of websites providing photo galleries, events listings and reviews of the main restaurants, bars and clubs. In addition, there are websites such as asiaxpat.com, which aim to be practical information portals for Shanghai's expat community.

Media & Communications

Great Firewall ◀

Mandarin may be the second-most common language used on the internet, but surfing the web can be a frustrating experience in China. Many websites popular elsewhere in the world are frequently blocked, with sites that are working one day inaccessible the next. A good deal of patience, or a good proxy, are handy assets for the Shanghai surfer.

Blogs

Blogs about everyday life in Shanghai have been springing up relentlessly over recent years and are now faithfully used by expats wanting to find local and international news, opinionated reviews and well-written articles. Controversial by their very nature, the blogs are regularly shut down by internet censorship brigades, but generally resume after a swift apology and slap on the wrist. Current popular blogs include *Shanghaiist*, *Shanghai Diaries* and *Mad About Shanghai* (see table below), which put into practice the freedom of speech often lacking in Shanghai's official publications. *Shanghaiist's* 'Contribute' feature allows anyone to send in information or articles they find interesting, and means that as well as being kept totally up to date, the website is more varied in content and style than the sometimes egocentric blogs of solo writers.

Websites

Business	
www.sbr.net.cn	Shanghai Business Review
City Information	
www.elong.net	China-based travel website with good flight and hotel deals
www.exploreshanghai.com	Interactive street and Metro maps
www.shanghai.gov.cn	Official website for the municipality of Shanghai
www.shanghaihighlights.com	China Travel Service's conventional tourist information site
Culture	
www.culture.sh.cn	Theatre, concert and events listings
www.mocashanghai.org	The independently operated Museum of Contemporary Art
www.shanghaijazzscene.com	Information on Shanghai's jazz scene
www.talesofoldchina.com	Pictures and writings about old Shanghai
Directories	
www.en.yellowpages.com.cn ▶ p.xviii	English language business listings, city guides and maps
www.enjoyclassifieds.com	Classifieds for the Shanghai area
www.mychinastart.com	Comprehensive Shanghai directory
News & Media	
www.danwei.org	Media, advertising and news site about urban life in China
www.iht.com	*International Herald Tribune*
www.shanghaidaily.com	Daily local and limited international news
Online Shopping	
www.ebay.com.cn	Local Chinese-language version of eBay auction site
www.sherpa.com.cn	Meal delivery from around 70 restaurants
Shanghai Life	
www.adweekly.cn	Classified ads covering personals, jobs and flats to rent
www.afroshanghai.com/shanghai	Info portal for the African community in Shanghai
www.asiaxpat.com	Expat portal with information, forums and jobs section
www.chinasnippets.com	Observations on living in Shanghai and China in general
www.expatsh.com	General expat guide with classifieds and A-Z directory
www.madaboutshanghai.blogs.com	City information
www.shanghaiexpat.com ▶ p.345	Trilingual site with classifieds for the French, German and English-speaking communities
www.shanghaidiaries.com	Dan Washburn's insightful Shanghai blog
www.shanghaiist.com	In-depth and well-run blog of the city
www.shanghai.alloexpat.com ▶ p.165	Global network of classifieds, property and forums
Listings & Going Out	
www.8days.sh	Weekly listings
www.cityweekend.com.cn/shanghai ▶ p.195	Restaurant and bar listings, reviews, listings and classifieds
www.smartshanghai.com	'Urban webzine' with listings and reviews
www.thatssh.com	Lifestyle articles, classifieds, weekly listings and expat forums

Shanghai Annual Events

Spring Festival

Various Locations
January or February

Marking the beginning of China's New Year, this important festival starts on the first day of China's lunar calendar, which can be anytime between late January and mid-February (see p.208). Festivities kick off with lavish family dinners the evening before, and the exchange of little red envelopes filled with money. Dragon and lion dancers perform throughout the city streets – and don't even think about travelling during this chaotic period of mass-migration. Instead, buy some firecrackers from the corner store and let loose.

The Lantern Festival

Yu Garden
Huangpu
Februrary

6328 2465

Marking the end of winter, the Lantern Festival (*Yuanxiao Jie*) falls on the 15th day of the first lunar month, and is a great time to visit Shanghai's Yu Garden (p.214) in the Old City, where at night you can see the hundreds of colourful paper lanterns that people have hung up. Traditionally, people put a red lantern by their door in the belief that it would encourage the Taoist Lord of Heaven to bring happiness and good fortune to their household. Nowadays, this custom is usually limited to Yu Garden which, during the festival, is filled with stalls selling sweet dumplings filled with red bean or black sesame paste. Try and get there before sunset in order to avoid the huge crowds. In 2008, the Lantern Festival occurs on February 21, while in 2009 it falls on February 9.

Nanhui Peach Blossom Festival

Chengbei Folk
Peach Orchard
Nanhui
March-April

5800 0521

For a spring break from Shanghai's smog, visit Nanhui district, an hour's drive from downtown, where hundreds of acres of peach trees in Chengbei Folk Peach Orchard are in full bloom. Together with the masses of other city dwellers gasping for a breath of fresh air, you can visit a model peasant's farm, watch pig races, participate in traditional folk dancing and singing or take a boat ride on the huge artificial lake.

Shanghai International Literary Festival

M on the Bund
Huangpu
March

A jewel in Shanghai's cultural calendar, this month-long festival brings together several famous foreign writers in intimate cocktail-bar settings where they lecture, discuss and eat with any interested Shanghai resident willing to pay a mere ¥50-¥200 for the pleasure. The 2007 line up included Gore Vidal and Booker Prize winner Kiran Desai. Big names sell out quickly, so book early.

Art Shanghai

Shanghaimart
Hongqiao
April

6209 0739 | www.artshanghai.com.cn

More than 100 galleries exhibit at this massive annual art fair in the Shanghaimart exhibition centre. Modern and contemporary art is displayed from both Chinese and foreign artists; 2007's fair included pieces by Salvador Dali, Chagall, Zhang Xiaogang and Zeng Fanzhi, among other big names. Lots of investors and collectors come especially to buy, and, as long as you trust the individual gallery and check the provenance of the artwork, you can often pick up pieces of art cheaper here than at auction.

BMW Asia Open

Tomson Shanghai
Pudong Golf Course
Pudong
April

5833 8888 | www.tomson-golf.com

Free entry to an international golf tournament in which famous players such as Ernie Els and Nick Faldo have regularly taken part should guarantee large crowds. Surprisingly, the stands of Pudong's Tomson Golf Club (p.252) are often only half full, proving that golf, although growing in popularity, is still very much an elite sport in Shanghai.

China International Boat Show

Shanghai
Exhibition Centre
Jing'an
April

www.cmpsinoexpo.com/boat

In 2007, Shanghai played host to Asia's largest nautical event for the 12th consecutive year. At least 22,000 people visit the Boat Show over a four-day period. The show features 350 different exhibits covering water activities such as canoeing, water-skiing and sailing. Don't miss the incredibly luxurious presentations from famous names in the world of boating, including Sunseeker, Feretti and Fairline.

International Tea Culture Festival

Songyuan Tea House
Zhabei
April

5633 4409

Although Shanghai grows no crop of its own, Zhabei district carries the torch for tea, reminding residents that Starbucks arrived on the scene a few thousand years later. To join in the festive spirit, visit the Songyuan Tea House for a perfectly brewed cup, or buy in bulk at the nearby Shanghai International Tea City. Zhabei Park, near the Yanchang Lu Metro station, acts as headquarters for the week-long festival, which includes seminars and tasting sessions.

Longhua Temple Fair

Longhua Temple
Xuhui
April-May

6436 5333 | www.longhuacity.com

The majestic Longhua Temple turns into a bit of a circus for this traditional three-week festival, which began during the Ming Dynasty as a celebration of the birth of the Laughing Buddha. It is now the largest folk gathering in eastern China, with hundreds of stalls surrounding the heavily decorated temple grounds, selling toys, folk art and every type of snack imaginable. It's relentlessly crowded, so be prepared to join the scrum.

Tomb Sweeping Day

Various Locations
April

On Tomb Sweeping Day (*Qingming* Festival), Chinese families clear the ancestral tombs, pray before the dead, and make offerings of food and drink. To provide greater comfort to their ancestors in the nether world, many also burn imitation banknotes or paper models of houses and furniture. In recent years, the selection has widened to include sacrificial refrigerators, mobile phones and even condoms. Unless you have (or had) relatives from Shanghai, you're not likely to participate, but you might wish to purchase a paper Mercedes or *mahjong* set at the Baoxing Lu funeral supply shops.

Birthday of Sakyamuni Buddha

Jing'an Temple
Jing'an
May

In the officially atheist country that is China, it is not often that you will see public displays of religious faith. But at the Jing'an Temple in May every year, you can see monks chanting prayers and brushing dust off the statues of Buddha, all in honour of the birthday of Sakyamuni, the founder of Buddhism. Some local Chinese believers will also visit the temple and light candles in celebration.

International Labour Day & Labour Week Holiday

Various Locations
May

The International Socialist Congress designated May 1 as an international 'labour day' in 1899. It remains the standard Labour Day worldwide and is of particular

53

significance in communist countries such as China, which traditionally celebrated the efforts of farmers, workers and the socialist movement of the 1930s. Today it marks the beginning of one of China's 'golden weeks'. Up to 100 million people travel to visit their families, causing unbelievable overcrowding and utter chaos on the transport networks. As a result, it's advisable to stay home during the break and take advantage of the special events put on by some of the bars, clubs and live music venues.

Dragon Boat Festival

Huangpu River
Huangpu
May or June

Held on the fifth day of the fifth lunar month, this festival honours the poet Qu Yuan (340-278BC) who drowned himself in a river on hearing that his state had been conquered. In commemoration, teams race on Huangpu River in boats with dragonheads and eat a traditional type of glutinous rice dumpling, or '*zongzi*', which legend says were fed to Qu's ghost by his distraught friends. For more information on dragon boats see p.246. In 2008, the dragon boat festival will take place on June 8 and the 2009 event will be on May 28.

Shanghai Jazzy

Fuxing Park
Luwan
May

www.jazzyshanghai.com

This popular weekend jazz festival is now allied with the Shanghai Spring International Music Festival. Foreign and local jazz musicians perform outside in Fuxing Park, where people bring picnics and pray for good weather. The 2007 line-up included Lisa Ono, Japan's most acclaimed bossa nova artist.

Shanghai Spring International Music Festival

Various Locations
May

6386 8686 | *www.culture.sh.cn*

Every May, various Chinese and international musicians come to Shanghai to play in a series of concerts and operas during this two-week festival. Performances are held in different venues across the city, the best of which are Shanghai's Grand Theatre and the Shanghai Oriental Art Centre, which opened in 2004 after building costs of approximately $120 million. The 2007 festival included Bizet's *Carmen*, conducted by the renowned Michel Plasson, as well as *Sound of Cloud*, which starred dancers and singers from several of China's ethnic minorities.

Shanghai International Film Festival

Various Locations
June

www.siff.com

Running for a week in mid-June, the Shanghai International Film Festival showcases a large range of Chinese and foreign films at several venues across the city. In its 10th year, the festival offers a chance to see some of the more obscure foreign films not easily found on DVD. The 2006 winner of the Golden Goblet award was the German film *Vier Minuten*, directed by Chris Kraus, and 2007 saw a special Israeli film festival included in the larger event, showing films such as Shemi Zarhin's *Aviva My Love*.

Shanghai International Television Festival

Various Locations
June

www.stvf.com

Now in its 13th year, this event gives Chinese and foreign television production companies and individual programme makers the chance to showcase their works to the Chinese media and TV industry. Hundreds compete for the Magnolia Awards, covering many categories ranging from best TV film and best director, all the way to best nature documentary. For a chance to watch screenings visit the website.

Millionaire Fair

www.millionairefair.com.cn/eng

This annual three-day international trade fair for the luxury products and services industry gives Shanghai's new 'millionaires' a perfect chance to flash their cash. Although the opening party is invite only, like anything in Shanghai you can buy your way in – tickets for the daily fair cost ¥600.

Mid-Autumn Festival

Always falling on the 15th day of the eighth lunar month (anytime between mid-September and early October), the Mid-Autumn Fetsival (*Zhongqiu Jie*) is also called the Moon Festival; it was traditionally a time when people honoured the moon, but now it is mainly seen as a chance for families to come together and make 'moon cakes.' These round pastries are stuffed with fillings ranging from the surprisingly tasty red bean and lotus paste to the slightly less digestible salty egg yolk. Originally offered to the moon as food sacrifices, the cakes are now more likely to be seen in fancy packaging at supermarkets and hotel gift shops.

Shanghai Sweet-scented Osmanthus Festival

Osmanthus is a popular flavouring in China, finding its way into wine, tea, cake and even cough syrup. Also known as fragrant olive, the local varieties of this shrubby tree bloom in the autumn. Up close, the scent is sweetly captivating; at a distance, it seems almost poignant. Several parks and gardens offer extensive plantings. Guilin Park (p.212), originally the private garden of a Concession-era gangster, boasts more than 1,000 trees. Grand View Garden (p.218), in suburban Qingpu, and the Shanghai Botanical Garden (p.219) are also popular scenting spots. Although the peak typically occurs near the beginning of October, weather can affect the timing by more than two weeks. Check *Shanghai Daily* for up-to-date news on the bloom.

China National Day

October 1 marks the start of one of the three 'golden weeks' in China (see p.14). China's National Day marks the event in 1949 when Chairman Mao stood up in front of 300,000 people during a ceremony in Tiananmen Square in Beijing and declared the founding of the People's Republic. In celebration, parades and firework displays are held around the city; a memorable place to see them is over the Huangpu River on the Bund. Most workers also take time off to visit their families, resulting in mass migrations across the country. This is a chaotic time to travel with tremendous crowding and high ticket prices.

Formula One Grand Prix

www.icsh.sh.cn

Arriving in Shanghai in 2004, the Chinese Grand Prix now tears its way around the ewly built Shanghai International Circuit every year (see p.280). The event attracts many visitors, including a high proportion of local glitterati, who come as much for the parties as for the races themselves. Tickets purchased online range from ¥160 to ¥3,980. Hotels tend to fill up over the F1 period so book in advance.

Shanghai International Arts Festival

www.artsbird.com

Every year, numerous venues in Shanghai play host to a month-long arts fest with everything from dance performances and concerts to art exhibitions. Hosted by the ministry of culture and organised by the Shanghai Municipal People's Government, the events veer more towards the conservative than the edgy, but the odd gem of a

55

performance can be found; 2006 brought in Sketch Mk1, the Australian Street Dance Company, as well as some stars of the New York City Ballet. Special events include an Asian music festival, an art fair and an international magic festival.

Shanghai Biennale

Shanghai Art Museum ◄
Huangpu
November

www.shanghaibiennale.org

This biennial contemporary art event, held at the Shanghai Art Museum, coincides with Shanghai's International Arts Festival and allows established, local and foreign galleries and artists to display their carefully selected collections to the media and general public. Although started way back in 1996, foreign artists were only allowed to enter after 2000. Subsequent biennales, like the one in 2004, saw some high-profile exhibits from Cindy Sherman and Yoko Ono. Since then, however, the number of big names has dwindled, leaving more space for emerging foreign artists and established Chinese names, such as Ding Yi and Chen Wenbo.

Shanghai Fashion Week

Various Locations ◄
November

www.fashionshanghai.com

Every November, most of the world's biggest designers flounce their way into Shanghai with dollar signs flashing in their eyes. A city of more than 20 million people, many with a growing dispensable income and an addiction to brands, presents a pretty juicy market for a major fashion house. In top-secret locations across the city, models strut the newest creations in front of Shanghai's fashionistas. Unless you can convince organisers that you are a fashion journalist, it will be difficult to gain entrance to these hallowed events – but fashion week parties do occur in nightspots around the city.

Shanghai International Marathon

Various Locations ◄
November

www.shmarathon.com

Traditionally held on the second Sunday in November, this annual event is a favourite in Shanghai's sporting calendar, now attracting at least 15,000 competitors from many different countries. Beginning at 08:00, the 26.2 mile slog follows a route all over the city and is open to all who are fit, or brave, enough.

Tennis Masters Cup

Qi Zhong Tennis Centre ◄
Minhang
November

www.masters-cup.com

Held at Shanghai's 15,000 seat Qi Zhong Tennis Centre, the Masters Cup is the culminating event of the men's professional tournament season. This occasionally means that some big names drop out due to exhaustion, but that's not to say you can't catch some famous faces competing in an exciting week of singles and doubles matches – Roger Federer took the men's singles title in 2006. Tickets cost ¥36-¥176.

Longhua Temple Bell Ringing Ceremony

Longhua Temple ◄
December

6328 2465

The monks at Longhua Temple (p.209) have demonstrated their adaptability to the Gregorian calendar by celebrating the western New Year since 1987. Hopeful supplicants toss wish-bearing ribbons into trees and an abbot presides as 108 lucky visitors get to ring the 3,000kg bronze bell. Along with these nominally religious observances, the festival offers fireworks, lion dances, a noodle-eating contest and a carnival atmosphere. In case you're wondering, the number 108 is considered especially significant in Buddhist ritual. Depending on your point of view, there could be 108 deadly sins – or 108 signs of perfection.

Are you always taking the wrong turn?

Whether you're a map person or not, these pocket-sized marvels will help you get to know the city – and its limits.

Explorer Mini Maps
Fit the city in your pocket

Shape your world!

Imagine a learning environment dedicated to inquiring young minds. A school that provides your child with the confidence and skills for 21st century success and an inquiry-based curriculum, exploring the International Baccalaureate (IB) Program.

Currently accepting applications up to Grade 8 for the 2007-2008 school year and expanding through to Grade 13.

Call (86 21) 6976 6388
Puxi Campus
No. 555 Lian Min Road, Xujing Town, Qing Pu District
上海青浦区徐泾镇联民路555号

Western International School of Shangha
The Shanghai College Preparatory School

上海西华国际学校

www.wiss.cn

Residents

Residents

Overview

If you're new to Shanghai, prepare to be surprised. The outside world may perceive the city as a grey industrial hub but to the foreign resident it is delightfully complex, with its unique history, remarkable architecture and cosmopolitan citizens. Shanghai startles newcomers with its beauty and street-level charm amid its alarming growth. Most expats experience an overall feeling of 'this is where things are happening'. The charm lies in the city's stunning vestiges of a colonial past combined with an unrelenting drive into the future. An expat in China always has to contend with being the *laowai* (old foreigner), but being an outsider doesn't preclude close friendships and respectful work relationships with local people.

Considering Shanghai

Expat Capital
More than 50% of mainland China's expats live in Shanghai. Not including Hong Kong or Taiwan, Japan provides the largest group while the rest come mostly from the US, Germany, the UK and Australia.

Living and working in Shanghai means amazing career opportunities, exciting language challenges and a fascinating cultural immersion. Living on the cheap is relatively easy here, but if you want a decadent night out there are plenty of choices. You can enjoy food from all over Asia, mingle among a large, diverse expatriate community and participate in the fastest growing economy in the world. Shanghai life, however, comes with frustrations: it's crowded, noisy and chaotic. People push on the Metro, bicycles squeal at unbelievably high decibels, and the language barrier frustrates. Also, Shanghai may be within a unique economic zone but don't forget you're still in China – foreigners must follow strict visa regulations and are seen as outsiders.

The last five years have brought incredible growth to the city but it's no longer a get-rich-quick destination – Shanghai real estate may be in danger of overheating and fewer companies enjoy open market share. The good news? Shanghai is now a much easier place to live as an expat – with world-class hospitals, a wide range of western-standard accommodation, and dozens of accredited international schools.

Before You Arrive

Congratulations on your decision to move to Shanghai! The process presents various administrative hurdles, so make sure your visa and work plans are in order. Ship any necessary items, but remember – pretty much everything can be purchased in Shanghai (except deodorant and good cheese) so feel free to leave unnecessary items behind. Here are some of the things to consider before you leave for China:

Documents – make sure you have all necessary documentation for your pet, visa, children's school applications and job search.

Visa – apply for an entry visa into the country for you and your family.

Finance – organise your finances, and check the status of tax and your pension.

Address – send change of address notices to banks and credit card companies.

Property – consider renting out your home property – many Shanghai expats live off tenants back home.

Schools – contact Shanghai's schools before you arrive – most international schools have very long waiting lists.

Language – buy a book or a CD on Mandarin Chinese – knowing a few phrases off the bat goes a long way.

Medical – check to make sure your medical insurance covers you in Shanghai – if not, buy expatriate health insurance or temporary travel insurance.

Work – start searching Shanghai's job sites (see p.74) or contact interesting companies to get a feel for what's out there.

Belongings – keep an inventory of all your packed, shipped or stored items.

When You Arrive

Finding and furnishing an apartment, securing a job and meeting new people can be an exhausting but fun process in Shanghai, but the city offers plenty of support from recent arrivals so don't be afraid of the challenge.

Visas/residency – report to the police station with your current address (hotels will do this for you) within the first 24 hours of your arrival. If you're working, your employer should begin to apply for your work visa and resident permit for you and your family (see p.62). If you're looking for work, know your options for staying in Shanghai longer-term (see p.65).

Consulate – register with your consulate for tax and safety reasons (see p.28).

Accommodation – take your time and pick the right realtor for your budget (see p.84).

Language – sign up for a Mandarin course or find a private tutor online (see Activities, p. 308). Explore your neighbourhood and try out new phrases on your Chinese neighbours.

Socialise – go out and explore the Shanghai nightlife, join an association that promotes a common interest, or attend a networking event (see Activities, p.236).

Essential Documents

Remember to keep a copy of all important documents in a safety deposit box (or with a trusted relative) in your home country. You should also keep a copy of your passport with you at all times. Other essential documents include:

Passport photos – if you forget, don't worry; most Shanghai Metro stops have cheap photo booths.

Entry visa

Diploma – original (or copy) of college or university diploma (needed for work visa application).

Family birth and marriage certificates – to process visa applications.

Children's school records

Insurance papers

Bank details – for transferring money back to home accounts.

Medical prescriptions

Pet health certificate and vaccination forms

When You Leave

For a graceful exit from China, keep the following in mind:

Pets – obtain a pet exit health certificate 30 days before departure.

Furniture – put any unwanted furniture up for sale or give it to friends.

Rent – receive two-month deposit back from landlord (or negotiate to use it for final two months of rent).

Shipping – research shipping options – use a relocation company if needed.

Money – plan on transferring currency ahead of time, keeping exchange regulations in mind.

Souvenirs – buy a backlog of gifts for friends (enjoy cheap souvenir shopping one last time). Get the tailored suit made that you always wanted.

Contacts – record friends' contact information so you can stay in touch.

Urban Myths

Mandarin is the common language of Shanghai
Yes, most city residents can speak Mandarin but the ambient noise on the street is Shanghainese – a completely different dialect from the national language. You can get by in Mandarin with no problems but proficiency in the local dialect brings a deeper understanding of the city.

Shanghai is dirty
On the contrary, the city boasts clean streets, beautiful parks and stunning neighbourhoods. The city employs hundreds of street cleaners and individual districts constantly spruce up shop fronts and building facades.

Shanghai has 5,000 years of history, like the rest of China
Shanghai as a major city has just over 160 years of history, roughly dating back to the establishment of the British port in 1842. Shanghai's past of foreign settlements, the opium trade, gambling, gangsters, and intrepid Chinese workers makes for an exciting tale, and an understanding of the city's rise and fall holds important insights into today's Shanghai.

Documents

Living and working in Shanghai as an expat requires wading through a fair share of red tape. Visa regulations are somewhat difficult to access and are under constant review – government officials can and do enforce rules on a whim. The best defence is to learn as much as you can and plead ignorance if caught in a difficult situation. Like most Chinese transactions, personal relationships trump any rulebook and most administrative conflicts can be eventually resolved with seemingly idle conversation. Remember you are now in the land of the middle man – so always use a trusted friend, colleague, employer or reliable agency to assist in any documentation errand; direct, straight-to-the-source problem solving does not work here. Issues are resolved through roundabout paper-heavy channels, so be patient and keep your cool.

Entry Visa

Having a Visitor

Remind any visitors to apply for a tourist visa at least two weeks before departing their home country. They will not be allowed on to a China-bound flight without a valid visa. Guests may also fly through Hong Kong, leaving at least a full day in the city to receive a China tourist visa at the embassy or a travel agency before moving on to Shanghai.

Entry into mainland China requires a valid visa – which needs to be obtained before landing in the country. Only transit travellers entering and exiting China within 24 hours can apply for a transit G visa upon arrival. A visa is required from all country nationals except Taiwan and Hong Kong residents. All the entry visas listed below can be obtained at Chinese embassies and consulates in your home country. Each visa requires specific documentation and the final processing fee depends on the country in which you reside, the number of entries you request, how long it takes to process, and the duration of the visa. Along with a visa, your passport must be valid for at least another six months and have one blank page to enter China.

Tourist Visa (L Visa) – tourist visas are the easiest to obtain. You may apply for a tourist visa in Chinese consulates and embassies abroad, or through private visa companies or travel agencies. You need two passport photos, an application form and the application fee. Tourist visas are granted for up to 60 days, but may be extended by another 30 in Shanghai. An L visa may be single or double entry.

Business Visa (F Visa) – intended for foreigners invited to China for short-term research or business, many freelancers, entrepreneurs or non-working foreign residents also depend on this visa to live long-term in Shanghai. However, it should be noted here that working under an F visa is illegal in China. To enter China on an F visa, you may apply at a Chinese consulate or embassy abroad or within a private visa or travel agency. Outside of China, F visas require a stamped invitation letter from a company in China. F visas are valid for single, double or multiple entries within a three, six or twelve-month period. Many travellers pick up long-term F visas in Hong Kong, where travel agencies (excluding CITS) don't require an invitation letter – only a passport and the fee. Applying for an F visa in Shanghai requires the original and a copy of the business licence of the sponsoring company, a temporary residence permit, and an invitation letter. In addition, the sponsoring company must have more than $3 million in investment capital (as reported on the business licence). Also, US citizens now have limits on the duration of consecutive days an F visa holder may stay in China. The standard is 30 days (meaning you have to leave the country every month and come back in) but you may ask for 60 days. Some visa agencies in Shanghai offer Americans no-restriction F visas for an added fee.

Student Visa (X Visa) – student visas are issued for six months or more and require an application form from the ministry of education, a letter of admission from an accredited Chinese university, and a physical examination form. Some students, unable to gather documentation in time, enter China with a tourist visa and change to a student visa once in China (with the help of the university). Student visas are valid for the time of study and universities can help extend if needed.

Permanent Resident (D Visa) – select individuals qualify for a D visa, which grants hassle-free stays for up to five years in China. These special visas are for significant investors in China (you may qualify if you have invested more than $2 million into China during the past three years, and you have been living in China during this period) or foreign children of Chinese citizens.

Work Visa (Z Visa) – work visas are granted to working foreigners. Employers should take care of all the paperwork. Requirements vary depending on the type of company you are working for. The documentation may include a copy of the work approval certificate, the original and copy of the business registration licence, work visa application, health certificate and four passport photos. Work visas can be obtained in your home country. However, an entry visa marked 'Z' is only valid for 30 days. During this 30 day period, the employer must process a year-long work permit and residence permit.

Foreign Correspondent Visa (J-1 Visa) or Short-term Foreign Correspondent Visa (J-2 Visa) – J visas are given to journalists or foreign correspondents on assignment. J-1 visas can sponsor family members' residence permits as well.

If you plan to join a company job immediately upon arrival, your employer should take care of all visa processing. Most companies issue a short-term Z visa before departing and convert these to a longer work visa and grant a residence permit once in the country. If you are a job seeker, your F or L visa can be extended in Shanghai for a certain period of time until you find a full-time job. At the time of writing, applicants must leave Shanghai and re-enter in order to change an L or F visa to a work Z visa. Most companies will pay for this required trip to Hong Kong for visa processing.

Nanjing Dong Lu

Using a Visa Agency

Chinese bureaucracy depends on middlemen, so it's appropriate to use an outside agent in these matters. Plus, it's a good way to avoid the hassles of waiting in line and filling out forms. Make sure that the visa consultancy is experienced and has good relations with the government. If you are working on your own or looking for a job, working with a visa agency to apply for a new visa or extend your current one is also a good solution. However, be wary of agencies that offer visas without proper documentation, such as automatic F visas without invitation letters. While many of them operate successfully, be aware that these services are borderline illegal and using them can be risky (these agencies simply sign you up as an employee of a random company). A raid on such firms in 2006 forced a number of foreigners in Shanghai to leave the country.

Overstaying Your Visa

If you don't extend your visa in time and are still in China, you may face stiff fines. For each day you stay past the expiry date, the fee is a minimum ¥500. The maximum fee is ¥5,000 (10 days). Some offenders have been able to negotiate a lower fee or get out of paying all together, but it's not guaranteed. Also keep in mind that visas expire when your passport does, so apply for a new passport well ahead of time.

Arriving in China

All foreigners are required to register with the local police upon arrival in Shanghai. Simply go to the nearest police station in your neighbourhood, present your passport, and report where you are staying and for how long. Once registered, you receive a pink form, which is your temporary residence permit and is needed when applying for a longer-term residence permit. For F or L visa holders, the temporary resident permit is your sole proof of residence. For short stays, your hotel or service apartment will register you without notifying you. You can also ask your landlord about registering – some housing compounds are willing to do it for foreign tenants.

Regulations state that foreigners are required to re-register every time they leave and re-enter the country. Foreigners in Shanghai rarely do this though and it's not usually enforced. However, if you're caught with an out-dated temporary residence permit and an over-zealous official, go to a cheap hotel and ask them to re-register you. Always re-register if you move house in Shanghai.

Health Certificate

In order to apply for a work visa and then a residence permit, you and your family members need a Chinese government-issued health certificate. To receive this documentation, you need to undergo a health evaluation at the Shanghai Health & Quarantine Verification Office on 15 Jinbang Lu (6268 8851) in Hongqiao. Report to the office with two passport photos, your company's business licence, and ¥800 (employers should cover all costs, prepare all necessary documentation and provide a visa agent to accompany you). The health evaluation involves roving from room to room in a gown with several other fidgety foreigners, having blood drawn, and undertaking an x-ray and an electrocardiogram (ECG). If you prefer to get checked in your home country, you need to deliver the following documentation to the Health & Quarantine Verification Office: a letter from your doctor stating that you are in good health, original copies of your chest x-ray, blood test results and ECG results, a completed application form, your company business licence, passport, and two passport photographs. After the health inspection, you will receive your certificate in one or two weeks.

Work Permit

Companies are required to provide work permits (Z visas) to all their foreign employees. Be wary of employers who delay in providing Z visas – they are simply saving tax money by not claiming you as an employee. If need be, tell your company you'll pay for all related fees if you do not stay longer than three months. Z visa applications are processed through the Shanghai Labour Bureau on 258 Wusong Lu in Hongkou (www.12333.gov.cn), and you'll need to accompany the HR person or visa agent to the office. In order to obtain a work permit, you need two copies of the application form (completed in Chinese), a copy of the business licence, a CV in Chinese, an employment certificate in Chinese, a Chinese version of your stamped contract, your health certificate, your passport and a photocopy of your passport, and two passport photos. Despite being illegal, living and working on an F visa is still tolerated, but beware – the government is starting to crack down on the practice.

Residence Visa

If you hold a valid D, Z, X or J1 visa and need to stay in China for one year, you and your family may apply for a residence permit at the Shanghai Public Security Bureau on 1500 Minsheng Lu in Pudong (p.64). These permits are valid for one to five years, depending on your visa, and family members must show proof of kinship (birth certificates, adoption papers or marriage certificates). China does not recognise same-sex couples or common law marriages. Residence permits also may not be extended to parents of foreign workers. In order to apply, you need an application form, temporary residence permit (pink form), passport, one passport photo, health certificate, official application letter from your employer, work permit and original foreigner employment register form, and a copy of your company's business licence.

Chinese Citizenship

China does not recognise dual citizenship so taking Chinese citizenship means giving it up in your home country. If a foreigner marries a Chinese citizen, he or she may apply for a one-year L visa. After being married for at least five years, and living in China for that period, the foreign spouse may apply for a D visa (permanent residence). However, it's rarely granted because of other stipulations concerning the foreign spouse's monetary investments in China.

Students

For most students living on campus, the school will register residence. However, if a student wishes to live off campus, he or she may apply for a residence permit. Foreign students need to show a completed application form from the ministry of education and a completed approval form for off-campus accommodation from the university.

ID Card

Every Chinese citizen has to carry a *shenfenzheng* (citizen's card), which must be presented whenever proper identification is required. A *shenfenzheng* is valid for 10 years. Prior to expiration, citizens must report to their district PSB station for a new one. A citizen's *hukou* (residence card) must be presented in order to reapply. The *hukou* assigns citizens to a specific area of residence and needs to be changed in order to move house or cities. *Hukou* is given at birth and doesn't expire.

Chinese citizens

Driving Licence

Other options **Transportation** p.158

Few expats drive around the city, but having a licence can afford you a sense of independence that taxis can't match, especially for exploring beyond city limits. In order to get a licence in Shanghai you must be at least 18 years old and have a residence permit. If you have a valid licence from your home country then you can easily convert it. Otherwise, you will have to enrol in a local driving school and take a test. Whenever you're on the road remember to keep your driving licence on you. If you're stopped for a violation and you don't have your licence with you, it will be suspended. Driving licence requirements can change, so check with the Shanghai Traffic Authority (6498 7070) for up-to-date information.

What's in a Name?

Chinese names are composed of three characters (one for the family name before one or two for the given name). Some foreigners create their own Chinese name, to the amusement of locals, particularly if it implies the wrong gender or sounds funny. Others play it safe by asking a native Chinese speaker for help or using a common Chinese equivalent to western names. There are free online resources (www.chinese-tools.com/names) that can help you convert your name.

Permanent Licence

If you have a licence from a foreign country and a Shanghai residence permit, you will have to take a theoretical driving test before you can get a Chinese driving licence. Belgium has a special agreement with China, which excuses people with that country's licence from taking the test, but it is still necessary to complete some paperwork in person and pass the health exam (see below). Licences in languages other than English will first have to be translated into Mandarin by either the Shanghai SISU Translation Service at 3, Lane 100, Dong Tiyuhui Lu (6587 7585) or by the Shanghai Interpreters' Association at 66 Nanjing Dong Lu (6323 3608). This should only take 10 minutes to complete and will cost around ¥50. English language licences can be translated on-site at the Traffic Authority's registration desk for free. For your Chinese driving licence, you will need a Chinese name, so create one beforehand if you don't have one already (see left).

At the Traffic Authority, you will have to register for the C1 licence for small passenger vehicles, have a photo taken, and undergo a vision and hearing evaluation. The Traffic Authority will then schedule a date for you to come back and take the theoretical test. Depending on how busy the Traffic Authority is, you might have to come back up to a month later to take the test. The test is available in a number of languages including English, Chinese, French, German, Spanish and Japanese. You are given 45 minutes to complete it and must answer 90 out of 100 questions correctly to pass. Beforehand, you will be given a booklet of the questions and their answers to study (the same questions you will see on the test, so it's worth reading them carefully). If you pass, the Traffic Authority will issue a licence to you straight away.

The entire process should cost a total of ¥155. Your Chinese licence will be valid for six years, and you must apply for a free renewal three months before the expiration date. To do this, go to the Traffic Authority with your old licence and residence permit to fill out the renewal form.

Driving Test

If you don't have a driving licence from your home country, you will have to attend a local driving school and pass the theoretical and practical exam. It is possible to find outside agencies that can complete the process for you for an exorbitant fee (without you having to take a test or go to a driving school), but their status ranges from dodgy to downright illegal.

In order to enrol in the mandatory driving school, you will have to take a theoretical exam. Driving school itself involves at least 35 hours of practical driving experience under instructor supervision, and all of Shanghai's driving schools have implemented a fingerprint ID card system to record the driving hours of trainees. The final practical driving exam is divided into three stages: a training site test, a basic driving test, and an on-road driving test. The tests come at different stages during the driving school process, with the on-road driving test signalling the completion of your education. Instruction and testing will all be conducted in Mandarin, and some instructors are more comfortable speaking Shanghainese so lessons may even be incomprehensible to Mandarin speakers. The road tests are not challenging and instructors are known for being lenient. If you fail, a retest can be arranged within 10 days after an appointment is scheduled. The Shanghai Traffic Authority runs around 100 reputable driving schools, and can supply you with a list. Driving courses cost around ¥4,000, and extra fees such as the fingerprint card and exam fees add up to ¥550.

Motorcycle Licence

Motorcyclists who already have a foreign licence must apply for a 'D' (all motorcycles including ones with side-cars or three-wheeled bikes) or an 'E' (two-wheeled motorcycles only) licence by following the same procedures as above.

Driving Schools

Driver Training Centre	5750 3942	www.shdriver.com
Erqi Driving School	6492 1508	www.sh-eqjx.com
Huanwei Driving School	6305 1087	www.honggang.org
Jinjiang Automobile Training Centre	6275 1818	www.jjqx.com
Jonghong Driving Company	5115 2221	www.zhonghang-sh.com
Qizhong Number One Driving School	5498 0666	www.qi-zhong.com
Shenghao Driving School	130 0213 0598	www.shjiaxiao.com
Shentong Driver Training Centre	6241 3321	www.shen-tong.com
Wanguo Automobile Training Centre	5897 1966	www.wgpx.com.cn
Yongda Driver Training	5896 8055	www.96818.com.cn

Birth Certificate & Registration

Red Eggs

Traditionally, Chinese families never named their children until their one-month birthday, due to high mortality rates. Today, a 'red egg and ginger party' is a banquet during which the baby's name is formally announced and guests celebrate over traditional foods. The baby receives red envelopes or jewellery while guests are given red-dyed eggs to symbolise vitality and happiness.

Foreign parents in Shanghai do not have to worry about any special childbirth laws, including the one-child policy. In fact, the birth and post-birth process is pretty streamlined. It only gets tricky when one parent is a Chinese citizen and the other is not. Before your child is even born, you should check with your consulate to determine the procedure for granting citizenship and obtaining your child's passport. Most consulates can supply you with a checklist of necessary documents.

Babies born in Shanghai will receive a Chinese birth certificate from the hospital. Some consulates will require the baby's western name to be written on the birth certificate in addition to their Chinese name (see p.66). You should go to your local Public Security Bureau (see p. 64) to get a Registration Form of Temporary Residence within a month of the baby's birth. This is vital for getting a valid endorsement in your baby's passport, so he or she can leave the country later.

A child with two foreign parents cannot be a Chinese national, so the parents will have to go to their respective embassies or consulates and fill out the required forms to register their child. Each country has different regulations regarding how long you can wait to declare your child's nationality. Acquiring your child's passport also differs according to your embassy's rules, so you should consult with them ahead of time to determine what documents you need and whether your child needs to go with you. Consulates often require you to bring the original Chinese birth certificate, your marriage certificate (if you are married), your birth certificate and your passport.

China does not recognise dual citizenship, so if a child has at least one parent that is a Chinese national, it will be automatically identified as a Chinese citizen (regardless of the other parent's nationality) unless the child is registered under another nationality.

67

While China's legalities may seem flexible, choosing a single nationality straightaway for your child will prevent any complications when trying to leave the country. Chinese citizenship will grant your child eligibility to the country's social welfare programmes, meaning cheaper education and medical costs, but will deny any rights to consular services.

Each birth certificate comes with a little slip of paper attached to it. If you decide that you want your child to be a Chinese citizen then you must apply to your local Public Security Bureau where your child will be entered into the family *hukou* (registration book), at which point the bureau will keep the slip.

If you don't want your child to be a Chinese citizen your embassy can write you a consular report of the birth, which you should take to the Entry-Exit Inspection Bureau in Pudong (1500 Minsheng Lu, Pudong; 2895 1900), and apply for an exit permit, which will allow your child to leave the country (if both parents are foreign citizens, then this step is avoided, and a visa can be obtained directly from the consulate). The Pudong PSB will then remove the slip on the side of the birth certificate. The first time you leave China after this, you need to obtain a tourist visa for your child at the nearest Chinese embassy while you are outside of the country. You can then legally re-enter China with your child, and transfer him or her on to your visa or residence permit as a dependent. Your child will always be a dependent on your visa type and residence permit while in China, and does not need his or her own.

There is no strict timeline for this; it depends on how quickly you need your child to be officially recognised under the passport's nationality. Again, if you and your partner are both foreign citizens, then you need not worry about your child's re-entry.

Adoption

China's historical partiality to boys and its one-child policy has created a high supply of orphaned girls, and many people from outside of China have chosen to adopt as a result. In order to adopt, you will have to connect with the China Centre for Adoption Affairs in Beijing (010 6554 5199; www.china-ccaa.org). It is a long and complex process involving family background checks and paperwork. Recently, regulations on who can adopt from China have tightened significantly to only include certain heterosexual couples in a specific financial bracket. If you choose to endure the red-tape system, you will have to wait an average of 10-12 months. Families with Children from Shanghai-China (FCC) is an adoption support group with monthly meetings. You can call 139 1795 1721 or email rponek@msn.com for details.

Marriage Certificate & Registration

Costly Ceremonies

In line with increasing consumerism, the average cost of urban wedding ceremonies in China has exploded in the past few years to nearly ¥600,000. The vast majority of these marriages are paid for by the parents.

Tying the knot in Shanghai is not that difficult for expats if you don't mind some paperwork, but most choose to fly home for the big occasion. If you're the partying type, you might consider having the formal ceremony in your home country and then a festive reception or two in Shanghai after the fact.

Top-notch hotels and restaurants are hot wedding venues for the Chinese population, but options in Shanghai are diverse. You can design your ceremony however you want, from a traditional church wedding to a fusion of western and eastern traditions. For more ideas, see Wedding Services on p.340 in the Shopping section.

The Paperwork

The wedding process for two foreigners in Shanghai differs from that of a foreigner and Chinese citizen getting married, although the basic laws remain the same. The eligibility age is 22 for men and 20 for women. Both members of a couple must provide statements indicating that they are single before the marriage, and any divorce annulment documents (or death certificates, if widowed) must be submitted to the

Hukou

Hukou is the household registration and residence permit that identifies a Chinese citizen and contains information such as the citizen's date of birth and the names of his or her parents, spouse or children. It has been used in China to control and monitor the general population, and citizens who move outside the place of their *hukou* have limited access to governmental services. Citizens from other provinces who buy property or marry a Shanghai resident can get a Shanghai *hukou*, and thus gain access to better healthcare, schools and real estate rates in the city.

Shanghai Marriage Registration Bureau (Shanghai Everbright Convention and Exhibition Centre, 82 Caobao Lu; 6432 5087; shhy@shmzj.gov.cn).

If the marriage is between two foreigners, one person must have a residency permit, and both must go with their passports to their respective consulates or embassies to obtain a Certificate of No Impediment (also known as a Certificate of Marriageability). No appointment is necessary. After checking over the forms and translations, staff will take a picture of both partners for the marriage licence and there will be a short ceremony where the certificate is presented to you. It will cost ¥50 (extra for photos), and your marriage will be recognised both inside and outside China. Since it is technically a formal wedding ceremony, you may want to invite some friends or bring some fancy attire.

If you are a foreigner marrying a Chinese citizen, you must go to your consulate to obtain the Certificate of No Impediment ($30 from the US consulate and ¥1,240 from the UK consulate). To marry in the city, the Chinese partner's *hukou* (residence permit) should be from Shanghai, and both members of the couple must apply for the marriage registration in person. Besides filling out an application, the foreigner must submit a current passport, Chinese residence permit, the Certificate of No Impediment and a certified translation. The Chinese partner must submit his or her *hukou* and Chinese National ID card. The whole process should cost around ¥40 in total. While Chinese students are technically able to marry a foreigner while enrolled in university, it is not uncommon for them to be expelled after completing their marriage registration. You must go to the Marriage Registration Bureau and have the registration process overseen by officials there in order to guarantee the marriage is recognised and protected by Chinese law.

Death Certificate & Registration

In the event of a family member passing away, you will first need to call a hospital. Ambulance services can be reached by dialling 120. A doctor can supply you with a medical death certificate, which you will need to register the death. Take this to the Department of Entry-Exit Administration at the Shanghai Bureau of Public Security (1500 Minsheng Lu, Pudong; 2895 1900) within 15 days.

If a close friend passes away and they have no family in Shanghai, a member of their host organisation, their employer or an official from their home country's consulate will have to go. Whoever takes on the responsibility will need to bring the passport and residence permit (if available) of the deceased, as well as the medical death certificate issued by a hospital, the report issued by the local Public Security Bureau (in the case of an accidental death), and any other relevant hospital or police documents.

At the Department of Entry-Exit, whoever is registering the death has to fill out a 'declaration of death for foreign nationals'. If registration is filed by non-family, the consulate or embassy of the deceased's country must first grant the representative power of attorney. The Department of Entry-Exit will then register the death and hand you a certificate that you will need for funeral arrangements. Funeral services can be arranged by Shanghai Fei Si Funeral Intermediary Centre (6240 0479), who will take care of the death certificate, transportation of the corpse, funeral and cemetery plot.

Death Rituals
Strange as they may seem, Chinese death rituals are a perfect example of the culture from which they come. Based on a hierarchy of respect and honour, the very detailed ceremony must be carried out exactly or else the mourning family could face disaster in the future. One such example is that the deceased must not be dressed in red during the funeral or else he will become a ghost.

Investigation & Autopsy

If the cause of death is undetermined or there are suspicious circumstances involved, the family of the deceased can request an autopsy. To apply for an autopsy, you must contact the Shanghai Public Security Bureau (see above) within 48 hours of the death, and it will send someone to perform the autopsy.

If the cause of death cannot be determined, the death registration must be notarised by Shanghai's Public Notary Office (660 Fengyang Lu; 800 620 4848). To do so, bring the medical death certificate from the hospital, the Declaration of Death for Foreign Nationals or an autopsy report, the deceased's passport, and your personal identification. The Public Notary Office will then issue a Death Notarisation for the death certificate.

In general, if there are suspicious circumstances involved in the death then the local Public Security Bureau or police department should be notified immediately to investigate (private agencies are illegal). They will then write up a report to supplement the medical records.

Returning the Deceased to Country of Origin

After following the above registration procedures, you will need to cancel the deceased's passport at their country's consulate. Procedures for writing up Reports of Death, which will be used for settling estate and insurance matters, differ with each country; make sure you are aware of the correct formalities. The consulate will provide an entry visa into the home country for the body. Besides arranging for the air tickets, which can be particularly expensive (around ¥50,000), you will need to organise the body's embalming or antisepsis treatment at a funeral parlour, which will then provide a Certificate of International Corpse Transport. Longhua Funeral Parlour (210 Caoxi Lu; 6464 7444) is competent in embalming techniques and offers a comprehensive funeral package for expatriates.

When you register the death, Shanghai Entry-Exit Inspection and Quarantine Bureau (1208 Minsheng Lu, Pudong; 6854 9999) will also schedule a sanitary inspection of the body, and can then issue a coffin exit certificate. Customs paperwork and procedures can be completed at the local airport.

Independent company SOS International (5298 9538) offers repatriation services for the deceased. It can make all the necessary arrangements for shipping the body home, but non-members may have to pay around ¥80,000 or more depending on their situation.

Troubled Youth

Suicide is now listed as the number one cause of death of Chinese people between 15 and 34 years of age, accounting for 26% of fatalities in that age group. Estimates claim that the number of people who have contemplated suicide has risen around 3% since 2002. A cultural reluctance to discuss emotions, familial and academic pressures, and relationship problems are given as the main reasons listed for the high suicide rate.

Organ Donation

The current organ donation system in China has a severe shortage, but the country's Confucian society is slowly embracing the concept. It is still an immature system at best, however, and expats are advised to consider carefully before getting involved. See p.130 for more details.

Working in Shanghai

Shanghai's expatriate workers have benefited from the city's rebirth and tremendous growth of the past 10 years – profiting from local real estate investments, manufacturing opportunities and market liberalisation. The optimistic mood among expats recalls the heady days of the 1920s and 30s when the Chinese port city boasted the most opulent lifestyles and seediest characters on the planet. However, unlike in Shanghai's heyday, the city is no longer an exotic outpost but a common global workplace, now home to more than 400,000 foreigners. That said, Shanghai remains a honeypot of opportunity – to start a business, develop professionally, pursue artistic endeavours, or just to take it easy and live well doing it. Because of the booming economy, most working expats put in long hours at their jobs – influenced, no doubt, by their live-to-work Shanghainese co-workers.

Chinese Language at Work

Many high-level managers recruited from abroad don't need Chinese in the workplace and often can't find the time to pick up the local language in the off-hours. Outside of these executive positions, however, proficient *Putonghua* (standard Mandarin) is extremely useful and can mean a better job at a better pay. Many companies only interview bilingual candidates and certain jobs require Chinese. However, don't let language skills be a deterrent from moving – non-Chinese speakers can still find good jobs if they have relevant experience and a willingness to work in a multicultural environment. Just start studying once you get to Shanghai.

Teaching English

Teaching English to Chinese students is a common occupation for foreign students, new arrivals, or other professionals seeking a change or some steady cash in Shanghai. Some schools require an English-language teaching certification while others merely

Huaihui Lu offices

check your pulse, but be wary of schools with an overly lax hiring policy. Teachers in Shanghai work under three basic arrangements: working for one school exclusively; working through middlemen to teach at several schools; or private tutoring. The first option is the most common, with many expats choosing to teach at supplementary evening schools such as Web International or Wall Street English on top of this. Most schools offer six-month or yearly contracts with salaries of ¥5,000 to ¥15,000 a month. High schools and universities offer less money but often provide housing. Full-time positions almost always offer work visas and residence permits (see p.62), at the expense of rigid supervision.

Freelance and private tutors usually make more money but sometimes have trouble obtaining the proper visas and permits. 'Educational consultants' advertise on the city's job sites and help teachers find work at multiple locations for about ¥120-¥200 per hour. Private tutors need to find students themselves, but native English speakers can make up to ¥300 per hour.

71

Starting a Business

The process of establishing a legal entity in China constantly changes. New businesses may set up a representative office, wholly-owned foreign enterprise (Wofe), foreign invested commercial enterprise (Fice) or a joint venture (JV) with a Chinese entity. Many industries, such as publishing or mining, require Chinese partners, while others call for a certain level of registered capital (funds from abroad brought into China). Most Wofes, for example, must raise a minimum of $200,000 registered capital. Foreigners often hire a China entry consultant to wade through the bureaucracy and prepare the necessary paperwork. Each entity has its own registration process and fees. For liquidity purposes, many expats choose to set up a company first in Hong Kong, then establish a mainland branch. Shanghai-based consultants offer this service.

Corporation Consultants		
Aberdeen Consulting	5117 6330	www.aberdeenconsulting.com.cn
JLJ Group	5211 0068	www.jljgroup.com
NCO Limited	6279 8595	www.ncochina.com
Willsonn Partners	6355 0060	www.willsonn.com

Expat Benefits

Benefit packages depend on whether the employee was hired in Shanghai or recruited from abroad, as well as on the particular company, the position, and the employee's home country. An executive in a large multinational who was asked to come to Shanghai will enjoy a generous housing allowance, children's school tuition (a must for Shanghai's prohibitively expensive international schools), continuing pension payments, medical insurance, relocation services, supplement for spouses, language and assimilation training, tax equalisation, trips home, hardship salary (which currently averages at 15% extra) and a large living stipend. In contrast, a foreigner hired in Shanghai (known as a 'half-pat') receives a much lower housing allowance and perhaps less health insurance and a lesser pension plan. The Chinese government doesn't tax allowances for food, housing, transportation, or laundry for foreign employees, so many companies rearrange salaries in order to save money.

A company's attitude towards time in Shanghai influences the package offered – some still consider Shanghai to be a hardship post, while others view a stint in Shanghai as a necessary developmental stage. As Shanghai grows, some luxuries afforded to expatriates have diminished. Certain benefits remain extremely valuable, however, and musts for executives include school tuition, medical insurance and pension plans. Try to find out what your company usually offers and negotiate for the best arrangement possible. Also, due to currency appreciation, try to have at least a percentage of your salary (your living expenses at least) paid in yuan.

Cost of Living

Shanghai was recently rated as the 26th most expensive city for expats by consultancy Mercer – meaning it's still pretty cheap. How expats spend their money has significantly changed, however. Five years ago, those on a high salary had no choice but to save a large percentage of their income. Now, with several high-end bars, restaurants, and nightclubs in town, expats can easily blow their monthly Manhattan salary right here in Shanghai. On the other hand, those who want to live frugally can still do so. Chinese groceries, standard Chinese restaurants, transportation, furniture, electronics, and mid-level rents all remain extremely affordable. Eating at home or at a cheap restaurant, living in a reasonably priced home, and rarely drinking can keep monthly living costs at ¥5,000-¥8,000.

Working Hours

The standard work week in China is Monday to Friday, 09:00 to 18:00. Overtime is the norm and most local companies don't compensate workers for staying late. Government and state-owned offices open from 08:30 to 16:30 and sometimes close for an hour or so in the afternoon. Many restaurants also close early, many by 21:00, as most Chinese people eat dinner around 18:00. All workers in China are entitled to three national holidays, each stretching into a week of vacation: Chinese New Year in late January to early February, International Labour Day in the first week of May, and National Day in the first week of October (see p.14). While employees get the week off, the government mandates that workers make up for the holiday by working through the previous weekend – so the result is effectively only three days off.

Guanxi Games ◀
Though the Chinese guanxi *(connections)* closely resembles the western idea of a social network, it differs in several subtle ways. Stemming from the core Chinese values of honor and respect, guanxi connections tend to be stronger, more personal, and longer lasting than western business contacts, which are often abandoned upon the completion of a transaction. Most importantly, guanxi *must* be constantly maintained and cared for.

Business Councils & Groups

American Chamber of Commerce	6279 7119	www.amcham-shanghai.org
Australian Chamber of Commerce	6248 5580	www.austchamshanghai.com
British Chamber of Commerce	6218 5022	www.britcham.org
Canada China Business Council	6359 8908	www.ccbc.com
China-Italy Chamber of Commerce	5407 5181	www.cameraitacina.com
European Union Chamber of Commerce	1709 1710	www.euccc.com.cn
Expatriate Professional Women's Society	na	www.epws-shanghai.org
Foreign Correspondents Club	na	www.fccsh.org
Fortune Cookie Club	na	www.fcclub.com
French Chamber of Commerce	6132 7100	www.ccifc.org
German Chamber of Commerce	5081 2266	www.china.ahk.de
Haigui	na	www.haiguish.com
Next Step Shanghai	na	www.nextstepchina.wetpaint.com
Oriented	na	www.oriented.com
Rotary Club of Shanghai	6415 5588	www.rotaryshanghai.org
Shanghai Entrepreneurs' Group	na	www.shanghaientrepreneurs.com
Shanghai MBA Network	na	www.shmba.org
Shanghai Singapore Business Association	na	www.ssba-scs.com
Swiss Chinese Chamber of Commerce Shanghai	6276 1171	www.sha.swisscham.org
XL Entrepreneur Club	5465 2144	www.resultsfoundation.com
Wai White Dragon's Who is Who ▶ p.89	5272 2525	www.waiwhitedragon.com
Young Entrepreneurs' Organisation Shanghai Chapter	na	www.yeo.org
Young Professionals Happy Hour	na	www.yphh.com

Finding Work

Shanghai remains a fast-moving dynamic job market: start-ups offer big responsibilities at the entry level, multinationals grow and change quickly, and local companies provide an invaluable cultural education. College degrees are required for most jobs, and a top university education opens a lot of doors. Many foreigners find their time in Shanghai allows for more job opportunity and advancement than in other parts of the world. Finding employment is more often than not about who you know, but job classifieds can give you a glimpse of what's out there. Reading the city's popular job sites for expats is a good place to start: www.shanghaiexpat.com/careers; www.enjoyclassifieds.com; jobs.amcham-shanghai.org; and shanghai.craigslist.com. The print editions of *City Weekend*, *that's Shanghai* and *SH* also have limited classified sections.

Finding Work Before You Arrive

If you want to move to Shanghai with a job secured, do your research. Most multinationals have offices in Shanghai and corporate websites often list global openings. Don't be afraid to cold call or email companies – just be honest about your qualifications and experience. Check Shanghai websites (see p.51) from your home country and try to contact a Shanghai expat for advice. If you want to teach, many education outfits provide flights, visa and accommodation for free or for a small fee (locking you into a long-term contract in return).

Finding Work While You're Here

Guanxi, guanxi, guanxi. Shanghai revolves around *guanxi* (relationship), and finding a job demands having good *guanxi* (building a good network of contacts). Attend networking events (look up events on the comprehensive Shanghai Networking News website *www.shanghainn.com*), go out at night, catalogue collected name cards, and call back important contacts. Print out English/Chinese name cards with your contact information (just remember to hand over your name card with two hands, as a casual one-hand pass is considered rude), and start shaking hands. Have coffee with people working in the industry you're interested in, which will lead to other contacts. Cold call potential companies or recruitment agencies. While HR departments are beginning to see the benefits of hiring 'half-pats', know that salaries and benefits are lower if you're hired locally (see p.72). Be realistic but be ambitious – in fast-moving Shanghai, you never know what may happen.

Recruitment Agencies

Fapiao
The Chinese version of an invoice, the fapiao *is not only the consumer's way of proving a purchase, but also the government's way of auditing companies for tax purposes. Most shops won't give a* fapiao *unless asked and this process can often be a hassle, especially in smaller shops. Freelancers whose clients require invoices often make deals with larger companies that can provide them for a fee.*

Only contact appropriate recruitment agencies – some work within certain markets or only handle executive appointments or local staff. Try establishing a personal relationship with the agent so you're not just another name on the list – more *guanxi*.

Recruitment Agencies

Boyden Global Executive Search Limited	6113 8558	www.boyden.com
Egon Zehnder International	6385 2118	www.egonzehnder.com
Horton International	6288 1808	www.hortonchina.com
Huijie Executive Search	5211 0068	www.huijiechina.com
Kienbaum Consultants International	5103 5351	www.kienbaum.de
Korn Ferry International	6256 7333	www.kornferry.com
MRI Worldwide	6390 6007	www.mri-china.com
Quadrant Asia	na	www.quadrantasia.com
Russell Reynolds Associates	6391 5511	www.russellreynolds.com
Spencer Stuart & Associates	6288 8989	www.spencerstuart.co.uk
Staff Service Company	5298 6298	www.staffservice.com
The Talent Business	5258 9881	www.thetalentbusiness.com
Templar International Consultants	6390 6618	www.templarsearch.com
Uphunt Executive Search	5079 1400	www.uphunt.com

Working as a Freelancer or Contractor

Shanghai is home to many freelance graphic designers, writers, editors, photographers, programmers, interior designers and architects, as well as a broad range of consultants. It's a great city to work for yourself – constant new businesses offer fresh batches of potential clients and a rough month requires minimal budgeting. Many freelancers live on F visas or receive a work visa through part-time jobs (see p.62). Most companies are flexible and can pay for services with petty cash. Find out what others in your field are charging, print out creative cards, and start meeting as many people as possible.

Voluntary & Charity Work

Shanghai-based charities need people's time and thoughtful donations. Organisations sponsor children's education, provide medical supplies or give care and time to local elderly people. Some groups don't have English-speaking staff, but welcome new volunteers despite any language barrier.

Volunteer Organisations in Shanghai

CereCare Wellness Centre Shanghai – a residential facility for young children suffering from cerebral palsy, offering treatment and education (www.cerecare.net).
Friends of Hope – volunteer to play with children on the cardiac ward of the Pudong Children's Hospital. Contact Kristen Harvey at kmdjeharvey@yahoo.com.
Half the Sky – foreign parents of adopted Chinese children help orphans who remain in China's social welfare system (www.halfthesky.org).
Hands on Shanghai – expat-run organisation that fills the needs of local NGOs by organising flexible volunteer programmes for Shanghai's busy professionals (www.handsonshanghai.com).
Lifeline Shanghai – volunteers work the phones to provide free and anonymous information and support to Shanghai expats (www.lifelineshanghai.com).
Loving Heart Association – inspires youth through various volunteer projects to love and care for others (www.lovesino.cn).
River of Hearts – run by the Shanghai community centre, River of Hearts collects and distributes used clothing, bedding, shoes and toys to those in need around China (www.communitycenter.cn).
Second Chance Animal Aid – expat-run organisation which facilitates the adoption of homeless or abandoned pets in Shanghai (www.scaashanghai.org).
Shanghai Community Centre – a community centre for expatriates living in Shanghai which organises various charities (www.communitycenter.cn).
Shanghai Lequn – social work service working with Shanghai migrant workers' children and the elderly. Contact director Shen Limin (Chinese-language only) by phone on 5851 7412, or email dir@lequn.org.
Shanghai Sunrise – with the belief that every student has a right to an education, Shanghai Sunrise provides sponsorships to students in the Shanghai municipal area (www.shanghaisunrise.com).
The Smile Train – provides free cleft surgery to thousands of children around China (www.smiletrain.org).
The Wheelchair Foundation – Shanghai chapter of the global organisation donates wheelchairs to those in need (www.wheelchairfoundation.org.cn).
The Zigen Fund – supports grass-root efforts to help the poor and underprivileged of China (www.zigen.org).

Need Some Direction?

The *Explorer Mini Maps* pack a whole city into your pocket and, once unfolded, are excellent navigational tools for exploring. Not only are they handy in size, with detailed information on the sights and sounds of the city, but also their fabulously affordable price mean they won't make a dent in your holiday fund. Wherever your travels take you, from the Middle East to Asia and beyond, grab a mini map and you'll never have to ask for directions.

Employment Contracts

An initial job offer can come in either verbal or written form. A formal offer should include your job title, salary (gross and net) and a start date. It's common to negotiate your salary and benefits, but Chinese HR managers may get frustrated with demands. Talk to someone higher up if necessary. A written contract is usually in Chinese and English (always request an English version if not given one, but bear in mind that the Chinese contract is the binding one). Contracts need to be signed and stamped with the company's seal to be valid. It should include terms of agreement, working hours, salary, holidays, training, benefits, rules of the company and termination policies. Contracts in China are valid for a year and include a probationary period (three months is the average, and it can't exceed six months by law). Chinese employees don't receive benefits during this time, but foreign workers should. Maternity leave is granted forat least than 90 days with pay (see p.139). Notification of dismissal is under the discretion of the company.

Labour Law

Employment regulations and procedures vary in different cities, although national labour law is applicable nationwide. For specific questions, contact the Shanghai Labour Bureau (12333). The Shanghai Expatriates Employment Resource, jointly sponsored by the local labour bureau and the Shanghai Foreigner Employment Centre, is also a good resource for employment questions (6365 0095).

Employment Lawyers		
Baker & McKenzie	6105 8558	www.bakernet.com
Duan & Duan	6219 1103	www.duanduan.com
Lehman, Lee & Xu	5298 5252	www.lehmanlaw.com
Squire, Sanders & Dempsey	6103 6300	www.ssd.com

If there is a labour dispute between employees and employers, both parties need to report to the district labour arbitration commission. These arbitration awards, however, are not binding. If either party is dissatisfied by the decision, they may initiate a court proceeding. Parties are not required to hire a lawyer for arbitration or court procedures (employees sometimes represent themselves while HR managers represent the company) but local legal experts advise foreigners to seek legal advice in any dispute. Attorneys are more likely to be involved in complicated cases.

Changing Jobs

Young Shanghainese are notorious for constantly changing jobs, especially recent graduates, and many foreigners follow suit. According to Shanghai labour laws, when an expat changes jobs, it must be cleared through visa channels and recorded in the work permit. Change of employment requires a statement of termination from your previous employer and your new contract. Your new employer should take care of all the necessary paperwork. If you leave your job early and have no immediate new job your employer needs to report your termination to the visa office, but this rarely happens and expats usually stay until their visa expires. If your Z visa is about to expire and you want to stay in Shanghai without a job, it's best to leave the country and re-apply for an L or F visa (see p.62). Once you have a work permit, it's much easier to extend or renew under a new employer – reapplying after holding an F or L visa requires a full medical check and application process once again.

After an employee leaves the company, employers have the right to enforce confidentiality and non-competition clauses, restricting work for the competition for a period of time.

Company Closure

Shanghai labour law states that if a company closes before any of its employees' contracts have expired, the employer is required to pay each employee one month's salary for each full or partial year of service given to the firm. If the company closes down and reports the termination of the employee's work permit, the Public Security Bureau will allow foreign employees to stay in China until their residency permit expires. If the expat finds a new employer during this time, the expat can apply for a new work permit without having to leave and enter China again. If a termination letter from the employer is not available, the labour bureau will accept a statement of de-registration from the Administration of Industry and Commerce to confirm company closure.

Financial & Legal Affairs

Bank Accounts

Shanghai's banking options expand every year – but domestic banks still dominate, with foreign banks operating under strict guidelines. Many expats choose domestic banks with an international focus, such as Bank of China or ICBC, for their personal banking needs. HSBC and Citibank offer good options for foreigners as both companies provide a wide range of international services. The main banks will offer a savings plan, foreign currency exchange services, security services, phone support, e-banking services and overseas and domestic remittance. Debit cards and ATM cards can be provided for a small fee (¥10 and up).

The majority of local banks will be open from 09:00 to 17:00 between Monday and Friday, plus a half day on Saturday.

Some local banks offer multi-currency accounts. A US dollar account at ICBC requires a residence permit and a minimum deposit of $300. At Bank of China, you don't need a residence permit (only your passport); there is a ¥5 set-up fee, and a US dollar bank account requires a minimum deposit of $500.

Common bank fees include an annual service charge, account transfer fees, and small service charges for ATM usage (¥5 to ¥10).

Overdrafts are a relatively new concept but are gaining headway. Banks are still reluctant to offer overdraft services to foreigners, and you will often need a local guarantor, such as your employer, to vouch for your financial stability.

Credit Where Due

China is still a cash-run society, but local credit cards are slowly catching on. China Union Pay is the transaction platform used by all state-run bank cards, including Bank of China and ICBC. To get a card as a foreigner you need to at least bring your passport and a certification of your salary to the bank.

Shanghai Banks

ABN Amro Bank	2893 9600	www.corporates.abnamro.com
Agricultural Bank of China	95599	www.abchina.com
Asahi Bank	6275 8111	www.asahibank.co.jp
ANZ	6841 0111	www.anz.com
Bangkok Bank	6323 3788	www.bbl.co.th
Bank of China	95566	www.bank-of-china.com
Bank of Communications	95559	www.bankcomm.com
Bank of East Asia	800830 3811	www.hkbea.com.cn
Bank of Montreal	5047 1066	www.bmo.com
Bank of New York Mellon	5879 6622	www.bankofny.com
Bank of Shanghai	962888	www.bankofshanghai.com.cn
Bank of Tokyo-Mitsubishi UFJ	6888 1666	www.bk.mufg.jp
China Construction Bank	95533	www.ccb.com
China Everbright Bank	95595	www.cebbank.com
China International Trust and Investment Co(CITIC)	95558	www.ecitic.com
China Merchants Bank	95555	www.cmbchina.com
China Minsheng Banking Corp	95568	www.cmbc.com.cn
Citibank ▶ p.IFC	2896 6000	www.asia.citibank.com
DBS Bank	3896 8888	www.dbs.com
Dresdner Bank AG	3866 5588	www.dresdner.com.cn
Hang Seng Bank	5882 1338	www.hangseng.com.cn
HSBC	3888 3888	www.hsbc.com.cn
Industrial & Construction Bank of China (ICBC)	95588	www.icbc.com.cn
Metropolitan Bank & Trust Co	6886 0008	www.metrobank.com.cn
Mizuho Corporate Bank	6841 0000	www.mizuhocbk.co.jp
Shanghai Pudong Development Bank	95528	www.spdb.com.cn
Standard Chartered	80 0820 8088	www.standardchartered.com.cn

Want A-Share?
Although foreigners are technically limited to dabbling in B-shares, there are a few ways to participate in the A-share rat race. You can buy through a trusted friend or family member's account (if they are a Chinese citizen), or through a bank with a QFII (qualified foreign institutional investor) designation that sells financial products related to the A-share market.

Financial Planning

For expats on comprehensive business packages, it can be tempting to live the high life without saving money. However, if you create a budget and stick to it, you can save a lot in a short amount of time (depending on your monthly salary and budgetary needs, of course). Experts expect the yuan to continue to appreciate in the immediate future, but no one can say how it will fare over the course of a few years.

Playing the stock market is a favourite hobby of almost every Chinese national. The country has two exchange markets: Shanghai and Shenzhen, both with two types of stock – A-shares and B-shares. A-shares are considerably more widely traded but can only be bought by a Chinese citizen, whereas B-shares can be bought by foreigners. If you want to trade in B-shares, international brokers such as BOC International (6860 4866) can help you from anywhere in the world.

If you are interested in buying property as an investment, you should first enquire about taxes. Selling the property may result in a value-added tax, and you will be taxed according to the house's appreciated value (see p.88).

Pension

Foreigners cannot receive funds from the government's pension system, but employers, especially multinational companies, can and do include provisions for pension schemes in their expat packages. The best packages will offer schemes comparable to a pension in your home country.

Offshore Savings Accounts

Transferring yuan out of China is a challenge for anyone, so most expats prefer to keep an offshore savings account as well as a local account. You can usually work out a payment plan with your employer so they deposit a certain amount of your salary in one account and a certain amount in the other. This allows you to legally avoid dealing with currency exchanges and wire transfers, as long as you continue to pay your income tax in full.

Taxation

Personal income taxes can range from 5% to 45% of your income, depending on how large your salary is. Income taxes are deducted automatically from your salary and the

Financial Advisors

AC Business Consulting	5187 9097	www.acbcshanghai.com
Asia Connect	6415 1181	www.theasia-connect.com
Austen Morris Associates ▶ p.vi	6390 1233	www.austenmorris.com
CITCC	5873 3545	www.citcc.com
Credit Suisse	6881 8418	www.credit-suisse.com
Deloitte & Touche	6141 8888	www.deloitte.com
Devere & Partners	na	www.devereandpartners.com
Ernst & Young	2405 2000	www.ey.com/china
Essential Finance ▶ p.79	+852 2893 3200	www.essential-finance.com
Financial Page International	6215 1333	www.fpi.cn
Financial Partners International	6288 0558	www.financial-partners.biz
Global Wealth Management	6327 7620	www.gwm-ltd.com
KPMG	5359 4666	www.kpmg.com.cn
PricewaterhouseCoopers	6123 8888	www.pwccn.com
Vocation International Certified Public Accountants	5840 2701	www.tzcpa.com
Shui Lun Pan CPAs	6339 1166	www.pcpa.com.cn
TA & Associates Asia	6103 7162	www.ta-asia.com

Money frees you from doing things you dislike.
Since I dislike doing nearly everything,

money
is handy

Groucho Marx

Money means choices. Where to buy a home,
how to educate kids, when to retire.
With a little planning, we can help you realise your
goals. It's time to look forward to your future.

Find out how at: www.essential-finance.com

essentialfinance

Cost of Living

Apples (per kg)	¥10-¥30
Bananas (per kg)	¥5-¥7
Beer (pint – restaurant or bar)	¥10-¥60
Beer (pint – shop)	¥2-¥10
Beer (six pack)	¥13-¥38
Bottle of house wine (restaurant)	¥400-¥800
Burger (takeaway)	¥50-¥80
Bus (10km journey)	¥5
Can of soft drink	¥1.5-¥2
Cappuccino	¥20-¥35
Car rental (per day)	¥200-¥500
Carrots (per kg)	¥20
CD album	¥5-20
Chocolate bar	¥5-¥20
Cigarettes (per pack of 20)	¥4-¥16
Cinema ticket	¥50-¥80
Dozen eggs	¥6-¥7
Fresh beef (per kg)	¥20-¥30
Fresh chicken (per kg)	¥15-¥20
Fresh fish (per kg)	¥20-¥80
Golf (18 holes)	¥300-¥600
House wine (glass)	¥50-¥80
Large bag of dogfood	¥30-¥40
Large takeaway pizza	¥40-¥70
Loaf of bread	¥5-¥10
Local postage stamp	¥0.6
Milk (1 litre)	¥8-¥10
Mobile to mobile call (local, per minute)	¥0.1
New release DVD	¥5-¥20
Newspaper (international)	¥20
Newspaper (local)	¥1
Orange juice (1 litre)	¥20-¥50
Pack of 24 aspirin/paracetamol tablets	¥50
Petrol (gallon)	¥5
Photo prints (50 prints)	¥35-¥100
Postcard	¥2
Potatoes (per kg)	¥8
Rice (1kg)	¥10
Salon haircut (female)	¥50-¥400
Salon haircut (male)	¥50-¥200
Strawberries (per punnet)	¥4
Sugar (2kg)	¥20
Taxi (10 km journey)	¥30-¥50
Text message (local)	¥0.1-¥0.5
Tube of toothpaste	¥2-¥12
Water 1.5 litres (restaurant)	¥15
Water 1.5 litres (supermarket)	¥2-¥5

average rate throughout the country is around 10% to 25%, but if you earn more than ¥100,000 per month then you can expect to be taxed up to 45%. The area you live in does not affect how much tax you pay. If you buy a house or apartment, you will have to concern yourself with property tax details, which include a 3% contract tax (determined by the sale price), a maintenance fund tax (2% of the sales price) and a stamp duty (0.05% of the sales tax). Taxes associated with selling personal property include a sales tax (5.5% of the sales price), the stamp duty (0.05% of the sales price), a value-added tax (VAT) of 1% of the sales price, and an income tax of about 20% of the property's appreciation (see p.88).

Whenever you buy items in shops, a sales tax of about 5.5% will be already included in the price. There is also an annual personal savings deposit tax, which equals 20% of the total interest for that year. Tax regulations now state that everyone, including foreigners, has to declare their worldwide income if they have been in China for longer than 183 days and earn more than ¥120,000 annually. The form for this individual income tax return is in both English and Chinese, and can be accessed online through the State Administration of Taxation website (www.chinatax.gov.cn).

There are no tax breaks or rebates for citizens, and even if an expat stays in China on a long-term basis, they shouldn't expect any special treatment in terms of taxation. Tax evasion can result in fines of up to five times the owed amount, and prolonged tax evasion can result in jail time.

Legal Issues

Since 1979, China has established and developed a legal system with a strong foundation in civil law. Courts do not have the power of judicial review that would let them reject legislation, and in all cases the legislative government always gets the final word.

The prison system in China is known for its strict policies, and although arrested expats are permitted visitation rights with consulate officials, courts on the whole are not tolerant towards misbehaving foreigners. Court proceedings are conducted in Mandarin, which presents obvious problems, and foreigners have been imprisoned and executed for drug-related offences and religious or political proselytising.

China's laws are in a constant state of flux, and it is a good idea to find a reliable lawyer who you can refer any legal concerns to. Some of the consulates' websites list international and local law firms that foreigners can turn to. If not, most consulates can provide a list of law firms if requested.

Divorce Deals

The divorce rate in China in 2006 was a notable 1.9 per 1,000, up 7% from 2005. The rise follows a recently relaxed divorce process, changing family values and 'fake' divorces. Recent investigations have revealed that more and more couples are getting divorced to take advantage of government-run relocation and welfare programmes.

Divorce

If you were married outside China and you and your spouse are both foreign passport-holders, then you cannot legally divorce here. Both members of a foreign-related marriage (any marriage with one non-Chinese citizen) must file for divorce through the Marriage Registration Authority (70 Caobao Lu; 6432 5087). After the Registration Authority verifies that both parties agree to divorce, and have made suitable arrangements for their children and shared property, they will issue the couple a certificate of divorce. The divorce process is not hugely expensive, and hiring a lawyer is not necessary.

If only one member of the couple applies for divorce, the case will be referred by the Marriage Registration Authority to a local court, which will try to mediate between the two parties but will consent to divorce if reconciliation fails. It's best to get a divorce lawyer for these proceedings.

Some reasons for divorce being approved are if one of the parties is proven to be a bigamist, physically violent, a gambling or drug addict, or if the couple has not lived together for more than two years. The court will also help settle estate, financial and child custody matters if the couple cannot come to an agreement. If the court finds a husband or wife guilty of bigamy, cohabitation with a person other than his or her spouse or physical violence, the partner is entitled to compensation. Fees for child support will cost around 20% to 30% of a partner's monthly income and will be mandatory until the child turns 18. If there is more than one child, this percentage increases to 50%.

Making a Will

A will can be drawn up with the help of a Shanghai law firm, and will then need to be notarised by Shanghai's Public Notary Office (800 620 4848; 660 Fengyang Lu) to be legally recognised in China. Even if you have a will drawn up by an international law firm, you should make sure that all your assets are protected and enforced under the will according to Chinese law. There may be exceptions, such as immovable properties like an apartment or house. To preserve the rights to these properties you will need to have the will rewritten by a Chinese lawyer and notarised at the local Public Notary Office.

Adoption

Adopting children from China is relatively common, although the government has recently tightened guidelines to specify who can and cannot apply for adoption, and also who can be adopted.

Prospective adoptive parents must closely follow the China Centre of Adoption Affairs' (CCAA) stipulations, which can be found on its website or by calling directly (010 6554 5199; www.china-ccaa.org). A social worker will conduct a 'home study report' and you will need a letter from your embassy that attests to your citizenship and work history in China for over a year. The CCAA will then review your application and notify you when a decision is reached. Application fees include social worker costs, authentication of dossier documents by lawyers or your embassy, and CCAA service charges. You should check with the individual institutions for specific prices, but you can expect to spend anywhere from ¥75,000 to ¥150,000 in total.

Housing

Accommodation in Shanghai can be frustrating. The converted lane house you rent for ¥24,000 a month may be close to the hub of the action, but it frequently loses hot water, while the expansive suburban villa your family needs leaves you isolated from city life. It's important to choose your housing carefully – in a city this big, and this sprawling, where you live really dictates your lifestyle. The best way to get a feel for Shanghai's varied residential worlds before you sign up is to stroll through the different neighbourhoods, and also give potential daily journeys a trial run. Speaking to a property agent that specialises in expatriate housing, as well as asking colleagues and friends about their areas, helps too.

Renting in Shanghai

Until the law changed in 2004, all local Shanghai residents received housing through their *danwei*, or work unit, and most Shanghainese still live in government-issued apartments. These houses were given on a 'user rights' basis, meaning the government can take the homes away at any time. Expats, however, have to find housing for themselves.

Many expats with children choose to live in suburban areas, such as Hongqiao or Pudong, in order to be close to the city's far-flung international schools, while younger foreigners tend to favour downtown areas such as the French Concession and Jing'an for their proximity to dining and nightlife.

Pudong housing

A large number of expat packages include housing budgets which, thanks to lingering perceptions of Shanghai as a hardship post, may prove substantial enough for pretty plush accommodation. Mid-range one-bedroom apartments in central areas range from ¥4,000-¥9,000 per month, while similar housing further out generally costs less.

Nicely renovated colonial apartments or new complexes in the same areas rent for ¥8,000-¥40,000 per month. Downtown also boasts some breathtakingly renovated lane houses and garden villas that fetch an astounding ¥45,000-¥80,000 per month or more. In the outer areas of the city, homes are usually confined to large gated complexes. A modest suburban villa in Gubei, for example, can be had for the same as a two-bedroom apartment of similar quality in the French Concession.

Negotiating the Lease

Rent, like everything else in China, is negotiable. It's common practice to bargain for a lower rent, customised lease terms or a furniture allowance. Lease agreements are typically made for one year (shorter leases are available for serviced apartments) but longer leases often lower the rent. A security deposit of two months' rent is generally expected to be paid upon signing. Rent is paid in yuan, and in cash, and does not usually include utilities (water, gas, electricity, phone, internet and cable or satellite TV). The landlord needs to specify what utility bills will arrive and when. Some landlords may ask for a property management fee, depending on the facilities of the building, and the use of a parking space also usually incurs an added cost. The landlord should be responsible for any and all property maintenance.

Sheshan Golf Estate

World Class Golf, Even Better Living

Luxury Residential Townhouses for Lease

118 luxury Tuscan themed townhouses for lease, on an exclusive private 18 hole golf course, close to Hongqiao airport.

Ranging from 245 sq m to 404 sq m, these houses are ideally situated in a quiet and tranquil country club community.

Golf & Country Clubhouse:

- Customer Service Centre
- Chinese & Italian Restaurants
- Coffee Shop & Bar
- Convenience Store
- Indoor and Outdoor Swimming Pools
- Bowling Alley
- Children's Playground
- Spa
- Gym and Sauna
- 2 floodlit Tennis Courts
- Basketball Court
- Squash Court

Property Leasing Line: (8621)5779 9888   www.sheshangolf.com

Add: Lane 288, New Linyin Avenue, Songjiang District, Shanghai 201602, PRC

UNIFRONT 优孚控股

SHESHAN
GOLF CLUB

Property Management Company:
Shanghai Unifront Hotel & Property Management Co., Ltd

Developer:
Unifront Holdings Limited

Golf Course Managed by:
Shanghai Sheshan International Golf Management Co., Ltd.

savills
第一太平戴维斯

IMG
Golf Course Management

Property Management Consultant by:
Savills

Golf Course Management Consultant by:
IMG

Finding a Home

Most foreigners find apartments through agents. If your budget is lower than ¥7,500 a month, you should work with a local real estate company to help you find something suitable. There are agencies on practically every city block; look for the apartment photos and profiles lining the windows. Most of these smaller operations only represent real estate in their neighbourhood, so pick the area in which you'd like to look and walk into any agency. Many are franchised and the service is standard throughout. It's best to bring a Chinese speaking friend since most local agents don't speak English, however. Agencies that cater specifically to expatriates with budgets larger than ¥7,500 abound and generally include an English-speaking service. Some of the most reputable ones are listed in the table below.

Besides agencies, there are plenty of resources for people looking to rent or share a flat. Sharing an apartment is common among younger expats in Shanghai and most of the listings mentioned below have a 'roommates wanted' section. While many new arrivals can afford their own place, sharing rent is a good way to save money as well as meet new people and perhaps learn from a more seasoned expat. Alternatively, some foreigners choose to live with locals – an excellent language and cultural opportunity. Check for property or roommate listings in *that's Shanghai* or *City Weekend* magazines. Online, you can find property listings on www.shanghai.craigslist.org, www.enjoyclassifieds.com, www.adweekly.cn, www.cityweekend.com.cn and www.shanghai.asiaxpat.com.

Housing Abbreviations	
A/C	Air Conditioner
Ba	Bathrooms
Br	Bedrooms
A/C-H	Heating
Lr	Living Room

Real Estate Agents

Real estate agents in Shanghai take 30%-100% of your first month's rent as commission. Make sure you come to an understanding with the agent before you sign on the dotted line. Only certain realtors, such as Space or Crispin Property Consultants, do sales. A real estate agent must be licensed by the local authorities, so check for their stamped business registration on the wall.

Real Estate Agents		
Ark International	6248 8464	www.ark-shanghai.com
Asia Asset	6288 3785	www.asia-asset.com
Autumn Leaves	3406 0273	www.autumnleaves.com.cn
BB House	5236 7766	www.bb-house.com.cn
Build Shanghai	5213 6309	www.buildshanghai.com
City Grand	6288 5502	www.citygrand.com
Crispin Property Consultants	3310 0077	www.cpcproperty.com
Easyhome Shanghai Property Agency	5117 4877	www.easyhome-shanghai.com
Fullhome Real Estate	5115 0101	www.fullhomechina.com
Kingseal	3401 1008	www.kingseal.net
Metropolis Property Consultants	6210 9150	www.metropolis-sh.com
Mid Sunshine Property	6380 9021	www.mid-sunshine.com
Pacific Relocations	6218 6660	www.worthenpacific.com
Phoenix Property Realty	6240 4052	www.shanghai-realty.com
Red Dragon Property Agency	5230 2979	www.reddragonproperty.com
Shanghai Kingswick Property Agency	6278 2929	www.sh-kingswick.com
Shanghai Pearl Property	5102 9172	www.shrelocation.com
Space	5404 0110	www.space.sh.cn
Supercity Property Consultant	6219 7110	www.supercity.com.cn
Transpac Real Estate	5835 9400	www.transpac.com

Long and Short of It

*Quickly disappearing,
Shanghai's* longtang
alleys and shikumen
*(stone gate houses)
define the city's
architectural heritage.
The trend arose in the
mid-19th century and
is a great example of
east meets west design;
traditional Chinese
courtyards
surrounding western
townhouses. At one
point* longtang
*accounted for 60% of
Shanghai's housing.
Most were occupied by
several families and
few had modern
luxuries such as
indoor plumbing.*

The Lease

After the tenant and landlord sign the lease agreement, the landlord is required to register the lease with the local district authorities. This rarely happens, however, because landlords want to avoid the resulting stamp duty of 0.1% of the rent (which, if required, is shared by both tenant and landlord). Municipal officials don't seem to press the matter. However, if you're on a housing budget, your company will require a monthly *fapiao* (receipt) from your landlord. This incurs a 5% tax for each *fapiao*, so your landlord may make excuses. You may have to bargain a small increase in rent.

Most leases require tenants to give one month's notice of early departure. Early lease termination usually means the tenant loses the two-month security deposit, unless there is a 'diplomatic clause' in the contract (originally for those in the diplomatic service who may be called away suddenly due to political problems, a diplomatic cause is also referred to as a 'break clause'). A break clause allows the tenant to leave without sufficient notice and still receive the original deposit.

If the tenant has fulfilled the lease obligations and has not damaged the property, he or she is entitled to have the full deposit returned no later than 30 days after moving out. A tenant may request an English version of the lease, but keep in mind that most local agents' English leases are merely poorly translated and abridged versions of the Chinese original. If disagreements arise during the lease period, only the Chinese version is legally binding so it may be worthwhile having someone translate the lease for you if your language skills aren't up to par. The real estate agent often arbitrates any disagreement. If no compromise can be reached, real estate conflicts can be hashed out at the China International Economic and Trade Arbitration Commission of Shanghai (28 Jinling Xi Lu; 6387 7878). Be forewarned, however, that if the disagreement escalates into a full-blown legal action, foreigners rarely get the upper hand in property disputes.

Main Accommodation Options

There are many different types of accommodation available in the city, from studio apartments downtown to sprawling villas in the far-reaching green suburbs. The type you opt for is largely dictated by your budget, and often determines your lifestyle, so choose carefully.

Duplex

Duplexes are new, two-level apartments found in western-styled complexes. Usually equipped with modern heating and kitchen facilities, they total at least 200 square metres. Expect to pay rents starting from ¥12,000.

Garden House

Garden homes offer stunning secluded surroundings in the heart of downtown Shanghai. Only former concession areas, such as the British or French Concessions, boast garden homes. These attractive colonial standalone houses have terraces and a large adjacent green space, a real rarity in the city. Expect homes to be two to three storeys, totalling at least 250 square metres. Garden homes have all been renovated to a degree, but some may still suffer from poor heating and structural problems. Rents for these exclusive properties begin at ¥45,000.

Lane House

A colonial lane house stands two-to-three storeys and abuts other homes on both sides. Rows of lane houses are found along downtown *longtang* lanes. The first floor entrance sometimes has a small lawn and some feature roof terraces or gardens.

85

Warming to Shanghai Winters

Heating is a major issue for a lot of foreigners. When the bone-chilling Shanghai winter sets in, many recent arrivals discover that the temperatures inside their homes are colder than outdoors. Due to long-standing government regulations, insulation, double-paned windows and central heating are largely unheard of in the city, even in modern apartments. Only recently have some overseas developers and savvy private owners begun to install these amenities. The Shanghainese, for their part, insist that the cold is good for the body. If you think differently, check that there are sufficient *kong tiao* (space heaters) and that the window frames form a seal with the glass – central heating and radiators do exist but usually raise the rent significantly. Some apartment buildings offer double-paned windows for an added fee (ask the landlord). Kitchens can also be a compromise. Chinese families usually cook with two burners and do not use ovens, so kitchens are often small, and located in outer rooms, especially in older apartments. Stove and oven units can be purchased at home appliance stores for ¥5,000-¥8,000 but landlords frequently agree to make the investment.

Narrow staircases connect the multiple floors so lane houses may not be the best place for young children. Closely packed neighbours and thin walls make lane homes noisy at times but the public spaces between the rows are a great place to interact with your neighbours and observe Shanghainese life. Rents start at ¥16,000 for 100-plus square metre homes.

New Apartment

Shanghai's real estate boom of the last 10 years produced thousands of new high-rise apartments across the city. Building quality varies wildly. Many new complexes start to have structural issues within two to three years of completion. Mid-to-high range apartment complexes, with rents starting at ¥16,000, usually have gyms, pools and community centres.

Old Apartment

Despite its habit of levelling the old to prepare for the new, the city government has spared several pockets of 1930s and 40s colonial housing. These apartments, some within lane houses, all suffer from drafty windows and poor heating but capture the true flavour of Shanghai with real wood floors, beautiful brick exteriors and lively neighbourhoods. Colonial apartments are not confined to downtown areas and can be found throughout the city. Rents start at ¥4,000.

New Villa

The farther out of the city you go, the larger the accommodation becomes. Property complexes in suburban areas such as Gubei, Hongqiao, Minhang and Pudong all have villa communities. Varying in quality and furnishings, these standalone houses are always within secure gated complexes. Design varies depending on the theme of the complex but many villas now boast open kitchens and central heating. The rent of a large, three-bedroom villa starts at ¥40,000 in Hongqiao and ¥20,000 in other areas.

Townhouses

A new incarnation of Shanghai's downtown lane houses, multi-storey townhouses are appearing in many recent suburban developments. Townhouses tend to be noisier but cheaper than their villa counterparts. Rents for a 200 square metre townhouse start at ¥16,000.

Other Rental Costs

Be prepared to pay the first month's rent, along with a two-month security deposit, upon signing a lease agreement. Tenants also need to pay the agreed real estate commission, unless they found the apartment through other means. Utility expenses should not begin until the start of the lease term, and do not require any initial deposits. If the apartment is new, the landlord should take on any set-up costs for water, phone lines and other such facilities. If the landlord chooses to register the lease with the local authorities, the tenant must share the resulting stamp duty (0.05% of the rent each).

Buying Property

Buying property in Shanghai, like anywhere else in the world, is a serious, long-term commitment. As the city's economy continues to boom and new apartment complexes stand purchased but empty, government officials are trying their best to cool the market and curb speculation. Regulations constantly change, especially where foreign buyers and sellers are concerned.

For now, foreigners can only purchase one residential property and must live in Shanghai (with a residence permit) for one year before the date of purchase. Additionally, you must pay a 20% capital gains tax if you sell within the first five years (capital gains is the term for the owner's remaining profit after the sale, minus sales costs and expenses). Buying space in Shanghai is no longer a short-term proposition, but experts say there is another 10 years of growth in the city's real estate market and money can still be made if the buyer is willing to hold on to the property. Regardless, an apartment in the downtown of a major world city will always be in demand.

Property Pitfalls

Shoddy construction work, continual repossessing of lands for municipal developments, and over-speculation are just a few of the problems in Shanghai's real estate market. Before buying, have a structural engineer or architect check out the foundations of the home – many hastily thrown-together complexes in the city will be lucky to last another 20 years.

If your home is suddenly in the way of a new Shanghai Metro line or mall, the government is obligated to buy the property back at the local market price (read: the minimum price you would pay for the property). The property owners are usually told five years ahead of time. To avoid purchasing an apartment not long for this world, buyers can view the next five-year city plan at the Housing and Planning Bureau. The Shanghai Municipal Housing, Land and Resource Commission (95 Beijing Xi Lu; 6319 3188) can guide you to your district's map. Your real estate agent should also be able to direct you to the proper district office. Buying in a municipal preserved building (*baohu jiance*), marked by a bronze plate on the building's exterior, also decreases the chances of an impending wrecking ball.

Property Rights

In Shanghai, there are two types of ownership rights: user rights (*shi yong quan*) and freehold rights (*chang quan*). The former grants rights to use the land and the latter offers rights to the property. Foreigners are not allowed to purchase user rights. Freehold rights are for a period of 70 years, at the end of which the owner may pay a tax to extend the period. The details of this policy have yet to be set forth by the government, but real estate experts predict a small, one-time tax will be sufficient to extend the period. Only a potential buyer of a garden home should be concerned about the amount of years left on a property, since the land tax for these properties may be quite steep (up to ¥3,000 per square metre).

The Process

The first step for a prospective buyer is to find a reliable and licensed agent. Even for expats armed with all the available information, the agent is an important go-between during the sometimes inscrutable purchasing process.

After making an offer on a home, the owner and prospective buyer will sign a stamped sales contract. This contract is needed to apply for a mortgage. The two parties also need to go to the District Property Exchange Centre to transfer the name on the property title. Your real estate agent should direct you to your district's office. At this time, you need to provide your residence permit to prove you have lived in

Shanghai for at least a year. New foreign owners then need to make a 30% down payment on the home. The whole sales and mortgage process should take two to three weeks.

Buying to Rent

Currently, no regulations or systems exist to stop foreigners from renting their property out in the fair market. Current rental yields hover around 7% and may be increased if the property's design and construction are done well and angled towards foreign renters.

Selling Property

Most sellers work through agents to advertise their property and facilitate the paperwork. Agents will ask for 1% of the sales price from the current owner. Make sure to have the title to the home, up-to-date tax documentation, and the original purchase receipt to hand. Also factor in renovation or refitting costs, depending on the state of the home and your desired selling price. Current regulations ask for a 20% capital gains tax if you sell the property within the first five years of purchase.

Moving Again?

If you like what the *Shanghai Explorer* offers, take a look at some of our other titles. Whatever the city, we'll tell you what you need to know for whatever it is you want to do.

Mortgages

Many Chinese banks offer mortgages to foreign homeowners. Foreigners can borrow up to 70% of the value of a recently built property and around 50% of an older property. Requirements and regulations differ from bank to bank, but most need to see proof of income as well as all visa and passport documentation. The majority of banks only offer adjustable rate mortgages so interest rates may change as the Central Bank adjusts the yuan. In 2007 the Chinese yuan interest rate hovered around the 5.5% mark. Everbright Bank remains the only one in the city to offer fixed-rate mortgages, although other banks say they're moving to do the same. Do some comparison shopping – a few Chinese banks have unfavourable early repayment policies or overly complicated application processes. HSBC and Standard Chartered offer a US or Hong Kong dollar mortgage (a great way to take advantage of the appreciating dollar to the yuan). Also, be wary of owners or developers who force you to use a certain mortgage provider – this often means they have some sort of kickback deal with the bank.

Mortgage Providers		
Bank of China	95566	www.bank-of-china.com
Bank of Communications	95559	www.bankcomm.com
China Construction Bank	95533	www.ccb.com
China Everbright Bank	95595	www.cebbank.com
HSBC	80 0830 2880	www.hsbc.com.cn
Industrial & Construction Bank of China (ICBC)	95588	www.icbc.com.cn
Shanghai Pudong Development Bank	6329 6188	www.spdb.com.cn

Other Purchasing Costs

Property agents usually charge 1% of the cost of the property. Taxes range from 3%-5% depending on the type of property. Construction costs for fitting out a house (any renovations minus furnishings) start from ¥1,000 per square metre thanks to a cheap labour force.

WAI WHITE DRAGON'S
Who is Who

Broadening your networking experience

Wai White Dragon's Who is Who

The Prestigious International Community and Guide in Shanghai

The exclusive biographical Encyclopedia and networking tool
1,300 entries of prominent people working and living in Shanghai
Publication available in printed and online database version

The concept of highlighting accomplished people and tool for building personal and professional relationships.

Wai White Dragon's Who is Who
Your networking platform:

- Get to know your business partners and their backgrounds
- Perfect corporate gift for your professional partners
- Meet CEOs, General Managers and entrepreneurs in Shanghai
- Share professional and personal interests
- Give the best exposure to yourself, your company and your projects
- Entry social elite and business circles

Find out about this elegant and functional Encyclopedia and explore our online database about notable people on our website www.waiwhitedragon.com, or e-mail us at info@waiwhitedragon.com

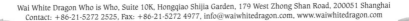

Wai White Dragon Who is Who, Suite 10K, Hongqiao Shijia Garden, 179 West Zhong Shan Road, 200051 Shanghai
Contact: +86-21-5272 2525, Fax: +86-21-5272 4977, info@waiwhitedragon.com, www.waiwhitedragon.com

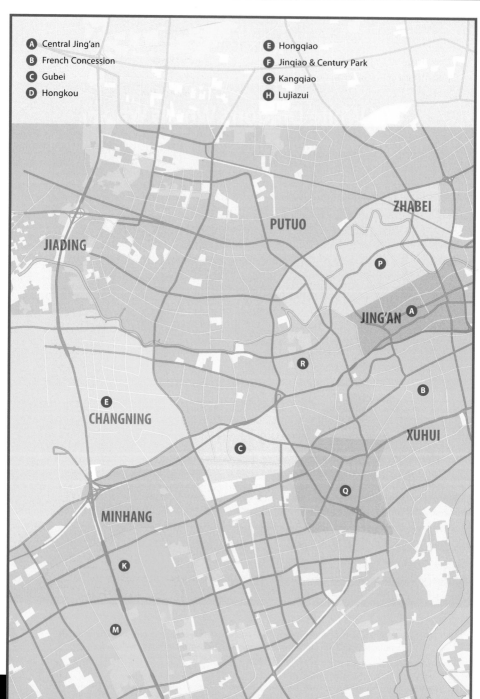

Ⓐ Central Jing'an
Ⓑ French Concession
Ⓒ Gubei
Ⓓ Hongkou
Ⓔ Hongqiao
Ⓕ Jinqiao & Century Park
Ⓖ Kangqiao
Ⓗ Lujiazui

ZHABEI

PUTUO

JIADING

JING'AN

CHANGNING

XUHUI

MINHANG

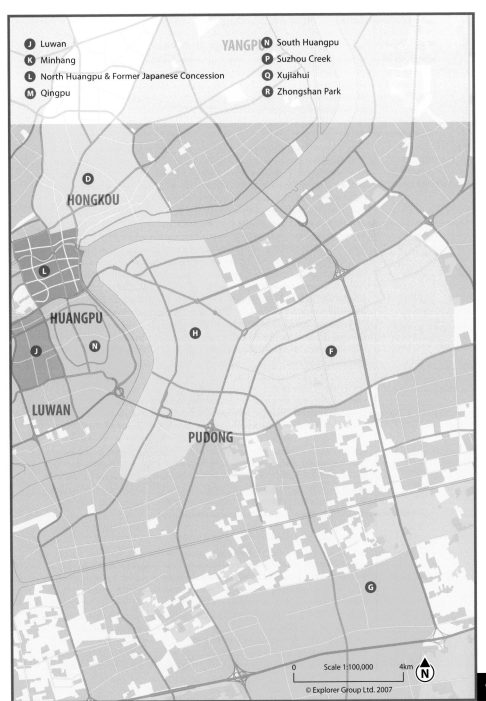

J Luwan
K Minhang
L North Huangpu & Former Japanese Concession
M Qingpu

YANGPU
N South Huangpu
P Suzhou Creek
Q Xujiahui
R Zhongshan Park

D
HONGKOU

L

HUANGPU

H

F

J

N

LUWAN

PUDONG

G

0   Scale 1:100,000   4km   N

© Explorer Group Ltd. 2007

Best Point

Convenient, in-the-thick-of-things living, with plenty of entertainment and eating options.

Central Jing'an

Central Jing'an is one of Shanghai's busiest business, shopping and entertainment hubs. The area runs from the Yan'an highway in the south up to Changping Lu in the north and stretches beyond the newly renovated Jing'an Temple to Zhengning Lu in the west and to the elevated Chengdu Lu highway in the east. This downtown district includes densely packed residential areas, high-end business and shopping centres, popular bar streets and the crossroads of the city's major Metro and bus lines. A very convenient but crowded home address.

Worst Point

Noisy with fewer high-end apartments and far from international schools.

Overview map, p.90

Accommodation

Central Jing'an has fewer residential options than other areas, and neighbourhoods tend to be noisier and more hectic. Modern high rises such as One Park Avenue on Lane 500 Chengde Lu or Manhattan Heights at 339 Xikang Lu offer fully furnished one and two-bedroom apartments with western kitchens, central air conditioning, parking facilities, and large clubhouses with indoor pools, gyms and tennis courts. The complexes almost exclusively attract foreigners. Rents begin from ¥8,000. The cavernous Shanghai Centre (6279 8600; www.shanghaicentre.com) – a business and residential enclave surrounding the Portman Ritz-Carlton hotel at 1376 Nanjing Xi Lu – houses 472 US-dominated high-end service apartments. Expect higher rents here, from ¥20,000 and up. The remainder of central Jing'an is home to older Chinese residential neighbourhoods which increase in density as you move north towards the creek. Accommodation is cheaper than in the complexes mentioned above, and foreigner friendly, with 24 hour security, public courtyards, and within walking distance of supermarkets and public transport. Colonial buildings from the former British Concession are found in the western half of the area and offer expats a feel of old Shanghai. South of Nanjing Xi Lu are tangles of expansive *longtangs*, divided by busy shopping streets. Rents vary in these older areas, from ¥3,000 to ¥8,000, depending on the home's condition.

Shopping & Amenities

Central Jing'an is divided by the city's premiere shopping street, Nanjing Xi Lu. Several malls and a surprising number of luxury shops, including Louis Vuitton, Tiffany's, and Chanel, line this portion of the famous street. Plaza 66 is the area's main upmarket shopping mall, and its expansive pavement is a popular spot for window shoppers, watch sellers, foreigners on the go and local fashionistas. For western food supplies such as meat and cheese, try City Shop in the Shanghai Centre (6279 8018), the mini City Shop on Chengde Lu, or Japanese import Freshmart in the basement of the Sogo mall at 1608 Nanjing Xi Lu by Jing'an Temple. Several Chinese supermarkets, including a large Park n' Shop in the basement of Westgate Mall, and wet markets north of Nanjing Xi Lu provide an ample supply of cheap produce.

Entertainment & Leisure

At night, Central Jing'an hosts hordes of locals and expats in the many bars on Tongren Lu and the adjacent blocks. Sport bars Malone's at 255 Tongren Lu (p.393) and Big Bamboo at 132 Nanyang Lu (p.305) offer pub grub and big-screen TVs while the after-work crowds enjoy happy hour at Blue Frog at 86 Tongren Lu (p.388). Young Chinese and foreign university students congregate for the ¥10 beer at Windows Too at 1699 Nanjing Lu (p.399). In addition to drinking options, Jing'an also offers a lot of great food – both western and Chinese. Try the basements of Sogo or Westgate malls for convenient lunch options, salads and smoothies at Element Fresh in the Shanghai Centre (6279 8682), great dim sum at Royal China on the eighth floor of Sogo, or cheap Cantonese on Wanghangdu Lu. After eating, take a stroll in the well-manicured Jing'an

Park across from the temple or check out a show at the Majestic Theatre at 66 Jiangning Lu behind the Westgate Mall.

Healthcare

World Link has a fully staffed medical (6279 7698) and dental facility (6279 8318) in the Shanghai Centre at 1376 Nanjing Lu. A quick walk over Yan'an Lu to the French Concession area brings Central Jing'an residents to Huashan Hospital at 2 Urumqi Zhong Lu, which has a 24 hour foreign clinic on the 19th floor (6248 3986). The American-Sino obstetrics and gynaecology clinic (p.139) is also located on the 14th floor of Huashan Hospital; the outpatient facility is a few blocks away at 800 Huashan Lu (6210 2299).

The Temple

Jing'an is named after the temple at its heart. The Buddhist Jing'an Temple dates back to the third century and is one of the oldest landmarks in the region. For more information see Exploring, p.180.

Education

Expat children in central Jing'an face a longer commute than their classmates in more suburban areas. No international schools have campuses in this area but many offer shuttle bus services from downtown complexes such as the Shanghai Centre. Check the school's website for pick-up and drop-off times and locations – most campuses design routes around their current student population, but also reserve the right to refuse bus service. Many parents in this area opt for a long commute for their kids out to the American and British schools in Hongqiao (around 45 minutes by car) rather than a Metro ride and taxi to Pudong locations.

Transport

Central Jing'an is by far the most convenient area in the city in terms of transport. Metro Line 2 follows Nanjing Lu with stops at Jing'an Temple and Nanjing Xi Lu. Several useful bus lines converge at Jing'an Temple. Take buses 20, 37 or 921 down Nanjing Lu. Bus 830 goes down Hengshan Lu for access to Xujiahui and 939 runs along Beijing Lu until turning north into Hongkou. Taxis are easy to grab (except when it rains) and you can find cab stands at the Shanghai Centre and the Westgate Mall. Motorbikes loiter around the malls and Metro stops during rush hour, looking for passengers.

Safety & Annoyances

This is a busy, crowded area and, if you live street-level, expect a lot of noise. The area is very safe, like the rest of Shanghai, although there are aggressive beggars and vendors along Tongren Lu and Plaza 66 in the evenings.

Nanjing Xi Lu offices

Jing'an apartments

Best Point
An attractive and
historic home address.

French Concession

The French Concession boasts tree-lined streets, quiet neighbourhoods, quaint housing and a central location. The attractive area includes most of the city's historic buildings and is the first choice for many foreigners, accommodating almost one third of expats.

Accommodation

Worst Point
Tough to get a cab
and few public
transportation options.

Gorgeous historic apartments, lane houses and garden homes line beautiful streets such as Wukang Lu, Hunan Lu, Gaoyou Lu and Jinxian Lu. Due to its popularity, rental prices for colonial properties from the 1920s have been rising steadily. For two-bedroom renovated apartments, expect rents to start at ¥25,000. Lane houses and garden homes in this area represent the highest downtown rents, from ¥50,000 and up. Several service apartments scatter the area, including the Summit, Ambassy and Forty One Hengshan Road.

Overview map, p.90

Shopping & Amenities

The area has several Chinese supermarkets and smaller wet markets for basic grocery needs. Expats travel to the large Parkson's department store at 918 Huaihai Lu (p.342) or the City Shop next door (6474 1290) for imported ingredients. There are pharmacies and banks along the adjacent section of Huaihai. Carrefour (6474 1290) has a branch in the Hong Kong New World department store at 939 Huaihai Lu, next to the Shanxi Lu Metro station. Boutique shops have sprung up along Changle Lu (mostly urban fashion), Xinle Lu (for the older crowd) and Sinan Lu. These lovely small stores are constantly changing hands and redefining themselves according to the city's fickle trends.

Entertainment & Leisure

Stroll through the French Concession's narrow streets admiring the art deco hotels such as Jin Jiang and the Okura Garden on Maoming Lu, or the area's many boutique shops. Fuxing Park (p.212) is a pleasant respite from the hordes on Huaihai. Listen to jazz in sultry JZ Club (p.392), bring your laptop to the popular Wi-Fi spot Coffee Tree (p.380), or enjoy the famous carrot cake at Ginger (p.381).

Healthcare

The New Pioneer Medical Centre on 910 Hengshan Lu has a foreign-friendly medical and maternity clinic (6469 3898) as does Ruijin Hospital at 197 Ruijin Er Lu (6437 0045). Huashan Hospital at 2 Urumqi Zhong Lu has a 24 hour foreign clinic on the 19th floor (6248 3986). The American-Sino obstetrics and gynaecology clinic (p.134) is also located in the Huashan Hospital, and the outpatient facility is on 800 Huashan Lu (6210 2299).

Education

The area houses a few international kindergartens and pre-schools, including a Montessori school (p.148). Older international students must commute to Hongqiao or Minhang campuses by bus, which takes between 45 minutes and an hour.

Transport

The French Concession is mostly dependent on taxis and cars, with Metro Line 1 only accessible at three stops: Shanxi Bei Lu, Changshu Lu and Hengshan Lu. The area is notorious for the lack of cabs in rush hour, and the twisting one-way streets often cause traffic jams. Taking motorcycles is a good option, as is buying a moped to avoid traffic.

Safety & Annoyances

The French Concession is safe, although there have been break-ins at first-floor colonial homes. The area is quieter than other downtown areas but has fewer public transportation options.

Boulevards and buildings of the French Concession

Best Point
Convenient, secure living for families.

Gubei

Located to the east of Hongqiao, this suburban outpost hosted Shanghai's first foreign apartment complex, built in 1994. Today, the area caters to mainly Asian expats, specifically Korean and Japanese. The residential area is a convenient and well-equipped compromise for expat parents with offices downtown and children in Hongqiao schools.

Worst Point
A lack of distinct personality in strip-mall suburbia.

Overview map, p.90

Accommodation

There are fewer villas in Gubei than in other suburban areas such as Hongqiao, with the accomodation consisting mostly of high-rise apartment complexes. Housing is cheaper in this pocket of the suburbs – expect a big range, from ¥4,000 low-end apartment buildings to ¥80,000 villa homes. The few high-end options are within larger gated complexes, usually with European-inspired names such as Vienna Plaza and Marseilles Mansion.

Shopping & Amenities

The city's largest Carrefour at 268 Shuicheng Nan Lu (6209 8899) is the focal point of Gubei's busy shopping area. There is also a Parkson's supermarket, which includes a popular western butcher counter, at 100 Zunyi Lu (6257 4518). Home supplies and speciality foods can easily be found in the shops of Gubei.

Entertainment & Leisure

The area has several excellent Korean and Japanese restaurants, such as De All Korean Cuisine and Bar at 768 Huangjincheng Dao (6219 7727), as well as Chinese and western fare. Although the area lacks nightlife, there are some nightspots like the classy bar The Door (6295 3737) at 1468 Hongqiao Lu. For daytime activities, the area around Gubei Lu hosts several yoga studios, massage parlours and spas.

Healthcare

Gubei is 10-20 minutes by car to the healthcare facilities in Hongqiao (see p.98).

Education

Yew Chung Shanghai International School (p.154) has two campuses in Gubei. The area also has several pre-schools and kindergartens. Gubei children have an easy commute to the schools in Hongqiao.

Transport

Right off the Yan'an Elevated Highway, Gubei is a straight drive into the city, but expect delays during peak hours. Metro Line 3 crosses the east edge of Gubei with a stop along Hongqiao Lu. It is also an easy 10-15 minute ride by car to Hongqiao Airport. Parking is plentiful within the expansive villa complexes.

Safety & Annoyances

Gubei is an extremely safe area with most residential areas locked and guarded at all times, but it can be boring for those used to fast-paced city life.

Gubei villas

Hongkou

Hongkou is in the north-eastern corner of Shanghai. The district's two universities, Fudan and Shanghai International Studies University (SISU), attract thousands of foreign students each year with their Chinese language programmes. The home of the former American Concession, Hongkou is a pleasant city district, with old homes, museums, parks and busy shopping streets. The area lacks direct public transportation links to the downtown, however, and a smaller number of working expats choose to live here.

Accommodation

Hongkou has some of the city's best mix of European and Chinese-style architecture and offers a blend of new high-rises, older homes and mid-range local communities. Duolun Lu, the area's famous cobblestone 'culture street', has smaller apartments, along with coffee shops, scroll stores and jewellery stalls. Near the universities, housing is mainly older apartment buildings for students. Expect rent to range from ¥2,000 for student housing to ¥15,000 for larger homes.

Overview map, p.90

Shopping & Amenities

The district has a large Carrefour at 560 Quyang Lu (5589 6076), north of the SISU campus. Hongkou's main shopping street, Sichuan Bei Lu, runs from Lu Xun Park in the north down to Suzhou Creek, and is lined with shops, banks and food stores. Smaller shops specialising in home goods, furniture and kitchen wares cluster around the university campuses.

Entertainment & Leisure

Shanghai's Hongkou Football Stadium hosts the city's football league as well as various concerts and cultural events. A rock climbing gym (5696 6657), laser tag centre (5560 0658) and swimming pool complex, which serves as an ice rink in the winter, surround the stadium. The adjacent Lu Xun Park (p.213) is one of the city's best, with boat rides, playing fields and singing locals. The Duolun Lu Modern Art Museum (p.197) features a collection of China's contemporary artists.

Healthcare

IMCC First People's Hospital at 85 Wujin Lu has a small foreign clinic (6306 9480).

Education

Shanghai International Studies University and Fudan University both offer semester or year-long programmes in Chinese language and culture. International schools for youngsters all require long commutes from Hongkou.

Transport

The Pearl Line (Metro Line 3) runs through Hongkou, stopping at Dong Baoxing Lu, Hongkou Football Stadium and Chifeng Lu. Line 8, arriving by 2010, will traverse the middle of the district, adding stops along Dalian Lu. Line 4 also skirts the bottom of the area. For now you have to switch lines at Shanghai Railway Station. To get into town, you're better off taking a taxi along the ring road, then connecting to the Yan'an Elevated Highway. The trip still takes 20-30 minutes – Sichuan Bei Lu can become extremely congested in rush hour. Many bus routes run along this street, making the route a time-consuming commute. Bus 21 runs from Beijing Lu to Lu Xun Park and several buses take commuters to areas around People Square, including lines 17 and 123.

Safety & Annoyances

Hongkou is a safe area, but is a lengthy commute into the city.

Best Point

Quiet, suburban living with all the conveniences.

Hongqiao

Originally an industrial zone inside Changning district, far-flung Hongqiao is now a city neighbourhood in its own right. Located east of Beihong Lu and Hongxu Lu, it is an extremely popular place for expats with families, close to several international schools, and has a well-developed infrastructure of housing, retail and entertainment for its largely foreign residents. Commuting into town, however, may take over an hour in heavy traffic.

Worst Point

Away from the centre and long commutes to downtown.

Overview map, p.90

Accommodation

Large villa communities such as Le-Chateau on Jianhe Lu (6262 2020) and Hongqiao Golf Villas at 555 Hongxu Lu dominate Hongqiao's housing market. These expansive villas offer gardens and come with pools, sports facilities and community activities. Many are close to supermarkets, cafes and clinics. Rents are more expensive than in Minhang or Qingpu, but families receive a lot more floor space for their money than in central areas. Expect villa rents to start from ¥32,000 a month. Popular complex Shanghai American Homes on Qingxi Lu (6291 1052) offers apartments from ¥20,000, and, a bit further out, you can even live on a golf course at Sheshan Golf Estate (see p.83).

Shopping & Amenities

The Carrefour in Gubei at 268 Shuicheng Lu (6209 8899) is easily accessible by taxi or shuttle bus. Hongqiao has many of its own western markets, including City Shop at 3211 Hongmei Lu. The multi-storey Hongqiao Friendship Store on Zunyi Lu houses a well-stocked supermarket, restaurants and clothing stores (6270 0000).

Entertainment & Leisure

The pedestrian section of Hongmei Lu in Hongqiao has developed into a popular restaurant and bar street, with American burger and fries at Moon River Diner (p.356), German fare at Papas Bierstube (6465 8880), and Indian Kitchen (6261 0377) all popular.

Healthcare

There are several healthcare facilities in Hongqiao, including a World Link medical centre at 2258 Hongqiao Lu (6445 5999), the Hongqiao Clinic in Mandarin City at 788 Hongxu Lu, the private Sun-Tec Medical Centre at 2281 Hongqiao Lu (6268 8811) and the Shanghai United Family Hospital, which offers 24 hour care (see p.136).

Education

Hongqiao is a popular address for families because of the easy access to international schools. The Livingston American School (p.154), Rainbow Bridge International School (p.148), Shanghai Community International School (p.154) and the Sino-Canada School (5111 3113) all have Hongqiao campuses. The area also has several pre-school and kindergarten programmes. Some residents bus their children west to the Shanghai American School (p.152), Shanghai Singapore International School (p.154) and British International School (p.152) in Minhang, or the Eurocampus in Qingpu.

Transport

The closest Metro is a 20 minute cab ride, so most residents depend on cars and taxis. Commutes into the city are simple enough, thanks to easy access to the Yan'an Elevated Highway. Easy doesn't mean fast, however, as rides downtown can take more than an hour at peak times. Drives into Minhang and Qingpu can be just as variable.

Safety & Annoyances

Life in the 'burbs is extremely safe, although you may feel isolated from the excitement of the city at times. Traffic can be testy, especially at peak hours.

Best Point◀
A great place for
families with schools,
parks and restaurants
near by.

Jinqiao & Century Park

Jinqiao (also called Green City) is much like the suburbs in the western world with its wide streets, green lawns and family-friendly neighbourhoods. Adjacent Century Park offers slightly more congested city blocks, with government buildings, art museums and strip malls. Both areas are convenient home addresses for those who work in the adjacent high-tech parks of Pudong, and for the nearby international schools. Isolated from the city, however, exposure to Chinese language and culture is limited.

Worst Point◀
A bit of a bubble and a
long ride into the city.

Overview map, p.90

Accommodation

Spacious high-end villa communities such as the Spanish-inspired Vizcaya Villas or the luxurious Green Villas dot the landscape in Jinqiao. The remaining residential blocks of Green City consist of mid-range apartments for locals and single foreigners. Villa rents range from ¥35,000 to ¥70,000. Expect smaller apartment complexes to start at ¥20,000. High-end property peaks around ¥95,000 a month. Ten minutes south of Green City lies Tomson Golf Court (5833 2288), which hosts a scattering of luxury villa homes around the golf course, housing mostly Asian expats. All these developments include community centres, pools and plenty of room to run and play for kids. Century Park offers slightly cheaper housing than central Jinqiao with smaller apartments and fewer villas.

Shopping & Amenities

Two large Carrefours service the Jinqiao area: one at 555 Biyun Lu (5030 6899) and the other at 185 Fengdian Lu (800 820 0871). Yanggao Lu connects the two shopping hubs. Next to the Biyun Lu Carrefour, Green Plaza at 633 Biyun Lu houses another western supermarket, Pines the Marketplace (5030 6971), as well as the sporting goods store Decathlon, B&Q and various gift shops. The Fengdian Lu Carrefour is smaller than the Biyun branch but within Thumb Plaza, which also hosts a wide range of restaurants and speciality shops. Seasons Villa at 1983 Huamu Lu, next to Tomson Golf Course, also houses a Pines (5030 6971).

Entertainment & Leisure

Many foreigners frequent Green Plaza's Blue Frog (p.388) and Italian Cameo (5030 5009) restaurants as well as the centre's giant gym, Megafit (5030 8118). Thumb Plaza has its own set of similar eateries, including popular American diner Moon River

Housing near Century Park

(p.356). Jinqiao's open spaces, rare in other parts of the city, are perfect for bike riding, rollerblading or impromptu sports games. Several golf courses, including the nearby Tomson Golf Course, keep Pudong's business set busy on the weekends. Century Park is one of the city's largest green spaces, and its formal, manicured grounds offer quiet walks and beautiful scenery. Locals and foreigners enjoy renting rollerblades from next to the Shanghai Science & Technology Museum and zipping around the roads surrounding Century Park.

Healthcare
World Link's Pudong branch is in the eastern end of Green City at 51 Hongfeng Lu (5032 5826) and houses a medical and dental clinic.

Education
Jinqiao exists because of the international campuses in the area, including the Shanghai Japanese School, Concordia International School (p.152) and Dulwich College (p.152). The area provides easy access to the Shanghai American School (p.152) and the British International School (p.150) to the east and Yew Chung International School's two campuses near Century Park (p.154).

Folding Bikes
One option to beat the taxi blues, and get some exercise in the process, is to commute to the nearest Metro by bicycle. If you have a considerable trip on both ends of the Metro ride, consider investing in a folding bicycle. See Shopping (p.311) to find out where's good for buying bikes.

Transport
Green City residents need cars or taxis to get around. The wide, spread-out city blocks, native to Pudong, make it difficult to walk longer distances. In the car, commuters can easily take Longyang Lu to Zhangjiang High-Tech Park or Yanggao Lu to Lujiazui and then across the river to Puxi. Metro Line 2 loops under Jinqiao, so you must take a cab to the nearest stop at the Science & Technology Museum.

Safety & Annoyances
Jinqiao is a very safe area, with residents having little interaction with those outside their close-knit communities. It's a bit of a bubble and those craving city life may get frustrated living in the far-flung suburbs.

Century Avenue

Kangqiao

Best Point ◀
Not too far from downtown by car, unlike other areas of Pudong.

Worst Point ◀
The area is still developing, and has very few stores or dining spots.

Overview map, p.90

Kangqiao is a new development on Pudong's south side, which has sprung up as a result of the nearby international schools and industrial parks. The area resembles Jinqiao a few years ago, with scattered housing and slowly developing infrastructure for expats.

Oriental Pearl Tower in nearby Lujiazui

Accommodation
Having had plenty of practice in built-up areas such as Hongqiao and Jinqiao, property developers offer new and improved villas in Kangqiao. Rents are in the ¥30,000-plus range for villa property. Smaller townhouses in developments such as Oasis Villas are cheaper than in other suburban areas, with rents from ¥20,000 to ¥40,000. Some accommodation looks out on the nearby industrial parks, which makes for an unattractive skyline.

Shopping & Amenities
Kangqiao shoppers head for the Lotus Supermarket at 3521 Shangnan Lu (6832 1188) and 1126 Yanggao Nan Lu (5873 1228) – both reachable in under 20 minutes by car.

Entertainment & Leisure
Kangqiao offers few entertainment venues other than the abundant green space. An easy 20 minute drive takes you to the shops of Lujiazui (pictured) or over Nanpu Bridge to the Bund and beyond.

Healthcare
Kangqiao is a short drive to the medical facilities in Lujiazui and Jinqiao (see p.102).

Education
There are two international schools: the British International School (p.150) and the Shanghai Community International School (p.154). Students can also commute by car to Jinqiao (see p.99).

Transport
Kangqiao residents depend on their cars to get around. Easy access to the ring road means fast commutes into southern Puxi.

Safety & Annoyances
Kangqiao is very safe as most housing is behind guarded gates. Kangqiao is still dependant on nearby areas for shopping and entertainment.

Best Point ◀

Close to the Metro and filled with entertainment and eating options.

Worst Point ◀

It's still Pudong: wide streets, empty blocks, and a distance from the bigger half of the city.

Overview map, p.90

Lujiazui

Pudong's business and financial centre and the district's most developed area, Lujiazui covers the eastern bank of the Huangpu River. The futuristic skyline is made of high-end business centres and five-star hotels. Only a few landmarks along the wide streets here are residential, but that's changing. The area is welcoming more upscale apartment complexes and filling up the once barren office-only landscape.

Accommodation

Expensive housing options such as Skyline Mansion and the new, exclusive Shimao Rivera Gardens (5882 6988) offer overseas Chinese citizens a solid investment and tenants a short commute home from their nearby finance jobs. These smaller apartments are usually in larger property developments and rents run from ¥8,000 upwards, including 24 hour security, pools, gyms and parking facilities. Lujiazui has fewer mid-range options than the adjacent Century Park or Jinqiao. Family-sized apartments are usually privately owned, and rent ranges from ¥14,000 to ¥60,000.

Shopping & Amenities

Super Brand Mall, right by the Lujiazui Metro stop, houses most of the area's shopping options (see p.342). Lotus Supercenter is in the basement of the mall (5047 0648), and the upper floors include dozens of clothing, cosmetic, toy and shoe shops. Carrefour has a branch at 33 Huayuanshiqiao Lu and there is also a City Shop in the Citigroup Tower on the same street (6267 4248).

Entertainment & Leisure

Known as the 'other Bund', Lujiazui's riverside is a very pleasant promenade to sit, have a coffee or meal and watch the tourists fight for elbow space across the river. The spruced-up walkway now boasts a park, Spanish restaurant La Verbena (5878 9837) and an obligatory Starbucks. More western and Chinese eating options encircle Super Brand Mall, and most of the office buildings have impressive basement cafeterias for an affordable lunch and dinner. Tourists crowd the Oriental Pearl Tower and Jinmao Tower observation deck, while locals take it easy inside the Grand Hyatt's cafe on the 54th floor. At night, the most expensive – but arguably the most delicious – meal in the city can be found at Jade on 36 (p.391) in the Shangri-La hotel.

Healthcare

The Shanghai East International Medical Centre on Pudong Dadao offers outpatient and inpatient medical care for expats (p.136).

Education

There are no international schools in Lujiazui, but the Pudong address makes for easy commutes by car to schools in Jinqiao or Kangqiao (see p.99 and 101).

Transport

Metro Line 2 runs through the area, with a Lujiazui stop across from Super Brand Mall, for easy access to Puxi. Driving in Pudong is relatively easy and stress-free, but cars often get stuck in traffic moving across the river into Puxi, especially during peak hours. Expect delays of 30-45 minutes in the Yan'an Tunnel.

Safety & Annoyances

Lujiazui is very safe, although pickpockets and aggressive vendors come with the tourist territory around the Oriental Pearl Tower and Jinmao Tower. The wide developing streets can leave residents feeling a little isolated.

Lujiazui's modern buildings

Best Point ◀
A lot of offices make for exciting dining and entertainment hotspots.

Worst Point ◀
Traffic and tourists.

Overview map, p.90

Luwan

The more subdued French Concession dominates half of Luwan district, but the remaining eastern portion of this central area offers lively downtown living, with some of the city's best shopping, entertainment and dining. The area described here runs from the Chengdu Lu highway in the west to Xizang Lu in the east, with the Xintiandi complex at its centre.

Accommodation

Luwan consists of new high rises, older Chinese apartment complexes south of Huaihai Lu, and exclusive complexes surrounding the trendy Xintiandi, including uber-luxurious apartments such as Lakeville Regency and 88 Xintiandi (5383 8833). Several service apartments with short-term stays available are scattered along Huaihai Lu, including Times Square Apartments (6391 0265) and Hong Kong Plaza Serviced Apartments (6390 8866). Construction continues in this area so old communities are being flattened to make room for newer high rises. Proximity to Xintiandi raises the rent – expect to pay ¥15,000 to ¥40,000.

Shopping & Amenities

Huaihai Lu offers some of the best shopping in the city, boasting malls including the upmarket Times Square at 99, and larger indoor markets such as the electronic goods stalls within Hong Kong Plaza. The street also houses mid-range clothing labels, including the extremely popular European imports of H&M and Zara (see Shopping, p.320). Tourists crowd inside the over-priced boutiques of Xintiandi. Retail shopping overwhelms grocery options, but the basement of Times Square has a City Shop, and the area hosts several smaller Chinese supermarkets south of Huaihai Lu.

Entertainment & Leisure

Several bars and nightclubs scatter along Luwan's eastern portion of Huaihai, including international DJ venues Rojam (6390 0877) and Club DKD (p.404), both popular with young locals and expats. Times Square has a cinema on its upper floors and Huaihai Park is a surprising respite from the shopping crowds. Most of the area's nightlife centres around the neon-lit bars and clubs of Xintiandi, with music at Ark Live House (p.387) and Luna (6336 1717).

Healthcare

World Link medical centre has a speciality and inpatient care centre on Danshui Lu (6445 5999), right next to Xintiandi. Ruijin Hospital's medical and maternity clinic is close by at 197 Ruijin Er Lu (p.131) and Body & Soul, the traditional Chinese medicine clinic for expats, is at 760 Xizang Nan Lu (5101 9262).

Education

There are no international schools in Luwan. Students living here must opt for a long bus commute to Minhang or Qingpu (p.108), or face a lengthy Metro ride out to Pudong.

Transport

Luwan is notorious for bad road traffic, as the intersection of Yan'an and Xizang Lu can get severely congested during rush hour, slowing commutes through the area. A scattering of one-way streets, including long sections of Fuxing Lu, also impedes traffic. Metro Line 1 travels through Luwan, and the continual expansion of the Metro system will see the north-south Line 8 and Line 5 intersect this part of town.

Right now, taking the Metro is the best transport option for people wanting to commute to northern parts of the city or Pudong. Several buses, including the 911 service, run along Huaihai Lu for access to Xujiahui, and the 23 service travels from the corner of Xizang Lu to Nanjing Lu. If you want to get to the Bund from here, take bus 126.

Safety & Annoyances

Luwan is a safe area on the whole, although there are many street vendors and a few pickpockets because of its central location and the crowds drawn to the tourist attractions. The call of 'watch, bag, shoes, DVD' is an all-too-familiar greeting for the foreigners who choose to live in this downtown area – you'll either grow to ignore it or hate it.

Luwan apartments

Xintiandi

Tian Zi Fang

Tian Zi Fang

Best Point
Doesn't feel like part
of China, so is a good
place to escape to.

Minhang

Minhang is a quiet green suburb to the south-west of the city, composed of a cluster of villa communities surrounding the area's international school campuses. Sporting better infrastructure than nearby Qingpu, Minhang now boasts its own healthcare clinic and supermarket. City shopping and nightlife, however, requires a 25-45 minute drive downtown, depending on traffic.

Worst Point
Doesn't feel like part
of China, so you may
feel like you're
missing out.

Overview map, p.90

Accommodation

The housing options here are almost 50% cheaper than those in adjacent Hongqiao. The up-and-coming area hosts mainly villa complexes, such as Forest Manor (5226 0878), which offers pools, a gym and tennis courts inside its green expanse. There are also large apartment complexes such as Rancho Santa Fe (5226 0888), which abuts the Shanghai American School campus. The rents are the same as in Qingpu, ranging from ¥20,000 to ¥60,000 per month.

Shopping & Amenities

Minhang's Shanghai Racquet Club (p.283) has a western Country Market on the grounds. For bigger shopping trips, Minhang also has a Carrefour at 7388 Humin Lu, and a Pines the Marketplace at 421 Jinfeng Lu. Many Minhang residents drive to the larger Gubei Carrefour for weekly shopping trips. May's Deli (5119 1289) on Gaojing Lu in Qingpu has a good selection of western meats.

Entertainment & Leisure

Children enjoy Minhang for its green parks and wide streets, perfect for biking, rollerblading or hosting an impromptu football game. Many families belong to the Racquet Club, where they can swim, play tennis and use the large gym.

Healthcare

The Shanghai United Family Clinic (p.136) is located on the ground floor of the Shanghai Racquet Club, and the expat-oriented traditional Chinese Medicine clinic Body & Soul (6461 6550) is on nearby Zhongyi Lu in Qingpu.

Education

Several international schools have campuses in Minhang, including the Shanghai American School (p.152), Shanghai Singapore International School (p.154) and British International School (p.152). Qingpu's Ecole Francaise (6405 9220), Deutsche Schule (6405 9220) and Western International School of Shanghai (p.154) are 10 minutes by car.

Forest Manor

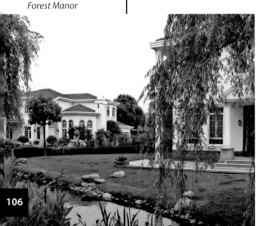

Transport

The Metro should reach the area with a new line by 2010, but meanwhile there's easy access to the A9 Expressway into the city or the Jiajin highway to Hongqiao. The area is only a 10-20km drive from Gubei via Yan'an highway. Expect a 25-45 minute drive into the city, depending on the time of day.

Safety & Annoyances

Minhang is a safe place for children and parents, although the feel of community only resides within the individual housing complexes. Not many signs of Chinese culture can be found out here, a common complaint of residents.

Best Point
The Bund – Shanghai's
most famous address.

North Huangpu & Former Japanese Concession

This area centres around Shanghai's often-photographed skyline, the historic Bund. Extending from Yan'an Elevated Highway, across Suzhou Creek and into the old Japanese Concession, this area offers few residential options but remains a diverse area for those who call it home.

Worst Point
Tourists,
underdeveloped
areas and few
residential choices.

Overview map, p.90

Accommodation

South of Suzhou Creek, the residences in the Westin Hotel (6335 1888) and Tianci Service Apartments offer the area's few high-end living options; rents start from ¥9,000. North of the creek, densely populated apartment buildings housing mostly locals line the winding narrow streets of the former Japanese Concession. Rents vary with the quality of the buildings, but start in the ¥2,500 range. A few decent high rises are now being built in this area, with rents starting from ¥4,000. There's a lot of construction in this area though, so buying anywhere in north Huangpu may be risky.

Shopping & Amenities

For now, the city doesn't seem to know what to do with the northern Huangpu area – there are scattered art galleries, a few tourist restaurants and the neon-lit razzle dazzle of the Nanjing Dong Lu. The historic Bund buildings are home to consulates, banks and a growing number of luxury shops and bars. Better shopping is found in the adjacent People's Square or across the river in Lujiazui. Western groceries are scarce, but smaller Chinese supermarkets line the streets south of Nanjing Dong Lu.

Entertainment & Leisure

The pedestrian walkway of Nanjing Dong Lu remains a favourite night-time hangout for locals to linger on the benches and watch the crowds go by. The Bund now hosts several of the city's hottest bars and restaurants in the Bund 18, Five on the Bund and Three on the Bund complexes, where the glitterati share cocktails at Bar Rouge (p.387), dance to the club music at Attica (p.403), or enjoy the city's best martinis at Laris (p.366).

Healthcare

The First People's Hospital International Medical Care Centre (p.131), north of Suzhou Creek at 585 Jiulong Lu, offers 24 hour medical emergency assistance and a dental clinic.

Education

North Huangpu is just one Metro stop away from Pudong – and from there it's easy to access the outer international schools.

Transport

Metro Line 2 follows Nanjing Dong Lu with a stop located at the end of the pedestrian street. Bus lines 910 and 22 travel up and down the Bund, and several that traverse the city have their terminus here. Parking is tight along the area's narrow streets, and you'll have to compete for precious space with the huge tourist buses.

Safety & Annoyances

Because of all the tourists, the Bund has its share of pickpockets and 'art students' strong-arming passer-bys to purchase poor quality paintings. Watch out for scamming young ladies who invite you for 'English practice' at local coffee shops – you may find yourself holding a hefty bill at the end with your new friend nowhere in sight. Tourists also bring crowds and foot traffic is congested.

107

Best Point
Very close to
international schools
and cheaper housing
than in other
suburban areas.

Worst Point
Still developing and
you may need to drive
a while to shop or
have fun.

Overview map, p.90

Qingpu

This area is a relatively new residential development south of Minhang. It has built up alongside the Ecole Francaise and Deutsche Schule, known as the Eurocampus. An extremely quiet suburban neighbourhood, Qingpu is now beginning to get its own share of shopping and entertainment spots.

Accommodation

Qingpu is mostly expansive villa communities such as Long Beach Villa, Golf King or Forest Rivera, which house many Europeans whose children attend the nearby Eurocampus. Rent is almost half the price of similar properties in Hongqiao – expect to pay from ¥20,000 and up, depending on the amenities and furnishings. Most villa complexes offer swimming pools, playing fields and community centres.

Shopping & Amenities

Most Qingpu residents drive to the Carrefour at 7388 Humin Lu in Minhang for grocery or home goods shopping. Minhang's Shanghai Racquet Club also has a closer expat-oriented Country Market, while May's Deli on Gaojin Lu has western meats. Bank ATMs accompany the Metro stop and Carrefour.

Entertainment & Leisure

Qingpu offers wide, quiet streets, plenty of green space, and community pools and clubhouses. If your own compound is not enough, Qingpu residents frequent Shanghai Racquet Club's pool, tennis courts and gym. Families enjoy dinner at the club's restaurants or Spanish fare at the cosy La Mesa (5119 1266) on Gaojin Lu. The Thirsty Monk is popular for drinks (5988 9983), or take the 20 minute drive to Hongmai Lu pedestrian street for an evening out. Le Meriden hotel in adjacent Songjiang, 20 minutes by car, boasts a large pool and generous weekend brunch. Next to the hotel is the Moon River Art Park, a popular destination for families with children featuring sculptures, mazes and a lagoon, as well as plenty of green space to play.

Healthcare

The United Family Clinic (p.136) is 10 minutes by car. Body & Soul Clinic (6461 6550) on Zhongyi Lu is a traditional Chinese medicine clinic geared towards expats.

Education

The Ecole Francaise and Deutsche Schule (see p.152) share facilities on the large Eurocampus in Qingpu. The area also hosts the Western International School of Shanghai (p.154) and a large Montessori kindergarten (p.148). Children in Qingpu have an easy ride by car (or even bike) to the numerous international schools in nearby Minhang (see p.106).

Transport

Although the city plans to extend Metro Line 1 and build Line 9 into the southern half of Minhang and the university campus of nearby Songjiang, cars and bikes are the only options for now. Easy access to the A5 expressway (which leads to Ya'an Elevated Highway) means a 30-45 minute drive to the city centre, depending on traffic conditions, and a 20 minute drive to Hongqiao or Gubei during off-hours. Parking is plentiful in these outskirts.

Safety & Annoyances

Qingpu is an extremely safe area, with most housing inside gated communities. Life may be a bit sleepy for some in this out-of-the-way neighbourhood.

Best point ◀

Rents are cheap in old Shanghai and there are still a few scenic areas left in which to glimpse the city's past.

Worst point ◀

A bit difficult to get into the city by public transport.

Overview map, p.90

South Huangpu

The southern half of Huangpu district includes the lower section of the Bund plus the part of town known as old Shanghai. Construction continues to spruce up the area, and many World Expo sites are being constructed along the southern banks of the Huangpu.

Accommodation

Older apartments and cheaper high rises make up the south Bund. Locals populate most of the residential space, although some foreigners who work in Luwan or People's Square appreciate the easy commute and the inexpensive housing. Expect rents in the ¥2,000 to ¥6,000 bracket. Construction disrupts the landscape and most apartment complexes abut some sort of renovation work.

Shopping & Amenities

Tourists and locals alike flock to the bonanza of handicrafts and knick-knacks surrounding Yu Garden. This neighbourhood is filled with every possible souvenir as speciality arts and crafts, jewellery and wedding markets crowd the narrow streets. The city's recently renovated fabric market is located on Lujiabang Lu, south of Yu Garden. The area does not have many western supermarkets but large Chinese food stores accompany every crowded neighbourhood. Wet markets, regulated to smaller spaces in other parts of the city, spread out a huge selection of fruits, fish and vegetables in south Huangpu.

Entertainment & Leisure

Most entertainment spots here are geared to tourists – Yu Garden, the docks along the Bund, or the fabric market. The best venues for relaxation are for the locals, with expansive teahouses and large KTVs along Lujiabang Lu and Fuxing Lu.

Healthcare

Those seeking healthcare need to travel to Luwan or Pudong. Nearest is the traditional Chinese medicine clinic for expats, Body & Soul, at 760 Xizang Nan Lu (5101 9262).

Education

If you live by the Nanpu Bridge, school commutes to Kangqiao (p.101) and other parts of Pudong are relatively easy by car.

Transport

South Huangpu is currently isolated from the city via public transport, but that will change. Metro Line 4 is being extended along the Huangpu River and into Pudong. By 2008, this line will connect with yet-to-be-finished Line 8, which will move up north to People's Square. For now, buses are the only public transport available. Bus 910 runs up and down the Bund, with access to Hongkou to the north. Bus 802 runs to People's Square and the 43 travels from the Nanpu Bridge to Xujiahui via Zhaojiabang Lu. Taxis are easily accessible and traffic on the Bund is surprisingly fast moving.

Huangpu housing

Safety & Annoyances

Pickpockets and other scammers hang out in the areas around Yu Garden. Poor public transport may isolate you from downtown venues.

Suzhou Creek

Unless you secure a spot on the Bund, the closest thing to waterfront living is Suzhou Creek. This area includes both banks of the waterway from Chengdu Lu in the east to Wanghangdu Lu in the west. The brackish creek that transverses the northern half of the city isn't much to look at, but city developers are hoping otherwise. Dense high-rise apartments go shoulder to shoulder with decaying but beautiful warehouses. A growing art community has taken up residence in the converted factory spaces, and architectural and advertising firms have followed suit. The northern bank of the creek is sporadically developed with neon overload at new shopping centres within Everbright City.

Accommodation

Large high-rise apartments dominate, housing foreigners and locals. Some offer newish accommodation with modern kitchens and clubhouses, while others were built too quickly for quality. Rents are cheaper than in adjacent central Jing'an (p.92), ranging from ¥4,000 to ¥12,000 for a two-bedroom place. Only a few high-end serviced apartments are in this area, including the Regalia Serviced Residences (p.38) on Lane 1161, Shanxi Bei Lu, with rents from ¥20,000. A precious few converted warehouses host dramatic but expensive studios overlooking the water. Densely populated local areas surround Everbright City on the north side.

Shopping & Amenities

Suzhou Creek holds a few surprises; don't be afraid to explore the neighbourhood's clothing stores, DVD markets and electronic shops. The bustling stores, restaurants and bars surrounding Shanghai Railway Station have earned the title Everbright City, Shanghai's self-proclaimed 'second Xintiandi'. This still-developing area has large Chinese supermarkets and stores, along with mixed-use buildings. South of the creek, stop for groceries at several smaller Chinese supermarkets and the Carrefour at 20 Wuning Lu.

Entertainment & Leisure

There are several art and photography studios south of the creek. A number of artists reside at 50 Moganshan Lu, a community of exhibition and studio spaces that include the well-known BizArt, ShanghART and Eastlink galleries (see p.196). Come for a stroll and then a drink at the adjacent coffee house. West of Moganshan Lu sits the impressive Pier One complex on 88 Yichang Lu (5515 8318). The elite entertainment and dining spot features the high-concept Mimosa Supperclub (p.370). The art deco-inspired scenic spot, however, can seem a bit too isolated even to those who live nearby.

Healthcare

Suzhou Creek is a taxi ride to the World Link healthcare facilities (6279 7698) in the Shanghai Centre in Jing'an and Huashan Hospital (p.132) in the French Concession.

Education

No international school has a campus in this area. A difficult commute for expat students, the closest option would be Hongqiao locations (more than an hour by car).

Transport

Taxis vanish at certain times of the day and travel can be slow on larger streets such as Jiangning Lu in rush hour. Metro Lines 1, 3 and 4 converge at Shanghai Railway Station.

Safety & Annoyances

The area is safe with most apartments gated. The far-flung location makes taxis scarce at times, while buses to downtown are slow and indirect.

Best Point ◀
A shopper's paradise and affordable housing.

Xujiahui

The heart of Xujiahui is a group of large shopping malls: Grand Gateway, the Oriental Department Store and Metro City. The area spreads out from here, housing many foreigners attracted to the hustle and bustle of the shopping hub. Western restaurants and bars are scarce but expats enjoy Xujiahui for its convenient transport options, stores and daytime activities.

Worst Point ◀
Loud and crowded.

Overview map, p.90

Accommodation
The area consists mainly of older apartment buildings, although there are newer developments off Nandan Lu. Expect cheaper rents in older housing complexes, starting from ¥3,500 for one bedroom. Foreigners pay around ¥10,000-¥14,000 for a decent three-bedroom flat in central Xujiahui. South of Shanghai Stadium, the building quality drops and housing is cheap but usually in poor condition.

Shopping & Amenities
Shopping is Xujiahui's biggest draw. Besides the malls and underground markets in the Metro stops, expats shop for groceries at Century Mart in Shanghai Stadium and the large Lianhua (Chinese supermarket) in the basement of the Pacific department store. The malls surrounding Xujiahui Metro station house electronic markets, furniture stores and supermarkets. IKEA (p.326), next to Shanghai Stadium, attracts thousands of shoppers, and Tianyaoqiao Lu hosts all the major Chinese banks and several pharmacies.

Entertainment & Leisure
Most entertainment options are housed in the area's malls: catch a movie in Grand Gateway or sing karaoke in Metro City. The city's biggest concerts and sporting events show at Shanghai Stadium, and the venue also houses a popular climbing wall (p.284). Several western and Chinese restaurants line Tianyaoqiao Lu and the large foodcourt in Metro City attracts the business-lunch crowd. The area lacks expat-oriented nightspots, although biker dive bar Harley's on Nandan Lu (5424 7317) is a popular hangout for locals and foreigners.

Healthcare
Xujiahui residents can go to the New Pioneer Medical Centre (6469 3898) and the International Peach Maternity Hospital (p.134), both in the Gure Building at 910 Hengshan Lu. There is also convenient access to the adjacent French Concession or nearby Jing'an for healthcare facilities.

Education
The Shanghai Singapore International School has a Xujiahui campus (p.154) as well as Little Eton Bilingual Kindergarten on Xietu Lu (6469 0445). It's not a bad commute to Minhang or Qingpu school campuses (15-30 minutes by car).

Transport
Lines 1, 3 and 4 converge at the busy Shanghai Stadium Metro stop, with easy access to downtown and beyond. Metro and taxis are the best way to get around. The area is a popular compromise for expat singles who work in more family-oriented areas like Minhang or Qingpu, with access to the highway for fast commutes by car. Several bus lines converge in Xujiahui: 15, 824 and 927 take you to Jing'an Temple and points north, while bus 43 travels east to south Huangpu.

Safety & Annoyances
Xujiahui is a safe area, but to some it's a noisy and overcrowded part of town.

111

Best Point
Attractive developing
area close to
central and
suburban locations.

Zhongshan Park

Zhongshan Park is an up-and-coming area for younger expats, with several accommodation options and convenient transport, plus a large green space. The local Metro stop connects Line 2 and 4, and it's an easy drive to Hongqiao and beyond.

Accommodation

Worst Point
Fewer bars and
restaurants than
adjacent areas.

Overview map, p.90

Colonial *shikumen* buildings from the former British Concession hide in lanes along Yuyuan Lu, housing locals and a few foreigners who pay rents from ¥4,000 a month. The condition of these old apartments vary, but renovated spaces make unique homes. Decent large apartment complexes are springing up around Jiangsu Lu, including Edifice at 888 Yuyuan Lu, with rents from ¥12,000 for one bedroom. Park View (5241 9828) is a comfortable two-building complex overlooking the park, and offers a wide range of rents starting from ¥20,000. Across the street, Belvedere Apartments at 833 Changning Lu (6312 2222) is one of the area's few all-inclusive serviced apartments, with one and two bedrooms for ¥18,000 to ¥28,000 a month.

Shopping & Amenities

Cloud Nine mall (p.342), attached to Zhongshan Park Metro station, has a large Carrefour in the basement, along with various clothing stores, Korean and Chinese restaurants, and KFC and Starbucks in the basement. The area surrounding Cloud Nine resembles Xujiahui, with large electronic and home goods markets on Changning Lu. Sizeable gyms are located in Cloud Nine and Regents Park.

Entertainment & Leisure

The city's first mini-golf centre, Lucky Greens (6382 0021), is in Cloud Nine – just don't have high expectations. The sprawling park offers boat rides and amusements for children, speedy go-karts for adventurous adults, and ample green space for a game of frisbee. The Metro, taxis or motorbikes make for a short ride to the bars and restaurants in the Nanjing Xi Lu area.

Healthcare

Zhongshan Park residents can take a 10 minute taxi ride to Hengshan Hospital's 24 hour foreign clinic in the French Concession or the International SOS branch at 55 Huaihai Xi Lu in Xujiahui (5298 9538).

Education

The city's only downtown international school, Shanghai Community International School, closed its Jiangsu Lu campus in August 2007 due to the government repossessing the land (the school welcomed its students back to a newly expanded Hongqiao location after the holiday). While not as convenient to downtown families, the Hongqiao campus offers bus services to several points throughout the city.

Transport

Metro Lines 2, 3 and 4 converge at Zhongshan Park, with easy access to People's Square and Pudong to the west or to Xujiahui to the south. The Yan'an Elevated Highway and the Zhongshan Er Lu mean short commutes to points in Hongqiao, Gubei or beyond. Many bus lines leave from Zhongshan Park – 20 and 921 go to the Bund, while bus 519 heads west to Hongqiao.

Safety & Annoyances

Zhongshan Park is a safe area. Traffic can get congested and the area still lacks a lot of night time entertainment options.

Small but indispensable…

Perfectly proportioned to fit in your pocket,
this marvellous mini guidebook makes sure
you don't just get the holiday you paid for,
but rather the one that you dreamed of.

New York Mini Visitors' Guide
Maximising your holiday, minimising your hand luggage

Setting up Home

The hard part is over; you've found a home and signed a lease. Now all you have to do is move, furnish and find some help. The abundance of cheap labour in China makes those tasks easier, with low moving costs, customised furniture and furnishings, beautiful Chinese antiques and reliable domestic help. Sometimes it's best to deny the urge to ship everything to your new home. Low prices and wide availability often mean it's cheaper to just buy the necessities after you've settled in. Much of your buying and ordering depends on the size of your home and how long you plan on staying there.

Moving Services

Multinational companies hire relocation services to move their employees overseas. Relocation firms assist in all aspects of the move, including visa registration, school consultations, and the packing and unpacking of possessions. If you want to hire a relocation or removal service as an individual, give a detailed scope of your requirements in order to get an accurate quote. Take fewer things or pack boxes yourself to save money.

China charges import tax on furniture and electronics; up to 20% for some items. Check with a removal or relocation company before you pack – smaller unnecessary electronics can rack up big bills in port. It's best to pack laptops, CDs and other smaller electronics in your personal luggage. Also remember that China only takes 220 voltage appliances, so some items may not be compatible.

Relocation Companies		
Asia Pacific Properties	6288 7333	www.asiapacificproperties.com
Bridge Worldwide Relocations	5422 5488	www.bridgerelo.com
Crown Relocation	6250 8820	www.crownrelo.com
Pacific Relocations	6218 6660	www.worthenpacific.com
Pricoa Consulting (Shanghai)	6122 6058	www.pricoarelocation.com
Santa Fe Relocation Services	6233 9700	www.santaferelo.com

Shanghai doesn't impose many restrictions on what you can bring into the country (barring of course the standard drugs or illegal goods). Shipping costs vary but the average quote of locally based relocation firms is around ¥75,000 for a container (40 cubic feet) travelling from the US or the UK to Shanghai.

If you only require a move across town, the cheapest option is to hire a small taxi van, known in Chinese as a 'loaf of bread van' (*mianbao che*) for its resemblance to the steamed bread for sale on the street. Call Dazhong Taxi (the turquoise cab) to hire a *mianbao che* (6258 1688). Fares for these smaller vans start at ¥20 and the driver will help you load and unload. Dazhong also has larger trucks and mover teams available, plus a 24 hour call centre (5275 3667). Fees start from ¥170.

Another low-cost moving team option is Gongxing Movers (6605 5185). These services are Chinese-language only so you will need to get a native speaker to make the call.

Removal Companies		
AGS Four Winds Shanghai	5213 6330	www.agsfourwinds.com
Allied Pickfords Shanghai	6332 0088	www.alliedpickfords.com.cn
Asian Express International Movers	6258 2244	www.aemovers.com.hk
Asian Tigers	3209 5561	www.asiantigersgroup.com
Doda International Moving Company	6413 1891	www.doda.com.cn
Eagles Moving Company	6228 6087	www.eaglesmoving.com
Hiboo	3307 0199	www.hiboo.com.cn
Prudential Moving Company	na	www.prudentialmovers.com
Relocasia	5228 3076	www.relocasia.com
Schenker China	2307 1188	www.schenker.com
Wilcan International Moving and Relocation	6328 2229	www.wilcan.com

While moving is cheap, keep an eye on the operation – movers here are notorious for damaging or destroying things, so it can be be safer to carry the important stuff yourself. All the firms listed in the table handle both international and domestic moves.

Furnishing Your Home

Most low to mid-range Shanghai rentals come fully furnished with beds, tables, couches, TVs and telephones. Landlords are keen to achieve a foreign-friendly decor, so ask to remove anything you don't like and negotiate a furniture allowance, if desired. Landlords are usually willing to part with up to one month's rent to cover furnishing. Expensive renovated homes geared to foreigners may be left empty, as most high-end tenants prefer their own furnishings. Most apartments are equipped with washing machines, although dryers or dishwashers are rare.

If you wish to refurnish your apartment, reasonable outlets and opportunities to order custom-made pieces abound. In Shanghai, furniture and soft furnishing markets such as the South Bund Fabric Market in Huangpu or the Qingfeng Market in Putuo offer negotiable prices, a vast selection of goods, and tailors and furniture makers willing to copy or create pieces. Cost and quality vary, with curtains ranging from ¥150 to ¥400. The city also has several large home marts along Yishan Lu, near the Xujiahui Metro stop. These multi-storey warehouses showcase a dizzying array of domestic and imported furniture and home goods. The gilded Victorian-style furniture loved by local Shanghainese is among the more expensive (bedroom sets start at ¥4,000) but slightly more subdued styles are cheaper – mid-range couches begin at ¥2,000 and bedroom sets cost ¥2,000-¥4,000. Some vendors in these buildings also do copies – just bring along a catalogue or photo. A copied three-person couch, for example, can be custom-made and delivered to your door for ¥1,800.

The third option is to pay a visit to the individual furniture stores in malls or on shopping streets. These outlets tend to be more expensive, but with higher quality items. Areas around Taikang Lu in the French Concession have several boutique furniture and home accessory suppliers. When all else fails, the IKEA store across from Shanghai Stadium in Xuhui (5425 6060) is an old standby for reasonably priced furniture, fabrics and kitchen equipment. Hordes of Shanghai families enjoy browsing the gigantic showrooms on the weekends. Any of the city's several Carrefour locations

Tailors		
Hanrong Interior Fabrics	831 Xinzha Lu	Jing'an
Hola Home Furnishing	Brilliance West Shopping Mall	Changning
Qingfang Market	1648 Cao an Lu	Putuo
Shanghai Home Expo	1263 Wuzhong Lu	Changning
South Bund Fabric Market	399 Lujiabang Lu	Huangpu

Furniture & Interior Design		
Build Shanghai	5213 6309	Real estate agency that offers design and build services for Shanghai homes
Casa Pagoda	5422 2974	Funky European and Asian-inspired home furniture on the boutique-filled Taikang Lu
Category of 1 Interiors	5466 0222	Expat-owned and operated American furnishing and interior design showroom
Design Republic	6329 3339	Exclusive designer pieces for the home
Henry's Studio & Antiques	5217 3833	Custom-made furniture and Chinese antiques in an airy warehouse next to Hongqiao Airport
Hu & Hu	3431 1212	Beautiful Chinese antiques and reproductions in a large warehouse space off the ring road
Norman and Karen Design Studio	6467 7223	Home interior design and furnishings on Taikang Lu

115

also have furniture and bedding sections, again for decent prices.

If you want the aid of a professional, several interior designers in the city specialise in residential space. Many have specific experience in renovating and restoring Shanghai's colonial homes, so it can be worth getting a quote for their services.

Buying furniture from another expat, however, remains the easiest route. The chances are that as someone is moving into the city, someone else is usually moving out. Check out local furniture listings in city magazines such as *that's Shanghai* or *City Weekend* to find good second-hand sales. Departing expats also post online at shanghai.craigslist.org, www.enjoyclassifieds.com, www.adweekly.cn, www.cityweekend.com.cn and www.shanghai.asiaexpat.com, and place furniture ads on the bulletin boards in City Shops or Pines.

Household Insurance

Break-ins are very rare in Shanghai, although they can happen, especially in first-floor apartments. Most apartments are in complexes that are guarded by some sort of 24 hour security, but nosy neighbours are often the best protection. For renters, the landlord is responsible for any household insurance for protection from fires or water damage. If you protect your valuables within the home, take out a personal goods insurance policy with a Shanghai-based insurer or one from your home country. These plans cover accidental damage or loss of personal possessions. Some may require an individual appraisal of each item. For Shanghai homeowners, household insurance policies should cover water damage and fires, two real dangers to the city's ageing buildings. All insurance providers listed are available and suitable for expats, but only Royal & Sun Alliance and Winterthur offer English-language service.

Household Insurance		
American International Assurance	6350 8180	www.aiu.com.cn
Ping An Insurance Company	6321 6698	www.paic.com.cn
Royal & Sun Alliance	6888 1999	www.royalsunalliance.com.cn
Winterthur Insurance	6882 3351	www.winterthur.com.cn

Laundry Services

Nearly all Shanghai apartments are equipped with washing machines, although dryers are rare – the Shanghainese prefer to use outdoor clothing lines and all apartments come with bamboo or metal poles hanging from the terrace or window. If you don't fancy air-drying your clothes, most appliance stores offer a range of domestic and imported dryers. Small shops offering dry cleaning and laundry services are found in many Chinese neighbourhoods – look for the sign marked *xi yi* (洗衣). These smaller operations charge by weight – around ¥8 per 500g (one *jin*) for dry cleaning, ¥3 for washing. Ironing is usually included, and same day or next day delivery is available. Other, franchised laundromats are usually adjacent to expat complexes, such as Elephant King (6407 3633) in Jinqiao or Jazz Cleaner in the Shanghai Centre on Nanjing Xi Lu (133 3193 5332). These usually have higher prices and charge by the item. Typical prices are ¥40-¥60 for a two-piece suit, ¥20-¥30 for trousers, ¥45-¥65 for a coat, ¥20-¥35 for a sweater, ¥20-¥30 for a T-shirt, ¥30-¥50 for dresses and ¥30-¥40 for a skirt.

Laundry, Shanghai style

Domestic Help

Most Shanghai expats (and local Shanghainese as well) have part-time or full-time *ayis* (which literally translates as 'auntie'). *Ayis* are older Chinese women (often with families of their own) who clean the house, cook, buy groceries, pay the bills, look after children and run other errands. Most *ayis* in Shanghai come from nearby provinces, although there has been a recent influx of Filipino domestic help. Having an *ayi* can mean much more than affordable housekeeping and childcare; for many expats, it's an important Chinese interaction. The best way to find an *ayi* is through friends or co-workers – one *ayi* often has several clients and can refer friends if she is unavailable. Announcement boards in western stores such as City Shop or in community club houses also advertise available *ayis*. Most do not speak English, so do some research if that's important. If you have several requirements, a relocation agency can find an appropriate match. Domestic help agencies provide household staff trained in western cooking, English or baby care. The rate for a part-time *ayi* is ¥8-¥12 per hour and it's customary to give a bonus at Chinese New Year.

Full-time *ayis* are less common. However, expats living in far-flung suburban areas sometimes rely on live-in domestic help. Many expats are now hiring live-in Filipino *ayis*, but when doing so it is important to check their visa status – it's illegal to house a foreign *ayi* without a work permit (see p.63). Some companies are willing to sponsor work permits for Filipino nannies, but without a Z visa, families can get in trouble for employing one themselves.

Domestic Help Agencies

American-Sino Research and Human Resource Consulting	5840 2563	www.aseap.com
Ayi Pro	5033 2544	www.ayipro.com
Ayi Service	6259 2933	www.ayiservice.com
Leyu4u	5879 6646	www.leyu4u.com
Sarah Home Service	6233 0955	www.sarahhomeservice.com
Shanghai Enjoy Housekeeping	6351 1438	www.enjoylife-sh.com
Shanghai GNI Housekeeping	6871 2199	www.chinagni.com
TianTian Housekeeping Service Company	5873 2918	www.shttjz.cn

Babysitting & Childcare

Most expat families rely on part-time or live-in *ayis* (see above) for babysitting and after-school childcare. Employing a local domestic helper means low-cost supervision of your children, as well as important language exposure and cultural interaction. When your children are not with the *ayi*, the city remains a kid-friendly place with several active parents' groups, play centres and easy-to-access childcare resources. Many expat-oriented housing complexes also have established playgroups, which help each other out with sitting when necessary.

Parent organisations such as the Shanghai Mamas, Shanghai International Family,

Babysitting & Childcare

Bridges Daycare	5882 8911	www.bridges-sh.com.cn
Bumps & Babes	6247 2880	peterandmary@msn.com
Fun Dazzle	6210 7288	na
Heart-to-Heart Parent Support Group	139 1731 9214	thomasf1@apci.com
International Mothers Support Group	6856 4758	groups.msn.com/IMSGShanghai
Koala Kids	na	www.awsg.org
Moms in Pudong	na	www.momsinpudong.com
Shanghai Mamas	na	www.shanghai-mama.com
Shanghai International Family	na	www.shfamily.com
Starbugs Children's Centre	6856 8611	www.starbugs.cn

117

International Mothers Support Group and Moms in Pudong provide expat parents with activities, practical information, online forums and child-rearing resources.
Most five-star hotels in the city offer babysitting for guests, including the Four Seasons in Luwan and the Ritz-Carlton in Jing'an. Many western eateries such as Blue Frog, Coffee Tree or Zentral – all with branches in Hongqiao – or SyZyGy in Pudong offer spacious playrooms with supervising staff. Sunday brunch spots such as the Westin in the Huangpu, O'Malley's in the French Concession and the Novotel in Pudong have friendly creches so parents can dine while their children play. Staff in large Chinese, Japanese or Korean restaurants throughout the city often offer to watch your child during the meal for an extra fee. When shopping, the playroom in IKEA in Xujiahui is a popular stomping ground for local and foreign children.

Domestic Services

For any home repair, always go through your landlord if renting. A landlord should take care of all property maintenance and be responsible for the charges incurred, and usually establish arrangements with a few local handymen. Like many other service industries in Shanghai, plumbing or carpentry is dominated by one-man operations rather than larger companies. These men work through real estate agencies or security guards and service a few neighbourhoods. If you have to tackle a problem on your own, ask your neighbours or security guard for the local contact. Property owners, likewise, should ask the previous owner, neighbours or property management group for references. Handymen rarely have official credentials but many have long experience and are competent.

If an appliance such as the air-conditioning unit or refrigerator is acting up, the manufacturer almost always has a service number to call. Look on the product information sheet (the landlord or previous owner should supply these brochures for every appliance in the house). Local workers charge by the visit plus any needed parts at cost. A plumber or carpenter will charge ¥30-¥50 per visit, while an electrician will charge ¥50-¥60.

When all else fails, call directory enquiries (114) for a domestic serviceman in your area (Chinese-language service only).

Pest control companies are a bit more organised, and those listed here are well equipped and professional. Ask your landlord before you call though – the property development may have regulations concerning this matter. Cockroaches and rats are the most common home intruders in Shanghai.

Pest Control Companies	
IPCS	6536 7350
Shanghai Wei Sheng	6276 5873
Shanghai Yin Wei	5078 8030

DVD & Video Rental

DVD rental is non-existent in Shanghai due to the oversupply of pirated movies. These clandestine operations squeeze in behind fruit stands, clothing stores and CD music shops all over the city. Prices range from ¥6 to ¥10 per DVD, depending on the store. Selection varies but with enough searching you can find just about any film or TV show. Some stores target expats with English signs and free coffee, but the best DVD store is the one in your neighbourhood. Proximity allows for easy returns and if you're friendly with the owners, they'll be sure to point out poor quality copies or mismatched subtitles. DVD stores usually organise their selection by language (Chinese, English and many European languages are available) but subtitles can sometimes be gibberish or missing – make sure to return bad copies. When in doubt, just ask the owner to check the DVD on the store's TV for you before taking it home. Newly released films are often bad copies for the first few weeks (these early versions are filmed in a cinema instead of being a digital rip from a DVD) so wait a while before you buy a new release. For a few extra yuan, most stores offer DVD9s – better quality discs with fewer problems. DVDs in Shanghai are not region-coded so you should be able to watch them in any player around the world. That said, regulations abroad have changed, so be wary when taking cheap movies back home. Hong Kong, for instance, may confiscate the discs or even fine people carrying pirated movies. For now, regulations in the city are lax, but piracy is a constant hot topic in China so things may start to change, and any attempt to resell the discs overseas is strictly forbidden.

Pets

Having a pet is becoming more popular among Chinese families. Chinese parents buy their children bunnies or turtles, and older Chinese couples often benefit from the companionship of a dog or cat once their only child moves out. Buying cuddly creatures in Shanghai is not recommended, however. Pet shops or pet markets usually do not feed or treat the animals well, and Shanghai pet stores are notorious for housing sick or malnutrioned dogs, cats and rabbits. It's common to see people selling these animals on the sidewalk. Rather than supporting the pet trade, it's better to adopt. Shanghai's Second Chance Animal Aid (www.scaa.org) is not an animal shelter or rescue team, but facilitates the adoption of rescued or abandoned pets and offers information for pet owners in the city.

Cats & Dogs

Shanghai neighbourhoods have their share of cats and dogs. Most locals prefer smaller breeds, and rarely lead dogs outside of the apartment complex. Many Shanghainese, especially young women, are scared of larger dogs and the sight of them can inspire a shriek or two. That's not to say that Shanghai is unfriendly to pets. Dogs can get plenty of space to run around in suburban areas or parks, and most apartment buildings allow animals.

Fish & Birds

Fish and birds are not allowed for import into China, although songbirds and fish are popular pets for children and adults in the city. Slightly safer bets than cats or dogs,

Rabbits for sale

you can easily purchase these pets in fish and bird markets around the city (one of Shanghai's largest is located on Xizang Nan Lu in Luwan). These markets also house a wide variety of reasonably priced fish tanks, filters and birdcages, and offer a fascinating look into another popular pet in China: the fighting cricket. Stroll through the stalls and learn more about the world of competitive cricket fighting, a popular pastime among retirees.

Bringing Your Pet to Shanghai

Importing a pet into Shanghai is not difficult, but many people opt to use a relocation company or pet service for help. Agencies such as AGS (p.114) or Pets in Shanghai (p.121) provide information and facilitate airport pick-up and registration. Most airlines offer pet transport as cargo or excess baggage, but some have special policies and hefty fees. Before a pet gets airborne, the animal must receive two government-issued certificates from its home country: health and vaccination (ask your local veterinarian). These certificates do not need to be translated into Chinese. All vaccinations and the international-standard health certificate have to be done within 30 days of departure to China.

After touching down in Shanghai, the pet owner must register his or her pet at the Animal and Plant Quarantine department of the customs office, for a fee of ¥150 (Pudong Airport, 3848 4500; Hongqiao Airport, 6268 8918). The owner must have two copies of the vaccination and health certificate plus the original, and two copies of his or her passport and Shanghai address ready.

According to Shanghai regulations, newly arrived pets need to be quarantined for 30 days. However, most of the time the pet is required to only spend the first seven days inside a government facility, after which it can spend the remaining three weeks in the owner's home. Once the pet is allowed home, the owner may have to fill out a form for the following three weeks, reporting on the pet's temperature, eating habits and general well-being. After the month is up, officials will visit the owner's home and do a final health inspection. If everything is fine, the animal will be issued a Chinese health certificate.

Dog Licences

Well before the first month is over, however, dog owners must register their canines with the local police department. A Chinese person is required to register the dog, so ask your landlord or a friend. The Chinese resident must bring their ID card, two photos of the dog (front and back view), and one photo of the owner. Within the ring road, a dog licence costs ¥2,000 per year and outside of the ring road it costs ¥1,000 per year. After presenting the money and documentation to the police station, a receipt for the required microchip and final vaccinations is handed over and you'll be informed of the vet you need to visit. Two weeks after getting the chip implanted and receiving the two shots, you can pick up your final registration papers at the police station.

Registering for a dog licence as soon as possible is important. If unlicensed, police may pick up the animal and bring it to a less-than-pristine outdoor kennel. With almost 75% of the city's dog population unlicensed, officials are keen to catch those who avoid the regulations. Be on the safe side and carry the licence around with you if you wander outside your compound while walking the dog. Also make sure to leave your registration papers with a boarding kennel when you travel – police check these facilities regularly and confiscate pets without papers. Other pet regulations mainly revolve around dogs: local families can now only raise one dog each (although multi-pet families merely register extra dogs under neighbours' or relatives' addresses).

Pet Shops

Imported and domestic pet food and pet supplies are readily available in most supermarkets. However, if a pet has a special diet, the owner should bring a large supply just in case. Speciality pet shops are springing up all over the city and niche services in pet clothing, pet holidays and even pet dating are gaining popularity among Shanghai's animal lovers. GouGou 50 (www.gougou520.com) purports to be Shanghai's first doggie matchmaking service, and Chinese owners love dressing up their pets at Tingting Pet Family at 205 Fuming Lu (5403 1527) or the Xiao Wanpi Pet Shop at 114 Weihai Lu (6327 8241).

Pet Boarding & Sitting

Jialiang Kennels	6411 0049	Kennel services for dogs and cats
Pets Are Wonderful Veterinary Clinic	5254 0611	Cat boarding
Shanghai Naughty Family Pets	6268 9507	Kennel services for dogs over one year old

Vets & Kennels

There's a wide range of well-trained and well-equipped veterinary clinics in Shanghai, both foreign and locally staffed. Most foreign clinics are located in Gubei or Pudong, but downtown local clinics also come recommended. Some facilities offer 24 hour emergency treatment, although none offer pet transport. While there are more and more kennels in Shanghai, many expats choose to leave their pets with friends or *ayis*. Stays at kennels range from ¥40 to ¥100 per night.

Grooming & Training

Both pet supply stores and veterinary clinics offer grooming and training services. Since pet ownership is just taking off in the city, check the facilities of any shop or clinic before dropping Fido off. The same goes for training – be wary of under-experienced dog trainers posing as experts and don't be scared to ask for a business licence.

Pet Grooming & Training

Bark Dog Grooming	Changning	5422 4457
Dog Ego	Jing'an	6359 5489
Jialiang Kennels	Minhang	6411 0049
Pets Are Wonderful (PAW) Veterinary Clinic	Changning	5254 0611
Pets in Shanghai	Various Locations	137 6146 7251
Shanghai Bon Bon Pet Home	Changning	6294 8543
Shanghai Naughty Family Pets	Xuhui	6468 9148
	Pudong	5875 0999
	Changning	6268 9507
Xiaojingling Pet Grooming	Luwan	6359 4649

Taking Your Pet Home

Before taking a pet to Shanghai, consider the trip home. Some countries have strict importing policies, while others, such as Australia or New Zealand, don't accept any animals from China. In these cases, only after a continuous stay of six months or more in an allowed country of export can an animal be accepted back home.

No matter the destination, in order to leave China, the pet needs an exit certificate from the Animal Bureau. One month before a pet's departure from Shanghai, the owner needs to take the animal to 361 Zhaojiabang Lu (6418 9236) for a round of shots costing ¥150. This service is Chinese-speaking only. Also make sure to bring all the pet's original certification and Shanghai licences. Two weeks later, with vaccination and health certificates in hand, the same bureau can issue a new health certificate for export after a final check-up (¥300).

Veterinary Clinics

Elite Garden	Changning	6446 0006
Guai Guai Pet Clinic	Hongkou	5696 9964
Jialiang Kennels	Minhang	6411 0049
Jianping Pet Clinic	Changning	6261 5904
Pets Are Wonderful (PAW) Veterinary Clinic	Changning	5254 0611
PetsHome Veterinary Hospital	Changning	6242 5599
	Jing'an	6226 1122
Ronson's Pet Centre	Minhang	5443 8071
Shanghai Animal Hospital	Changning	6268 8191
Shanghai Guoxing Pets' Clinic	Changning	5218 9959
	Xuhui	5489 0009
Shanghai Shenpu Pet Clinic	Xuhui	6418 9236
Shanghai United Animal Hospital	Minhang	5485 9099
Western Veterinary Service	Changning	3223 1498
Xiaojingling Pet hospital	Luwan	6327 6108

121

Electricity & Water

The Shanghai Electricity Company and Shanghai Tap Water Company provide the city with electricity and running water. As Shanghai's electricity needs grow, the city depends on neighbouring provinces to supply power. As a result, Shanghainese residents enjoy air conditioning all summer long with no outages, while Zhejiang province may be in the dark for hours at a time.

Electricity and water costs are not normally included in the rent. Utility bills usually peak in summer, when expats leave air-conditioning units on all day and night. Don't be surprised if your neighbours have lower utility charges – Shanghainese don't use the heat as much in the winter and tend to use less water. There's no reconnection fee when you move into your Shanghai home, as landlords are responsible for all connection and installation utility costs.

Your building's conditions influence the effectiveness of your hot water heater or air-conditioning units. In older houses, turning the shower or faucet down to a slower stream usually heats things up faster. Older apartments easily blow fuses if too many appliances are on at once. Often a hot water bottle and some extra blankets may be the only solution to keeping warm in the dead of winter.

Fuse News

Make sure to identify fuse boxes when you move in, in case of a power shortage. Fuses in older buildings are made of large porcelain bases with two wires – turn off the main fuse before touching these and make sure you have a replacement in the house. You can buy these old-style fuses at any electrical market (see Shopping, p.321).

Electricity

Each city district has its own Shanghai Electricity Company (95598) branch office. Look at the back of your monthly electricity bill for the list of addresses and phone numbers. Offices open from 08:30 to 11:30 and 12:30 to 17:00. Utility offices usually don't offer an English service, so ask your landlord for help if needed.

China uses 220 volts and 50 cycles. American or Canadian 110 volt appliances will burn out if plugged into a Shanghai socket. You can buy adapters in the city for any overseas appliance, but bring at least one to get started. Some appliances don't work well with adapters and you may save money by leaving smaller items such as hair dryers and irons at home and buying replacements in China. As for outlets, a Shanghai apartment may have a variety of three-pronged, two flat, or two round sockets. For a small apartment with one or two people, expect monthly electricity costs to average ¥100-¥300, although bills can reach up to ¥500-¥800 per month in the summer with the air conditioning running all day long.

Water

Shanghai Tap Water Company (6298 8544) has branch offices in every city district. As with electricity, look at the back of your monthly water bill for addresses and phone numbers. Water is inexpensive, (around ¥100 per 1,000kg) and one or two people average a monthly water bill of ¥30-¥50. Neighbours in old lane houses sometimes share the water bill (splitting the cost according to each apartment's meter).

Water Companies	
Drinking Water Suppliers	6427 7474
Nestle Water (English service)	5854 5854
Nongfu Springs	800 620 5888
Sparkling Water	5891 4195
Water Delivery	96858

Shanghai tap water is unsafe to drink. Neither foreigners nor locals drink it, although you may use it in cooking. Avoid using tap water for cleaning uncooked vegetables or fruits, making tea or brushing your teeth – it won't make you sick but the chemicals and hard metals used to treat the water may be bad for you in the long term, and some people complain of skin reactions.

Most people in the city have water dispensers in their homes and order water jugs for them. You can purchase water dispensers at any home appliance store or supermarket – the cost ranges from ¥200 upwards. Some come with filtration systems, although quality and reliability vary. Water jugs range from ¥7-¥25 per five-gallon jug, and a ¥50-¥60 refundable deposit is required. Most offer a Chinese-only service, but the operator's questions are always the same so with practice you can order yourself.

Gas

Shanghai Dazhong Gas (co-owned by Dazhong Gas Company and Shanghai Gas Group) is the centralised provider of natural gas, coal and liquefied petroleum to Shanghai. Dazhong Gas installs and delivers gas to Puxi and Pudong residents. Call the 24 hour Shanghai Gas hotline (962777) or look on the back of your bimonthly bill for district branch offices.

Gas bills to your house may vary, as gas workers often estimate your monthly usage (based on the previous year) then 'catch you up' on your bills when they have time to check your meter. Some buildings require you to check the meter yourself and report to building management on a public bulletin board. Gas bills for one or two foreigners in a small apartment is around ¥75-¥150 per month – much less if you don't cook.

Sewerage

Shanghai's 60-year-old sewerage system is being revamped, and the city's new treatment facilities should be open by the time of publication. The construction aims to stem the flow of millions of cubic metres of untreated water pouring directly into nearby rivers, causing pollution and disease. Residents pay for the cost of the project with raised water treatment fees (a nominal fee included in your monthly water bill).

Rubbish Disposal & Recycling

Rubbish disposal is organised by district, and every apartment complex or lane has a designated dumpster. A municipal truck empties these nightly and carries them to landfills outside the city or to river barges.

Everything is recycled, although it may not look like it on the surface. Shanghai's recycling system is a multistep process that involves a lot of hands. A sorely needed source of income for a lot of people, several different groups pick through the trash every night to collect glass and plastic bottles, cardboard and metal to sell to reprocessing centres or middlemen for around ¥0.1 per piece. If you want to be helpful, separate the recyclables and put them next to the dumpsters to aid the collectors. You can also sell it yourself – collectors roam the streets (often on bikes or three-wheeled carts) yelling and ringing bells for recycling materials, although some only collect items such as old TVs, phones or furniture. Some expats give their recycling to their *ayi* for selling.

Telephone

Shanghai Telecommunications, a subsidiary of China Telecom, is the city's leading landline provider. The competition, China Netcom, has fewer customers and higher rates. Shanghai Telecom's basic plans have a monthly fee of around ¥2, ¥0.15 per minute for calls within your district, and an average of around ¥0.25 per minute for domestic long-distance calls. Shanghai Netcom charges ¥35 a month and ¥0.22 per

Utility Melt ▶

Despite the amazing progress that has enveloped China in recent years, one area that seems to have been left lagging is Shanghai's notoriously disorganised utility providers. Nearly any expat can tell you stories of skipped bills, mixed up water lines and non-working gas meters. There's not much you can do to speed up such problems, so the best advice is to keep your cool until the heat comes on.

minute in the first three minutes of a local call, and ¥0.11 for every additional minute.

Call 10000 to install or change your Shanghai Telecom plan. Installation is free. Cancellation or change of a Shanghai Telecom plan costs ¥10 and changing your number costs ¥100. Call-waiting and caller ID are standard services for both providers. Your monthly bill will not list individual calls. Dial 170 for a detailed breakdown of your Shanghai Telecom bill.

SMS Saviour

Stuck for directions in Chinese? Make sure you put Guanxi's number into your phone's memory (9588 2929). All you need to do is send a text with the name or partial details of the establishment you're looking for and you'll receive a reply containing the address, cross-street and phone number. Need to show the directions to a taxi driver? Reply to the message with 'C' and the same details are sent back to you in Chinese (see advert, p.vii).

Most foreigners use IP cards (Internet Phones) or other calling cards to dial internationally, rather than using a Shanghai Telecom long-distance plan. The majority of hotel rooms offer free local calls, but dialling internationally without a phone card is also very expensive. IP cards are available at small stalls (look for an IP sign) on the street or online at www.cnard.com. Every mobile phone provider in China offers an IP card. Unicom 17910 IP Card, for example, is ¥0.30 per minute domestic long distance, or ¥2.40 per minute to the US and Canada and ¥3.60 per minute to other countries. Street vendors sell these cards at a 30%-40% discount (a ¥100 card for ¥60), and they can be even cheaper if bought in bulk, so always negotiate. English service is usually available for these

Mobile friendly city

cards – just dial the number on the back followed by the pin code and the number you want to call.

Telephone Companies

China Netcom	10060	www.chinanetcom.com.cn
Shanghai Telecom	10000	www.sh.ct10000.com

Public phones are located in local neighbourhoods on the street or inside smaller stores – look for signs with the letters 'IC'. These public phones are either coin operated (¥0.5 or ¥1 coins only) or take IC cards. Cards can be purchased here or at the post office in ¥20, ¥50 or ¥100 denominations. IC cards can only be used for domestic calls. Just insert the card into the phone after the dial tone. Both IC and IP cards expire after a period of time, so check the date when purchasing.

Mobile Phones

Shanghai is home to more than 15 million mobile phone subscribers. Practically everyone in the city has one, including young children and the elderly. Young Shanghainese feel compelled to buy the most up-to-date model and city residents constantly find new ways to incorporate mobile technology into their lives – paying bills, playing games, selling stocks, even reading books.

Dual-band phones (GSM 900 and GSM 1800) are compatible in Asia, Australia, and Europe, but not in the US or Canada. North America only accepts tri-band phones (GSM 1900). It's easy to pick up tri-band and dual-band mobiles in Shanghai. You'll find a broad range of models and brands in home electronic stores, electrical markets, and street-side stalls. Used phones sell for as little as ¥300 while the newest models cost upwards of ¥4,000. SIM cards and phones are sold separately so you can choose any provider.

Mobile Service Providers

China Mobile	10086	www.chinamobile.com
China Telecom	10000	www.chinatelecom.com.cn
China Unicom	10010	www.chinaunicom.com.cn

Despite growing competition in China's cellular sector, there remains two main mobile service providers: China Mobile and China Unicom. Both offer a pay-as-you-go or subscription service.

Monthly Subscription

Don't Lose Your Pals
Make sure you save your contact list in another place besides your mobile phone, unless you want to end up cut off from all you know in Shanghai. If it's lost or stolen, you can easily update the new one, and you don't have to lose friends over it.

A monthly plan means never running out of money, and can be cheaper if you use your phone frequently. However, expats need a Shanghainese friend or colleague to sponsor a mobile-phone plan (in case you skip town without paying). He or she needs to show their Chinese ID at the time of application, and you will need your passport too. Apply at any China Mobile, China Telecom or China Unicom branch – check the companies' websites for branch locations. Providers offer several different plans, so look for the one that fits your needs. If you lose your phone, bring your passport and your Shanghainese friend's ID to get a new SIM card at a branch office (the usual fee is around ¥20). Your number will not change.

Overseas with world-wide roaming, Chinese mobile providers charge local and international service rates for calls you make and receive so, if you travel often, it's best to purchase separate SIM cards and numbers for the countries you frequent.

China has incredible domestic mobile phone coverage and you are rarely out of touch, even in the mountains of Sichuan or the valleys of Hunan.

Cheap Overseas Calls

In addition to IP cards (see previous page), internet options such as Skype or Gizmo Project offer popular alternatives for expats to talk to friends and family back home. Skype costs approximately ¥0.20 per minute to landlines around the world, while calling other online users is free. Other websites listed here sell cheap international calling cards.

Cheap Overseas Calls	
Cell Wireless	www.cellwireless.com
Expat Call	www.expatcall.com
Gizmo Project	www.gizmoproject.com
Skype	www.skype.com
Virtual Calling Cards	www.china-mobile-phones.com

Internet

There are several options to get online at home in Shanghai. China Telecom (10000) boasts the most dial-up subscribers in China and can be accessed by any phone line by having the modem dial 16300 (the username and password you'll need is also 16300). No fee is necessary, and the internet charges are then included in your next phone bill. Other internet service providers offer internet access cards, which can be bought on the street at IP vendors. Just dial the number on the card for a given period of internet access time. Another option is high-speed cable internet. Shanghai Cable Network Company (800 820 7700) delivers cable modems to your home, but remember that some areas don't have cable internet access, so check with the company first before ordering. To get the modem you'll need to show your passport and cable TV receipt (your landlord should be able to provide this). You also need a domestic bank account as the bills will be deducted directly.

Internet Service Providers		
1st China	5108 3389	www.1stchina.com
Haplink Communications	800 620 0098	www.haplink.com.cn
Shanghai Guomai Telecom	10010	www.guomai.sh.cn
Shanghai Online	85160	www.online.sh.cn
Sonic Communications	897271	na
Uninet	6217 1229	www.uninet.com.cn

Certain new buildings are wired for broadband. Check with your landlord to see if your apartment has broadband already installed and the name of the provider. One of the leading providers of broadband in Shanghai is Great Wall (6122 6600).

China Telecom is the city's leading provider of ADSL, which is quickly becoming the most popular option for homeowners, and most downtown neighbourhoods are ADSL-compatible. Subscribers can pay either for unlimited access or a set number of hours, plus an installation fee.

For internet access outside of the home, Wi-Fi hotspots are popping up all over the city in cafes and restaurants. Internet cafes, smoky and loud hideaways for the city's teenagers to play countless hours of *Counterstrike*, are located throughout town – look for the characters 庫勘 (*wang ba*). These cafes usually charge ¥2-¥4 per hour for internet access.

The Chinese government does block certain sites that are deemed inappropriate, but major newspapers and email servers are left alone. Government sites of foreign countries, certain blog servers and large media sites (such as the BBC) are blocked.

Bill Payment

Monthly utility bills can be paid at post offices, and Kedi and Family Mart convenience shops (between 13:00 and 16:00). Banks, such as the Shanghai Construction Bank have ATM machines in select branches that pay bills (just scan the bill, insert your bank card, type in your pin and confirm bill amount). Ask the bank's security guard for help. To pay online, visit the government-sponsored bilingual site online.shfft.com/fftweb/welcome.jsp. If you don't have a local bank card, the site accepts pre-paid cards (available at Kedi convenience stores or Family Marts).

If you miss the final pay date, you must go to a branch office (listed on the back of the bill) to pay – post office and convenience stores don't accept late bills. If you don't make an initial payment, you will receive a reminder bill two weeks after the due date (an added reminder appears on the following month's bill). For electricity, if you don't pay within the following month, the company posts 24 hour or 48 hour warnings on your door prior to shutting off power. The electricity companies also have automated phone messages that call (very early in the morning) after a late payment. Late electricity bills incur a small charge (less than 2%) on the following month's bill.

Post & Courier Services

China Post offices (www.shpost.com.cn) are located throughout the city (look for the green sign) and are open 09:00-17:00 Monday to Friday, and part of Saturday. Services vary – smaller postal centres only handle mailing letters, selling stamps and paying bills, while larger branch offices also offer international Express Mail Service and registered letters. Most postal workers cannot speak English – head to the second floor of the Shanghai Centre at 1376 Nanjing Xi Lu for English service.

China Post letter box

When posting a letter, make sure to include the country name in Chinese. The boxes in the upper left corner are for the zip code of the address you are sending it to (the return address goes on the bottom right). Airmail letters and postcards usually take one to two days to domestic cities, two to four days to Hong Kong, 10 days to Europe and two weeks to North America.

If you're sending a package, it is best bring the contents unwrapped as postal officers will want to know what's inside. Contents cannot exceed ¥1,500 if going overseas (the officer will assess the value).

Depending on your apartment complex, mail is delivered to individual boxes in the building's lobby, to your door, clipped to the wall in a public area, or given to the security guard – and only an address written in Chinese guarantees delivery.

If someone sends you a package, you'll receive a small card in the mail telling you to pick the item up as well as the address of the receiving centre, where you'll need to show your passport to collect the package.

The growing number of reliable private mail carriers in Shanghai includes UPS (800 820 8388), DHL (800 810 8000); Fedex (800 988 1888) and TNT (800 820 9868). They provide a more expensive but reliable service.

Courier Companies

Local *kuaidi* (辦華) services in Shanghai offer a cheap and easy way to send printed material, money and parcels around the city. Light packages cost ¥10 to

Courier Companies	
Lebang Squirrel Express Company	5465 7326
Shanghai Guangling	6468 4093
Shuan Feng Shuyun	5463 4567

send across the city, while heavier packages or suburban destinations may bring the price up to ¥15-¥20. When you call the *kuaidi*, tell them where to pick up the parcel and the delivery address. The company will give you the price over the phone and pick up the parcel within an hour. Delivery is usually same day, except if it's a late pick up (after 15:00).

Radio

The government controls the radio waves, but there's a growing number of English-language and international stations available on Chinese national radio. Try FM87.90, China Radio International, or listen to the *Live It Up Shanghai* show on weeknights (22:15-23:00) on 94.4FM and 990AM. Another option is to try to access your favourite show online, if it's not blocked.

Television

Stars of CCTV

Currently running 16 channels, CCTV has come a long way from its one channel origins, when it broadcast only in the evenings. Originally called 'Beijing Television', the government-run company started in the late 1950s and is run by the State Administration of Radio, Television and Film.

Watching Shanghai cable television provides a fascinating insight into Chinese culture. Cable offers 60 local channels, comprised of several government-owned CCTV channels, provincial channels, and music or news channels. The only English-language channel, CCTV 9, plays travel documentaries and news broadcasts. All news is heavily censored so stories are confined to dignitary visits and economic statistics. Chinese-language soap operas, talk shows, movies and late-night 'infomercials' dominate the choices. Movie channels, such as CCTV 6, sometimes play films in English. Many foreigners prefer to buy their favourite TV series on DVD (see p.331). Local Chinese viewers love foreign TV – *Friends* was a monster hit with youngsters here.

Satellite TV

Satellite TV is hugely popular among expats in Shanghai. Unfortunately, having a satellite dish is illegal so foreigners subscribe to one of the many black-market satellite services in the city. Installation requires unobtrusive small dishes, ranging from 0.35m to 1.5m in diameter, and an access card. Packages vary, but many expats like to borrow signals from the Philippines and Hong Kong.

The devices are cheap and have no annual fees. However, cards may need to be replaced often as satellite companies change codes and some dealers scam customers with fake access cards or service hotlines.

Expat compounds get littered with flyers advertising satellite services. Two of the most popular providers are Pacific TV (www.shanghai-tv.com.cn) or Angel Satellite (www.tvinshanghai.com). Outside of the home, four and five-star hotels offer international channels such as CNN, BBC, and Starworld. Expats can catch international sports games at several bars around the city, including Malone's, Big Bamboo, British Bulldog and O'Malley's (see Bars, p.394).

General Medical Care

Shanghai has a reputation for having the best medical facilities in all of mainland China, and expats should have no worries in finding quality healthcare when needed. Western-style clinics and hospitals have been especially set up to serve the ever-expanding expat population. Facilities at these institutions are improving every year, and some include 24 hour care and accident and emergency departments with trained international staff at hand.

A good number of public hospitals have set up VIP clinics, which cater specifically to expats. Foreigners are technically required to go to either a western-operated clinic or one of these VIP clinics, although some expats go to their local neighbourhood hospital. VIP perks include English-speaking staff, a nurse that will escort you around the hospital, and no waiting.

Attending a public hospital means you will have to pay a registration fee before treatment; this can cost ¥10 to ¥15 for local hospitals and roughly ¥100 for VIP clinics. VIP sections vary – some will charge fees comparable to local services, but some will charge five times this amount.

If you're looking for a warm and inviting attitude from a doctor you should probably refer to the list of internationally focused western hospitals and clinics (p.134), where the doctors will be trained to provide the bedside manner you expect. Otherwise, Shanghai's medical services do not emphasise human relations, and you might find staff to be unfriendly, blunt or uncommunicative.

A reliable general practitioner (GP) can be good for annual check-ups and can serve as a reference whenever you have a health-related concern. When looking for the right doctor for you and your family, it's best to listen to the recommendations of your friends and colleagues.

Before you come to China, you're advised to get the following immunisations up to date: hepatitis A and B, tetanus, polio and typhoid. If you are considering venturing to more rural areas, you should look into getting a rabies vaccination and the series of Japanese encephalitis shots. Travellers from South America, central Africa and other vulnerable areas are required to provide a yellow fever vaccination certificate upon arrival into China. Be sure to consult your physician before you get the vaccinations; women who are pregnant or breastfeeding are advised not to receive any of the above immunisations.

Government Healthcare

There is no formal government healthcare system in place for Chinese citizens. Uninsured and insured alike have to largely pay out of their own pockets. About half of Shanghai's local residents are part of the government's social welfare insurance plan, through which citizens pay an insurance premium via their employer and in turn receive money for their public hospital fees. For expatriates though, there is really no choice. Company packages will often include a comprehensive health insurance plan or individuals can choose to buy their own plan.

Emergency Services

If you can safely transport the victim without causing further injury, then it is almost always a good idea to find your own fastest way of getting to the hospital, either by driving yourself or by taxi. Ambulance response times are typically slow; Shanghai traffic does not yield to emergency vehicles and they may have trouble finding you. The ambulance service can be reached by dialing 120. The operator will most likely not speak English, so it's useful to learn a couple of Chinese phrases such as where you live and the address of whichever hospital you want to go to. Ambulance workers are not required to know basic procedures like cardiopulmonary resuscitation (CPR), so you

Homesick?
Have a friend come visit and hand them the mini equivalent of this behemoth. The Shanghai Mini packs everything a tourist could want to know in a pocket-sized parcel... Complete with maps.

might want to take a class yourself. First Aid China (www.firstaidchina.com) is a good place to learn.

Before an emergency even occurs, you should work out a plan of action with your family. This includes deciding on a facility that is open 24 hours a day, calling to pre-register your details with the hospital (so you won't have to worry about paperwork during an emergency), and practising an emergency run-through with your family where you drive to the hospital. Additionally, you can prepare an emergency folder listing all of your family's medical conditions, allergies, medications and surgical histories. Even if you primarily go to a western hospital, it's a good idea to have the folder's contents in both English and Chinese.

You also might want to make a card with the hospital's address and contact information that you and your children can keep with you at all times. Shanghai United Family Hospital (p.136) supplies cards that allow parents to give the hospital power of attorney. This can be important in avoiding delays if the child is brought to the hospital by someone other than their parent, and the parent is not available.

Private Healthcare

Private hospitals tend to be smaller, with friendly service and specialised equipment. Hospital bills at a private institution will generally be much heftier than a public hospital's and can add up to as much as a hospital fee in a western country. You may find yourself paying tens of thousands of yuan for a week's worth of tests and medication, even if your condition is not that serious, compared with ¥1,000 at a public hospital for similar treatment. A regular check-up costs around ¥500, but will usually total ¥1,000 or more when basic medicine is provided.

Health Insurance

Take Cover

Nearly 45,000 people are injured in China every day from traffic-related accidents. In a city where cars and buses share the roads with millions of taxis, cyclists and hand carts, even if you walk around in neon orange clothes and wear a helmet, you're still at risk – better to be covered than clobbered.

If medical insurance is not supplied by your employer, no one will force you to buy it. Rates vary dramatically based on your personal situation and what type of insurance plan you want to buy. For a free quote on expat packages, you can go through an insurance broker such as International Medical Group (www.imglobal.com), Medibroker (www.medibroker.com) or Expatriate Insurance Services (www.expatriate-insurance.com). A basic insurance plan can be bought for as little as ¥4,000 per year, but premium annual insurance can cost as much as ¥40,000 (see p.130).

Pharmacies

Many kinds of medicine can be obtained over the counter in Shanghai and prescriptions are rarely needed. Be wary of fake drugs or mislabelled products and always buy from reputable pharmacies that are government-run or associated with a hospital. Look out for bad spelling on packages and suspicious labels that appear inauthentic. Medicine will often be sold under different brand names here, so write down the chemical or pharmaceutical that you are looking for as well as the Chinese brand name.

In recent years, the government has tried to regulate over-the-counter medicines, so you should bring a prescription from your GP for antibiotics and more serious drugs. Painkillers, cough and allergy medicines, digestive remedies, skincare medication and vitamins or dietary supplements are all available over the counter. Huashan Pharmacy (12 Wulumuqi Lu; 6248 5674) and Huifeng Pharmacy (973 Central Huaihai Lu; 6473 6810) have 24 hour service with a large selection of both western and Chinese medicine. Wuyao Pharmacy (619 Panyu Lu; 6294 1403) is also 24 hours, takes phone reservations and offers a delivery service. Other pharmacies can be found throughout the city and are marked by large green crosses.

Many of the reliable brands you may be accustomed to using don't exist in

Shanghai, so stock up whenever you're back home. If bringing prescriptions from overseas, be sure to have a medical certificate from your doctor. World Link's pharmacies can order and import special overseas medication for patients on an individual basis if necessary.

Health Check-Ups

Regular medical checkups are offered by all the major hospitals and clinics. Well-woman and well-man checkups are provided by some hospitals and clinics under the guise of 'health screening' services. The Shanghai East International Medical Centre (p.136) offers a comprehensive check-up that requires two sessions to complete. The first session involves diagnostic evaluations that include an eye screening, x-ray, ECG, ultrasound, stress test, blood drawing and urine collection. The second session concludes with a physical evaluation by a health screening doctor, and a review of test results, as well as lifestyle counselling.

Health Insurance

Health insurance is not mandatory for expats, but it is advised. If you have a sudden accident and need rehabilitation or long-term treatment, you'll be grateful to have insurance as a financial safety net.

A basic coverage scheme will generally involve inpatient care, post-hospital treatment, emergency dental care and pregnancy complications. A comprehensive plan will additionally cover outpatient care, specialist services and regular maternity or dental costs. Insurance plans usually exclude pre-existing conditions that the applicant has had for two or more years, as well as drug abuse, infertility, cosmetic surgery and injuries resulting from a risky pastime such as bungee jumping. Insurance plans and costs differ dramatically according to your personal situation and the type of coverage you're interested in (see p.129 for a list of brokers).

All expats should look for health insurance that includes repatriation or emergency relocation and treatment outside of China. When you are deciding on an insurance plan, consider any future lifestyle choices, such as pregnancy, and choose accordingly. You might want to look into which plans hospitals will direct-bill with, so you don't have to pay out of your own pocket initially. Also, reflect on payment methods and how flexible the insurance company is: some offer monthly payment plans, while others have annual plans. Read over the details until you understand it completely, so there are no surprises.

Liver Lot Longer

China's transplant surgeons carried out more than 10,000 liver transplants between 2005 and 2007, with Shanghai's hospitals leading the way. Since 2003, the three-year survival rate for liver transplants has doubled to 75%.

Donor Cards

Most Chinese citizens still adhere to Confucian principles of keeping the body intact after death, but with a critical organ shortage for patients needing transplants, views on organ donation are changing. There is still a major lack of regulation with the donation system though, and it is recommended that foreigners do not get involved.

Giving Blood

Blood donation is becoming increasingly regulated and standardised, which is good news for anyone worried about safety issues in a hospital's blood supply. The Shanghai health department has helped enforce high national standards that include screening systems similar to those of western nations, regulating who gives blood and how often. If you have rhesus negative blood you might want to consider donating to help your fellow expats. Less than 1% of Chinese prople have this blood group, meaning that there is a limited supply available for expats who need transfusions. Not only will donating help others, but blood donors are given priority for transfusions. There are regular volunteer drives, with donation points in various spots around the city.

Giving Up Smoking

Various local hospitals offer clinics to help addicts quit smoking, including Xuhui, Zhongshan and Jing'an. These clinics are aimed more at the local population, and expats generally seek help for addiction through Alcoholics Anonymous (www.aashanghai.com) due to a lack of other support groups.

Some people swear by alternative methods such as acupuncture and hypnotherapy to help them quit. Wales Psychological Clinic (6255 2588) offers clinical hypnosis specifically aimed at smoking cessation. Acupuncture is another option, and can help reduce the unpleasant side effects of withdrawal, such as depression (see p.142).

Main Government Hospitals

Shanghai has more than 500 public hospitals, so it should be relatively easy to find a local hospital near your residence. While foreigners are technically not allowed to set foot into a hospital without a special foreigners' ward, it can be done as long as you are willing to endure long lines and put up with aloof service.

If you decide to go to a local hospital without a foreigner clinic and can't speak Chinese, be sure to bring a translator or Chinese-speaking friend. Even the majority of the personnel at VIP foreigner branches will often only speak Chinese. Nevertheless, there are expats that stay loyal to their local hospitals and especially enjoy the economical prices when compared with the costly foreign-owned clinics.

Other Government Hospitals

Changzheng Hospital	Huangpu	6361 0109
Chenxin Hospital ▶ p.133	Changning	6225 3456
First Maternity and Infant Hospital	Luwan	5403 5206
Guangci Hospital	Luwan	6466 4483
Guanghua Western and Chinese Medical Hospital	Changning	6280 5833
Huadong Hospital	Hongqiao	6248 3180
Ninth People's Hospital	Huangpu	6313 8341
Tongji Hospital	Putuo	5605 1080

585 Jiu Long Lu
Hongkou
九龙路585号
虹口
🚇 *Dalian Lu*
Map p.422 C4 1

First People's Hospital International Medical Care Centre
上海市第一人民医院国际医疗保健中心
6306 9480 | www.firsthospital.cn
This hospital is said to be one of China's best. It is affiliated with Shanghai Jiaotong University and has a 24 hour emergency clinic available. Specialised research includes organ transplants, ophthalmology, anaesthesiology and cardiovascular surgery. You can pay by cash, card or through insurance. The average consultation fee is around ¥100 to ¥200 (not including the cost of medication).

145 Shandong Lu
Huangpu
山东中路145号
黄埔
🚇 *Nanjing Dong Lu*
Map p.431 D3 2

Renji Hospital 上海仁济医院
6326 0930
Like the First People's Hospital, Renji is also affiliated with Jiaotong University, and was Shanghai's first when it was established in 1844. It has a second campus in Pudong New District, known as East Renji Hospital (1630 Dongfang Lu; 5875 2345). The Clinical Centre for Rheumatic Disease and the Clinical Centre for Digestive Disease are its main focuses.

197 Ruijin Er Lu
Luwan
瑞金二路197号
卢湾
🚇 *Shanxi Nan Lu*
Map p.436 B2 3

Ruijin Hospital 瑞金医院
6437 0045 | www.rjh.com.cn
A leader in the Shanghai healthcare system, Ruijin Hospital serves as a teaching hospital under Shanghai Jiaotong University. Established in 1907, it has a staff of over 3,300, and around 1,774 sick beds. You can pay by credit card or be billed directly to your insurance. Services are available in English, French and Mandarin. The average consultation fee is ¥300 for outpatient service and ¥450 for emergency service.

1111 Xianxia Lu
Hongqiao
仙霞路1111号
虹桥
🚇 Yan'an Xi Lu
Map p.434 A2 4

Shanghai Changning Central District Hospital
上海市长宁区中心医院
6290 9911 | www.cnchospital.com

This hospital provides basic medical care as well as services from its ophthalmology, orthopaedic, dermatology and traditional Chinese medicine departments, among others. It is known for its cardiovascular and orthopaedic specialists. In 2004, it formed a joint-venture with Chindex International to establish the Shanghai United Family Hospital.

128 Guangdong Lu
Huangpu
广东路128号
黄埔
🚇 Nanjing Dong Lu
Map p.431 E3 5

Shanghai Huangpu Central District Hospital
上海市黄浦区中心医院
6321 2487

Huangpu's main public hospital has a range of expertise from breast cancer and cardiovascular disease to endocrinology, urology and ophthalmology. There is also an immunisation specialist on staff and a traditional Chinese medicine outpatient clinic. Check-up packages available include a comprehensive medical examination with ECG and blood tests for around ¥200.

1068 Changle Lu
Jing'an
长乐路1068号
静安
🚇 Jing'an Temple
Map p.435 E1 6

Shanghai Huashan Worldwide Medical Centre
华山环宇保健医疗中心
6248 3986 | www.huashan.org.cn

Huashan hospital has a reputation as one of Shanghai's best places for medical care. It combines traditional Chinese medicine with western practices, and has a strong neurology department. Research institutions associated with the hospital include the Huashan School of Clinical Medicine and the WHO Collaborating Centre for Neurology. There is 24 hour emergency service available, and patients can pay with cash or card. Consultation fees vary – outpatient service is ¥250, emergency service between 17:00 and 22:00 costs ¥350, and emergency service between 22:00 and 8:00 is ¥450.

259 Xikang Lu
Jing'an
西康路259号
静安
🚇 Jing'an Temple
Map p.429 F3 7

Shanghai Jing'an Central District Hospital
上海市静安区中心医院
6247 4530

Jing'an's central public hospital is a teaching establishment affiliated with Shanghai's TCM and Tongji Universities. Besides its traditional Chinese medicine department, it is also known for treating digestive disorders, and has a range of outpatient services including gynaecology, infertility and general physical examinations. The hospital also has a number of internationally manufactured machines, such as a CT scanner.

301 Yanchang Lu
Zhabei
延长中路301号
闸北
🚇 Shanghai Circus
Map p.422 A3 8

Shanghai Tenth People's Hospital 上海市第十人民医院
6630 0588 | www.shdsyy.com.cn

Founded in 1910, this teaching hospital is affiliated with Tongji University and its focus lies with a traditional Chinese medicine approach to cardiovascular disease. The university has also done intensive research on throat cancer and haematosis, in addition to offering services from its departments in ophthalmology, orthopaedics, endocrinology and traditional Chinese medicine.

1665 Kong Jiang Lu
Yangpu
控江路1665号
杨浦
🚇 Dalian Lu
Map p.423 E3 9

Xinhua Hospital 新华医院
6579 0000 | www.xinhua-scmc.com.cn

This hospital is affiliated with Jiaotong University's School of Medicine, and specifically concentrates on paediatric care and research. It's most well-known for its Centre for Paediatric Congenital Heart Disease and its Centre for Paediatric Surgery of Abnormalities. There are more than 1,300 patient beds and it regularly sees over two million outpatients per year.

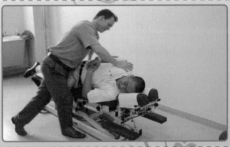

180 Fenglin Lu
Xuhui
枫林路180号
徐汇
🚇 *Xujiahui*
Map p.436 A4 🔟

Zhongshan Hospital 中山医院

6404 1990 | www.zshospital.com

Affiliated with Fudan University, this is a general hospital that specialises in cancer research and treatment. The focus is on diagnosing and curing liver cancer, as well as heart, kidney and lung disease. There is a 24 hour emergency service and clinic available, and patients can pay with cash or card. An average consultation fee is around ¥100 to ¥300.

Main Private Hospitals

Since Shanghai's first private hospital (Bo'ai Philanthropism Hospital) was established in 1999, the sector has grown rapidly, and seemingly everyone wants to cash in. These private hospitals are foreign-invested companies or joint ventures, and advertise themselves as offering lots of one-on-one attention as well as intimate and clean facilities. Clinics offer similar but more limited services, generally reserved to outpatient care. Some are designed to look more like hotels than hospitals. Still, the quality of service, training of staff and amenities vary and you should always visit the hospital yourself before deciding on whether to be treated there. Private hospitals and clinics are more and more in demand, especially with the expat community, and unless it's an emergency you should call ahead to make an appointment.

Other Private Hospitals

Canadian Evergreen Family Health Centre	Hongqiao	6270 6265
CanAm International Medical Centre Shanghai	Luwan	5403 9133
International SOS	Xuhui	5298 9538
Ren'ai Hospital	Xuhui	6468 8888
Shanghai Bo'ai Hospital	Xuhui	6433 3999
St John's Health Clinic	Luwan	6304 7175
St Reiss Medical Centre	Xuhui	5404 8771
Sun-Tec Medical Centre	Changning	6268 8811

800 Huashan Lu
Xuhui
华山路800弄丁香公
寓6号裙楼
徐汇
🚇 *Changshu Lu*
Map p.435 E1 🔟

American-Sino OB/Gyn Service 美华妇产服务

6210 2299 | www.americanobgyn.com

American-Sino was co-founded by New York-based New Life OB/Gyn Group and Huashan Worldwide Medical Centre with the aim of providing the best women's healthcare in Shanghai. It offers comprehensive services in obstetrics, gynaecology, infertility and pre-teen care. There is 24 hour service available, and insurance as well as major credit cards are accepted.

**301 Shanghai
Kerry Centre,
1515 Nanjing Xi Lu**
Jing'an
南京西路1515号
静安
🚇 *Jing'an Temple*
Map p.429 F4 🔟

Global HealthCare 全康医疗

5298 6339 | www.ghcchina.com

This health centre provides a wide range of services to the expatriate community including general check-ups, paediatrics, rheumatology, cardiology, neurology and plastic surgery. A 24 hour hotline is available to patients, although general services require an appointment. A first consultation will cost around ¥500 including exams and the second visit will cost ¥300, while for pregnant women it is slightly more expensive, around ¥500.

910 Hengshan Lu
Xuhui
衡山路910号
徐汇
🚇 *Hengshan Lu*
Map p.435 E4 🔟

International Peace Maternity Hospital 国际和平妇婴保健院

6438 2452 | www.ipmch.com.cn

Established by the China Welfare Institute, this hospital specialises in healthcare for women and children, and comes highly recommended by the expat community. Clinics include services for obstetrics, gynaecology, mammography and pregnancy. There is also a centre dedicated to birth control with specialists available to give guidance and recommendations. Services are available in English, French and Mandarin.

ParkwayHealth – international healthcare where you need it

To provide you with comprehensive services and the best international healthcare possible, Shanghai's two most internationally renowned healthcare providers, Shanghai Gleneagles International Medical & Surgical Center and World Link Medical & Dental Centers have come together as ParkwayHealth – The name renowned for clinical quality, superior medical expertise and an extensive Asia-wide network that includes ParkwayHealth's internationally eminent Singapore hospitals – Gleneagles and Mount Elizabeth.

ParkwayHealth is continuously raising the standards of medical excellence – Offering a comprehensive range of services and specialties from a dedicated, multilingual medical team, all within easy reach through ParkwayHealth's Shanghai network and 24 HOUR HEALTHLINE.

Services and Specialties

- Family Medicine
- Pediatrics
- Women's Health
- OB-Gynecology
- Gastroenterology
- Dermatology

- Endocrinology
- Plastic Surgery
- General Surgery
- ENT (Ear, Nose & Throat)
- Neurology
- Counseling

- Psychiatry
- Dentistry
- Physiotherapy
- Sports Medicine
- Orthopedics
- Rehabilitation Medicine

- Diagnostic Radiology
- Clinical Laboratory Testing
- Preventive Medicine
- Health Screening
- Speech Pathology
- Occupational Therapy
- Nutrition

Tomorrow Square International Medical & Surgical Center: 4th Floor Tomorrow Square (same building at the JW Marriott Hotel), 389 Nanjing West Road. Specialty & Inpatient Center: 2/3 Floor, 170 Danshui Road (near Xintiandi). Hong Qiao Medical Center: 2258, Hongqiao Road. Shanghai Centre Medical & Dental Centers: Units 203-4, West Retail Plaza, 1376 Nanjing West Road. Jin Qiao Medical & Dental Center: 51 Hengfeng Road, Jinqiao Pudong. s e r v i c e s @ p a r k w a y h e a l t h . c n • w w w . p a r k w a y h e a l t h . c n Singapore • Malaysia • India • Brunei • Vietnam • China

551 Pudong Nan Lu
Pudong
浦东南路551号
浦东
🚇 **Dongchang Lu**
Map p.432 B3 **14**

Shanghai East International Medical Centre
上海东方国际医院
5879 9999 | www.seimc.com.cn

A comprehensive healthcare facility designed to create a calming hospital environment for international families. There are outpatient, inpatient and surgical services available, with onsite digital x-ray, mammography, ECG and laboratory resources. Inpatient and outpatient services are available 24 hours a day. The average consulting fee (excluding medication) is ¥500 to ¥1,000.

120 Yunjian Lu
Pudong
云间路120号
浦东
🚇 **Century Park**
Map p.440 B2 **15**

Shanghai Ruidong Hospital 上海瑞东医院
5833 9595 | www.ruidong-hospital.com

Ruidong Hospital was established as the result of a Sino-Japanese joint venture, and serves as a branch of Puxi's Ruijin Hospital. It offers clean, high-quality facilities and specialises in infertility treatment and digestive diseases, in addition to physical examination services. There is a 24 hour emergency clinic available, and costs for a consultation (excluding medication) will be around ¥50 upwards. Besides accepting insurance, you can also pay with cash or by card.

1139 Xianxia Lu
Changning
仙霞路1139号
长宁
Map p.427 E3 **16**

Shanghai United Family Hospital 上海和睦家医院
5133 1900 | www.unitedfamilyhospitals.com

Shanghai United aims to provide expats with an international standard of healthcare. The latest technology is used for surgical procedures, and the hospital also has dental facilities, a modern birthing centre and a pharmacy with imported medicine. There is also a Shanghai United Family Clinic in Minhang district, a sister organisation that covers paediatrics, mental health counselling, obstetrics and gynaecology, and family medicine. An international staff allows for some services to be conducted in various languages, including English, Spanish, Swedish, Cantonese and Swahili. Cash, credit card and direct billing to Shanghai United's approved insurance providers are all viable forms of payment.

Shanghai Centre,
1376 Nanjing Xi Lu
Jing'an
南京西路1376号
静安
🚇 **Jing'an Temple**
Map p.429 F4 **17**

SinoUnited Health 中国联合卫生中心
6279 8920

This is an international hospital that was established by American physicians, and aims to provide quality western-style care to expats. The hospital's emphasis is on physical therapy, pain management and neurology. All of the physicians and therapists are expats or have international training and work experience, and languages spoken include English, Japanese, French, Spanish and Mandarin.

Various Locations

World Link International Medical Centres
世界联合医疗中心 ▶ p.135
6445 5999 | www.worldlink-shanghai.com

This international company offers extensive expat medical services, with clinic locations around the city. Different specialities are catered for at various centres, covering specific issues such as internal medicine, gastroenterology, neurology, dermatology and women's health. Dental check-ups, visa health screenings, vaccinations, basic health check-ups and a 24 hour observation room are also available – check the website to find the locations. A pharmacy with imported medication and a traditional Chinese medicine clinic including acupuncture are also offered. Language assistance is available, including English, Japanese, German, Malay, Taiwanese and Mandarin. You should contact each clinic individually to learn about their specific services.

Dermatologists

Bioscor Shanghai Clinic	Xuhui	6431 8899
Shanghai Skin Disease & STD Hospital	Pudong	5889 2700
Shanghai Skin Disease & STD Hospital	Changning	6252 2721
World Link Specialty & Inpatient Centre	Luwan	6385 9889

136

Maternity

Other options **Baby Items** p.310

Postnatal Depression

Experiencing postnatal depression is a completely natural phenomenon. Postnatal courses are a good way to seek assistance, since midwives and doctors closely work with mothers during this time to ensure they fully recover from pregnancy both physically and mentally. Shanghai United Family Hospitals and World Link have professional therapists on staff, who can provide support and information on how to cope after giving birth.

With modern, quality hospital care readily available, few non-citizens find any medical reason to leave Shanghai to give birth. A number of hospitals and clinics approach birth from a western point of view, including United Family Hospitals, Huashan Hospital, Peace Maternity, Shanghai East International Medical Centre and World Link Clinic. This means that they should be approachable and offer open communication through the entire birthing process. Many of the doctors will be competent, if not native, English speakers, who have been trained in western countries or worked abroad.

Local hospitals will be efficient, but won't offer the type of birthing experience that expat mothers-to-be might expect. Most Chinese women prefer a painless birth, which leads to many local doctors recommending Caesarean sections. Doctors favour Caesareans because they can schedule their day and the hospital can charge about ¥20,000 more for the birth. The Chinese ideal of a painless pregnancy is helpful if you are interested in an epidural, which are readily available.

For expats in search of alternative birthing options, Shanghai can be a frustrating place. Hospitals here are more comfortable dealing with birth in a clinical environment, and the medical community has only recently become more open to natural birthing choices involving midwives and even water birth. Currently Shanghai Changning District Maternity and Infant Care Hospital (934 Yan'an Xi Lu; 6252 1865) has a birthing pool, where a water birth will cost around ¥4,000. Jacuzzis and tubs are also sometimes supplied for pain relief, including in Shanghai United Family Hospital's delivery rooms. Some mothers have unassisted home births after hiring midwives for prenatal training. If you're interested in homebirths, you should network through a mothers' club such as La Leche League (www.llli.org) to find an independent *doula* (a trained person providing support during labour and after childbirth) and to get advice from any women who have had a homebirth experience in Shanghai.

Maternity Care in Government Hospitals

If choosing to give birth in a local hospital, make sure you are comfortable with the doctor you are dealing with, and that they are willing to create the birthing experience you want. Some hospitals don't provide open communication, refuse partners to be present, are overcrowded, have strict policies and staff with minimum or no English. Some have long waiting lists to serve mothers-to-be, so you will have to check to see if doctors are even available. That said, public hospitals can be cheaper alternatives to the private sector, and many now have VIP sections for expatriate clients, with private rooms and more one-on-one attention. VIP clinic prices can be comparable to private hospitals (¥40,000 to ¥60,000 for a maternity package).

Maternity Hospitals & Clinics

American-Sino OB/Gyn Service (Huashan Hospital)	Jing'an	6249 3246	Government
Changning Maternity and Infant Care Hospital	Changning	6228 8686	Government
International Peace Maternity and Child Health Hospital	Xuhui	6407 5328	Private
Shanghai East International Medical Centre	Pudong	5879 9999	Private
Shanghai First Maternity and Infant Hospital	Luwan	5403 5206	Government
Shanghai United Family Hospitals and Clinics	Changning	5133 1900	Private
World Link International Medical Centres	Various Locations	6445 5999	Private

Maternity Care in Private Hospitals

Private hospitals and clinics are pricier but operate on western standards. Most clinics offer a pregnancy package, which costs around ¥40,000 to ¥60,000 for a natural birth (as opposed to a Caesarean), and usually includes prenatal care, the hospital stay, medication, newborn shots and postnatal care. Ultrasound appointments and doctor check-ups will cost around ¥500 to ¥1,000 without a package. The price depends largely on the delivery room you choose, ranging from ¥15,000 to ¥21,000. Shanghai United Family Hospital will cost around ¥80,000 for check-ups leading up to the birth, the birth itself, and a three-day stay in one of the hospital's private rooms.

Abortions

Abortion rates are high in China due to the 'one child' family planning policies and a lack of sex education. Since abortion is a popular option for the local population, hospitals do not judge and will not ask a lot of questions. All the main hospitals are able to perform legal abortions in a clean, safe manner. Depending on where you go, an abortion can cost ¥200 to ¥500 or more. Private western institutions are not allowed to perform abortions and do not offer these services.

Going Back to Your Home Country

If you choose to give birth in your home country, there are a few things to keep in mind. Unless your doctor specifically warns you against it, you should be able to fly up to 32-36 weeks into a pregnancy, and four weeks after giving birth. Airlines have different policies for flight during pregnancy and after, so confirm your details before booking. You should get your Shanghai physician to give you a record of all the monitoring sessions conducted for your pregnancy and pass it on to your home doctor. After the birth, you'll have to obtain a passport and visa for your new baby. Remember to bring your child's birth certificate and any medical records of vaccinations, blood tests or health evaluations since its birth. Once you land in Shanghai, don't forget register your baby at your local Public Security Bureau within a month of the birth (see p.64).

Antenatal Care

While you're receiving your antenatal care you have a good opportunity to assess the hospital you are going to give birth at. If you buy a maternity package from a hospital, the costs of antenatal care will be included. If not, American-Sino offers antenatal care

Local hospital

for about ¥5,000 per trimester, and complete antenatal care at Shanghai United is roughly ¥14,000. If you pay by individual visits, prices can range from ¥150 to ¥2,500 each. Antenatal classes are also offered by the western-style clinics, and they can be a good way to prepare for parenthood and learn about the birth process.

Postnatal Care

Postnatal care differs for each hospital and clinic, but some offer home visits if requested. World Link's birthing services provide an experienced, expatriate midwife to visit you and your newborn at home and answer any questions you may have, and it also provides a 24 hour nurse hotline, while American-Sino provides six weeks of postnatal care. You should bring your baby back to the hospital a month after the birth so it can receive a basic check-up and receive any booster vaccines, if needed. If you're interested in breastfeeding your child, La Leche League (p.144) is a welcoming network of mothers that support or are interested in breastfeeding and can supply plenty of information on pregnancy and raising children in Shanghai.

Maternity Leave

Foreigners and Chinese citizens receive 90 days' paid maternity leave – 15 days before giving birth, and 75 days after. During maternity leave, the employer is legally obligated to ensure that the mother's job will be available for her return. Employers are reimbursed through the government's social insurance policy, which all businesses pay for on a monthly basis. After the 90 days of paid leave, some women choose to continue to stay at home, in which case you should work it out with your employer to make sure you have a job to come back to. Otherwise, women are not obligated to compensate their employer for the maternity leave costs should they decide to stay at home indefinitely. Maternity leave regulations may vary according to your business contract, so you should verify the details with your employer.

Gynaecology & Obstetrics

Finding a proper gynaecologist who makes you feel at ease is important. Before you start the hunt to narrow down potential doctors, think about your expectations and the traits you would expect in a personal physician. Any of the doctors who work with expats should be aware of different cultural requirements. There are male gynaecologists available, so decide if you would be alright with a male doctor or would prefer a female. Once you have a list of doctors, ask the hospitals about each one's medical experience and educational background. Also, factor in where they are located and how available they are for appointments. The easiest way to get an accurate sense of which gynaecologist you should go to is by getting references from friends and trusted acquaintances.

Mammograms

Having a mammogram every year or two can significantly reduce a woman's risk of difficulties from breast cancer, according to the World Health Organisation and National Cancer Institute. Shanghai East International Medical Centre offers high-tech digital mammography services that detect abnormalities. Call 5879 9999 to schedule a breast exam and mammography, which costs around ¥1,600.

Fertility Treatments

American-Sino OB/Gyn and World Link's Birthing Centre both have modern facilities and comprehensive services aimed at helping infertile couples. Ruijin Hospital and Ji Ai Fertility Centre (588 Fangxie Lu; 6345 4244) both specialise in in-vitro fertilisation (IVF) services. Since most insurance does not cover fertility treatment, you will most likely have to pay for IVF services yourself. While it varies from hospital to hospital, IVF services cost around ¥18,000 to ¥30,000, ultrasounds cost from ¥100 to ¥300, and blood tests will cost from ¥100 all the way to ¥1,500.

Gynaecology & Obstetrics		
American-Sino OB/Gyn Service	6210 2299	www.americanobgyn.com
Dr Katherine Chu	6334 3666	www.drkatherinechu.com
Dr Michelle Lu-Ferguson	6445 5999	www.worldlink-shanghai.com
Dr Ninni Ji	5133 1900	www.unitedfamilyhospitals.com
Dr Yvette Kong	6445 5999	www.worldlink-shanghai.com
Ji Ai Hospital	6345 9977	na
Ruijin Hospital	6437 0045	www.rjh.com.cn
VIP Maternity & Gyn Centre	6407 4887	www.upmg.us

Contraception

It is recommended that you consult your physician before choosing a birth control brand. One of the most popular contraceptive pills on the market is Marvelon, which comes in packets of 21 tablets, and Minulet, which is divided into 28 tablet packs. Various morning-after pills, which act as emergency contraceptives, are also available. All of these contraceptive pills may cause side effects. The morning-after pill has the worst effects, so should only be used as a last resort. Your gynaecologist can also help you vary dosages if side effects are causing you problems.

Contraception is available at pharmacies, hospitals, some local shops, and a few larger department stores, while condoms are available in all convenience stores.

Paediatrics

Special Needs

While there are limited professional therapy options for children faced with learning disabilities, there is a tight-knit community of special needs families that can offer advice and support. The Heart-to-Heart Support Group (139 1731 9214) provides emotional backing for parents of children with special needs. World Link (6445 5999) has a few specialists, and Shanghai Children's Medical Centre holds a weekly special needs clinic. Shanghai Special Education Consulting is a good contact to have. It provides professional support, evaluations and treatment. See p.157 for more details.

Finding a good paediatrician usually involves asking for recommendations from friends, co-workers or other doctors. You can also ask your insurance company for referrals that they have worked with. Once you have the name of a doctor, you can contact them and schedule a meeting with your child to see whether he or she is at ease, and if the doctor is suitable. If you have a family health plan, then your child's regular hospital appointments should be covered by insurance. Children are given a tuberculosis vaccine and a hepatitis B vaccine at birth, and the Chinese vaccination schedule calls for a polio vaccine at two months, a DPT1 vaccine (for diphtheria, pertussis and tetanus) at three months and a measles vaccine at eight months of age. This schedule is unique to China, but is not enforced, so keep a close eye on your child's vaccination schedule. Besides these vaccinations, a meningitis vaccine is recommended at six months, rubella and mumps at between eight and twelve months, and Japanese encephalitis is recommended at the year mark. The chicken pox vaccine is also available.

Paediatrics		
Dr Morgan Jenkins	Luwan	6445 5999
Dr Robert Kohlbacher	Luwan	6445 5999
Shanghai Children's Hospital Jing'an	Huangpu	6247 4880
Shanghai Children's Hospital of Fudan Hospital	Xuhui	5452 4666
Shanghai Children's Medical Centre	Pudong	5873 2020
Shanghai Pudong Children's Heart and Thorax Surgical Dept	Pudong	5835 9353
Shanghai United Family Hospital and Clinics	Changning	6291 1635
Sunshine Children's Clinic	Gubei	5477 6480
Xinhua Hospital	Yangpu	6579 0000

Dentists & Orthodontists

A good basic dentist is not that hard to find in Shanghai. Costs range from ¥200 to ¥750 for a regular cleaning, depending on where you go. The general services offered are comparable to western countries, including x-rays, fillings and extractions. International clinics offer cosmetic services such as teeth whitening, orthodontics and even oral surgery. Equipment is also normally imported from abroad. When thinking about major dental surgery, remember that some hospitals are not permitted to provide anaesthesia. Dental clinics operate on a 'fee-for-service' basis, and patients pay in cash, by credit card or through direct billing arrangements with international insurance companies.

It is recommended that children begin visiting the dentist at least six months after their first tooth appears, but before the child has reached its first birthday. The first visits are less of a formal check-up and more to ensure that your child's mouth development is OK. A dentist can also advise you on preventative care and instil in you and your child healthy cleaning habits.

Dentists & Orthodontists		
Arrail Dental	Luwan	5396 6538
Bioscor Shanghai Clinic	Xuhui	6431 8899
Cidi Dental Clinic	Jing'an	5115 4575
DDS Dental Care – Hongqiao	Hongqiao	6876 0409
DDS Dental Care – Pudong	Pudong	5465 2678
DDS Dental Care – Puxi	Xuhui	6445 6099
Dr Harriet Jin's Dental Surgery	Hongqiao	6448 0882
DUZ Dental Clinic	Changning	6247 3247
Garden Dental Clinic	Xuhui	6445 6099
Liwei Dental	Jing'an	6271 5707
Orthodontics Asia	Xuhui	6473 7733
Sino-Canadian Dental Clinic	Luwan	6313 3174
Tokushinkai Dental Clinic	Hongqiao	3431 7387
World Link International Medical Centres	Various Locations	6445 5999

Opticians & Ophthalmologists

Opticians can be found throughout the city. Service is relatively cheap and consistent across the board, but costs vary from ¥150 to over ¥6,000 depending on the frames and lenses. Most opticians will also do prescription sunglasses, such as Paris Miki and American Eyes. For a Chinese driving licence, you will have a short eye exam at the testing centre, which is of a questionable standard.

For more serious eye-related procedures, ophthalmologists are available through all the major medical clinics, and even if there is no specialist ward doctors can refer you to a reliable ophthalmologist.

If you are worried about your baby's vision, you can visit the Shanghai Children's Medical Centre (see p.140), which offers paediatric ophthalmology.

Laser eye surgery is becoming increasingly popular, and the larger eye health clinics and hospitals with ophthalmology departments all offer laser vision correction with similar results. Costs vary according to clinic and procedure, but expect to be charged from ¥4,800 to ¥20,800 for lasik surgery.

Opticians & Ophthalmologists		
American Eyes	Jing'an	6258 4838
Fudan Vision Medical and Healthcare Centre	Jing'an	6334 3666
Huangpu District Eye Clinic	Huangpu	5382 1270
Mancang Optical	Huangpu	6322 2113
Paris Miki	Luwan	5382 4882
Shanghai Changhai Hospital	Yangpu	2507 1114
Shanghai Ocular Clinic	Jing'an	6271 7733
Shanghai Peace Eye Hospital	Hongkou	5589 0118
Shanghai Wuliangcai Optical	Huangpu	6351 4540
Sino-America Ocular Clinic	Xuhui	6248 9999

Cosmetic Treatment & Surgery

Shanghai is becoming a key city for cosmetic surgery, with its reputation for highly professional medical service and its consistently low prices. Foreign surgeons tend to be in high demand, but there are claims that many local surgeons are said to not have professional qualifications. Wherever you decide to go, be aware of your doctor's professional history and education. Ren'ai Hospital is known for its highly qualified South Korean surgeons and Bioscor International is popular for its expat-oriented service and varied face-lift methods.

The most popular procedures are double eyelid surgery (particularly among Asian women), breast augmentation, rhinoplasty and liposuction. Non-invasive and alternative techniques are also popular, including botox, skin peels and microdermabrasion.

Cosmetic Treatment & Surgery		
Bioscor Shanghai Clinic	Xuhui	6431 8899
Ren'ai Hospital	Xuhui	6468 8888
Shanghai East Hospital Cosmetic Surgery	Pudong	5876 4134
Ye Medical Centre Shanghai	Hongqiao	6208 8088

Alternative Therapies

Shanghai has some of the most well-known traditional Chinese medicine and alternative therapy institutions in China, but they are sometimes not as easily accessible to expats as you might expect. English-language services are limited, and that's really what you end up paying for most of the time.

The principles of traditional Chinese medicine are still adhered to in Shanghai society, although the growth of western hospital facilities has forced it to take a back seat during critical medical emergencies. Traditional Chinese medicine involves maintaining the body's balance between yin and yang. This Chinese philosophy states that the world is composed of a balance between yin (characterised as female, dark, negative, cold) and yang (characterised as male, light, positive, hot). This balance extends to individuals, determining how they behave and feel. Many people still swear by its dietary theories. Body & Soul (see table) is a good place to start on your path to a more balanced lifestyle. An initial consultation will cost you ¥500.

Alternative Therapies	
Body & Soul TCM Clinic	5101 9262
Cai Tong De Tang Medicine	6322 1160
Dr Li's Chinese Medicine Clinic	3424 1989
Longhua Hospital	6438 5700
Shanghai Chinese Medical Hospital	5663 9828
Shanghai East International Medical Centre	6887 1189
Shanghai Huadong Hospital	6248 3180
Shanghai Yueyang Integrated Medicine Hospital	6253 6300
Tong Ren Tang Medicine	6294 9837

141

Acupressure & Acupuncture

Acupressure and acupuncture are both popular alternative therapies for everything from quitting smoking and treating asthma to fighting depression and providing antenatal and postnatal care. As one of the central forms of healing in traditional Chinese medicine, acupuncture involves sticking thin needles into specific areas of the body to stimulate meridians (energy channels). This can revitalise or calm a person, depending on the type of treatment. Many Shanghai hospitals have traditional Chinese medicine clinics with acupuncture and acupressure services, as do the universities that teach TCM. The most popular acupuncturists can be booked up for months, so call as much in advance as possible to make an appointment. Sessions can range from ¥80 to ¥600.

Acupressure/Acupuncture	
Body & Soul TCM Clinic	5101 9262
Dr Kelly Clady	137 7177 2431
Mediterranean Sauna	63531430
Shanghai Chinese Medicine Clinic	62588203
Shanghai Research Institute of Acupuncture	64684215
Shanghai University of Traditional Chinese Medicine	64171226
Shuguang Hospital	53821650
World Link TCM and Acupuncture	64451515
Xiangshan Chinese Medicine Hospital	53061730

Addiction Counselling & Rehabilition

There are limited options when expats are faced with serious addictions. The best place to turn is the Community Centre Shanghai (476 Ming Yue Lu, 5030 3313; 568 Julu Lu, 6247 2880), which has regular support groups and services with professional therapists on staff. Alternatively you can turn to LifeLine Shanghai, which has a database of qualified counsellors around the Shanghai area. The latter will offer support over the phone, and refer you to relevant specialists who will help you face the addiction. For those battling alcohol addictions, Alcoholics Anonymous meets regularly, with both English and Chinese groups available. There is also an AA women's group, and Al Anon, a weekly support group for family members of Alcoholics Anonymous.

Addiction Counselling & Rehabilition	
Al-Anon	137 6109 0877
Alcoholics Anonymous	137 0171 5848
Dr Debi Yohn	138 1787 8973
Lesley Bainbridge	159 0095 4347
Lifeline Shanghai	6279 8990

Aromatherapy

This form of therapy enhances your moods and cleanses your system through the use of natural essential oils. Aromatherapy massage is available at many of the major spas, and prices can range from ¥100 to ¥500 depending on the place and type of treatment. Aroma Garden offers an 'aroma body therapy' that consists of three sessions, meant to gradually balance your hormones and rid your body of toxins. Aromatherapy is also said to be benificial for skin problems.

Aromatherapy		
Aroma Garden	Xuhui	6466 2064
Beauty Farm	Jing'an	6391 6789
City Legend Aromatherapy	Luwan	5385 8305
The Herb Store	Xuhui	5403 4458
Yi Mei Studio	Luwan	6305 1735
Yinlin Aromatherapy	Xuhui	6439 2967

Healing Meditation

Meditation can help release stress and overcome any physical or mental difficulties. Yoga centres encourage meditation circles and can connect you to other people interested in holistic methods of healing. Reiki, which heals the body through the opening of energy paths, is practised at the

Healing Meditation		
Ashtanga Yoga Shanghai	Luwan	139 1623 8614
Breeze Yoga	Hongqiao	6295 9068
Frank'n Sense	Various Locations	5465 7275
Hatha Yoga	Luwan	138 0197 7749
Incense Reiki Space	Various Locations	6276 5092
Karma Yoga	Pudong	3887 0669
Kundalini Yoga Asia	Jing'an	6267 6842
Y+ Yoga Centre	Xuhui	6433 4330
Yoga Moon Studio	Luwan	2252 4433

142

Incense Reiki Space. Frank'n Sense offers reiki sessions, as well as other forms of therapy such as sekhem (a healing art that focuses on the use of positive energy), crystal healing therapy and aromatherapy massage.

Rehabilitation & Physiotherapy

Physical therapy is still a relatively new field in China, and patients with minor to serious injuries are usually encouraged to stay in bed and not move for long periods of time. If you are in need of physiotherapy, there are only a few options. These clinics can develop a treatment plan with you to decrease pain and steadily restore your body's functions to normal, in addition to recommending ways for you to prevent future complications. One session can cost roughly ¥800, but prices change according to the individual situation.

Rehabilitation & Physiotherapy		
Chinafit Health Centre	Pudong	135 6482 8970
Shanghai Spinal and Sports Clinic	Jing'an	2281 1822
SinoUnited Health	Jing'an	6279 8920
World Link Specialty and Inpatient Centre	Luwan	6385 9889

Back Treatment

One of the largest and most reputable of the chiropractic clinics is Shanghai East International Medical Centre's ESI Spinal unit, which provides American chiropractors at affordable rates. Craniosacral therapy is also available through ESI Spinal. SinoUnited Health focuses on sports physiotherapy and back injuries, and has a team of orthopaedic specialists addressing conditions such as ruptured discs, sciatica, low back pain and scoliosis.

Back Treatment		
Alexander Technique Lessons	Hongqiao	136 8162 5540
Chiropractic-ESI Spinal Clinic	Pudong	5879 9999
Mandara Spa	Huangpu	5359 4969
Shanghai Chiropractic & Osteopathic Clinic	Jing'an	5213 0008
Shanghai Spinal & Sports Clinic (Chenxin Hospital)	Hongqiao	5213 0008
SinoUnited Health	Jing'an	6279 8920
World Link Specialty and Inpatient Centre	Luwan	6385 9889
Xiangshan Chinese Medicine Hospital	Luwan	5306 1730

A typical visit will take 15 minutes to an hour depending on the type of treatment your chiropractor is using. Initially you may find yourself meeting a chiropractor up to three times a week, and then decreasing the number of visits over time. International clinics will charge around ¥800 per session, but prices depend on your personal treatment.

A more relaxing option for back treatment is a shiatsu massage or herbal back treatment, which you can get at many of the spas around town (see Well-Being, p.289).

Nutritionists & Slimming

There do not tend to be a vast number of options when looking for nutritionists or dieticians in the city. Other than the nutritionist centres at Shanghai Xinhua Hospital and Gleneagles Shanghai, the best bet is an expensive membership at a luxury health club, which often employ professional nutritionists. Some hospitals have specialists for digestive disorders, and many of the upscale spas offer slimming treatments. These can range from massage therapies to the application of plant extracts to the body.

Nutritionists & Slimming	
Amanda Miller	135 8560 6477
Dragonfly	6327 1193
Evian Spa	6321 6622
Gleneagles Shanghai	6375 5588
Portman Ritz-Carlton Fitness Centre	6279 8888
Renji Hospital	5875 2345
Ruijin Hospital	6437 0045
Shanghai Hilton Health Club	6248 0000
Xinhua Hospital	6579 0000

143

Counselling & Therapy

Mental health facilities are still lacking in China, and most Chinese people with depression avoid proper treatment because of social stigmas attached to mental illness. While Shanghai has several local psychiatric centres, the doctors usually lack English-speaking skills, or don't have a proper grasp of expat issues. Shanghai's Mental Health Centre is one of the biggest and best in the city with a few English-speaking specialists. Psychiatrists tend to be hard to come by. If you're in need of a therapist, it's usually best to refer to the private western-focused clinics, which are familiar with western culture and problems that can arise from the expat experience. LifeLine, a hotline dedicated to supporting the expat community, constantly updates its database and can refer callers to therapy resources and suitable counsellors that specialise in specific areas. Besides calling a hotline, couples counselling is available through the Community Centre.

The lack of resources means organisations you might not expect are involved in counselling. Body & Soul, the traditional Chinese medicine clinic, has counselling services available for domestic abuse cases. Al Anon (see Addiction Counselling, p.142) is also a place where people can look to for help with eating disorders and self-mutilation. The international schools all have a psychologist or child therapist that can help you with any child behavioural problems. More serious issues should be addressed at an international clinic or hospital through inpatient care. Shanghai United Family Hospital is a supportive place to go to in these situations. Not being covered by insurance or not owning any insurance can be a hindrance in getting treatment, since therapy can be pricey due to a large demand and limited supply of professionals. Check your plan to see if you have coverage.

Counsellors & Psychologists	
Body & Soul TCM Clinic	5101 9262
Community Centre Shanghai	5030 3313
Dr Cecilie Kolflaath Larsen	136 3631 7474
Dr Debi Yohn	138 1787 8973
Lesley Bainbridge	159 0095 4347
LifeLine Shanghai	6279 8990
Ruoqing Mental Health Clinic	5238 6061
Shanghai United Family Hospitals	5133 1900
Shanghai's Mental Health Centre	3428 9888
Wales Psychological Clinic	6255 2588
World Link International	6445 5999

Support Groups

Living in Shanghai isn't all fun and games, and can mean facing cultural adjustments, language barriers and loneliness. Although resources are still limited, the past few years have seen a growth in services and support groups aimed at helping expats cope with culture shock, homesickness and depression. Shanghai residents are generally open people who are always willing to make new connections and new friends, and wherever your interests lie, you should be able to find a group that will make you feel at home. The Community Centre Shanghai also has a 'newcomer orientation programme' (see p.144) aimed at helping you get settled. Each programme is tailored to family, business, or individual needs, offering an insight on how to adapt to the cultural landscape and business world. Ongoing support is offered for six months.

Many groups are set up to help parents and families network, but illness support groups are rare. Group listings and descriptions are regularly printed in all the expat magazines, such as *City Weekend*, *SH*, *that's Shanghai*, and *Shanghai Talk* (see p.50).

Social Groups

Chinese society runs on *guanxi* (relationships), and it's no different for Shanghai expats. There are numerous groups that regularly meet and can help you settle into the city while you make new friends. Some revolve around a shared nationality or alma mater. Others can help you meet people with like interests, and some groups have no particular theme, but are just meant as social get-togethers for Shanghai residents. See Social Groups in Activities on p.271 for details.

Support Groups	
Alcoholics Anonymous	130 0329 8376
Bumps & Babes	6247 2880
Heart-to-Heart Parent Support Group	139 1731 9214
International Mothers Support Group	6856 4758
La Leche League	130 2210 7202
Lifeline Shanghai	6279 8990
Shanghai Community Centre	6247 2880

144

Education

Education

Home Work

Home schooling is not condoned by the Chinese government as it conflicts with the country's compulsory education system, and home-schooled children may have a hard time finding their way into Shanghai high schools or universities later as they lack official certifications from other schools. If you're set on this as an educational approach, however, you can find further information on Shanghai's homeschooling groups at www.shanghai homeschool.com.

A good education is highly prized in Chinese culture, but in recent years has been harder for local families to pay for due to rising costs and lowered government spending. A nine-year compulsory education system is in place for citizens (from age 6 to 15), and the local school curriculum keeps most Chinese parents bragging about their child's study habits. During the period of compulsory education, tuition is free for Chinese citizens, although parents still need to pay for some small fees such as books. In recent years a number of local schools have opened up to expat children, and some expats without education allowances are giving it a go. Not only can local schools be easier on the wallet by ¥8,000 per month, but they present an ideal opportunity for children to become immersed in the language and culture. Children aged six and older should have a good grasp on Mandarin before entering, as everything is conducted in Chinese. Local schools have class sizes ranging from 20 to 30 pupils. Registration procedures must be handled by parents in person at whichever authorised local school they choose. Necessary items to bring include your child's passport and a Chinese-issued health form. Also, the parent should bring his or her work and residence permits.

The Chinese school system concludes with the intense National University Entrance Examinations, which are recognised internationally. In general, foreigners stop attending Chinese schools some time in early primary stages due to China's teaching methodologies, which conflict with western techniques.

For expat families wanting a more international education, there is a diverse range of international schools offering International Baccalaureate programmes, the English National Curriculum and American-based curricula. Class sizes change according to age, with younger children getting more one-on-one attention. An average class can contain anywhere beteween 12 and 25 students.

With more and more expats arriving in Shanghai, the most popular schools are finding themselves increasingly in demand, and waiting lists are a constant presence in the admissions process. You should send in your child's application by early March, as most schools begin finalising their rosters at that time. Enrolment procedures differ according to the school, but most ask for your child's passport information, medical records, previous school records and sometimes a copy of their birth certificate.

If you have a child of pre-school age and you move to Shanghai in the middle of an academic year, you should have no problem enrolling them. Most pre-schools that have space are open to taking in a new student any time of the year. Primary and secondary schools usually require students to start at the beginning of a school year.

Shanghai has a good number of after-school activities to keep your kids busy too. Local after-school programmes called 'children's palaces' were established after the Cultural Revolution to help entertain offspring of working parents, and many are still running today. There are also various scout groups that have social get-togethers, which can be a valuable use of time (www.shanghaiscouts.org).

Shanghai school children

Nurseries & Pre-Schools

New pre-schools spring up every year as the number of expats increase, which means it can be a competitive system – but there are a variety of programmes on offer. Busy mums and dads tend to keep their child under the personal care of an *ayi* (a maid and/or babysitter) when they're young, but pre-school can be a good opportunity to nurture your child's social skills and ease them into the school system. Most pre-schools emphasise character building and playing, and are not that formal. Enrolling in pre-school can also get your child's foot in the door to the more competitive primary school programmes. Children are generally accepted from 2 to 6 years old, although there are exceptions. Shanghai's pre-schools and international schools will sometimes set up free playgroups for mothers and children to meet, but details often change, so check with schools for specifics. The most in-demand schools have waiting lists, and admission fees can be steep. Expats with education packages usually pay by term or year, but if fees are coming out of your pocket a monthly payment system can usually be worked out. Yearly fees can range from ¥23,000 to more than ¥100,000, and there may be additional costs such as application or food fees.

Most schools have full-day programmes, but some have set up half-day options as well. Smaller kindergartens such as Learning Habitat Bilingual Kindergarten (p.148) will accommodate parents and work out a schedule.

If qualifications matter to you, then you should always ask schools about their hiring criteria. When shopping around, arrange a playtime meeting to speak with teachers and allow your child to interact with some of the pre-school's students. Bilingual pre-schools are popular picks with parents, and many advertise themselves as such. Be aware though that some exaggerate, and only designate an hour each week to English classes with a native English teacher. When ready to apply, bring a copy of your child's passport, any previous school records, medical records and the child's birth certificate.

2151 Lianhua Lu
Minhang
莲花路2151号
闵行
🚇 **Hongqiao Lu**

Fortune Kindergarten 海富幼儿园　▶ p.147

5458 0508 | www.fkis.com.cn

Fortune aims to prepare students for the primary school system while incorporating fun activities such as storytelling and games to encourage communication skills. It prides itself in its dedication to a 50-50 bilingual progamme, in which half of the lessons are conducted in Chinese and half in English. The school also operates a Pudong campus at 1361 Dongfang Lu.

Various Locations

Gymboree 金宝贝

www.gymboree.com.cn

This US-founded franchise company offers classes for parents and their children, from birth to the age of 5. Programmes include fitness, play, arts and crafts, and musical exploration. Classes last around 45 minutes and are relatively unstructured, but involve a lot of music and singing. You'll have to pay for sessions in bulk, so ask for a free trial before starting. Sessions are held in Pudong, Gubei, Xuhui and Xintiandi.

75 Wuxing Lu
Xuhui
吴兴路75号
徐汇
🚇 **Hengshan Lu**

Julia Gabriel Centre for Learning
上海徐汇区民办嘉宝幼儿园

6437 3773 | www.juliagabriel.com

Originally from Singapore, and with venues in India, Indonesia and Malaysia, this new Shanghai branch of the Julia Gabriel Centre offers children up to the age of 6 structured learning programmes that encourage inspiration and leadership. Creative curricula, such as EduPlay and EduDrama, provide a comfortable environment for children as young as 18 months to express themselves. Julia Gabriel schools also pride themselves in their extensive reading rooms, which house hundreds of children's books.

海富幼儿园
Fortune Kindergarten

LIFELONG LEARNING BEGINS HERE

真正的国际化双语教育

ACCOMPLISHING BILINGUALISM THROUGH AN INTERNATIONALLY RECOGNIZED CURRICULUM

A Caring and Positive Learning Environment
An International, Open, Supportive Curriculum accredited by CITA
Experienced dedicated team of foreign and Chinese teachers
Enrolling Children from 2 to 6 years of age
Open Year Round

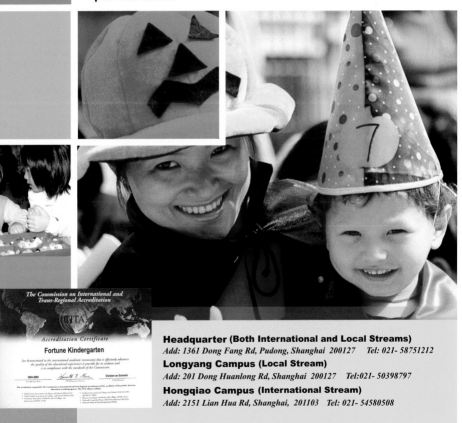

The Commission on International and Trans-Regional Accreditation

CITA

Accreditation Certificate

Fortune Kindergarten

has demonstrated to the international academic community that it efficiently advances the quality of the educational experience it provides for its students and is in compliance with the standards of this Commission.

2004-2005   Division on Schools

Headquarter (Both International and Local Streams)
Add: 1361 Dong Fang Rd, Pudong, Shanghai 200127   Tel: 021- 58751212
Longyang Campus (Local Stream)
Add: 201 Dong Huanlong Rd, Shanghai 200127   Tel:021- 50398797
Hongqiao Campus (International Stream)
Add: 2151 Lian Hua Rd, Shanghai, 201103   Tel: 021- 54580508

http://www.fkis.com.cn   Email:fortunek@online.sh.cn

Blue Sky Villa,
1980 Hongqiao Lu
Hongqiao
虹桥路1980号
蓝天别墅
虹桥

Learning Habitat Bilingual Kindergarten 学之园双语幼稚园
6262 7668 | www.learninghabitat.org.cn
Using large-scale group projects, field trips and art projects, this school aims to encourage analytical thinking, communication and creativity. Days are split into mornings, which are taught in English, and afternoons, which are taught in Chinese, so the structure is completely bilingual. Staff members keep continuous, open communication with parents and there are regular social evenings for parents and children to talk about the school.

21 Donghu Lu
Xuhui
东湖路21号
徐汇

Montessori School of Shanghai 上海私立蒙特梭利幼儿园
5988 6688 | www.montessorisos.com
Established in 2005, this school offers authentic Montessori programmes to children aged 18 months to 6 years. The school's directors all hold international certifications and, following the Montessori philosophy, students determine their own independent educational focuses and learning levels. Classes also encourage children of different ages to interact and work together in small groups. There is another campus in Qingpu at 1258 Zhuguang Lu.

Floor 2,
2-10 Meihua Lu
Pudong
梅花路2-10号
浦东

Play School Choo Choo 上海易趣爱幼儿园
5059 6248 | www.ichooi.com
This US-based programme encourages its 2 to 6 year old students to explore and make their own discoveries. Teachers enhance social skills and help build self confidence with personable student-to-teacher ratios (a maximum of eight children attend each 2-3 year old class). Friday is 'event day', where parents and children participate in activities oriented towards learning about different communities.

2381 Hongqiao Lu
Hongqiao
虹桥路2381号
虹桥

Rainbow Bridge International School 上海虹桥国际学校
6268 9773 | www.rbischina.org
Located within the Shanghai Zoo, Rainbow Bridge has created a unique curriculum emphasising interpersonal skills and cross-cultural understanding. The US-based programme encourages students from 18 months to 10 years to apply their maths, science and reading skills to their unique surroundings. There are also ample opportunities for learning about the environment through an annual Earth Day celebration and regular participation in Roots & Shoots, a scheme that encourages social service projects.

81, Lane 3297,
Hongmei Lu
Changning
虹梅路3297弄81号
长宁
🚇 *Hongqiao Lu*

Shanghai Victoria Kindergarten 上海维多利亚幼儿园
6405 6668 | www.victoria.sh.cn
Managed by the Hong Kong Victoria Educational Organisation, this kindergarten follows the International Baccalaureate Primary Years Programme and also offers a bilingual structure for children aged 2 to 6. The Primary Years Programme aims to develop each child's strong points and nurture a well-rounded intelligence. After-school and summer programmes are also available, and there are campuses in Xinzhuang, Xuhui and Pudong.

3908 Hongmei Lu
Hongqiao
虹梅路3908号
虹桥

Soong Ching Ling Kindergarten 宋庆龄幼儿园
6242 9851 | www.sclkids.com
With a focus on bilingual language development and reading, this kindergarten trains children from 2 to 6 to be self confident, inquisitive and well behaved. The school uses the heavily structured British Oxford Reading Tree and has a wealth of facilities, including a pool and music room. There is another campus in Qingpu.

Is getting lost your usual excuse?

Whether you're a map person or not, this pocket-sized marvel will help you get to know the city like the back of your hand – so you won't feel the back of someone else's.

Shanghai Mini Map
Fit the city in your pocket

138 Yingbin San Lu
Hongqiao
迎宾三路138号
虹桥

Stars and Stripes American Kindergarten
新世纪虹桥幼儿园
6268 3957 | *www.starsandstripes.com.cn*

All the teachers at Stars and Stripes are from the US and hold Early Childhood Education degrees. The teaching philosophy revolves around student-centred 'discovery learning' and utilises several methods to help each individual child gain self confidence in preparation for primary school. The school accepts children from the age of 2 and focuses much attention on American culture and language.

43 Fuxing Xi Lu
Xuhui
复兴西路43号
徐汇
🚇 *Changshu Lu*

Tiny Tots International Pre-School and Kindergarten
泰宁国际幼儿园
6431 3788 | *www.tinytotschina.com*

This English-led school emphasises close attention – average student to teacher ratio is less than 5:1 – to encourage self confidence through personal success. Children are able to choose their own activities in order to rouse creativity and passion. Tiny Tots offers daily student reports and a parent-child after-school group three times a week. There is also a sandbox, computer room and music room.

Primary & Secondary Schools

Shanghai's international primary and secondary school community boasts programmes with increasingly elaborate facilities and various academic offerings. Many of the most popular have waiting lists, although some only apply to specific grades. Admissions departments are constantly updating these, so check back often to see if a certain school has space. Formal admissions interviews are rare.

Most do not require an entrance exam, unless the student's maths or English skills seem shaky, in which case an assessment may be required. Otherwise, parents and students must fill out an application form, and provide previous school records, medical records, standardised test scores and sometimes a letter of recommendation. Shanghai's international schools have adopted the world's most popular curricula so students can easily make the transition to another country's school system. In recent years, the International Baccalaureate (IB) programme has been gaining popularity with secondary schools thanks to its global appeal and recognition by top universities. American-based curricula are also popular, with students churning out Advanced Placement (AP) exams and often choosing US universities upon graduation. The English National Curriculum, which includes GCSE and A Levels, is offered at the British International School. For government-sponsored curricula, the Ecole Francaise, Deutsche Schule, and Japanese School (6406 8027) have all been established by their respective countries for citizens to receive an authentic national education while abroad. A regular day at an international school runs from 08:00 to 15:00, or from 09:00 to 16:00, Monday to Friday. Schools mainly break for major Chinese holidays as well as Christmas and the western New Year. Most expats can usually only afford the pricey tuition fees of primary and secondary school if their employers pay for them, which often happens. Fees escalate by grade, with grade 12 (year 13) the most expensive. The least expensive schools ask for around ¥60,000 per year, while the priciest charge more than ¥180,000 plus extra fees.

**600 Cambridge
New Forest Town**
Pudong
康桥半岛600号
浦东

British International School 英国国际学校 ▶ p.151
5812 7455 | *www.bisshanghai.com*

The relatively new and flashy campuses in Puxi (111 Jinguang Lu, Huacao Town) and Pudong offer students aged 2 to 18 the standard English National Curriculum. Secondary students can opt for an IB diploma, GCSEs or A levels. Facilities include a dance studio, music technology suite and impressive sporting areas.

150

999 Mingyue Lu
Pudong
明月路999号
浦东

Concordia International School 上海协和国际学校
5899 0380 | www.ciss.com.cn
Offering classes from pre to high school, Concordia adheres to an American college preparatory curriculum and nurtures spiritual and Christian religious values. The Advanced Placement system aims to present high-school classes in a more challenging, university-like way. Facilities include a wireless laptop programme, through which students and staff can borrow computers with wireless capabilities for up to two hours at a time.

30, Lane 399,
Zhu Guang Lu
Qingpu
诸光路399弄30号
青浦

Deutsche Schule Shanghai 上海德国学校
3976 0555 | www.ds-shanghai.org.cn
Accredited by the German government, the Deutsce Schule offers a standard German national curriculum from kindergarten to high school. A third of the teachers, including the headmaster, are German government employees. High school instruction concludes with the Abitur, the final exams and degree given to German students.

222 Lan'an Lu
Pudong
蓝桉路222号
浦东

Dulwich College Shanghai 上海市德威英国国际学校
5899 9910 | www.dulwichcollege.cn
Dulwich is an International Baccalaureate World School establishment that follows the strict standards of the British National Curriculum, leading up to the International Baccalaureate diploma. There is also a programme for toddlers that has an emphasis on language acquisition. Facilities include several music rooms, a pool, gymnastics hall, basketball court and science labs.

30, Lane 399,
Zhu Guang Lu
Qingpu
诸光路399弄30号
青浦

Ecole Française Shanghai 上海法国学校
3976 0555 | ef.shanghai.online.fr
Established by the French government, this school provides citizens from France with the country's national curriculum. Students must be fluent in French and take part in the standard exams, such as the Baccalaureate, at the end of their high school experience. The majority of teachers and staff have been certified in France. The school shares a 'Eurocampus' with the Deustche Schule.

1600 Sanjiagang Lu
Pudong
三甲港路1600号
浦东

Shanghai American School 上海美国学校
6221 1445 | www.saschina.org
The American curriculum at this and the Puxi campus (258 Jinfeng Lu, Zhudi Town) is available for under 5s through to age 18. Along with providing impressive facilities, such as a 600 seat performing arts centre and large gym, the school also has a policy of limiting each class to 18 students and strives to balance class make-up across ethnic borders. The majority of teachers here are American.

800 Xiuyan Lu
Pudong
秀沿路800号
浦东

Shanghai Community International School
上海长宁国际学校
5812 9888 | www.scischina.org
Founded in 1990 by the International Schools Foundation, Shanghai Community provides an American college preparatory curriculum with Advanced Placement exams. The school is accredited with the Western Association of Schools and Colleges and has two campuses, the other in Puxi (1161 Hongqiao Lu). It has recently established an online records system so parents can easily follow their child's academic progress. Extracurricular activities include various sports leagues and a model UN.

We Know Where You'll Live

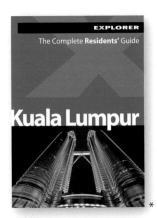

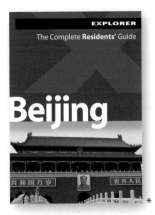

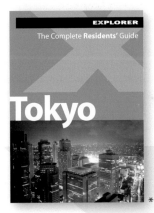

New Explorer Residents' Guides available Spring 2008

* Covers not final

580 Ganxi Lu
Changning
甘溪路580号
长宁

Shanghai Livingston American School 海李文斯顿美国学校
6238 3511 | www.laschina.org
Created to provide an American, and Californian in particular, education for US citizens living in Shanghai, the majority of the student population is surprisingly non-native English students attracted to the school's full-immersion English language techniques. With classes for under 5s through to age 18, Livingston prides itself on intimate class sizes, with one teacher for every 10 students.

189 Dongzha Lu,
Xinzhuang Town
Minhang
莘庄东闸路189号
闵行

Shanghai Rego International School 瑞金国际学校 ▶ p.155
5488 3431 | www.srisrego.com
This school teaches for GCSE and A-Levels through the UK National Curriculum, and has recently added a fully integrated Dutch curriculum programme. Academics are supplemented with daily Chinese instruction, and there are a range of after-school activities on offer including sports and drama.

1455 Huajing Lu
Xuhui
华泾路1455号
徐汇

Shanghai Singapore International School 新加坡国际学校
6496 5550 | www.ssis.cn
This school strives to maintain Singaporean academic standards and testing. The kindergarten and primary school follow the Singaporean curriculum, while secondary students follow the International Baccalaureate programme. Core classes are taught in English and the arts in Mandarin. Those with less proficient English skills attend bilingual core classes. There's also a campus at 301 Zhujian Lu in Minhang.

999 Hongquan Lu
Minhang
虹泉路999号
闵行

Shanghai United International School 协和双语学校
3431 0090 | www.suis.com.cn
A co-ed international day and boarding school with a curriculum that follows the International Baccalaureate programme. The ethnically broad student body interacts closely with teachers through a technologically advanced interface. Facilities include a heated indoor swimming pool, a lecture hall, and indoor and outdoor sports areas.

169 Qing-Tong Lu
Pudong
青桐路169号
浦东

SMIC Private School 上海市民办中芯学校
5855 4588 | www.smic-school.cn
What began as a school for children of Semiconductor Manufacturing International Corporation's (SMIC) employees has expanded into a popular, economical private school for expat and local families. Classes serve children from kindergarten all the way through to grade 12/year 13, with students choosing between English learning (based on the US curriculum) and Chinese learning (based on Shanghai's local curriculum).

555 Lianmin Lu,
Xujing Town
Qingpu
徐泾镇，
联名路555号
青浦

Western International School of Shanghai ▶ p.58
上海西华国际学校
6976 6388 | www.wiss.cn
Opened in 2006, this school is in the trial phases of all three International Baccalaureate programmes (primary, middle and diploma). With nine levels in operation, starting from pre-school (age 3), Western International will open a new grade each year until it reaches grade 13. Facilities include large recreation areas and computers in every classroom.

Regency Park,
1817 Huamu Lu
Pudong
花木路1817号
浦东
🚇 *Century Park*

Yew Chung International School 上海耀中国际学校
5033 1900 | www.ycef.com
This bilingual school strives to create graduates who are prepared to enter an increasingly globalised world. Yew Chung uses a modified UK National Curriculum that focuses on teaching children Mandarin. There are more than 1,800 students across five campuses (in Gubei, Hongqiao and three in Pudong), with varying grades on each campus.

To strive, to seek, to find
And not to yield

-- Tennyson

SRIS is proud to offer
an Integrated Dutch
Curriculum for Native Dutch Speakers

- Fully licensed UK National Curriculum School
- Catering for 3-18 years olds
- All British teaching staff
- Daily Mandarin Chinese lessons

For more information, please contact Ruth at Tel: 5488 3431 / 5498 5072 or email: info@srisrego.com
Shanghai Rego International School,189 Dongzha Road, 201100 Minhang
www.srisrego.com

Shanghai Rego International School

University & Higher Education

Shanghai is the home of a number of China's most famous universities, including Fudan, a humanities-oriented institution, and Jiaotong, which specialises in engineering. For locals, the university admissions process is extremely stressful and based solely on nationwide examinations held in July. Luckily, foreigners are exempt from these tests, although they have to pay higher fees to attend. Instead, expats with foreign passports can enrol in certain Chinese universities' undergraduate or graduate programmes by filling out a simple application form and sending in their school records, passport photos, physical examination record and proof of their language proficiency. Some schools will ask you to designate a sponsor in China, but most often this is optional, and student visas are fairly easy to obtain through the reputable university channels. Chinese students currently pay an average of ¥5,000 per semester, while foreigners can expect to pay around ¥10,000. The majority of expat students, when they finish secondary school, choose to study in the US or Europe, but more and more are choosing to study at a Chinese university for at least a year before transferring.

Further Education

With Shanghai's reputation as China's economic boomtown, it's no surprise that Master of Business Administration (MBA) and Executive Master of Business Administration (EMBA) courses have been popping up everywhere. University of Maryland, Washington University, Rutgers Business School and USC Marshall have all established high-ranking Shanghai EMBA programmes aimed at senior management with a global focus. A growing number of international universities have teamed up with local universities to create effective MBA programmes that can be completed within 18 months to two years. For people interested in more creative studies, the Institute of Fashion (IFA Paris) has recently opened a branch in Shanghai with French-trained instructors. Jiaotong University's International Continuing Education classes can give you the opportunity to dabble in subjects including painting and graphic design.

Higher Education

699 Hongfeng Lu
Pudong
红枫路699号
浦东
🚇 *Century Park*

China Europe International Business School
中欧国际工商学院
***2890 5890** | www.ceibs.edu*
This school has run top-ranking MBA and EMBA programmes since 1994. Jiaotong University is one of its joint-venture partners and it is financially supported by the Municipal Government of Shanghai and the European Union. Both English and Chinese classes are available, and there is an emphasis on international business.

220 Handan Lu
Yangpu
邯郸路220号
杨浦

Fudan University 复旦大学
***6511 7628** | www.fudan.edu.cn*
One of the most reputable universities in China, this school is located 30 minutes to the north of Shanghai on a grassy, sprawling campus. You'll find some of the best university living conditions here, especially for foreign students. Tuition costs approximately ¥19,000 a year for expats.

Floor 1,
435 Xincun Lu
Putuo
新村路435号
普陀

IFA Paris Shanghai 中法埃菲时装设计师学院
***3605 0654** | www.ifa.cn*
A French-based fashion design institute, this establishment connects its students with influential designers through internships and trainings. Classes are taught in English, and students receive the same degree as graduates of the Académie Internationale de Coupe de Paris. Tuition is €7,500 (around ¥78,000) per year.

580 Nanjing Xi Lu
Jing'an
南京西路580号
静安
 Jing'an Temple

Rutgers Business School 美国新泽西州立大学商学院

6217 6067 | *www.rutgers.cn*

A branch of the high-ranking US business school, this curriculum combines business management and accounting knowledge with discussions on policies and industry strategies. There is a part-time course that allows hard-working executivess to keep a full-time job and study on the side.

550 Dalian Xi Lu
Hongkou
大连西路550号
虹口
Hongkou Stadium

Shanghai International Studies University 上海外国语大学

6536 0599 | *www.shisu.edu.cn*

One of the country's top universities that specialises in foreign languages, Shanghai International Studies University offers a wide variety of study programmes for foreigners, provided they meet the language and admission requirements. Concentrations include Chinese language, international business, law and broadcast journalism. Undergraduate study for one year costs ¥18,000.

1954 Hua Shan Lu
Xuhui
华山路1954号
徐汇
Xujiahui

Shanghai Jiaotong University 上海交通大学

6282 1079 | *www.sie.sjtu.edu.cn*

One of the oldest and most prominent universities in China, this school is run jointly by both the Shanghai government and ministry of education. Though Jiaotong specialises in the sciences and engineering, it does have degrees in law and social studies. Tuition for the undergraduate programme will cost around ¥24,800 a year.

Room 710,
670 Guoshun Lu
Yangpu
国顺路670号
杨浦

Washington University/Fudan University 华盛顿大学/复旦大学

5566 4788 | *www.olin.wustl.edu/execed/shanghai.cfm*

The *Financial Times* named this one of the top 10 EMBA degree courses worldwide, and the number one programme in China. Curriculum strengths include helping students develop their strategic, leadership and organisational skills when coaching foreign and local managers. The course concludes with a two-week residency on the Washington University campus in the US.

Special Needs Education

Social awareness about mental disabilities has been increasing in China, but there is still little access to information and few support systems for special needs children throughout the country. No Shanghai school has been able to establish a fully integrated special needs programme with the right professionally trained staff yet. Some establishments, such as the British International School (p.150) and Tiny Tots kindergarten (p.150) will accept special needs students, depending on how severe the child's requirements are. Other schools will make concessions to students who have relatively minor needs, including learning disabilities such as dyslexia. Serious special needs cases almost always get turned away.

600 Tian Shan Lu
Changning
天山路600号
长宁

Special Education Consulting Services 上海特殊教育咨询服务

5206 6273 | *www.specialedchina.com*

Special Education Consulting Services provides qualified staff to help all families with special needs. Besides providing children with one-on-one specialised care and establishing tutorial programmes for professionals, parents and schools, the company also offers daily group sessions for students that are tailored to their needs. International schools are slowly making progress in this area, and most schools are working in conjunction with Special Education Consulting to admit more special needs students each year.

157

Transportation

Other options **Getting Around** p.42

Whether you're on an expat package or a student scrimping for change, transportation in Shanghai can be as affordable or convenient as you want it to be. Most people living close to the city centre take advantage of cheap, ubiquitous taxis, the efficient Metro system, or the bus network. Bicycles and scooters are also a

Shanghai traffic

popular way to get around and explore the streets. For people in the suburbs, where everything is more spread out, a car and driver is by far the most practical mode of transportation. Driving yourself around town as a newly arrived expat is not recommended. While the number of vehicles on the road is rising every year, the streets around the city remain narrow, and when shared with taxis, buses, cyclists and cart pullers, can be difficult to manoeuvre around. Roadworks are frequent and can aggravate an already disorderly system. Additionally, the layout of the city can be confusing, with roads weaving in unforeseen directions or turning into one-way streets. Parking garages are increasing in number with the rise of each commercial building, but a space can still be hard to find and street parking is often non-existent. Drivers are handy when trying to solve this dilemma since they can stay with your car all day and meet you when and where you need them to.

Go With The Flow ◀

The Shanghai traffic radio station AM648 provides up-to-date reports in Chinese. If you're driving on the inner ring roads, keep a look out for the display board posting information on driving conditions. Green means the traffic flow is smooth, while red indicates congestion. It also provides a time estimate for reaching the Bund.

Driving in Shanghai

China's car market is rapidly expanding and cars have become major status symbols. For customers, this growth means a wide selection and increasingly competitive prices. Even so, most expats opt to lease a car with a driver due to the expenses and long bureaucratic process involved in buying.

A driver can be hired to work for one day only, or work on a daily basis and be paid monthly for their services. Employing a full-time driver is affordable, and will cost somewhere around ¥2,500 per month (plus overtime), whereas a day trip around the city with a driver will cost more. A personal driver can charge around ¥600-¥700 for eight hours in the city. This cost increases if the driver goes beyond the city borders. Driving is on the right side of the road with automatic left-hand drive cars. Road signs are in Chinese characters, plus a mix of English and Pinyin.

Driving Habits

Drivers are aggressive, frequently honk their horns, swerve around the lanes and rarely signal. Although local driving techniques may make you wince, it's rare to see a serious car accident with injuries.

Traffic patterns can switch rapidly from a frantic pace with cars zigzagging between lanes to a stop-and-go situation. The traffic can get especially frustrating during rush hours, which are 07:30-09:30 and 17:00-19:00. To curb congestion on the highway, the local government has made it illegal for cars with licence plates from outside Shanghai to use the elevated highway during peak times. It's also illegal to honk your horn – although that doesn't seem to deter most drivers.

Non-Drivers

Traffic police are located on various street corners to stop jaywalkers and cyclists from crossing at the wrong time. Still, pedestrians do not commonly heed traffic signs, and cyclists often follow their own rules. The Shanghai Police Department estimates that around 400 pedestrians and cyclists are killed each year from traffic accidents, 90% of which occur because of jaywalking or cycling violations. Shanghai laws state that the driver is always responsible for an accident involving a pedestrian, so drivers should be especially wary of people strolling across the street. Large intersections have overhead bridges for pedestrians to safely cross.

Crash Course

Lane divisions, traffic lights and general road regulations are often taken as suggestions rather than rules by Shanghai drivers. Don't let constant honking or erratic car weaving upset you. Instead, drive defensively and be prepared for sudden stops.

Parking

Prime real estate and central commercial buildings are likely to have underground garages, but free parking is very limited (with the exception of some malls and hotels). Most of the time, parking won't be that expensive and can cost around ¥10 per hour or less. Offices often supply employees with parking passes. Monthly parking in the pricier garages can reach up to ¥2,000, while other buildings will only cost a few hundred yuan.

Garages attached to office buildings generally close at the same time as the offices, so you might need special access for after-hours. Parking areas associated with retail shops will close later according to shop hours, and valet parking is sometimes available.

Petrol Stations

Compared with most other countries, the government-subsidised and regulated petrol in China is relatively cheap. SinoPetrol and Sinopec are the two main stations around Shanghai, and have a general monopoly on energy services in China. Attendants will always fill the vehicle for you, and the stations often have subcontractors who will offer car wash services or simple maintenance checks. All types of petrol are unleaded. Prices vary but expect to pay less than ¥5 per litre. Petrol stations are harder to find closer to the city centre, but are plentiful in the suburbs. If in dire need of a refill, ask a taxi driver or chauffeur to point you in the right direction.

Driving Licence

If you hold a residence permit and own a driving licence from another country, you will be able to get a Chinese licence (a mandatory step to enable foreiners to drive in Shanghai). For step-by-step instructions on how to do so, see p.66.

Traffic Rules & Regulations

Speed limits are between 40 and 60kph within the city, while the highway and inner rings allow speeds of up to 80kph. Speed signs are identifiable by their black digits within red circles. Drivers are most often fined for traffic irregularities, such as running a red light. Main intersections have speed cameras recording your every move, and any illegal activity will be fined and sent to the address that the car is registered under. If you don't pay on time, you will have to pay at your annual car inspection (see p.163). Luckily, there are no late fees. If the cameras don't get you, traffic cops with radars could be waiting at intersections and will fine you immediately. Although there are formal traffic laws that give the illusion of lane protocol, the attitude on the streets is that of 'anything goes'. Overtaking on the right is a common phenomenon although technically prohibited, and drivers never hesitate to make right-hand turns on red lights even if pedestrians are trying to cross.

Vehicle Leasing

Leasing a vehicle to drive yourself around requires a Chinese licence (see p.66). In terms of leasing companies, Avis has obvious international appeal, and is a good bet if you want reliable service. Otherwise, old-hand taxi services such as Dazhong offer monthly renting deals with drivers that companies and individuals can take advantage of. If you pay to lease a Dazhong car, the vehicle is the company's full responsibility, so you won't have to worry about anything except where you're going and when. If you're leasing, all additional costs such as maintenance and recovery should be covered, and many companies offer 24 hour emergency services.

Vehicle Leasing Agents		
ASD Shanghai	6428 0535	www.carrenting.cn
AsiaLimo	5358 0168	www.asialimo.com
Avis	6229 1119	www.avischina.com
Bashi Rental Company	6835 5556	na
Dazhong Car Rental	6318 5666	dzzc.96822.com
eHail Limo	6468 0365	www.ehail.cn
Haisun Car Rentals	135 8552 1272	www.shzuche008.obm.cn
Hertz (Hershi)	6252 2200	www.hertz.net.cn
Jin Jiang Car Rental	6275 8800	www.jjauto.com
Longhui Car Rental	130 0322 2327	www.longhuicar.com
Qiangsheng Car Rental	6258 3799	www.qszlc.com
Rising Shanghai Car Rental	5447 8361	www.risingsh.com
Yongda Auto Group	96818	www.yongdaauto.com

Take your time to figure out which leasing situation is best for you. Most leased cars come with drivers, but if you're driving yourself you might want to look into companies that offer emergency towing services and in-depth insurance options.

Company Cars

Expats are often given a leased company car and driver upon arrival, or a cash allowance to pay for a leased car or general transportation fees. Companies enjoy the freedom of having a leased car rather than a bought one because it means less work for them. If you're interested in buying a car instead of leasing one, ask your employer if they're willing to switch you to a cash allowance system.

Buying a Vehicle

In order to purchase a car, you must have a residence permit (see p.65) and brave the same bureaucratic system that locals go through. Most foreigners buy their cars through their company. The upside of the Chinese car market is that you can find a wide range of brands from Mercedes-Benz and Bentley to Toyota and Jeep. International brands are more expensive because of the duties involved, and you should expect a 40%-50% premium rate in most cases. With the current car boom, competition means better prices for consumers, and you can find small cars (under 800CC) such as local brand Chery Automotives' QQ for as low as ¥50,000, while a Honda Civic should cost about ¥160,000. Around the city you'll mostly see GMs and Volkswagens, since they both have manufacturing plants in China and are economical. Each brand has its own showroom and dealerships representing them, so picking the type of car you want is usually the first step in deciding where to shop. Otherwise dealerships are all relatively standardised, and you should choose the one that is most convenient to you location-wise. When entering a dealership, it's best to have

New Car Dealers		
Shanghai Auto Industry Group	2201 1888	www.saicmotor.com
Shanghai Changjiang Chuansha Auto Sales	5859 3722	na
Shanghai General Motors	6875 8833	www.gmchina.com
Shanghai Heping Automobiles Sales	6893 0000	www.hepingauto.com
Shanghai Volkswagen	800 820 1111	www.csvw.com
Yongda Auto Group	96818	www.yongdaauto.com

Driving tensions

studied what you want beforehand, as salesmen aren't overly knowledgeable. Don't sweat too much over bargaining, as prices are pretty uniform if you're using a legitimate dealer, and negotiations only occur over small things such as accessories.

Other car-purchasing options include a growing number of second-hand dealerships with cars that are rarely good value. The used car system is new, and the cost of depreciation and terms of agreement are not that clear cut. Many of the second-hand car dealerships sell specific makes. Precautions should be taken when dealing with second-hand car dealerships. Bring an expert to check everything out before you buy and always test drive. Used cars do not come with the same guarantees as new cars, so you will have to read the contract carefully and you might have to negotiate for a refund or repair clause in case the car has a problem after you purchase it.

In order to formally transfer car ownership and (most importantly) the car's licence plate, you will need to go through the Motor Vehicle Administrative Office. The office can then give you another licence plate number, so you can avoid the painful bidding process (see Registration, p.162). If you are selling a car back to a dealership, then you will need to hand over the car and licence all at once, and forgo the rights to an automatic licence plate from the Motor Vehicle Office.

Private Sales or Importers

Buying cars from non-authorised dealers in China is often known as buying from the 'grey market'. If you choose this option be aware that the warranties offered are not honoured by the actual car companies. If you still decide to buy through a private importer, be sure to look over the car and make sure everything is in order. If you want a car but don't want to go through a dealership, you can ask within your company and see if any fellow employees are leaving the country and want to sell their car. The company will be able to help you with the paperwork, and the transfer of ownership will be relatively simple because the car and both employees are under the umbrella of the same company. Otherwise, a private sale with another individual is a complex process and it's better to find an agent or dealer who will do the work for you.

Importing a Vehicle

Importing a car can cost you half or more of the car's worth in tariffs and taxes, depending on who is processing your documents and what the ever-changing regulations involve. Unless you're a diplomat, car-related importation laws are strict and complicated. Check with the Shanghai Traffic Police Authority in Minhang (179 Qinchun Lu; 6498 7070) and the Shanghai Entry-Exit Inspection and Quarantine Bureau for an assessment of your situation (bring a Shanghainese-speaking friend).

Used Car Dealers

Manheim China	Pudong	6866 9922	www.manheimchina.com
Secondhand Car Market	Jiading	6950 2364	www.52921234.com/ershouche
Shanghai Old Car Market	Putuo	6257 1111	www.jcsc.com.cn
Xin Zhuang Old Car Market	Minhang	6492 9599	www.sh-2sc.com
Yongda Feng Chi Auto	Pudong	6893 8020	www.yongdaauto.com
Yongda Old Car Market	Pudong	5897 2468	na

161

Vehicle Finance

Buying your car in Shanghai often means setting up a finance plan with a bank. You will need to show a residence permit and prove that you have a stable income. You will also probably find yourself paying in cash, since China is still very much a cash-based society. Recently some dealers are able to offer customers finance options, but only because manufacturers are establishing finance programmes that work directly with their dealerships. GM's joint venture with the Shanghai Automotive Industry Corp has created GMAC-SAIC Automotive Finance, which provides retail finance for buying GM cars.

Vehicle Finance		
Agricultural Bank of China	95599	www.abchina.com
Bank of China	95566	www.bank-of-china.com
China Construction Bank	95533	www.ccb.com
Industrial & Construction Bank of China	95588	www.icbc.com.cn
Shanghai Pudong Development Bank	6329 6188	www.spdb.com.cn

All the big banks offer finance schemes, so you can shop around for rates, which vary depending on the car, your financial situation and each bank's policies. Shanghai Pudong Development Bank's finance plan requires clients to pledge one of three guarantees, including a warranty or mortgage. Make sure you have a clear understanding of what's involved to prevent having to deal with any surprise payments.

Vehicle Insurance

In order to legally own your own vehicle you'll need insurance, which is calculated based on the value of your car. Full coverage for a car costing ¥245,000 would come out to about ¥3,800 per year, while a ¥100,000 car's insurance policy costs roughly ¥2,000. Of course, rates of insurance also vary according to the company's policies, the level of insurance coverage and your driving history.

Vehicle Insurance		
AIU Insurance	2893 8000	www.aiush.com.cn
China Pacific Insurance	5877 6688	www.cpic.com.cn
The People's Insurance Company of China	95518	na
Ping An Insurance Company	6321 6698	www.paic.com.cn
Tian Ping Insurance Company	6355 5599	www.tpaic.com

Policies must include third-party liability insurance. Leasing agencies in the city will usually cover this type of insurance for you, but if you want something more substantial you'll have to go elsewhere for your policy. In Shanghai, where anything could happen on the road or in the street, it is recommended that you look into a comprehensive coverage plan. AIU provides a 24 hour hotline for clients so that a claim handler can come and assess damage to your vehicle at anytime.

Registering a Vehicle

The registration process occurs once in a car's lifetime, and can cost almost half as much as the car itself. In order to control pollution and the number of cars on the road, Shanghai auctions a limited number of licence plates to the public. Registering your car involves signing up for this auction, and then engaging in a bidding war with everyone else in Shanghai who wants to buy a car. You can opt out of the auction by having the car dealership handle the entire registration process for a fee. If you want to participate, you will need two forms of ID and will have to pay a ¥2,000 deposit.

The auction occurs once a month in the town of Anting (at the Secondhand Car Market at 1000 Moyu Nan Lu, one hour west of Shanghai's city centre).

Bids can be placed over the phone (9696 8222) or online (toubiao.alltobid.com), but most prefer to see the competition and enter their bids in person. The price of a plate fluctuates according to the market demand. Expect to pay at least ¥30,000. If your bid doesn't win, then you'll have to repeat the process.

Some people try to get around the system by buying incredibly cheap licence plates in bordering Zhejiang or Jiangsu provinces for a few hundred yuan, but the government is making this practice harder with increased restrictions on cars with foreign plates.

All cars must obtain official car registration within one week of purchase. While you're waiting on the real licence plate, your dealer will supply you with a temporary one that is good for one week. The temporary licence plate prohibits you from using the elevated roads, and you should drive as little as possible until you get the actual plate (any fines you incur during this week will be higher than normal).

You must also go to your local Motor Vehicle Administrative Office for a yearly car inspection, and pay the road maintenance tax, which will cost around ¥250 per month (¥3,000 per year). If you're short on time, or don't want to do it yourself, it's fine for expats to send their driver to complete these inspections on their behalf.

Rein-car-nation

If an old car dies on you, you might still find a buyer from a second-hand dealership or auction marketplace. You probably won't get a good price, but if it's too old it won't pass the annual inspection and the government will scrap it for you. The amount of licence plates available for auction is determined by a formula involving the number of scrapped cars to monthly car sales in the city, which means your car's death might mean another car's birth.

Traffic Fines & Offences

Despite the chaos on its streets, Shanghai has an indepth system for penalising drivers and assigning fines, although these regulations change on a regular basis. Most often drivers who offend will find themselves faced with a small fine, but make the wrong move and you could have your licence revoked or, in the worst case-scenario, find yourself jailed.

The majority of fines are for speeding violations, and traffic irregularities such as ignoring a 'no U-turn' sign. Speeding can cost ¥200 or more, while not wearing a seat belt incurs a relatively small fee of around ¥5. Other minor offences include running a red light, ignoring street signs and crossing the white traffic line at a stop light. Illegal parking can cost ¥200 or more. If it is towed in the process, getting your car back will cost you around ¥300 and several hours of waiting. Driving without a licence can result in an instant visit to the police department. Likewise, drunk driving is one of the more serious offences and can lead to an immediate suspension of your licence at the least.

Cameras are located at many main intersections around the city, and can catch you running red lights, speeding or neglecting traffic lines. You can pay your fees at the local traffic police station that is specified by the ticket.

Seatbelt and safety laws are constantly developing and changing. Currently the law only requires that the driver fasten up; all cars are fitted with seat belts, but you'll find the backseats of many taxis will have their seatbelts covered or in disrepair.

Breakdowns

In the event of a breakdown, stay relaxed. If you're in a high-traffic area, try to move your car out of the way. Depending on how dire the situation is, call the police (110), a friend to pick you up, or a mechanic. You can always collect your car at a later time as long as it's not blocking traffic.

Emergency phones are placed on the highway every couple of kilometres or so. Whenever you're travelling, whether it's around the

Recovery Services & Towing (24 hour)	
Jiehong Auto Towing	6592 9066
Lingdun Towing Service	5833 5655
Shanghai Rescue Auto Service	5911 9119
Xingan Auto Repair Shop	6488 1136

city or to a remote location, it's a good idea to always have your charged mobile phone with you and a dependable map. Car leasing companies usually offer 24 hour recovery services, but if you're far from the city, there is no established towing or recovery service for you to call, so you will have to rely on your phone, your wits and the kindness of local strangers.

Drink Driving ◀

There is a virtual zero-tolerance policy in Shanghai on drink-driving, and drivers caught driving under the influence will get pulled over and may have their license confiscated. In the event of a bad accident where alcohol is a factor, the driver will probably be arrested for drunk driving.

Traffic Accidents

Other options **Car** p.44

In 2006, more than 9,000 car accidents were reported in Shanghai. Surprisingly, serious traffic accidents around the city are not as common as you might expect, although close calls seem to occur every second.

In the case of an accident, you should call the police at 110, and state your location; a traffic officer should arrive within 10 minutes. If one party takes responsibility, then you should both clear the road as soon as possible. If it's a small bump people tend to settle matters on the spot to avoid the hassle of paperwork. After some haggling, a few scratches can be settled for around ¥300. If it's a bigger dispute, then it's best to call the police, especially if there is potential for future insurance claims. Make sure you mark the positioning of the cars and, if you have a camera, use it to snap some photos of the scene before you move your car out of the way of traffic. It's not uncommon for people to feign injuries, so be prepared to argue.

If you are involved in a serious traffic accident, remain calm. Dial the police at 110, and if someone is injured, make sure you call an ambulance at 120. Keep the accident scene as preserved as possible. Any witnesses should also remain at the scene so they can recount the accident to police. Always keep the car's registration information, any certifications, and insurance in the vehicle.

By law, the driver is always held accountable in an accident involving a pedestrian, even if the pedestrian was in the wrong, and in the cases where it is clearly the driver's fault, the penalties will be much higher. Most penalties in an accident scenario are monetary and even a severe accident scenario does not mean jail time.

Just like friendly Shanghainese chatter often sounds like a screaming match, angry outbursts are a part of the local driving demeanour and shouldn't be taken too seriously. Don't give in to road rage, and take the yelling and honking with a pinch of salt.

A driver's level of traffic offences are monitored through a points system. Every driver has 12 points, and every traffic offence results in a loss of points as well as a fine. Points are renewed at the end of each year, but losing all 12 points within a year will result in a suspension of your licence.

Vehicle Repairs

Dealerships can help you with the paperwork and can refer you to approved repair workshops that will conduct a reliable, warranty-friendly check-up. If you're using a private mechanic then you should bring all of the car's information with you, including any documents regarding its history, such as police reports and warranty. The mechanic should refer to these documents in order to stay within the manufacturer's guidelines.

Make sure that you always comply with your insurance company's requirements if you need repairs for damage caused through a traffic accident. This might include gathering the formal traffic report, the police statement or the full accident statement. If you happen to be leasing a car when an accident occurs, then the damage and repairs fall under the responsibility of the leasing company. Warranties differ, so check over their policies so you know when the company should pay for damages or defects and when you're responsible. If you decide to install after-market parts, go to your dealer first to make sure the add-ons won't void the warranty or devalue the car.

Vehicle Repairs		
Dongchang Auto Services	Various Locations	96800
Shanghai Auto Repair	Xuhui	6404 9385
Shanghai Benz Co	Changning	5870 5171
Shanghai Jinjiang Auto Repair	Minhang	6438 4259
Volkswagen	Jing'an	6230 1808
	Xuhui	6487 8457

上海海洋水族馆
SHANGHAI OCEAN AQUARIUM

An Ocean in the City

Shanghai Ocean Aquarium

f inding an "ocean" within Shanghai's concrete jungle? Sounds impossible but you better believe it as it is located right in the midst of the city's bustling financial district of Lujiazui and right beside the Oriental Pearl Tower – Shanghai Ocean Aquarium (SOA).

Divided into 9 different zones, the theme of SOA is to bring visitors "Across Continents – Through the World of Water with a wide display of unique aquatic species from the five continents and four oceans. SOA is currently the only aquarium in the world to have a separate exhibition zone that displays aquatic animals from China, particularly rare and precious species from the famous Yangtze River. Main highlights from the China Zone includes the Chinese sturgeon, Yangtze alligator, Giant Salamander, etc. If you are brave enough you can even have the opportu-nity to come into close contact with sharks in an "I Love Sharks" exhibition held in the aquarium's marine classroom.

With two feeding performances scheduled everyday visitors will be able to catch the fishes and aquatic animals "live in action". You should also try one of SOA's most popular tour – "Underwater Night Camping", which allows visitors to spend the night sleeping beneath one of the world's longest underwater viewing tunnels. A truly unforgettable night under the sea!

The aquarium is easily accessible, just take Metro Line 2 and get off at Lujiazui station, you will find Shanghai Ocean Aquarium right in sight. Visit SOA soon and experience for yourself the beauty of an "Ocean in the City".

No.1388 Lujiazui Ring Road Pudong New Area
Shanghai(Beside Oriental Pearl Tower)
86-21-58779988   www.sh-aquarium.com

Exploring

Decoding the Bund
Although businesses on the Bund often give their addresses as a building number – Three on the Bund, for instance – the actual street name is Zhongshan Dong Yi Lu, or Zhongshan East No.1 Road. The locals refer to the Bund as waitan, *which translates roughly as 'outer bank'.*

Exploring

Once famed as the Paris of the East, the Orient's 'whore' as well as its 'pearl', Shanghai has reclaimed its hold on the world's imagination. Almost everything you've heard about it is true, in some sense or some circumstances. It is a frontier and a fantasyland; meticulously planned and unnervingly chaotic; a sophisticated banquet and an appalling stew.

More cosmopolitan than any other mainland city, Shanghai serves as the regional headquarters for at least 150 multinational companies. It is also a tourist destination for both Chinese and outlanders. Listen to the shoppers on Huaihai Lu and you're likely to overhear a mix of Shanghainese, Mandarin, Cantonese and other dialects. Of course, you also might catch a few sentences of German, Italian, Swedish or Hungarian. Shanghai's status as a capital of international finance and object of global fascination creates an atmosphere that you can see and taste, even on the smoggiest days. On a stroll beneath the plane trees in the former French Concession you could come across the white dome of a Russian Orthodox church. Built in 1933, after an initial stint as a place of worship, the stained glass windows subsequently shed light on a washing machine factory, a community cultural office and at least two different eateries.

Besides the dizzying array of restaurants and cuisines, there is an intriguing convergence of the forged and the fashionable, the bold and the bulldozed. Bootstrap entrepreneurs hawk dubious Rolex watches a few steps from a genuine Hermes boutique. The city's most vibrant gallery district, 50 Moganshan Lu, is housed in a warren of renovated warehouses surrounded by a neighbourhood of drab apartment blocks.

The city's colonial past and expansive present have combined to forge the sort of optimism that inspires big dreams and big risks. Look down an alley and you might spot a freelance photographer reclaiming Qing Dynasty bricks, hoping to build his own penthouse someday. Look to the skyline and you'll glimpse a surreal jumble of the retro and the futuristic. More landmarks are scheduled, including, in 2008, Pudong's 101 storey World Financial Centre, with the planet's highest hotel and tallest observation deck, among other superlatives.

As the first developing nation to host the World Expo (in 2010) China is determined to make a showcase of its most populous city. But with an estimated population of 20 million and growing, Shanghai is more than just a city. The planning bureau's '1-9-6-6' document describes the future of the metropolis in terms of these numbers: one primary city, nine new nearby cities, 60 small towns, and 600 villages. And if the current frenzy of building is a reliable indicator, this plan will easily be met.

By 2020, a series of expressways should link any two points in the municipality in under an hour, while 17 Metro lines, six light rails and a Maglev extension will improve public transport.

District Guide
We've included a Shanghai district by each entry in this section to help you locate the galleries, parks and museums. The map on p.416 shows which area of town each one covers.

All of which is good news for Shanghai residents. Not quite halfway through 'the plan', it is already possible to lunch on traditional recipes in a 1,000-year-old water town, sip cocktails on the deck of a Moroccan-themed bar in People's Park, take in the opening of an international art exhibition, and dine at the Bund outpost of an acclaimed New York chef. All on the same day.

Sprawling, cosmopolitan Shanghai

Buy a Bike

Bicycles allow you to navigate the city at a more human pace than modern modes of transport. And because Shanghai is entirely paved and reliably flat, almost any bike will do for short jaunts. Your nearest Decathlon outlet (see p.337) will offer reasonable prices and a range of styles. Dedicated cyclists should visit Giant (p.311) or Bohdi (www.bohdi.com.cn). Don't forget to wear a helmet, despite the local disdain for headgear.

Circumnavigate the Bund

You can begin wherever you like (it's a circle after all) but don't start until sunset, when Shanghai's lights and shadows are at their atmospheric best. Proceeding clockwise from Three on the Bund, use the elevated crosswalks over Yan'an Lu and Zhongshan Lu, the Huangpu ferry, the Riverside Promenade, and the Bund Sightseeing Tunnel. You'll emerge, bedazzled, near the entrance to the underground passage at Nanjing Lu. And when you've worked up a thirst, there are plenty of world-class watering holes to visit.

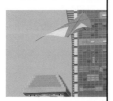

Dine at Altitude

Shanghai's skyscrapers provide more than just eye candy. For innovative cuisine with inspiring views, try Jade on 36 at the Shangri-La (pictured; see p.391). On the 56th floor of the Grand Hyatt (p.34), take your pick from grilled, Japanese, or Italian dining. At a somewhat lower elevation, New Heights (p.370) offers an eclectic menu – and the city's favourite outdoor deck – on the seventh floor of Three on the Bund.

Fly a Kite

Chinese people have raised both kite making and flying to a high art. Buy your own colourful bird, butterfly or dragon, then join the locals. Head to People's Square, north of the Shanghai Museum, or the open plaza between Century Park and the Shanghai Science & Technology Museum, and see how high you can go (see Activities, p.235). Some experts can make their kite soar to such great heights that you can barely see it.

Exercise in the Park

Shanghai's residents prefer to exercise outdoors, among company. Tai chi is by far the most popular activity, but badminton, ballroom dancing, running backwards, and therapeutic shouting all have their fans. The French Concession's Fuxing Park (p.212) provides the most scenic initiation to these morning rituals – but you'll have to be up early, and probably postpone that tea and toast until afterwards.

Catch the Acrobats

Acrobatics flourished during China's Tang Dynasty, more than 1,200 years ago, and is no less entertaining today. See the traditional Shanghai Acrobatic Troupe at the Shanghai Centre Theatre (see Going Out, p.409) or reserve tickets for the multimedia 'ERA' at Shanghai Circus World (p.409). Some of the stunts seem to defy physics; prepare to gasp, laugh and wince as nimble performers leap, tumble and fly before your eyes.

Visit a Water Town

Although Shanghai itself is not an ancient city, there are several nearby villages that are centuries old. The town of Xitang (p.193) stands out, with its well-preserved core of narrow lanes and tile-roofed homes. Go early to avoid the coach-loads, and look beyond the souvenir shops to get a glimpse of life lived along a network of canals linked by ancient stone bridges.

169

Take in a Temple

Foreign tour groups favour the Jade Buddha Temple, but the City Temple (also known as Temple of the City God, or *Chenghuang Miao*, p.208) is where local Taoists go to offer prayers to Shanghai's home-grown deities, including the scholar Qin Yubo. You'll see tourists there too, of course, photographing the smoke of incense as it fades like wishes in the air. It's all very calming, and mystical too.

Light Fireworks

Although any occasion will do for setting off fireworks in Shanghai, the Spring Festival, or Chinese New Year (see Annual Events, p.52), offer your best opportunity to launch bangers the size of mortar shells into the night sky. These are pyrotechnics that make normal rockets seem like sparklers. Make sure to remember your ear plugs, keep your pets indoors, and stand well back after lighting that fuse.

Cruise the Huangpu

Short ferry rides can be fun, but to truly appreciate the wonders of the Huangpu, you need at least an hour-long cruise between the banks of Puxi and Pudong, with drinks and snacks. Sit back and relax as 20th century Shanghai passes you by on one side of the river, and 21st century Shanghai towers above you from the other. Shanghai Huangpu River Cruise Company offers one-hour or three-hour trips (see p.221).

Buy Antiques

Because Chinese law prohibits export of any objects more than 200 years old, the goods for sale to tourists are generally much newer, with some fresh from the factory. That said, some relatively youthful pieces of provincial furniture can be astonishingly beautiful. Visit Henry's Studio & Antiques (see Shopping, p.306) to begin developing your connoisseur's eye.

View the Master Plan

The masterpiece of the Shanghai Urban Planning Exhibition Centre (p.203) is its third-floor scale model of the city, which shows every house, tower and mall (including the building you're standing in) set to be built in Shanghai by 2020 rendered in fanatical detail. One circuit of the grand display will take you from Pudong to the outer ring road – and leave you staggered at the size of it.

Follow in the Chairman's Footsteps

Mao Zedong – one of the past century's most venerated and feared men, depending on your perspective – was a frequent visitor to Shanghai. Trace his path in the city, beginning with the site of the first national congress of the Communist Party of China (p.204), and ending up at his former residence at 120 Maoming Lu (p.206), where he lived for nine months in 1924.

Eat Dumplings

Shanghai is particularly proud of two different types of dumplings, and for good reason. Each of these tasty morsels contains soup along with a filling of pork or crab, and you need to try both. Taste the smaller, steamed *xiaolongbao* at Jiajia Tangbao (90 Huanghe Lu), and savour the larger, pan-fried *shengjian mantou* at Yang's Fry Dumplings (54 and 60 Wujiang Lu) – then start combing the neighbourhood for your own favourites.

Ride the Maglev

Thanks to Chinese ambition and German technology, a ¥10 billion magnetically levitating train runs from Pudong International Airport to the Longyang Lu Metro station (p.44). So what if it's not a practical means of transportation – where else can you go from 0 to 350 kilometres per hour in two minutes flat, while tilting so much that you're almost looking vertically down at the crawling cars beneath you? Hold on tight...

Attend the Opera

Chinese opera comes in an incredible variety of forms, most determined by region of origin. Popular shows can involve elaborate costumes, swordplay, acrobatics – or just old-fashioned singing. At least two Shanghai theatres stage regular performances of classic works: the Yifu and the Lyceum (see Going Out, p.408). You can also get a dose of amateur warbling in some of the city's parks – Lu Xun in particular is a good place to immerse yourself in a tuneful (and sometimes tuneless) cacophony.

Speak Mandarin

It is certainly not easy for most foreigners to master Mandarin's rising and falling tones, but you don't need to speak like a native to get by. Get the pronunciation reasonably close and you will have much more satisfactory experiences with taxi drivers, produce vendors and dry cleaners, among others. See p.258 for a school or course near your home, or download podcasts from www.chinesepod.com and www.mandarinhill.podomatic.com to get practising.

Walk the Old Lanes

Shanghai's narrow lanes and *shikumen* architecture once provided more than half of the city's housing. That percentage is dwindling fast, as old areas are cleared and high-rises sprout up in their place, but there are still old neighbourhoods between Nanjing Xi Lu and the western portion of Weihai Lu, north of Suzhou Creek, and in the Old City (p.184), among other places. Visit these historical remnants before the jackhammers find them.

Shop at the Fabric Market

Officially known as the South Bund Soft Spinning Material Market (see Shopping, p.339), this palace of fabric represents your chance to purchase tailored clothes at prices much lower than the department store racks back home. A long woollen overcoat is a typical first order (Shanghai winters are damp and cold), but the market's resident tailors can copy almost any item of clothing – go on, treat yourself to some smart togs. Silk King (pictured) on Huaihai Zhong Lu is another great option (p.339).

Dine on Hairy Crab

In October and November, Shanghai's markets come alive with the bubbling, scrabbling carapaces of hairy crabs. Raised in fresh water lakes, these fist-sized crustaceans have tasty and delicate meat protected by an exasperatingly tough shell. Many of the city's restaurants will offer some sort of crab special. Shanghai Lao Fandian (242 Fuyou Lu) employs a team of 46 professional pickers to separate the shell from the meat.

Get Arty

Thanks to the increased foreign interest in Chinese contemporary art, Shanghai has become a major player in the avant-garde scene – and 50 Moganshan Lu is the city's hub. The seemingly empty warehouses collected in the northern-most bend of Suzhou Creek house some of the most innovative galleries in the east. Once there, don't bother asking directions – these are the type of galleries that should be 'discovered' (p.196).

171

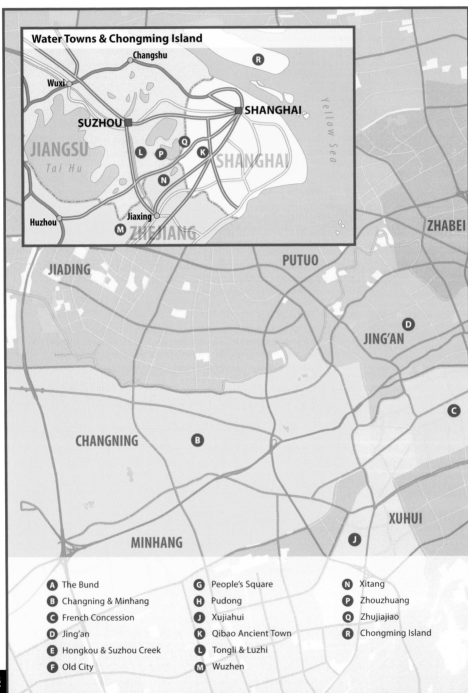

Water Towns & Chongming Island

Changshu

Wuxi

R

SUZHOU

SHANGHAI

JIANGSU
Tai Hu

Q

L P K

SHANGHAI

Yellow Sea

N

Huzhou

Jiaxing

M ZHEJIANG

ZHABEI

JIADING

PUTUO

D
JING'AN

C

CHANGNING

B

XUHUI

J

MINHANG

Ⓐ The Bund	Ⓖ People's Square	Ⓝ Xitang
Ⓑ Changning & Minhang	Ⓗ Pudong	Ⓟ Zhouzhuang
Ⓒ French Concession	Ⓙ Xujiahui	Ⓠ Zhujiajiao
Ⓓ Jing'an	Ⓚ Qibao Ancient Town	Ⓡ Chongming Island
Ⓔ Hongkou & Suzhou Creek	Ⓛ Tongli & Luzhi	
Ⓕ Old City	Ⓜ Wuzhen	

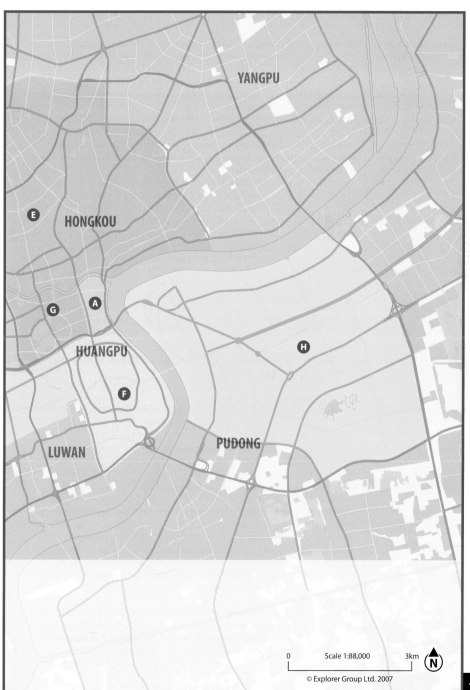

YANGPU

HONGKOU

E

G **A**

HUANGPU

F

LUWAN

H

PUDONG

0   Scale 1:88,000   3km   **N**

© Explorer Group Ltd. 2007

The Bund

The Lowdown

Turn of the century pomp and splendour, once neglected but now revitalised.

Originally ceded to the British in 1845, Shanghai's Bund did not derive its name from the German word for 'bond' or 'association' as commonly thought – it actually comes from a Hindi term for 'embankment.' In those days, the Bund was a dirt path along the Huangpu River. By the 1920s, it was an imposing mile of banks and hotels, one of the world's great concentrations of financial capital and urban sophistication. The transformation was impressive, but no less astonishing than the Bund's rebirth since 1990, after 50 years of economic stagnation.

The Good

Colonial architecture and modern high-end glitz and glamour, all within gazing distance of new Shanghai on the other side of the Huangpu.

Fans of early 20th century architecture or latest-fashion cuisine will find themselves returning again and again, but even if you fall in neither category, it's worth revisiting to walk the promenade in all seasons and at different times of the day. The watery light, the passing ships and the cheerful crowds all change by the minute – and so, it seems, do the Bund's attractions.

A good place to start is the red-striped meteorological signal tower at 1 Zhongshan Dong Er Lu (the official name name for the Bund) opposite the Yan'an Dong Lu overpass. Built in 1907, the tower once warned river traffic of approaching storms. As recently as 2006, its base housed the Bund Museum. Now it's a pleasant bar named Atanu (3313 0871), with truly panoramic views; the third-floor deck is a fine spot to get your bearings. To the south, you can see the turnstiles for the Huangpu ferry. The ticket office is in a little booth, and a one-way passage to Pudong is ¥2.

The Bad

The Bund is not a friendly place for cyclists. Try riding along Zhongshan Dong Yi Lu pavement and you're likely to be fined, or at least lectured. Keep your wheels on Sichuan Lu, one block to the west.

Looking north, you can see the graceful curve of the promenade and the grand institutions across Zhongshan Dong Yi Lu, each built facing east towards the river. At the corner of Guangdong Lu, the seven-storey structure topped by a cupola is Three on the Bund. The former Union Assurance building has become a temple to high fashion, contemporary art and fine dining, including Jean Georges (p.365) and The Whampoa Club (p.364).

The top two floors of its neighbour, the former Nisshin Shipping Building, are occupied by the flashy M on the Bund (p.366) and Glamour Bar (p.390), and also play host to the Shanghai International Literary Festival (p.52).

The Must-Dos

See the Bund under changing light: set aside at least one afternoon and evening to circumnavigate the Bund using the Huangpu ferry and the Sightseeing Tunnel, with occasional pauses for refreshment.

Whether you are sustained by drink or by literature, cross Zhongshan Lu on the overpass and walk north. Step inside the lobby of the Pudong Development Bank, at number 12, and turn your eyes to the ceiling. The intricate mosaics show scenes from eight world cities, along with the signs of the zodiac. Next door at number 13 is the Shanghai Customs House. Its impressive clock tower, the third highest in the world, was silenced in summer 2007 as it underwent renovations, but was due to have resumed chiming by October. The American International Assurance (AIA) building, at number 17, once housed the *North China Daily News*, the most influential foreign publication in China for nearly a century. Its publisher in the 1920s and 30s, Harry Morriss, also owned the villas that are now the Ruijin Guesthouse (p.37). The paper's motto, etched in stone, is suitably noble, but the masons should have checked with a proofreader – see if you can spot the error.

Overview map, p.172

Then again, who has time for spelling when you're setting the world on fire? Bar Rouge (p.387), on the seventh floor of no.18, has built a reputation for regaling a hip crowd with ethanol-fuelled pyrotechnics. And there are sure to be plenty of traditional fireworks when the venerable Peace Hotel (p.206), at number 20, reopens in 2009. The underpass at Nanjing Dong Lu will return you to the river's edge. Note the sign for the Bund Pedestrian Sightseeing Tunnel as you reach the stairs – you can't walk through it, and there are no sights to speak of, but the surreal experience is worth the ¥40 trip, at least once. Emerge from the underpass just south of Huangpu Park (p.212), where you can jostle with affectionate couples and amateur photographers for a place at the rail. The carved stone relief at the base of the Monument to the People's Heroes is a revolutionary history named 'One Hundred Years of Shanghai Wind and Clouds.' With its historical galleries under renovation, the nearby Bund Museum has been reduced to a long, narrow gift shop, but is due to reopen in 2008.

Behind the Bund

If you call a halt to your exploring here, where Suzhou Creek enters the Huangpu, make plans to walk Sichuan Nan Lu, one block inland, on another day. The red bricks of Holy Trinity Church, at the corner of Jiangxi Lu and Hankou Lu, have indeed witnessed more than a century of Shanghai winds. Another block south, on Fuzhou Lu, Noah's Bar (p.394), on the top floor of the Captain Hostel, provides river views with happy hour prices less than half of other Bund bars.

If you're ready for extravagance, on the other hand, stroll two blocks further inland on Guangdong Lu to The Stage at the Westin Bund Centre (6335 0577), where Sunday brunch includes caviar, foie gras, lobster, and an endlessly refilled flute of Piper Heidsieck champagne.

Around the corner at 260 Yan'an Dong Lu is the Museum of Natural History (p.201). This aging science museum houses a well-seasoned collection of the taxidermist's art in the former Cotton Exchange, built in 1923. The cracked walls and peeling paint won't quite transport you to the era of the dinosaurs, but you'll get close. If the sight of a mummy's parched lips makes you thirsty, march back to Sichuan Nan Lu for a pint at Henry's Brewery (p.222), where the lunch special includes a tasty combination of barbecued ribs, fries and baby *bok choy*.

Finally, when the sun's long gone and the lights of Pudong begin to induce that trance-like state, join the beautiful people on the dance floor at top-end club Attica (p.403).

Sights of the Bund

Changning & Minhang

The Lowdown

The place where many of Puxi's expats live and play, with more than enough shops, parks and restaurants to keep you entertained.

Changning and Minhang districts, part of Shanghai's western suburbs, include Gubei, Hongqiao Airport, and a formidable array of expat housing compounds. The Metro network is gradually extending to these areas but, for now, much of your exploring here must take place by bicycle, taxi or private car. Most attractions involve shopping or eating, with the emphasis on comfort food for homesick internationals, including many Taiwanese, Japanese and Korean places.

The Good

The major roads near Hongqiao Airport, including Wuzhong Lu and Huaxiang Lu, are prime hunting grounds for antique furniture, both genuine and reproduction.

Hongmei Lu

One street where walking offers a few hours of diversion is Hongmei Lu, which is bisected by the six-lane Yan'an elevated expressway. Lane 3338, a block south of the expressway and three blocks west of Carrefour, conceals the Hongmei Entertainment Street. Limited to pedestrians only, the lane offers dozens of drinking and dining options, including the expat favorites Moon River Diner, Blue Frog and Simply Thai (see Going Out, p.377). Across the road, at 3717 Hongmei Lu, is Hongqiao Pearl City. The first floor is a hive of commerce in Shanghai souvenirs such as silk bags, pashmina scarves and bargain sets of knock-off golf clubs. The second floor, as advertised, is packed with jewellers who will turn that idea you had for a necklace into something you can wear in minutes. Negotiate firmly – and with a smile – to get a price both buyer and seller will be happy with. The same building also harbours more choices in cuisine, including vegetarian (Zentra; 6446 0230) and Indian (Bukhara; 6446 8800).

The Bad

Shoppers descend on Gubei's Carrefour supermarket on weekend afternoons like a plague of locusts, producing unnavigable aisles, interminable checkout lines and shouting matches in the parking lot.

Walk north under the expressway to find another assortment of restaurants in and around the lane at 3911 Hongmei Lu. Cafe Montmartre (6261 8089) delivers authentic French cooking, while Hatsuhana (6261 6179) provides all-you-can eat Japanese. Retracing your steps south on Hongmei Lu will lead you to one of Johnny Moo's burger outlets at 3219, and the largest of Shanghai's City Shop supermarkets at 3211. Above City Shop, the fourth-floor Kidtown (p.217) promises a respite for weary parents.

Beyond Hongmei Lu

The Must-Dos

Although technically in Putuo district, indoor racetrack Disc Kart provides the perfect antidote for pent-up passengers. Behind the wheel of a Honda go-kart, you can replicate every risk your taxi driver taught you.

Other options for kids in the wider neighbourhood include the Shanghai Discovery Children's Museum on Songyuan Lu (p.201), inside the Shanghai Kids Museum. Further west, the Shanghai Zoo (p.220) is large enough to exhaust even the most energetic eight year old. For older kids, and the young at heart, try a few laps in a go-kart at Disc Kart (809 Zaoyang Lu; 6222 2880). If you prefer a chillier thrill, Minhang's Yinqixing Indoor Skiing Site (1835 Qixin Lu; 6272 7910), south-west of Hongqiao Airport, offers skiing and snowboarding, with a drop of 45m and a snow depth of up to 50cm. A few blocks away, the Aloha Marine Fishing Club (1555 Qixin Lu; 5488 5785) provides more pensive recreation. The staff enthusiastically applaud every catch and will cook the fish to your taste. Anyone with an interest in Chinese antiques should devote a couple of weekends to the furniture warehouses near Hongqiao Airport. Henry's Studio & Antiques (p.306) is a good first destination. The same building also contains a workshop where the antiques are refurbished, a design studio, and the Chinese traditional furniture centre of Tongji University. Huaxiang Lu, between the Huqingping and Beiqing highways, hosts at least a dozen furniture shops, including Mary's Shanxi Art (239 Huaxiang Lu; 5227 0085).

Overview map, p.172

Another cluster is located on Wuzhong Lu, between Hongxu Lu and the A20 expressway. One expat favorite is Hu & Hu Antiques (p.326). For a family outing, check out the Hongqiao Flower Market at 718 Hongjing Lu, a few blocks west of Hongmei Lu. In addition to plants, the market's several buildings sell toys, aquarium supplies and, in season, a wide selection of Christmas decorations. Veering back to the east, the Shanghai Sculpture Space (p.199) merits a visit. The former No.10 Steel Plant of the Shanghai Steel Company held its first sculpture festival in 2007 and promises innovative exhibits to go with its landscaped site.

Overview map, p.172

French Concession

There's something about Shanghai's former French Concession that corresponds with the notion of graceful urban living. Its tree-lined streets are amply populated, but not overcrowded; peaceful in the morning, spirited at night. The residential areas include only a handful of high-rise towers, but are liberally supplied with boutiques and bars, restaurants and street markets.

Established in 1849, the French Concession remained a relatively sleepy protectorate for decades, overshadowed by the International Settlement to the north. That changed quickly in the early 1900s, when its reputation for laissez-faire capitalism attracted an unholy trinity of drug-runners, gamblers and prostitutes. The colony expanded to the west, becoming a refuge for wealthy Chinese, White Russians, gangsters, and the Communist Party, which held its first meeting here in 1921. Newly minted fortunes – some legitimate, others less so – financed a building boom in *shikumen* row houses and art deco mansions along the winding thoroughfares shaded by plane trees. By 1932, the French Concession had a population of nearly 500,000 Chinese and about 16,000 foreigners, with the French themselves ranking fourth after Russians, British and Americans.

Although the Chinese government has long ceased to recognise the colonial borders, most residents would describe the area as bounded by Yan'an Lu in the north and Jianguo Lu in the south, extending west to Xujiahui and east to Xintiandi.

Xintiandi

Since its opening in 2002, Xintiandi has been hailed as both an unqualified success and an extravagant sham. Designed by American architect Benjamin Wood, this two-block shopping and entertainment complex required the relocation of more than 1,600 families. Wood appropriated the *shikumen* style of the razed homes, building stone-gated facades for trendy shops and restaurants, and creating a neighbourly ambience for outdoor cafes. Despite the token museum, it's not the sort of model typically envisioned by historical preservationists. Nevertheless, the city's affluent consumers have enthusiastically embraced the concept, inspiring other real-estate developers and spawning the verb 'xintiandi' to describe this blueprint for gentrification.

Strangely enough, one of Xintiandi's chief tourist attractions is the site of the First National Congress of the Chinese Communist Party (p.204). You should visit that exhibit at least once, if only to view the wax models of 13 Party members seated around a table, with a young Mao Zedong standing at the centre of attention. As for Xintiandi itself (the name translates as 'new heaven and earth'), you will no doubt return again and again.

Marx and Engels in Fuxing Park

Huaihai Lu & Fuxing Lu

Before Xintiandi entered the lexicon, shoppers emptied their wallets on Huaihai Lu, a block to the north. The former Avenue Joffre bisects the French Concession from east to west, and its popularity rivals that of Nanjing Lu. It remains a fine venue for both shopping and people watching, but for more contemplative browsing you should try Huaihai's flanking roads: Fuxing Lu and Changle Lu.

Near its intersection with Chongqing Lu, Fuxing Lu represents the southern boundary of Fuxing Park (p.212). Shanghai's most elegant green space hosts a thriving rose

garden, the occasional jazz festival and a large sculpture of that inseparable left-wing duo, Marx and Engels. It's a wonderfully theatrical place in the early morning, when hundreds of local residents gather to practise tai chi. Leaving the park's western gate, on Gaolan Lu, you'll pass the chic clubs at Park 97 (p.406). Just ahead is the dome of St Nicholas Church, christened in 1930, and now vacant.

One block south, on Sinan Lu, the Former Residence of Sun Yatsen (p.207) has been transformed into a multimedia shrine to the first president of the republic. Two blocks farther south, Zhou Enlai's old home (p.207) presents a much quieter face to the populace (just be careful not to wake the napping security guards.) If you'd rather peruse art than history, continue two blocks south and another block west. At 210 Taikang Lu, an eclectic sampling of shops, galleries and restaurants has fused into an

French Concession

alternative Xintiandi – less calculated, more hip. True, you're still expected to buy things, but you could make that a beer at the Kommune Kafe (p.381), an Australian-accented establishment that serves Brooklyn lager. On the left-hand side of the lane's entrance, the Pottery Workshop at 220 (6445 0902) houses a ceramics studio with classes for adults and children.

Returning to the north on Ruijin Er Lu, you'll pass the Old China Hand Reading Room (27 Shaoxing Lu; 6473 2526). Photographer Deke Erh's peaceful coffeehouse and bookshop is a fine place to spend an afternoon. The same comment applies to the grounds of the Ruijin Guesthouse (p.37), once the home of the Morriss family, publishers of the *North China Daily News*. Except that here, you're likely to linger until sunset, sipping cocktails outside the impeccably furnished Face Bar (p.390). After the sun's long gone, step upstairs to Lan Na Thai (118 Ruijin Er Lu; 5466 4328), perhaps the city's best Thai restaurant.

Select another day to explore the western reaches of Fuxing Lu. More than most of Shanghai's other neighbourhoods, the French Concession rewards long strolls or casual rides. Although Huaihai Zhong Lu is closed to bicycles, other roads are designed to allow cars to travel in one direction, while bikes proceed in the other. If you're on two wheels, use Fuxing Lu to travel east and Jianguo Lu to travel west.

The area south of the intersection between Fuxing Lu and Hengshan Lu has been colonised by a multinational conglomerate of pubs and restaurants. In the space of three blocks, you'll encounter dozens of expat hangouts, including Simply Thai (p.377), the tapas bar Azul (p.366), and Haiku (p.373), which offers California-style sushi by way of Beijing.

At 11 Dongping Lu, Sasha's (6474 6628) offers food and drink in one of the legendary Soong family's mansions. The intimate third floor is an especially congenial place for cognac and a cigar. The two-storey cobblestone structure at 9 Dongping Lu, inside the Shanghai Conservatory of Music, is the famous *Ai Lu*, or 'Love Cottage'. The red-tiled villa was the favourite home of Nationalist leader Chiang Kaishek and his wife Soong Mei Ling, the younger sister of Soong Ching Ling. Before becoming a classroom building, it also served briefly as the residence of Jiang Qing, more infamously known as Madame Mao.

A block to the east, at 79 Fenyang Lu, you'll notice the former mansion of the French consul general and other Shanghai notables, including the city's first post-liberation mayor. This 'Little White House' is now home to the Shanghai Museum of Arts and Crafts (6437 3454).

Changle Lu

North of Huaihai, charming Changle Lu offers another leafy corridor to explore. The eastern section, near its junction with Maoming Lu, provides an ever-changing mix of shops and restaurants. One reliable option is Eddy Tam's Gallery (20 Maoming Nan Lu; 6253 6715), which offers stylish custom framing and stocks a reasonably priced selection of Jinshan peasant art. The Lyceum Theatre (57 Maoming Nan Lu; 6217 8530), built in 1930, stages regular performances of Chinese opera and hosts an annual rendition of Handel's *Messiah* by the International Festival Chorus (www.ifcshanghai.org). A block to the west, Garden Books (p.313) tastefully complements its inventory of English books and magazines with coffee and ice cream. Nearby Shanxi Nan Lu is famous for its seemingly endless array of shops selling dresses, shoes and handbags.

Farther to the west, a visit to the Chinese Printed Blue Nankeen Exhibition Hall (637 Changle Lu; 5403 7947) will feel like a voyage of discovery. Follow the narrow lane until it turns into a small courtyard hung with drying cloth. Inside the shop, one small room displays some sun-bleached samples of the dyer's handiwork, while the other offers blue-and-white cotton tablecloths, runners, bags, shirts and shoes. Prices are relatively high and bargaining is discouraged, but the intricate wood-block patterns are hard to resist.

North on Fumin Lu, the cavernous Bao Luo, also known as Paul's (271 Fumin Lu; 5403 7239), serves Shanghainese specialties such as red-cooked river fish and – believe it or not – Swiss steak. Nearby Madame Mao's Dowry at 207 (p.308) is the authoritative setting for purchasing vintage memorabilia.

South on Donghu Lu are the haunts of the concession-era's pre-eminent power broker, Du Yuesheng. Big-eared Du possessed all the talents of a banker, labour leader, mafia godfather and party boss. His former home is now the four-star Donghu Hotel (p.34). Continuing west on Changle Lu to its intersection with Huashan Lu will bring you to the President Apartments, where the Propaganda Poster Art Centre (868 Huashan Lu; 6211 1845) lurks in the basement of building B. Admission is ¥20 at this hard-to-find gallery of ephemeral art, where prices range up to ¥1,000 for images that were once printed by the millions. Another block west on winding Huashan Lu is Xian Yue Hien (849 Huashan Lu; 6251 1166), an expansive dim sum restaurant at the edge of the Ding Xiang Garden. The pleasures of the garden itself, named after a general's favourite concubine, are now reserved for government officials only.

Xintiandi

Jing'an

The Lowdown
An area full of Shanghai's consistent contradictions: counterfeit versus authentic, old colonial versus new entrepreneurial, elevated intentions versus baser instincts.

The Good
The Fenshine Fashion Accessories Plaza at 580 Nanjing Xi Lu is a fine place to practise your bargaining skills on imitation handbags, pashmina scarves and souvenirs.

The Bad
Ghost-town malls with their many luxury brands but few active shoppers. You'll find yourself a target for hucksters peddling fake Rolex watches.

The Must-Dos
If the rumours are true, the Wujiang Lu food street has been targeted for gentrification within the near future. Get there for a plate of Yang's dumplings before it's too late.

Overview map, p.172

Believe it or not, fresh water once bubbled from the ground near Jing'an Temple – hard to imagine given the area's modern urban guise. In 1862, when the British built a road from what is now People's Square to the temple, they named it Bubbling Well Road. The neighbourhood became fashionable, replete with green lawns and lavish mansions. But the well was paved over in 1919, most of the foreign residents fled in 1937 with the Japanese invasion, and after liberation the road was renamed Nanjing Xi Lu. Forty years later, liberalisation supplanted liberation, and another building boom began. For most of the 1990s, the Jing'an district served as the hub of expat life in Shanghai, with the Shanghai Centre (www.shanghaicentre.com) – also known as the Portman – at 1376 as its focus. Although that's changed in recent years, many longer-term residents still measure distances from the Portman, and several housing compounds dutifully dispatch their shuttle buses to its front doors. In addition to its popular salon, medical clinic and restaurants, the Shanghai Centre's tenants include seven international airlines, along with the British,

Jing'an Temple

Canadian and Australian consulates – and the Ritz-Carlton hotel (see p.36). The Shanghai Centre Theatre hosts regular performances of the acclaimed Shanghai Acrobatic Troupe (p409).

Across Nanjing Xi Lu looms the back gate of the Shanghai Exhibition Centre (6279 0279). Inspect its Russian domes and spires, then imagine what Shanghai might look like if the Bolsheviks had overwhelmed Asia. The building now hosts trade fairs, including the over-the-top Millionaire Fair in June, a Dutch 'luxury lifestyle event'.

A few steps to the west is a branch of the inexpensive Cantonese restaurant chain Bi Feng Tang at 1333 (6279 0738). Menu items are numbered, and you indicate your selections by checking the appropriate boxes on an order sheet. Its versions of roast goose and shrimp dumplings are particularly tasty. In good weather, the open-air booths on the sidewalk are preferable to the chaotic din inside. This outlet is open until 04:00, making it a welcome sight for pubgoers trundling around the corner from Tongren Lu's occasionally raucous strip of bars.

The West

Two blocks further to the west are Jing'an Temple station, Jing'an Park (p.213) and Jing'an Temple (p.209) itself. Inside the park, through a shady alley of plane trees, Bali Laguna (p.372) offers some of the best outdoor seating in town. For some reason, this Indonesian-themed restaurant feels absolutely appropriate in Shanghai. Then again, so does the remodelled temple, despite the contradiction of Buddhism and billboards. If you can't get enough of the colourful juxtaposition of east and west, pay the ¥10 admission fee and take a picture of a succession of upturned eaves, the smoke of incense, and the benign gaze of Tiffany's latest blonde poster goddess.

If you're in need of a budget makeover, there's a large indoor clothes market behind the temple, on Yuyuan Lu. If you've been craving sashimi-grade tuna or can't find your favourite brand of extra virgin olive oil, try the Fresh Mart in the basement of the City Plaza shopping mall at 1618 (3217 4838).

The East

Walking east from the Shanghai Centre, the first corner is Xikang Lu, where you can find relaxed Italian dining at Bella Napoli (p.372). The next intersection is Shanxi Lu (also written as Shaanxi Lu in some places). Besides its mysteriously alternating spelling, this street features several fine examples of Concession-era architecture. Two blocks south is the fairytale Hengshan Moller Villa (p.207); two blocks north is the former Ohel Rachel Synagogue, at 500 Shanxi Bei Lu.

Continuing east along Nanjing Xi Lu for several more blocks will lead you past a mix of high-rise shopping centres and fashionable stores. Although it has no English sign, you can find Wang Jia Sha (6258 6373) at 805, near Nanjing Xi Lu station (formerly Shimen Yi station). Just follow the lunchtime traffic. It's an old reliable, revered by both locals and tourists. Remodelled in 2006, Wang Jia Sha offers traditional Shanghai snack food in a clean, well-lit place. Watch, point, pay and eat. For faultless dim sum in a more elegant setting, ride the escalators to floor seven in Westgate Mall and try Crystal Jade (p.359), where tables are much easier to find than in the Xintiandi outlet.

Beyond Nanjing Xi Lu

Heading south, near the corner of Maoming Lu and Weihai Lu, is the former residence of Mao Zedong (p.206). When you've finished contemplating the cult of Mao, walk north across Weihai Lu, turn right, then enter the gate at number 590. This quiet lane conceals some beautiful *shikumen* houses, and feels inhabited and enjoyed in a way that will revive your spirits considerably. Heading north will return you to the Nanjing Xi Lu station.

At 580 Nanjing Xi Lu, the Fenshine Fashion Accessories Plaza (also known as the Feng Xiang Clothing Gift Plaza) has emerged as a worthy successor to Xiangyang Market, the notorious bazaar of counterfeit goods which closed in 2006. Wujiang Lu, the alley just to the south, between Shimen Yi Lu and Qinghai Lu, was once Shanghai's most popular destination for combining shopping and eating. The street vendors were cleared out in April 2007, but many of the restaurants remain open for now. Don't let the long lines outside Yang's Fry Dumplings (6267 6025) scare you off – it's definitely worth the wait. The pan-fried dumplings, or *shengjian mantou*, are simultaneously crisp, succulent, tender and savoury. At ¥3.5 for a plate of four, Yang's qualifies as one of the city's most satisfying bargains – although eating them can be a bit tricky. The preferred technique involves a judicious lift with the chopsticks, a prudent nip in the wrapper, then a pensive slurp – all before taking that first bite. You can spot the amateurs by the stains on their shirts.

Jing'an wall and park

Hongkou & Suzhou Creek

In the opening sequence of Lou Ye's award-winning film *Suzhou River* the narrator says: 'If you watch it long enough, the river will show you everything.' He's right, in this case, because Suzhou Creek is more than a body of water. It's an artery and a boundary; a stream of effluent and a stream of consciousness.

Trade goods and freight have followed its winding course for centuries, from its origin at Taihu Lake all the way to the Bund. During Shanghai's early years as a treaty port, the creek marked the line between the British and American concessions. After the 1937 Japanese invasion, it provided the northern border for the International Settlement. And since the 1920s, Suzhou Creek has been a stinking, polluted mess.

Today it is a success story of sorts. The first two phases of its decade-long clean-up are over. In June 2007, workers began dredging the river bottom of silt. Fish and birds have returned to some sections, as have the real-estate developers. Locals now stroll in the many riverfront parks, admiring the barge traffic, and the creek is no longer a psychological barrier to tourists or urban explorers.

Moganshan Lu

Art and artists have taken the lead in this rediscovery. At 50 Moganshan Lu, across the river from the Shanghai Railway Station, a maze of Concession-era lofts and warehouses now serve as an eclectic assemblage of studios and galleries. ShanghART (see p.199) was one of the first to move in and Art Scene Warehouse (p.196) is one of the largest, representing more than 40 painters, sculptors and photographers. It's easy to spend an afternoon here, wandering among the galleries and cafes. A former flour mill at nearby 120 Moganshan Lu hosts the non-profit Island6 (p.198). Across the river and two bends downstream, Creek Art (101 Chang'an Lu; 6380 4150) combines contemporary art and modern dining with fine views of the city.

Further north and east are two Hongkou district neighbourhoods that receive less attention than the grand sights at People's Square or Lujiazui.

Duolun Lu

To the north is Duolun Lu, an L-shaped road, closed to vehicles, that begins and ends on Sichuan Bei Lu, between Lu Xun Park (p.213) and the Dongbaoxing Metro station. Many of China's best-known writers made their homes here in the 1930s, which explains the sequence of genial bronze statues and the dutiful school groups with their electronically amplified tour guides. The Meeting Place of the League of Left-Wing Writers (p.206) is down the lane at 201 Duolun Lu. Within walking distance are writer Lu Xun's former residence (p.208) and the Lu Xun Museum (146 Dongjiangwan Lu; 6540 2288), which respectfully displays many of the author's personal effects, including a purple V-neck sweater, his pocket watch and lighter, and a pair of socks. The book shop on the second floor sells some inexpensive English translations of his work.

An outdoor table at Old Film Cafe (p.382) makes a good seat for soaking up the literary atmosphere. If the terrace is full, open a window on the second floor and let the street noise drift upward. Listen to the waitress's suggestion and order a fresh waffle, served hot with chocolate syrup and sprinkles, a smear of whipped cream on the side.

The northern portion of the street is lined with curio shops, some of which are more like small museums. The southern end features Hongde Tang, a 1920s Christian church with Chinese architectural sensibility, and a genuine museum: the Shanghai Duolun Museum of Modern Art, also known as the Doland Museum (p.197).

For an altogether otherworldly experience, walk north and west on Baoxing Lu from the Dongbaoxing Lu Metro station. Along the 700 and 800 blocks of Xibaoxing Lu, you'll encounter a procession of funeral supply shops. These shops peddle flowers, caskets and incense, along with various items meant for burning at an ancestor's tomb.

Paper money – guaranteed by the Bank of the Underworld – is the most commonly burnt offering, but you can also honour and equip your forebears with houses, whisky, watches and mobile phones.

Former Jewish Ghetto

East of the Dalian Lu Metro station, closer to the Huangpu River and north-east of the Bund, lies Shanghai's former Jewish ghetto. At 62 Changyang Lu, Ohel Moishe Synagogue (p.210), founded by Meir Ashkenazi in 1926, now houses a small museum. There is a row of picturesque homes around the corner on Zhoushan Lu, and another across from undersized Huoshan Park (p.212). For more information about Shanghai's Jewish community, past and present, visit www.chinajewish.org.

If you walk north on Zhoushan Lu from Ohel Moishe, you'll find a bustling street market at the intersection with Yuhang Lu. Colourful umbrellas shade the fruit, vegetables, crayfish and eels, while narrow lanes lead mysteriously into warrens of tenement housing. Try a *zongzi* – a ball of sticky rice wrapped in leaves – from the stall on the corner. It's ¥2 for the most expensive version, which contains an egg yolk along with a chunk of sweet and salty pork. Very few foreigners venture here so be discreet with your camera – the frog vendor is particularly jumpy.

Duolun Lu

Old Film Cafe

Hongkou housing

Moganshan Lu

183

The Lowdown

Old City

The Old City is among Shanghai's favourite destinations for tourists, photographers and souvenir hunters, with unforgettable sights of both the ephemeral and the timeless.

Look at any map of Shanghai and your eyes are drawn to the Old City, a densely packed area of crooked lanes ringed by broader streets. From above, the neighbourhood resembles a rough oval situated between the more rectangular grid of the former French Concession and the wide curve of the Huangpu River. The oval traces the path of the former city wall, built to repel 16th century pirates, but dismantled in 1911 during Shanghai's first boom. In those days, tourists ventured into the teeming alleyways to witness the stink and squalor of an alien culture.

Life has changed considerably since then, but not uniformly. Recent developments have imposed only a patchwork pattern of modernity. There are still some lanes, lacking indoor plumbing or other modern amenities, where tenants brush their teeth at sidewalk spigots and tote chamber pots to a public toilet.

The Good

During the Lantern Festival (p.52), the Yu Garden Bazaar becomes a veritable menagerie of lights, featuring elaborate displays of illuminated fish, dragons, rabbits and other beasts.

While most lifelong residents have little nostalgia for the discomforts of a bygone age, some do lament the loss of community that occurs when their old homes are demolished to make way for impersonal apartment blocks. So go now and go often to see for yourself how change comes to China.

Northern Section

The Bad

The reconstruction of Shanghai Old Street and Fuyou Lu veer dangerously toward commercial excess.

Begin with Fangbang Zhong Lu, which runs from west to east across the northern third of the Old City. Just inside the arch at Henan Nan Lu is the multi-level Cangbao Lou antique market (459 Fangbang Zhong Lu). Inside the ageing building, traders have staked their claims on hundreds of tiny stalls. Some specialise in porcelain, some in jade, others in pearls or bronze or embroidery. It's a bewildering jumble of the odd and the uninteresting, partially segregated by type and geography of origin. Come prepared to bargain – and be aware that nearly all the real treasures have already been purchased by wiser eyes than yours.

Moving east, Fangbang Lu is reborn as Shanghai Old Street, the southern boundary of the Yu Garden Bazaar, a theme park version of a 19th century Chinese market. If you continue east, the glitz gradually diminishes, and the streets are lined with produce vendors and snack stands. But you really should turn in at the bazaar, if only to visit the City Temple of Shanghai (p.208) and Yu Garden (p.214).

The Must-Dos

In early spring, Yu Garden (p.214) blushes with the fleeting sight and scent of plum blossoms. Try to visit early in the morning, during a persistent drizzle, while the tourists linger safely at their hotels.

Both of these renovated Ming Dynasty relics are distinctly beautiful in the absence of crowds, but both are almost always crowded. If you arrive at a fortunate time, buy some pellets to feed the shoals of goldfish beneath the Bridge of Nine Turnings. Otherwise, escape the crush by entering the Mid-lake Pavilion, or *Huxinting* (257 Yuyuan Lu; 6373 6950). Built in 1784, this authentic teahouse has played host to many foreign dignitaries, including the Queen and Bill Clinton. Although the tea might seem expensive at up to ¥90 per glass, you can sit as long as you like, order a few sweet or salty snacks, and ask for a fresh infusion of hot water when your cup runs dry.

Overview map, p.172

From the pavilion's second-floor windows, you also can monitor the lines at the original Nanxiang Mantou Dian (85 Yuyuan Lu; 6355 4206). The soup dumplings at this legendary restaurant attract a dedicated following, although some *xiaolongbao* aficionados rank them relatively low on the scale. Wandering among the shops in the bazaar, you might notice several other historic brand names. Tong Han Chun Traditional Chinese Medicine (20 Yuyuan Lu; 6355 3027), established in 1783, is the oldest pharmacy in Shanghai, while Starbucks and McDonald's represent a somewhat more recent vintage.

The northern boundary of Yu Garden Bazaar is Fuyou Lu. Unless you've committed to buying souvenirs for the extended family, you can safely ignore the acres of trinkets on display and concentrate on two addresses. The restaurant at the Shanghai Classical Hotel, also known as Shanghai Lao Fandian (242 Fuyou Lu; 6355 2275), has satisfied diners since 1875. During each autumn's hairy crab season, it employs a team of 46 professional pickers to extract the succulent meat. At 378 Fuyou Lu, the city's oldest mosque welcomes visitors for a glimpse of its modest and expressive interior.

If you're not yet weary of temples, walk one block south to Chenxiangge Lu and its small monastery (p.208). Otherwise, flee west across Henan Lu, then turn south on Jiucang Jie until you reach Dajing Lu. This street offers a busy wet market, the relocated White Cloud Taoist Temple (p.210), and – at its intersection with Renmin Lu – the Dajing Pavilion (p.204), the last remnant of the Old City's protective wall.

For antique shopping in the open air, cross Renmin Lu to Shouning Lu, continue west across Xizang Lu (also known as Tibet Road), then turn south on Luilin Lu, where you'll be rewarded with the Dongtai Lu antiques market (p.344), several blocks of stalls backed by a secondary layer of shop fronts. Although many of the items for sale are newly made, a small percentage seem genuinely dusty. The atmosphere in this market varies from day to day – sometimes sleepy, other times frantic. Try to modulate the ferocity of your bargaining based on the number of other foreigners in evidence. Shopkeepers seem less inclined to deep discounts when fresh faces (and wallets) meander into view.

Southern Section

Most visitors to this part of Shanghai head for the Fabric Market, officially known as the South Bund Soft Spinning Material Market (p.339). Relocated from nearby Dongjiadu Lu in 2006, this market offers expat residents the luxury of a tailored wardrobe at prices much lower than the department store racks back home. The typical purchases include wool overcoats, tuxedos and ball gowns, but the market's resident tailors can copy almost any item of clothing. If choosing between silks or

Old City street and Dongtai Lu

三十年代影星周璇

tweeds gives you an appetite, walk across the road to Xiao Wei Yang Hot Pot with Magic Broth (436 Lujiabang Lu). Order the 'nourish broth,' some mushrooms, vegetables, and 'handiwork noodles', along with several mutton kebabs. After your meal, you'll have plenty of energy for a walk north on Nancang Jie, then east on Dongjiadu Lu, the site of the first Catholic church in Shanghai, the Dongjiadu Cathedral (p.209).

Retracing your steps to the intersection with Nancang Jie, continue west until you re-enter the boundaries of the Old City. Between Xiaoputuo and Nanqu Lu, behind the blue-and-white police station, a clean and well-lit wet market offers appetising displays of fish, pickles, eggplants, melons and other produce.

Thread your way north and east, passing residents lounging on wooden stools or shopping in their pyjamas, to Wenmiao Lu. There you'll find more street vendors, extending in both directions from the gate of the Wenmiao Confucian Temple (p.210), with its courtyards, pagoda and intriguing collection of root carvings. On Sundays, the temple hosts the biggest second-hand book market in the city. Around the corner is Kongyiji restaurant (36 Xuegong Jie; 6376 7979), recognisable by the rows of traditional wine jars and the smell of fried fish.

South of the fabric market, near the site of the upcoming World Expo 2010, are the newly renovated Penglai Park and the Sanshan Guild Hall (1551 Zhongshan Nan Lu; 6313 5582), patriotically preserved as 'the south Shanghai headquarters of worker pickets in the city's third armed uprising' in 1927. Built in 1909, the guild's rooms surround a central courtyard with a traditional raised stage for dramatic productions. The building now houses the Museum of Folk Collectables, an eclectic assemblage of watercolour paintings, blue-and-white porcelain, woodcarvings, postcards and Metro tickets. The museum contains very little English signage, except for a plaque noting the contributions of the US ambassador in the restoration of the stage.

Yu Garden

The Lowdown ◀
*People's Square
provides its own
cityscape within a city.
You can traverse the
area in 15 minutes on
foot, and encounter
the full range of
Shanghai's varied
architecture and
inhabitants.*

The Good ◀
*The Shanghai
Museum, though often
beset by tour groups,
deserves its reputation
as one of the best
collections in Asia.
Don't miss the galleries
of ancient jade or
Buddhist sculptures.*

The Bad ◀
*Visitors to People's
Square suffer a higher
rate of pick pocketing
than in other districts.
Many locals hold their
bags or purses in front
of them, with one
hand on the clasp.*

The Must-Dos ◀
*The scale model of
Shanghai in the Urban
Planning Exhibition
Centre astonishes
everyone who sees it.*

Overview map, p.172 ◀

People's Square

Once the International Settlement's Recreation Ground, the area around People's Square has become the commercial, municipal and cultural heart of modern Shanghai. Bounded by Nanjing Xi Lu on the north and Xizang Lu (Tibet Road) on the east, it consists of two large green spaces – People's Park and People's Square itself – bisected by Renmin Dadao (People's Avenue), and studded with monumental architecture. Huangpi Lu, with its row of skyscrapers, defines the western boundary, while the elevated Yan'an expressway noisily fences the southern edge. You can traverse the area in 15 minutes on foot, and in that interval encounter the full range of the city's varied inhabitants: students, tourists and bureaucrats, labourers lugging heavy loads, old men playing cards and young women with high heels clacking on the path.

During the height of the city's Concession era, the Recreation Ground offered facilities for swimming, cricket, golf, baseball, tennis, rugby, soccer and – most famously – horse racing. Although the racing ended in 1941, when the Japanese took temporary control of the city, the square remained prime real estate for public gatherings, including a three-day bash for the coronation of Britain's King George VI in 1937, and a victory speech by the Nationalist leader Chiang Kaishek, after Japan's defeat.

People's Square Metro Station

Already the busiest Metro station in the city, the scheduled opening of Line 8 in October 2007 (see p.10) will add a third source of congestion to the overflowing intersection of Lines 1 and 2. A new interchange hall promises to ease the rush-hour crush, when the walk from one line to the other can become a 10 minute ordeal. But whether it fulfils that promise or not, the people will keep on coming – and not just to browse at the cavernous underground Hong Kong Shopping Centre, packed with stalls selling inexpensive clothes, jewellery, and cosmetics.

Your first stop after stepping off the subway and through the crowds should be the Shanghai Urban Planning Exhibition Centre (p.203), located at the southern edge of People's Park. The underground level – accessible from the Metro station – houses a replica of a 1930s street that has yet to become a big attraction. The mezzanine displays black-and-white photographs of what the curators have translated as the 'vicissitudes of the Bund.' But the centre's undisputed treasure is the third-floor scale model of Shanghai, from Pudong to the outer ring road, with every highway, apartment building, and tennis court rendered in painstaking detail.

People's Park

In People's Park, you'll find the clock tower of the former Shanghai Race Club, now the Shanghai Art Museum (p.199), and the former greenhouse reborn as the Museum of Contemporary Art (p.198). These are both worthy destinations in their own right, but each also offers a place to eat and drink with a view of the park: Kathleen's 5 (6327 2221) and MOCA Caffe (6327 0856). Between them lies Barbarossa (p.387), with an enticing open-air deck, extravagant Moroccan pillows, but only average martinis.

With refreshments in hand, keep your eyes roving over the nearby terrain. It's a pleasure during the day, but a neon distraction at night, when the surrounding skyline acquires an almost kinetic fascination. Depending on your table, you might be able to spot two or three more of the city's temples to high culture, including the arching roof of the Shanghai Grand Theatre (p.408) or the evocative urn handles of the Shanghai Museum (p.203) – both within easy walking distance.

With a dozen different galleries, the Shanghai Museum rewards repeat visitors with beautiful and unexpected discoveries. Among the beaded and embroidered garments

187

in the Chinese Minority Nationalities Gallery, for instance, is a suit of clothes fashioned from salmon skin. The plaza north of the museum is a favourite spot for kite flying, and its popular fountain can provide a pleasant place to watch the locals at play – until the roving street peddlers find you.

Around People's Square

Although you could easily spend hours within the grassy confines of the square, the nearby roads, though often choked with traffic, have attractions of their own. The Park Hotel (170 Nanjing Xi Lu; 6327 5225) was the tallest building in Asia in the 1930s. Now dwarfed by its glass-and-steel competitors, including the 60 storey Tomorrow Square, which houses the JW Marriott (p.35), the hotel remains the geographical centre of Shanghai. Look for the 'zero point' on the lobby floor, said to be located directly beneath the flagpole.

Just to the west of the Park Hotel, the gate of Huanghe Lu beckons hungry locals to taste everything from chicken hotpot to crabmeat tofu. At 90 Huanghe Lu, Jiajia Tangbao (6327 6878) serves what many consider Shanghai's best *xiaolongbao* (small, soup-filled dumplings) for ¥6 per steamer. There's no English sign, but you can spot the building number and, more often than not, the long line of hopefuls waiting outside the door. Nanjing Dong Lu provides the busiest shoppers' corridor to the Bund, including a branch of legendary tourist trap Madame Tussauds (6358 7878; www.madame-tussauds.com.cn). But for a more meditative route, try Fuzhou Lu. Only three blocks south of the fake-Rolex touts and the sightseeing trolley, this street hosts a mix of bookstores and stationery shops, including the Shanghai Foreign Languages Book Store (390 Fuzhou Lu; 6322 3200), which stocks the largest selection of English books in the city.

Walking to the west, Jiangyin Lu, opposite the Shanghai Grand Theatre, will transport you back at least several decades and architectural styles. Just to prove that almost everything that typifies Shanghai, both old and new, can be found in this central hub, this narrow market street features a chirping, splashing display of crickets, fish, and turtles, along with a handful of *shikumen* houses in fine repair, all within a hop of People's Square's towering developments.

Nanjing Dong Lu

People's Square

Pudong

Pudong is cited as evidence of China's miracle of modern urbanisation. It boasts the world's fastest train – a magnetically levitated wonder – but the ride lasts only seven minutes and ends at the Longyang Lu Metro station, far from any legitimate transportation hub. Nearly all foreign visitors arrive at Pudong International Airport, but very few use the Maglev to reach their hotels. Like much of what is novel and exciting about Pudong, it was built to impress on first glance, not for the long haul. Viewed from the Bund, across the Huangpu River, Pudong's skyline alternately stabs and dazzles. The 89 storey Jinmao Tower radiates an undeniably grand beauty, but the pink-and-purple Oriental Pearl seems scarcely more than a towering bauble. In any case, the Lujiazui area represents only a small fraction of the district. Four bridges link Pudong with Puxi, along with five tunnels and 15 ferries. Covering more than 500 square kilometres, from the east bank of the Huangpu to the shores of the East China Sea, Pudong is larger than all of Shanghai's other urban districts combined. Some locals like to describe it as a boggy wasteland before development began in 1990, but old maps and photographs show that factories and warehouses once occupied the ground beneath the new structures.

Pudong does have some historic sites, including a Ming Dynasty fortress, but many are difficult to access or in poor repair – for more information about Pudong's heritage, visit www.english.pudong.gov.cn. A car and driver can help shrink the distances between developed areas, but even within them, the wide avenues and soaring towers often feel beyond the human scale, and the long walks between shopfronts can become disheartening rather than invigorating.

Lujiazui

The obvious place to begin your explorations is the unignorable Oriental Pearl Tower, easily accessed from the Lujiazui Metro station. The view from the observation decks is pretty breathtaking, but unless you enjoy waiting in endless queues, ascending the tower can make for a trying afternoon. Descend to the basement instead for a visit to the Shanghai History Museum (p.202). Strangely enough, Pudong's sometimes overlooked gem is the city's best place to learn about Concession-era Puxi. The intricately detailed dioramas provide a fascinating look back at 'the metropolis infested with foreign adventurers'.

For a superior perspective, ride to the 87th floor of the Jinmao Tower (p.34). You'll have to change elevators twice before entering Cloud 9 (p.389), the Grand Hyatt's rooftop lounge. There's a minimum charge for a seat or barstool, easily consumed by two drinks. (If you're not the thirsty type, there's a dedicated observation platform with its own ¥50 admission fee and a separate ground-floor entrance.) With glass in hand, make a panoramic tour of Cloud Nine's windows, which offer the expected bird's-eye views, as well as a unique look at the nearby Shanghai Hills World Financial Centre (www.shanghaihills.com). Scheduled for completion in early 2008, its 101 floors are projected to surpass the height of Taiwan's competitor, Taipei 101. On your way back down, take a peek into the Hyatt's atrium, a vertigo-inducing 115m from top to bottom. Back at ground level, take your pick from the Shanghai Ocean Aquarium (p.218), north-east of the Oriental Pearl Tower, or the Shanghai Natural Wild Insect Kingdom (p.220), to the west. The aquarium is first rate, with an interesting exhibit of Yangtze River specimens such as sturgeon and paddlefish. The insect collection offers entertainment of a lower order, involving nets and buckets and caged chinchillas. The massive, eight-storey building south of the Pearl is the Super Brand Mall (p.342). It's a popular place with both locals and expats, featuring a basement supermarket, a branch of Chaterhouse Booktrader (p.312), which specialises in English-language books, and a wide range of restaurants. For free wireless and a taste of Asian fusion, try

Element Fresh (p.381), where ocean-going freighters seem to pass the second-floor deck at precisely eye level.

On the eighth floor, Super Rink provides the rare opportunity for Shanghainese to practise their axels and lutzes. Admission is ¥50 for two hours, plus ¥10 for skate rental. This actually entitles you to about 90 minutes of skating, because the ice closes periodically for resurfacing. The rink offers group and private lessons, as well as skating-plus-meal packages with five different restaurants.

If you'd rather walk to your meal, the Riverfront Promenade adorns the east bank of the Huangpu for more than a kilometre. On sunny afternoons, an outdoor table at the Paulaner Brauhaus (p.396) supplies the perfect platform for pilsner. Later in the evening, the Pudong Shangri-La's Jade on 36 (p.391) delivers high style at correspondingly high prices. Both food and decor are memorably inventive. Months after your meal, you might still recall that first bite of lemon tart.

Puxi, Pudong

Literally 'west of the Huangpu,' Puxi was synonymous with Shanghai – until the 1990s, when Pudong (east of the river) emerged as the site of China's new financial centre. Except for Pudong and the water towns, every area and district mentioned in this section is located in Puxi.

Beyond Lujiazui

Three stops west on Metro Line 2, the Shanghai Science & Technology Museum (p.202) anchors another fleet of attractions. Its spacious halls contain an artificial rainforest, two Imax cinemas, a troupe of dancing robots, and more than you ever wanted to know about the human digestive system. If you go, don't miss the small exhibit devoted to Suzhou Creek's rehabilitation on the second floor.

On the basement level, adjacent to the Metro station, the Shanghai AP Xinyang Fashion and Gifts Market hosts many vendors displaced by the closing of Puxi's infamous Xiangyang Market in 2006. If you're looking for cold-weather gear, the selection of bibs, gloves and parkas is particularly good. Don't respond to the smiling touts though unless you want to be steered to your new friend's designated stall.

The open plaza between the museum and Century Park (p.211) is a favorite spot for kite flying, while the colourful buildings on the opposite side of the Zhangjiabang River are intended to house an art and design enclave: the Yifei Originality Street. Still in its early days, the area has yet to capture the imagination (or the commerce) on display at Puxi's Moganshan Lu and Taikang Lu.

Century Park itself, Shanghai's largest park, is spacious enough to repay repeated visits. Bikers, rollerbladers and birdwatchers all appreciate its tree-lined paths. A pleasant stroll beside the weedy ponds might introduce you to a flock of azure-winged magpies, along with an odd duck or two.

Leaving the park by its north-east gate will place you within walking distance of Thumb Plaza (199 Fangdian Lu), named for the shiny sculpture that appears to signal at least two thumbs up, perhaps more. Intermingled with an assortment of upscale boutiques are the American-style Moon River Diner (p.356), the French patisserie Paul (p.348) and three pizza parlours, along with Chinese, Japanese and Indian restaurants. On the west side of the plaza, the Shanghai Zendai Museum of Modern Art (p.200) offers exhibits of thought-provoking work by contemporary Chinese and international artists.

Oriental Pearl Tower

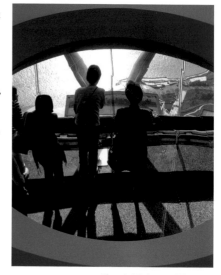

The Lowdown ◀

Unlike the luxury-brand malls on Nanjing Lu, Xujiahui is the place to buy the things you really need, from an office chair to a wireless router or a bar of Belgian chocolate.

The Good ◀

The museum in Xu Guangqi Memorial Park provides a historic reminder of the value of looking outside your own culture for knowledge.

The Bad ◀

Xujiahui's five-way intersection can become a nightmare of clogged traffic, even during off-peak hours.

The Must-Dos ◀

Go to the swarming hive of electronics shops in Metro City. Bargain hard if you want the best possible price on those noise-reduction headphones or that iPod sock.

Overview map, p.172 ◀

Xujiahui

Xujiahui arises from an intersection of five busy roads: Hongqiao Lu, Huashan Lu, Hengshan Lu, Zhaojiabang Lu and Caoxi Lu. This confluence has attracted a critical mass of shopping centres, which in turn have lured shoppers. Most of these are young and middle class, including many students from nearby Jiaotong University.

The glossiest mall resides in the lower levels of the Grand Gateway (1 Hongqiao Lu), twin 52 storey towers that resemble gigantic lipstick tubes. The Paradise Cinema City (6407 6622), on the sixth floor, often screens first-run English-language films.

Across the intersection to the south-east, Metro City (1111 Zhaojiabang Lu) is recognisable for its huge dome, set to be transformed into a video screen. Besides the ordinary complement of shops and restaurants, Metro City hosts Shanghai's largest agglomeration of electronic gadgets. The prices are higher than in Hong Kong or the US, but the selection of computers, mobile phones and MP3 players will bewilder most adults and even some teenagers.

Somewhat less popular than its two neighbours, the Orient Shopping Centre (8 Caoxi Bei Lu) conceals a basement market with a comprehensive selection of imported cookies, chocolates and liquor. All three malls can be reached by the underground passageway radiating from the Xujiahui Metro station.

South

Walk one block south on Caoxi Bei Lu to admire the red-brick Xujiahui Cathedral. Its graceful spires are a reminder of the area's long history as a Jesuit settlement. Mathematician and philosopher Xu Guangqi, author of *A Memorial in Defence of Western Learning,* was one of Chinese Catholicism's most interesting converts. In fact, the name Xujiahui refers to the 'Xu family gathering place'. You can visit Xu's tomb at the nearby Xu Guangqi Memorial Park (p.213). A small museum in the park's south-west corner documents his life and displays some interesting scientific artefacts.

Several blocks to the south, near the Shanghai Stadium, Swedish home-furnishings warehouse IKEA (126 Caoxi Lu; 5425 6060) is a favourite of Shanghai's young professionals and many newly relocated expats. Venturing even further south from Xujiahui, either by taxi or Metro, will reward you with two of Shanghai's more far-flung attractions: Longhua Temple (p.209) and the Longhua Martyr's Cemetery (p.206). At the temple, you can visit an octagonal pagoda built more than 1,000 years ago, then view a plump and jovial Buddha. At the cemetery, you can tread the same underground passage where Kuomintang captors led Communist prisoners to their deaths.

West

If you haven't the appetite for either of these experiences, return to Xujiahui. Heading west through the intersection, Ya Wang (20 Tianyaoqiao Lu; 6464 9169) serves a version of Beijing roast duck, carved at your table. Across Zhaojiabang Lu, the tall brick chimney marks the former site of the Great China Rubber Works, now part of Xujiahui Park (p.214). For a different perspective on Shanghai, walk the pedestrian bridge that extends nearly the length of the park, or play a few games of pickup basketball on the public courts. At 598 Hengshan Lu, O Spa (5466 0505) specialises in toxin-removing ionic foot baths.

Also within walking distance, at 1843 Huaihai Lu, is Soong Ching Ling's Residence in Shanghai (p.208). The widow of Sun Yatsen – and one of the three famous Soong sisters – is a beloved figure in China. An exhibition hall displays many of her possessions and documents, including a statement calling for 'a government to which all people may contribute their ideas' and a congratulatory letter, in English, addressed to 'generalissimo' Joseph Stalin. At 1555 Huaihai Zhong Lu, the Shanghai Library (p.261) manages a collection of 13 million volumes, including many rare English books on China.

The Lowdown ◀

*China's water towns
give visitors a glimpse
into an older world.*

The Good ◀

*Exploring the narrow
alleys and romantic
canals in the early
morning, before the
crowds arrive.*

The Bad ◀

*During peak season
and after lunch, the
towns become packed
with hordes of tourists
and hawkers.*

The Must-Dos ◀

*Visit Chongming's
nature reserve before the
island becomes home to
an eco city – and
500,000 more people.*

Overview map, p.172

Water Towns & Chongming Island

Shanghai's relative youth as an international port does not mean that the surrounding area lacked either inhabitants or commerce. The Yangtze is China's greatest river, and its delta region is the terminus of 6,000km of flowing water.

Recent construction projects have unearthed evidence of small settlements several thousands of years old, while many nearby villages maintain recorded histories of 1,000 years or more. These old towns were typically built along a network of narrow rivers and canals, crossed by arched bridges built of wood or stone. For centuries, the water provided a source of shrimp and fish, a means to transport goods and visit neighbours, a place to rinse vegetables and wash clothes.

To the gratitude of tourism promoters, this picturesque way of life persists within day-tripping distance of People's Square. Development has encircled the communities with parking lots and infiltrated them with souvenir shops, but much of the old charm remains. Even today, you might see a short clothesline hung with a damp mop, a skewered carp, and a suit of long underwear. Ride in a wooden boat propelled by a single oar, or dine on traditional recipes in a second-floor restaurant, its plaster walls rising upward from a canal, and you'll begin to understand the appeal. If you become addicted to water-town specialties such as barley candy and marinated pork knuckle, there are many relatively undiscovered villages, such as Nanxiang to the north and Fengjing to the south, along with other, more developed destinations farther west, including Tongli and Wuzhen. In the other direction, to the east of the mainland, is Chongming Island, currently a nature reserve an ear-marked to become a pioneering eco-city.

Qibao Ancient Town

Qibao means 'seven treasures'. Only 18km from People's Square, it's the most convenient introduction to Shanghai's outlying water towns. Cynics will snort that Qibao is not a real village, but a touristy re-creation of the market that flourished on this site nearly 1,000 years ago. It's a legitimate complaint, but Qibao's architecture is traditional, if newly built, and the lively crowds crossing the 700-year-old bridge are genuinely Chinese. Many of the snacks for sale – such as preserved pork and glutinous rice – are old favorites, and the wine shop uses a time-honoured method to distill *qibao daqu* (seven treasures liquor) from sorghum and bran. A full glass is not for the faint of heart, although it appears to have few lasting ill effects.

No admission fee is required to dine or shop. A ¥45 ticket permits entrance to eight exhibits, including the bell tower, cricket house, cotton textile mill and a gallery of miniature carvings. It's also possible to purchase separate tickets at each attraction.

Tongli & Luzhi

One of the prettiest and liveliest of the water towns, Tongli is worth at least one day by itself – although it can be combined with Luzhi. Before 1985 the old town was only accessible by boat. It is fed by a river which has been turned into 15 canals and is surrounded by five lakes. The many Ming and Qing buildings are adorned by intricate tile patterns on their roofs. Three old stone bridges – colloquially called Peace, Luck and Lasting Celebration – form a circuit, around which tourists and brides-to-be are borne in a wedding sedan chair accompanied by high-pitched reed instruments. At the canal junction in the centre, a fisherman demonstrates cormorant catching for tourists from his boat. A gondola tour costs ¥60 per boat. Other highlights include the pretty Tuisi (Retreat and Reflection) Garden (¥40) and the sumptuous Chen family residence (¥5). The most incongruous of attractions is the Chinese Sex Culture Museum (¥20), which moved to a former primary school in Tongli from Shanghai in early 2004, although a small branch has reopened back in town (see p.202). Entry to Tongli is ¥80. Luzhi, 25km east of Suzhou, has 41 bridges and is also surrounded by five lakes. A bus from Tongli costs about ¥12. Luizhi's Buddhist Baoshen Temple was originally built in 503AD but rebuilt in the Song Dynasty after being destroyed during the Tang Dynasty. It's well worth getting to Tongli, and indeed any of the other water towns, early enough in order to appreciate them without the crowds who flock there by mid-morning. Locals wash clothes and pots and pans, and even prepare food on the steps by the canals. Early-morning markets are also worth visiting, if you have a strong stomach. Be prepared to see sights including pigs' heads, scooped-out turtles and jumping frogs.

Wuzhen

Open to visitors since 2001, Wuzhen appears less artificial than some of the other water towns because of the sympathetic restoration it has undergone instead of wholesale rebuilding and renovation. The town lies on the Grand Canal in the north-east of Zhejiang province, about 140km from Shanghai and 90 minutes by road. Entry is ¥100, or ¥145 including return bus travel from Shanghai. A private car and guide costs ¥1,500. Besides its many old waterside houses, Wuzhen's main attractions include the Qing-era former residence of celebrated writer Mao Dun, the Xiu Zhen Guan Taoist Temple, dating back to the Northern Song Dynasty, and a pair of old bridges – Tongji and Renji – each of which can be viewed through the other. Fanglu Pavilion is one of Wuzhen's most noted teahouses.

Xitang

About a two-hour drive west of Shanghai, the well-preserved town of Xitang survived relatively unscathed until its discovery by Tom Cruise and the producers of *Mission Impossible: III*. Since the publicity generated by the filming in 2005, Xitang's impossibly narrow alleys (including Shipi Lane, which is just a metre wide at its widest point), Ming Dynasty homes and black slate-tile roofs have witnessed such indignities as the Miss Tourism International Bikini Contest. Nevertheless, its covered walkways, elaborate button museum, and tasty local dishes – try the river shrimp subtly flavoured with tea – keep it a favoured destination among many locals and a few expats. Xitang has also long been associated with yellow rice wine and China's largest manufacturer, Zhejiang Jiashan Rice Wine Company (www.jshjgf.com), is located in the old town. Admission is ¥60, which includes entrance to a dozen historic sites.

Typical water town bridge

Zhouzhuang

Unesco World Heritage Site Zhouzhuang has declared itself the nation's number-one water town – and has the tour buses to prove it. As soon as you set foot on the pavement, rickshaw drivers and map vendors will vie for your attention. And because it's a bit of a walk from the parking lot to the old town's gate, you might want both. Hucksterism aside, the cobblestone lanes and arched bridges invoke dreamy images of the past, and you'll see many traditional artisans at work, including embroiderers, woodcarvers and blacksmiths. The tourist museums, including a hall of fishing tools, are generically bland. You'll find it much more interesting to walk down the side alleys, away from the endless rows of souvenir shops, where you might spot a quartet of old women mending real fishing nets. Admission is ¥100, which includes 16 exhibits. The best way to see the old buildings lining the waterways is on a gondola trip, costing ¥80 per boat, which take up to eight people. Among sites are the Zhang (Ming) and Shen (Qing) family houses, Chengxu Taoist Temple and Qanfu Temple.

Zhujiajiao

Zhujiajiao is Shanghai's nearest authentic water town – only 30km west on the A5 expressway. This well-preserved little town (admission ¥60) is often used as a setting for films and has a number of stone bridges crossing streams, and canals lined with old courtyard houses. Package tours typically visit more distant Zhouzhuang in the morning, then stop here in the afternoon, so plan accordingly. The town's slender passageways can go from peaceful to congested in a matter of minutes. The Shanghai Ancient Culture Exhibition Hall contains some interesting artefacts from the area's Neolithic past, while you might hear monks chanting and praying inside the small Buddhist temple. Xizhou Woodcarving (5923 0831) creates unusually intricate reliefs, some of them strikingly painted. The town's most popular attraction is the monumental Fangsheng Qiao Bridge, where tourists gather to toss goldfish into the water (according to some Buddhist sects, releasing fish is thought to confer merit). Admission to the town is ¥10; each museum or temple requires an additional fee.

Chongming Island

Chongming Island, just north of Shanghai, is the world's largest sandbar. Formed by the deposit of millions of years of Yangtze River silt, its shoreline is constantly evolving. Even though the recently completed Three Gorges Dam has blocked the downstream progress of much of the river's sediment, Chongming's eastern end continues to lengthen by about 150m per year.

With less than 700,000 people scattered over more than 1,000 square kilometres, Chongming has room to roam. The local government has been busy promoting the island's ecological attributes, hoping that bicyclists and birdwatchers will contribute to its development as a tourist destination for Shanghai's city dwellers, starved for nature. Dongping National Forest Park (5933 8028) offers camping, rock climbing, and grass skiing. Dongtan Nature Reserve (p.219), on the island's eastern edge, provides a crucial waypoint and wintering ground for migratory waterbirds.

A few kilometres from the nature reserve, construction has begun on the world's first eco-city. The green community of Dongtan will permit only non-polluting vehicles, recycle all of its wastewater, and generate all of its own power through wind, solar and the burning of rubbish. Planners expect the city's population to reach 500,000 by 2050. Access is currently by ferry from Shidongkou in Baoshan district, which can involve waits of an hour or more in addition to the hour-long passage. The Changjiang tunnel and bridge project, scheduled for completion in 2010, aims to cut the travel time from Shanghai to 40 minutes. Call the Chongming Island tourist information centre on 6969 5888 for the latest developments.

Museums, Heritage & Culture

Shanghai may not quite have the cultural prominence of Beijing, but it still houses a surprising wealth of attractions. Historic houses document the growth of both the city and the nation, modern museums provide educational distractions, and contemporary art galleries define China's metamorphosis into a 21st century country. Individually, the following highlights are all worthy of a visit; collectively they act as a reflection of the past, present and future of a city that is constantly changing.

Art Galleries

Other options **Art** p.309, **Museums** p.201

Traditionally, Beijing is where artists go to create and Shanghai is where they go to sell. This makes sense, considering that the huge number of highly paid foreigners in Shanghai make up 80% of the buyers of Chinese contemporary art. It means, however, that many of Shanghai's galleries tend to be largely market-dominated with exhibitions often focussing on established names. Slowly, though, a new breed of (nominally) not-for-profit galleries are emerging, whose aim it is to support younger artists. Establishments such as Island6 and BizArt are particularly well known for putting on shows that venture out of the commercial comfort zones. If you are new to Chinese contemporary art, then a good starting point would be ShanghART. From there, spend an afternoon wandering around the rest of Moganshan Lu, a former industrial park north of the city centre near Suzhou Creek, that since the late 1990s has become the hub of Shanghai's underground art community. Other funky areas are cropping up around the city too. Especially worth a visit are the small boutiques, art-inspired shops, and little artsy bars of Lane 210, Taikang Lu in Luwan. And for a more conventional approach to art viewing, try one of the four new art museums that have been built in Shanghai since 2002. An older one, the Shanghai Art Museum, plays host to the Shanghai Biennale (see Annual Events, p.56). In contrast to the museums, entrance to Shanghai's art galleries is generally free.

Lane 37,
8 Fuxing Xi Lu,
French Concession
Xuhui
复兴西路37弄8号，
法租界
徐汇
🚇 *Changshu Lu*
Map p.435 E2 ❶

Art Scene China 艺术景画廊

6437 0631 | www.artscenechina.com
Begun purely as a website in 1997, Art Scene China provided an online gallery in which contemporary Chinese artists could show their work to a larger public. Its success led to the establishment of a gallery in Hong Kong followed by two in Shanghai. The first is housed in a colonial-style 1930s villa in the French Concession and specialises in small to medium-sized contemporary Chinese artworks that are relatively conservative in content, making them suitable buys for the home. Don't expect to pick up anything cheap and cheerful here though, as the gallery represents established artists who sell for prices at the higher end of the spectrum. The gallery regularly exhibits different works by the 25 or so artists that it represents, including established names such as Qing Qing, Morgan and Peng Wei. It's open from Tuesday to Sunday,10:30 until 18:30. The other gallery is at 50 Moganshan Lu (see below).

Floor 2, Building 4,
50 Moganshan Lu
Putuo
莫干山路50号
普陀
🚇 *Shanghai Railway*
Station
Map p.429 F1 ❷

Art Scene Warehouse 艺术景仓库

6277 4940 | www.artscenewarehouse.com
Needing more space to exhibit larger works, Art Scene China took over a warehouse space in the Moganshan Lu area of Suzhou Creek in 2003 and aptly named it Art Scene Warehouse. As well as regularly exhibiting avant garde works by both Chinese and international artists, the gallery hosts the Dragonair Emerging Chinese Artist Awards every January, which aims to find the best in up-and-coming talent from across China. Recent winners include Chen Jiao and Zhang Jie. You can visit it from Tuesday to Sunday; it's open from 10:30 until 18:30.

Floor 4, Building 7,
50 Moganshan Lu
Putuo
莫干山路50号
普陀
🚇 **Shanghai Railway**
Station
Map p.429 F1 3

BizArt 比翼艺术中心

6277 5358 | www.biz-art.com

With a mission to support young local and international talent, BizArt is essentially a not-for-profit art centre that survives on income made from its art residency programmes and arty event organising. Taking up the fourth floor of Building 7 at 50 Moganshan Lu, the gallery is divided into an exhibition space and a studio area for artists in residence, from both China and abroad. These residency programmes, usually lasting about two months, welcome artists working in all media, from painting to video art to dance performances. Recently the centre has decided to focus more on the process of making art than the final product itself, and has begun to host workshops, performances and symposiums that are open to the public. You can enjoy what it has to offer from Monday to Saturday, 11:00 until 18:00.

Floor 3,
713 Dongdaming Lu
Hongkou
东大名路713号
虹口
🚇 **Linping Lu**
Map p.431 F1 4

DDM Warehouse 东大名创库

3501 3212 | www.ddmwarehouse.org

Established in 2000, DDM Warehouse occupies a converted space filled with dramatic pillars and staircases. Its urban style is just as suited to hosting art exhibitions as underground raves and the gallery often transforms itself into a live music venue. It hosts the annual Rock for Charity gig every May, at which local bands play to raise money for Shanghai Sunrise, a charity for the education of underprivileged kids. The music is accompanied by video art, a platform particularly supported by the gallery, as well as other new artistic media such as installation and performance. Chosen to collaborate with 2007's prestigious Venice Biennale, the gallery is raising its profile, and has begun to hold exhibitions by some very well-established artists. These include Beijing's Zhang Dali, whose works are now being collected by Charles Saatchi among others. Open Tuesday to Sunday from 11:00 until 19:00, with late openings for special events.

27 Duolun Lu
Hongkou
多伦路27号
虹口
🚇 **Dong Baoxing Lu**
Map p.422 B4 5

Duolun Museum of Modern Art 上海多伦现代美术馆

6587 2530 | www.duolunart.com

The Hongkou district Cultural Bureau built this rather ugly, seven-storey cube-shaped museum in 2003, making it the first publicly funded, state-owned contemporary art museum in China. It sits in Duolun Lu, an interesting little street with a rich cultural history, which was once home to writers such as Lu Xun (credited with having pioneered modern Chinese vernacular literature). Under the early guidance of respected curator Bilijana Ciric, the museum received rave reviews for its exciting exhibitions (such as the Jean-Michel Basquiat retrospective in 2006). However, a transfer of power to the state-owned Changyuan Group in 2004 saw the beginning of problems including cuts in funding and the closure of exhibitions due to censorship. It's still too early to predict the future of Duolun, but early reports see a shift towards more conservative, but still well-organised, exhibitions. Worth keeping an eye on. Admission costs ¥10 for adults, and it is open every day (except Monday) from 10:00 until 18:00.

Catch modern art in Shanghai

197

Floor 5, Building 6,
50 Moganshan Lu
Putuo
莫干山路50号
普陀
🚇 Shanghai Railway
Station
Map p.429 F1 6

Eastlink Gallery 东廊艺术

6276 9932 | *www.eastlinkgallery.cn*

As the first gallery to take up residence in the old factory district of Moganshan Lu, the Chinese-owned Eastlink has always been a pioneer. In 2000, it staged a controversial protest exhibition against the Shanghai Biennale. The organisation of the Biennale had been dominated by the Shanghai government, which had angered artists who felt that the resulting show had been so censored that it failed to paint a true picture of the Chinese contemporary art scene. Eastlink has always pushed the boundaries of censorship in a quest to find and support emerging and established Chinese artists. Many of the major players in the Chinese contemporary art scene, such as the Gao Brothers and Ji Dachun, got their first representation at Eastlink. The venue's 'white cube' exhibition space is a great platform for all mediums of art, ranging from painting to installations. Open daily from 10:00 to 18:00.

Floor 2, Building 6,
120 Moganshan Lu
Putuo
莫干山路120号
普陀
🚇 Shanghai Railway
Station
Map p.429 F1 7

Island6 六岛艺术空间

www.island6.org

Situated in a red brick, four-storey renovated flour warehouse with its own little sculpture garden, the Island6 art centre stands out from the crowd of other warehouse galleries on Moganshan Lu. Completely not for profit, and sadly sometimes struggling, it hires only voluntary staff under the guidance of French director and co-founder Thomas Charveriat, and is devoted to supporting young and emerging artists who produce innovative works. Island6 runs an active artist-in-residency programme and represents a large number of Chinese and foreign talents, including, in 2007, New York University students in an exciting exhibition called *Laugh Now, Cry Later*. Open 10:00-18:00 daily, or by appointment.

Building 2,
97 Moganshan Lu
Putuo
莫干山路97号2号楼
普陀
🚇 Shanghai Railway
Station
Map p.429 F1 8

m97 Gallery

6266 1597 | *www.m97gallery.com*

Canadian photographer Steven Harris started m97 Gallery in early 2007, with a desire to create the best and largest space in Shanghai dedicated solely to photography. Although not huge, it is well laid out and bright. Exhibitions in the main hall change every four to six weeks, while those in the smaller back rooms show for a little longer. A major aim of m97 is to promote photography as a medium worthy of consideration as 'fine art'. It is already moving some way towards this goal by hosting excellent early exhibitions by well-known British artist Nadav Kandar and German artist Michael Wolf. Open Tuesday to Sunday, 10:30 until 18:30.

231 Nanjing Xi Lu
Huangpu
南京西路231号
黄埔
🚇 People's Square
Map p.430 C3 9

Museum of Contemporary Art Shanghai 上海当代艺术馆

6327 9900 | *www.mocashanghai.org*

Housed in what was originally the greenhouse of People's Park, this museum became the first independently run, not-for-profit contemporary art institution in Shanghai in 2005. Intended as a platform for both Chinese and international contemporary art, the museum has no permanent collection and instead has regularly changing temporary exhibitions. Leaving the challenging and overly provocative shows to the more avant-garde of Shanghai's galleries, the Museum of Contemporary Art puts on aesthetically pleasing and often flashy exhibitions to draw in both the sponsors and the crowds, such as events enabling visitors to download contemporary art on to mobile phones. There are, however, more substantial displays too. The top floor's MOCA Caffeé serves half-decent Italian food on an attractive terrace overlooking the park. Entrance for adults costs ¥20. The museum is open daily from 10:00 until 18:00, and stays open until 22:00 on Wednesdays.

Shanghai Art Museum 上海美术馆

325 Nanjing Xi Lu
Huangpu
南京西路325号
黄埔
🚇 *People's Square*
Map p.430 C3 **10**

6327 4030 | *www.cnarts.net/shanghaiart*

The Shanghai Art Museum has a large permanent collection of fine traditional and modern art ranging from ink-wash calligraphy to kitsch late 1990s pop art. Works are exhibited in 15 exhibition halls over five floors in a lovingly restored building that was owned in the 30s by the British Racing Club. The connection to the British Isles seems, however, to stop there: the lack of an English language website or explanation of the artworks can prove frustrating. Every two years the museum takes its place on the international art stage when it hosts the Shanghai Biennale and invites contemporary artists from all over the world to participate in a month-long festival (see p.56). For a bite to eat and a lovely view of the park, head up to Kathleen's 5 (6327 2221), a glass-encased, fine dining restaurant serving modern American cuisine. General admission to the museum is ¥20, and it is open daily from 09:00 until 17:00.

Shanghai Gallery of Art 沪申画廊

3 Zhongshan
Dong Yi Lu
Huangpu
外滩三号,
中山东一路3号3楼
黄埔
🚇 *Nanjing Dong Lu*
Map p.431 E3 **11**

6321 5757 | *www.shanghaigalleryofart.com*

Situated on the third floor of the glamorous Three on the Bund, the impressive Shanghai Gallery of Art is immaculately laid out with a dramatic atrium suited to the large-scale art installations it often exhibits. The gallery's aim is to showcase works by well-established Chinese contemporary artists who have already gained international recognition, and acts both as their agent and a dealer. Perhaps not as cutting-edge as some of the grittier galleries in Moganshan Lu, it nevertheless puts on challenging shows. In April 2007, Beijing artist Gu Dexin transformed the main hall into a 45 degree slope covered in concrete slabs and manhole covers to resemble a city pavement, and in a trough under the atrium he placed thousands of life-sized artificial fruit flies, a sweeter-smelling alternative to the piles of real rotting fruit that he installed back in 2005. Open 11:00-23:00 daily.

Shanghai Sculpture Space 上海城市雕塑艺术中心

570 Huaihai Xi Lu
Xuhui
淮海西路570号
徐汇
🚇 *Hongqiao Lu*
Map p.434 C4 **12**

6280 5629 | *www.sss570.com*

More a museum than a gallery, Shanghai Sculpture Space is seriously impressive in both its size and its shows. A converted steel factory surrounded by residential complexes, it has two huge exhibition halls plus a large outdoor space. Opened with the help of government funding, it inevitably houses the statues of many past leaders, but also makes space for younger, more innovative artists. Spring 2007 saw a highly acclaimed exhibition entitled *Communication Between Sculptures and the City*, which showcased 120 emerging and established artists, and which was the first exhibition celebrating Shanghai's World Expo 2010. Occasionally it also hosts special one-off exhibitions of famous foreign sculptors such as the August Rodin show in 2006, for which tickets cost a mere ¥20. Open 10:00-16:00 daily, except for Mondays.

ShanghART Gallery & H-Space 香格纳画廊

Buildings 16 & 18,
50 Moganshan Lu
Putuo
莫干山路50号
普陀
🚇 *Shanghai Railway*
Station
Map p.429 F1 **13**

6359 3923 | *www.shanghartgallery.com*

The first serious contemporary Chinese art gallery in Shanghai and arguably the finest, ShanghART was started in 1996 by Swiss gallerist Lorenz Helbling. The enormous size of his permanent collection of Chinese contemporary art is the biggest of any gallery in Shanghai. It includes iconic works from over 30 artists including Zhao Bandi's tongue-in-cheek panda photographs and Zeng Fanzhi's disturbing Mask Series oil paintings, which now fetch as much as $1.5 million at auction. Helbling's incredible collection occupies two warehouse spaces in Moganshan Lu: the first is the ShanghART Gallery in building 16 which plays host to paintings and small exhibitions; the second, H-Space at number 18, exhibits installations and large-scale projects in its larger cubical space. In 2007, ShanghART was the first gallery in China to take part in the prestigious Art Basel, where it had its own booth showing works by Xu Zhen and Huang Hui as part of a project called Focus Shanghai. The ShanghART Gallery is open daily, from 10:00 to 19:00, and H-Space is open 13:00-18:00 every day except Monday.

Stir Art Gallery 搞艺术画廊

172 Jinxian Lu, French Concession
Luwan
进贤路172号，
法租界
卢湾
🚇 Shanxi Nan Lu
Map p.4430 A4 **14**

5157 5985 | www.stir-art.com

A relatively small but exciting newcomer to Shanghai's art scene, Stir Art Gallery sits in Jinxian Lu, a funky little street housing artsy cafes and boutiques in the middle of the French Concession. The gallery aims to exhibit young, up-and-coming local and foreign artists who experiment with different types of media. Recent shows include Nicky Broekhuysen's 'Urban Crust' series of Shanghai-inspired photographs and Chris Rekrutiak's 'I Love Dream & Romance' series of quirky paper-cuts. And after all of this cultural exertion, you can take a break at the classy little Citizen Café (6258 1620) just down the road at 222. Open daily from 10:30 until 21:30.

Studio Rouge 红寨

17 Fuzhou Lu
Huangpu
福州路17号
黄埔
🚇 Nanjing Dong Lu
Map p.431 E3 **15**

6323 0833 | studiorougeshanghai@yahoo.com

Proving that good things can come in small packages, Studio Rouge's minimalist space just off the Bund is a good starting point for anyone wanting to learn more about Chinese contemporary art. Director George Mitchell is both knowledgeable and well connected, having initially set up the gallery as an offshoot of Beijing's godfather of contemporary art spaces, The Redgate Gallery. In 2006, needing more space, the gallery took up a second venue in Moganshan Lu called Studio Rouge M50 (138 0174 1782) which continues to put on interesting exhibitions by well-established and commercially friendly artists, including Xue Song, Wang Yuping and Han Qing. Both venues are open daily from 10:30 until 18:30.

Unique Hill Studio 奇岗草堂

Tian Long Apartments, 907 Tianyaoqiao Lu
Xuhui
天龙公寓，
天钥桥路907号301室
徐汇
🚇 Shanghai Stadium
Map p.443 F1 **16**

5410 4815

If you are craving a little bit of old, decadent Shanghai, then check out the hundreds of 1920s and 30s advertising posters at the Unique Hill Studio. Wonderfully kitsch pictures of Shanghai's risque, *qipao*-wearing, cigarette-smoking ladies of the decadent heyday hang alongside taxi adverts from the colonial age. Collectors will be enthralled, and the casual visitor should find it intriguing. Passionate owner Jiang Qigang will understandably not sell the originals, but there are some decently priced replicas on offer.

Zendai Museum of Modern Art 上海证大现代艺术馆

28 Zendai Thumb Plaza, 199 Fangdian Lu
Pudong
大拇指广场，
芳甸路199弄28号
浦东
🚇 Century Park
Map p.440 A2 **17**

5033 9801 | www.zendaiart.com

Zendai Museum of Modern Art (MoMA) somehow manages to break away from the commercial restraints often plaguing Shanghai's other art museums and regularly puts on exciting contemporary exhibitions. The calendar often includes edgy shows, for example the 2005 inaugural exhibition Electroscape, which tried to marry the concepts of 'electronic' and 'landscape', and 2006's Strange Attractors that explored connections between art and science. What really helps Zendai stand out from the crowd is the attention it places on the academic side of art: only half of its 3,000 square metres is dedicated to exhibitions, with the rest given over to research facilities and academic exchanges. Entry costs ¥20. Open Tuesday to Sunday from 10:00 until 18:00.

Museums

Other options **Art Galleries** p.196, **Heritage Sites** p.204, **Religious Sites** p.208

Shanghai has a wealth of private and state-owned museums dedicated to culture, art, history and science. Times have certainly changed since the Cultural Revolution, which saw countless historical and cultural artefacts destroyed. The government now actively supports the preservation of its rich heritage by funding new museums and renovating some of those already in existence. The enormous Science & Technology Museum in Pudong and the brilliant Shanghai Museum in People's Square have both received huge amounts of government funding, the latter becoming a world-renowned institution as a result. Part of the motivation behind this generous support is commercial, especially with regards to the art museums (see Art Galleries, p.196); following the hyperinflation of the Chinese contemporary art market in recent years, and the huge attention it has gained on the world stage, the government has established four new art venues since 2002. Although a welcome addition to the city's cultural landscape, these museums are often limited to putting on exhibitions that attract revenue-generating sponsorship deals.

The future is promising though. By the World Expo 2010, the Shanghai Municipal Government hopes that at least 150 private and state-run museums will be in operation, all geared towards attracting the millions of tourists expected to descend on the city. Most museums charge entry ranging from ¥5 for older establishments such as the Shanghai Natural History Museum to ¥60 for modern ones such as the Shanghai Science & Technology Museum.

61 Songyuan Lu
Changning
宋园路61号
长宁
🚇 *Hongqiao Lu*
Map p.434 A4 18

Discovery Children's Museum 上海互动儿童探索馆

135 0180 3125 | *www.shanghaidiscovery.org*
Reopened in 2007 after intensive renovations, the Shanghai Discovery Children's Museum is a fantastic hands-on, interactive play area for kids up to the age of seven and their families. Children can play in different sections of the museum, including the planetarium, the theatre, the discovery hall and the cute miniature markets and doctors' surgeries. All of these contain interactive games, masterfully designed to subconsciously teach children the basic skills of maths and science while they have lots of fun. Bilingual signs also help language learning. A few hours of fun, well worth the ¥20 entrance price for both children and adults. Open Tuesday to Sunday from 08:30 until 16:00.

260 Yan'an Dong Lu
Huangpu
延安东路260号
黄埔
🚇 *Nanjing Xi Lu*
Map p.431 E3 19

Museum of Natural History 上海自然博物馆

6321 3548
There is no denying the beauty of the former Cotton Exchange building that now houses the Museum of Natural History, but one step inside will show you an interior as dusty and musty as the specimens it exhibits. This old-fashioned quaintness will appeal to some adults, but children may be easily bored given the lack of flashy, interactive displays now found at most of Shanghai's museums. That said, little dinosaur fans will not be disappointed by the first floor's collection of skeletons, including a complete specimen of a 140-million-year-old dinosaur displayed in the main atrium. On the third and fourth floors you will find a plethora of invertebrates, birds, amphibians and mammals, many of which are stuffed and have been known to give very small children a fright. Of particular interest are the Ming Dynasty mummies excavated from local sites in Shanghai. Pay ¥5 for a ticket and expect to spend about an hour there, most of which may be spent viewing the lovely mosaic floors and stained glass windows. The museum opens every day except Monday, from 09:00 until 17:00 (last entrance at 15:30).

Floors 3-5,
518 Ruijin Nan Lu
Luwan
瑞金南路518号
卢湾
🚇 *Damuqiao Lu*
Map p.436 B3 20

Museum of Public Security 上海公安博物馆

6472 0256 | www.policemuseum.com.cn

Novels and films about 1930s Shanghai are often filled with references to its former reputation as the 'whore of the Orient', simmering with gangsters, opium dealers and all types of unsavoury sorts – and this museum documents how the powers that be tackled such criminals. It contains several thousand artefacts and documents describing the rise of the Shanghai police force following its formation in 1854, with particularly interesting exhibits covering the post-Opium War period and the Cultural Revolution. Proving that spy gadgets do exist outside James Bond movies, there are exhibits showing guns disguised as pens, guns hidden in violin cases and gadgets formerly used by captured spies or government bodyguards. Also explained are the modern methods of capturing criminals, from DNA testing to hi-tech computer surveillance. Covering three floors in a fittingly communist-style concrete building, the museum is certainly worth around an hour or two of your time and ¥8 of your money. Open daily from 09:00 until 16:30.

2000 Shiji Dadao
Pudong
世纪大道2000号
浦东
🚇 *Shanghai Science*
& Technology
Museum
Map p.439 E1 21

Science & Technology Museum 上海科技馆

6854 2000 | www.sstm.org.cn

Give yourself (and definitely your kids if you have them) at least a whole afternoon to explore the vast Science & Technology Museum near Century Park in Pudong. You can play on the hundreds of games in the six newly added interactive exhibition halls – including the hugely popular World of Robots, where visitors can test their skills against robot chess masters or indulge in a little duet karaoke with the metal divas. Going on a weekday may help you avoid the huge queues for other fun activities such as the Iwerks 4D movie theatre. Here, in addition to 3D technology, members of the audience are treated to wind and rain simulators. For those interested in 'what's really out there', it may be worth paying an extra ¥40 (on top of the original ¥60 entrance fee) to watch a film in the museum's Space Theatre. But be aware that, as yet, none of the films have subtitles in English. Open Tuesday to Sunday from 09:00 until 17:00.

Bund
Sightseeing Tunnel,
2789 Binjiang Dadao
Pudong
外滩观光隧道,
滨江大道2789号
浦东
🚇 *Lujiazui*
Map p.431 F2 22

Sex Culture Museum 性文化博物馆

5888 6000 | www.chinasexmuseum.com

Liu Dalin, former professor of sociology at Shanghai University and China's leading expert in sexology, has amassed over 4,000 sex-themed artefacts, many of which are displayed in his two museums. The larger of the two is in Tongli, Jiangsu province (p.192), but recently a second branch was reopened in Shanghai after the 1999 original on Nanjing Lu was closed due to lack of public support. Now it occupies a high-profile space at the Pudong end of the Bund Sightseeing Tunnel. People come to view the small exhibitions covering many areas of China's sexual history, including ancient marriage customs and prostitution. The aim of the museum is not to amuse, but to educate. Although information on current sexual practices and issues such as Aids is scarce, the first museum in China devoted to sex is certainly worth a visit, and a ticket price of ¥20. Open daily from 08:00 until 22:00.

Oriental TV Tower,
1 Shiji Dadao
Pudong
东方明珠电视塔,
世纪大道1号
浦东
🚇 *Lujiazui*
Map p.431 F2 23

Shanghai History Museum 上海市历史博物馆

5879 1888

Underneath the futuristic skyline of Pudong lies a world time forgot, in the form of the excellent little Shanghai History Museum in the basement of the Oriental Pearl Tower. The vivid visual displays, including small-scale models of 19th century shops and houses, are brought to life by a number of full-sized wax mannequins. There are some remarkable artefacts on show, including an early bus and a sedan chair in the transport section, plus an original bronze lion that used to guard the HSBC Bank on the Bund.

This holistic take on Shanghai's recent history is truly engrossing and helped by the well-annotated displays in Chinese and English. Give yourselves about an hour at the museum and then shock yourselves back into reality by paying ¥50 for a ticket to take you up to the Oriental Pearl Tower's 263m high viewing platform. Open daily from 09:00 until 21:00, the museum is well worth the ¥35 entrance ticket.

201 Renmin Dadao
Huangpu
人民大道201号
黄埔
🚇 *People's Square*
Map p.430 C3 24

Shanghai Museum 上海博物馆

6372 3500 | *www.shanghaimuseum.net*

Originally established in 1952, the Shanghai Museum was reopened to much acclaim in 1996, following an estimated $700 million reconstruction. Now it stands proudly in the centre of People's Square in a striking building, its round roof and square base symbolising the traditional Chinese philosophical belief of a square earth sitting beneath a round sky. Each beautifully laid-out floor can take up to two hours to explore. Highlights include the compelling Minority Nationalities Art Gallery on the fourth floor, which displays art, jewellery, dress and handicrafts from China's 56 different ethnic minorities, and the Ming & Qing Furniture Gallery where mock-up houses let you imagine what it was like to live in a traditional Chinese home. To assist you around this wealth of information, it is worth getting an audio guide that comes in eight languages for ¥40 (on top of the ¥20 entrance charge). The museum is open daily from 09:00 until 17:00.

250 Suzhou Bei Lu
Hongkou
北苏州路250号
虹口
🚇 *Nanjing Dong Lu*
Map p.431 D2 25

Shanghai Postal Museum 上海邮政博物馆

6362 9898

Despite opening in January 2006, the Shanghai Postal Museum is sadly still much overlooked – but it is an interesting place to visit. Friendly staff guide you around the beautiful 1931 District Post Office building, which is split into well-designed zones covering the origins of the postal system in China. Some interesting displays show ancient tortoise shells inscribed with pictures of men beating drums – the method of relaying messages in ancient times. The atrium of the restored old building is breathtaking but the biggest delight comes in venturing up to the charming rooftop garden which, as well as housing an old clock tower, grants visitors some of the best views of the city. Entry was originally free of charge, but there is talk of a ¥10 charge being introduced. Open on Wednesdays, Thursdays, Saturdays and Sundays from 09:00 until 16:00.

100 Renmin Dadao
Huangpu
人民大道100号
黄埔
🚇 *People's Square*
Map p.430 C3 26

Shanghai Urban Planning Exhibition Centre
上海城市规划展示馆

6318 4477 | *www.supec.org*

Despite its lacklustre name, the Shanghai Urban Planning Exhibition Centre is surprisingly compelling and strangely addictive. For a ¥40 fee, you can enter a world of past, present and future Shanghai, documented over five floors in exhibits ranging from old photographs to videos, models and interactive displays. If your time is limited then go directly to the museum's key attraction: the world's largest model of urban planning. Covering over 100 square metres at a scale of 1:2000, this incredible model shows what Shanghai will look like in the year 2020 – and gives you a sense of the sheer size of the metropolis as you stand at its very heart. Open daily from 09:00 until 16:00.

Urban Planning Exhibition Centre

203

25, Lane 181,
Taicang Lu, Xintiandi
Luwan
太仓路181弄新天地
广场北里25号
卢湾
📍 *Huangpi Nan Lu*
Map p.430 C4 27

Shikumen Open House Museum
石库门博物馆
3307 0337 | www.xintiandi.com
Shikumen, or 'stone gate' houses, were the traditional forms of middle-class residential architecture in 1920s and 30s Shanghai. Arranged in tightly packed, south-facing terraces, each house had five rooms upstairs and five downstairs. Sadly, few have survived in construction-crazy Shanghai, but to see a meticulously restored version, visit this museum in Xintiandi, which is filled with original photos, beds, cutlery and toys, all with explanations in Chinese and English. The entrance fee is ¥20, and the museum is open daily from 10:30 until 22:30 (11:00 until 23:00 on Saturdays).

Heritage Sites
Other options **Art Galleries** p.196, **Museums** p.201, **Historic Houses** p.206

Shanghai can retrace its history as a trading port for more than 700 years. However, not much remains of the dynastic past. The Dajing Pavilion, in the Old City area, represents the sole vestige of the city's 16th-century defences against marauding pirates. The most distinguished resident of that period, Xu Guangqi, is memorialised by a small park (p.213) hidden behind the Xujiahui Cathedral. Longhua Temple, in the city's south-west, is another 1,000 years older, but the original foundations have endured repeated reconstructions.
Shanghai's more recent cultural heritage breaks down into two broad categories: colonial and communist. Although rampant development threatens many of these historic sites, some have been transformed into self-contained tourist attractions, and several others are currently undergoing much needed renovation.

269 Dajing Lu
Huangpu
大境路269号
黄埔
📍 *Nanjing Dong Lu*
Map p.431 D4 28

Dajing Pavilion 大境阁
6326 6171
The Dajing Pavilion preserves the only remnant of Shanghai's Old City wall. It's part of the western gate, built in 1553, a tower where archers could take aim at the sort of foreign invaders who didn't come armed with credit cards. The rest of the wall was demolished in 1912 because the Shanghai government believed it had become 'an obstacle in the city's economic development and communication'. On the second floor, a stone bears an inscription that translates as 'His majesty's good faith lasts eternally.' The ground floor houses a small historical exhibit, including a scale model of the old city, with signs in Chinese only. Admission is ¥5.

374 Huangpi Nan Lu
Luwan
黄陂南路374号
卢湾
📍 *Huangpi Nan Lu*
Map p.436 C1 29

The First National Congress of the Chinese Communist Party
中国共产党第一次全国代表大会会址
5383 2171 | www.shcrm.com
Call it irony or call it fate, but the geographical convergence of fashionable Xintiandi and the first meeting place of China's Communist Party seems like more than mere coincidence. Located just around the corner from numerous temples to consumerism, this *shikumen* shrine to the Party's creation presents its rise to power as the 'inevitable outcome' of history. The congress began on July 23, 1921, when 13 representatives from secret communist, socialist and marxist societies gathered for their first meeting. Seven of these eventually quit or were expelled; a few others died young. One of the survivors, of course, was Mao Zedong. The artefacts on display include the swords and pistols of revolutionary heroes, a Concession-era boundary marker, and several examples of colonial currency, including a note issued by the Sino-Belgian Bank for '10 Mexican dollars.' Admission is ¥3.

Great things can come in small packages…

Perfectly proportioned to fit in your pocket, these marvellous mini guidebooks make sure you don't just get the holiday you paid for, but rather the one that you dreamed of.

Explorer Mini Visitors' Guides
Maximising your holiday, minimising your hand luggage

180 Longhua Xi Lu
Xuhui
龙华西路180号
徐汇
🚇 *Longcao Lu*
Map p.443 F1 30

Longhua Revolutionary Martyrs' Cemetery 龙华烈士陵园
6468 5995
Located near Longhua Temple (p.209), this cemetery looks and feels more like a park than a traditional graveyard, with trees, flowers and heroic sculptures. Visitors are even welcome to walk on the grass. The former site of a Nationalist prison, it commemorates the deaths of hundreds of local Communists over many years of war. The memorial hall, completed in 1995, resembles a glass pyramid. Admission to the park is ¥1, with an additional ¥5 for the memorial hall.

No. 2, 201 Duolun Lu
Hongkou
多伦路201弄2号
虹口
🚇 *Dong Baoxing Lu*
Map p.422 B3 31

The Meeting Site of the Chinese League of Left-Wing Writers 中国左翼作家联盟成立大会
Although the League of Left-Wing Writers is not likely to ascend to the ranks of superheroes, this group attracted several of modern China's most popular and influential authors, including Lu Xun and Ding Ling. They debated the function of literature during dangerous times (1930 to 1936), and several members were imprisoned or executed by the Nationalists. The exhibit includes historical pictures, documents and movie adaptations. The building itself is located near the end of a quiet lane, and a weekday visit might require the attendant to turn on the lights especially for you. Admission is ¥5.

20 Nanjing Dong Lu
Huangpu
南京东路20号
黄埔
🚇 *Nanjing Dong Lu*
Map p.431 E2 32

Peace Hotel 和平饭店
6321 6888 | www.shanghaipeacehotel.com
Although nearly every building along the Bund has a story, the tale of the Peace Hotel reads more like an epic, complete with heroic deeds and grand events. Sun Yatsen was welcomed here in 1911, on his way to Nanjing to assume the presidency of a new China. In 1930, Noel Coward finished his play *Private Lives* in a penthouse suite while battling the flu. The north building was constructed in 1929 by Victor Sassoon, one of Shanghai's richest men, and originally named the Cathay Hotel. Its jazz age luxury attracted many famous travellers over the years, including Charlie Chaplin, George Bernard Shaw and Muhammad Ali. But the dated furnishings inside the granite facade have made it increasingly difficult for the current owners to compete in a market dominated by international chains. In April 2007, the Jinjiang Group joined forces with Fairmont Hotels and Swatch to start on two years of renovations.

Historic Houses

81 Yuyuan Lu
Jing'an
愚园路81号
静安
🚇 *Jing'an Temple*
Map p.429 E4 33

Former Residence of Liu Changsheng 刘长胜故居
6255 5377
One of Shanghai's many sites for patriotic education, this three-storey brick and wood building held both shops and apartments. The owner of the ground floor cigarette shop was Liu Changsheng, a leader in the Communist Party's battles with the Kuomintang in the 1930s and 40s. Meeting under the cover of *mahjong* games, Liu and his comrades – including the owner of the third-floor rice shop – helped plot the course of the revolution. The memorial recreates the atmosphere of both shops, with vintage furnishings and memorabilia. Admission is ¥5.

120 Maoming Lu
Jing'an
茂名路120号
静安
🚇 *Nanjing Xi Lu*
Map p.430 A4 34

Former Residence of Mao Zedong 毛泽东故居
6272 3656
Mao lived in this typical two-storey lane house for nine months in 1924, with the second of his four wives, Yang Kaihui, their two young sons, and Yang's mother. He was 31 years old, and the Chinese Communist Party had only been in existence for three years. The exhibit reproduces the young family's drawing room and bedroom,

populated by thoughtful wax mannequins. Mao's figure sits at the desk, his writing brush poised at the edge of the paper. The second floor galleries display period photographs, brief biographies of two other revolutionaries who shared the house, a map of Mao's subsequent activities in Shanghai, and the leather sofa on which the Chairman sat when visiting the Shanghai Machine Tool Works. Admission is ¥5.

Mao's Residence

7 Xiangshan Lu
Luwan
香山路7号
卢湾
🚇 *Shanxi Nan Lu*
Map p.436 B1 **35**

Former Residence of Sun Yatsen 孙中山故居

6437 2954 | *www.sh-sunyat-sen.com*

Sun Yatsen, doctor and revolutionary, became modern China's first president and most influential thinker. He made this former Rue de Moliere residence his home from 1918 until his death in 1925. His widow, Soong Ching Ling, remained here until 1937, then moved to a house on Huaihai Lu. You can don plastic shoe covers and tour the rooms where they ate, slept and entertained. Although the bookcases contain only pictures of books, the genuine-looking furniture is arranged in original positions. The museum next door opened in November 2006 and threatens to overshadow the house. Its climate-controlled galleries thrum to theatrical narration with piano accompaniment. The artefacts include Sun's copy of Aulard's *The French Revolution*, his croquet mallets, and an unidentified man's long, twisted braid of hair, shorn on the president's orders. The T-shirts in the souvenir shop bear the message: 'The world for all.' Admission is ¥20.

73 Sinan Lu
Luwan
思南路73号
卢湾
🚇 *Shanxi Nan Lu*
Map p.436 B1 **36**

Former Residence of Zhou Enlai 周恩来故居

6473 0420 | *www.shcrm.com*

China's 'beloved premier' from 1949 until his death in 1976, and the country's foreign minister from 1948 to 1959, Zhou Enlai is remembered fondly in Shanghai. He was a general when this gracious, four-storey home, covered with ivy, served as his residence from 1946 to 1947. It also functioned as the Shanghai office of the Communist Party, as well as a kind of revolutionary dormitory, with rows of cots in the attic rooms. A proud sign points out the former Kuomintang spy post across the street. Admission is ¥2.

30 Shanxi Nan Lu
Jing'an
陕西南路30号
静安
🚇 *Nanjing Xi Lu*
Map p.430 A4 **37**

Hengshan Moller Villa 上海衡山马勒别墅饭店

6247 8881 | *www.mollervilla.com*

The former home of Swedish shipping magnate and racehorse owner Eric Moller, this surreal collection of gables and spires lurks in the shadows of the Yan'an elevated expressway and is rather like something from a fairy tale or a hallucination. The Moller family fled Shanghai after the city's liberation, and from 1949 until 2001 the house served as the Shanghai headquarters of the Communist Youth League. It has since been transformed into a boutique hotel, but was temporarily closed for renovation in 2007. The best long-range views are from the pedestrian crosswalk over Yan'an Lu.

207

64 Yan'an Xi Lu
Jing'an
延安西路64号
静安
🚇 **Jing'an Temple**
Map p.429 E4 38

Kadoorie Residence 嘉道理住宅
6248 1850
Sir Elly Kadoorie, a Jewish philanthropist, was the leading member of one of pre-war Shanghai's legendary families. Originally from Baghdad, the family passed through Bombay before Sir Elly settled in Shanghai and built this mansion. Popularly known as the 'marble palace' due to its inlaid floors and stone colonnade, it is now owned by the local government. Situated in the same enclosure as Jing'an Children's Palace, with a multi-level climbing maze, it periodically teems with schoolchildren. Sir Elly's grandson Michael currently oversees the family's holdings, which include Hong Kong's Peninsula Hotel. In a symbolic return to Shanghai, a new Peninsula is currently under construction near the Bund. Admission is free but typically restricted to organised groups. Try calling first or asking politely at the front gate for a brief look inside.

132 Shanyin Lu
Hongkou
山阴路132号
虹口
🚇 **Hongkou Stadium**
Map p.422 B3 39

Lu Xun's Former Residence 鲁迅故居
5666 9711
Author of *The True Story of Ah Q* and *The Good Hell That Was Lost*, Lu Xun is often referred to as the father of modern Chinese literature. This narrow, three-storey row house was the writer's last home in Shanghai; he died of tuberculosis in 1936. Worth a visit for a glimpse into the living conditions of the 30s, at least for a successful author. Look out of the windows at the neighbouring terraces with their laundries and bonsai; listen to the distant honks of horns and the decades melt away. You buy your ticket next door at number 8, which entitles you to a surly guide. Admission is ¥8.

1843 Huaihai Lu
Xuhui
淮海中路1843号
徐汇
🚇 **Hengshan Lu**
Map p.435 E3 40

Soong Ching Ling's Residence in Shanghai 上海宋庆龄故居
6437 6268
The widow of Kuomintang founder Sun Yatsen was known in the west as Rosamonde Soong. After her death in 1981, this home became a lovingly detailed shrine to her memory, complete with her government limousines, dovecote and pistol. The bedroom is preserved intact, as though she has only just left, with her typewriter resting on a small desk beside the bathtub. The sitting room carpet was a present from Chairman Mao. Admission is ¥20 and includes a guided tour.

Religious Sites

29 Chenxiangge Lu
Huangpu
沉香阁路29号
黄埔
🚇 **Nanjing Dong Lu**
Map p.431 E4 41

Chenxiang Temple 沉香阁
6328 7884
Built in 1600 by the same official who commissioned Yu Garden, this temple was damaged during the Cultural Revolution, then restored in 1994. Its most memorable icon is a large golden Buddha with blue hair, looming behind an offering table strewn with apples and melons. The Buddha's right hand is raised with the thumb and middle finger touching, suggesting the 'middle path' between extremes. A vault of disciples looms above him, rising in circular tiers. Admission is ¥5.

249 Fangbang Lu
Huangpu
方浜中路249号
黄埔
🚇 **Huangpi Nan Lu**
Map p.431 E4 42

City Temple of Shanghai 上海城隍庙
6386 8649 | www.shchm.org
Shanghai's 'city god', Qin Yubo, began his career as a scholarly official under the last Yuan and first Ming emperors. He was reputably a reluctant servant of the Ming Dynasty, but the emperor conferred godly status

Lunar Calendar
Though most Chinese people use the Gregorian (western) calendar for their daily lives, the Chinese lunisolar calendar still determines the dates for traditional holidays. Unlike the western version, the Chinese calendar continues in 60 year cycles based on two components: the five Celestial Stemms and the 12 Terrestrial Branches (the animal names). Years are determined by lunar months and solar orientations.

upon Qin after his death in 1377. The original Taoist temple, built in the 15th century, has been destroyed and rebuilt several times. The most recent renovation of the red walls, black tiles and gracefully upturned eaves of City Temple (also known as Temple of the City God) occurred in 2006. Located next to Yu Garden in the Old City (p.214), it's a popular pilgrimage for both tourists and locals. Admission is ¥5

City Temple of Shanghai

185 Dongjiadu Lu
Huangpu
董家渡路185号
黄埔
🚇 **Nanjing Dong Lu**
Map p.438 A1 **43**

Dongjiadu Cathedral
董家渡天主堂
6378 7214

Built in 1853, this wood and brick structure was the first Catholic church in Shanghai. It was originally called St Xavier's Cathedral, after the Spanish Jesuit missionary Francisco Xavier, who died of fever in 1552 while trying to smuggle himself into China. Mass is celebrated behind the white baroque facade at 07:00 on weekdays, and 06:30 and 08:00 on Sundays. If you visit at other times, ask the security guard for a look inside. The vaulted interior provides a peaceful sanctuary.

170 Anyuan Lu
Putuo
安远路170号
普陀
🚇 **Zhenping Lu**
Map p.429 E2 **44**

Jade Buddha Temple 玉佛寺
6266 3668 | www.yufotemple.org

On any given day, the Jade Buddha Temple is a veritable Babel of tour groups: French, Italian, German, English, Japanese and Chinese to name but a few of the nationalities of sightseers. While it remains a working temple, the grounds also include two vegetarian restaurants, a tea house that invites you to 'taste the Buddha's tea', several gift shops, and a fish-feeding pool. Admission is ¥20. An additional ¥10 is required to glimpse the Jade Buddha's beautiful downcast eyes and smoothly gleaming shoulders, plus another ¥10 for entry to a gallery of ancient stone carvings. Arrive early, before the tour groups, and you won't regret any of these costs.

1868 Nanjing Xi Lu
Jing'an
南京西路1868号
静安
🚇 **Jing'an Temple**
Map p.429 F4 **45**

Jing'an Temple 静安寺
6256 6366 | www.shjas.com

Flanked by glass and steel shopping plazas, the contrast of the traditional architecture of Jing'an Temple really catches your eye. But then you notice that the paint seems a bit too glossy to be truly authentic. Although restoration began in 1997 and should be completed by 2009, the site remains a work in progress. All that bare concrete can make parts of this urban sanctuary feel more like a warehouse than a place of worship. And yet the worshippers are still here, hands clasped and bowing, burning incense, tossing coins into a multi-tiered bronze vessel for good luck. Admission is ¥10.

2853 Longhua Lu
Xuhui
龙华路2853号
徐汇
🚇 **Longcao Lu**
Map p.443 F1 **46**

Longhua Temple 龙华寺
6456 6085

This is by far the oldest temple in Shanghai, with a history of more than 1,700 years. The octagonal brick and wood pagoda, restored in 2006, is 40m high and leans slightly to the east. A popular place during festivals, the temple is particularly lively on December 31, during the bell-ringing ceremony (p.56), and during the Longhua Temple Fair in the spring (p.53). Admission will cost you ¥10.

209

62 Changyang Lu
Hongkou
长阳路62号
虹口
🚇 *Dalian Lu*
Map p.423 D4 47

Ohel Moishe Synagogue 摩西会堂

Ohel Moishe, completed in 1927, is located near the heart of the former Jewish ghetto, where more than 25,000 European refugees found shelter from Nazi persecution. Mr Wang, the 88-year-old volunteer head guide, grew up in the ghetto himself and is eager to reminisce. The building was shrouded by scaffolding in the first half of 2007, but was due to reopen to the public by late August or September. If you're in the neighbourhood, walk around the corner and south along Zhoushan Lu to see the beautiful row houses with their black iron doors; then pause in tiny Huoshan Park (p.212), where there is a memorial tablet for stateless refugees.

52 Xiaotaoyuan Jie
Huangpu
小桃园街52号
黄埔
🚇 *Nanjing Dong Lu*
Map p.431 E4 48

Peach Garden Mosque 小桃园清真寺
6377 5442

This unassuming mosque, also known as Xiaotaoyuan Masjid, was built in 1925 (the number 1343 on the facade refers to the same year in the Islamic calendar). Inside the gate, you walk across worn tiles and past walls of cracked yellow plaster. Although the mosque can hold 500 worshippers, its central golden dome is nearly invisible from the courtyard. To appreciate its understated beauty – along with the four surrounding green domes – walk back out to Henan Lu or Fuxing Lu.

Sheshan Hill,
Songjiang County
Songjiang
佘山山顶,
松江风景区
松江

Sheshan Cathedral 佘山天主堂
5765 1521

Sheshan Cathedral looms like a mirage on the crest of some low hills about 45km west of the city centre. At 97m above sea level, the largest of these hills is the highest peak in Shanghai. The cathedral can hold 3,000 worshippers and is a favourite destination for Catholic pilgrims in May. The site anchors Sheshan National Holiday Resort (5765 3235), which is divided into two forest parks and a host of other attractions, including Moon River Art Park, home of Shanghai's most expensive toilet (built in 2004, its construction costs reached ¥5 million). Admission is ¥30 for the West Hill, including an astronomical observatory and the Sheshan Cathedral. Admission for the East Hill is ¥45, including the sand sculptures as well as the bird and butterfly aviaries. A cable car that connects the two peaks is an additional ¥10.

215 Wenmiao Lu
Huangpu
文庙路215号
黄埔
🚇 *Nanjing Dong Lu*
Map p.437 E1 50

Wenmiao Confucian Temple 上海文庙
6377 9101 | www.confuciantemple.com

Shanghai's Confucian Temple was established in 1294 and moved four times, most recently in 1855. A place of study as well as a place of worship, on certain days you will find a courtyard alive with the twittering of caged birds and the disputations of scholars. Outside the main hall, students tie wishes for favourable exam scores to trees. In the gallery of root carvings, don't miss the 500-year-old figure of a dancing crane. The street outside is lined with vendors selling everything from mobile phone covers to watermelons. Admission is ¥10.

239 Dajing Lu
Huangpu
大境路239号
黄埔
🚇 *Nanjing Dong Lu*
Map p.431 D4 51

White Cloud Taoist Temple 上海白云观
6377 2800

Now located near the Dajing Pavilion, this historic temple was moved north from its former home on Xilinhou Lu in 2004. Inside the gate, you might witness monks in heavily brocaded robes, chanting to the accompaniment of drums, horns, cymbals, flutes and wood blocks. The sound rises to a near-frantic cacophony before falling calmly away. Climb the stairs to the second floor for a good view of the surrounding neighbourhood (partially demolished in 2007), along with the trio of pinnacles on the Pudong skyline. Admission is ¥5.

Parks

Other options **Beaches** p.216, **Botanical Gardens** p.218

Considering Shanghai's population density, the city's parks are surprisingly clean and well tended, with paved paths, tranquil ponds and manicured flower beds. Shanghai residents use their neighbourhood parks like leafy community centres. They nap on quiet benches or deal cards under shady pavilions, and they play badminton, practise fan dancing or waltz to portable sound systems. An early morning at Fuxing Park can feel like the world's largest tai chi class, a windy afternoon on the plaza outside Pudong's Century Park like a kite-flyer's convention. There are at least 140 green spaces in Shanghai, 122 with free admission, and more are unveiled each year. In 2008, three new parks will open in Pudong alone. According to the city's comprehensive plan, every resident should live within 500m of a park by 2020.

The following list features some of the city's notable parks and gardens. Most unlock their gates around 07:00 and close at sunset, although those that contain popular nightspots remain open much later. Most prohibit dogs, football and private bicycles, although a few rent tandem bikes. When looking for an open playing field, you're better off at a nearby international school or an expat housing compound.

Century Park 世纪公园

1001 Jinxiu Lu
Pudong
锦绣路1001号
浦东
🚇 *Shanghai Science & Technology Museum*
Map p.439 F1 🔢

3876 0588 | www.centurypark.com.cn
Shanghai's largest park at nearly 350 acres, this is the place to go for unobstructed views. The government intended it to be an equivalent to New York's Central Park, as you can see from the grand scale of investment. Although the planned golf course is closed indefinitely, the park offers paddleboats and electric motorboats on a long stretch of the Zhangjiabang River, as well as a fishing pond and tandem bike rentals. Admission is ¥10. Kite flyers congregate near the Shanghai Science & Technology Museum (p.202), on a plaza where no admission fee is required.

Changfeng Park 长风公园

25 Daduhe Lu
Putuo
大渡河路25号
普陀
🚇 *Jinshajiang Lu*
Map p.427 F2 🔢

6245 3270 | www.sh-cfpark.com
This large park north of Suzhou Creek aims to entertain. Ocean World aquarium (p.218), with its sharks, penguins and performing whales, occupies the centre stage. The accessible fun also includes carnival rides, calligraphy artists, and vendors who fashion rabbits, dragons and other beasts from caramelised sugar. In the north-east corner, Disc Kart (6222 2880) offers racing with the same invigorating absence of rules as the city's mean streets – plus an upstairs bar. A biennial flower show occurs in April of even-numbered years and is an impressive affair for horticultural fans – the 2006 incarnation boasted one million tulips.

Daning Lingshi Park 大宁灵石公园

288 Guangzhong Xi Lu
Zhabei
广中西路288号
闸北
🚇 *Shanghai Circus*
Map p.421 F3 🔢

5665 3229
This walled park, the largest in Puxi, offers alternating doses of solitude and spectacle. In some areas, you can sit undisturbed on the grass, with only birds for company. In others, you'll be entertained by a parade of uniformed school groups, grandparents pushing strollers, and Chinese wedding photographers commanding their subjects – in English – to get 'closer, closer.' A triumphal arch provides a grand stage for ballroom dancers to polish their moves, while the substantial lake offers designated areas for anglers, boaters and even beachgoers. It's not Thailand by any means, but children dig happily along a 100m strand of coarse white sand, fringed by a few anaemic palms. No swimming allowed, though you can get your ankles wet. Admission is ¥2.

211

Fuxing Park 复兴公园

2 Gaolan Lu
Luwan
皋兰路2号
卢湾
🚇 **Shanxi Nan Lu**
Map p.436 B1 **55**

6372 0662

Near the eastern boundary of the French Concession, Fuxing Park's plane trees and rose garden would remind you of Paris, if Paris was the capital of tai chi. Visit this park early in the morning to see the many groups exercising along the wide avenue on the park's east side. Some groups are larger than others, some less formal in their demeanour, but all move with an enviable grace. To the west, as you approach the rose garden, the range of activities widens to include calisthenics, badminton, fan dancing and sword displays. Return in the evening to watch a well-heeled percentage of Shanghai's party crowd climb the stairs for food and entertainment at Park 97 (see p.406), then emerge on the balcony, champagne in hand.

Gongqing Forest Park 共青森林公园

2000 Junggong Lu
Yangpu
军工路2000号
杨浦
🚇 **Songfa Lu**

6532 8194 | www.52921234.com/gongqing

Despite its inconvenient location in the north-east portion of Puxi, about 15km from the city centre, Gongqing Forest Park remains a regular pilgrimage for many residents. As the name suggests, there is an actual forest here, with more than 300,000 trees. It's not wilderness, of course, but you can ride a horse (¥15 for one trip around the corral) or fire up a rented barbecue (¥20 per hour). And if that doesn't entertain the kids, you can fall back on those old forest standbys: the carousel and the roller coaster. Admission is ¥12. If you're travelling by Metro, you'll need to take a taxi from Songfa Lu station.

Guilin Park 桂林公园

188 Caobao Lu
Xuhui
漕宝路188号
徐汇
🚇 **Caobao Lu**
Map p.443 D2 **57**

6483 0910

Originally the private garden of a distinguished gangster, 'Pockmarked' Huang, the grounds were partially destroyed by the invading Japanese army in 1937, then restored, then damaged again by the Kuomintang. The meandering paths have been returned to their Concession-era splendour, as have the elaborate pavilions, one of which features 88 windows, considered an especially lucky number because the sound of the Chinese word for 'eight' resembles that for 'fortune'. Attendance swells during the Osmanthus Festival (p.55), when crowds gather to walk among more than 1,000 specimens of the flowering plants.

Huangpu Park 黄浦公园

28 Zhongshan Dong Lu
Huangpu
中山东一路28号
黄埔
🚇 **Nanjing Dong Lu**
Map p.431 E2 **58**

6329 2636

Situated at the head of the Bund, where Suzhou Creek empties into the Huangpu River, Huangpu Park occupies a prominent place in both history and imagination. Non-Europeans were excluded until 1928, but most scholars agree that the legendary sign 'Dogs and Chinese Not Admitted' was just that: an urban myth. Foreign tour groups and fond couples now gaze across at Pudong's epic skyline, or pose beneath the Monument to the People's Heroes. The available refreshments are decidedly more upscale than in most other city parks. Options include a teahouse that dubs itself The Treasure Museum (5308 2637) and a branch of the Parisian ice cream parlour Amorino (5308 2330).

Huoshan Park 霍山公园

118 Huoshan Lu
Hongkou
霍山路118号
虹口
🚇 **Dalian Lu**
Map p.423 D4 **59**

This tiny park in the middle of the former Jewish ghetto teems with ageing fan dancers and elderly exercise groups. Many of these senior citizens spent their childhoods among foreigners, so don't be surprised if they greet you in English. Because Huoshan Park lies around the corner from the Ohel Moishe Synagogue (p.210), you also might encounter tourists taking photos of the memorial tablet to 'stateless refugees,' inscribed in Chinese, English and Hebrew.

189 Huashan Lu
Jing'an
华山路189号
静安
🚇 **Jing'an Temple**
Map p.429 F4 60

Jing'an Park 静安公园

6248 3238

For a small parcel of land, Jing'an Park leaves a big footprint on Shanghai. Located across the street from Jing'an Temple, and directly above the Metro station of the same name, it lies midway between the Hilton Hotel and Portman Ritz-Carlton. A tourist information centre is strategically positioned near the Nanjing Xi Lu entrance, but many of the park's regulars are students or office workers, stretching their legs along its tree-lined thoroughfare or relaxing on shady benches. Admission to the park itself is free, but a ¥3 ticket gives you entrance to a further realm of serenity. Inside an encircling barricade of rock and bamboo, the Eight-Scene Garden boasts a replica of the historic Bubbling Well that no longer bubbles (see p.180), a goldfish pond, at least two feral cats, and a teahouse populated by an air of sleepy dissolution. Near the Huashan Lu entrance, Bali Laguna (p.372) offers Indonesian cuisine amid water lilies and birdsong.

146 Jiangwan Dong Lu
Hongkou
东江湾路146号
虹口
🚇 **Hongkou Stadium**
Map p.422 B3 61

Lu Xun Park 鲁迅公园

6540 0009

Lu Xun Park's initial incarnation, in 1896, was as a shooting range. The first park, known as Hongkou Park, opened 10 years later, exclusively to foreigners, with Chinese people not admitted until 1928. It was renamed in honour of Lu Xun, widely considered the founder of modern Chinese literature, and has since become a favourite of dancers, painters and musicians. Located in the former American Concession, the park still retains an international feel. Besides the Lu Xun Museum (p.208), it contains a Korean plum garden (admission ¥15), a memorial clock dedicated to friendship with Japanese youth, and the so-called English Sunflower Garden – an unusual description as there are no sunflowers to be seen.

231 Nanjing Xi Lu
Huangpu
南京西路231号
黄埔
🚇 **People's Square**
Map p.430 C3 62

People's Square (Renmin Park) 人民广场

6327 1333

You can spend an entire day or evening here just gazing about in wonder. During the Concession years, it was a thoroughbred racetrack; during the Japanese occupation, a holding camp for enemy prisoners. The Shanghai Art Museum (p.199) is now housed in the Shanghai Race Club, and eye-catching, neon-lit towers encircle the lawns and gardens. The Urban Planning Exhibition Centre (p.203) gleams in the park's south-east corner, displaying a scale model of Shanghai so astonishingly detailed that real estate buyers use it to scout for potential purchases. From its top-floor cafe, you can sip cocktails or coffee while admiring the kites soaring over the trees. If you prefer a more stylish setting for your drinks, try Kathleen's 5 atop the Art Museum, or the second-floor deck of the Moroccan-themed Barbarossa (6318 0220). When you're back on your feet again, the trees and flowers continue to the south at People's Square, and to the west in several greenbelts along the Yan'an Expressway. Beneath the park, adjacent to the swarming Metro station, a former air-raid shelter has been transformed into the vast hive of the Hong Kong Shopping Centre.

17 Nandan Lu
Xuhui
南丹路17号
徐汇
🚇 **Xujiahui**
Map p.435 D4 63

Xu Guangqi Memorial Park 光启公园

6468 9252

This park honours one of Shanghai's most distinguished sons, the scholar Xu Guangqi. It's a contemplative spot, easily overlooked, a place for quiet games of chess or cards. Born in 1562, Xu converted to Catholicism in 1603. Over a long and amazingly productive career, he completed the first Chinese translations of Euclid's *Elements*, and wrote influential books on agriculture, astronomy, military training and the Pythagorean theorem, among other topics. Although his star might have dimmed over the centuries, his name lives on in Shanghai: the area Xujiahui means 'Xu family gathering place'. Admission to the small museum in the park's south-west corner is ¥3. The rooms provide a fascinating portrait of Xu's life and work, with signs in English and Chinese.

Xujiahui Park 徐家汇公园

Tianping Lu
Xuhui
天平路
徐汇
🚇 *Xujiahui*
Map p.435 E4 64

The former site of the Great China Rubber Works, Xujiahui Park provides a green oasis by the clamour of Metro City (p.321), Shanghai's biggest electronic market, and the Grand Gateway, a high-rise mall. The landscaping incorporates an iconic brick chimney, a serpentine lake, and an elevated walkway that creates a sort of pedestrian flyover. The park's perimeter offers three different options for stylish dining, including former EMI recording studio La Villa Rouge (811 Hengshan Lu; 6431 9811). Although the food can be unreliable, it's worth at least one drink amid the record company memorabilia and bluesy soundtrack. For a dependable game of pick-up basketball, head to the courts along Wanping Lu.

Yu Garden 豫园

218 Anren Jie
Huangpu
安仁街218号
黄埔
🚇 *Nanjing Dong Lu*
Map p.431 E4 65

6328 2465

Shanghai's famous Yu Garden (*Yuyuan*) can become intolerably busy on sunny weekends and during traditional festivals. Try to visit early in the day, during the week, when it's not crowded. Without the hordes, you can quietly set about evading your demons (and the trinket-filled bazaar) by crossing the Bridge of Nine Turnings, built to prevent the nasty imps from keeping up with your changes of direction. Once inside the walls, you'll be pleased by the picturesque scenes of Ming Dynasty order and their extravagant names, such as the Hall of Jade Magnificence. Linger among the pavilions and rocky alcoves for perfectly framed glimpses of trees and ponds. Admission is ¥40.

Zhabei Park 闸北公园

400 Pingxingguan Lu
Zhabei
平型关路400号
闸北
🚇 *Yanchang Lu*
Map p.422 A3 66

5633 4565

Just one Metro stop away from Daning Lingshi Park (p.211), Zhabei Park has an entirely different personality. On a typical afternoon the benches are filled with senior citizens, and talk, laughter and song fill the air. A paint-by-numbers artist usually attracts an appreciative crowd of onlookers, while the jingly tunes of carnival rides provide a tinny counterpoint. As you might have guessed from the giant golden teapot standing outside the entrance on Gonghexin Lu, this neighbourhood park also serves as the home of the annual Tea Culture Festival (p.53), held in April. Luochuan Lu, on the park's southern boundary, is lined with cavernous seafood restaurants. With the main courses displayed live in their tanks, it's easy to order a 'point and eat' lunch.

Zhongshan Park 中山公园

780 Changning Lu
Changning
长宁路780号
长宁
🚇 *Zhongshan Park*
Map p.428 B4 67

6210 5806

Zhongshan Park's location on Metro Line 2 makes it a convenient meeting place for both locals and tourists. Ballroom dancers prefer the paved area in front of the Marble Pavilion, while kite enthusiasts claim the large open lawn. A maze of paths conceals a few secluded tables for chess playing or conversation. In the far north-west corner stands a sycamore tree planted in 1866, reputed to be the oldest in east Asia. Children will appreciate the indoor play area, amusement rides, and the shop selling sugary treats.

Tranquility and activity in Shanghai's parks

215

Beaches

Other options **Parks** p.211, **Swimming** p.273

Shanghai's location near the mouth of the mighty Yangtze River, one of China's most polluted waterways, means that the city's surf culture remains dormant. To the south, shorelines along the East China Sea tend toward murky tidepools and gritty mudflats. When knowledgeable locals crave the beach, they make a pilgrimage to Putuoshan (p.226) or Taohua Island in the Zhoushan archipelago, a few hours away by ferry. Nevertheless, the coast is within an hour's drive of downtown, and a few outlying communities have seized on artificial beaches as potential tourist attractions (the demand is certainly there, enhanced by years of *Baywatch* reruns). If you're hoping for an approximation of Tahiti or Thailand, then you'll be sorely disappointed by Shanghai's seaside. But if you can't wait to feel the sand between your toes, here are three options.

5 Xincheng Lu
Jinshan
新城路5号
金山

City Beach 金山海滨浴场

Built with sand from Dongting Lake in Hunan province, the Jinshan City Beach opened in 2004. About 2.5km long, it has played host to both the men's and women's world beach volleyball tours. Water quality in the enclosed swimming area has improved steadily, as scientists have transplanted seaweed, shrimp, crabs and more than 100,000 fish. In May 2007, Shanghai's first recreational divers reported a visibility of six metres. Admission is free.

Fengzian
奉贤

Golden Beach 上海奉贤海滩

5712 1919 | *www.baystar.cn*

Shanghai's newest beach, this one imported 120,000 tonnes of golden sand from Hainan Island. Enclosed by a concrete levee, the water is treated to remove silt and pollutants from the surrounding bay. The developers have completed a 2,000-space car park, and future plans include hotels, restaurants and a yacht basin. This golden idyll can suffer from overcrowding, with more than 10,000 packing in over one sweltering July weekend. Admission is ¥50.

Huaxia Dong Lu
Pudong
华夏东路
浦东

Sanjiagang Beach 三甲港海滨乐园

6890 9803

Just north of Pudong Airport, this more or less natural 1.3km strip of sand is part of the Sanjiagang Sea Paradise. The resort offers water-bike rentals and other amusements, and occasionally hosts matchmaking parties and rock concerts of rare homegrown talent. The beach actually fronts on a tidal portion of the Yangtze, where swimming is not recommended. Admission to the separate bathing area, which contains filtered and treated water, is ¥20.

Amusement Parks

Other options **Water Parks** p.219

Although both Universal Studios and Walt Disney have contemplated building grand theme parks in Shanghai, no ground has yet been broken. That might be because their accountants remember the $50 million American Dream Park. Launched in 1996 with great ambition, it has long since passed from the city's memory. Those who seek more diversion than their neighbourhood park's ageing collection of carnival rides must content themselves for now with the Jinjiang Amusement Park. Parents and children with lower expectations will find gratification at small-scale arcades such as Tom's World or the newly opened Kidtown, aimed specifically at expat families.

Fun Dazzle 翻斗乐

6210 7388

This is the largest and most popular of the Fun Dazzle outlets around the city. Just inside the main entrance to Zhongshan Park, it offers a warren of tunnels, slides and ball pits for the younger set to crawl, jump and fly around, along with some more focused, refined activities for older children. All equipment is child-safe, and birthday parties can be arranged. The place can be overcrowded at the weekends and chilly during the winter months. Admission is ¥30.

Zhongshan Park,
780 Changning Lu
Changning
中山公园，
长宁路780号
长宁
🚇 *Zhongshan Park*
Map p.434 B1 71

Jinjiang Amusement Park 锦江乐园

5420 4956 | www.jjlysh.com

Opened in 1984, this theme park drew 2.4 million visitors in its first year, setting a Chinese attendance record that lasted for nearly two decades. It now boasts more than 30 attractions, including old favourites such as bumper cars, plus a 'huge wheel' (Ferris wheel), and a 'layered merry-go-around' (carousel). The rollercoaster breaks no records but does turn you upside down both coming and going. Admission is ¥70 and includes six rides, and there are several eating options within the park.

201 Hongmei Lu
Minhang
虹梅路201号
闵行
🚇 *Jinjiang Park*
Map p.443 D4 72

Kidtown 可童探索城

6405 5188

Located above a popular branch of City Shop, one of the expat community's favourite supermarkets, Kidtown targets English-speaking and bilingual families. Opened in April 2007, it is laid out like a 'miniature town' and aims to educate and entertain children of up to 10 years old by mixing exploratory play with music, movement and read-aloud activities. It also hosts birthday parties. Admission is ¥120 for a full day pass. If you're travelling by Metro, you'll need to take a taxi from Hongqiao Lu.

Floor 4,
3211 Hongmei Lu
Minhang
虹梅路3211号4楼
闵行
🚇 *Hongqiao Lu*
Map p.442 C1 73

Shanghai Film & TV Amusement Park 上海影视乐园

5760 1627

Not really a theme park in the same bracket as Universal Studios, but movie fans will appreciate the chance to check out – and photograph – the well-known Shanghai Film Studio's sets and props. These have featured in many familiar movies, including James Ivory's *The White Countess*, the recent adaptation of Somerset Maugham's *The Painted Veil*, and the irresistible *Kung Fu Hustle* by director Stephen Chow (Zhou Xingchi). The park reportedly spent ¥25 million to build an impeccable copy of old Nanjing Lu for Ang Lee's *Lust, Caution*, based on Eileen Chang's novel of 1940s Shanghai. Admission is ¥50.

4915 Beisong Lu
Songjiang
北松公路4915号
松江

Tom's World 汤姆熊娱乐世界

3878 0139

Tom's World will look familiar to any teenager. It's your classic mall arcade, though perhaps a little bit bigger and a little less expensive than the western varieties. Video games and other distractions cost ¥1 or ¥2 per play, with many games returning tickets for high scores. You can redeem your tickets for candy or trinkets, as well as some decidedly adult amenities, including beer, wine and home appliances. Tom's World is also found in other parts of Shanghai, with branches at 685 Nanjing Dong Lu and Lanxi Lu in Putuo.

Super Brand Mall,
168 Lujiazui Lu
Pudong
正大广场，陆家嘴西
路168号
浦东
🚇 *Beixingjing*
Map p.431 F2 75

Chinese Film

Founded in 1949, the Shanghai Film Studio has released more than 600 films and is one of the three largest film studios in China, along with the Beijing Film Studio and the Xi'an Film Studio. The current output from Chinese film makers, especially in Xi'an, has been in the 'amateur' style, with gritty production techniques and edgier themes. More than any other medium, current Chinese cinema is taking advantage of relaxed censorship.

217

Aquariums & Marine Centres

Because aquariums have become synonymous with urban renewal, you probably won't be surprised to learn that Shanghai hosts more than one collection of fish tanks. The city's two aquariums have divided the market between them – in geographic terms, if not financial ones. Although neither facility is yet a decade old, Pudong's Ocean Aquarium has captured most of the splash. It's newer, bigger, and blessed with a lucrative location near the Oriental Pearl Tower. Puxi's Ocean World is buried in Changning district's Changfeng Park, several blocks from the nearest Metro station. If you are not expecting to be astounded by architectural design or ecological awareness, both make fine destinations rain or shine, with children or adults.

451 Daduhe Lu,
Changfeng Park
Putuo
大渡河路451号，
长风公园
普陀
🚇 *Jinshajiang Lu*
Map p.427 F2 **76**

Ocean World 长风海洋世界
6223 8888 | www.oceanworld.com.cn

Opened in 1999 as Aquaria 21, Ocean World seems to be holding its own against the competition. Along with the ever popular sharks and reef fish, it also features otters, penguins and two beluga whales. The whales can fetch balls, perform arithmetic and paint with brushes (watercolors, of course). For an extra fee, they even do weddings. Although reasonably spacious on the whole, some of its narrower corridors can become stiflingly congested at the scheduled feeding times, when visitors contend for prime viewing spots. The 2,000 seat stadium can be reached by a speedy shuttle or a leisurely walk across the park. Admission for the aquarium and whale show is ¥110 for adults, ¥80 for children under 1.4m tall, and free for kids under one metre.

1388 Lujiazui
Huan Lu
Pudong
陆家嘴环路1388号
浦东
🚇 *Lujiazui*
Map p.432 A2 **77**

Shanghai Ocean Aquarium 上海海洋水族馆 ▶ p.166
5877 9988 | www.sh-aquarium.com

With more than 10,000 specimens, the Shanghai Ocean Aquarium hosts one of the largest collections of aquatic animals in the world. Themed displays cover a range of habitats from the Yangtze River to the Amazon and Nile, and a huge saltwater tank allows visitors to walk beneath sharks, rays and other ocean dwellers. If you get hungry watching all that seafood, skip the bland snack bar and walk to the nearby Super Brand Mall for its rousing selection of restaurants. Admission is ¥120 for adults, and ¥80 for children between 0.8m and 1.4m.

Botanical Gardens

Although Shanghai has been designated a 'national garden city' by the Chinese government, this refers strictly to the green coverage (36%) and per capita green space, (currently nine square metres), rather than its horticultural achievements. Not content to rest on its laurels, the city vowed to add three million pots of flowers in 2007 and at least two million each year after that until the World Expo in 2010. Nevertheless, the opportunities to visit a formal garden in the city proper are limited to Yu Garden (p.214) in the Old City and the Botanical Garden, south of Xujiahui. If you have the right connections, however, you might be able to visit the French Concession's elegant Ding Xiang Garden (849 Huashan Lu), open only to government officials.

701 Qingshang
Gong Lu
Qingpu
青商公路701号
青浦

Grand View Garden 上海大观园
5926 2831

Unlike the authentically classical Guyi Garden, the Grand View Garden's ancient charms are all of recent vintage. Built in 1979, its principal showpiece is an imitation landscape modelled on Cao Xueqin's 18th century novel *A Dream of Red Mansions*. Other attractions include a cultural village and an osmanthus garden, which is a popular spot during autumn's Sweet-Scented Osmanthus Festival (p.55). Located about 50km west of the city, off the A9 expressway. Admission is ¥60.

218 Huyi Lu
Jiading
沪宜公路218号
嘉定

Guyi Garden 古漪园

5912 2225 | www.guyigarden.com

Guyi Garden, also known as the Garden of Ancient Splendour, is located in the suburban town of Nanxiang, about 20km north-west of People's Square. Built between 1522 and 1566, during the Ming Dynasty, it contains historic pavilions, bamboo forests, lotus ponds and a captive crane. One of the newer pavilions, built during the Japanese occupation of Manchuria, is purposefully – and symbolically – missing one corner of its roof. Just inside the gate, the Guyi Garden Restaurant (5912 1335) is a good place to try the original version of Shanghai's famous soup dumplings, *nanxiang xiaolongbao*. The skins are a bit thicker here than at Jia Jia Tangbao (p.170), but the filling is quite tasty. Even the crane likes them. Admission to the garden is ¥12.

1111 Longwu Lu
Xuhui
龙吴路1111号
徐汇
🚇 *Shilong Lu*
Map p.443 F3 80

Shanghai Botanical Garden 上海植物园

6451 3369 | www.shbg.org

This expansive garden in the city's far south-west is worth the trek, especially in the spring. Peonies and peaches bloom in April; roses, cherry blossoms and azaleas in May. The 200 acres of grass and trees give you room to stretch your legs and fill your lungs. There are bamboo forests, multi-storey greenhouses, an extensive display of bonsai (*penjing*), and ponds for fishing. To appease the crowds, which can grow noisy during festivals, the garden also offers several restaurants, snack stands and toy vendors. Admission is ¥40 for all exhibits, including the bonsai and greenhouses; access to just the garden is ¥15.

Nature Reserves

Dongwang Lu
Chongming
东旺大道
崇明

Shanghai Chongming Dongtan Nature Reserve
上海崇明东滩鸟类自然保护区

6273 3855 | www.dongtan.cn

Shanghai's only nature reserve is a notable staging ground for migratory waterbirds, including tundra swans, hooded cranes and black-faced spoonbills. Established in 1998, it includes more than 80,000 acres of reeds, marshes, creeks and mudflats. These diverse habitats support at least 288 species of birds and 73 species of fish, including the endangered Chinese sturgeon. Thanks to its global importance, the reserve has attracted international support from the World Wildlife Fund and The Nature Conservancy, among others. The number of visitors is currently limited to 1,000 per year, so phone ahead. Although the city is only 45km away, the journey requires a one-hour ferry ride, and often involves another hour of waiting at the ferry port.

Water Parks

Other options **Amusement Parks** p.216, **Beaches** p.216

78 Xinzhen Lu
Minhang
七宝镇, 新镇路78号
闵行
🚇 *Shanghai Stadium*

Dino Beach 上海热带风暴水上乐园

6478 3333 | www.dinobeach.com.cn

Dino Beach is Shanghai's only water park, and features an imported filtration system, wave pool, artificial river and eight water slides. It's popular with both locals and expats, with family day trips giving way to breakdancing and bikini contests in the evenings. Admission ranges from ¥60 to ¥150, depending on the time of day and day of the week. The park is open from late June to early September. To get there by public transport, take the Metro to Shanghai Stadium then take a shuttle bus.

219

Zoos & Wildlife Parks

China's zoos and wildlife parks do not have an admirable reputation for animal welfare, but conditions have been improving in Shanghai. In 2006, Pudong's wildlife park cancelled its 'Animal Olympics' – which included kangaroo boxing, bear fights, and elephant tug-of-war – after a barrage of complaints from animal rights groups. Across town, the venerable Shanghai Zoo has been gradually upgrading its enclosures, replacing the traditional cages and concrete with more spacious and naturally landscaped settings. As international scrutiny intensifies before World Expo 2010, you can expect additional government action to improve Shanghai's image on the world stage.

1 Fenghe Lu
Pudong
丰和路1号
浦东
🚇 *Lujiazui*
Map p.431 F2 83

Shanghai Natural Wild Insect Kingdom 大自然野生昆虫馆
5840 6950 | www.shinsect.com

Neither natural nor wild, this place contains more than just bugs, and is more fun than you might think. Despite its convenient location, in the shadow of the Oriental Pearl Tower, the galleries can be peaceful even on weekends. The display of lizards is particularly comprehensive. Visitors can feed goldfish, rabbits, goats and chinchillas, or rent equipment for capturing fish in the concrete pond for ¥20 per hour. On the basement level, children can select insect specimens and display cases to make customised souvenirs. Admission is ¥40 per adult and ¥25 per child, with discounts for families.

178 Nanliu Gong Lu
Nanhui
南六公路178号
南汇

Shanghai Wild Animal Park 上海野生动物园
5803 6000 | www.shwzoo.com

Notorious for its cancelled 'Animal Olympics', the practice of feeding live ducklings to crocodiles (¥10 each), and a worker mauled by lions in 2005, Shanghai Wild Animal Park remains a popular attraction among locals and expats. There are more than 200 different species – including giraffes, takins, rhinos and tigers – divided between two areas, one viewed by bus, the other on foot. The park is located on the Pudong side of the river, about 35km from the city. Admission is ¥90.

2381 Hongqiao Lu
Changning
虹桥路2381号
长宁
Map p.427 D4 85

Shanghai Zoo 上海动物园
6268 7775 | www.shanghaizoo.cn

Originally a horseracing track, then a golf course, the rambling grounds of the Shanghai Zoo adjoin the expat enclave of Sassoon Park. During the past 50 years, more than 150 million people have visited the animals here. Chuan Chuan, the zoo's lone panda, is approaching 30 years old and is a father of five. His designated mate lives in Chongqing. If you don't enjoy pondering the fates of mammals in cages, it's worth a visit for the aquariums, aviary and water birds. In fact, birdwatchers will appreciate the early opening time (06:30 in summer) and the numerous wild birds attracted to the feeding areas. For a dramatic view, take a turn on the creaky Ferris wheel (¥8), where you can watch herons, egrets, and pelicans soaring freely above the central lake and its shady pavilions. The zoo also offers animal shows, other amusement rides and several restaurants. Admission is ¥30. Each adult can bring one child under 1.2m tall for free.

Need Some Direction?
The **Explorer Mini Maps** pack a whole city into your pocket and, once unfolded, are excellent navigational tools for exploring. Not only are they handy in size, with detailed information on the sights and sounds of the city, but also their fabulously affordable price mean they won't make a dent in your holiday fund. Wherever your travels take you, from the Middle East to Asia and beyond, grab a mini map and you'll never have to ask for directions.

Tours & Sightseeing

Other options **Weekend Breaks** p.225, **Exploring China** p.231

From specialised, private heritage tours to massive citywide bus tours, Shanghai's growing status as a visitor destination means there are more touring options than before, although many are primarily conducted in Chinese. Still, there are a few interesting options, and even long-time residents can appreciate a private art or *shikumen* tour.

Bicycle Tours

Floor 1, Block 25,
1984 Nanjing Xi Lu
Jing'an
南京西路1984号25座
静安
 Jing'an Temple
Map p.435 E1 86

Cycle China 骑车中国

6248 2146 | www.cyclechina.com

Cycle China is more a travel agency than a club, with an older branch in Beijing. The company designs hiking and biking tours specifically for expats. Their regular trips include day-long outings to Xitang and Suzhou – and a midnight jaunt in Shanghai. Prices vary depending on the number of people in the group.

2918 Zhongshan
Bei Lu
Putuo
中山北路2918号
普陀
Caoyang Lu
Map p.428 B2 87

Shanghai Bike Club 上海自行车俱乐部

5266 9013 | www.bohdi.com.cn

The Shanghai Bike Club is operated by Bohdi, a manufacturer of sleek, high-end mountain bikes. The club organises rides in several outlying areas, including Hangzhou, Moganshan, Dianshan Lake and Chongming Island. You can rent a bike or bring your own, and tour leaders will accommodate beginners as well as more experienced riders.

Boat Tours

Eleven companies operate cruises on the busy Huangpu River, with more than 30 boats. The city sets requirements for size, safety equipment and sanitary conditions. Very few accidents have been reported in recent years, though in late June 2007 a cruise ship was struck by a cargo vessel, injuring 23 tourists. Longer cruises typically sail to the Huangpu's confluence with the Yangtze, while shorter trips shuttle between the Yangpu and Nanpu bridges. Only 2% of passengers are locals. It's also possible to cruise in five-star luxury from Shanghai to Chongqing, eight days away on the Yangtze River. Visit www.yangtzeriver.org for more information.

219 Zhongshan
Dong Er Lu
Huangpu
中山东二路219号
黄埔
Map p.431 F3 88

Shanghai Huangpu River Cruise Company
上海船游黄浦江公司

6374 4461 | www.shpjyl.com

Located at the south end of the Bund promenade, this is the largest cruise company in Shanghai. It offers boats that look like comfortable ferries, boats bearing the heads of dragons, and boats that resemble ornate floating teahouses. You can choose a one hour, three hour, or evening cruise, with varying levels of seating. Onboard snack bars sell food and refreshments.

221

Brewery Tours

Although Shanghai currently offers no brewery tours, the city has a small but growing number of brew-pubs where you can drink within sight of the vats. Try Henry's Brewery & Grill (33 Sichuan Zhong Lu; 6321 7127), whose brewmaster produces five beers, including an unusual take on the 'honey brown' variety. Another good option is the German-themed Castle Oktober (39 Taojiang Lu; 6431 2668), which produces a few wheat and dark beers.

Bus Tours

59 Maoming Nan Lu
Luwan
茂名南路59号
卢湾
🚇 *Shanxi Nan Lu*

Shanghai Jin Jiang Tour Bus Lines 上海锦江观光巴士
6270 1667
Jin Jiang tour buses depart opposite the Jin Jiang Hotel every 45 minutes from Monday to Friday, 09:00 to 17:15, and Saturday and Sunday from 08:45 to 17:45. The bus makes eight stops, including People's Square, the Oriental Pearl Tower, Yu Garden and the Bund – before returning to the hotel. You can hop on or off at any stop. Tickets cost ¥18 and can be purchased on the bus.

Various Locations

Shanghai Sightseeing Bus Centre 上海旅游集散中心
6426 5555 | www.64265555.com
This municipal office operates regularly scheduled, no-frills bus tours to water towns, gardens and other suburban tourist destinations. In the past, most routes departed from Shanghai Stadium or Hongkou Stadium, but some are set to move to the city's new long-distance bus stations. Check the website for up-to-date information.

City Tours

476 Mingyue Lu
Pudong
金桥明月路476号
浦东
Map p.440 C2 **9I**

Community Centre Shanghai 上海国际社区中心
5030 3313 | www.communitycenter.cn
In addition to a newcomer orientation programme and a range of classes for expats, the Community Centre Shanghai offers several different city tours. These include a Suzhou Creek bike tour, a hidden market tour, and a Pudong wet market and flower market tour. As of June 2007, the centre's Puxi office, formerly on Julu Lu, was planning a move to the Hongqiao area. Visit the website to sign up for the weekly newsletter.

Various Locations

The Shanghai Expatriate Association 上海外派人员协会
www.seashanghai.net
Membership of the Shanghai Expatriate Association is open to foreign passport holders only. The annual family membership fee of ¥300 permits you to sign up for walking tours of Yuyuan, Moganshan Lu and the French Concession, day trips to Suzhou, and other events. An additional fee is required for each tour.

Farm & Stable Tours

Da Ye Gong Lu
Songjiang
大叶公路虹洋路2号
松江

Shanghai Organics 上海崇本堂农业科技有限公司
6249 2118 | www.shorganic.com
Shanghai Organics is the first certified organic farm in Shanghai, and its fruits and vegetables available in most expat supermarkets. About a 45 minute drive from the city centre, the farm offers customised tours, barbecues and birthday parties. Rates begin at ¥100 per adult and ¥50 per child. The company also operates a weekly farmer's market on Sundays from 10:30 to 13:30, at 2 Dongping Lu, near the Hengshan Lu Metro station.

Not big, but very clever…

Perfectly proportioned to fit in your pocket,
this marvellous mini guidebook makes sure
you don't just get the holiday you paid for,
but rather the one that you dreamed of.

Shanghai Mini Visitors' Guide
Maximising your holiday, minimising your hand luggage

Other Tours

461 Tianshan Lu ◀
Changning
天山路461弄18号
长宁
Map p.427 F3 94

Gang of One Photography 上海中加摄影图片社

6259 9716 | *www.gangofone.com.cn*

Photographer Gangfeng Wang grew up in the old Shanghai lanes between Weihai Lu and Nanjing Xi Lu, in a neighborhood that is unfortunately scheduled for destruction in December 2007. His award-winning work has been exhibited in the United Kingdom, Japan and Canada. He leads energetic half-day tours of Shanghai's *shikumen* housing for ¥300 per person.

Various Locations ◀

My Shanghai: Art Tours & Talks
我的上海：艺术之旅与对话

136 8160 7815

Robert Davis offers tours to students and adults at the Shanghai Art Museum, the Shanghai Museum of Contemporary Art, and the Shanghai Museum. A dedicated and talented teacher, his tours focus on helping people understand and appreciate art. Three-hour tours cost ¥500 per person. You can email him at deeppeaceone@ yahoo.com.

1065 Zhaojiabang Lu ◀
Xuhui
肇嘉浜路1065号
徐汇
🚇 *Xujiahui*
Map p.435 E4 96

W Patrick Cranley

3368 0055

A resident of Shanghai since 1997, Patrick Cranley is a co-founder of the Shanghai Historic House Association. He offers customised tours on Shanghai history, architecture, economics or politics. Half-day tours cost around ¥4,600 for up to 12 people. Email him at wmpatrick.cranley@asiamedia.net.

Shopping Tours

Various Locations ◀

Shop My Shanghai 血拼在上海

www.shopmyshanghai.com

Shop My Shanghai is a small, American-run company that specialises in customised tours for individuals and groups. Guides serve as interpreter, consultant, negotiator and concierge. Tours include visits to the fake markets, fabric markets, luxury clothing outlets and more. Visit the website for a description of the hourly rates.

Tours Outside Shanghai

1558 Dingxi Lu ◀
Changning
定西路1558号
长宁
🚇 *Yan'an Xi Lu*

Spring International 春秋航空旅游网

6252 0000 | *www.tour.china-sss.com*

One of the largest travel agencies in China – and operator of its own low-fare airline – Spring International has 55 outlets in Shanghai alone. It offers domestic and international tour packages, hotel reservations and airline tickets. Tours are conducted in both Mandarin and English and are often attended by both locals and expats.

Various Locations ◀

Travel Professionals Shanghai 上海旅游专业人士

6485 2218 | *www.travel-professionals.cn*

Travel Professionals' English-speaking agents offer air tickets and tours within China and beyond. Ranging from three days to over two weeks, these guided tours can be geared to both active travellers as well as those looking for a relaxing break from city life. The company also provides customised tours of Shanghai and its outlying areas.

Weekend Breaks

There are many options for weekend breaks from Shanghai. Neighbouring provinces Jiangsu and Zhejiang have a wealth of towns and cities with historic and cultural attractions. Shanghai's extensive air connections make more distant breaks an easy option as well. Most Chinese people travel during the three Golden Weeks – the seven-day holidays around Spring Festival (Chinese New Year), Labour Day (May 1) and National Day (October 1). Avoid travelling then if at all possible, as planes, trains and buses are usually packed and fares are much higher.

That's Grand

Stretching from Beijing to Hangzhou, the Grand Canal of China is the longest in the world, at 1,794km. It is also the oldest – some sections have existed since 486BC.

Beijing

You could spend weeks in the Chinese capital and still not do it justice, but the city is also ideal for a short break to get a quick fix. If you haven't been before, you need to spend one day at the Forbidden City (¥40-¥60) and Tiananmen Square, and watch the People's Liberation Army soldiers raising the flag at dawn or lowering it at dusk. Marvel at the majestic royal palaces, then walk a couple of blocks to the department stores of Beijing's premier shopping street, Wangfujing Jie.

If you're peckish, try a snack in the night markets to the side or at the end of the street, where you'll find such delicacies as fried scorpion and silkworm. More substantial and appetising fare is on offer at the 143 year old Qianmen Quanjude Roast Duck Restaurant – the place to go for Beijing duck.

Some of Beijing's top hotels are in the Wangfujing area, including the venerable Palace Peninsula and the former Raffles Beijing Hotel (see p.230). Among other excellent hotels are the Shangri-La Beijing in the north-west, sister property China World Hotel and the Kempinski Hotel, close to the Sanlitun bar district.

Other must-dos from Beijing include visiting the Great Wall (¥40-¥45) and Ming Tombs (¥30-¥60), (which can be combined in a one day trip), Beihai Park (¥5-¥10), where you can watch people doing tai chi, calligraphy or ballroom dancing in the early morning, the Temple of Heaven (¥30-¥35), where locals gather to play music and *mahjong*, and the Summer Palace (¥25-¥35). A good alternative is a pedicab tour of Beijing's fast-disappearing *hutong* neighbourhoods. And for some unusual presents, Panjiayuan market offers everything from crafts and coral jewellery to secondhand bric-a-brac.

Winters are bitter but can be a good time to get clear skies, and very few crowds. Spring brings flower blossoms but also sandstorms from the Gobi Desert, and summers are hot and humid. Autumn is when Beijing enjoys its most settled weather – but avoid the incredibly crowded National Day holiday.

Hangzhou

Established during the Qin Dynasty over 2,000 years ago, Hangzhou was one of the world's largest cities with a million-plus population when Marco Polo visited in the 13th century. He described the city as 'beyond dispute the finest and the noblest in the world'. During the Taiping Rebellion of 1861, the city walls, gates and many of its fine buildings were razed, and the Cultural Revolution brought more destruction 100 years later.

But its most famous and alluring attraction has endured for many centuries; West Lake is a magnet for visitors, especially lovers and honeymooners. It has spawned some three dozen similarly named lakes across China and inspired the well-known Chinese phrase: 'In heaven there is paradise; on earth there is Suzhou and Hangzhou.' West Lake has four islands, pavilions, pagodas, gardens and a pair of causeways with humpbacked bridges large enough for boats to pass under. A cruise on the lake costs ¥45 per person, and you can also watch a spectacular night show set on an extending, floating stage.

Other attractions include the Temple of Hidden Souls, which dates back to the Qing Dynasty (¥35), the Zhejiang Provincial Museum, Mausoleum of General Yue Fei and the

225

60 metre high Six Harmonies Pagoda, which visitors can climb for an extra ¥10 on top of the ¥20 admission.

On the Water
Overnight boats operate on the Grand Canal between Hangzhou and Suzhou. However, as it is at night you miss much of the scenery and the conditions on board leave much to be desired. Instead, hop on a boat in Suzhou to see the pretty canal-side houses and arched bridges. An hour-long cruise costs about ¥70.

There are numerous snack stalls around West Lake, but for a more substantial meal try a Sichuan hotpot at one of the three Hangzhou branches of Chuanweiguang restaurant (www.hzcwg.com), or dine in one of the three restaurants at the Shangri-La Hangzhou overlooking West Lake. There is also high-end shopping around Wulin Square, in Hangzhou Tower and on Euro Street.

The cheapest and quickest way to get to Hangzhou is by bullet train from Shanghai South Station; the journey takes just over 90 minutes and costs ¥44. Weekends are very busy from spring to late autumn, holiday periods impossibly so. Even bad weather won't put off crowds; the lake is said to be at its best when the rain is falling.

Nanjing

The capital of Jiangsu stands on the south bank of the Yangtze River and is three hours by train from Shanghai. It has served as the capital of several dynasties in its 2,500 years and played a pivotal role in China's history. The city walls were constructed between 1368 and 1398, before the third Ming emperor shifted the capital to Beijing. They were among the longest city defences ever created, and two-thirds of them still stand today. The grand Zhonghua Gate (¥20) is one of the few Ming city gates still standing. The Tomb of Zhu Yuanzhan (¥60), east of the city in the Purple and Gold Mountains, has an avenue of giant stone statues and animals. The mountains also contain the huge mausoleum complex built to honour revolutionary hero Sun Yatsen (¥40). He became the first provisional president of the fledgling Republic of China in 1912, when the dynastic period ended. Among the city's most impressive structures is the Nanjing Yangtze River Bridge. Visitors can go up to a viewing deck on one of its mighty towers (¥12).

Nanjing successfully blends its old treasures with the high-rise towers, shopping centres and other trappings of a city in the fast lane. The Confucius Temple (*Fuzi Miao*) area is kitsch but fun after dark, with lively nightlife, bright lights and boat trips on the Qinhuai River as well as a vibrant street market. You can sample a selection of Nanjing's traditional *xiaochi* snacks at the Wanqinglou restaurant, also in the Confucius Temple area. At the Nanjing Brocade Museum & Research Institute (¥15), you can see how silk was woven for emperors on huge wooden looms that still produce expensive brocade. For more affordable items, head for the department stores and shopping centres of downtown Xinjiekou.

Putuoshan

This tiny island, measuring little more than 6km long, is one of the most revered sites for Buddhist pilgrims because of its mountain, which is one of the four sacred Buddhist peaks. The island is famed for its beautiful coastal scenery, beaches and mountain landscape, and is virtually traffic free (except for minibuses, which drive between the main tourist areas). It is also a religious centre featuring numerous temples and monasteries, including Puji Temple (¥5), which dates back almost 1,100 years. You have to pay ¥110 to get on to Putuoshan as it is a national park. You can climb the steps up to the 279m peak, or just explore the island at leisure and relax on its lovely beaches. Seafood, especially shellfish, is the local speciality, but ensure you settle on the price before you eat or you could end the meal with indigestion from the inflated bill. There are several medium-quality hotels, mostly small. To get to Putuoshan, you can take a slow ferry from Shanghai, which takes 12 hours. Alternatively, you can catch a bus to Luchao Wharf and then a fast ferry to the island for a total journey time of four to five hours.

Qingdao

Few cities are immortalised in the name of a drink, but Qingdao's fame has spread far and wide thanks to beer. Tsingtao has been produced in the town since the Germans annexed the city and brought their brewing skills with them more than 100 years ago, not relinquishing control for a quarter of a century. The city remains the largest beer production centre in China, and an international beer festival is held each August. A tour of the Tsingtao brewery costs ¥50. The German influence goes beyond just the famous tipple. The residence of the former German governor is perhaps the best example of the well-preserved European buildings. The city is also set to benefit from the 2008 Olympics; it is hosting the sailing races for the games, and a lot of investment is being ploughed into developing the seafront area and enhancing its beaches. The Qingdao Museum is worth a visit for its carved Buddhas and paintings, and, if you have time, take a trip beyond the city to scenic Laoshan Mountain. Qingdao's bustling port and growing reputation as a tourism destination mean there are plenty of hotels. Top of the crop are the Hai Tian, Shangri-La and Crowne Plaza (see p.230).

Pincer Movement

The Shanghai hairy crab, or Chinese mitten crab, is an autumn delicacy. Despite the name, the crabs mainly come from Yangcheng Lake, north-east of Suzhou, in Jiangsu province. They are caught and harvested while migrating to the Yangtze delta. The crabs' shells and claws are chewed to extract the meat.

Suzhou

Suzhou's position on the Grand Canal established the city as a key trading waypoint from the seventh century. It had also been the temporary capital of the Wu state during the Warring States period a millennium earlier. A series of canals cross the city, connected to the main arterial canal and a moat around the city walls, hence the nickname 'Venice of the east'.

Other than trade, Suzhou's fortune was built on the silk industry. It also became an important cultural centre; wealthy merchants and government officials built ornate gardens, with pavilions, rockeries, bridges and miniature landscapes of lakes. By the 16th century there were nearly 100 gardens. Of the few surviving examples, the largest is the Humble Administrator's Garden (the entrance fee is ¥50-¥70, depending on the season). But it is the smallest, the exquisite Master of the Nets Garden (¥20-¥30), which is the real gem.

The Panmen Scenic Area (¥25) contains Suzhou's only remaining city gate and the Auspicious Light Pagoda (¥6), as well as the ancient, arched Wumen Bridge. Immortalised in a Tang-era poem, the Maple Bridge is another evocative spot, near Hanshan Temple. The Song Dynasty leaning pagoda on top of Tiger Hill (¥40-¥60) is brick-built but made to imitate wood.

A day trip should also include the new Suzhou Museum, the Silk Embroidery Research Institute, (where you can watch artisans at work), and the Suzhou Silk Museum, which traces the history of silk production in China.

A roundtrip express train ticket costs ¥44 and the journey takes less than 50 minutes from Shanghai Railway Station. A day trip for two people with a car and an English-speaking guide, including entry to some gardens and a canal cruise, costs ¥1,500.

Wuxi

About 90 minutes by road from Shanghai, Wuxi straddles the Grand Canal and is close to Taihu Lake, the third-largest freshwater lake in China. While it can be done in a day trip, an overnight stay allows you to explore the canal-side streets, appreciate its 3,000 years of history and experience the beauty of the lake. Wuxi is known for its chubby Huishan clay figurines, made with self-curing clay that does not need to be fired. You can watch them being hand-painted at the Wuxi Clay Figurines Museum and Research Institute. The other clay product this area is famous for is the purple teapots from nearby Yixing, where a ceramics festival is held every May.

The Xihui Scenic Area houses several historic sites, including the Jichang Garden and several springs, temples and bridges. A novel attraction is the Wuxi CCTV Film & TV

Studio (¥120), where stunt shows are staged among film sets used for well-known Chinese productions. More serene is the Lingshan Scenic Area (¥88), which has the world's tallest bronze statue of the Sakyamuni Buddha. There is also a smaller Buddha that appears out of the opening petals of a giant lotus flower. Taihu Lake's picturesque tree-festooned rocky headlands are best enjoyed in Turtle Head Peninsula Park. Traditional sailing boats still sail on Taihu Lake, but for tourists only. A sailing cruise costs ¥105.

City centre hotels such as the Sheraton Wuxi or New World Courtyard are handy for sightseeing (p.230), while lakeside resorts like the Wuxi 1881 Peninsula Hotel and Taihu Hotel offer a tranquil escape.

Yangzhou

Located on the northern side of the Yangtze River, close to its junction with the Grand Canal, Yangzhou has a very important position. Its significance through the years is underlined by mausoleums of emperors from the Han and Sui Dynasties. It is also the site of an ancient Tang and Song city. Geyan Garden is on the site of the much earlier Shouzi Garden and is noted for its rock gardens, while Heyuan Garden is a Qing masterpiece. Tianning Temple houses the Yangzhou Museum and has a hall dedicated to Marco Polo, who is said to have been governor of Yangzhou for three of his 17 years

Sights of Beijing and beyond

in China. A bronze lion sculpture was given to the museum as a gift by the city of Venice. Daming Temple, on Slender West Lake, is a must for tourists. The temple, along with humped bridges, the White Pagoda and the Five-Pavilion Bridge, are the highlights of a ¥80 lake cruise.

In a province famed for its arts and crafts, Yangzhou's speciality is red lacquer ware. Some huge examples are on display at the Yangzhou Arts and Crafts Museum. Food is its other claim to fame. Yangzhou is home of the Huaiyang cuisine style, known for its delicate flavours, liquid-filled steamed buns and *yung chow* fried rice, a corruption of the city's name. Breakfast at Fuchun Teahouse is not to be missed. The once-exclusive Yangzhou State Guesthouse is now open to all and serves excellent food. Yangzhou can be reached by road across the Yangtze. A weekend visit could also take in historic Zhenjiang, across the river on its southern bank.

Weekend Break Hotels

Beijing	Grand Hyatt Beijing	10 8518 1234	www.beijing.grand.hyatt.com
	Kempinski Hotel Beijing Lufthansa Centre	10 6465 3388	www.kempinski-beijing.com
	Raffles Beijing Hotel	10 6526 3388	www.beijing.raffles.com
	Shangri-La Hotel	10 6841 2211	www.shangri-la.com
	St Regis Hotel	10 6460 6688	www.starwoodhotels.com
	The Peninsula Beijing	10 8516 2888	http://beijing.peninsula.com
Hangzhou	Best Western Hangzhou Richful Green Hotel	571 8792 9999	www.bestwestern.com
	Four Points by Sheraton Hangzhou	21 6391 8251	www.starwoodhotels.com
	Hyatt Regency Hangzhou	571 8779 1234	www.hangzhou.regency.hyatt.com
	Lakeview Hotel	571 8707 8888	www.lakeviewhotelhz.com
	Radisson Plaza Hotel Hangzhou	571 8515 8888	www.radisson.com/hangzhoucn
	Shangri-La Hangzhou	571 8797 7951	www.shangri-la.com
Nanjing	Crowne Plaza Nanjing Hotel & Suites	25 8471 8888	http://holidayinn.com.cn
	Mandarin Garden Hotel	25 5220 2555	www.njzyl-hotel.cn
	Nanjing Jinling Hotel	25 8471 1888	www.jinlinghotel.com
	Sheraton Nanjing Kingsley Hotel & Towers	25 8666 8888	www.starwoodhotels.com
	Sofitel Galaxy	25 8371 8888	www.sofitel.com
	Xianwu Hotel	25 8335 8888	www.xianwu.com.cn
Putuoshan	Citic Putuo Hotel	580 669 8222	www.citicpt.com
	Luyuan Holiday Inn	580 669 0588	na
	Putuoshan Hotel	580 609 2828	na
	Xilei Xiao Zhuang Hotel	580 609 1505	na
Qingdao	Best Western Premier Qingdao Kilin Crown Hotel	532 8889 1888	www.bestwestern.com
	Crowne Plaza	532 8571 8888	www.ichotelsgroup.com
	Grand Regency Hotel	532 8588 1818	www.regencyhotelqd.com
	Hai Tian Hotel	532 8387 1888	www.hai-tian-hotel.com
	Hotel Equatorial Qingdao	532 8572 1688	www.equatorial.com
	Shangri-La Hotel	532 8388 3838	www.shangri-la.com
Suzhou	Regalia Serviced Apartments ▶ p.41	512 6825 8118	www.regalia.com.cn
	Shangri-La Hotel	512 6808 0168	www.shangri-la.com
	Suzhou Sofitel Hotel	512 6522 2222	www.sofitel.com
Wuxi	New World Courtyard Wuxi	510 8276 2888	www.marriott.com
	Sheraton Wuxi Hotel & Towers	510 8868 8688	www.starwoodhotels.com
	Taihu Hotel	510 8551 7888	na
	Wuxi 1881 Peninsula Hotel	510 8868 1881	www.1881hotel.com
Yangzhou	Grand Metropole Hotel	514 732 2888	na
	Xiyuan Dajiudian	514 734 4888	na
	Yangzhou State Guesthouse	514 780 9888	na

Exploring China

Flight time: 3 hours
Best time to visit:
April to October, but
winter snow and ice is
beautiful in Jiuzhaigou.

Chengdu, Leshan, Emeishan & Jiuzhaigou

Fiery Sichuan cuisine, some of China's best street snacks and teahouses, and a distinctive Chinese opera style are just some of Chengdu's attractions. It is also the home of the giant panda. They live in the wild in Sichuan's mountains and can be seen close-up at a breeding research centre. The Giant Buddha of Leshan and the holy Buddhist mountain, Mount Emeishan, can be visited on a day trip, but the spectacular forested valleys, waterfalls and pools of Unesco-listed Jiuzhaigou to the north deserve a few days.

Flight time: 2.5 hours
Best time to visit:
Spring and autumn. Avoid
high summer. Winters can
be drab and cold.

Chongqing & Yangtze Cruise

Yangtze cruises have been some of the most popular tourist trips since China opened up to visitors. The completion of the towering Three Gorges Dam will raise the water level 156m when the project is finished in 2009, and a number of historic sites are being submerged. But the majesty of the cliffs remains and a visit to the dam has become a highlight on cruises. Boats sail between Chongqing, a vast city perched on cliffs, and Wuhan, downstream.

Flight time: 2 hours
Best time to visit:
Any time, but it gets hot
and humid in summer.

Guangzhou

Formerly known as Canton and famed for its cuisine, the capital of Guangdong province lies on the Pearl River Delta close to Hong Kong. It is often overlooked as a tourist destination but has many interesting sights. Shamian Island, where British and French traders were once confined, has wonderful European architecture. Nearby is fascinating Qingping Market, with its dried insects and animal parts. Yuexiu Park has the Statue of the Five Goats, the city's symbol, plus 600-year-old Zhenhai Tower and the Sun Yatsen Memorial Hall. The decorative Chen Family Temple, Six Banyan Tree Temple and a night Pearl River cruise are other highlights.

Flight time: 2 hours
Best time to visit:
Autumn – spring is the
rainy season, winter is cool
and summer is hot.

Guilin & Yangshuo

The sharp limestone peaks of this area of south-west China rise up dramatically out of the flat paddy fields to create one of the country's most iconic landscapes. They punctuate Guilin in a series of evocatively named hills, stretching either side of the Li River to laid-back Yangshuo and beyond. Other than taking a river cruise, you can explore the area by bike, venture into caves, go rock climbing, watch cormorant fishermen or chill out in bars and cafes.

Ice and Snow Festival, Harbin

Flight time: 2.5 hours
Best time to visit:
January, for the ice and
snow festival.

Harbin

China's most north-easterly city has a strong Russian influence. It was founded by Russian railway builders constructing the trans-Manchuria rail line and settled by refugees of the Bolshevik Revolution. The onion-domed Church of St Sophia is among the period buildings which survived the Cultural Revolution. But the city's real highlight is the spectacular Ice and Snow Festival, featuring snow sculptures and colossal buildings carved from the frozen Songhua River and lit by multi-coloured fluorescent tubes.

Hong Kong

Flight time: 2.5 hours
Best time to visit:
Any time, although
summers are hot
and sticky.

A decade on from its hand-over to China, the former British colony has retained its vitality and character and is thriving under the 'one country, two systems' policy. The opening of Hong Kong Disneyland has bolstered its appeal, which centres on shopping, nightlife, culture and cuisine. Victoria Peak gives spectacular views and is a perennial favourite, along with open-air markets, Ocean Park, Repulse Bay's beaches and bistros, the Big Buddha on Lantau Island and the Symphony of Lights show. The *Explorer Mini Hong Kong* guide is the perfect companion for a visit.

Huangshan

Flight time: 1 hour
Best time to visit:
Autumn is pretty because
of the foliage colours but
any time of year is good,
even winter.

The pine-tree-clad craggy pinnacles of Huangshan, or Yellow Mountain, are an iconic Chinese scene gracing countless paintings and porcelain designs. Clouds often cloak the mountain, enhancing its beauty. Climbing it takes a full day, but a cable car whisks more sedentary visitors to the summit. The mountain can be combined with a visit to the nearby preserved historic villages of Xidi and Hongcun, which starred in the movie *Crouching Tiger, Hidden Dragon*.

Kashgar

Flight time: 7 hours
Best time to visit:
Spring and autumn.
Summer brings fierce heat.

China's western outpost feels very much like a frontier city. It grew into an important staging point on the Silk Road, having been established at an oasis at the junction of the trading route's northern and southern arms. Under Islamic rule for eight centuries, it has several important Muslim edifices including the Id Kah Mosque and Abakh Hoja Tomb. The Sunday bazaar is a lively and colourful affair. A Silk Road trip may take in historic Urumqi and Turpan, where grapes grow in a fertile valley and where the ground plunges to the second-lowest point on earth.

Lhasa

Flight time: 4 hours
Best time to visit:
May to October

The opening of the Qinghai-Tibet Railway has brought an unprecedented rush of tourists and settlers to the Tibetan capital – so much so that authorities have had to restrict tickets to the fortress-like Potala Palace, the former winter home of the Dalai Lama, which stands on a hill overlooking the city. Among Lhasa's other historic treasures are the ancient Jokhang Temple and neighbouring Barkhor district, with its lively market and prayer-wheel-spinning pilgrims. The impressive Sera and Drepung monasteries and the Dalai Lama's summer palace, Norbulingka, from which he fled in 1959, are also worth a visit.

Lijiang, Dali & Kunming

Flight time: 2.5 hours
(Kunming), 4.5 hours
(Lijiang).
Best time to visit:
Spring and autumn.

An ancient town of cobbled streets and alleys lined by ornate wooden buildings and laced by streams, Lijiang, in north-west Yunnan, is a delight, despite becoming increasingly overrun by tourists. The town is home to the Naxi minority group, whose traditions, culture and music remain strong. More minority culture can be experienced among the cafes and environs of Dali (the Bai people) and in provincial capital Kunming, where the main attraction is the Shilin Stone Forest, two hours outside the city.

Macau

Flight time: 2 hours
Best time to visit:
Any time, but summers
are hot and humid.

Macau was the oldest European colony in China, having been under Portuguese rule for more than four centuries, before it was handed back to China in 1999. Its Historic Centre has been declared a World Heritage Site by Unesco and encompasses 28 buildings and monuments, and eight squares. Gambling has been licensed for over 150 years and gaming revenue now exceeds that of Las Vegas thanks to the opening up of its casino industry and the building of new mega casino resorts. More are in the pipeline.

Flight time: *2.5 hours to Jinan, then two hours by bus to Qufu.*
Best time to visit: *April to October.*

Qufu

The Shandong town of Qufu has left its mark on the world as the birthplace of philosopher Confucius, whose teachings have been followed for 2,500 years. At the heart of the old town, which is Unesco listed, is a walled complex encompassing the Kong Family Mansion and Kong Miao, or Temple of Confucius. Just beyond the town is Kong Lin, or Kong Family Cemetery, a huge forested area where the great man, his sons and more than 100,000 descendants are buried.

Qufu life

Flight time: *3 hours*
Best time to visit: *Any time, but October to March is the peak season.*

Sanya

Set on the southern-most tip of tropical Hainan Island, Sanya has become China's premier beach resort. International resort hotels line sandy bays lapped by the warm, clear waters of the South China Sea. Activities include diving in the coral-rich sea and golf on palm-fringed courses designed by star players. Yalong Bay nestles between two peninsulas and is where most of Sanya's top hotels are located.

Flight time: *2.5 hours*
Best time to visit: *Spring and autumn.*

Xi'an

The Terracotta Warriors, buried for 2,000 years and discovered by two farmers in 1974, are one of the world's greatest treasures and have made Xi'an a must-visit destination. The burial chambers do not disappoint, but the city has other attractions worth visiting; Xi'an was the starting point for the Silk Road and was the capital for 13 dynasties. The Ming Dynasty city wall and moat run for more than 15km around its historic heart, enclosing sights such as the Drum Tower and Great Mosque, in the Muslim quarter. Beyond the wall are delights including the Big Wild Goose Pagoda.

Travel Agencies

China Merchants Group Shanghai International Travel Service	6120 3601	www.cmit.com
China Youth Travel Service	6433 0000	www.scyts.com.cn
Classic Travel	6416 0808	www.classictravel.net.cn
East Shanghai International Travel Service	5888 5681	na
Easy Tours International Travel Service	6203 7070	www.easytours.cn
Great West Travel	6279 8489	www.great-west-travel.com
Great World International Travel Service	6360 2939	na
Happy Travel Service	5835 7434	www.gohappytravel.com
New World Travel Service	6351 6346	na
Poloair Holidays	6334 6118	www.poloair.net
Redfrog Travel	6271 7432	www.redfrogtravel.com
Shanghai China International Travel Service	80 0820 8286	www.scits.com
Shanghai CITIC International Travel	5292 5277	www.shcitictravel.com.cn
Shanghai Ctrip International	3406 4880	www.ctrip.com.cn
Shanghai Dazhong International Travel Service	6353 2130	www.dzit.com
Shanghai FASCO International Tour & Travel Co	6350 0170	www.efasco.com
Shanghai New Comfort International Travel Co	5116 8155	na
Shanghai Shihua International Travel Service	6853 6853	www.ssits.com.cn
Spring International	6252 0000	http://tour.china-sss.com

Davids camp
men's spa & skin care

Websit: www.davidscampapa.com
Email: dcsh@davidscampspa.com

David's Camp
Men's SPA & Skin Care

戴维营专业男子SPA护理中
David's Camp Men's SPA & Skin Care C

Shanghai Store

No.200,West Yan An RD (Near Urumqi Rd)
Shanghai ,PRC
Tel:021-62473602, 62486704

Nanjing Store

No2 Buiding, No.54, North Taiping RD
Nanjing, PRC
Tel: 025-84537316, 84537318

Managed By David-Belle SPA Investment Co.,Ltd
website: www.david-belle.net

Activities

Sports & Activities

While it may seem as though the main pastimes for most of Shanghai's population are donning a tracksuit to do tai chi in the park or flying a kite in a public place, the city offers both the athlete and the creative a wealth of opportunities to exercise their muscles and their brains. From cricket and football to yoga and cooking courses, there are options for virtually all tastes, ages and wallets.

Sport is becoming increasingly popular in Chinese culture, especially among the young. Interest has been inspired, in part, by the country's increased status on the global competitive stage, particularly Beijing's hosting of the 2008 Olympics and the national team qualifying for the football World Cup for the first time in 2002 (although they didn't make it to Germany in 2006). Volleyball, gymnastics, badminton, weightlifting and the much-loved table tennis – all Olympic events – remain the most popular sports nationwide, and it's no different in Shanghai. Table tennis is synonymous with China, and with a large number of the city's apartment blocks providing tables, it's easy to see why the country produces some of the world's best players.

For expats looking to get physically and mentally active, the language barrier can be problematic. However, there's certainly no reason to let that discourage you from getting out – the growing number of westerners in Shanghai has resulted in a boom in international activities and clubs, many of which form the fabric of expat social life in the city. Smaller neighbourhood sports clubs and traditional Chinese cultural activities usually do not have English-speaking instructors (although this doesn't mean that English speakers are not welcome). To find out about language, check out the club's website (where available) or call ahead and ask if anyone speaks English ('You hui shuo ying yu de ma?' is the crucial phrase).

Shanghai weather can be extreme, with cold, wet winters and hot, humid summers, so most activities have set seasons, and some have indoor options. Cricket, for example, limits the number of matches during the hottest months of July and August – check

District Guide

We've included a Shanghai district by each entry in this section to help you locate the clubs, sports centres and spas. The map on p.416 shows which area of town each one covers.

Activity Finder

out www.asas.com.cn for year-round indoor and outdoor sports leagues. If the thought of running around under a gym roof instead of the summer sun makes you nauseous, follow the locals' lead and use early mornings or late evenings to avoid the warmest periods of the day, particularly for strenuous activities such as running and cycling. Shanghai's poor air quality can also have a negative effect on outdoor activities, so one way to get some welcome relief is to try to get out of the city with one of the cycling groups that take trips to less polluted areas.

The free and widely available expat publications, such as *Shanghai Talk*, *that's Shanghai*, *City Weekend* and *SH*, contain listings and contacts for many of the international clubs, leagues and forthcoming events.

Aerobics & Fitness Classes
Other options **Sports & Leisure Facilities** p.281, **Well-Being** p.289

Plenty of Shanghai's gyms and health clubs offer aerobics and fitness classes. The larger places usually have English-speaking instructors, while members of smaller, Chinese-run gyms fare perfectly well mimicking the unintelligible class leaders. Classes are typically common activities: aerobics, step, dance and spinning, as well as heavier options such as body pump. In addition, Chinese gyms tend to specialise in relaxation and stretching classes such as Pilates, body balance (a mixture of tai chi, yoga and Pilates) and yoga. Most gyms require a membership to attend the classes, although some places allow the public to pay per class without joining. Hotel gyms tend to be less crowded but membership is usually more expensive and classes less frequent.

Aerobics & Fitness Classes

BodyTech	Changning	6281 5639	Aerobics, ballet, belly dancing, Chinese dancing, hip-hop, karate, Pilates, salsa, step, yoga
Clark Hatch Fitness Centre	Changning	6212 9998	Aerobics, kick boxing, Pilates, step, yoga
Fitness First	Jing'an	6288 0152	Aerobics, body balance, body combat, body jam, body pump, cycling, RPM, Pilates, step, yoga
Kerry Gym	Jing'an	6279 4625	Tai chi, yoga
Megafit 1	Luwan	5435 6399	Ballet, body balance, body conditioning, cardio-burning, spinning, step, all types of yoga
Megafit 2	Pudong	5030 8118	Ballet, body balance, body conditioning, cardio-burning, spinning, step, yoga
Physical Fitness	Luwan	6390 8188	Aerobics, dance, hip-hop, step, yoga
Portman Ritz-Carlton Fitness Centre	Jing'an	6279 8888	Latin dance, Pilates, swimming class, yoga
Star Gym	Jing'an	6271 7944	Aerobics, body pump, dance, hip-hop, kick boxing, Latin dance, Pilates, spinning, step
Total Fitness	Jing'an	6255 3535	Aerobics, body combat, body jam, body pump, dance, karate, Pilates, spinning, step, Thai boxing
Total Fitness Club 1	Putuo	6276 2922	Aerobics, body combat, body pump, body jam, boxing, dance, spinning, step, tai chi, yoga

Archery

Various Locations

Daoshun Archery 道顺射箭馆
www.daoshun.net

This archery chain, which also offers badminton, darts and table tennis, has branches in different areas of Shanghai, all of which are affordable and kid friendly. Daoshun has equipment to rent and the instructors are extremely helpful, if not overly attentive. Most of them don't speak English, so you'll have to brush up on your Mandarin for

237

detailed tuition. There are branches at 293 Yunnan Nan Lu in Huangpu (6320 0062), 96 Zhaojiaban Lu in Xuhui (6473 6819) and on Zhangyang Lu in Pudong (5835 0307).

Art Classes

Other options **Art & Craft Supplies** p.310, **Art Galleries** p.196

Traditional arts and crafts

[the studio] 创意灵感空间

6247 2765 | www.thestudio.cn

2, 796 Julu Lu
Changning
巨鹿路796号，
长宁
 Jing'an Temple
Map p.435 F1 1

This funky studio offers various types of art classes, conducted in English, for both beginners and pros. Sketching classes are on Tuesdays and painting classes on Thursdays (both from 10:00 to 12:00 and 19:00 to 21:00). On Sundays, there is an 'anything goes' creative class (13:30-15:30), as well as an 'art attack' where you can meet for drinks and finger food from 16:00 to18:00, but check beforehand as this one is sporadic. All classes cost ¥250 per lesson including materials, except for art attack, which is ¥150 including pizza and a beer. Classes rotate every five or seven weeks, so call in advance.

Chinese Folk Art Club 中国民艺俱乐部

2886 8712 | info@myfolk-art.com

Room 1001,
Building 11,
883 Shuicheng Lu
Pudong
水城路883号
浦东
Changshu Lu
Map p.427 F3 2

Anyone interested in learning some traditional Chinese art will like the two courses on offer here: Jinshan peasant painting and knot making. The painting class provides indoor and outdoor training in traditional art, with beginner, intermediate and advanced sessions available. The course consists of six two-hour classes held once a week and costs ¥1,530-¥2,125, including all the necessary materials, and spot training in Fengjing water town. For something different, try the four-week traditional knotting programme, which also caters for varying levels of experience and costs ¥355-¥545. There is another campus on Shuicheng Lu in the Changning district, near Zhongshan Park station.

Shanghai Expat Learning Centre 上海外派教育中心

6467 6875 | www.shanghai-classes.com

580 Yongjia Lu
Xuhui
永嘉路580号
徐汇
Hengshan Lu
Map p.435 F2 3

The highly popular Expat Learning Centre offers various courses in art and painting. The classes start with sketching and drawing and then move on to cover various tools and techniques, including pastels, watercolours, acrylics and oils. Courses are broken up into seasonal 10-week sessions and usually cost ¥3,200 plus the price of materials. The quality of the instructors reflects the slightly high course rates. Interested creatives can research and register for classes online.

Sharp+Focus 锐变艺术文化生活会馆

6275 5179

Room 301,
601A Honggu Lu
Changning
虹古路601A号
长宁
Map p.427 E3 4

This little creative gem runs a programme of varied art classes in Chinese painting, oil, watercolour and sketching, as well as knitting, professional quilting and jewellery making. There is even a class for making teddy bears. As well as the art classes, Sharp+Focus offers music classes and flower arranging (see p.264 and

238

p.248). Prices per class range from ¥80 to ¥280, depending on the subject and whether or not materials are included.

Australian Rules Football

Australian Rules Football has its origins in both rugby and Gaelic football, with a heavy dose of Antipodean bravado thrown in for good measure. The game is being gradually exported from Australia to various parts of the globe, and Shanghai is no exception. For the uninitiated, matches are played on an oval-shaped field between teams of 18 players. Players can't run with the ball without dribbling it in some way and passes, as well as opponents, are either kicked or punched, but never thrown. The game is physically demanding, but the camaraderie is amiable and an integral part of the sport.

Shanghai Rugby Football Club, 222 Lan'an Lu
Pudong
上海橄榄球俱乐部,
蓝按路222号
浦东
Map p.440 C1 **5**

The Shanghai Tigers 上海虎之队

138 1818 7975 | www.shanghaifootballclub.com

Shanghai's Australian Rules Football team is the Shanghai Tigers, and it invites anyone, non-Aussies included, to join up. The team plays on Saturdays at 15:00 from March to October at the Shanghai Rugby Football Club in Pudong. In addition to matches within the club, there are also periodical tours across Asia for tournaments. Although there is no cost to play with the team itself, the Shanghai Rugby Football Club does have a ¥1,800 membership fee (concessions and family rates are also offered).

Badminton

Known in the west as a leisurely pastime, badminton in China is a ferociously fun alternative to other racket sports. When you see locals slamming the shuttlecock back and forth and lunging for impossible volleys, you'll forget everything your grandma taught you about the game. The best way to get acquainted with this sport is to find a playing partner (take a look through the message boards on www.shanghaiexpat.com) and book an hour at one of the several sports centres that have courts. Some of the best include Hongkou Stadium (p.283) and Shanghai Stadium (p.284). Hourly rates are low, around ¥30-¥40, and most centres rent rackets for about ¥15. Outside of formal facilities, a leading pastime in Shanghai is to find a patch of grass and have an impromptu game – a practice easily observed in the city parks throughout the summer.

East China Normal University, 3663 Zhongshan Lu
Xuhui
中山西路3663号
徐汇
Map p.428 A4 **6**

Shanghai Badminton Club 上海羽毛球俱乐部

139 1610 4066 | www.shbadminton.com

Anyone can join this friendly badminton club, from beginners to experts, English and non-English speakers. The club meets on Tuesdays, Thursdays and Saturdays, and the monthly membership fee starts at ¥200 for one session per week. Group coaching is free, with membership and private tuition available at an additional charge. Other higher-priced packages are available for those wanting to play more regularly.

Ballet Classes

Other options **Dance Classes** p.244

Xi Jiao Sports Centre, 1949 Hongqiao Lu
Changning
虹桥路1949号
长宁
Map p.427 E4 **7**

Ballet Tian Tian 天天芭蕾

6479 1925 | www.tiantianballet.cn

This simple, lively ballet studio has classes for children aged 3-14 and is led by a graduate of the prestigious state-run Beijing Dance Academy. Youngsters learn the basic steps and then continue with more advanced pirouettes and tiptoeing. You can pay per individual class (¥75) or per month (four classes for ¥300). Sessions are held every day of the week and organised by age group.

239

Jin Bao Long Ballet Studio 金宝龙芭蕾舞工作室

6278 1361 | www.jblballet.com

The Jin Bao Long Ballet Studio is based in Changning but offers classes at various locations around town, including Pudong, to students of all ages, from children to adults. With an emphasis on fun and basic exercise, children's and junior classes are held every day of the week and cost ¥320 for four sessions, or ¥115 for one class. Adults can buy a 10 ticket pass for ¥950.

Basketball

Basketball is an increasingly popular sport in China, and Shanghai has a large number of decent courts scattered throughout its districts. Many serviced apartment buildings and school grounds have open outdoor courts that are free to use, while the courts in sport centres are another option for finding a pick-up game or perfecting your jump shot (although typically demand a small fee for their use).

Melody Women's Basketball Club

http://melodybasketball.spaces.live.com

This girls-only club is open to anyone interested in playing basketball and having a good time. Two of the more experienced players in the group act as coaches for the monthly exhibition games against other teams in Shanghai, mostly universities. The team also meets for outdoor half-court games on Tuesday and Thursday evenings and indoor full court games on Sunday evenings, as well as holding regular social events. Membership is ¥50, plus court reservation fees.

Shanghai International Basketball League
上海国际篮球联赛

139 1731 6770 | www.asas.com.cn

Organised by Active Sports Active Social (ASAS), Shanghai's biggest basketball league offers three levels of competition, from casual to highly competitive. All players are welcome but a basic understanding of the game is recommended. You can sign up as a team, or if you want to join as an individual, ASAS will place you with a side that corresponds to your skill level. The cost for a season is ¥450 and training games are held every week for ¥40. The league plays at four locations throughout Shanghai. The best way to get involved is by contacting the club through its website. Once you've joined, you'll receive scheduling updates via email.

Shanghai Liqiuping Basketball Club
上海李秋平篮球俱乐部

6445 0489 | www.liqiuping.com

This basketball club offers fun and professional training for kids and teenagers. Created in 2000 by the head coach of the Shanghai Sharks, Liqiuping has hired several English-speaking coaches to teach expat youngsters the fundamentals of the game. There are two leagues: one for kids between 8 and 12 and another for 13-18 year olds. Sixteen classes cost ¥1,900, and sessions are conducted once a week for two hours at a time. The club also organises weekend, summer and winter camps. Liqiuping has a second location at Luwan Stadium (p.283).

Birdwatching

Other options **Environmental Groups** p.248

Thanks to the dense city environment and lack of open green spaces, Shanghai's birdwatching options are limited, but not altogether absent. With increasing awareness of environmental issues and the threat of extinction for some rare species, public interest in this sedate pastime is steadily growing. Shanghai Botanical Garden in Xuhui, Century Park in Pudong, and Gongqing Forest Park in Yangpu offer the highest concentrations of birds, while Jing'an Park and Lu Xun Park might also house some pretty garden birds. Even Yu Garden, with its green spaces and twisting walkways, is a nice place for watching in early mornings, before the hordes of tourists arrive. Outside Shanghai, Chongming Island (p.192), with more than 300 recorded species, is well work the day trip. For more information check out www.chinabird.org or turn to the Parks section on p.211.

Bowling

Ten-pin bowling used to be very popular among locals during the 1990s, resulting in alleys popping up all over the city. Although interest has declined in recent years, and some lanes have disappeared, it's still easy enough to find somewhere to skittle. Costs start from ¥15 per game during the day, rising to about ¥25-¥30 in the evening. Shoe rental can be extra at some venues.

Bowling			
Orden Bowling Centre	10 Hengshan Lu	Xuhui	6474 6666
Sakura Bowling Alley	580 Jiangning Lu	Jing'an	6227 1088
Shanghai High Score Bowling Alley	456 Dongjiangwan Lu	Hongkou	5671 1111
Tong Ling Bowling Alley	123 Caoxi Lu	Xuhui	6468 5858

Boxing

Shanghai Xiaolong Boxing Club 骁龙拳击俱乐部
5671 1380 | www.xsmgym.com

Hongkou Stadium,
444 Dongjiangwan Lu
Hongkou
东江湾路444号
虹口
Hongkou Stadium
Map p.422 B3 12

Boxing in China is growing, although it is still dwarfed by the much more popular kung fu. The country won its first Olympic medal in Athens in 2004 and many believe that it will soon become a boxing powerhouse. Despite the fact that the coach teaches in Chinese, this club offers traditional western boxing classes for both Chinese and expat adults. Xiaolong offers two different memberships: 36 classes for ¥1,800 or a 104 class membership for ¥2,400. Sessions are held Monday to Thursday from 19:00 to 20:30.

Camping

Other options **Outdoor Goods** p.332

Camping probably isn't the first activity that comes to mind when thinking about the mega-metropolis of Shanghai, but a short trip outside the city limits can offer a respite from the towering concrete canyons and roaring traffic. Pitching your tent is best suited to spring, early summer and autumn, as winter can be bitterly cold and the peak summer months too hot. One of the closest options is Qingpu's Meadowbrook Centre (p.254). Only 35 kilometres outside Shanghai, Meadowbrook offers horse riding, trekking and low-key camping. Further afield, Zhejiang province, Chongming Island (p.192) and the Zhoushan archipelago have campsites in some beautiful scenery.

Generally camping in and around Shanghai is very safe, but it's always worth being prudent about where you pitch up. For equipment, a few shops sell camping and hiking gear in Shanghai. Try Yehuo and the competitively priced Decathlon (p.332).

241

Various Locations

Turen Club 土人登山俱乐部

5466 5056 | www.turenclub.com

Turen Club arranges camping, hiking, trekking and climbing activities for people wanting to get away from the bustling city and discover the surrounding areas. Activities are mainly arranged for weekends, but there are some trips during the holiday weeks too. Weekend outings cost around ¥300. Excursions vary in difficulty, but everyone is welcome. Call for full details of forthcoming programmes.

Chess

Chess matches can be seen all over Shanghai, but the game most people are playing may not be the one you're used to. It's *xiangqi*, or Chinese chess, which has some notable differences from the western version. The biggest variation is the layout – Chinese chess has a rectangular board divided by a 'river' which limits how some pieces can move. The pieces themselves are flat discs with characters painted on them – there is no queen, instead players manoeuvre pieces such as elephants and cannons. *Xiangqi* is considered more fast-paced and aggressive, and many believe this makes it more difficult than western chess. Players locked in battle over

Mahjong and chess are played all over the city

the board are a common sight in parks throughout Shanghai (along with other games such as *mahjong* and cards), but taking on an experienced local usually results in disappointment as the easily understood game is extremely difficult to master. Formal, expat-friendly clubs are tough to find and serious chess-players in parks are rarely amused by anxious expat beginners. The best way to learn the game is to befriend some locals and have them show you the ropes.

Climbing

Hongkou Stadium,
444 Dongjiangwan Lu
Hongkou
东江湾路444号
虹口
🚇 *Hongkou Stadium*
Map p.422 B3 **14**

Masterhand Rock Climbing Club 攀岩俱乐部

5696 6657

A fun and friendly place for the entire family, this big indoor climbing wall is open every day between 10:00 and 22:00. Entrance costs ¥40 for adults and ¥30 for children, and is valid for the entire day (provided you don't leave). There is often a climbing instructor on site to help those who want guidance, and there is always a supervisor for safety reasons. Masterhand is rarely packed so there is no need to reserve.

666 Tianyaoqiao Lu
Xuhui
天钥桥路666号
徐汇
🚇 *Shanghai Indoor*
Stadium
Map p.443 F1 **15**

Shanghai Stadium Rock-Climb Sports Centre 上海体育场攀岩中心

6426 5178 | rokclimb@ssc.sh.cn

This sizeable wall, 24 metres wide by 20 metres high, has several climbing routes of various difficulty, which are often changed. The centre is open between 10:00 and 22:00 and you can just rock up and climb without booking. Entrance is ¥50 and shoe and harness rental costs ¥15 extra.

Cookery Classes

Floor 3,
1 Yan'an Dong Lu
Huangpu
延安东路1号3楼
黄埔
🚇 **Nanjing Dong Lu**
Map p.431 E3 **16**

Ayi Training and Lunch Classes

6330 8098 | www.shuiyuan-restaurant.com

With the majority of expats employing the services of indispensible *ayis*, this is a concept that could catch on. The restaurant Shui Yuan on the Bund can teach your *ayi* to cook healthy and delicious meals using less oil than in traditional local fare, without missing out on the taste. Your *ayi* can accompany you to Shui Yuan at lunchtime, and while you enjoy a nice lunch, the chef will teach your *ayi* how to cook one of the restaurant's signature Chinese dishes. The lunch-lesson combo costs ¥158. Make sure you book in advance as spaces in the popular classes are limited.

Floor 1, 35,
Lane 865, Yuyuan Lu
Jing'an
愚园路865弄35号
静安
🚇 **Jiangsu Lu**
Map p.435 D1 **17**

Chinese Cooking Workshop 中华料理教室

137 0187 3243 | www.chinesecookingworkshop.com

This highly popular, friendly course offers English-speaking cooking lessons for several different cuisines, including Chinese, Japanese, Thai and Indian. The workshop holds signature dim sum classes once a month and constantly changes its teaching menus. The Chinese cooking class covers all the major food regions of the country and is held a couple of times a week. One lesson costs ¥200, and reduced rate packages and at-home lessons are available. Group or private classes are also held in the Pudong kitchen, at 10, Lane 910, Dingxiang Lu, near the Science & Technology Museum station.

Cricket

Shanghai Rugby
Football Club,
222 Lan'an Lu
Pudong
上海橄榄球俱乐部,
蓝桉路222号
浦东
Map p.440 C1 **18**

Shanghai Cricket Club 上海板球俱乐部

135 0179 9365 | www.shanghaicricketclub.org

The sole expat cricket club in Shanghai has a distinguished history dating back to the 1850s. It has more than 200 members, and offers leagues, tournaments, coaching and overseas tours to cricketers, male and female, of all standards all year round. In summer, experienced players are allocated into one of four teams that make up the club. They then compete in the annual limited overs league, held at the club's home at Shanghai Rugby Football Club, which houses a synthetic wicket, astroturf nets and a decent clubhouse. For beginners, indoor cricket is a great way to learn the basics. The highlight of the year is the International Sixes tournament, which draws teams from all over Asia for a weekend of six-a-side cricket and a gala dinner. Club nights out are a regular occurrence, and the monthly quiz evening draws a good crowd.

Cycling

Other options **Mountain Biking** p.264, **Sports Goods** p.337

Cycling is one of the most common forms of transportation in Shanghai and hordes of bike riders dominate the city streets at every hour of the day. Most Shanghainese see the bicycle as nothing more than a way to get from A to B, but recreational pedaling is popular among Shanghai's expats. Although cycling is generally safe within the city limits, the lack of open space and fresh air tends to push leisure riders towards more scenic destinations such as Taiping Lake in Anhui province, Chongming Island and Zhejiang province. Although these places require bus transportation they offer a great alternative to the congested streets of Shanghai. If city riding is more your cup of tea, there are a few guided tours (see Bicycle Tours, p.221), and the French Concession has several quiet tree-lined streets to cruise through. Despite the lack of helmet-wearing locals, Shanghai's chaotic traffic makes it wise to put safety before style.

243

Various Locations

Flying Hairy Legs Cycling Club 飞毛腿自行车俱乐部

http://sports.groups.yahoo.com/group/FlyingHairyLegsCyclingGroup

Offering fast-paced training rides (50-100km) on Tuesdays, Thursdays, Saturdays and Sundays, this club is meant for serious road cyclists only. Some of the members compete at high levels, so if you are a beginner you might want to get in some training before joining. Setting out from both Puxi and Pudong, the groups usually separate into two – one for slower riders and another for faster cyclists. The club also organises races every month in the summer. Membership is free.

395 Dujuan Lu
Pudong
杜鹃路395号
浦东
🚇 *Longyang Lu*
Map p.440 A4 20

SISU Cycling

5059 6071 | *info@sisucycling.com*

Revolving around a bike shop of the same name in Pudong, this club arranges free cycling tours in and around Shanghai a few times a week, ranging in length from 25 to 100km. The guides are mostly English-speaking expats and tailor the rides to the ability of the cyclists that sign up. SISU also organises family-oriented 'escape' packages to destinations outside the city such as Chongming Island. Rental bikes are available through the shop for ¥120 per day.

Dance Classes

Other options **Ballet** p.239, **Music Lessons** p.264

Dancing isn't all jazz hands and tights – it can act as a creative outlet, a fitness tool or a romance igniter. From pole dancing to the waltz, Shanghai boasts a wide range of classes that cater to every need and style. Many of the studios schedule dance parties that complement classes. Belly dancing in particular has become popular among expats in Shanghai, with many studios offering classes, and one particular studio, ISIS Belly Dance Club, specialising in the art.

518 Sichuan Bei Lu
Huangpu
四川北路518号
黄埔
🚇 *Baoshan Lu*
Map p.431 D1 21

Blackpool Dream 黑池梦国标会所

6393 1808 | *www.clubtbd.com*

Named after the British 'Blackpool Dance Festival,' this nostalgic ballroom is more of a club than a studio. All skill levels are welcome and professional instructors teach both modern styles (waltz, tango, foxtrot and quick-step) and Latin (rumba, cha-cha, samba, paso and jive). Blackpool offers one-on-one, couples' or group classes, which start at ¥480 per 16 class term. The club also provides nightly dance parties, dance master seminars and workshops, as well as wedding services.

Super Brand Mall,
168 Lujiazui Lu
Pudong
陆家嘴西路168号
浦东
🚇 *Lujiazui*
Map p.431 F2 22

City Art Centre Dance Studio 都市舞工厂

5047 2175 | *www.cityartcenter.com*

With several international dance instructors, this funky studio conducts classes in Latin, belly dancing, street, tap, ballet, jazz and modern, as well as yoga sessions. City Art Centre spreads its classes over three modern studios; its flagship studio is in the Super Brand Mall, while the others are at 45 Guangyuanxi Lu in Xuhui and Mingrenyuan Sports Centre on Zhangyang Lu in Pudong.

Floor 2,
321 Kangding Lu
Jing'an
康定路321号
静安
🚇 *Nanjing Xi Lu*
Map p.429 F3 23

iDancing 爱跳舞学校

6271 4952 | *www.idancing.cn*

A cool, modern dance studio with lots of classes. The international instructors are passionate about their dancing and do their best to make you shake it with them. Courses range from contemporary favourites such as hip-hop, 'MTV dance' and pole dancing to traditional styles such as ballet and ballroom. The studio also offers fitness classes including aerobic-dance, yoga and Pilates. Sessions are available for beginner,

244

intermediate and advanced dancers, and students can choose between group classes or one-on-one lessons. One class costs ¥100, eight classes ¥580 and 16 classes ¥980. A private class costs ¥400-¥500, and the studio frequently offers deals.

Various Locations

ISIS Belly Dance Club 艾希丝俱乐部
5382 7238 | www.isisclub.cn

Well known in Shanghai, ISIS specialises solely in belly dancing and offers classes for beginner and experienced wigglers. The instructors are well versed in several styles, including Egyptian and tribal. Lessons led by an English-speaking teacher cost ¥75 and full courses consist of 8-10 classes. Chinese-taught lessons are available at a lower price. The classes are held at various dance studios throughout the city – call to find the one closest to you.

Building C,
UDC Innovative Plaza,
125 Jiangsu Bei Lu
Changning
江苏北路125号
长宁
🚇 *Jiangsu Lu*
Map p.428 C4 **25**

Jazz Du Funk 爵士风度
5239 9922 | www.jazzdufunk.com

This popular dance school offers classes in jazz, hip-hop, ballet, belly, flamenco, tap, samba, jive, swing, contemporary dance and 'lady freestyle', as well as fitness classes such as Pilates and dance-aerobics, all taught by a big pool of professional instructors. There are classes for adults and children of all abilities. The joining fee is ¥100, with prices ranging from ¥100 for one class to ¥1,600 for 20 classes and ¥2,800 for 40 classes. There are also monthly (¥850-¥900) and annual cards (¥9,000). Eight classes for children cost ¥650.

28B Huijia Plaza,
41 Caoxi Bei Lu
Xuhui
漕溪北路41号
徐汇
🚇 *Caoxi Lu*
Map p.430 B4 **26**

Salsa Shanghai 莎莎舞在上海
6464 9264 | www.salsashanghai.com

Shirley and Bob, the passionate teachers behind the Salsa Shanghai dance group, started giving lessons in 2001 and their hard work has paid off. Salsa Shanghai meets several nights a week at both Huijia Plaza and Xiangming High School. There are five levels of instruction for all abilities, and students can choose between New York or Cuban salsa. To complement the classes, members are invited to salsa parties held throughout the city.

Floor 2,
1 Maoming Nan Lu
Jing'an
茂名南路1号
静安
🚇 *Nanjing Xi Lu*
Map p.430 A4 **27**

Souldancing
6256 4400 | www.souldancing.cn

This modern dance club with international instructors conducts classes in belly dance, pole dance, jazz, salsa, tango and hip-hop, plus several yoga styles. There are group and private classes, while kids too can enjoy lessons in ballet and hip-hop. You can choose to pay for a single class at ¥60-¥80 or buy eight for ¥544.

Early-morning dance lessons

245

Floor 4,
350 Changning Lu
Changning
长宁路350号
长宁
🚇 *Jiangsu Lu*
Map p.428 C4 **28**

Tango In Shanghai 探戈在上海
135 6485 3169
Tango in Shanghai offers classes for beginners on Mondays and for more experienced dancers on Thursdays (both 20:00 to 21:00). The real treat comes after the class when there is an hour of free dance. No partner? Don't worry – although it takes two to tango, dancers rotate frequently so everyone has someone to pair up with. Classes cost ¥30, and the club also arranges tango parties at Le Royal Meridien on Nanjing Dong Lu.

Various Locations

Tangoshanghai 上海阿根廷探戈
138 1786 4703 | oficial_tangoshanghai@yahoo.com.cn
This member-run club organises a 'milonga' dance party every Saturday evening (21:00-01:00) at various locations, when expats and local Shanghainese can work on their tango skills in a lively atmosphere. Call for more on the group's eight-week courses on this classic dance. The regular parties cost ¥70 and entrance includes two drinks.

Darts

Various Locations

Shanghai Darts League 上海飞镖联盟
1332198 7907 | www.shanghaidarts.com
This big expat league has 24 teams and is open for anyone, regardless of ability. Teams play every Tuesday at 20:00 in various bars across Shanghai. Check out the website for exact venues. Despite being a relatively new competition, it's pretty well organised; league play is free and the best shooters get complimentary drinks while the rest can enjoy happy hours and snacks.

Diving

Changfeng Park
451 Daduhe Lu
Putuo
大渡河路451号，
长风公园
普陀
Map p.427 F2 **31**

Aquaria 21 Dive Club 长风海洋世界的潜水俱乐部
6223 5280 | www.oceanworld.com.cn
Ocean World is a huge aquarium that offers two-day CMAS diving instruction on weekends. The courses are available for all levels, from beginner to experienced, and cost from ¥2,800, which includes a dive in the shark tank. The aquarium also offers a yearly membership for ¥980 that gives you one shark dive and half-price diving. Book at least two weeks in advance for the courses.

Dragon Boat Racing
Dragon boat racing originated in China, and remains a celebrated sport. Traditional races are held in honor of Qu Yuan, a famous poet who died in 278 BC by committing suicide in the Miluo River. According to fable, the villagers used drums and paddles to scare the evil spirits away from his body. Today, races are organised annually to commemorate the legend and have become very popular. Similar to a very large canoe, dragon boats usually hold 20 rowers whose movements are dictated by a large drum at the front of the boat. In Shanghai, races take place in May or June, on the fifth day of the fifth Chinese lunar month, and are held on the Suzhou River with teams from all over China (see p.54).

2 Shuicheng Nan Lu
Qingpu
水城南路2号
青浦

Shanglong Dragon Boat Team 尚龙龙舟队
136 6144 7145 | dragonboatsh@yahoo.com
Racing dragon boats isn't solely for locals; this friendly team welcomes expats to its sessions every Sunday morning on the Dian Shan Lake, just outside Shanghai. The team meets at the Starbucks at 2 Shuicheng Nan Lu at 08:00 from May until August, and at 09:00 from September through to April. There is an annual fee of ¥1,000 and a weekly charge of ¥50, which includes transport to and from the lake, plus boat rental.

246

Drama Groups

The Acting Workshop 表演工场

Downstream Garage,
Building 100,
200 Longcao Lu
Xuhui
龙漕路200弄100号
徐汇
🚇 *Longcao Lu*
Map p.433 F2 33

138 0180 2384 | www.taw.cabanova.com

After appearing in several TV shows, films and stage performances, LA-born Paul Cascante started these theatre workshops in 2004. His sessions, all based on western-style drama, focus on character development and making the actors feel as natural as possible on stage. The workshops are held on Sundays from 15:00 to 18:00, and there are also film acting courses on Tuesdays between 18:00 and 21:00. Both courses cost ¥450 per month and prospective students can try two classes before joining.

East West Theatre Group 东西方舞台剧团

Various Locations

131 6242 5652 | east.west.info@gmail.com

This non-profit theatre group is split into two parts: one is a more serious section that produces up to six plays a year, for which you have to audition; the other welcomes both beginners and old hands, and stages improvising workshops and a few plays. Both sessions are held once a month at different venues and attract locals and expats. It is also a good organisation for those who like to watch theatre, with tickets for most productions costing around ¥100.

Shanghai Dramatic Arts Centre 上海话剧艺术中心

288 Anfu Lu
Xuhui
安福路288号
徐汇
🚇 *Changshu Lu*
Map p.435 E1 35

6473 4567

For Mandarin-speaking expats, Shanghai's major theatrical venue, the Shanghai Dramatic Arts Centre, offers Chinese-led drama courses for members of the theatre. The course lasts for six weeks, with one class a week, and usually focuses on traditional Chinese plays. Theatre membership costs ¥60, and the course itself will set you back ¥288.

Shanghai Expat Learning Centre 上海外派教育中心

580 Yongjia Lu
Xuhui
永嘉路580号
徐汇
🚇 *Hengshan Lu*
Map p.435 F2 36

6467 6875 | www.shanghai-classes.com

The Shanghai Expat Learning Centre organises a wide variety of courses in all kinds of creative areas, including a comprehensive acting class suitable for beginners as well as more advanced actors. There are exercises in scene study, improvising, reading and performance. The course lasts for 10 weeks (one class per week), and costs ¥3,200.

Shanghai Theatre Academy 上海戏剧学院

630 Huashan Lu
Jing'an
华山路630号
静安
🚇 *Hengshan Lu*
Map p.435 E1 37

6248 5215 | www.cinaoggi.it/shanghai-theatre-academy

This prestigious drama institution is well known in China, providing courses in acting, directing, broadcast and TV editing, opera, Chinese and modern dance, and other interesting options. The courses range from single-term workshops to four-year degrees and postgraduate studies. Keep in mind, however, that all classes are conducted in Chinese, so language could be a barrier. One year's tuition costs ¥30,000. The school regularly holds performances ranging from Shakespeare and traditional Chinese opera to experimental dance and student-written productions.

Anything Missing?
Did we miss anything out? If you have any thoughts, ideas or comments for us on things to include in the Activities section, drop us a line, and if your club or organisation isn't in here, let us know and we'll give you a shout in the next edition. Visit www.explorerpublishing.com and tell us what's on your mind.

Environmental Groups

Other options **Voluntary & Charity Work** p.75

Grassroots Community Association
热爱家园青年社区志愿者协会

Room 701,
2, Lane 827, Datong Lu
Hongkou
大统路827弄2号
虹口
🚇 *Hangzhong*
Map p.430 A1

5663 3338 | *www.glinet.org*

Grassroots, which was started at Fudan University by a group of students, is an active environmental and human rights association. It runs volunteer projects throughout the year that tackle issues such as Aids, environmental protection, community labour, and educational support to migrant children. University students largely run the organisation but anyone is welcome to join. Contact the group directly to see what you can do to help.

Roots & Shoots 上海根与芽青少年活动中心

Floor 15,
Ocean Towers,
550 Yan'an Dong Lu
Huangpu
延安东路550号
黄埔
🚇 *People's Square*
Map p.431 D3

6352 3580 | *www.jgi-shanghai.org*

This branch of the international Jane Goodall Institute welcomes everyone who wants to contribute to a better world. The association runs programmes for young people about issues of environmental, human and animal welfare. In addition to working with other groups in China, the institute is also involved with local schools (both Chinese and international) in Shanghai, teaching the importance of recycling and taking care of nature. There's also the possibility for students to start their own group, with training and coaching from Roots & Shoots.

Wildlife Conservation Society 国际野生生物保护学会

East China
Normal University,
3663 Zhongshan Bei Lu
Putuo
华东师范大学,
中山北路3663号
普陀
Map p.428 A3 🔢

6223 2361 | *www.wcschina.org*

The China branch of this worldwide organisation works to protect wild animals in the country, as well as raising awareness and educating more people to do the same through workshops, debates and educational activities in schools and universities. The group also carries out bigger projects and advertising campaigns in collaboration with local governments and companies. One of its recent successes has been a drive to save the tiger, which resulted in the building of new protected areas for the species.

Fencing

It may be seen as a niche activity, but fencing has been steadily gaining fans who see it as a sport requiring a combination of skill, poise and stamina. Shanghai offers two main venues for beginners and professionals. Equipment is expensive but the clubs have extra kit for those without. Janus Fencing (1900 Tianshan Lu; 6228 1891) offers group classes and private lessons for anyone over 10 years old, while Shanghai Power Fencing Club (456 Xietu Lu; 6301 9639) holds classes for all levels and offers 20 lessons for ¥999.

Flower Arranging

Other options **Flowers** p.322, **Gardens** p.325

Sharp+Focus 锐变艺术文化生活会馆

Room 301,
601A Honggu Lu
Changning
虹古路601A号
长宁
Map p.427 E3 🔢

6275 5179

This multi-art organisation offers a flower-arranging course in which students are taught how to create beautiful bouquets, as well as learning the history behind this traditional art form. The 12 class programme covers different types of arrangement, including Chinese, European and Japanese designs. The two-hour sessions cost ¥200 each, including materials.

Foosball

You might think that foosball, or table football as it is known in some parts of the world, is just another simple pub game, but there are actually thousands of clubs all over the globe, huge competitions and millions of dollars of prize money available in the sport. For anyone interested in improving their skills and eventually taking on one of the real experts in Shanghai, there are several places to practise, notably Big Bamboo (132 Nan Yang Lu; 6256 2265), Baby Bamboo (3338 Hongmei Lu; 6465 9099), Wunderbar (300 Liaoyuan Xi Lu; 3377 3373) and The Spot (331 Tongren Lu; 6247 3579).

Suite 21E, Building 1,
515 Yishan Lu
Xuhui
宜山路515号
徐汇
 Yishan Lu
Map p.443 E1 **42**

Shanghai Foosball Club 上海手足球俱乐部

138 1897 2009 | www.shanghaifoosball.com

While you'll see tables in many of the expat bars, the Shanghai Foosball Club is the place to find serious players, as well as those just looking for some organised fun. At the club's home (near Zhongshan Xi Lu), the limited number of tables means the more serious competitors tend to have priority. The club sometimes organises games at other venues for anyone to join, including beginners. Check out the website for news and upcoming events.

Football

Some claim the beautiful game was actually invented here several thousand years ago, and there's no denying that today's China is well and truly wrapped up in modern-day football hysteria. Public interest has grown considerably over the last decade, and money has been flowing into the sport as a result. China may not have qualified for the last World Cup, in 2006, but viewing audiences were up significantly from their appearance in 2002 and Chinese players are beginning to be recognised on the world scene. In Shanghai, league matches draw decent crowds of passionate locals and children are increasingly interested in the sport, playing at school and in their spare time. Options to take part are numerous. Leagues are organised for adults and children of all standards across the city; some are mixed local and expat teams, while others are more expat oriented. If you want to play with a couple of friends you can either join in with the students at one of the universities for free or book a field for your own game. At Shanghai Stadium (see p.284), for example, one hour on the pitch costs around ¥700.

Zhangjiang Stadium,
Guang Lan Lu
Pudong
张江体育馆,
广兰路
浦东

QiLin FC 麒麟足球俱乐部

138 0190 9471 | www.qilinfootball.com

This is one of Shanghai's premier youth football clubs, training children and teenagers between 6 and 16 years old. The club offers two different programmes: the first is a skill-building course which is open to all levels; the second is an 'academy' programme, which competes at a high level and consists of invited players only. Both hold three training sessions a week, with match play every weekend, and cost ¥3,000 per season.

Tianma Golf &
Country Club,
3958 Zhao Kun Lu
Songjiang
赵昆公路3958号
松江

Shanghai International Football League
上海国际足球联赛

www.eteamz.active.com/sifl

This relatively large expat football league has 10 teams, several of which are 'international' (among the current crop of competitors are sides such as Japan, Oranje, Krauts, Azzuri and Les Bleus). What started out as a pick-up game in the 1990s has gradually evolved into today's 11-a-side format. The organisation offers both friendly and competitive leagues, plus cup tournaments, with matches played on Saturdays from September through to May. You can find details on how to join a particular team on the league's website.

249

Jinhui Stadium,
462 Jinhui Lu
Minhang
金汇球场,
金汇路462号
闵行

Shanghai International Youth Soccer League
上海国际儿童足球联赛
6418 1236 | www.siyslchina.org

This international football league has lots of teams to join for any youngster interested in getting involved in the beautiful game. Players range between 3 and 16 years old, but there are plans to extend eligibility to 18 year olds. Once a player joins, he will be allocated to an appropriate side, based on age and experience. The price to join is ¥1,050 for a three-month period, playing once a week, and ¥1,900 to play twice a week. Games also take place at the Shanghai United International School field on Hongquan Lu in Minhang.

Huo Che Tou Stadium,
955 Gonghe Xin Lu
Zhabei
火车头体育场,
共和新路955号
闸北
 Zhongshan Bei Lu
Map p.422 A4

Super Seven Soccer League 超级七足球联赛
139 1731 6770 | www.asas.com.cn

The seven-a-side football league is organised by Active Sports Active Social, Shanghai's largest sports league. There are teams for all levels, so anyone is welcome to join. Players can form their own side or enter the league as an individual and be placed in a team. The price is ¥50 each time you play – contact ASAS for more information on how to join.

Frisbee

Shanghai Rugby
Football Club,
222 Lan'an Lu
Pudong
上海橄榄球俱乐部,
蓝按路222号
浦东
Map p.440 C1 47

Shanghai Ultimate Players Association 上海极限飞盘协会
www.shanghai-ultimate.com

Born in the US and slowly creeping around the globe, this team sport requires a wide range of frisbee skills and endurance. The game is relatively easy to pick up; players can't run with the disc, only pass it, and points are awarded when a player catches a pass within the opposing team's 'endzone'. Shanghai Ultimate holds weekly league games in which all skill levels are welcome. Meetings are on Saturdays and require a small fee for field rental. Shanghai Ultimate also organises a yearly tournament that attracts teams from all over the region.

Gaelic Football

Shanghai Rugby
Football Club,
222 Lan'an Lu
Pudong
上海橄榄球俱乐部,
蓝桉路222号
浦东
Map p.440 C1 48

Shanghai Gaelic Football Club 上海爱尔兰足球俱乐部
www.shanghaigaelic.com

Gaelic football is often said to be a mix of soccer and rugby, but is most similar to Aussie Rules Football in that players can't run with the ball without some sort of dribble, and passes must be made by kicking or 'bumping'. Points are scored by kicking the ball through two uprights (one point) or into a guarded goal (three points). Unlike rugby, full-on tackles are not allowed, only heavy shoulder bumps. The Shanghai Gaelic Football Club has two men's and two women's teams and welcomes any interested participants to join. Offering competitive games, training sessions and introductions for the newbies, the club costs ¥600 per season and trains twice a week in Pudong and once a week at Luwan Stadium in Puxi.

Golf

On paper, Shanghai is not the most attractive city in the world for playing golf – uninterestingly flat terrain, scorching, humid summers and cold winters are all ingredients for bland golf offerings. But despite these hindrances, the city offers some of the most impressive golf in China, if not Asia, and has firmly established itself as a key port of call for professional events. Some 20 courses surround the city, and while getting to many of them can involve an hour or more in the car, the journey is often rewarded by some great golf. World-renowned designers have created some exquisite layouts which, in general, are well maintained and manicured. It's crucial to always call ahead when planning a round in Shanghai. Many of the courses are for members only (with huge annual fees), but they do offer public days from time to time, so a bit of investigation is always worthwhile. For those in need of a quick golf fix, or who want to correct that dodgy swing, there are several driving ranges in and around the city offering both memberships and walk-ins. Some of the notable options are Shanghai Dong Zheng Golf Club in Minhang (6420 6666), Shanghai Fei Hong Golf Club in Jiading (5270 2222), Shanghai Lujiazui Golf Club in Pudong (6887 1700) and Silport Citygolf Club in Minhang (5976 6666).

6555 Boyuan Lu
Jiading
博园路6555号
嘉定

Enhance Anting Golf Club 上海颖奕安亭高尔夫俱乐部
6950 6555 | www.enhancegolf.com

Designed by Robert Trent Jones Jr, heavy bunkering and water features are used to carve an interesting 18 hole, 7,266 yard course out of this otherwise flat and featureless site. A relative newcomer on the Shanghai golfing scene, Enhance Anting has good facilities, including a driving range and pro shop. The club doesn't accept unaccompanied visitors, but if you know someone who is a member you can play for ¥750-¥1,050.

6655 Hutai Lu
Baoshan
沪太路6655号
宝山

Lake Malaren Golf Club 美兰湖高尔夫俱乐部
5659 0008 | www.lmgolfresort.com

Roughly 30 minutes' drive from central Shanghai, this aesthetically pleasing golf complex has two 18 hole courses, both constructed by the celebrated US designer Peter Thomson. The tight, tree-lined North Forest course looks likely to hold professional international events in the next few years. Non-members can play on weekdays for ¥560 (Mondays and Tuesdays) and ¥810 (Wednesdays and Fridays).

**Dongda Highway,
Nanhui**
Pudong
南汇滨海,
东大公路东首
浦东

Shanghai Binhai Golf 上海滨海高尔夫
5805 8888 | www.binhaigolf.com

Binhai offers two excellent courses, a large pro shop, chipping green and two driving ranges. The Peter Thomson-designed Lakes course is typified by deep bunkers and numerous mounds, and the prevailing wind off the East China Sea adds to the links-style challenge. The second 18 holes, the Forest course, provides a more tree-lined experience. Binhai is members only, but offers good value for money. A one year membership costs ¥4,800, and individual rounds then cost between ¥240 and ¥980.

961 Yingzhu Lu
Qingpu
盈朱路961号
青浦

Shanghai Country Club 上海国际高尔夫球乡村俱乐部
5972 8111 | www.shanghaicountryclub.com

Another Robert Trent Jones Jr-designed course, opened in 1990, this club set the benchmark for many of the rivals that have since opened in the area. Located 30 minutes from downtown Shanghai, this par 72, 7,025 yard layout is complemented by a three-hole mini course, driving range and extensive leisure facilities. Membership is reportedly full, but non-members can book and play on certain days for ¥480 to ¥780. Ladies' day is on Mondays.

**12 Shuangtang
Village,
Tang Hang Town**
Jiading
唐行镇双塘村12号
嘉定

Shanghai Golf Club 上海高尔夫俱乐部
5995 0111

About 50km from downtown Shanghai, this 18 hole, par 72 course is characterised by water, with the wet stuff confronting you on 16 of the holes. Add to this relatively undulating terrain, and Shanghai Golf Club makes for a stern challenge. A driving range, pro shop and Japanese restaurant complete the facilities at this members-only club.

251

**9988 Zhongchun Lu,
Qibao Town**
Minhang
七宝镇中春路9988号
闵行

Shanghai Grand City Golf Club 大都会高尔夫培训中心
6419 3676 | grandcity@online.sh.cn

If you are short on time, or your short game is in need of some work, this nine hole, par three course is the ideal choice. A steal at ¥130, including caddy, Grand City has holes ranging from 85 to 240 yards and an abundance of water hazards to add to the challenge. The centrally located club also has a driving range and teaching facilities. No membership is required.

1600 Ling Bai Lu
Pudong
凌白路1600号
浦东

Shanghai Links Golf & Country Club
上海林克斯高尔夫乡村俱乐部
5897 3068 | www.shanghailinks.com.cn

It's hard to gain access to this club as a non-member, but if you do play, the Jack Nicklaus-designed links course will challenge your game to the limits. Deceptively wide in places, the layout will consistently test your accuracy. A driving range and pro shop sit alongside some fantastic leisure facilities in this community, about 35 minutes from central Shanghai.

**1366 Huqingping Lu,
Kunshan**
Jiangsu
沪青平公路1366号，
江苏省昆山市淀山
湖镇

Shanghai Silport Golf Club 上海旭宝高尔夫球俱乐部
512 5748 1111 | www.silport.com.cn

It's well worth the 90 minute drive to Silport, one of Shanghai's finest courses. Having hosted four consecutive Volvo China Masters professional events, Silport is renowned for its fast, undulating greens, and the Ming and Qing Dynasty sculptures that adorn the course and bring 'good fortune' to golfers. The 56 holes, covering a total of 10,344 yards, feature an abundance of water. The members-only club regularly offers public access on weekdays.

**128 Huanzhen Xi Lu,
Zhouzhuang Town**
Jiangsu Province
江苏省昆山市周庄镇
环镇西路128号

Shanghai West Golf Club 上海光明高尔夫俱乐部
5720 3888 | www.shanghaiwest.com

Close to the historic water town of Zhouzhang, Shanghai West is about 80km from central Shanghai, and in 2001 joined the association of The Finest Golf Clubs of the World, a collection of 200 luxurious golf resorts. The par 72, 7,001 yard layout has tricky greens and is complemented by a driving range, pro shop and further leisure facilities. The club is members-only but holds public days for ladies and a weekly open day; call for details of times.

3958 Zhao Kun Lu
Songjiang
赵昆公路3958号
松江

Tianma Country Club 天马高尔夫球场
5766 1666 | www.tianmacc.com

Located in the beautiful Sheshan Natural Reserve, Tianma has a large, cosmopolitan membership community. The course is flat but by no means straightforward, and the excellent non-golf facilities complete the country club feel. Guests are welcome from Tuesday to Friday when ¥885 gets you 18 holes and a set lunch.

1 Longdong Dadao
Pudong
龙东大道1号
浦东
Map p.440 B2 59

Tomson Shanghai Pudong Golf Course
汤臣上海浦东高尔夫球场
5833 8888 | www.tomson-golf.com

Located in the heart of Pudong, Tomson Golf is one of the most central courses in Shanghai. While the Pudong skyline is a dramatic backdrop, the course itself has plenty to interest and test the golfer too. The par 72, 7,400 yard layout is famed for its obstacles, notably the metre-high 'Great Wall' that crosses the fourth fairway. Host of the BMW Asia Open for the past three years (see p.278), Tomson Golf is a must-play for the serious golfer, if you can get past the members-only policy. Additional facilities include driving range, pro shop, tennis courts and a swimming pool.

Gymnastics

China is proud of its gymnastics heritage and has produced many successful athletes within the field. It's a common sport in Chinese schools, teaching children to build strength and flexibility. The most talented kids are sent to the infamous specialist gymnastics schools, which have a reputation outside of China as places of long hours of hard daily practice. Fortunately, less rigorous alternatives are available in Shanghai. Quite a few after-school programmes offer gymnastics for expat children, aiming to combine training with a healthy dose of fun. Multisports (6466 3710; www.multi-sport.com.cn), Active Kidz (6406 6757; www.activekidz.org) and Sport for Life (6282 1762; www.sportforlife.com.cn) all offer recognised gymnastics programmes.

Hashing

Other options **Running** p.269

Invented by a bunch of British colonials in Kuala Lumpur in 1938, hashing consists of a group of runners who follow a trick-laden path created by human 'hares' 15 minutes ahead of the pack. Though fitness is a key component of the sport, hashing is primarily a social activity, which means food and beer usually play a large role. Like most cities with large expat communities, Shanghai has several hashing groups to choose from, many of which are connected to one another.

Shanghai Centre,
1376 Nanjing Xi Lu
Jing'an
南京西路1376号
波特曼
静安
🚇 *Xinzhuang*
Map p.429 F4 60

Drunken Dragons Hash House Harriers
中国醉拳小饭馆猎狗队

138 1837 5573 | www.drunkendragonhhh.com

Drunken Dragons Hash House Harriers is a club for all fitness levels, from serious runners to joggers and walkers. The group organises hashes every other Saturday and participants meet across the street from the Shanghai Centre (also known as the Portman) at 13:00, where a bus then takes them outside of the city to one of the outlying parks. Hashes are usually followed by a dinner and one or two drinks back in Shanghai.

Various Locations

Pudong Full Moon Hash 浦东满月跑步俱乐部
139 1853 3716

If you think Shanghai is too busy or hot for daytime running try this club, which meets once a month at midnight for intense runs through the relatively empty Shanghai streets. The runs always stop at Metro stations and are quite long, offering hashers a view of their city rarely seen. As usual, the group of 10-40 people reward themselves with drinks afterwards.

Various Locations

Shanghai Hash House Harriers 上海小饭馆猎狗队
137 6138 0687 | www.shanghai-hhh.com

The original Hash House Harriers club in Shanghai is a large group of happy runners of all levels. The club emphasises fun, and the beer and food served after the run is just as integral as the run itself. With anywhere between 25 and 100 runners, the hashes take place every Sunday at 15:30 and start from various locations (information is posted on the website). Each run costs ¥60 for locals and ¥80 for expats.

Various Locations

Taiping Hash 太平小饭馆猎狗队
139 1853 3716 | jeffrey.wilson@bakernet.com

Created for runners who fancy mountains and nature trails, the Taiping Hash club meets once a month on Saturdays. These long affairs are held out of Shanghai in neighbouring Zhejiang or Jiangsu and combine scenic landscapes with routes for all

253

abilities. There are usually around 100 people per hash, and the group provides buses for transport to and from the city for all the exhausted participants.

Hockey

Other options **Ice Hockey** p.254

Shanghai Hockey Club 上海曲棍球俱乐部

139 0191 9394 | www.shanghaifieldhockeyclub.com

Offering fun and competitive field hockey for both men and women, this club meets on Saturdays from 17:00 to 19:00. It welcomes all levels and usually has a few extra sticks to borrow for complete beginners. Along with the weekly games, the club regularly participates in regional tournaments in Hong Kong. Quarterly membership is ¥300, half that for students and interns. See the website for details of how to get involved.

Minhang Hockey Stadium, 540 Xin Dong Lu
Minhang
闵行区曲棍球赛场,
莘东路540号
闵行
🚇 *Xinzhuang*

Horse Riding

Other options **Farm & Stable Tours** p.222, **Polo** p.267

Jialiang Equestrian Club 佳良马术俱乐部

6411 0049 | www.jialiang.com

This organisation doesn't claim to offer picturesque surroundings, rather its real value lies in its proximity to central Pudong. With 30 horses, a 500 metre track, a jumping course and an indoor riding area, it's a perfect club for trying out the sport. You need to join in order to train here, and the cheapest membership costs ¥2,000 per year. Members can take private 45 minute lessons with a Chinese tutor for ¥190 on weekdays and ¥230 on weekends. English tuition is available, but costs more.

1858 Sanlu Highway
Pudong
三鲁公路1858号
浦东

Meadowbrook Shanghai 伟图种马发展有限公司

6983 0022 | www.meadowbrookshanghai.com

This horse riding range is perfect for anyone who wants to get out of the city for some authentic equestrian action in natural surroundings. The club, located 35km west of Shanghai, is part of an activity centre that also offers fishing, camping and hiking. There are group and private lessons for children, as well as one-on-one classes for adults. Children's group courses are six weeks long (once a week) and cost ¥2,180. Private classes for adults (45 minutes long) cost upwards of ¥370. Individual and family riding memberships are also available.

3088 Shen Zhuan Highway
Qingpu
沈巷沈砖公路
3088号
青浦

Ice Hockey

Shanghai Ice Hockey Association 上海冰球俱乐部

139 1866 0783 | www.icehockeyshanghai.com

There are currently six teams competing in the Shanghai ice hockey league. Organised matches are played on Sundays and pick-up games are held twice a week at different ice rinks throughout Shanghai. The league fees are approximately ¥1,000, and the ice fee for pick-up games varies. In addition, the club organises trips to regional and international tournaments and weekend getaways. The season usually starts in October and finishes in May.

500 Dongjiangwan Lu
Hongkou
东江湾路500号
虹口
🚇 *Hongkou Stadium*

Ice Skating

500 Dongjiangwan Lu
Hongkou
东江湾路500号
虹口
🚇 **Hongkou Stadium**

Hongkou Swimming Pool Leisure Rink 虹口游泳俱乐部
5696 0676

This large ice rink is built over the Hongkou swimming pool from November every year. Although it may not live up to the standards of top rinks, it still provides some good skating. Courses are available for adults and children, but only in Mandarin. Opening times are from 10:00 to 22:00 daily, and admission is ¥30 for 90 minutes.

Super Brand Mall,
168 Lujiazui Xi Lu
Pudong
陆家嘴西路168号,
正大广场
浦东
🚇 **Lujiazui**
Map p.427 E4 69

Super Brand Mall Ice Rink 司凯特正大真冰溜冰场
5047 1711

Located on the eighth floor of the huge Super Brand Mall in Pudong, this rink offers some fun ice skating for those who are tired of shopping (or other people shopping). The arena is quite compact and almost always packed with skaters, no matter what time of day or night you go. If you're feeling a bit rusty, there are private classes on offer for ¥100 per hour. Entrance is ¥50 for two hours, skates cost ¥10 extra. The rink is open between 10:00 and 22:00 every day.

Kids' Activities

Expats have little to worry about when it comes to keeping youngsters busy. There are a multitude of activities on offer for children and teenagers, providing great opportunities to make new friends. Since many expat families opt for housing in Pudong, several activities can be found in this part of town. The majority of the options here are aimed towards foreign children and most offer summer programmes.

Nice Year Villas,
Building A1-0,
3333 Hong Mei Lu
Changning
虹梅路3333号
长宁
Map p.427 E4 70

Active Kidz Shanghai
6406 6757 | www.activekidz.org

This community-based expat organisation offers lots of sports activities for children. Parents pay a ¥300 annual membership fee and activity prices range from ¥50 per session for bigger sports such as soccer and basketball to ¥120 per session for more intimate sports such as gymnastics and tennis. Active Kidz accepts children aged 3-14, and also offers both full and half-day camps for ¥1,800 and ¥1,100.

Hong Kong Plaza,
282 Huaihai Zhong Lu
Luwan
淮海中路282号
卢湾
🚇 **Huangpi Nan Lu**
Map p.430 C4 71

Azure Drama Kids 碧空儿童英语戏剧社
6554 8738 | www.kidsdrama.cn

Offering weekend drama workshops, 10 week drama and arts and crafts courses, and multi-activity summer camps, Drama Kids strives to create 'passion and creativity.' Workshops are available for children aged 6-12 and other programmes accept children aged 2-14. Courses are offered all year round, and the organisers often hold free trial classes for curious parents.

255

6, Lane 270,
Wu Yuan Lu
Xuhui
五原路270号6楼
徐汇
🚇 *Changshu Lu*
Map p.435 E2 **72**

JZ School 爵士学校
5403 6475 | *www.jz-school.cn*

This 'after-school school' focuses on music and English language classes for kids of all ages. Offering group and private music lessons, as well as weekly ensemble classes for a variety of styles, JZ teaches with an emphasis on creativity and improvisation. The 12 week classes are taught by both Chinese and expat teachers and prices vary; a private music course costs ¥4,200, while a group course is ¥1,800. The school occasionally holds promotions too, so check the website for more information.

5, Lane 650, Biyun Lu
Pudong
碧云路650弄5号
浦东
🚇 *Shanghai Science &*
Technology Museum

Kids Gallery 儿童艺廊
6105 9336 | *www.kidsgallery.com*

This international creative kids' club offers plenty of activities for all ages, including visual and performing arts, acting, music, singing and dance. It also holds early learners courses for children starting to read. Most activities run for eight-week terms and cost between ¥1,400 and ¥2,000, including materials. Each activity has different timings; check the website for schedules and registration information.

Various Locations

MultiSport 外国儿童体育活动中心
6466 3710 | *www.multisport.com.cn*

This professional expat sports organisation holds classes for 3-12 year-olds in locations across Shanghai. There are lessons in swimming, trampolining, basketball, short tennis, soccer, gymnastics and 'gym for tots' – all aiming to keep your young ones active and entertained. The trainers are all qualified in physical education and first aid. Depending on the activity, week-long classes cost between ¥425 and ¥1,000; discounts are available to multi-week students.

Various Locations

Sport for Life 生命来自运动
6282 1762 | *www.sportforlife.com.cn*

This British and Australian-run sports club puts on a variety of activities for children of different ages (as well as adults). Covering everything from cricket and basketball to football and tennis, the expat instructors aim to teach the children the techniques, rules and skills of the sport while keeping the focus on fun. The club also organises tournaments and holiday camps. Check out the website for schedules and registration. Fees depend on the activity as well as the length of the course – a seven-week soccer course for 4-5 year olds costs ¥420.

Kite Flying

Kite flying in China dates back some 3,000 years, when kites were made out of silk and bamboo, and emperors used them during the ancient wars in order to send signals to their troops. Today, kite flying is a more peaceful pastime, and remains one of the most popular activities in both Shanghai and China. At any time of the day you can see men, women and children flying their kites in the city's parks. Some are just there for fun; others have their kites soaring higher than the Oriental Pearl Tower, manoeuvring them in ways that suggest years of practice. Kites can be bought almost anywhere in Shanghai, so grab one, grab a partner and head to the park.

When you're lost what will you find in your pocket?

Item 71. The half-eaten chewing gum

When you reach into your pocket make sure
you have one of these minature marvels to
hand – far more use than a half-eaten stick of
chewing gum when you're lost.

London Mini Map
Fit the city in your pocket

Language Schools
Other options **Language** p.20

Despite Shanghai's most prevalent spoken language being Shanghainese, Mandarin is the form most widely taught. If you are keen to learn there are two options. One is to enrol at a university where the larger and cheaper classes generally focus on reading and writing Chinese characters. The other is to take classes at one of the many language schools, which offer both full-time and part-time courses. Classes tend to be smaller and most schools offer private tutors. Though they are often more expensive, language schools tend to be more flexible, offering programes that suit personal schedules. Another difference is that language schools often avoid the Chinese characters in the introductory levels, choosing instead to teach oral Mandarin using the Pinyin system (Chinese written in the western alphabet). Oral learning is easier and faster so, for those in need of some 'survival' Chinese, it is probably the best option.

Various Locations

Ease Mandarin 益习商务咨询有限公司 ▶ p.259
5465 6999 | www.easemandarin.com
With seven years of experience servicing Shanghai's expats, this school focuses its lessons on spoken Mandarin. The teaching method combines experienced tutors, custom materials and online practice. Private and group lessons are available for both adults and children. The 32 hour courses start at ¥2,900, and there are other learning locations in Pudong (58 Xinjinqiao Lu) and Hongqiao (8 Zunyi Nan Lu).

Various Locations

Enjoy Mandarin 欢乐中国语培训中心
6258 6885 | www.enjoymandarin.com
Fun learning is easy learning, according to Enjoy Mandarin. The school offers language and cultural learning, as well as fun activities designed to put the theory into practice, at its three branches across Shanghai. The beginner class focuses on Pinyin writing and basic conversation, while the more advanced courses introduce students to Chinese writing and continue with conversation-based topics. Each level consists of 60 hours of instruction. Private lessons are available and discounts are offered for students registering for multiple levels.

220 Handan Lu
Yangpu
邯郸路220号
杨浦
🚇 *Jiangwan Zhen*
Map p.423 D1 78

Fudan University 复旦大学
6564 2258 | www.fso.fudan.edu.cn
This university, located on the outskirts of Shanghai, was one of the first in China to enrol international students. There are two terms for language students, starting in September and February, and, once enrolled, students are put in a group that suits their level. Most students live on campus but you can of course choose to stay in central Shanghai and commute. The cost for a year is ¥21,000; six-month courses are also available.

Various Locations

iMandarin 爱马德汉语培训
3222 1028 | www.imandarin.net
Another popular option for expats, iMandarin is one of the biggest language schools in Shanghai. It offers group and private classes, or a combination of both, that teach Chinese, in Pinyin form, from basic to advanced levels. There are two different courses: standard and academic. The standard option puts more energy into speaking in order to acquaint learners with simple conversation as soon as possible. The academic classes develop writing skills, preparing students for university courses in Chinese. IMandarin also has courses specialising in teaching children, as well as classes in business Chinese. An 80 hour programme costs ¥5,700.

Conversational Mandarin Training (Adult)

Online Supplementary Learning Support

Private Group Corporate

Journey of a kite

Camp & Tutoring

Children's Program

All year round

EASE Mandarin

TEL: 8621-5465-6999

EMAIL: learn@easemandarin.com

★ SHANGHAI ★ BEIJING ★ SHENYANG

SHANGHAI: ★ Pudong ★ XuHui ★ Hongqiao

www.easemandarin.net

Various Locations

Mandarin House 美和中国语学校
6288 2308 | *www.mandarinhouse.cn*

This language school is an expat institution in both Beijing and Shanghai. Its courses, which cater to all skill levels, are available in group and private formats, or a mix of the two. Group sizes are small, with three to six people on average per class. At beginner levels, Mandarin House concentrates on Pinyin with a focus on speaking and basic conversation. As well as language lessons, Mandarin House also organises internship programmes in Chinese companies, as well as after-class activities and excursions. Each 40 hour course costs ¥3,000, with a 5% discount for every subsequent programme you take.

Xin Zha Mansion,
1851 Xinzha Lu
Jing'an
新闻大厦,
新闻路1851号
静安
🚇 *Jing'an Temple*
Map p.429 E4 **81**

Master China 中国通公司
6253 5239 | *www.masterchina.com.cn*

Master China offers a mix of language and cultural training as well as an online course. Available at all hours of the day, the language programmes are broken up into three groupings: survival, veteran and expert. The survival classes start with the basics of conversation, while the veteran course brings Chinese characters into the equation. The cost for a group programme starts at ¥3,500 for 50 hours and varies depending on the number of students enrolled.

50, Lane 90,
Qinghai Lu
Jing'an
青海路90弄50号
静安
🚇 *Nanjing Xi Lu*
Map p.430 A3 **82**

Miracle Mandarin Language Centre 奇迹中文
6218 3629 | *www.miraclemandarin.com*

This language school, technically a part of Shanghai Ligong University, limits its classes to six students. It has long-term academic Mandarin courses as well as short-term intensive and part-time options. Participants can select conversational, reading or business Chinese. Class prices vary depending on the number of hours per month, starting from ¥2,300 for 40 hours. Private lessons are available. There is a second facility near the Shanxi Nan Lu Metro in Xuhui.

1954 Huashan Lu
Xuhui
华山路1954号
徐汇
🚇 *Xujiahui*
Map p.435 D3 **83**

Shanghai Jiaotong University 上海交通大学
6282 1079 | *www.sie.sjtu.edu.cn*

This university offers half and full-year Mandarin courses that use Chinese characters and a Chinese-only teaching format, a method rarely utilised in language schools in Shanghai. Students study with other internationals in relatively large classes, and students are placed according to their existing level of Chinese comprehension. Semester-long courses cost ¥9,100 plus various enrollment fees.

Libraries
Other options **Books** p.312

There are numerous libraries in Shanghai – at least every district has its own local branch – but don't build up too much hope of finding a huge selection of reading matter if you can't understand Chinese. A few, such as Shanghai and Pudong libraries, offer a fairly good collection of international books. Most tend to be dictionaries and reference books, although there are some science and history volumes, plus a few old classics. All libraries with international sections will have an up-to-date selection of newspapers such as *The Times*, *New York Times*, *The Washington Post* and *USA Today*. In addition, there are usually big, quiet reading rooms that offer some good spots for studying. Students at the large universities in Shanghai can use the libraries on campus, which tend to have good collections.

3663 Zhongshan Bei Lu
Putuo
中山北路3663号
普陀
🚇 *Zhongshan Park*
Map p.428 A4 84

East China Normal University 华东师范大学

6223 2317 | www.ecnu.edu.cn

This is a huge library with a collection of more than 3.5 million books, but unfortunately it's only open to students and staff of the university. One section is dedicated to foreign books, containing a sizable amount of reference volumes. The library also has a book and database exchange with around 40,000 partners across the globe. Language students can only use the books on the premises, while degree students can borrow books to take home.

220 Handan Lu
Yangpu
邯郸路220号
杨浦
Map p.423 D1 85

Fudan University Library 复旦大学图书馆

6564 3173 | www.fudan.edu.cn

The Fudan library, only open to the students and staff of Fudan University, has an extensive collection of Chinese and foreign literature. It is actually made up of three smaller libraries: liberal arts, science and medical. Each has a vast selection of books, journals, papers and audio-visuals. Several big reading rooms offer the perfect environment for studying. Students or staff can use their card to visit other libraries around the city, such as Shanghai Library or other university libraries.

324 Yingchun Lu
Pudong
迎春路324号
浦东
🚇 *Shanghai Science & Technology Museum*

Pudong Library 浦东新区图书馆

5833 9529

This big library has a small section of international books and papers. The books, located in room 323 on the third floor, range from reference and dictionaries to science, history and fiction. Newspapers, in room 322, are mainly English and American, and there are also a selection of German and French titles. The rooms are comfortable and airy, so make good places for a study session. There's no need for a library card but books are read-only. Opening times are from 07:00 to 20:00.

1550 Wenxiang Lu
Hongkou
文翔路1550号
虹口
🚇 *Hongkou Stadium*

Shanghai International Studies University
上海外国语大学

6531 1900 | www.shisu.edu.cn

The Shanghai International Studies University has two libraries for staff and students to use (partner universities can also use the facilities). There is an average collection of Chinese and foreign books. Most are reference, and there are also some science and technological books. Other facilities include an internet centre and fax machine for members to use.

1555 Huaihai Zhong Lu
Xuhui
淮海中路1555号
徐汇
🚇 *Hengshan Lu*
Map p.435 E2 88

Shanghai Library 上海图书馆

6446 5555 | www.library.sh.cn/english

There is an extensive collection of Chinese books and a decent array of international titles at the largest public library in Shanghai. Although you shouldn't expect a comprehensive choice when looking for English publications, it is worth checking out for those in need of a fresh read. The library also houses several reading and seminar rooms and a few exhibition halls. Visiting requires that you bring your passport in order to get a ¥25 library card. Borrowing books requires a residence visa and a special ¥50 card, plus a ¥1,000 deposit.

Martial Arts

China has a long history of martial arts covering a variety of genres. Originally based on survival and self-defence, martial arts not only develop physical strength, coordination, flexibility and enhanced reflexes, but also teach inner strength, willpower and a deeper connection between mind and body. Every morning in Shanghai, locals can be seen performing tai chi in parks and streets all over the city.

One option for expats is to find a group of locals and try to mimic their movements, although having an English-speaking teacher is usually more informative. For this there are two options: sign up for a membership at one of the many gyms or health clubs and take classes there, or join one of Shanghai's martial arts clubs. Gym memberships tend to cost more but include other facilities. Martial arts clubs, many of which conduct outdoor morning classes, offer specialised instruction from top-tier teachers and generally cost less.

Aikido Shinju-Kai 合气道

2, Lane 591,
Nanjing Xi Lu
Jing'an
南京西路591弄2号
静安
Nanjing Xi Lu
Map p.430 B3 **89**

139 1707 3111 | www.aikidoshinjukai.com
This club offers classes in aikido, a harmonious type of self-defence originating in Japan. Aikido has no offensive actions; instead it relies on soft but efficient movements alongside mental calm and body control. Classes are held three times a week: in Jing'an, on Tuesdays from 19:00 to 21:00, and Sundays from 13:00 to 15:30, and in Pudong, off Puming Lu, on Wednesdays from 19:00 to 20:30. Classes cost ¥250 per month and are open to anyone.

Chinese International Martial Arts Training 国际中国武术培训

People's Park,
Nanjing Lu
Huangpu
人民广场, 南京路
黄埔
People's Square
Map p.430 C3 **90**

139 1634 4184 | jeremybiglas@hotmail.com
Perfect for early birds, these morning classes are held in People's Park on Tuesdays, Thursdays and Saturdays from 06:00 to 08:00 and from 08.30 to 10:30. The school specialises in the 'internal' martial arts of tai chi, xing yi and tong bei, and welcomes all levels. One month costs ¥800 and includes three classes per week.

Longwu International Kungfu Centre 龙武国际功夫中心

1 Maoming Nan Lu
Luwan
茂名南路1号
卢湾
Shanxi Nan Lu
Map p.430 A4 **91**

6287 1528 | www.longwukungfu.com
One of the most well-known and respected martial arts centres in Shanghai, the Long Wu Kungfu Centre offers a variety of classes to choose from. Aside from kung fu, the centre offers tai chi, shaolin, taekwondo, karate, boxing, kickboxing, mixed martial arts and a few other disciplines. Longwu instructs through group and private classes, and also runs special courses for children.

Mingwu International Kungfu Club 明武国际功夫馆

Floor 3,
359 Hongzhong Lu
Minhang
虹中路359号
闵行

6465 9806 | www.mingwukungfu.com
With several locations around the city, Mingwu International is one of the larger-scale kung fu specialists in Shanghai. Offering classes in other martial arts as well, the club not only teaches combat, but also stresses the importance of self protection, increased body strength, fitness and stress relief – all with the aim of boosting self confidence. Classes are conducted in English and Chinese. Yoga, ballet and belly dancing are also available.

Peter's Wing Chun 佩德咏春武馆

Room 102, Building 1,
118 Panyu Lu
Changning
番禺路118号
长宁
Yan'an Xi Lu

6282 5159 | www.phwingchun.com
New Yorker Peter Hsu has been practising martial arts for more than 14 years. At his Shanghai club he teaches wing chun, the art of close contact combat. Pupils start by learning the discipline's three fundamental principles and then progress through more advanced techniques. Classes are held on Tuesdays and Thursdays between 19:00 and 21:00 and on Saturdays between 13:00 and 15:00. One month of group lessons (twice a week) costs ¥600 and private lessons cost from ¥200 to ¥300 each.

227 Puyu Dong Lu
Huangpu
普育东路227号
黄埔
🚇 *Huangpi Nan Lu*
Map p.437 F2 94

Shanghai Shotokan Karate Association
上海松涛馆空手道协会
136 0177 7137 | sunknight1974@163.com

The main instructor of this club is the technical adviser of China's national karate team. He sets high standards, which means tough training for participants. The classes are for beginners as well as more advanced students and are held on Wednesdays, Fridays and Sundays between 19:00 and 21:00. Three classes a week for one month costs ¥200.

Lane 372,
21 Xingguo Lu
Xuhui
兴国路372弄21号
徐汇
🚇 *Hengshan Lu*
Map p.435 E3 95

Wu Yi Guan 武易馆
6281 0783 | www.chinamartialart.com

With classy studios and experienced, professional trainers, this tai chi club is a popular choice. By learning the techniques and ancient thoughts behind tai chi, participants should be able to overcome inner stress and psychological limitations. Wu Yi Guan offers classes in each of the six major styles of tai chi: chen, yang, sun, zhao bao and two different styles of wu. Free practice time is allotted to each student. Schedules and prices vary depending on the style of tai chi chosen.

Mother & Toddler Activities

Various Locations

Gymboree Shanghai 金宝贝
6121 3618 | www.gymboree.com.cn

This friendly club has stimulating and educational classes in music, fitness, yoga and baby singing for infants of all ages. The club has four locations across Shanghai, so finding a site that suits shouldn't be a problem. Some interesting and fun events include icecream parties and baby crawling competitions. Classes are organised by age (starting with newborn), and are typically 45 minutes long. A course of 12 classes (one class per week) costs ¥2,880.

666 Tianyaoqiao Lu
Xuhui
天钥桥路666号
徐汇
🚇 *Shanghai Indoor*
Stadium
Map p.443 F1

I Love Gym 运动宝贝
6426 5090 | www.ilovegym.com.cn

This isn't a place for toddlers to get bulky muscles – I Love Gym is actually a fitness programme designed to develop balance, flexibility and coordination as well as collaboration and social skills. There are nine different levels depending on your baby's age, and classes are held on Wednesdays through to Sundays. Each class is 50 minutes long. A three-month course, with classes once a week, costs ¥3,180, plus an upfront membership fee of ¥100.

Various Locations

Sport for Life 生命来自运动
6282 1762 | www.sportforlife.com.cn

A welcoming sports organisation that offers lots of activities for children of all ages and which has a 30 minute swim class for babies between 18 and 36 months. The aim is to build confidence in water through various games and activities. Successful swimmers are recognised through the 'Ducklings' awards scheme. Check out the website for the schedule and location.

Need Some Direction?
The *Explorer Mini Maps* pack a whole city into your pocket and once unfolded are excellent navigational tools for exploring. Not only are they handy in size, with detailed information on the sights and sounds of the city, but also their fabulously affordable price mean they won't make a dent in your holiday fund. Wherever your travels take you, from Asia and the Middle East to Europe and North America, grab a mini map and you'll never have to ask for directions.

263

Mountain Biking
Other options **Cycling** p.243

Prodigy Mountain Biking Club 骑迹自行车俱乐部

**Room 302,
205 Wulumuqi Nan Lu**
Xuhui
乌鲁木齐南路205号
徐汇
Xujiahui
Map p.435 F3

6437 7559 | info@mtb.com.cn

This club of dedicated mountain bikers has about 200 registered members. Anyone is welcome to join, from beginners to more advanced cyclists. The club, which is a non-profit organisation, offers free training trips every Wednesday. There are also outings at weekends to the more mountainous destinations of the Zhejiang and Jiangsu provinces. Trips vary by difficulty, so it's easy to choose one that suits you. There is a small cost for transportation, food and accommodation for the weekend trips. If you don't have a bike of your own, the club can help you get in contact with shops where you can rent one. Occasionally, the club organises other activities such as biking lessons and barbecues. Check out the website for information on upcoming events or register for the club's email newsletters.

Shanghai Bike Club 上海自行车俱乐部

**Room 2308, Building 2,
2918 Zhongshan Bei Lu**
Putuo
中山北路2918号
普陀
Caoyang Lu
Map p.428 B2 100

5266 9013 | www.bohdi.com.cn

Shanghai Bike Club is run by Bohdisattva Mountain Bikes, a shop that sells equipment and accessories. These friendly guys organise bike tours of various lengths in and around Shanghai. Half-day, full-day (mainly at the weekend) and five-day tours are all on offer. Anyone is welcome to join and you can choose the difficulty and length of ride. While many of the routes are suited to mountain bikes, they are not extreme and you can probably get away with using a normal bike. You don't have to have your own either as you can rent one for ¥150 per day, using your passport or ID as a deposit. Check out the schedule on the website for upcoming tours. The price for a half-day trip is ¥200, and ¥300 for a full day.

Music Lessons
Other options **Singing** p.270, **Orchestras** p.265

Music Pavilion 乐亭

**Building 5,
200 Taikang Lu**
Luwan
泰康路200弄
卢湾
Shanxi Nan Lu
Map p.436 B2 101

6445 8688 | www.musicpavilion.com.cn

The Music Pavilion is a music school, a music shop, a recording studio and an art gallery, all under one roof. The place is right at home on Taikang Lu, the 'arty' street of Shanghai, which brings together lots of creatives of all genres. The classes teach beginners and more advanced musicians how to play western and traditional Chinese instruments. You can try Chinese *er hu* (a two-stringed fiddle), *gu zheng* (a zither with movable bridges and 16-25 strings) and *pi pa* (a four stringed lute), together with drums, trumpet and double bass. The aim is not only to teach the practical side of playing

Drumming practice

instruments, but also to learn how to appreciate them. One eight-week group course costs ¥2,000. A private course costs ¥2,400

Rainbow Music Studio 彩虹声音

16 Zhu Xin Yi Cun,
165 Baole Lu,
Zhudi Town
Minhang
诸翟镇保乐路165号
诸新一村16号
闵行

5226 5185 | rainbowmusicstudio@gmail.com

The Rainbow Music Studio offers classes for people of all ages, aiming to help them understand, create and perform music with the aid of professional teachers. Sessions cover piano, drums, violin, guitar, saxophone, flute, clarinet, voice and traditional Chinese instruments. There are also classes in music appreciation, music theory and music composition for both individuals and groups. A one-hour private class costs ¥200, although shorter, cheaper sessions are available. Group classes are ¥160 but reductions are offered when purchasing more than one at a time. Beginner music lessons for toddlers cost ¥80 per hour. The studio provides a drum set and piano to practise on, but all other instruments must be provided by the student.

Shanghai Conservatory of Music 上海音乐学院

International Students'
Office, 20 Fenyang Lu
Xuhui
汾阳路20号
徐汇
🚇 *Changshu Lu*
Map p.436 A1 **103**

6431 0305 | www.shcmusic.cn

As the country's first higher education music academy, the Shanghai Conservatory, founded in 1927, is a well-known institution in China. The school offers undergraduate and postgraguate programmes, and courses include practical classes (various types of Chinese and western instruments, singing and opera) as well as theory lessons (music history, literature and writing). You'll need to be able speak Mandarin in order to attend a course.

Sharp+Focus 锐变艺术文化生活会馆

Room 301,
601A Honggu Lu
Changning
虹古路601A号
长宁
Map p.427 E3 **104**

6275 5179

As well as art and flower courses, Sharp+Focus offers classes in instruments including piano, violin and guitar. Lessons are for all abilities, and timings vary, so call ahead to arrange a private class and discuss prices. Sometimes the club organises group lessons which are advertised in the main expat magazines. A group lesson normally starts from ¥150.

Orchestras & Bands

Other options **Singing** p.270, **Music Lessons** p.264

Shanghai International Youth Orchestra 上海国际青年乐团

Various Locations

137 6102 0546 | www.shiyo.net

This new orchestra aims to provide an opportunity for young and talented string players of all nationalities to share and exchange culture, as they explore an advanced musical repertoire in a large ensemble setting. Participants are typically between 13 and 19 years of age, and must have their own private instructor. Rehearsals, which are held on Sunday afternoons, cost ¥175 each. Contact the orchestra or check out the website for upcoming auditions.

Shanghai Opera 上海歌剧院

10, Lane 100,
Changshu Lu
Changning
常熟路100弄
10号
长宁
🚇 *Changshu Lu*
Map p.435 F1 **106**

6248 5368 | www.shanghaiopera.com.cn

Founded in the 1950s, this opera group has developed some of China's most respected singers. The group performs all styles, including musical theatre, dance and drama. Operas are performed in both Chinese and English but, at the moment, all participants are Chinese and you will need to know the language in order to join. Openings for new members are fairly rare but if you are interested in taking part send in your singing CV by email.

265

105 Hunan Lu
Xuhui
湖南路105号
徐汇
🚇 *Hengshan Lu*
Map p.435 E2 107

Shanghai Symphony Orchestra 上海交响乐团

6431 3018 | www.sh-symphony.com

This highly respected orchestra dates back to 1879, making it the oldest in Asia. Today, it holds regular concerts, performing classics as well as modern pieces, and has put on shows in many famous venues across the world. Numerous internationally famous artists, including Andrea Bocelli, have collaborated with the Shanghai Symphony Orchestra. It also featured on the soundtrack of the movie *Crouching Tiger, Hidden Dragon*. You can apply for an audition online by submitting a resume of your previous work.

Paintballing

388 Chenhua Lu
Songjiang
辰花公路388号
松江

Weicheng Paintball Shooting Sports Centre 伟成彩弹射击运动中心

5769 0500 | boss@sh-paintball.com

The Weicheng Centre offers a fun and exciting paintball experience for beginners and pros. There are four outdoor playing fields with trenches, sandbags and jungle cover, and experienced instructors on hand to help out and explain how the equipment works. Ninety balls costs ¥130, and every extra ball an additional ¥1. Opening times are 08:30 to 22:00. Call in advance to book.

Paragliding

Room 801, 12, Lane 6780, Humin Lu
Minhang
沪闵路6780弄12号
闵行

Flying Heart Paragliding Club 我心飞翔滑翔伞俱乐部

5103 5123 | www.flyingheart.net

This Pudong club offers a number of packages for anyone interested in paragliding. Single elementary classes start at ¥300. A full course is about ¥3,000 and will provide you with a recognised certificate enabling you to paraglide in 74 countries worldwide. The length of the course depends on how fast you learn and how much you practise, but most people tend to complete it in half a year. Motorised paragliding is also available. If you're not sure about committing to the whole course, the club sometimes organises trial classes. Call directly or check out the website (in Chinese only) for more information on dates.

729 Pujian Lu
Pudong
浦建路729号
浦东
🚇 *Longyang Lu*

Jim Qin's Joyvario 滑翔伞课程

133 1174 0909 | joyvario@gmail.com

Jim Qin's offers paragliding courses for beginners. You'll start by having 10 hours of classroom instruction, followed by 30-35 hours of practical learning, both spread over several days. The cost for the whole course is ¥5,000, including all the materials and equipment you'll need. The theory lessons are normally held in Pudong but can be changed to Puxi if it's more convenient for you. Make sure you book at least one month in advance.

Photography

580 Yongjia Lu
Xuhui
永嘉路580号
徐汇
🚇 *Hengshan Lu*
Map p.435 F2 111

Shanghai Expat Learning Centre 上海外派教育中心

6467 6875 | www.shanghai-classes.com

The Shanghai Expat Learning Centre offers a number of classes for expats, ranging from art and design to business, language and computer skills. The photography course provides you with all the basic techniques you need to shoot professional pictures. Students with either digital or traditional cameras can join as tuition covers both. Teachers are experienced, and you can see profiles and examples of their work on the centre's website. The course is divided into two parts; beginners to intermediates, and a more advanced level that includes black-and-white photography. The beginner classes are held on Thursdays (mornings or afternoons) and Saturday mornings. The more advanced classes are held on Tuesdays (mornings or afternoons) and Sunday mornings. A 10 week course costs ¥3,200.

Polo

Other options **Horse Riding** p.254

Nine Dragons Hill Resort & Tourism Park
Jiaxing
九龙山庄园
嘉兴区

Nine Dragons Hill Polo Club
九龙山马会俱乐部
6467 5252 | *www.ndhpolo.com*

Shanghai's sole polo club, which is a part of the luxurious Nine Dragons Hill Resort, is located an hour from the city centre in lush green surroundings. As well as the polo, members can enjoy a multitude of sports facilities (spa, gym, swimming pool and equestrian), and also fine dining. Polo is played between March and November, with the club organising regular tournaments and events for players and their friends. At the end of the season, Nine Dragons Hill also hosts an international championship.

Members of the club can either be selected to join the club's team, enter one of the growing numbers of private teams within the club, or start their own. The club has a wide range of horses available for players to use.

Pool

A popular pub game among expats and locals in China, pool attracts a decent number of players in Shanghai. The city has many pubs and bars with tables, all of which you can just rock up to and shoot some eight-ball without booking in advance. Big Bamboo (132 Nanyang Lu; 6256 2265) has pool tables, foosball and big flat screens for spectator games. Wunderbar (300 Liaoyuan Xi Lu; 3377 3373) is another fun venue with tables, as are Koala Bar (280 Huaihai Xi Lu; 5258 8779) and The Spot (331 Tongren Lu; 6247 3579).

Various Locations

Shanghai Pool Club 上海台球俱乐部
138 1730 9937 | *www.southside8ball.leaguerepublic.com*

This big community of pool players boasts 16 teams, with 12 bars involved in hosting games and training sessions. Participants meet at different venues every week to practise and compete against each other. New teams are always welcome to join the league, which is free to enter. See the website for membership details and upcoming matches.

Pottery

If you think pottery looks easy, then think again – unlike for Demi Moore in the film *Ghost*, it demands a great deal of work in order to get your bowls looking good enough to be on display. In China, clay pottery has been around for more than 7,000 years and is still a crucial part of Chinese art. Shanghai has lots of shops and galleries where you can find traditional pottery, notably the Shanghai Museum (p.203), which has a large ceramics section.

267

Lane 188, Changshu Lu
Xuhui
常熟路188弄
徐汇
Changshu Lu
Map p.435 F1 **114**

Hanguang Pottery Studio 汉光玩陶制陶俱乐部

133 8607 0268

This pottery studio has group classes to suit all levels. If your bowls and plates need some extra attention, there are private sessions as well. The children's classes on offer aim to get kids using their creativity and imagination, as well as teaching them the basics of working with clay. Call for details of upcoming courses.

Floor 2,
220 Taikang Lu
Luwan
泰康路220号
卢湾
Map p.436 B2 **115**

The Pottery Workshop 乐天陶社

6445 0902 | *www.potteryworkshop.com.cn*

A friendly and professional studio staging exhibitions and classes to which everyone is welcome. If you are a beginner, simply tell the instructor that you need some help and you'll be shown everything you need to know. Classes start with sculpting and throwing, before progressing to the wheel. There are lessons for children as well as adults, all with English-speaking instructors. The sessions for kids are held on Tuesdays, Thursdays and Saturdays and cost ¥100 per class, materials included. Adult courses are held on Mondays, Fridays and Saturdays and cost ¥600 for four classes, also with materials.

Rollerblading & Rollerskating

Other options **Parks** p.211

Although the heavy traffic in Shanghai makes some of the streets less safe (and less fun) for rollerblading, there are some areas that are perfect to explore on wheels. The quiet streets of the French Concession, as well as the long stretch of the Bund are good spots. In addition, word on the street is that some of the many construction sites around the city are something of a mecca for one or two of Shanghai's more extreme rollerbladers. This illegal activity may get the adrenaline going, but cannot be recommended as safe for obvious reasons. Skaters also have to watch out for security guards, who are not likely to be keen to let them get away with it. For the more traditional skater, there are some rinks where you can rent wheels and pay for an hour of skating, such as Century Park in Pudong (p.211).

Roller-disco revival

554 Anyuan Lu
安源路554号
Jing'an
静安
Map p.429 E2 **116**

Roller-disco! 轮滑迪斯科

136 7199 3664 | *www.rollerrevival.com*

If you're into oversize shoulder pads, neon-coloured miniskirts, David Bowie and roller skates, then this annual roller-disco is a true nostalgia trip. The booted boogie is held in a traditional roller rink with wooden floors, and features a raised round stage for anyone really wishing to show off. Dozens of expats come here every year to 'skate-dance' to 1980s hits. Entrance is ¥100, including boots or skates and a free bar for the night. The party is held during the spring, normally in May. Look out for the exact date in expat magazines or online – and don't forget the blue eye shadow and retro Adidas tracksuit.

Rugby

222 Lan'an Lu
Pudong
蓝桉路222号
浦东
Map p.440 C1 **117**

Shanghai Rugby Football Club 上海橄榄球俱乐部
6210 7977 | *www.shanghaifootballclub.com*
Shanghai Rugby Football Club is one of the most well-established expat organisations in the city. Most players have some experience, although beginners are welcome too. Matches take place every Saturday, year round (weather permitting). Timings vary, but sessions typically consist of round-robin games of touch rugby, followed by full-contact games for the more serious players. The club also plays larger tournaments a couple of times a year, where players are split into sides that compete against each other. Teams include the Shanghai Hairy Crabs, Japanese Twin Dragons, Shanghai Rhinos, Shanghai Sport Institute and Shanghai Knights, and it's easy enough to get involved with one of them. There are also junior teams for children and teenagers. Check the website for timings, tournaments and information on the club, and for a list of email addresses to contact committee members.

Running

Other options **Hashing** p.253

Shanghai is not the ideal city for running, due to its sprawling concrete make up, busy roads and pollution. You'll soon discover that running along the pavement is an uncommon sight for many locals. However, find the right place and it can be a rewarding experience. Pudong, Century Park and Fuxing Park are popular locations, while Zhongshan Park is just about big enough for a nice trot. One of the most pleasant experiences is running around the Shanghai Botanical Garden (p.219). Don't be surprised if you see some unusual activities while heading for a morning run in the park. Walking or jogging backwards, for example, is a common exercise for locals, designed to warn away evil spirits, and train the muscles in the back, waist, thighs, knees and lower legs. Tree slapping, performed to get rid of bad energy (and aggression) is being phased out due to the damage it can cause to the defenceless trees, but is still a common sight for now. See Parks on p.211 for more venue inspiration.

Sailing

Dianshan Lake,
Parkland's East Bank,
Huqingping Highway
Qingpu
淀山湖风景区东岸,
沪青平高速公路
青浦

Shanghai Boat and Yacht Club 上海游艇俱乐部
www.shanghaibyc.org
Started by a small group of sailing enthusiasts, this non-profit organisation has around 80 members and 20 boats. Anyone who loves sailing, or wants to see what it's like, is welcome to join. The club organises regular events such as casual sailing, racing and other social get-togethers. At the moment, there are no formal training classes, but you are welcome to accompany one of the experienced sailors for a trip and learn as you go. The joining fee is ¥500 plus an annual membership price of ¥2,000. Families pay a yearly fee of ¥3,000. If you want to visit the club before you join, you can attend one of the free open days (see the schedule on the website).

269

Singing

Other options **Music Lessons** p.264

Various Locations

International Festival Chorus Shanghai
上海国际节日合唱团
www.ifcshanghai.org

The International Festival Chorus in Shanghai started in 2003 as an extension of the organisation in Beijing. Today, it has around 70 members and holds concerts at least three times a year, including collaborations with other choirs from around the world. Recent performance venues include the Lyceum Theatre in Maoming Lu, the Shanghai Conservatory of Music, and Pudong Oriental Arts Centre (see Entertainment, p.407). The music ranges from favourite classical composers such as Beethoven and Bach through to opera, and also includes seasonal performances of Christmas carols. There are no regular weekly session, instead there is an intense period of rehearsals during the month before a performance. Although an amateur choir, given the focus on performance, members need to be of a certain singing standard in order to join. Auditions for new recruits are held regularly throughout the year; if you are interested email to arrange one. Non-singers are also welcome as there are many administrative and behind-the-scenes jobs. The choir is not for profit, but there is an annual fee of ¥500 (¥150 for students) in addition to some smaller, extra costs for clothing (for women only) and music scores.

Greenfield
Kindergarten,
1980 Hongqiao Lu
Changning
格林菲尔幼儿园，
虹桥路1980号
长宁
Map p.427 E4 **120**

Shanghai Voices   上海之声合唱团
136 8173 2582 | shanghai.voices@gmail.com

Open for anyone who loves singing, this choir started in 2005 and has grown significantly. Today, Shanghai Voices holds weekly rehearsals and puts on concerts as often as possible, at embassies, community centres and other locations across the city. The choir doesn't take itself too seriously and although many members do read music, about a fifth of the current group had never sung before they joined. There are mooted plans to divide the choir into beginners and more advanced singers. A six-month membership costs ¥500.

Skateboarding

880 Yinhang Lu
Yangpu
殷行路880号
杨浦
🚇 *Jiangwan Zhen*
Map p.422 B2 **121**

SMP Skate Park   滑板公园
6590 7622 | www.smpskatepark.com

This is one of Asia's, if not the world's, largest extreme sport skate parks. Its size makes it a must for anyone into rollerblading, roller skating, skateboarding or BMX biking. The park has huge ramps, 40-metre-long half pipes and flat training areas, suitable for all abilities. The nearest Metro stop is Jiangwan Town but you'll have to take a taxi from there (or get your skates on).

Skiing & Snowboarding

Although China can't offer the reputable skiing and boarding slopes of neighbouring Japan (a popular skiing venue for expats) there are some decent resorts in the country. The premier spot is at Yabuli in the north-eastern Heilongjiang province, where you can find some good slopes for all levels. The attractive resort was a venue for the third Asian Winter Games in 1996. Another popular ski resort is Beidahu, in Songhuahu Lake Nature Reserve in Jilin province.

Given the topography and climate, there are no outdoor skiing options in Shanghai but, to brush up on your technique or just try something different, head to the indoor slope at Yinqixing. Don't be put off by the erratic Chinese skiing style, which focuses on speed and minimal turning. As the saying goes, when in China ski as the Chinese do, who, no matter how many snowdrifts or pile-ups they end up in, always manage to see the funny side.

1835 Qixin Lu
Minhang
七莘路1835号
闵行
🚇 *Xinzhuang*

Yinqixing Indoor Skiing Site 银七星室内滑雪场

6478 8666 | www.yinqixing.com

The city is extremely proud of its indoor skiing centre, evidenced by the huge number of people swishing down the slopes every day. The slope, which has fake snow (not a carpet), is 380 metres long and 80 metres wide and divided into two sections of varying steepness. The lifts are not the quickest – some impatient people walk up with their skis just as quickly, so this probably won't satisfy the more experienced skier. But for a fun afternoon out, or for beginners, Yinqixing is worth a look. One hour costs ¥98 on weekdays and ¥118 on weekends, including skis, clothes and boots. You can hire the services of an instructor for ¥120 per hour. The nearest Metro stop is Xinzhuang, but from there it's a cab ride to the slope.

Social Groups

Other options **Support Groups** p.144, **Business Councils & Groups** p.73

Considering the large expat crowd in Shanghai, the numerous social clubs that exist shouldn't come as a surprise. Most people will find others with similar interests – from shared nationalities, business contacts or people to have dinner parties with, there is a group catering for pretty much everything. Many of these groups interact in an informal fashion, as in 'let's meet on Friday night at the local pub', rather than having memberships, websites or consistent contact people. The best way to keep updated on groups and their meetings is to check out the main expat magazines (*City Weekend*, *SH*, *Shanghai Talk* and *that's Shanghai*). The online forum on www.shanghaiexpat.com is also a good place for more information.

Various Locations

American Women's Club of Shanghai 上海美国妇女公会

www.awcshanghai.org

This non-profit social club organises events, lunches and other get-togethers for American women, as well as hosting charity galas and fundraisers. It also hosts a popular 'Welcome to Shanghai' programme called *Huan Ying* ('welcome' in Mandarin). This three-week course, offered every month, focuses on discovering the city and meeting other newbies. The club's membership year runs from October to September and costs ¥200. If you are interested in joining and want to know more about the club, you can visit one of the monthly coffee mornings, or send an email to membership@awcshanghai.org.

4, Lane 289,
Weihai Lu
Jing'an
威海路289弄4号
静安
🚇 *Nanjing Xi Lu*
Map p.430 B4 124

Australian Women's Social Group 澳大利亚妇女公会

139 1608 5723 | www.awsg.org

Although most of the members of the Australian Women's Social Group come from Down Under, anyone with a foreign passport in Shanghai is welcome to join. The group arranges morning teas, lunches, 'pamper days' and shopping trips, as well as other fun events for women. It also organise a kids' playgroup, which meets every Thursday from 10:00 to 12:00. If you are interested in joining, the group holds regular newcomers' coffee mornings where you can get to know some of the members and see what the club offers. Take a look on the website for dates and venues. Membership costs ¥200 per year, activities are extra.

271

Floor 1, 3,
Lane 100, Xinle Lu
Xuhui
新乐路100弄1楼3室
徐汇
🚇 *Shanxi Nan Lu*
Map p.436 A1 **125**

Cercle Francophone de Shanghai 中国法国工商会

5403 2338 | *www.cerclefrancophonedeshanghai.com*

French in Shanghai? *Vous n'êtes pas toute seule*. This friendly organisation has regular get-togethers for anyone interested in joining, although the majority of participants are French. Events range from dinners, dance lessons and cooking courses to sports, language practice, trips and much more. Check out the calendar on the website for a full update on the events. Call or email if you are interested in joining.

2099 Yan'an Xi Lu
Changning
扬子江万丽大酒店,
延安西路2099号
长宁
🚇 *Zhongshan Park*
Map p.427 F4 **126**

Deutscher Club Shanghai 上海德国俱乐部

134 8239 7145 | *www.schanghai.com/deutscherclub*

The Deutscher Club arranges activities for Germans in Shanghai. There is a coffee morning (*kaffemorgen*) at the Renaissance Yangtze Hotel every third Monday of the month from 10:00 to 12:00. Newcomers or longer-term residents interested in joining can enjoy a special event in which they get introduced to the club and its members. Check out the website for listings of upcoming get-togethers and other events.

Various Locations

ShanghaiNZ Community Group 上海新西兰社区俱乐部

www.shanghainz.com

Although the majority of the ShanghaiNZ group are New Zealanders living in the city, anyone with an interest in the country is welcome to join this association. The relaxed, informal and friendly club meets every month on a Friday for a get-together at various clubs in Shanghai. Email or join the discussion board to get information on when and where. Also view the website for an out-of-date slice of New Zealand news.

Room 301,
Sports Mansion,
150 Nanjing Xi Lu
Huangpu
南京西路150号
体育大厦301室
黄埔
🚇 *Nanjing Xi Lu*
Map p.431 D3 **128**

Toastmasters Shanghai Leadership Club
上海英文领导力演讲俱乐部

135 6464 5047 | *http://shleadership.freetoasthost.info*

This fairly new organisation is the local branch for Toastmasters International. The aim is to develop members' public speaking, presentation and leadership skills, and anyone is welcome to join. You will learn by watching others as well as practising yourself – members give speeches and conduct meetings, then receive feedback from the other participants. Sessions, which are relaxed and informal, are held from 19:00 to 21:00 on Wednesdays. The cost is ¥800 for the first six months, then ¥400 for half a year.

Squash

Other options **Leisure Facilities** p.281

Squash is a popular sport for expats in Shanghai. Some apartment blocks provide courts as part of their onsite fitness provisions. There are also lots of gyms and health clubs with squash facilities but you'll need to have membership to play. Shanghai International Tennis Club (516 Henghan Lu; 6445 8899) and Jinqiao Megafit Sports Club (600 Lantian Lu; 5030 8118) have excellent courts. Another option is to pay by the hour at one of the many gymnasiums and sports centres. Shanghai Stadium (666 Tianyaoqiao Lu; 6426 6666) has good courts on offer. One hour at a sports centre is normally around ¥50 and you can rent a racket for an additional small cost. Some hotels, such as the Hilton (250 Huashan Lu; 6248 0000) and Equatorial Hotel (65 Yan'an Lu; 6248 1688) also have courts to rent by the hour, although these are typically more expensive.

Various Locations

Shanghai Squash Association 上海壁球协会

137 0184 9343 | *www.shanghaisquash.com*

The Shanghai Squash Association welcomes experienced players, or anyone who wants to learn how to play. If you are interested in a class, simply call and book with one of

Sports & Activities

the instructors who operate at venues all over Shanghai. The club also offers group sessions. A private class costs between ¥100 and ¥200, depending on the experience of the teacher. Sometimes the club participates in leagues and competitions around Shanghai; information about this is sent out by email.

Swimming
Other options **Beaches** p.216, **Leisure Facilities** p.281

Swimming is a popular way to exercise in Shanghai. Many apartment buildings have indoor or outdoor pools for residents, as do some gyms (for members). There are also public pools that can be used by anyone for a small fee. These are clean and safe, and typically have lifeguards on duty. The more advanced complexes have different areas for serious swimming and more recreational activity, with fun toys and slides for children (and sometimes grown-ups). During the summer, the outdoor pools offer a well-needed break from the heat in the city, and are busy with residents trying to cool off.

Swimming Pools

Dino Beach	78 Xinzhen Lu	Minhang	6478 3333	Outdoor
Jing'an Sport Centre	151 Kangding Lu	Jing'an	6272 7277	Indoor
Le Royal Meridien	789 Nanjing Dong Lu	Huangpu	3318 9999	Indoor
Mandarine City	788 Hongxu Lu	Minhang	6405 0404	Outdoor
Mayfair Hotel	1555 Dingxi Lu	Changning	6240 8888	Outdoor
Pudong Swimming Pool	3669 Pudong Nan Lu	Pudong	5889 0101	Indoor
Purple Mountain Hotel	778 Dongfang Lu	Pudong	6886 8888	Outdoor
Shanghai International Tennis Centre	Regal International East Asia Hotel, 516 Hengshan Lu	Xuhui	6415 5588	Indoor
Shanghai Racquet Club	Lane 555, Jinfeng Lu, Huacao Town	Minhang	2201 0888	Outdoor
Shanghai Swimming Pool	1300 Zhongshan Nan Er Lu	Xuhui	6438 2372	Indoor

Table Tennis
Other options **Leisure Facilities** p.281

It should come as no surprise that China is extremely proud of its tradition in table tennis. After all, it first enabled the country to gain world recognition as a serious sporting nation. Since then, millions of Chinese kids have grown up with a table tennis bat in their hand, idolising icons such as Wang Liqin (winner of the world championship in 2005), female player Deng Yaping, and Sweden's JO Waldner (or *Lao Wa* – 'Old Wa' as he is called locally). Table tennis is set to be a big draw at the Beijing Olympics – China missed out on the gold medal in 2004, so will be determined to do better this time round on home turf.
It is estimated that more than 200 million people play the sport regularly in China, and a fair number of those are in Shanghai. Almost every accommodation block has a

Olympic Fever
The news of Beijing winning the bid to host the Olympics in 2008 was met with huge excitement and an overwhelming sense of national pride. With an estimated four billion TV viewers across the world set to turn their attention to China for the games, it's a golden opportunity to showcase the country's new stature. Shanghai has got itself a slice of the action too as host for nine of the preliminary games in the Olympic football tournament. The 80,000 seat Shanghai Stadium underwent a ¥200 million makeover in advance of the games. The Olympics is also being credited with changing the country's sporting scene, as more and more Chinese citizens take an interest in both playing and watching.

273

The Complete **Residents'** Guide

table for residents to use, as do some of the gyms, which are free to use if you go with a member. In addition, there are numerous table tennis venues that you can rent for a small cost, usually around ¥30 per hour. Bats are also available for hire at most places for a small additional cost.

Table Tennis

Jing'an Sport Centre	151 Kangding Lu	Jing'an	6272 7277
Luwan Gymnasium	128 Zhaojiabang Lu	Luwan	6467 5358
Shanghai International Tennis Centre	516 Hengshan Lu	Xuhui	6415 5588
Shanghai Stadium	666 Tianyaoqiao Lu	Xuhui	6426 6666
Xianxia Tennis Centre	1885 Hongqiao Lu	Changning	6262 8327
Yuanshen Sports Centre	1458 Zhangyang Lu	Pudong	5860 2330

Tennis

Other options **Leisure Facilities** p.281

Tennis is a common sport for overseas residents in Shanghai, and there are many places to have a knock about, both outdoor and indoor. If you've never played before, or just feel a bit rusty, there are tutors on hand at most clubs to help get the deuces flowing. Compared with western rates, lessons are fairly cheap in Shanghai – usually around ¥200 an hour for a private session. You can either take classes through a tennis club, which often means a certified tutor and a fixed price, or find a trainer yourself on websites such as www.cityweekend.com.cn and www.shanghaiexpat.com, where negotiation on cost may be possible.

Tennis

Changning Tennis Court	1038 Huashan Lu	Changning	6252 4436
Fuxing Tennis Centre	1380 Fuxing Lu	Xuhui	6437 0766
Luwan Tennis Centre	128 Zhaojiabang Lu	Luwan	6467 5245
Shanghai International Club	Hotel Equatorial Shanghai, 65 Yan'an Xi Lu	Jing'an	6248 1688
Shanghai International Tennis Centre	Regal International East Asia Hotel, 516 Hengshan Lu	Xuhui	6415 5588
Shanghai Racquet Club	Lane 555 Jinfeng Lu, Huacao Town	Minhang	2201 0888
Xianxia Tennis Centre	1885 Hongqiao Lu	Changning	6262 6720
Yuanshen Sports Centre (Pudong Sports Park)	1458 Zhangyang Lu	Pudong	5860 2330

Luwan Tennis Centre,
128 Zhaojiabang Lu
Luwan
肇嘉浜路128号
卢湾
🚇 *Xujiahui*
Map p.436 B2 **130**

Crossover Tennis Club 上海围城网球俱乐部

138 1862 2562 | crossover.tennis@gmail.com

This unofficial club plays at Luwan Tennis Centre during the spring and autumn season. The team often plays doubles 'speed tennis', where players change partners and opponents every 30 minutes to keep sessions fresh and interesting. Most players are intermediate level or better, but anyone is welcome to join. Call or email to find out about upcoming games.

Shanghai Racquet Club

Various Locations

Pro Tennis Coaching 专业网球教练

138 1610 4242 | www.protenniscoaching.com

This association of professional tennis coaches offers classes for adults, children and groups – simply call and a coach will come to your local court, or check out the websites for full course programmes. Coaches speak English, French and Dutch. New players can have a free assessment where the coach will test your ability and then advise on a programme that suits you best. Private lessons cost ¥200 per hour (10 lessons are ¥1,800), while the group lessons are ¥100-¥150, depending on the number of players.

Volleyball

Hunan Stadium,
515 Fang Xie Lu
Luwan
方斜路515号
卢湾
🚇 **Huangpi Nan Lu**
Map p.437 D1 132

Active Sports Active Social 体育大联盟

139 1731 6770 | www.asas.com.cn

This multi-sports organisation (see Football p.249, and Basketball p.240) is one of the largest sport clubs in Shanghai, and has a volleyball team open for anyone to join. Teams cover different age groups, genders and abilities, and there are training games a couple of times per week. Each session costs around ¥30. Sign up for the email newsletter and you'll be notified when and where games and training are held.

251 Baoshan Lu
Zhabei
宝山路251号
闸北
🚇 **Baoshan Lu**

VoVo Volley Club VoVo排球俱乐部

136 0197 1699 | www.vovo-club.com

This expat organisation is made up of many different nationalities and aims to provide a fun place to play volleyball, as well as somewhere to make new friends. Games are normally indoors but during the summer the club tries to organise outdoor sessions and beach volleyball. Meets are on Fridays between 19:00 and 22:00. One session costs ¥50. Call before to confirm your attendance.

Watersports

25 Daduhe Lu
Putuo
大渡河路25号
普陀
🚇 **Jinshajiang Lu**
Map p.427 F2 134

Changfeng Park 长风公园

6245 3270 | www.sh-cfpark.com

Ever fancied walking on water? In Changfeng Park you can do just that. Together with fishing and paddleboats, this park offers you the chance to clamber inside a large plastic bubble and actually stroll across the water surface. Other activites include fishing and rowing in fairly small pools. You can also find the Ocean World aquarium here (p.218), which is located under the Silver Axe Lake.

Wine Tasting

Shanghai Exhibition
Centre,
1000 Yan'an Zhong Lu
Jing'an
上海国际展览中心,
延安中路1000号
静安
🚇 **Jing'an Temple**
Map p.429 F4 135

China International Wine and Liquor Expo
中国国际葡萄酒蒸馏酒博览会

5223 4951 | www.cpexhibition.com

China's first wine exposition was held in 2006 as a result of the country beginning to establish itself on the global vino map, both for its domestic production and consumption levels. The debut expo focused on international varieties, and went down so well that it's now an annual event held every May. Although the exhibition is tailored to professionals within the industry, anyone who has an interest in the grape is welcome to attend. There are classes and workshops held by international experts on wine making, pairing and investment, and, importantly, there is also a huge selection of tipples to sample.

98 Xinle Lu
Xuhui
新乐路98号
徐汇
Shanxi Nan Lu
Map p.436 A1 136

Epicvre 飨爱主义

5404 7719 | www.epicvre.com

This shop, which also sells delicious sweets and snacks, has an extensive, handpicked wine list which is quite famous among connoisseurs in Shanghai. It also organises tasting sessions once a week where you can try some new varieties for ¥40 per glass. Some of these events are also attended by experts who speak on various grape-related subjects. Visit the website for details of forthcoming events.

376 Wukang Lu
Xuhui
武康路376号
徐汇
Hengshan Lu
Map p.435 E2 137

Globus Wine 阁乐葡

6466 8969 | www.globus-wine.com

This fine-wine retailer has a cute little shop in a beautiful

Globus Wine

renovated lane in the French Concession. It holds wine and champagne-tasting events each month, giving participants the chance to sample six to seven varieties for ¥150-¥180. Globus sometimes collaborates with the Coffee Tree cafe next door (p.380), offering dessert and wine tastings. For ¥150, you get to try seven wines and up to five desserts. Make sure to book in advance as it's a popular evening, and go easy on lunch to leave room for all those sweets.

41B, Tian Shan 2, Zunyi Lu
Changning
遵义路天山二村41号乙地下酒窖
长宁
Loushanguan Lu
Map p.434 A2 138

Ruby Red Wine Cellar 红樽坊葡萄酒专卖

6234 3031 | www.rubyred.com.cn

Ruby Red has classes for every type of vino fan, from glugging novices to quaffing connoisseurs. For beginners, a two hour course, taught in both English and Chinese, includes a brief introduction to wine-making before moving on to the basics of tasting. Sessions cost ¥60, which gets you five wines to taste. Intermediate classes (also two hours) focus on one variety per class, and cost ¥120. Other events, such as tastings at bars around the city and country-focused sessions, are also held.

118 Xingye Lu
Luwan
兴业路118号
卢湾
Huangpi Nan Lu
Map p.436 C1 139

VIN ▶ p.277

6385 2127 | www.vin-world.com

With hundreds of wines from around the world on display, this shop is a popular stop for expats. VIN's own expert, himself an export from France, holds regular vino and champagne courses. A wine class costs ¥200, which includes the tasting of four or five varieties. VIN also organises tasting dinners in collaboration with some of the city's more interesting restaurants. These range in price from ¥350 to ¥1,200. Check out the website for dates and restaurants.

Vintage Stuff

Grape wine first appeared in Chinese poetry nearly 1,000 years ago, and China's vineyards are currently expanding by nearly 30% each year. Whether or not they'll be able to compete on the international level has yet to be seen. Currently, Chinese wines account for 90% of the domestic market and are often compared to early Chilean and Argentinian vintages.

276

A World of Fine Wines

- More than 500 fine wines from around the world
(French Great Chateaux, rare Burgundy and Rhone wines,
boutique Italian and California wines,
large selection of rare Champagnes and dessert wines)
- Wine accessories
(glassware, decanter, wine stain remover, wine pump and stopper…)
- Free home delivery 7 days a week
- Professional advice on how to purchase,
store and enjoy wines

For any inquiries, please contact us at **info@vin-world.com**
Visit our website to download our most updated wine list
www.vin-world.com

Spectator Sports

As witnessed by the excitement generated by the hosting of the Olympics, China has really opened up to top class international sporting events. As one of the country's more cosmopolitan cities, Shanghai has little trouble attracting some fantastic events, with the jewel in the crown being the Formula One Grand Prix. China is yet to produce a world-class driver of its own but this has not served to dampen interest in the race, held at Shanghai's new international circuit. The track also hosts the popular Moto GP and A1 Grand Prix races. The Masters Tennis tournament brings together the finest servers and vollyers in the world, and the HSBC World Championships and BMW Asia Open golf tournaments are beginning to draw quite a crowd. Be warned though, tickets for major events sell out early. The expat listings (*Shanghai Talk*, *SH*, *City Weekend* and *that's Shanghai*) publish upcoming events, so keep your eyes peeled to avoid disappointment. There are also regular matches for some of the bigger local football and basketball teams, but interest in these tends to be more locally based.

Basketball

Luwan Stadium,
128 Zhaojiabang Lu
Luwan
肇嘉浜路128号
卢湾
Map p.436 B2 140

Shanghai Sharks Basketball 上海大鲨鱼篮球
6467 5358

Best known as the team that developed the iconic superstar Yao Ming before his move to the NBA, the Sharks are Shanghai's representatives in China's principal basketball league, the CBA. Regular matches are played in front of a locally dominated crowd at Luwan Stadium. Tickets cost ¥30-¥200.

Football

Yuanshen Stadium,
1458 Zhangyang Lu
Pudong
源深体育馆,
张杨路1458号
浦东
🅜 *Dongchang Lu*

Chinese Football Association Super League
中国足球协会超级联赛
6853 5533 | *http://csl.sports.cn*

The Chinese Super League, made up of 15 teams, is the country's premier football competition. Shanghai Shenhua United Football Club is the city's only club in the league after it merged with the second local side, Shanghai United, at the start of the 2007 season. With many internationals in their ranks, Shenhua draw decent, local-dominated crowds to games at the 16,000 capacity Yuanshen Stadium, and were runners up in the league in 2006. To get there by Metro, get off at Dongchang Lu then take a taxi.

Golf

Tomson Shanghai
Pudong Golf Course
Pudong
汤臣上海浦东高尔夫
球场
浦东

BMW Asia Open 宝马亚洲高尔夫公开赛
5833 8888 | *www.tomson-golf.com*

Originally held in Taipei, one of Asia's most celebrated golf tournaments moved to Shanghai's Tomson Golf Course in Pudong in 2004. The annual event, normally held in April, attracts many of the sport's best players, who entertain and impress the world's fastest growing golf market. Hugely popular Ernie Els has been the biggest draw in recent times, although emerging local favourites are also always present.

Sheshan Intl Golf Club
Songjiang
佘山国际高尔夫俱乐
部,
松江

HSBC Champions 汇丰银行冠军高球赛
5765 5765 | *www.sheshangolf.com*

Since its inception in 2005, the HSBC Champions golf tournament has been held at the picturesque Sheshan Golf Club (see advert, p.83), around an hour outside of Shanghai. The tournament features winners from the four leading golf tours and players ranked in the world's top 50, meaning all of the game's biggest names are

Written by residents, the Singapore Explorer
is packed with insider info, from arriving
in the city to making it your home and
everything in between.

Singapore Explorer Residents' Guide
We Know Where You Live

present. Tiger Woods has finished second in both 2005 and 2006, so is probably a decent bet to go one better in the near future. The event is held in November, and tickets range in price from ¥300 for the Pro-Am event on the Wednesday to ¥2,000 for a pass for entry from Wednesday to Sunday. Under 18s are admitted free if accompanied by a valid adult ticket holder.

Motorsports

Shanghai International Circuit
Jiading
上海国际赛车场
嘉定

A1 Grand Prix

6330 5555 | www.icsh.sh.cn

With the first race held in 2005, the A1 Grand Prix is a relative newcomer on the motorsports scene. As one of the first countries to sign up to the 'Grand Prix of Nations,' China has been part of the event from the word go, and the China team's fortunes are followed closely by locals. In the 2006-07 season, China finished 15th out of the 22 teams, but this has not dampened enthusiasm, and the annual race at the impressive Shanghai International Circuit draws a good crowd. The schedule is subject to change, so check the website for timings and ticket information. Entry is available from upwards of ¥150.

Shanghai International Circuit
Jiading
上海国际赛车场
嘉定

Chinese Formula One Grand Prix

6330 5555 | www.icsh.sh.cn

Shanghai International Circuit opened in May 2004, billing itself as the most advanced and challenging racetrack in the world. The circuit is certainly impressive, covering 5.4 miles, with a series of tricky turns and some great vantage points. The annual showcase is undoubtedly the spectacular Chinese Grand Prix which, since 2005, has become a regular on the Formula One calendar, usually in autumn. Race day tickets range from around ¥160 for seats on the grass banks to ¥2,000 for a basic grandstand seat. The best seats (up to ¥4,000) are reserved for three-day passes and enable you to watch the practice sessions, qualifiers and race from key parts of the track. The circuit is around 30 kilometres out of town, so grab a taxi or look for shuttle buses which run from Shanghai Stadium. Ear plugs are not on sale at the circuit so take your own if you want the use of your hearing for the next few days. The 200,000 capacity venue fills to the rafters, so get your tickets well in advance. For the full Formula One experience, check listings for race-related parties that happen all weekend in the city.

Shanghai International Circuit
Jiading
上海国际赛车场
嘉定

Moto GP

6330 5555 | www.icsh.sh.cn

The Moto GP brings together talented and fearless motorcycle racers from across the globe, who reach speeds of over 340kph. The Shanghai circuit again plays host, and this increasingly popular annual event draws quite a crowd. Three-day tickets range in price from ¥180 for grass seating to ¥6,500 for the full paddock club (pit lane) experience. The event is normally held in May.

Tennis

Qi Zhong Tennis Stadium, 5500 Yuanjiang Lu
旗忠森林体育城网球中心，
元江路5500号
Huangpi Nan Lu

Masters Tennis 网球大师杯赛

www.masters-cup.com

The 15,000 seat, state-of-the-art stadium at Qi Zhong is the venue for the Tennis Masters Cup, the annual season showdown for men's professional tennis. The world's best players battle it out over several days of intense competition each November. Large prize money attracts the top names, and the likes of Roger Federer and Rafael Nadal mean that the event is exceptionally popular. Book early to avoid disappointment. Daily tickets start at around ¥300, while series tickets can cost in excess of ¥4,000.

Leisure Facilities

China does not have a long tradition in western sport and leisure clubs. However, Shanghai is leading the charge to reverse that trend and new clubs are popping up all over the city. Indeed, the arrival of international fitness chains, and an increasing awareness of health and body, means gym membership is becoming an essential part of modern Shanghainese life. Given the poor air quality and the lack of green open spaces, many sports clubs are based around indoor activities. Outdoor options are only offered at the bigger country clubs and in some of the more up-market hotels that have open-air swimming pools and tennis courts.

Western-style gyms and health clubs almost always have English-speaking staff. The language barrier, though, is more significant at local clubs, and many of the sport and recreational centres do not have English speakers. Normally though, a few actions should set you up with your sport or activity of choice.

As far as costs go, it's not expensive to stay in shape in Shanghai. Although membership prices vary depending on the club's facilities (and its reputation), there are many budget options and it's worth doing a bit of an investigation before you sign up. Most gyms and health clubs also offer the possibility to pay for a single visit without being a member, although this is often expensive and probably only good for finding out whether you like the club or not. Sports centres typically operate on a 'pay and play' basis.

Health Clubs

Other options **Sports Centres** p.283, **Gyms** p.286

In addition to an increasing interest in health and fitness in Shanghai, rising incomes and international influences have seen citizens demand more upscale facilities for working out. This has resulted in new health clubs popping up across the city, offering fitness facilities (cardio machines, free weights, and fitness classes such as aerobics, yoga and body pump) together with swimming pools, tennis courts and spas. As with many things in Shanghai, these clubs offer accessible luxury with membership prices that might not be cheap, but are often considerably less than you'd pay back home. Choose between becoming a member, which often means at least a three month commitment, or pay for each visit. The latter is often considerably more expensive.

Floor 3, Lane 123,
6-7 Xingye Lu,
Xintiandi
Luwan
兴业路123弄新天地
6-7号
静安
📍 *Huangpi Nan Lu*
Map p.436 C1 148

Alexander City Club 亞力山大会馆

5358 1188 | www.alexander.cn

This exclusive club has established branches in Xintiandi and Xujiahui, with new additions in Hongqiao and Gubei. The modern oriental-style interiors are beautiful, and house a wide range of facilities ranging from a spinning room to a wealth of fitness and cardio machines. The Hongqiao branch also has a swimming pool and squash court. After the training session, you can have a meal in the club's Thai restaurant or a massage in the spa. A one year membership costs ¥8,000, entitling you to use all the branches in the city. Opening times are 06:00 to midnight.

Floor 6, 2 Yuyao Lu
Jing'an
余姚路2号
静安
📍 *Nanjing Dong Lu*
Map p.429 E2 149

Eternity Fitness Retreat 泳泰健身中心

6215 1519 | www.eternity-retreat.com

Eternity Fitness has a wide range of facilities, including a gym and classes in yoga, tai chi and Pilates – all of which are held in an ornate glass-topped penthouse. There is also a spa offering massage and aromatherapy treatments, and the smoothies served at the juice bar are also notable. The emphasis at the gym is on working out with one of the personal trainers – if you want to train on your own, it still costs ¥100 per session and you need to book in advance. Opening times are 10:00 to 22:00.

281

Floor 15, Mayfair
Hotel, 1555 Dingxi Lu
Changning
定西路1555号
巴黎春天大酒店15楼
长宁

🚇 *Zhongshan Park*
Map p.434 C1 150

Mayfair Hotel Fitness Club 香榭丽舍

6240 8888 | www.newworldmayfair.com

The Mayfair Hotel's health club offers a fully equipped gym with cardio machines and free weights, as well as fitness classes. The outdoor pool is very popular during the summer, offering a great setting and a perfect place to catch some rays. For further indulgence there's a hot tub, a steam room and saunas, as well as great massages in the spa. There's also a hair salon. A one year membership will cost you ¥6,800. Opening times are 06:00 to midnight.

Pudong Shangri-La,
33 Fucheng Lu
Pudong
富城路33号
浦东香格里拉大酒店
浦东

🚇 *Lujiazui*
Map p.431 F3 151

Pudong Shangri-La Health Club 浦东香格里拉健体中心

6882 8888 | www.shangri-la.com

This luxury hotel has two fitness gyms (one in the Grand Tower and one in the River Wing), both with a good range of cardio machines and free weights. There are also two swimming pools and tennis courts. After a workout, you can relax in the sauna, have a steam bath or use the Jacuzzi. The Chi spa (p.292) has a range of beauty treatments and massages. A one year membership costs ¥15,500, allowing access to both branches. Opening hours are 05:30 to 23:00, and massages are available from 10:00 to 01:00.

Holiday Inn,
700 Changshou Lu
Putuo
长寿路700号
普陀

🚇 *Jing'an Temple*
Map p.429 D3 152

The Rooftop Health Club 健身中心

6276 8888 | www.holiday-inn.com.cn

This health club, located in the Holiday Inn Vista Hotel, has a well-equipped gym with cardio machines and free weights, as well as a medium-sized indoor swimming pool. There's also an aerobic room where classes are held. Other facilities include steam bath, Jacuzzi, sauna and a virtual reality golf simulator. The joining fee is ¥3,600 and annual membership is ¥4,800. Opening times are 05:30 to 23:00.

Hilton Hotel,
250 Huashan Lu
Jing'an
华山路250号
静安

🚇 *Jing'an Temple*
Map p.435 F1 153

Shanghai Hilton Health Club 希尔顿酒店健身俱乐部

6248 0000 | www.hilton.com

The Hilton's health club has a pretty broad appeal. The gym features a good range of cardio equipment, machines, free weights and an indoor pool. In addition, members and non-members can book a tennis or squash court for an additional cost. Spa facilities include massage, sauna and hot tub. Membership doesn't come cheap – the joining fee is ¥5,000 and the annual price is ¥20,000. Opening times are 06:00 to 23:00.

Hotel Equatorial,
65 Yan'an Xi Lu
Jing'an
延安西路65号
上海国际贵都大饭店
静安

🚇 *Jing'an Temple*
Map p.435 F1 154

Shanghai International Club 上海国际俱乐部

6248 1688

The Shanghai International Club in the Hotel Equatorial dates back to the 1970s. Today, however, things look very different and the club has undertaken extensive renovations. Facilities include a gym, aerobics room, swimming pool, spa and a massage room. In addition, the club has squash and tennis courts which can be booked by the hour. There's also a bar for some healthy refreshments after your fitness session. An annual membership costs ¥11,800. Opening times are 06:00 to 23:00.

Regal International,
516 Hengshan Lu
Xuhui
衡山路516号
徐汇

🚇 *Hengshan Lu*
Map p.435 E3 155

Shanghai International Tennis Centre 上海国际网球中心俱乐部

6415 5588

This exclusive sports club at the Regal International East Asia Hotel has many facilities to choose from. There are seven high-quality outdoor tennis courts and two indoor ones. A swimming pool, an indoor squash court, well-equipped gym with fitness classes, golf simulator, solarium, 12 lane bowling alley, and spa with hot tubs, sauna and massage completes the facilities on offer. You need membership in order to indulge, which costs a rather steep ¥30,000 per year, plus extra for lessons.

Lane 555, Jinfeng Lu,
Huacao Town
Minhang
华漕镇金丰路555弄
闵行

Shanghai Racquet Club　上海网球俱乐部
2201 0888 | www.src.com.cn

The Shanghai Racquet Club is a luxury health club out in the western suburbs, with a wide range of facilities, including a gym, tennis and squash courts, and outdoor and indoor pools. The gym has all kinds of cardio machines and free weights, as well as regular fitness classes. If you want personal training, you can book one of the staff coaches for ¥180-¥200 per lesson. Tennis classes are on offer, if you're feeling a bit rusty, as are swimming lessons. For beauty treatments, there's expat-favourite Dragonfly Hair and Nail, while for food there's fine dining, a terrace bar, a poolside bar, and a cafe.

Sports Centres

There are a number of sport centres and clubs all across the city, so you won't have any problems finding one that's close to home. Many of these are fairly basic, offering a couple of tennis or squash courts, table tennis facilities and not much else. A few bigger stadiums have more on offer, including outdoor and indoor courts, swimming pools and gyms. Generally, there is no need for membership as you can pay for each visit or by the hour. Prices are cheap – an hour on the tennis court or a few in the swimming pool normally costs around ¥50. The only problem you might experience is the lack of English-speaking staff, which makes it difficult to call in advance to book courts. However, there's often no queue at the centres, so your best bet is often just to show up and try your luck.

715 Dongtiyuhui Lu
Hongkou
东体育会路715号
虹口
 Hongkou Stadium
Map p.422 B3 `157`

Hongkou Stadium　虹口体育馆
6540 0009

This huge stadium, one of China's biggest venues, hosts national league football games and other large-scale sporting events. But visitors can do more than watch since the stadium has plenty of sports facilities for hire. In addition to the football pitch, badminton, table tennis, rock climbing and boxing are all on offer, along with a traditional gym, an indoor swimming pool, archery, billiards and darts.

777 Wuyi Lu
Changning
武夷路777号
长宁
Yan'an Xi Lu
Map p.434 B1 `158`

International Gymnastic Centre　国际体操中心
5108 3583

This sizeable stadium, which looks like a compressed golf ball, hosts games and competitions on a regular basis. As for sport facilities, you can go swimming in the International Gymnastics Swimming Centre, just next to the stadium. There's also a Star Gym (see p.287) attached to the same building.

151 Kangding Lu
Jing'an
康定路151号
静安
Nanjing Xi Lu
Map p.429 F2 `159`

Jing'an Sport Centre　静安区体育中心
6272 7277

The Jing'an Sport Centre has good training facilities for karate and martial arts, as well as table tennis, but the main reason to go here is for the swimming pools. There are four different indoor options, including a kids' pool, play pool and one for serious lap training. Entrance costs ¥25-¥30. Opening hours are Monday to Friday, 15:30 to 21:00, and Saturday to Sunday from 13:00 to 21:00.

128 Zhaojiabang Lu
Luwan
肇家浜路128号
卢湾
Shanxi Nan Lu
Map p.436 B2 `160`

Luwan Stadium　上海卢湾体育场
6466 2776

This medium-sized stadium has good facilities and is easily reached from downtown Shanghai. There is a big hall, perfect for martial arts, gymnastics and badminton, along with tennis courts, table tennis, an indoor swimming pool and a football pitch. There's often no need to book in advance.

283

1108 Husong Lu
Minhang
沪松公路1108号
闵行

Olympic Garden Sports Centre 奥林匹克花园游泳馆

6763 7985 | www.sholympicgarden.cn

This big sports centre has everything you need to have an active time, including tennis, squash and badminton courts, table tennis, snooker tables, rock climbing, a big swimming pool and archery. In addition, there's a gym with cardio and resistance machines and free weights. Eighty minutes in the swimming pool costs around ¥30. Opening times are 10:00 to 21:30.

1111 Caoxi Bei Lu
Xuhui
漕溪北路1111号
徐汇
 Shanghai Stadium
Map p.443 F1 162

Shanghai Stadium 上海体育馆

6438 5200 | www.shanghai-stadium.online.sh.cn

The impressive Shanghai Stadium is more than just a huge professional sporting arena – it's also a great place for members of the public to play. The stadium offers an indoor swimming pool, table tennis, badminton, indoor and outdoor tennis, squash, rock climbing and billiards. In addition, the Regal Shanghai East Asia Hotel, which is an integrated part of the complex, is also home to the well-equipped Shanghai International Tennis Centre, (see p.282). Most activities are open between 09:00 and 22:00. Prices vary, but an hour of tennis or squash costs between ¥40 and ¥50. A swim in the pool costs ¥25.

655 Yuanshen Lu
Pudong
源深路655号
浦东
 Shiji Dadao

Yuanshen Sports Centre (Pudong Sports Park) 源深体育场（浦东体育公园）

5860 0871

This huge sports park in Pudong consists of numerous facilities, including a large football stadium with a running track, basketball courts, indoor tennis, badminton, table tennis, billiards and a fitness gym offering classes. There's also a 'kids' gym' and a martial arts centre. The facilities and studios are not brand new, and prices can seem on the high side – ¥120 for an hour on the tennis court. Opening times vary across the different facilities, but most don't close until at least 22:00.

2100 Gonghexin Lu
Zhabei
共和新路2100号
闸北
 Yanchang Lu
Map p.422 A3 164

Zhabei Stadium 闸北体育馆

5662 8210

The Zhabei Stadium is not only home to Shanghai Stars football club, but also hosts major sports events on a regular basis. In addition to the huge football pitch, there's a running track, decent basketball and volleyball courts, table tennis and bowling. Opening hours are 08:30 to 18:00.

Country Clubs

Upmarket country clubs are a relatively new addition to the Shanghai scene. Demand for luxury clubs has grown significantly with the emergence of a growing population of high net-worth individuals and also a business entertaining culture. Shanghai's clubs are generally based around high-quality golf courses, combined with other health, fitness and dining facilities. Most are located outside Shanghai, offering a getaway from the city's bustling environment. Accommodation is generally provided on site too. Memberships usually cost around ¥60,000 a year plus tee time fees. Members can normally introduce guests, and non-members can occasionally visit on public days.

Yangcheng Lake
Holiday Zone
Kunshan
昆山市阳澄湖旅游
度假区，昆山

Grand Shanghai International Golf & Holiday Resort 大上海国际高尔夫球度假村

5789 1999 | www.grandshanghaigolfresort.com

The 18 hole golf course makes full use of the rolling terrain and is worth the 60km drive from central Shanghai. Facilities include Chinese and Japanese restaurants, a member's lounge, a spa and saunas, a dance hall and pro shop, and a five-star hotel.

961 Yingzhu Lu
Qingpu
盈朱路961号
青浦

Shanghai Country Club 上海国际高尔夫球乡村俱乐部
5972 8111 | www.shanghaicountryclub.com

This exclusive club is located by the Dian Shan Lake, about 30 minutes' drive outside Shanghai. As well as a par 72 golf course, a driving range, putting green and three-hole practice course, there are two clubhouses with three tennis courts, an indoor swimming pool, saunas, billiards, a restaurant and bar, *mahjong* and reading rooms, and a pro shop. There is also accommodation for members. With its classic colonial-style interior, this is as close as you can get to the full western country club experience.

1600 Ling Bai Lu
Pudong
凌白路1600号
浦东

Shanghai Links Golf & Country Club 上海林克斯高尔夫乡村俱乐部
5897 3068 | www.shanghailinks.com.cn

Set in picturesque surroundings, 35 minutes' drive from Shanghai, this members-only club offers everything you need for a relaxing time away from the city. The 18 hole golf course is the main attraction, and you can also take boat trips on the lake. There are plenty of other activities available too, such as outdoor swimming, tennis courts, a restaurant, bar and a pro golf shop. Children and toddlers are provided with their own playground and playroom. An individual annual membership costs ¥60,000.

1366 Huqingping Lu, Kunshan
Jiangsu Province
沪青平公路1366号，
江苏省昆山市淀山湖镇

Shanghai Silport Golf & Country Club 上海旭宝高尔夫球俱乐部
5749 8758 | www.silport.com.cn

Very close to Dian Shan Lake at Kunshan, this club is set in green surroundings about 90 minutes' drive from Shanghai. In addition to a 36 hole golf course, which has a reputation as one of one of Shanghai's best, there is a Spanish-style clubhouse with a Chinese and western restaurant and a big terrace overlooking the golf course. The club currently has around 1,000 members and is very international. Fewer additional facilities are on offer at Silport – mainly steam rooms, saunas and hot tubs

2588 Shentai Lu, Zhujiajiao Town
Qingpu
朱家角镇沈太路
2588号
青浦

Sun Island Golf & Resort 上海太阳岛国际俱乐部
6983 3888 | www.sunislandclub.com

Located on the River Mao, about 55 kilometres from Shanghai, Sun Island has a 36 hole golf course as well as a luxurious recreation and leisure centre. This means swimming pools, tennis courts, horse riding, bowling and a hot-spring spa. Water-based activities are also on offer, including speed and cycle boats, as well as the club's luxury yacht cruise. For members wanting to stay for a weekend or longer, there are fairly good holiday chalets. There are many dining options, including Korean, Yunnan and western restaurants. Make sure to book ahead if you are planning to visit.

Jincheng Lakeside Luzhi, Suzhou
Jiangsu
江苏省苏州市吴中区
用直镇金澄湖畔

Suzhou Sanyang Golf & Country Club 苏州三阳高尔夫乡村俱乐部
6501 0980 | www.sanyang-golf.com

Located in Jiangsu province, it's a bit of a trip from Shanghai to this club. However, once there it's the perfect place for relaxing in comfortable surroundings. Facilities on offer, in addition to the 18 hole golf course and driving range, include saunas and hot tubs, a pro shop, a cafe, and Japanese and Korean fine dining. There is also family and standard accommodation plus KTV and poker rooms.

3958 Zhaokun Lu
Songjiang
赵昆公路3958号
松江

Tianma Country Club 天马高尔夫球场
5766 1666 | www.tianmacc.com

Located in the Sheshan Natural Reserve, the Tianma Country Club has a 27 hole golf course, indoor and outdoor swimming pools, two football pitches, tennis courts, a fitness centre and a beauty salon with massage and saunas. The pleasant surroundings are perfect for cycling, walking and fishing. For the evenings, fine dining, billiards and a video library are available. A year's individual membership costs ¥57,000, while a family membership costs ¥82,000.

Gyms

Other options **Aerobics & Fitness Classes** p.237

It's more and more common for 21st century Shanghinese to build the gym into their daily routines, and a significant number have opened recently in the city. Smaller gyms offer a limited selection of machines, and in some cases a fitness room where classes such as aerobics and yoga are held. Larger, international gyms have all the machines you can think of, in addition to a multitude of fitness classes such as aerobics, spinning, body pump, dance, yoga and Pilates. A few even have swimming pools and tennis courts. Personal trainers are available at most of these establishments, but it's always a good idea to ask to see the instructor's qualifications before you embark on anything strenuous. If you are thinking of becoming a member, it's also worth trying before you buy – take advantage of the free trials or 'pay as you go' sessions available at many of the top locations.

Memberships often range between three months and 12 months, varying in price from ¥2,500 to ¥18,000 per year. It's worth noting that while the hotel gyms might have fantastic decor and offer bottled water whenever you need it, the facilities rarely warrant the extra price.

BodyTech 康丽健身中心

387 Fanyu Lu
Changning
番禺路387号
长宁
Yan'an Xi Lu
Map p.435 D2 **172**

6281 5639

This fairly spacious gym, with cardio and resistance machines, free weights and fitness classes, offers good value for money (¥2,000 for a year). Fitness classes include aerobics, step, karate, yoga and various dance types including ballet, belly dancing, hip-hop and Chinese dancing. If you need a private trainer to boost your motivation, a session costs ¥150. After your workout, you can enjoy a healthy meal or a drink in the bar. Opening times are Monday to Thursday from 08:00 to 23:00 and Friday to Sunday from 10:00 to 22:00.

Clark Hatch Fitness Centre 克拉克海奇健身中心

Floor 3,
Xing Guo Hotel,
78 Xing Guo Lu
Changning
兴国路78号兴国宾馆
长宁
Map p.435 D2 **173**

6212 9998 | www.clarkhatch.com.my

This international chain has five branches in Shanghai, offering a good range of machines, free weights and fitness classes such as aerobics, step, kickboxing, Pilates and yoga. The club at the Radisson Plaza also has a swimming pool, bowling alley and a squash court, in addition to the spa. A one year membership here costs ¥12,880, including the joining fee. Opening times are 06:00 to 23:00.

Fitness First

Plaza 66,
1266 Nanjing Xi Lu
Jing'an
南京西路1266号
恒隆广场B1
静安
Map p.430 A4 **174**

6288 0152 | www.fitnessfirst.com

With its convenient downtown location in the basement of popular shopping mall Plaza 66, international chain Fitness First is one of the better gyms in Shanghai. It has a large range of modern cardio and resistance machines, an area for weightlifting, a spinning room and a room for fitness classes such as aerobics, step, body pump, body combat, Pilates, yoga, body balance and body jam. Personal trainers can be hired by the hour for ¥350. A year's membership costs ¥3,975. There's also a small spa with massage and treatments for an additional cost. Opening times are Monday to Thursday 06:30 to 23:00, Friday 06:30 to 22:00 and Saturday and Sunday 08:00 to 22:00.

**Shanghai Kerry Centre,
1515 Nanjing Xi Lu**
Jing'an
嘉里中心,
南京西路1515号
静安
🚇 *Jing'an Temple*
Map p.429 F4 **175**

Kerry Gym 嘉里中心健身房
6279 4625

Located in the Kerry Centre, this club's membership is dominated by residents of the apartment block or workers from the large office building. The gym itself is excellent – all the machines you need, an activity room housing punch bags, and a climbing wall. Though not as frequent as some of the other gyms, yoga, Pilates and tai chi classes are available, and there is a rooftop tennis court and indoor swimming pool. The gym is quiet, so there is not usually an issue waiting for a machine. Full membership costs ¥12,000 per year, with a ¥1,000 joining fee. There are shorter memberships available as well as family packages. Opening hours are 06:00 to 23:00.

**Hong Kong
New World Tower,
300 Huaihai Zhong Lu**
Luwan
淮海中路300号香港
新世界大厦B3层
卢湾
🚇 *Huangpi Nan Lu*
Map p.430 C4 **176**

Megafit 美格菲健身中心
5383 6633

There are four branches of Megafit in Shanghai (Xuhui, Luwan, Yangpu and Pudong). The Pudong branch is the largest, providing a large gym area as well as a swimming pool and courts for badminton, basketball, tennis and squash. The Luwan branch on Huaihai Lu is very spacious too, making it a popular city centre venue. All branches have fitness classes (dance, aerobics, step, yoga, body pump, Pilates, aerobics-kick, belly dancing, rumba, boxing, salsa, jazz, ballet and spinning). Frequency varies though, so check before you sign up. Annual membership at the Luwan club costs ¥2,950, including the joining fee. Opening hours are 06:30 to 23:00.

**Floors 4-6, Metro City,
1111 Zhaojiabang Lu**
Xuhui
肇嘉浜路1111号
徐汇
🚇 *Xujiahui*
Map p.435 E4 **177**

Physical Fitness 舒适堡美罗店
6426 8282

Physical Fitness has three branches in Shanghai (Xuhui, Huangpu and Luwan) – all with a large selection of cardio and resistance machines as well as free weights. Ladies Club, which is a part of Physical Fitness in Metro City, is one of the best options for women in Shanghai. Guys are welcome too, but men and women have separate reception rooms, and there's also a beauty centre for the fairer sex. One year's membership of the Metro City branch costs ¥3,200. Opening times are Monday to Saturday 06:30 to 23:30 and Sunday 07:00 to 22:00.

**Floor 7,
Portman Ritz-Carlton,
1376 Nanjing Xi Lu**
Jing'an
南京西路1376号
波特曼大酒店
静安
🚇 *Jing'an Temple*
Map p.429 F4 **178**

Portman Ritz-Carlton Fitness Centre
波特曼丽姿卡尔顿酒店健身中心
6279 8888

The location is perfect – right in the big Shanghai Centre on busy Nanjing Xi Lu. The gym itself is medium sized and, while the machines are not state of the art, they will be more than adequate for most people's needs, with cardio and resistance machines, bicycles, and free weights. There's also a great recreational area with an outdoor and indoor swimming pool, plus a fitness room where classes (Latin dance, Pilates, yoga) are held. One year's full membership costs ¥18,000 and includes access to the squash, basketball and racketball courts. Opening times are 06:00 to 23:00 every day.

428 Jiangning Lu
Jing'an
江宁路428号
静安
🚇 *Nanjing Xi Lu*
Map p.429 F2 **179**

Star Gym 星之健身俱乐部
5228 3818

This modern and spacious gym, with four branches in Shanghai, offers a wide range of new equipment, with cardio and strength machines as well as free weights available. In addition to the gym, there are fitness classes including aerobics, martial arts, spinning and yoga. There's also a great swimming pool which members can use free of charge. Membership costs ¥2,600 per year. Opening times are 07:00 to 22:00.

287

*Floor 5, Zhong
Chuang Building,
819 Nanjing Xi Lu*
Jing'an
南京西路819号
中创大厦5搂
静安
🚇 *Nanjing Xi Lu*
Map p.430 B3 180

Total Fitness　力美健健身俱乐部
6255 3535

There are two branches of this popular gym, but the one at Nanjing Xi Lu is the biggest and best. Equipment is not brand new, but there is plenty of it, offering cardio and resistance as well as free weights. The gym runs lots of fitness classes, and if you're into boxing there are punch bags and a boxing ring. After the session you can relax with a game of pool, a drink in the cafe or use one of the computers in the reception. A year's membership at the Nanjing Xi Lu branch costs ¥3,500. Opening times are Monday to Friday 07:30 to 22:30, and 08:00 to 22:00 on Saturday and Sunday.

5 Yinxiao Lu
Pudong
银霄路5号
浦东
🚇 *Century Park*

Will's Gym　上海威尔士健身中心
5045 6257 | www.willsgym.com

Will's Gym has eight branches across Shanghai, all of which offer well-equipped facilities with modern cardio and resistance machines and free weights. There's also a good range of fitness classes including aerobics, yoga, Pilates and martial arts. Some of the branches have an indoor swimming pool for laps. Single-branch annual membership costs ¥2,800 for the gym and fitness classes (there's an additional fee for yoga classes). More expensive packages offer membership to all of the branches. Opening times are 07:00 to 22:30.

2000 Jian He Lu
Changning
剑河路2000号
长宁
🚇 *Hongqiao Lu*

XPat Gym　国际健身房
6261 8982 | www.xpatgym.com

Run by a small number of professional trainers, this club offers a wide range of fitness classes and a well-equipped gym. Personal training is available with experienced trainers. Fitness classes include different levels of core training, aerobics, power training, Pilates, yoga, flexibility, balance and stress, martial arts, karate and spinning. One year's gym membership plus 20 classes costs ¥5,000 (students get a discount). This also gives you 20% discount on additional fitness classes, private training and sports massage. There are shorter memberships available too. Opening times are 06:00 to 21.00.

Chi at the Shangri-La

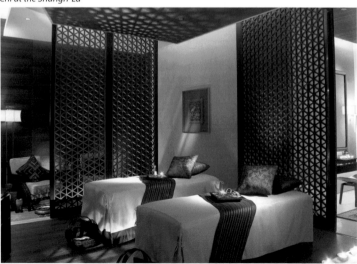

Well-Being

Living in a frenetic, sprawling metropolis such as Shanghai can take its toll, and it's important to take time out of your week for some well-deserved pampering. Shanghai has a myriad of options to get primped and preened, calm your inner being, and relax and refresh you in preparation for a new day. The Chinese strongly believe that the key to good health lies in the free flow of *qi*, the vital energy force thought to exist in all things. Chinese massage and tai chi both encourage the flow of *qi* and thus play a significant part in the lives of locals. Massage parlours in particular, are ubiquitous in the city, ranging from the no-frills bed and masseur to the more luxuriant options that the flourishing spa culture has to offer. With the high disposable incomes sloshing round in Shanghai, people have more to spend on such luxuries, as well as their appearance, health and fitness.

Beauty Salons

Other options **Perfumes & Cosmetics** p.333, **Health Spas** p.291

Keeping up appearances is important in the city, particularly in China, where so much emphasis is placed on 'face.' Facials are a popular treatment, offered by all the beauty salons and spas, but steer clear of the 'whitening' treatments, unless you aspire for a porcelain doll complexion. Waxing is also becoming more widely available thanks to western influences. For top choices, try Maylis de Gardelle (6433 1344) or Only Beauty (5238 3777), both in Xuhui, see the entry for Pola The Beauty below, and refer to Health Spas on p.291.

While there's nothing more agreeable than losing yourself for a couple of hours in one of the city's first-class salons or spas, there's also something appealing about being beautified in the privacy of your own home, particularly when the weather's bad. There are now a number of beauty services specialising in house calls, including At-Home (below), so you can get your beauty fix without stepping foot outside.

Shanghai Times Square, 99 Huaihai Zhong Lu
Luwan
淮海中路99号
大上海时代广场
卢湾
🚇 *Shanxi Nan Lu*
Map p.431 D4 183

At-Home 时尚肌肤专家

5382 8221 | www.at-home.com.cn

Make the call and within the hour, a professional therapist will appear at your door – no further effort on your part is required. They oversee all transport, products and tools – right down to the fold-up massage bed. At-Home offers a full menu of treatments, including facials, massages, waxing, slimming and simple cosmetic procedures. All are based around its three lines of imported products – Jurlique (organic essential oils), Bodrega and Skin Ceuticals (with anti-oxidant properties designed to defy the signs of aging). Its signature massage-plus-facial treatments (¥434 to ¥550) will give you the boost you need. A minimum treatment of 90 minutes is required for a house visit.

Room A9, 3, 156 Xingye Lu
Luwan
兴业路156弄3号A9
卢湾
🚇 *Huangpi Nan Lu*
Map p.436 C1 184

Pola The Beauty 颇丽美容

6385 6485 | www.pola.com.cn

Your visage is in good hands at this Japanese aesthetics salon. You begin with a full consultation and skin analysis to determine the programme suited to your skin type. This involves taking a swab of your skin cells to test moisture and protection levels under the microscope. The advanced computer software analyses the results, organises them into a series of tables and graphs, and awards you a final skin score. A basic one-hour facial costs ¥330 and a two-hour course ¥600. Whisked off into a serene treatment room, further new-fangled equipment blasts hot steam and pummels your face while you sink into the world's comfiest computerised massage chair. Up the ante by shelling out for a VIP room (an extra ¥150) and get your own mini bar. A 25% discount is given to first-time customers, and there is another location in at 788 Hongxu Lu in Changning (5422 1603).

289

Hairdressers

If you're used to paying an arm and a leg for a decent cut in your home country, Shanghai's agreeable rates might turn you snip happy. Hairdressers are aplenty, all offering a similar menu of services including colouring, perms, straightening, up-dos and moisturising treatments. If you're brave enough to trust your tresses to the hands of the locals, you can get a quick chop for around ¥10-¥30. If you can't speak Chinese, take along a photo of the style you want. Another word of warning – some stylists may not be accustomed to cutting and styling western hair so don't demand anything too drastic as you may end up with more than a bad hair day. Do visit the local salons for a *xi tou*, which involves a head massage and shampoo for around ¥30. Alternatively, treat yourself to a session at one of the more upmarket salons. Many of them have VIP memberships, which are worth inquiring about if you like to get your hair done regularly.

Hairdressers		
Barbers by Three	Huangpu	6321 6622
Beijing Hair Culture	Luwan	6340 6822
Benson Salon	Changning	6276 2653
ID hair	Luwan	3406 0490
J & Eleven	Xuhui	5405 2181
Juno Hair	Pudong	5047 1835
La Prime Hair & Beauty	Changning	6219 8855
Salon Esprit	Jing'an	5292 8800

4 Hengshan Lu
Xuhui
衡山路4号
徐汇
Ⓜ Hengshan Lu
Map p.435 F3 **185**

ERIC Paris Salon 爱丽克美容美发沙龙
6473 0900 | www.ericparis.com
This sexy salon captures the essence of Parisian chic with its lush padded cream-and-red walls, flawless staff and slick styles. First-class styling products from Wella, L'Oreal, Kerastase and Schwarzkopf are used and available to buy. A cut ranges from ¥340 to ¥385, depending on the length of your hair, and it specialises in non-Asian hair. Men can get a chop for ¥230, and there are special rates for children. While you're waiting for your colour to set, you can treat yourself to a manicure (¥100). For those on the Pudong side, there's also a branch in the Jinmao Tower (88 Shijia Dadao; 5047 1738).

208 Xinle Lu
Xuhui
新乐路208号
徐汇
Ⓜ Shanxi Nan Lu
Map p.435 F1 **186**

Hip Hair Culture 发型文化
5403 5827 | www.hairculture.com.hk
Hot pink is the colour scheme in this hip and happening little hairdresser. Settle down with a glossy rag and a coffee while the hair-savvy team gets to work with the scissors. If the stylists' own hair-dos are anything to go by, you won't leave disappointed. It's a popular haunt for both locals and expats, as patrons receive top-notch treatment at China prices. Haircuts start at around ¥90. Party hairdressing and make-up (¥250-¥380) for special occasions is also offered.

Room 102,
Lane 134, 2 Xinle Lu
Xuhui
新乐路134弄2号102
室
徐汇
Ⓜ Shanxi Nan Lu
Map p.436 A1 **187**

Michael Yeung
139 1800 0306 | www.mhair.cc
If you'll only settle for star treatment, Michael Yeung is your man. When he's not busy doing the hair for A-list celebs, or styling for a *Vogue* shoot, his nimble fingers are ready to give your locks a lovely new look. This famed stylist offers a very personal service, working from an exclusive boutique salon by appointment only. He offers the full works, but a simple cut and blow dry costs around ¥600. His holy scissors are in high demand so be sure to book well in advance.

Floor 3, Le Passage,
299 Fuxing Xi Lu
Xuhui
复兴西路299弄1号3楼
徐汇
Ⓜ Changshu Lu
Map p.435 E2 **188**

Pius 4 Workshop 派4工作室
6466 8814 | www.o4orient4.com
More than just a salon, this 'workshop' boasts a rooftop, kitchen area and VIP room, and is the perfect place to relax, chat, have a glass of wine, and receive first-class hair treatment. An offspring of the Orient 4 Hair Styling Group from Hong Kong, this group provides the official stylists at Hong Kong Fashion Week and is a popular choice with the stars. Teams of professional stylists visit Shanghai from Hong Kong on a rotational basis. A specific stylist will be assigned to your hair, depending on your requirements and hair

290

type. Set aside a good couple of hours for them to meticulously chop, trim and tousle your hair down to the very last strand. A cut and blow dry ranges from ¥320 to ¥2,000.

Toni & Guy 汤尼英盖

5351 3606 | *www.toniandguy.co.uk*

This British institution needs no introduction. These 40 year veterans are trusted the world over for the latest cutting-edge styles, asymmetrical looks and bold colours. The two industrially appointed salons (also at 1376 Nanjing Xi Lu; 6279 8806) are as swish as the well-coiffed stylists that work there. If you're thinking of making that drastic move from blonde to brunette, or taming those long locks to short and snappy, consult these hair gurus for their advice. A cut and blow dry starts at ¥180 and goes up to ¥520 for an appointment with the senior creative director.

**Shanghai Times Square,
99 Huaihai Zhong Lu**
Luwan
淮海中路99号
大上海时代广场
卢湾
🚇 *Huangpi Nan Lu*
Map p.429 F4 189

Vidal Sassoon 沙宣

6311 2201 | *www.vidalsassoon.com.cn*

Some of the world's most talked-about hairdressers have come out of Vidal Sassoon's London academy. In Shanghai there is a team of eight German, Italian and Asian stylists, ready to spice up any head put in front of them. The airy, light salon is one of the smartest in Shanghai, set out over three floors, with the school taking up residence on the top floor. Free cuts are offered for those willing to allow budding hair students free reign of their locks (call 6311 1606 for an appointment). Not recommended for fidgety types, it takes three to four hours for the students to be guided through every snip. For paying customers, hair cuts start at ¥390. A full head of highlights rings in at ¥1,450.

**Building 16,
181 Taicang Lu,
Xintiandi**
Luwan
太仓路181弄新天地
北里16号楼
卢湾
🚇 *Huangpi Nan Lu*
Map p.436 C1 190

Health Spas

Other options **Massage** p.293, **Health Clubs** p.281

To fully recharge your batteries, sacrifice your body and soul to a thorough cleansing at one of the city's luscious spas, a fashionable retreat for the posh set. Whether you're on the run and need a quick boost or have a whole day to spare, there are plenty of options. Seek out pure escapism at one of the five-star hotels for a small fortune, or settle for one of the more affordable independent spas scattered around town. All are decadently decorated and themed to make your milk bath, four-handed massage or body wrap as comfortable and other worldly as possible. It's always advisable to reserve ahead of time. Many spas also offer membership or VIP deals, which could save you serious money.

Health Spas			
Apsara Spa	457 Shanxi Bei Lu	Jing'an	6258 5580
In One Spa	J-Life, Jinmao Tower, 88 Shiji Dadao	Pudong	5103 6767
Jumpmale	879 Fahuazhen Lu, 578 Gonghexin Lu	Changning	6282 8656
Le Spa	789 Nanjing Dong Lu	Huangpu	3318 9999
Life Spa	Century Metropolis Upper East Club Spa, 128 Hongqiao Lu	Xuhui	6439 3408
Living Room	55 Xiangyang Bei Lu	Xuhui	5404 6007
Lotos Spa	West Tower Somerset Grand Shanghai, 8 Jinan Lu	Luwan	3308 0088
O'Rola Spa	563 Changyi Lu	Pudong	5879 8567
Peony Aromatherapy Retreat	426 Dagu Lu	Luwan	5666 1776
The Spa at the Hilton	250 Huashan Lu	Jing'an	6248 0000
Spa Chakra (L'institut de Guerlain Paris)	The Regent Shanghai, 1116 Yan'an Xi Lu	Changning	6115 9605
Wellness Spa	JC Mandarin Hotel, 1225 Nanjing Xi Lu	Jing'an	6279 1888

291

3, Lane 89,
Xingguo Lu
Xuhui
兴国路89弄3号
徐汇
🚇 *Changshu Lu*
Map p.435 E2 **191**

Aqua Villa 水泽堂
3423 0038

Aqua Villa is a home away from home, with a well-trained team of therapists. This four-storey villa has a more intimate, friendly feel than the more high-end establishments that the city is inundated with. Boasting dark wood furnishings and burnt orange and crimson decor, it's a perfect spot to go with a group of friends for a pampering party in a Japanese Jacuzzi, and there's also a nail bar. You can relax on the top of the house looking out over the rooftops if you choose. Treatments range from ¥500 to ¥600.

The Westin,
88 Henan Zhong Lu
Huangpu
威斯汀大饭店，
河南中路88号
黄埔
🚇 *Nanjing Dong Lu*
Map p.431 E3 **192**

Banyan Tree Spa 悦榕庄
6335 1888 | www.banyantreespa.com/shanghai

This five-star sanctuary offers treatments fit for a king. Stroll down the stately red carpet and immerse yourself in a Thai-inspired paradise, a mix of art deco and traditional south-east Asian trappings. This spa is characterised by the five elements, the life forces linked with *yin* and *yang*. Once you've selected from the huge menu, including hand and foot treatments (¥380), facials (¥620) and massages, pick your herbal tea and incense and lie back among the blooming lotus flowers. The signature Balinese massage gently soothes strained muscles with the help of aromatic oils, while the *gui shi* hot stones massage treatment involves heated river stones and sesame oil.

Floor 5,
5 Zhongshan Dong
Yi Lu
Huangpu
中山东一路5号
外滩五号5楼
黄埔
🚇 *Nanjing Dong Lu*
Map p.431 E3 **193**

Bund Five Spa Oasis 绿韵SPA外滩五号
6321 9135 | www.oasis-spa.net

Imagine lying in a deep, warm scented bath filled with rose petals, sipping on a refreshing cup of herbal tea and eating juicy slices of watermelon. In front of you is a sweeping window overlooking the Bund and the dazzling skyline of Lujiazui. Sound like heaven? Book yourself into a double VIP room at Bund Five Spa and this is exactly what you'll get. This is one of nine palatial treatment rooms at this grandiose Bund-side spa, all equipped with luxuriant showers and lavish furnishings. Each treatment incorporates all natural ingredients, including fresh fruit. The Body Purification Therapy will leave you feeling utterly refreshed and ready for anything.

Pudong Shangri-La,
33 Fucheng Lu
Pudong
富城路33号
浦东香格里拉大酒店
🚇 *Lujiazui*
Map p.431 F3 **194**

Chi 气’水疗中心
5877 1503 | www.shangri-la.com

This award-winning spa scores a five for bliss factor and is the only place in Pudong where you could kid yourself that you're actually in Tibet. Snuggling into a cosy bathrobe in one of the opulent, roomy suites will help you forget your responsibilities for a few hours. There are more than 35 therapies available, including a divine Himalayan healing stone massage.

200 Yan'an Xi Lu
Changning
延安西路200号
长宁
🚇 *Yan'an Xi Lu*
Map p.435 E1 **195**

David's Camp 戴维营专业男子SPA护肤中心 ▶ p.234
6247 3602 | www.davidscampspa.com

There's a new breed of image-conscious males emerging in Shanghai – the metrosexual – and they're embracing the spa culture as much as their female counterparts. David's Camp is a luxuriant haven where men can enjoy a menu of treatments tailored specifically to them without feeling like they're sacrificing their manhood. Treatments include a moisturising facial and manicure (no polish required). It's reasonably priced, ranging from around ¥150 to ¥600. Once you've given in to your feminine side, it'll become part of your weekly routine.

Well-Being

20 Donghu Lu
Xuhui
东湖路20号
徐汇
🚇 *Shanxi Nan Lu*
Map p.436 A1 196

Dragonfly Therapeutic Retreat 悠庭保健会所

5405 0008 | www.dragonfly.net.cn

With a Dragonfly in nearly every neighbourhood, this familiar Shanghai brand is a more convenient, cheaper escape than its five-star competitors. Elegant south-east Asian decor, ambient lighting and the strum of musical chords relax you as you enjoy a traditional Chinese massage (¥135) or an oriental foot massage (¥135). In a city that never sleeps, a foggy head is a weekly occurrence – and Dragonfly has just the ticket for recovery with its two-hour Hangover Relief massage. It also offers manicures, pedicures and waxing services.

Floor 2, 3 Zhongshan Dong Yi Lu
Huangpu
中山东一路3号2楼
黄埔
🚇 *Nanjing Dong Lu*
Map p.431 E3 197

Evian Spa 依云水疗中心

6321 6622

Straying from the formulaic south-east Asian theme, Evian Spa in Three on the Bund opts for a more continental approach. Allow yourself to be cleansed and refreshed by pristine Evian water straight from the French Alps. The menu of treatments for face, hair, body, hands, feet and nails incorporates top-notch products from France including Darphin, Sothys and Kerastase. There's also a special line of treatments tailored by Clarins. Warm herbal pillows greet you as you wait for the preparation of your themed treatment room. If you're tired of the same old choices, try the 'colour hydrotherapy underwater' massage (¥320 for 30 minutes), where you're met with underwater massage jets and coloured lights. There are also special therapies for expectant mothers.

JW Marriott, Tomorrow Square, 399 Nanjing Xi Lu
Huangpu
南京西路399号明天广场JW万豪酒店
黄埔
🚇 *People's Square*
Map p.430 C3 198

Mandara Spa

5359 4969 | www.mspa-international.com

After a deluxe session in this Indonesian-themed sanctuary, you'll leave feeling 10 years younger. There are a number of double suites, providing the perfect setting for a romantic date for two. Couples can indulge in packages such as Romantic Getaway or Shared Moments. End your treatment in one of the oversized terrazzo bathtubs, taking in the elegant timber and ceramic decor. And if you've only ever had one masseur working on you at one time, try out their four-hand Mandara Signature Massages (¥990), which combine five massage techniques.

Massage

Other options **Leisure Facilities** p.281, **Health Spas** p.291

After a hard day's work, a massage is one of the best ways to relax and unwind. Along with the luxuriant massage treatments offered by the health spas (see Aroma Garden, p.294), there's a sea of massage parlours (see table) where you can pay around ¥60 to ¥300 for a session. Avoid those places with a red light in the window – the scantily clad women lounging in the foyer should be a giveaway. The most common form is the Chinese massage which involves prodding and pummelling of the main pressure points to encourage the positive flow of *qi* around your body, great for sore muscles and niggling knots. Some of the best are performed by the city's blind masseurs, who are allegedly more in tune with your senses. Try out the cluster of Chinese massage places along Fuxing Lu, near Maoming Lu, where a one hour session with a blind masseur is just ¥60. Oriental foot massages are also great if you've been on your feet all day, providing you're not ticklish. Aromatherapy massages are another popular form,

Massage Parlours			
Double Rainbow Massage House	47 Yongjia Lu	Luwan	6473 4000
Ito Massage	158 Huaihai Zhong Lu	Luwan	6386 3101
Jade Massage	367 Zizhong Lu	Luwan	6384 8762
Magpie Massage	685 Julu Lu	Xuhui	5403 3876

293

offering a gentler touch and relying on the potent powers of essential oils that work their magic once absorbed into the skin. While many places offer aromatherapy treatments, there are few trained aromatherapists in the city – try Aroma Garden or Frank n' Sense (p.295).

496 Xiangyang Nan Lu
Xuhui
襄阳南路496号
徐汇
Shanxi Nan Lu
Map p.436 A2 199

Aroma Garden 贵阁保健
6466 2064

Greeted by sweet smells, greenery and the sound of birds, let your senses take over when you cross the threshold of Aroma Garden. With more than 500 oils to choose from, there's a vast range of treatments available, from head to toe massages to specific area massages. Full body massages range from around ¥430 to ¥450.

Nail Bars

Nice nails are mandatory for the urban dweller – it's often common to have your nails touched up on a weekly basis. Wherever you are in town, you're not far from a nail bar, stall or salon. You can treat yourself to an indulgent 60 minute manicure or pedicure in one of the many high-end salons (around the ¥100 mark), or you can sit yourself down at a stool and have your nails prettified for cheap, in record time, at one of the numerous little stalls. Nail art has caught on in a big way here, and you can choose from a gallery of intricate images and patterns. Acrylic and gel nails are also a recent popular trend requiring low maintenance, and the more you pay, the more real they look.

Nail Bars

Balsamine	33 Shaoxing Lu	Luwan	6474 1369
Finger Show	86 Shimen Yi Lu	Jing'an	6327 1696
Helen Nail Spa	120 Nanchang Lu	Luwan	5383 8957
I-Nail	89 Xingguo Lu	Xuhui	3423 0038
Nail Story	Shanghai Legend Shopping Arcade, 635 Bibo Lu	Pudong	5027 3836
Q-nail	411 Weihai Lu	Luwan	6340 1170
Rose Nail Spa	Floor 2, Corporate Avenue, 202 Hubin Lu	Luwan	5306 8581
T & E Nail Studio	No. 41, Lane 1487 Huaihai Zhong Lu	Xuhui	6431 8446

266 Ruijin Er Lu
Luwan
瑞金二路266号
卢湾
Shanxi Nan Lu
Map p.436 B2 200

Diva Life 美甲店
5465 7291 | www.mydivalife.com

This nail lounge-cum-beauty parlour caters to divas and their daughters. A charming old lane house has been made over into a deliciously decadent violet boudoir steeped in chiffon curtaining. Settle into one of the comfy armchairs, with a pile of girly magazines at your side, while indulging in guilty pleasures such as an icecream pedicure (¥300), where your feet sit fizzing in a scoop of bath salts before being scrubbed, smoothed and tucked snuggly in heated booties. Bored housewives can take advantage of the Tai Tai afternoon package, including mani, pedi, fruit and bubbly (¥500 for two people). There is also a full waxing menu covering all imaginable areas.

Shanghai Centre, 1376 Nanjing Xi Lu
Jing'an
南京西路1376号
静安
Jing'an Temple
Map p.429 F4 201

Fiori by Nail Plus
6279 8118 | www.nailplusconcept.com

Calling all girls to this very pretty boutique nail bar – Fiori's forte lies in nail art, and there's a dazzling choice of intricate designs to choose from. Opt for a blinging cluster of rhinestones in the corner of each nail, daisies on your big toes or a set of gel nails painted with 3D strawberries. Art is charged per nail (¥10 to ¥30). You'll pay ¥130 for a basic manicure and ¥230 for a basic pedicure, and these prices include moisturising treatments and massages. There is also an express service for those needing a last-minute fix before that important function.

76 Fuxing Xi Lu
Xuhui
复兴西路76号
徐汇
🚇 *Changshu Lu*
Map p.435 E2 **202**

Frangipani Nail Bar

6437 0310 | www.frangipani-shanghai.com

What better way to spend the afternoon catching up with friends than over a drink and a manicure? Frangipani is a homey hangout with a living-room style treatment area where you can put your feet up in true comfort. Parties of mums or teens are catered for, as is a bit of quiet time for you and your book. Your nails are done up with Frangipani's eponymous varnishes and treatments, which are also available for purchase. Try the invigorating paraffin hand and foot treatments for moisture-starved paws.

Pilates

Other options **Aerobics & Fitness** p.237, **Yoga** p.296

Also known as 'contrology,' this form of exercise targets your 'core' power (the abdomen), helping you to develop a supple, flexible body, without the added muscle bulk. It's also said to help with muscular injuries and back pain. It's a good complement to yoga or cardiovascular sporting activities, and you'll find that many yoga studios and gyms around town offer it.

Pilates incorporates both mat and machine exercises, focusing on one muscle group at a time. Mat Pilates is most common and costs about the same as a yoga session; check out the schedules at Breeze, Karma, Shanghai Fan Liang (see table, p.247) and the Orange Room (6406 3642) which is located in the Saint Laurent Hotel in Changning. Namaste (p.297) also offers machine sessions and has a range of equipment to test and stretch your muscles, including the Trap Table, Spine Corrector and Wunda Chair. Individual sessions cost ¥580.

The Synapse Studio (5876 3307) in Pudong is devoted to Pilates. Led by a team of professional instructors, it offers one-on-one and group sessions. Small groups have no more than 10 people in each class. It is recommended that beginners should have at least five private machine sessions (¥500 per session) before progressing to more challenging workouts. The qualified instructors will tailor a personalised programme based on an individual assessment.

Reiki

Reiki is based on the belief in the existence of a universal energy that can be manipulated and spread through the body helping to boost your energy levels and, in some cases, heal emotional and physical problems. Reiki therapy normally involves lying down fully clothed, while the therapist lays hands on you or just above you in response to your body's reactions. Starting with your head, the hand movements focus on realigning and balancing the seven 'chakras' of the body. During a reiki session anything can take place and every consultation is different, depending on your mood and health. A reiki attunement calls on an even higher form of energy, which helps to remove any negative forces and blockages. There are three stages of reiki and, with the help of a reiki master, you can learn to practise on yourself.

24 Xinhua Lu
Xuhui
新华路24号
徐汇
🚇 *Xujiahui*
Map p.435 D3 **203**

Frank n' Sense

6280 7751 | www.franknsense.cn

Reiki flows freely through this humble sanctuary. A professional team of Asian and western therapists rely on the holistic powers of crystals and the manipulations of reiki, in the hope of bettering your physical and emotional state. This is one of the only places in town where you'll find qualified reiki masters and aromatherapists. Along with reiki attunement, this tranquil retreat offers Egyptian Sekhem, Ayurvedic Shirodha and bio-energy (other forms of energy manipulations) applied to a range of facials and massages. A session of reiki therapy with a western master, including a consultation, costs ¥430, while an attunement costs ¥480.

Stress Management
Other options **Support Groups** p.144

Like any big city, Shanghai can be trying on your stress levels. If you're not averse to group sessions, the Shanghai Expat Learning Centre (p.238) offers comprehensive courses in stress management. The 10 session programme examines some common causes and effects of stress and how to alleviate it. If you'd prefer one-on-one sessions, contact life and business coach Alex Wu (138 1718 1403).

An alternative option worth considering is a course of acupuncture; a needle in the right pressure point is touted to help the positive flow of energy and eliminate feelings of strain and stress. Body & Soul TCM Clinic (760 Xizang Nan Lu; 5101 9262) performs one hour sessions for ¥500 and recommends a course of five to six appointments to see positive results.

Tai chi in the city centre

Tai Chi

If you ever find yourself in Shanghai's parks at dawn, you'll be in the company of elderly locals engrossed in their morning exercises, most likely a form of tai chi. Taijiquan (a branch of tai chi) is the ancient Chinese martial art that combines meditative actions with slow circular movements and balancing positions to help strengthen your muscles, internal organs and mind. It relaxes your muscles and joints and is good for high blood pressure. If you're not a morning person and don't fancy joining the locals in the park, there are a number of tai chi centres around the city that offer coaching.

Train with 50 year master Jiang Lin Ma of Chian Chuan Tai Chi Chuan Association (Lane 1295, Fuxing Lu; 6433 4084), who has travelled the world as a teacher and offers hourly sessions for ¥80. You can choose to do it in a group or one on one, and he's happy to work around your schedule. Alternatively, sign up for classes at the Hong Wu Kong Fu Centre (Lane 210, Taikang Lu; 137 0168 5893). Learn one movement per class twice a week for three months and you'll have mastered the first set of 24 movements. From there you can progress if you wish. A one month set of classes costs around ¥600 (based on two classes per week). If you want to take it a notch higher, learn tai chi in the luxury of Eternity Fitness Retreat (p.247).

Yoga
Other options **Pilates** p.295

One of the best ways to find inner harmony is through the practice of yoga, a pastime that's becoming increasingly popular in the city. While the elderly are all in the parks doing tai chi, the younger generations are getting all bendy in the yoga studios across the city. There are a number of different styles to choose from: for sedentary types,

Meditation

Yoga and meditation go hand in hand, and most instructors encourage meditation at the end of every class. Some yoga centres also offer weekly meditation classes. It's a very personal thing, and can be carried out anywhere at any time.

296

Yoga

Breeze Yoga	120 Xi Zang Zhong Lu	Changning	6350 1086
Karma Yoga	172 Pucheng Lu	Pudong	3887 0669
Kundalini Yoga Asia	495 Jiangning Lu	Jing'an	na
Shanghai Fan Ling Yoga	Zhaoyi Building, 1281 Dingxi Lu	Changning	6251 4885
Yoga Space	35 Gaoan Lu	Xuhui	6431 3164
Yoyo Yoga Spa Club	Big Thumb Plaza, Lane 199, Fangdian Lu	Pudong	5033 9990

Hatha yoga focuses on postures and breathing, while Vinyasa is based on movement from one position to the next. And for those who enjoy sweating it out, bikram (hot) yoga gets you to bend and stretch in room temperatures of 35C to 40C. For beginners, two to three sessions a week is probably enough, but yoga experts do recommend practice every day. Many yoga studios offer workshops and teacher training courses, and invite guest yoga masters from around the world to lead classes.

Floor 6, 2 Yuyao Lu
Jing'an
余姚路2号
静安
🚇 **Nanjing Dong Lu**
Map p.429 D3 204

Eternity Fitness Retreat 泳泰健身中心
6215 1519 | www.eternity-retreat.com

If you want to mix it up and give your body an all-round workout, join the fitness freaks at Eternity Fitness Retreat. You can improve your yoga, take up Pilates and learn the basics of tai chi all in one place. In addition there's a small adjoining spa where you can get your tired muscles massaged at the end of a tough workout.

1400 Beijing Xi Lu
Jing'an
北京西路1400弄
29号
静安
🚇 **Jing'an Temple**
Map p.429 F4 205

Namaste (Yoga Shala)
6247 2488 | www.namasteyoga.com.cn

This delightful yoga sanctuary is tucked away in the heart of local Shanghai, taking up residence in an old house dating back to 1949. The homely rooms are decorated in purple, pink and green, and feature quirky Japanese lamp shades that hide the glare when you're flat out on your back. There is also a fully equipped Pilates studio with an array of machinery. Namaste is led by two yogic experts, one of whom was Madonna's personal trainer, and also coached Bjork and Sting. In addition to teaching you all the moves, they'll help you find your inner warrior and awaken your source power through chanting, meditation sessions and Thai massage. Drop-in sessions cost ¥200, and there are various membership plans available.

299 Fuxing Xi Lu
Xuhui
复兴西路299号
徐汇
🚇 **Changshu Lu**
Map p.435 F2 206

Y+ Yoga Centre Y+瑜伽健身中心
6433 4330

Y+ Yoga's studio provides the perfect setting for a serious session of yoga. The colour scheme, decor and facilities in both of the centres are all conducive to finding inner harmony, whether you'd prefer to practise in the old villa house or more modern surroundings of the Xintiandi outlet. As one of the most expensive and luxurious stretching spots in town, it's not only the place to work up a sweat, but also take time out, meditate and relax. The teaching team brings a diverse range of backgrounds, including a focus on the healing powers of yoga. A range of membership plans are offered, and a drop-in session costs ¥200. If you're a member and ever find yourself in Hangzhou, you can also visit the studio by Westlake.

50, Lane 1487,
Huaihai Zhong Lu
Xuhui
淮海中路1487弄
50号
徐汇
🚇 **Hengshan Lu**
Map p.435 E2 207

Yoga Shala 大唐瑜珈
6437 5915 | www.yogashalashanghai.com

Pregnant women, kids and beginners are all welcome in this peaceful lane house themed around the elements. And when you're finished getting all sweaty and centred in one of the spacious wooden rooms, relax in the rest area, surf the internet and rehydrate yourself with the free juice. Beginners can familiarise themselves with the basics of Hatha and meditation before progressing to the more complex flow movements. Special rates are offered for first timers, and drop-in sessions after that cost ¥150.

297

Shopping

Shopping

Shopping

New York, London, Paris, Milan – now Shanghai is hot on their trails. Monikers such as 'China's fashion capital' are helping the city to shape a name for itself as a shopper's paradise. While Hong Kong used to be the place to go for shopping in China, and is probably still your best bet for cheap electronics, Shanghai now has much more to offer in other areas. There is a vast choice in the way of clothing, as well as a diverse selection of antiques, home furnishings, arts, ethnic crafts and speciality foods. In fact, there's little you won't find in this cosmopolitan jungle. In addition to high-end designer shops, international chain stores, countless markets and shopping malls, Shanghai is a hotbed for up and coming designers, and there is a strong presence of independent shops and showrooms – western and Chinese alike – cultivating a wealth of unique offerings.

There are two ways to live your life in Shanghai: like a local or like an expat – and the two peacefully exist side by side. Which you choose will affect how much you spend. Expenditure on amenities can be kept to a minimum if you frequent the markets, local shops and supermarkets. But, if you're a brand junkie and crave western luxuries, throwing your money around becomes easy.

Shanghai's Top Shopping Spots

For residents of the city's newer east side, Pudong, there's a Carrefour, a Wal-Mart (p.343), several large malls and plenty of international retail outlets to suffice. But if you're looking for all that and more – idyllic, leafy shopping streets lined with charming little boutiques, decadent designer emporiums and markets aplenty – stay Puxi side. Huaihai Lu, transecting Xuhui and Luwan, and Nanjing Lu, which runs through Jing'an and Huangpu, are the main shopping streets, and both serve up a wide selection of well-known international brands (see p.346). The leafy streets of the elegent French Concession boast a network of independent clothing shops selling an assortment of home-grown designs, cheap factory rejects and designer overruns. Then you have your pick of the markets, including electronics, fabrics, flowers and antiques (see p.343).

On Sale

While bargains can be found all year round, the shops and department stores have their biggest sales and promotions around the national holidays, particularly in the run up to Chinese New Year. If you can handle the frenzied crowds and the long queues, you're bound to find some great reductions.

Shoppers Beware…

Shanghai is a haven for fake goods, and if you don't know your designer brands it can sometimes be difficult to spot the rip-off Gucci sunglasses from the real McCoy. Vendors vie for attention at every street corner while trying to entice you into alleys with calls of 'DVD, watch, bag'.

The city recently lost the much talked about 'fake' market along Xiangyang Lu, only to be replaced by two new contenders – one on Nanjing Xi Lu and the other underground at the Shanghai Science & Technology Museum station in Pudong (see Markets, p.343). In all these places, the sellers will invariably attempt to rip you off, or certainly charge you over the odds, so be prepared to haggle and don't be intimidated (see Bargaining, p.302). Finally, remember that most stores in Shanghai don't carry much of a stock of large sizes.

Clothing Sizes

The biggest problem Shanghai's foreign shoppers come up against is sizing. Chinese men and women are typically petite, certainly in comparison to westerners, so there is a distinct lack of larger sizes to cater for broader, more rounded people. In some shops, the assistants will make reference to this (with a shake of their head or a polite remark) before a westerner even makes it into the changing rooms. The likes of H&M and Zara do stock larger sizes, but even their supplies are limited. There is also no standardised sizing system. Depending on where you shop, you'll find garments come in European, US or UK sizing. The moral of this section is to always try before you buy.

Online Shopping

Cyber shopping is gaining popularity in Shanghai. A favourite site among Chinese people is www.taobao.com, where you can buy new and second-hand goods, as well as trade items. There is also a Chinese eBay (www.ebay.com.cn), but both of these sites are in Chinese only. There is a general lack of China-based English-language websites, although more are appearing. Some international sites will deliver here, but the terms and conditions will vary, and you will probably need to pay with a foreign credit card.

Shopping Lingo
When shopping in the markets, the greatest bargaining tool you can have is a decent grasp of Mandarin. Check out the language chart on p.21 for some essential phrases.

Refunds & Exchanges

Refunds and exchanges aren't as widely available as in other countries – it all depends on where you shop. Unless the street vendor happens to remember you and is feeling generous, you're stuck with the faulty DVD and the broken zip on your fake Louis Vuitton bag. Large retail outlets will exercise a policy, but these will vary from place to place. For independent shops, there's unlikely to be an official rule, and it will probably be left to the sales assistant's discretion. Ask to see the manager, as it may be that the assistant on duty doesn't understand, or isn't really sure how to deal with your requests. To prevent any complications, it's best to inquire before you buy anything – and always make sure that you get a legible receipt.

Consumer Rights

There'll be times when you come up against difficult, unresponsive staff, and you'll find communication particularly difficult if you don't speak Chinese. If you encounter any problems with quality or service, contact the manager of the shop first. Should this measure prove futile, you can file a complaint by calling the national consumer rights hotline on 12315. This is a government organisation with English-speaking staff available to take your complaint. The issue should be dealt with within 20 working days of making the phone call.

This same organisation is also responsible for China's Consumer Rights Day held annually on March 15. Any serious problems with quality or service are brought to the public's attention on this day, through the media. In the months leading up to it, a number will be advertised that you can call if you have any issues that you'd like to raise yourself. Brands and shops will be named and shamed in the hope that they'll change their ways. In the weeks following this event, the government body will follow up to see if the situation has improved.

Shipping

Shipping goods overseas is pretty straightforward, as long as what you're shipping is permitted to be taken out of the country. Antiques from 1795 or before are not allowed out (although this rule can sometimes be overlooked) and large volumes of jade and porcelain can be near-impossible to export. Shipping companies will sometimes send government inspectors round before packing to check your goods.

301

Some stores may assist you with arrangements but it is easy to do it yourself. The cost of shipping is determined by weight, time of arrival and destination. Export taxes are included in the cost, but incoming VAT might be added at the other end.

China Post is the cheapest means of shipment but takes longer than private shipping companies. Their Express Mail Service is usually reliable and has a tracking system, but it's not as efficient as those of other companies.

FedEx, UPS and DHL all have various drop-off points around Shanghai (check their webpages), and they will also send someone to come and pick up your goods for around ¥10. See p.126 in the Residents section for contact information.

How to Pay

Paying with plastic is less common in Shanghai than other developed cities in the world. The best way to pay for goods is by cash, in the local currency. Many smaller stores will only accept cash or local Chinese bank cards. Chinese banks are part of the Union group, and if you see the Union sign advertised you can pay with your bank card. Credit cards (MasterCard, Visa and American Express) and debit cards are accepted in most major retail stores, supermarkets and department stores, while paying by cheque is very rare. If you're unsure, check for signs in the window or at the checkout. Some places will require your pin number; others will just swipe your card and ask you to sign. Luckily, card fraud isn't a major problem in Shanghai.

Bargaining

Bargaining is an integral part of shopping on the streets and markets of Shanghai and with a bit of practice you'll soon learn the tricks of the trade. Be bold – a lot of market vendors are well aware of the money you are used to spending and will hit you with outrageous prices. Accustom yourself, as soon as possible, to thinking in the local currency so that you don't get caught out paying four times more than you should. Even if you think you're getting a good deal, you're probably paying more than your Asian counterparts, and the fake Rolex you're eyeing up might not even last a week.

Start out low and aim to pay around a third of the asking price. Walk away if your offer is turned down, as you'll usually be called back. Your luck will vary depending on where you are. At tourist haunts such as Yu Garden, it's harder to get a good price. Knowing your Chinese numbers and some stock phrases can help (see the language table on p.21). Bargaining in stores is not common practice, but if you're shopping for luxury goods such as electronics or jewellery it's worth trying for a discount.

What & Where to Buy – Quick Reference

Alcohol	303	Clothes	314	Lingerie	328	Shoes	335
Antiques	304	Computers	320	Luggage & Leather	330	Souvenirs	336
Art	309	Electronics/Appliances	321	Medicine	330	Sports Goods	337
Art & Craft Supplies	310	Eyewear	321	Mobile Telephones	331	Stationery	337
Baby Items	310	Flowers	322	Music, DVDs & Videos	331	Tailoring	338
Beachwear	311	Food	323	Musical Instruments	332	Textiles	339
Bicycles	311	Gardens	325	Outdoor Goods	332	Toys, Games & Gifts	339
Books	312	Hardware & DIY	325	Party Accessories	333	Wedding Items	340
Camera Equipment	313	Health Food	326	Perfumes & Cosmetics	333		
Car Parts	313	Home Furnishings	326	Pets	334		
Carpets	313	Jewellery & Watches	327	Second-Hand Items	335		

Alcohol

Other options On the Town p.384

With the steady invasion of bars, nightclubs and boozy westerners, Shanghai is developing more of a taste for the drink. The legal age for buying alcohol is 16, but it is generally possible for anyone to purchase booze from the local 24 hour convenience stores.

Beer comes cheap in China – a big bottle of Tsingtao will set you back around ¥4, while spirit drinkers can get a bottle of Johnnie Walker Red Label whiskey for around ¥120. Western supermarkets such as Carrefour, City, Freshmart and Parkson (see p.343) all stock good ranges of wine and liquor, with bottles of Absolut Vodka costing just over ¥100 and a simple bottle of chardonnay from ¥75. If you have a taste for ouzo, you can find bottles at the Greek deli Amphora (p.325) for upwards of ¥100.

Up until recently wine was considered a luxury, and while it's still relatively expensive, appreciation for the grape is ripening. Fancy boutique wine shops have sprung up all over town to cater to an increasing demand. Fans can pick up three-litre boxes for ¥168 at Vins Descombe. And the ultimate wine buff can relish in the exclusive cellar at Jointek Fine Wines, separate from the rest of the shop, where vintage bottles start off at ¥1,000.

Well-stocked Globus Wine

Cheese & Fizz 奶酪美食店

6336 5823

119 Madang Lu, North Block, Xintiandi
Luwan
马当路119号
新天地北里
卢湾
Huangpi Nan Lu
Map p.436 C2 **1**

This is one of Shanghai's oldest and finest wine shops, ready to satiate the palates of serious grape-lovers. There is a large selection of French, Italian and New World plonks on offer, and a decent bottle of French red or white can be picked up for ¥300 to ¥400. When it's time to break out the bubbly, bottles of chilled Veuve Clicquot and Tattinger start at around ¥700. Knowledgeable English-speaking staff are on hand to guide you in your choosing, and if this is the beginning of a long and fruitful relationship with the grape, you can invest in a smart range of Atelier du Vin wine glasses, bottle stoppers and other accessories. There are also outlets in the Shanghai Centre (1376 Nanjing Xi Lu) and Super Brand Mall (see p.342).

Alcohol		
Aux Millesimes	415 Shanxi Bei Lu	5213 7880
D&G	627 Huaihai Zhong Lu	5382 8139
Enoteca	53-57 Anfu Lu	5404 0050
Globus Wine	376 Wukang Lu	5465 2774
Jointek Fine Wines	403-409 Weihai Lu	6340 0955
Joymax	333 Guangdong Lu	6416 5238
VIN	118 Xingye Lu	6385 2127
Vins Descombe	372 Dagu Lu	6340 1590

303

Epicvre 飨受主义

5404 7719 | www.epicvre.com

For Francophiles and French nationals alike, Epicvre has arguably one of the best selections of French wines in town. Bottles are picked from some of France's most affluent vineyards, and wine connoisseurs can test the savvy staff on their extensive knowledge of what is currently in stock, from bordeaux to the newest beaujolais. Price tags are subtly hidden, but most wines are priced around the ¥200 to ¥300 mark. This rustic little bar and cafe also holds regular wine tastings, so the thirsty masses can sample their new, imported stock.

Grace Vineyard Wineshop 怡园酒庄

**97 Ruijin Er Lu,
French Concession**
Luwan
瑞金二路97号,
法租界
卢湾
Shanxi Nan Lu
Map p.436 B1 **3**

5382 0633 | www.grace-vineyard.com

If the only Chinese wine you've sampled is the ¥30 bottle of watery Great Wall at your local Kedi or Lawson's, this is the place to go for a decent bottle of the country's very own harvest. Founded in 1997, Grace Vineyard is a family-owned winery located up on the yellow plateau of Shanxi province (in north-west China), a region famous for its sandy loam soils. You can find wines to suit all tastes, from a fruity pinot noir to a citrusy chardonnay. Bottles range from around ¥60 to ¥368 for a bottle of chairman's reserve.

Just Grapes 萄醉

462 Dagu Lu
Jing'an
大沽路462号
静安
Nanjing Xi Lu
Map p.430 B4 **4**

3311 3205 | www.justgrapes.cn

For a fool's guide to wine, check out the slick imitation cellar at Just Grapes. Here, bottles and shelves are clearly labelled with characteristics and flavours, making the often intimidating selection process a hundred times easier. Work your way down the rack and decide what you're after, whether it's 'fresh', 'rich', 'nutty', 'minerally' or 'spicy'. After a few visits, you'll have taught yourself the basics. There's also a lounge upstairs, where you can order a bottle and polish it off at your leisure over a tannin discussion. Look out for the regular promotions on select wines and frequent wine-tasting events.

Antiques

Shopping for untouched antiques in Shanghai is a risky business if you're not an expert in the field. The Chinese have a great talent for making things look old and weathered, even when they're not – you will find few genuine articles in any of the markets about town (see p.343). The best places to look are the government-owned shops such as Shanghai Antique and Curio Store (192-242 Guangdong Lu; 6339 2684), which deals exclusively in Chinese artefacts, including jade, porcelain, ceramics and mahogany furniture. Its pieces carry the official red stamp of authenticity. It also offers foreign exchange services, insurance, packing and shipping services.

Dongtai antiques

Casa Pagoda

15 Taikang Lu
Luwan
泰康路15号
卢湾
Map p.436 C2 **5**

6466 7521 | www.casapagoda.com

Casa Pagoda has struck a balance between ancient and modern and boasts the old 'east meets west' design aesthetic, which has proven popular across its three outlets in Asia. It markets its style as 'neo zen', which

BIG BAMBOO

SPORTS ★ BAR ★ GRILL

Relax. Unwind.

GUINNESS DRAUGHT

★ Happy Hour Daily 2pm-8pm
★ Full Food Menu from 10am-2am
★ 15 Flat Screens & Big Screen
★ Private Functions
★ Live Music

 #1 *Voted "Best Sports Bar" in Shanghai!*

132 Nan Yang Lu, Shanghai, China (021) 6256 2265

Directly behind Shanghai Center

www.bigbamboo.cn

translates as a mix of Parisian chic and Asian tradition. The smart single-floor showroom is regularly updated and rearranged to offer different interior solutions, whether you're outfitting a bachelor pad or a love nest. Find classic Chinese styles updated with striking colours, as well as grand French baroque armchairs, fluffy rugs and top-grain Italian leather sofas for around ¥5,500. There's also the odd piece of artwork to complement the charms of your newly decorated room. The team is trained to offer you advice on the remodelling of your home.

Design Republic　设计共和

*5 Zhongshan
Dong Yi Lu*
Huangpu
中山东一路5号
黄埔
🚇 *Hulang Lu*
Map p.431 E3 6

6329 3339 | www.thedesignrepublic.com

There are no copies to be found in this trendy showroom, housed in the same building as M on the Bund. Design Republic brings in exclusive designer pieces from all over the world (Alessi, Akari, Erik Joergensen and more). Pioneering the modern era of design, it serves as a platform for experimental furnishings. More like an art gallery than a furniture shop, new-fangled chairs, tables and other avante garde pieces are artily displayed around the room against a simple, wooden backdrop and funky beats. The lighting fixtures in particular are jaw-dropping. Unfortunately, so are the prices.

Hari Rabu　东南亚精品店

*Floor 2, Lane 6,
210 Taikang Lu*
Luwan
泰康路6弄210号
卢湾
🚇 *Shanghai Indoor
Stadium*
Map p.436 C2 7

6445 5413

Enter through a make-believe bazaar of wooden stalls, which offer a little taste of what's to come from the incense-infused hideaway upstairs. South-east Asian hand-crafted trinkets abound in this exotic boho atelier. Sprays of reeds have been woven into various shapes to make charming lamps, which start at around ¥200. In a separate nook, find incense sticks and aroma oils, ceramic statues and coconut crafts. It's cheap and cheery and will have you pining for a holiday to Thailand or Indonesia in no time.

Henry's Studio & Antiques　上海汉瑞古典家具有限公司

796 Suining Lu
Xuhui
绥宁路796号
徐汇

5219 4871 | www.antique-designer.com

This palatial furniture emporium sits on the outskirts of the city, a lengthy cab ride away for most residents. Founder Henry Wang divides his time between restoring a vast range of antique pieces from all over China, designing his own furniture and providing an interior design service. Unlike other furniture dealers, Henry strives to capture and preserve the beauty of the antique pieces he finds, ranging from attractive elm wood side tables to walnut chairs dating back to the Ming Dynasty, while making them more fitting for the modern day home. The huge showroom could see you whiling away more than a few hours, dreaming about your new Chinese-themed abode.

Home & Garden　好饰家建材园艺超市

285 Tianlin Dong Lu
Xuhui
田林东路285号
徐汇
🚇 *Shanghai Stadium*
Map p.443 E2 9

If you're economising, but don't want your home to resemble a page from the IKEA catalogue, venture a bit beyond the Swedish warehouse to House & Garden. Tucked away down Tianlin Lu, a little off the beaten track, this gigantic compound of warehouses has all you need and more. You'll find yourself lost in a dizzying maze of stalls within seconds – there's one building devoted to lighting alone. Delve deeper and you'll find outdoor furniture, stone and wood sculptures, paintings, toilets, carpets, beds and sofas. There are prices attached but bargaining down that ¥3,000 sofa is acceptable. Persist and you're sure to come away with some fantastic deals.

Fashion Boutiques p.123
Financial Advisors p.95

Written by residents, the New Zealand Explorer is packed with insider info, from arriving in a new destination to making it your home and everything in between.

New Zealand Explorer Residents' Guide
We Know Where You Live

EXPLORER

115 Jiangxi Zhong Lu
Huangpu
江西中路115号
黄埔
🚇 **Nanjing Dong Lu**
Map p.431 E3 🔟

Ma.Design House 一风阁

6321 6611

Everything about Ma.Design House screams art deco. An old renovated house just a street behind the Bund has been transformed into a showroom and studio for Hong Kong designer and artist Simon Ma. Going by the nickname 'Mad Designer', he's a pioneering figure on China's contemporary art circuit, experimenting with pushing the boundaries of art and design. The brick walls have been left bare and splashed with metallic colours, on which his abstract canvases hang haphazardly. His high-back wooden chairs (¥7,000) and other furnishings are customised with swirls of oil paint. There's also an adjoining bar where you can settle back and marvel at his artistic engineering over a long drink or two.

207 Fumin Lu,
French Concession
Xuhui
富民路207号,
法租界
徐汇
🚇 **Changshu Lu**
Map p.435 F1 🔟

Madame Mao's Dowry 毛太设计

5403 3551 | *www.madame-maos-dowry.com*

What started as a personal collection for the shop's owner has mushroomed into a prosperous business. With its China-blue painted exterior, this showroom really stands out along Fumin Lu. Inside is a treasure trove of hand-picked finds, each one with a story behind it. The shop specialises in north provincial styles and memorabilia from the Mao period (1930-1950). You can browse through original 1960s propaganda posters from the Cultural Revolution (¥600-¥6,000, depending on rarity) and artsy 1950s black-and-white photographs from the Xinhua News Agency (¥150). Also keep an eye out for coffee tables made from Golden Bricks (these once tiled the floors of the homes of famous Chinese officials) and their customised enamelware. To see more of Madame Mao's antique furniture, pay a visit to the shop's warehouse on Moganshan Lu. The owners are careful to make sure that everything they sell is authentic, but will provide a full refund on anything later discovered not to be. For its furniture warehouse, head to Eastlink Gallery at Building 6, 50 Moganshan Lu (6276 9932).

410 Wukang Lu
Xuhui
武康路410号
徐汇
Map p.435 E3 🔟

Magazine 万佳轩

6431 9971 | *www.kennethcobonpue.com*

There's an earthiness about Magazine's furnishings. Designer Kenneth Cobonpue demonstrates a fresh sensibility, influenced by his time spent on the exotic island of Cebu in the Philippines. He works with a range of natural materials including bamboo, wood and rattan, which is hand-woven around steel frames to create functional, simple, yet striking pieces. Soft curvy shapes are countered by rigid lines. Baskets are moulded into chairs and low-lying rattan beds resemble large cradles (¥11,500). If you're going for the minimalist approach, these furnishings are just the ticket. Worth a note is the fact that if you order items 90 days in advance, you're entitled to a reduction on the price.

321 Weihai Lu
Luwan
威海路321号
卢湾
🚇 **Nanjing Dong Lu**
Map p.430 A4 🔟

Nancy's Lifestyles 南希家具商业有限公司

6340 1681 | *www.nancyslifestyles.com*

Nancy not only has an immaculate two-floor show home of American-style furnishings, she also has airtime on Chinese television, with a view to educating her audience about stylish, comfortable living. For those who aspire to live the iconic lifestyles of homeowners in Manhattan, Cape Cod, Aspen, Hollywood and Beverly Hills, Nancy has designed five complete collections. Each offers everything you need to outfit your whole house, down to the table lamps, cutlery and place mats. All that's left is to ship over your chihuahua.

30 Hunan Lu
Xuhui
湖南路30号
徐汇
🚇 *Hengshan Lu*
Map p.435 E2 **14**

Paddy Fields 稻

6437 5567 | www.paddy-field.com.cn

Get yourself a custom-made piece of modish Indonesian furniture in just three weeks from this popular furniture store. You can also select from the collections of exotic wood furnishings, from understated teak wood pieces to striking angular elm tables and chairs. The two stores have a very rustic feel to them – think a jumbled array of goods with no surface left bare. If storage and beauty are your heart's desires, you can pick up a sturdy Asian-style chest for around ¥4,800. There is another branch at 273 Jianguo Xi Lu (6467 4128).

604-608 Jianguo Xi Lu
Xuhui
建国西路604-608号
徐汇
🚇 *Hengshan Lu*
Map p.435 F3 **15**

Shenhui Vintage Exchange Centre 申汇调剂中心

6433 3897

Unbeknown to many a foreigner, this store is a true gem. Second-hand beds, tables, lamps, chairs, flatscreen TVs and decorative items are squashed in wherever there's space. Take along your own cast-offs and come away with someone else's. Most stuff is in good condition. If you're used to shelling out for second-hand collectibles, the price tags here are sure to bring a smile to your face. Score an elegant freestanding lamp for the living room for around ¥100 and a set of speakers for just ¥250.

Art

Other options **Art Galleries** p.196, **Art Classes** p.238, **Art & Craft Supplies** p.310

You've Been Framed
To get your new investments framed, try Eddy Tam's Gallery. You'll find a range of options, from the inexpensive and simple, to more high-end woods, all ready to make your pictures and certificates even more satisfying to look at. Service takes a week and prices range from ¥80 to ¥700.

Shanghai's art scene is buzzing, much like the metropolis of which it is a part. Only since the end of the Cultural Revolution in 1976, however, have China's artists been given full reign to express themselves freely. The city is teeming with independent art galleries, and traditional ink paintings and calligraphy have been replaced by a flourishing contemporary art scene.

Some of the most commercially successful artists to emerge from this new era include Zhang Xiaogang (whose work has auctioned for close to $1 million), Yue Minjun and Zhou Tiehai. Photography art is also gaining ground, and there are a number of local and foreign up-and-coming photographers on the scene.

Number 50 Moganshan Lu is the modern art mecca of Shanghai, where a cluster of disused warehouses have been converted into a myriad of independent art galleries. One of the oldest is Art Scene Warehouse, who make it their mission to promote the work of less mainstream artists, like Xue Jiye and Zhong Biao. To get your hands on work from some of the newest up-and-coming artists, look out for its annual Chinese Art Prize competition (www.chineseartprize.com). ShangART, Eastlink, Studio Rouge and BizArt galleries are also worth a look, as are the multiple galleries along Taikang Lu and Anfu Lu, and the Museum of Arts and Crafts at 79 Fenyang Lu.

Prices for art have soared in recent years and certain places will mark up the prices significantly. You can invest in a piece for anything between ¥2,000 and ¥750,000, depending on the artist and background. There are also a number of art fairs in Shanghai now (see Annual Events, p.52). An emerging phenomenon, still in its teething stages, is the concept of art auctions. Eastlink Gallery currently hosts one of the only ones in town (www.shanghaiartauctions.com).

Museum of Arts and Crafts

309

Art		
Art Scene Warehouse	4, 50 Moganshan Lu	6277 4940
BizArt	7, 50 Moganshan Lu	6277 5358
Eastlink Gallery	6, 50 Moganshan Lu	6276 9932
Eddy Tam's Gallery	20 Maoming Nan Lu	6253 6715
Shanghai Ju'Roshine Arts & Crafts Centre	56 Maoming Nan Lu	6253 3556
ShanghART Gallery & H-Space	16 & 18, 50 Moganshan Lu	6359 3923
Stir Art Gallery	172 Jinxian Lu	5157 5985
Studio Rouge	17 Fuzhou Lu	6323 0833

If you're looking for something in a lower price bracket, IKEA (p.325) sells a wide range of generic prints, and you may find something to catch your eye in the one of the many other home furnishing stores in the city. For more traditional Chinese ink paintings and other art, head to Yu Garden or Duolun Lu.

Art & Craft Supplies

Other options **Art** p.309, **Art Classes** p.238, **Art Galleries** p.196

If you're a budding artist, or indeed fancy yourself as one, the city is a good place to exercise your talents. For economical supplies, walk east from People's Square down Fuzhou Lu. The bustling street is lined on either side with small shops selling canvases, paints, pens, easels, paper and other

Art & Craft Supplies		
Crayola	200 Fujian Zhong Lu	6375 7841
Espace Pebeo	0, 50 Moganshan Lu	6266 2101

necessary items. You can buy a canvas, a set of acrylics and brushes for less than ¥100. For more specialist supplies, try Espace Pebeo. It offers a range of fine materials, including oils, acrylics, fabric paints, 3D paints and children's provisions. A fabric paint kit is around ¥100 and, to give you a kick-start on the right artistic path, you can also sign up for art classes.

If you're after kid-friendly art supplies, you can't go wrong with Crayola. In this small office and shop space, you can find everything Crayola has ever made, from its signature wax crayons to felt pens and poster paints, as well as reams of brightly coloured paper, pipe cleaners and other craft items.

If knitting is next on your list of hobbies to try, there's a cluster of good yarn shops along Ruijin Lu (between Jianguo Lu and Fuxing Lu), selling cheap balls of wool for ¥3 to ¥15. Also try Fuyou Street Merchandise Mart at Yu Garden (see p.333) for threads and yarn.

Baby Items

These days, tots are looking trendy, some even trendier than their parents. High-street havens H&M (p.319) and Zara (p.320) offer the latest fashion fads in miniature without burning a hole in your pocket. But if you're after short-term baby-grows, head to Nihong Kids' Plaza. This noisy underground market is entirely devoted to children, who populate the aisles, running circles around their worn-out mothers. Stalls are jam-packed with clothing and shoes, all for around ¥10 to ¥30, including the bottomless trousers commonly worn by Shanghainese babes. There are also stacks of cheap toys and learning implements.

For good quality fabrics and understated styles, Bonpoint is a high-end French boutique selling adorable apparel, but cute cotton smocks and the like go for a tidy sum of ¥800. Independent French boutiques Shanghai Trio and Rouge Baiser also

Need Some Direction?
The *Explorer Mini Maps* pack a whole city into your pocket and, once unfolded, are excellent navigational tools for exploring. Not only are they handy in size, with detailed information on the sights and sounds of the city, but also their fabulously affordable price mean they won't make a dent in your holiday fund.

design small collections of Asian chic children's wear in beautifully soft and natural fabrics. At the other end of the spectrum, for mothers who favour labels and a touch of bling, Abebi stocks mini D&G, Kenzo and Moschino sets.

For all other baby supplies, head to cutesy store Goodbaby. If you don't go in feeling broody, you'll certainly leave feeling so. Within this homely three-floor kids' world, there's a great choice of reasonably priced baby garments and maternity wear, cots, playpens, bottles, toys and other amenities. For local expectant mothers, Changle Lu, between Xiangyang Lu and Shanxi Lu, is a popular destination for cheap maternity wear. For day-to-day amenities and foods, all big supermarkets and Watson's outlets stock a range of imported goods, including Johnson & Johnson, Pampers and Huggies. Also browse the children's department at Isetan (p.342).

Baby Items		
Abebi	Plaza 66, 1266 Nanjing Xi Lu	2576 0776
Bonpoint	207-209 Shanxi Nan Lu	5228 0884
Folli Folli Baby	1065 Nanjing Xi Lu	6258 8316
Goodbaby	Various Locations	6351 1558
Les Enphants	Various Locations	5382 2269
Nihong Kids' Plaza	10 Pu'an Lu	na
Rouge Baiser	299-2 Fuxing Xi Lu	6431 8019
Shanghai Trio	Lane 181 Taicang Lu, Xintiandi	6335 2974
Xiangyang Kidworld	993 Nanjing Xi Lu	626 7030

Another organisation that might help is www.shanghaitoyclub.com.cn, where you can hire or buy toys and equipment for newborns to 5 year olds, such as swim nappies, car seats and pushchairs. You can also buy a selection of cheap child-care products, which may not be available elsewhere in Shanghai, including wipes and lotions.

Beachwear

Other options **Sports Goods** p.337, **Clothes** p.314

Shanghai summers may be sweltering, but there are few places in the city where you can don your swimsuit and soak up the sun. Nonetheless, you'll still need beachwear for your next trip to Thailand, or beyond. Quiksilver (921 Huaihai Zhong Lu; 54656291) has the ultimate in baggy surfer shorts and exotic string bikinis from ¥500.

If that's a little out of your price range, keep an eye out for the seasonal swimwear in H&M (p.318), where you can pick up a trendy two-piece for around ¥250. Another good place to look is around the many lingerie shops (see Lingerie, p.328). Bao.d sells a random, cheap collection of imported bathers in larger sizes, and Lingerie & Me offers haute-couture cossies for a small fortune. Kids can find cheap water wear from Nihong Kids' Plaza and UV-protective swimwear from Shanghai Toy Club (www.shanghaitoyclub.com.cn). For water babies, Decathlon (p.333) stocks everything you'll need, from sporty suits to goggles and hats.

Bicycles

When the weather's right, a bicycle is one of the best ways to shoot around town. Unfortunately, bike theft is common, so be sure to invest in a few hardy bike locks. Giant is one of the most popular and reliable brands around, and there are a number of small shops dotted around the French Concession selling various bikes for around ¥350 to ¥550.

You can also pick up a bike at Carrefour (p.343) for around ¥200 and an electric bicycle (which is another popular mode of transport) for around ¥1,500. For additional parts, accessories and protective gear, try the Bicycle Shop in Jinqiao (1011 Zaozhuang Lu), which also offers repair and rental services. Similarly, Decathlon (p.337) stocks a small range of bicycles (¥400 upwards) and accessories, as

Bicycles		
Bicycle Shop	Various Locations	5070 1326
Giant	743 Jianguo Xi Lu	6437 5041
La Bici	241 Wanping Lu, French Concession	6473 4039

311

well as an in-house repair centre. Also try the locally operated Bodhisattva Bikes (www.bohdi.com.cn) for high-end titanium and aluminium bikes. For second-hand bikes, try the second floor of Modern Electronics City on the corner of Fuxing Lu and Xiangyang Lu (p.321).

If you're serious about cycling and looking for a bike that can handle more than the gentle flats of Shanghai, call in to La Bici. This snappy metal showroom displays all manner of mountain-friendly frames. The inventory of exclusive brands includes Sunn, Commencal and The Shadow Conspiracy. Standard models range from ¥5,000 to more than ¥20,000.

Books

Other options **Second-Hand Items** p.335, **Libraries** p.260

While English-language book stores are few and far between in Shanghai, the city does demonstrate an appreciation for its literature, mostly through the annual International Literary Festival that has been running since 2003. The event invites prolific writers from all corners of the world to discuss a range of literature and topics, from fiction to travel writing, culture and cookery. The event takes place at Glamour Bar on the Bund (see p.390).

If you've never tackled works from the likes of Thomas Hardy, DH Lawrence and Oscar Wilde, now may be your opportunity, as classic paperbacks like these are available for around ¥20. Bookworms can briefly bury themselves in the small foreign sections at Shanghai's City of Books and SBT, but the choices are limited. Cookery books, travel guides and children's picture books are available, as well as a small collection of modern-day fiction. You may also find the odd copy of *The Economist* and *Cosmo* here (¥70 to ¥90).

For specialist art and design books, and magazines covering fashion, contemporary art and architecture, peruse the shelves of Point to Life Books Company, part of the artsy Bridge 8 complex, or sit down for a coffee and a good read at Timezone 8 bookshop and cafe. It also specialises in arty books and magazines, including *Flash Art* and *Icon*.

Books

Bookazine	Citic Square, 1168 Nanjing Xi Lu	5292 5214	www.cnpiecsb.com
Point to Life Books Company	Bridge 8, 8-10 Jianguo Zhong Lu	6137 9388	www.pointolife.com.cn
SBT Bookstore	Isetan, 527 Huaihai Zhong Lu	5351 0989	www.sbt.com.cn
Shanghai's City of Books	465 Fuzhou Lu	6391 4848	www.bookmall.com.cn
Timezone 8	3, 50 Moganshan Lu	6227 1467	www.timezone8.com

Shanghai Times Square,
93 Huaihai Zhong Lu
Luwan
淮海中路93号
大上海时代广场
卢湾
Map p.431 D4 🔢

Chaterhouse Booktrader 外文书店

6391 8237 | www.chaterhouse.com.cn

Touted as the best English-language book shop in town, there's a plethora of books on these informed shelves. Sections include science fiction, crime and history. Find the newest paperbacks (¥200 to ¥300) and hardbacks, bestselling fiction and non-fiction, coffee table books (around ¥300) and celebrity biographies. You can cook up a treat with a little help from Nigella Lawson, or learn the deepest, darkest secrets of Victoria Beckham. There are also children's books and a decent offering of special interest and glossy rags such as *Vogue*, *Wallpaper* and *The Economist*. Unfortunately, the floor space is a little cramped and not conducive to an afternoon spent browsing. The staff can help you locate what you're looking for, or pre-order titles on the computer system. You can also place an order by calling its Shanghai Times Square branch and have it delivered to your door for ¥20. There's another shop in Pudong's Super Brand Mall (5049 0668).

325 Changle Lu,
French Concession
Luwan
长乐路325号，
法租界
卢湾
🚇 *Shanxi Nan Lu*
Map p.436 A1 **17**

Garden Books 韬奋西文书局

5404 8728 | www.bookzines.com

For literary fiends, Garden Books is a close second behind Chaterhouse Booktrader. This English-language bookshop boasts a pleasant, airy environment in which to leisurely leaf through texts of interest and enjoy afternoon refreshments in its cafe. The book selection is also impressive and accounts for a broad range of interests, from business matters to Chinese culture to the newest trashy romance. Modest selections of French, Italian and German reads are also available. There is a charming little garden out back where a flea market is held during the warmer months on the last Saturday of every month (see Second-hand Items, p.335). You can also subscribe to international magazines and newspapers here.

Camera Equipment

Other options **Electronics & Home Appliances** p.321

While many people save their camera shopping for their next trip to Hong Kong (where they're markedly cheaper), Shanghai isn't lacking in selection or quality. For the latest slimline, pocketsized options on the market, head to Cybermart (p.321) or Xujiahui. You'll find all the mainstream brands available in the latest models, including Olympus, Sony, Nikon and Canon. Shop around to find the best deal, as you can sometimes barter the price down significantly.

There's also a market dedicated to cameras and related equipment on the corner of Luban Lu and Xietu Lu. It has second-hand dealers on the fourth, fifth and sixth floors. For dusty, vintage box cameras, take a trip to the third floor of Modern Electronics City (see p.321). Say cheese.

Car Parts & Accessories

Considering the numerous transport options available to you in Shanghai, there is little incentive to buy a car. Aside from the complications of obtaining a Chinese driving licence, the prospect of navigating Shanghai's congested downtown roads and busy highways is enough to put the most capable drivers off getting behind the wheel. That said, if you do decide to invest in a car, and some expat families do, Wuzhong Lu has all you need in the way of cheap car parts and accessories, including second-hand goods. There's also a warehouse of automobile accessories out in Jinqiao, at Autro Automobile Department Store (518 Lantian Lu; 5030 1675).

Carpets

Other options **Souvenirs** p.336

19 Shaoxing Lu,
French Concession
Luwan
绍兴路19号，
法租界
卢湾
🚇 *Shanxi Nan Lu*
Map p.436 B2 **18**

Mortazavy 圣菱画廊

6467 3556 | www.mortazavy.cn

This large, inviting house on the beautiful Shaoxing Lu houses a collection of exquisite hand-knotted Persian carpets and rugs, ranging from traditional nomadic styles to more intricate tribal and city designs – all lovingly hand crafted from cotton, wool or silk. Hung from the walls, lining the floors and piled up in corners, they vary in age and value and make for an elegant addition to any home. For a three to four square metre rug, expect to pay anywhere between ¥6,000 and ¥450,000. All you need now is a genie in a lamp.

Carpets			
Bokhara Carpets ▶ p.298		679 Xianxia Lu	6290 1745
Golden Silk Road		1394 Beijing Xi Lu	6289 2260
Mandarava		38 Maoming Nan Lu	6215 4233
Pak Persian		3721 Hongmei Lu	6446 8122

313

1, Lane 180,
Shanxi Nan Lu,
French Concession
Luwan
陕西南路180弄1号,
法租界
卢湾
🚇 *Shanxi Nan Lu*
Map p.436 A1 19

Torana House Shanghai 图兰纳家苑
5404 4886 | www.toranahouse.com

This grandiose two-floor emporium could be mistaken for a museum. Carpets are grandly exhibited next to their vital stats and detailed information about their background (in English and Chinese). The colourful offerings are 100% hand-made by the rural artisans of Tibet. Designs are based on traditional motifs but hold a noticeably timeless appeal, sure to instil character into the blandest of rooms. Prices are markedly lower than overseas. A six-to-nine-foot masterpiece costs between ¥6,000 and ¥18,000, and the store is also happy to custom-produce carpets on request.

Clothes

Other options **Tailoring** p.338, **Sports Goods** p.337, **Shoes** p.335, **Lingerie** p.328

Walk the streets of Shanghai and you'll soon notice that virtually anything goes in the fashion stakes – Dior and Gucci from head to toe, chintzy *qipaos*, Japanese schoolgirl fashions, and, in the summer months, pyjamas. While the city used to nurture a taste for copies and knock-offs, it's gradually growing more fashion conscious. There's now

Clothes		
Benetton	1018 Nanjing Dong Lu	6115 5295
Diesel	Plaza 66 and Grand Gateway Mall	6288 4464
Dutch Items Shanghai	111 Ferguson Lane, 376 Wukang Lu	6126 7661
Esprit	Various Locations	www.esprit.com
Fornarina	688 Huaihai Zhong Lu	5306 3461
Fragile	222 Madang Lu	6387 9977
Giordano	Various Locations	6322 9901
Guess	Infiniti Mall, 138 Huaihai Lu	6375 6119
Hotwind	Various locations	www.hotwind.net
http://www.izzue.com	Various locations	6336 5719
Kenzo	Citic Square, 1168 Nanjing Xi Lu	5292 5233
Mango	823 Huaihai Zhong Lu	5465 2862
Marc Jacobs	Shanghai Centre, 1376 Nanjing Xi Lu	6279 8321
Pcode	232 Jinxian Lu, French Concession	5157 5505
Qiu Hao	158 Jinxian Lu, French Concession	6256 0134
Sisley	Raffles City, 268 Xizang Zhong Lu	6340 3903
Star Place	1251 Fuxing Zhong Lu	6433 6761
Sungu Village Girl's Embroidery	155 Anfu Lu, French Concession	5403 5754
Unreplaceable	15, 339 Changle Lu, French Concession	5404 7787
Vivienne Tam	6, Lane 123, Xingye Lu, Xintiandi	5383 3133

18 on the Bund

Nanjing Lu window shopping

an annual Fashion Week (p.56), which, while disorganised and not of the same calibre as London and Paris, still attracts a number of high-profile designers.

For brand addicts who want the real Prada and Chanel, darling, Plaza 66 (p.341) is the place to shop and be spotted shopping. It's where many of the world's most prestigious designers have their flagship stores, including Salvatore Ferregamo, DKNY, Karl Lagerfeld and Paul Smith. Other famed designers such as Giorgio Armani, Dolce & Gabbanna and Hugo Boss have created kingdoms for themselves in grandiose spaces along the Bund.

Street Wear

Fit in with all the cool kids by picking up some of the latest streetwear at 5cm (p.316) and Source (p.319).

If pricey labels are not your thing, there's a huge range of high-street shops including Europe's celebrated H&M and Zara, Hong Kong's www.izzue.com and 5cm, and Japan's Uniqlo. Trendy independent boutiques sit densely along the French Concession's network of picturesque streets, namely Changle Lu, Xinle Lu, Julu Lu and Nanchang Lu. You can spend the best part of a day wondering up and down these leafy sidewalks stumbling upon small undiscovered boutiques selling affordable Marc Jacobs' dresses and other coveted pieces. The quality and authenticity of this clothing varies from shop to shop – some are knock-offs, others may be factory rejects or designer overruns. There's also a pack of local designers worth checking out. Canadian-born Megan Fischer creates smart, sexy designs for the classy lady, available from her showroom (6433 8029; www.matsudesign.com). For really cheap fashions, head to Qipu Lu Market (near Henan Lu in Zhabei), a favourite with the younger crowd of fashion followers.

Local Designers

Look smart Shanghai style by checking out some of the city's best local designers: Cha Gang No. 1 p.316; Eblis Hungi p.317; Eno p.317; Even Penniless p.317; Insh p.318; Poesia p.318; Shion by Choichangho p.319; Shirt Flag p.319; The Thing p.320; Younik p.320

Accessories

Most clothing designers offer their own range of desirable accessories, but for something different to spruce up your look check out local design studio Jooi. It offers an array of shoulder bags in quirky and elegant designs, embroidered purses, and other trendy touches suited to the modern mum. Woo Scarf and Shawl has

Accessories

Jooi Design	3, Lane 210 Taikang Lu	6473 6193
Kate Spade	Plaza 66, 1266 Nanjing Xi Lu	na
Shanghai Trio House	6, Lane 37, Fuxing Xi Lu	6433 8901
Shanghai Trio House	181 Taicang Lu, Xintiandi	6355 2974
Woo Scarf and Shawl	3, Lane 210, Taikang Lu	6445 7516

sumptuous cashmere scarves, cosy woollen wraps and delicate embroidered silk shawls in a sea of rich colours to match the shades in season – plain cashmere pieces start at around ¥240. Shanghai Trio and Lerosin Tree's ethnic-chic fabric bags, purses and name card holders are a snappy alternative to the same old styles churned out by all the high-street shops. And for the bag-carrying metropolitan male, The Gloss (p.336) offers Freitag shoulder bags (¥1,500) engineered from recycled tarpaulin and seatbelts (www.freitag.ch).

Designer Boutiques

Serious fashinistas should be right at home in these designer boutiques: Aiaia p.316; Anne Fontaine p.316; Curiosity p.317; Giorgio Armani p.317; I.T p.318; Joyce p.318; Shiatzy Chen p.319

The clothing and fakes markets (p.344) are well stocked with covetable accessories too. Your local street vendor is also likely to have a whole room down an alley stuffed with fake Balenciaga and Chloe bags to tempt you. Don't pay more than around ¥60 to ¥100.

Ethnic Clothing

Bohemians will find their niche in the numerous ethnic minority boutiques scattered about town. Find cheap gypsy-style skirts and traditional *Miao* attire that's been updated for everyday wear at Brocade Country (616 Julu Lu; 6279 2677). Shanghai Harvest Studio (Lane 210, Taikang Lu; 6473 4566) has a group of *Miao* girls in traditional costume in-shop busily hand-embroidering brightly coloured attire, bags, wall hangings and cushions. They'll customise their apparel to fit you. For

315

ethnic patterns with a funky twist, try Larosin Tree (127B Maoming Nan Lu; 5403 3202), where cute wax-printed dresses and cropped jackets can be snapped up for ¥300 to ¥400.

Floor 3, Plaza 66,
1266 Nanjing Xi Lu
Jing'an
南京西路1266号
恒隆广场
静安
🚇 *Nanjing Dong Lu*
Map p.430 A4 **20**

5cm
6288 4270 | www.ithk.com
An offspring of the Hong Kong-born I.T group, 5cm is a hipster's paradise and a favourite with the metrosexual, artistic male. Find preppy blazers (around ¥700), fitted button-down shirts, polo shirts and funky canvas shoulder bags in this urban chic shop. Guys can piece together whole outfits – hat, trainers and all – before heading to one of the city's hipster hangouts (think Boona Cafe on Fuxing Xi Lu, p.380) to spend an afternoon drinking coffee and surfing the net on the iBooks.

1, 165 Taiyuan Lu
Xuhui
太原路165号-1
徐汇
🚇 *Changshu Lu*
Map p.436 A2 **21**

Aiaia
艾艾娅时装设计师精品沙龙
6467 9102 | www.aiaia.cn
Ring the doorbell to be ushered into this homely boutique villa, quietly residing along the tranquil Taiyuan Lu. The walls are all painted warm violet hues, and one-off designer pieces for women are carefully displayed on low-lying tables or hung from single rails against the walls. The shop is select in its offerings and shows support for fashion's latest prodigies, including the everyday wear of Japanese designer GVGV (¥800 plus), floaty pieces from Anne Valerie Hash and edgy cuts from Matthew Williams. For most items, there will only be one in stock, so if you can't squeeze yourself into it, then tough luck. This exclusive fashion house offers personal style advice and also hosts regular trunk shows to introduce lesser-known designers to their very affluent female clientele.

Shop 2, 222 Hubin Lu,
Xintiandi
Luwan
湖滨路222号
新天地
卢湾
🚇 *Huangpi Nan Lu*
Map p.430 C4 **22**

Anne Fontaine
6340 6211 | www.annefontaine.com
Who would have thought there were so many variations on the classic white shirt? This Parisian designer breathes new life into this wardrobe mainstay, prettifying it up with ruffles, bows, oversized collars and a variety of other subtle details. A small selection of the shirts are on display, the rest are neatly packaged and ready for sale in a pristine space. The simplest design goes for around ¥1,350. For all available styles, it's best to flick through the catalogue and then try for size.

1 Lane 299,
Fuxing Xi Lu,
French Concession
Xuhui
复兴西路299弄1号,
法租界
徐汇
🚇 *Changshu Lu*
Map p.435 E2 **23**

Cha Gang No. 1 茶缸
6466 1089 | www.chagang.cn
Quiet, intelligent types will be drawn in by Wang Yi Yang's conceptual clothing and household items. Inspired by everyday objects from 'China of the 70s', such as enamelware and cloth shoes, he has captured an equal sense of tradition and fashion in his understated, cleverly thought-out designs. Wang works simple cottons and deconstructed shapes into his clothing lines, and these covetable pieces start at around ¥800. The designer's other brand, Zuc Zug, represents his alter-ego (Floor 2, South Block, 123 Xingye Lu, Xintiandi) – it's clothing with a funkier edge, suited to a more urban type.

316

366 Julu Lu
Luwan
巨鹿路366号
卢湾
🚇 **Shanxi Nan Lu**
Map p.430 A4 **24**

Curiosity

What started life as a showroom for the popular French urban label Homecore/Lady Soul has now expanded into two small multi-label boutiques – one for him and one for her, within just 100 metres of each other (the women's store is at 373 Julu Lu). In the men's den, you'll find the latest trendy designs, from Homecore to a small collection by Jean-Paul Loyson (previously part of Kenzo fashion house), plus a table of imported accessories and treats. The women's store sees covetable Ladysoul slouchy dresses and T-shirts (¥300 to ¥500), select pieces from Li Hong's collection (head designer at Insh as well as other lesser-known French designers.

**Shop 18,
139 Changle Lu**
Luwan
长乐路139号
卢湾
🚇 **Shanxi Nan Lu**
Map p.430 B4 **25**

Eblis Hungi

5382 6807 | www.eblis-hungi.com

This young Chinese designer is one of Shanghai's best homegrown talents. His quirky apparel is recognisable through the bandaged mummy face that's splashed across his collection of jeans, T-shirts and accessories. This low-key store occupies a sizeable space along Changle Lu's crowd of fashion boutiques and should be duly noted. His eerie yet light-hearted T-shirt designs (starting at around ¥120) and his finely engineered jeans (ranging from ¥480 to ¥980) have a personality and edge that stand them apart from the rest.

**139-23 Changle Lu,
French Concession**
Luwan
长乐路139-23号,
法租界
卢湾
🚇 **Shanxi Nan Lu**
Map p.430 B4 **26**

Eno

6386 0120 | www.eno.cn

Eno pools the creative talents of Shanghai's freshest designers, inviting each of them to use plain T-shirts as their canvas. The concept store houses a huge mechanical conveyor belt structure, spanning the two floors, along which the finished T-shirt designs are slowly paraded. All items are available in men's and women's sizes and range from ¥180 to ¥290. There's a cafe, and Eno also hosts regular social events, providing a platform on which up-and-coming musicians and artists come to be seen and heard.

**139-3 Changle Lu,
French Concession**
Luwan
长乐路139-3号,
法租界
卢湾
🚇 **Shanxi Nan Lu**
Map p.430 B4 **27**

Even Penniless

5306 0466

Japanese design aesthetics feature strongly in local Chinese designer Goa Xin's monochrome black-and-white collection. In a stark white edgy space, his female pieces hang from industrial piping, characterised by masculine lines, fraying edges, unusual folds, zips and strips of material – all heavily reminiscent of Yohji Yamamoto. Invest in one of the shop's deconstructed dresses for around ¥1,500 and it's sure to turn the heads of the fashion crowd.

**Floor 1,
3 Zhongshan
Dong Yi Lu**
Huangpu
中山东一路3号
黄埔
🚇 **Nanjing Dong Lu**
Map p.431 E3 **28**

Giorgio Armani 乔治阿玛尼

6339 1133 | www.threeonthebund.com

Giorgio Armani's sartorial elegance is displayed in full glory in his flagship emporium on the ground floor of Three on the Bund. Mirrored ceilings, walls and pillars add extra dimension to this slick, stylised space. There's an impressive skill to his men's and women's deconstructed blazers and an unmatched beauty about his evening dresses and other party wear, which amount to ¥5,000-¥6,000 (and upwards) per piece. If you're feeling particularly thrifty, it's well worth shelling out for some of his handmade chocolates and rich jars of jam and marmalade.

Mini Marvels

Explorer **Mini Visitors' Guides** are the perfect holiday companion. They're small enough to fit in your pocket but beautiful enough to inspire you to explore. With detailed maps, visitors' information, restaurant and bar reviews, the lowdown on shopping and all the sights and sounds of the city, these mini marvels are a holiday must.

317

651 Huaihai
Zhong Lu
Luwan
淮海中路651号
卢湾
🚇 *Shanxi Nan Lu*
Map p.436 B1 29

H&M 海恩斯莫里斯

5383 8866 | *www.hm.com*

The average 18 to 30 year old is more than likely to have something in their wardrobe from this Swedish high-street tycoon. Keeping a keen eye on the latest fads from the catwalk, H&M adapts each trendy newcomer for everyday wear. This ever-bustling fashion emporium stocks a range of styles, from casual jeans in up-to-the-minute colours and cuts for just ¥300-¥500 to plain-coloured tees and work shirts, as well as party dresses and accessories. Look out for limited-edition lines from international designers and celebrities. There is another H&M in Super Brand Mall, Pudong (5047 2196).

Lane 123,
Xingye Lu,
Xintiandi
Luwan
兴业路123弄
新天地
卢湾
🚇 *Huangpi Nan Lu*
Map p.436 C1 30

I.T

6336 5131 | *www.ithk.com*

While the city's sense of style remains a bit fuzzy round the edges, the I.T chain of boutiques, hailing from Hong Kong is a driving force in Shanghai's developing fashion scene (for those who can afford it). Each outlet across the city takes on its own character, right down to the artistic tableaux of mannequins occupying the window space or entranceways. The roster of designers include the ready-to-wear collections of Costume National, D-squared, Miu Miu and Stella McCartney. High fashion doesn't come cheap, however. Expect to drop a couple of thousand yuan in one trip.

200 Taikang Lu,
French Concession
Luwan
泰康路200号
法租界
卢湾
🚇 *Huangpi Nan Lu*
Map p.436 C2 31

Insh

6466 5249 | *www.insh.com.cn*

Insh embodies the spirit of Shanghai, a juxtaposition of old and new, and this small boutique sits fittingly at the entrance to Shanghai's artsy Taikang Lu. You'll find interesting and unique men's and women's casual T-shirts (¥200), shirts, jackets, sweaters, bottoms and accessories, rich with vibrant colours and prints. Head designer Helen Lee has made quite a name for herself on China's fashion circuit, and her talents shine through her funky, affordable items.

Room 225, Plaza 66,
1266 Nanjing Xi Lu
Jing'an
南京西路1266号,
恒隆广场
静安
🚇 *Nanjing Dong Lu*
Map p.430 A4 32

Joyce

6288 8383

For those who want to spend extravagantly in style, this decadent Hong Kong boutique is the place to do it. A large dome-shaped fixture resembling golden beeswax, laced with white fairy lights, is the centrepiece of a candy-apple red room, where you can find women's collections from Viktor & Rolf and Oscar de la Rente. Men are directed to the ante room, where they'll find the latest talked-about offerings from Yves Saint Laurent, John Galliano, and Yohji Yamamoto. Spoilt for choice, you can take a meditative moment in one of the gilted baroque-style armchairs, before digging deep into your bag for the credit card.

301 Guangyuan Xi Lu
Xuhui
广元西路301号
徐汇
🚇 *Xujiahui*
Map p.435 E3 33

Poesia

6448 3401

If you've spent any time in the US and you're familiar with children's designer clothing, you might recognise the label Poesia. Designer Chris Chang, who spent several years working for Prada, has now set up shop in Shanghai, selling her children's finery in addition to a colourful female collection – exclusive to Shanghai. In a fresh and funky space, done up with fuchsia pink floors, pink and green mannequins, floral wallpaper and a grand wrought iron dome, she merges a pastiche of Chinese and European traditions and styles. Verging on the theatrical, there are some unusual constructions here, which might be better suited to the catwalk than the sidewalk. Her flirty feminine dresses are a particular standout and remain the most wearable items in the collection (¥1,000 and upwards).

Shanghai Tang 上海滩

15 North Block, 181 Taicang Lu, Xintiandi
Luwan
太仓路181弄，
新天地
卢湾
🚇 *Huangpi Nan Lu*
Map p.436 C1 34

6384 1601 | www.shanghaitang.com

Tourists come here for what they consider to be tasteful mementos of China, while local residents look upon purchasing anything from this Chinese lifestyle brand from Hong Kong as a faux pas. Embodying the hackneyed 'east meets west' concept, traditional Chinese styles are taken and updated with electric colours and more daring cuts from the west. While the clothing is by no means suited to everyone's tastes, there are some smart-looking *qipaos* and slinky Chinese-print nightwear (¥2,500) made of finely spun silks that would make perfect gifts to send home.

Shiatzy Chen 夏姿陈

9 Zhongshan Dong Yi Lu
Huangpu
中山东一路9号
黄埔
🚇 *Nanjing Dong Lu*
Map p.431 E3 35

6321 9155 | www.shiatzychen.com

Taiwanese designer Shiatzy Chen ups the ante on your traditional Chinese apparel at this Bund establishment. Sole occupier of an austere colonial mansion along the Bund, this flagship store cultivates an air of extreme elegance. High ceilings, dim lights and dark wood set the stage for this designer's sophisticated range of Chinese-tinged men's and women's fashions in exuberant silks, satins and velvets. Her finely beaded clutch bags start at ¥5,000.

Shion by Choichangho

13 Taikang Lu, French Concession
Luwan
泰康路13号，
法租界
卢湾
Map p.436 C2 36

6467 1866 | www.choichangho.com

Another pioneer of the Japanese minimalist aesthetic, this Korean-born fashion maven turns out covetable, elegant designs. The narrow intimate floor space offers women's wear on one side and menswear on the other. Dresses and shirts hang twirling on hooks, suspended from the high ceilings. Good quality soft fabrics, simple cuts and solid colours are a running theme throughout her understated designs. Simple T-shirts go for ¥500 and men's suits range from ¥3,000 to ¥6,000.

Shirt Flag 杉旗帜

330 Nanchang Lu, French Concession
Luwan
南昌路330号，
法租界
卢湾
🚇 *Shanxi Nan Lu*
Map p.436 A1 37

5465 3011 | www.shirtflag.com

Shirt Flag has become an institution among the city's urban cool cats, and there are numerous branches across town. Founded by a small collective of streetwise Chinese designers, the Cultural Revolution is their muse. Propaganda images, slogans and ideals are splashed across plain coloured T-shirts (¥99), bags (¥199) and other accessories. New designs appear regularly, in addition to the timeless favourites. There is another branch at 336 Changle Lu (6255 7699).

Source

158 Xinle Lu
Luwan
新乐路158号
卢湾
🚇 *Shanxi Nan Lu*
Map p.436 A1 38

5404 3808

As one of the coolest-looking ateliers on the Xinle Lu strip, Source is hard to miss. This large industrially appointed space stocks must-haves from around 40 international streetwear and skater brands, including Addict (UK), Insight (Australia), Jesus (Holland) and Onitsuka Tiger (Japan). Its piece de resistance, however, has to be the onsite denim factory on the second floor, where you can get bespoke jeans for only ¥888 – tailored to your needs in terms of size, cut, wash, pockets and buttons. Within just 24 hours, you'll have yourself a pair of these personalised denims. There's also an exhibition space and cafe area, making it a sociable hang-out for the cool crowd.

Heels, Suzhou Cobblers style

266 Changle Lu
Luwan
长乐路266号
卢湾
🚇 *Shanxi Nan Lu*
Map p.430 B4 39

The Thing

6384 5207 | *www.thething.cn*

Hot on the trails of Shirt Flag is this neighbouring streetwear den – China's more affordable answer to Bathing Ape. Edgy graphics is The Thing's thing, inspired by technology, art, movies, music and Chinese traditions. The T-shirts cost around ¥100 and come in a range of sizes for girls and boys. There are also smart record bags, hats, belts and sweatshirts bearing their computerised images.

Floor 1, Hong Kong New World Centre, 300 Huaihai Zhong Lu
Luwan
淮海中路300号
香港新世界大厦
卢湾
🚇 *Huangpi Nan Lu*
Map p.430 C4 40

Uniqlo 优衣库

3308 0427 | *www.uniqlo.com*

Japan's answer to Gap, this is one of the few places in Shanghai where cheap doesn't compromise quality. Polo shirts, T-shirts, jeans, strappy tops, khakis and other no-frills items are available in a wide palette of colours and simple designs to suit all moods. To help you in the sizing process, there are conversion charts posted all over the shop. The comfy ¥300 jeans are indispensable, and if you find them to be too long, they'll alter them in-shop in 15 minutes flat. Now that's good service. There is also a Uniqlo in the Super Brand Mall in Pudong.

Floor 2, 18 Zhongshan Dong Yi Lu
Huangpu
中山东一路18号
黄埔
🚇 *Nanjing Dong Lu*
Map p.431 E2 41

Younik

6323 8688

Younik has a mission – to spotlight Shanghai's up-and-coming designers. Some of the city's best talents are given show space in this fancy Bund 18 boutique. Local names Jenny Ji, Zhang Da and Ling Ya Li all offer select items from their latest collections, vastly differing in style. Jenny Ji favours exotic floral prints while Zhang Da experiments with shape. Ling Ya Li specialises in striking couture gowns which are sure to pack a punch at the right occasion.

Shanghai Times Square 99 Huaihai Zhong Lu
Luwan
淮海中路99号大上海
时代广场
卢湾
🚇 *Huangpi Nan Lu*
Map p.431 D4 42

Zara

6391 0666 | *www.zara.com*

While Zara customers in Shanghai don't enjoy quite the same prices as Zara customers in Spain, this Iberian retail chain still has a lot to offer in the way of everyday and business wear for young adults and children. Versatile frocks for around ¥300 to ¥500 can be dressed up or down, depending on the occasion. The winter coats are a good seasonal investment, reflecting the latest fashions, and gentlemen can pick out one coordinating shirt-and-tie combo from the vast collection for every day of the week. There's another store at 1193 Nanjing Xi Lu (6279 3282).

Computers

Other options Electronics & Home Appliances p.321

Computers just keep getting niftier. Shell out for the latest PC on the market and it'll be out of date within six months, and unless you know your Compaq from your Sony, it's difficult to decide which brand to go for. You can shop for a new laptop or computer at Cybermart and Metro City (p.321), but you'll find that prices for big brands aren't much cheaper than in the US or Europe. Go with an idea about what you're looking for otherwise you'll quickly get lost in the myriad of stalls beckoning you from all corners. All international brands come with multilingual instruction booklets and a warranty, though how valid these slips of paper are varies from stall to stall. A lot of the major companies also have their own customer service centres in Shanghai to assist with any technical difficulties. You can purchase second-hand computers and printers on the fourth floor of the Modern Electronics City (p.321), including Macs.

Electronics in Hong Kong

Hong Kong is a hot spot for technophiles. Its range of tax-free electronics draws shoppers from all over. If you're coming from mainland China, expect to save at least 10% on cost. If you're looking to buy a new camera or laptop, Fortress and Broadway are very dependable stores and have branches across the city. Avoid tourist traps like Tsim Sha Tsui market. Instead, opt for the Wanchai Computer Centre and Mongkok Computer Centre, where prices are generally fixed. Everything you purchase should come with an international warranty; most DVD players are multi-regional. A copy of the Hong Kong Mini Explorer is the ideal companion for any trip to the SAR.

Electronics & Home Appliances

Other options **Camera Equipment** p.313, **Computers** p.320

With LCD display screens on virtually every street corner and talking at you in every taxi, not to mention hidden speakers blasting out music in the parks, it's clear that the city has fully embraced the world of technology.

To invest in this culture yourself, make your way to the concrete kingdom of Xujiahui, where you'll find malls, markets and stores overflowing with the goods. It's probably best to set yourself aside a decent chunk of time and be prepared for crowds. Head out of exit 10 of the Xujiahui Metro station and you'll be standing in the giant shadow of Metro City, one of Shanghai's best electronics spots. Small stores and counters are densely packed over several floors, offering computers, cameras, games systems, home entertainment systems, mobile phones, electrical appliances and all related accessories. You'll find all the brands imaginable under one roof.

There is scope for bargaining and, if you have a Chinese credit card, you can sign up for some great monthly price plans. Always check whether your DVD player or TV is multi-regional, so it will still work if you ever decide to take it back to your home country. Cybermart is another electronics market worth checking out before you secure a deal on an Xbox – it's much the same as Metro City in terms of products and prices. For all home appliances, Yongle and Gome are reliable Chinese stores. Irons, kettles and other smaller items can also be purchased for around ¥150 in supermarkets such as Carrefour (p.343) and Hymall (p.343).

If you're interested in trading your electronics or you want cheap or second-hand goods, try Modern Electronics City or Baoshan Lu Market. You run the risk of purchasing stolen or faulty goods, but you'll be paying a fraction of the price. They have everything from electric fans, refrigerators and shower heads to speakers, portable DVD players, PDAs, memory sticks and cards.

Electronics & Home Appliances

Bang & Olufsen	Unit 426, Plaza 66	6288 3378
Baoshan Lu Market	Baoshan Lu Metro Station	na
Best Buy	1065 Zhaojiabang Lu	400886 8800
Cybermart	282 Huaihai Zhong Lu	6390 8008
Gome	984 Changning Lu	5239 5962
Metro City	1111 Zhaojiabang Lu	6426 8393
Modern Electronics City	1255 Fuxing Zhong Lu	na
Pacific Digital Plaza	1117 Zhaojiabang Lu	5490 5900
Studio FH	520 Yuyuan Lu &	
	121, Lane 1520, Huashan Lu	6252 0082
Yongle	505 Guebi Lu	6229 5355

Eyewear

Other options **Sports Goods** p.337

Gone are the days when wearing glasses was a drag. Today, sporting a pair of specs or shades is a fashion statement. Nanjing Lu is full of opticians, selling a range of inexpensive and designer glasses and sunglasses. Most places will perform on-the-spot eye tests free of charge. Check out Eyes for modest frames ranging between ¥200 and ¥500. Trusty American chain LensCrafters has numerous outlets about town, stocking up-to-the-minute styles from a list of famous designers. You can pick up a pair of slick, dark-rimmed Prada frames for around ¥2,000.

For cheap Chinese eyewear and fake brands, there's an enormous underground glasses market at Shanghai Railway Station, at the junction between Metro Line 3 and 4. For basic prescriptions this market is fine, and frames and lenses together are around ¥150 to ¥300, but it's probably better to get tested elsewhere, particularly if you don't speak Chinese. The stalls are all competing so you can bargain for a good price. The fake frames aren't always on display, so ask the vendor to bring them out. The best thing is that the whole process takes only about 30 minutes.

Eyewear		
Aier Eye Hospital	1286 Hong Qiao Lu	6295 6699
Eyes	515 Huaihai Zhong Lu	5386 0110
LensCrafters	Hong Kong Plaza, 283 Huaihai Zhong Lu	5306 5265
Moscot	Raffles City, 268 Xizang Zhong Lu	6340 3029
New Vision Eye Clinic	Building 4, 197 Ruijin Er Lu	6437 7430
Paris Miki	500 Huaihai Zhong Lu	5382 4882
Redstar Optical Co	594-598 Huaihai Zhong Lu	5306 5069
San Ye Glasses Market	Exit 3, Line 3, Shanghai Railway Station	na

Flowers
Other options **Gardens** p.325

In a city where green space is scarce and the air is stale, flowers are the perfect way to introduce some of mother nature's touches to your home. There are a whole bunch of flower and plant markets in the city, along with a prominence of street side carts, all selling simple bouquets, cacti and other random house plants. Yongjia Flower Market is a convenient downtown market to get your floral fill. Since fresh flowers quickly die in smogville, fake ones are also popular and can be picked up at most of the florists and markets. For more exotic flowers and plants, there are a number of upmarket florists around. Rosa Gallica, for example, has beautiful potted orchids for ¥100 and larger potted plants from around ¥300 to ¥500.

Flowers		
Art Flower Shop	202 Wukang Lu	5466 8657
Gubei Flower Market	1778 Hongqiao Lu	na
Rosa Gallica	Ferguson Lane, 376 Wukang Lu, French Concession	2821 2241
Rose Theatre	284 Anfu Lu, French Concession	na
Secret Garden	347 Zizhong Lu, Xintiandi	6384 1605
Wanshang Flower & Bird Market	405 Xizang Lu	na
Yongjia Flower Market	406 Shanxi Nan Lu	na

1148 Changshou Lu
Jing'an
长寿路1148号
徐汇
Map p.428 C3 **43**

Caojiadu Flower Market 曹家渡花市
5239 7777
Probably the biggest and the best of Shanghai's flower markets is Caojiadu. Occupying three floors of an enormous warehouse, there's a redolent array of stalls and small shops offering floral delights. The first floor is devoted to freshly cut flowers and house plants – roses, lilies and carnations are the most common, in every colour imaginable. Small bunches start at around ¥10. Most stalls offer flower arranging services for you and will deliver on request (delivery fees start at around ¥15, depending on area). There are also stalls specialising in wedding bouquets. The second and third floors are for faking it, offering a range of plastic and silk flowers, some tasteful, some not. There's also an assortment of cheap home accents, outdoor plastic, stone and metal pots.

Food

Other options **Health Food** p.326, **Supermarkets** p.342

When the novelty of eating out every night wears off, you'll start to crave home-cooked food and, more than likely, a few western delicacies. Shanghai has an abundance of markets, western supermarkets and independent grocery stores. There are a large number of family-run businesses producing goods from their homelands, and some of the western restaurants also offer a portion of their culinary delights to go – try Italian restaurant Nuova Vita's famous pesto (350 Yushan Lu; 5860 8170). For those with a sweet tooth, City Shop (p.343) has a colourful collection of imported sweets and chocolates. It also has one of the best and most reasonable selections of cheeses, including big chunks of mature cheddar and creamy gouda. For stinky French fromage, stop by Cheese & Fizz (p.303) – but savour the taste; a 100g block of soft, ripe saint romain goes for around ¥60. Epicvre (p.304) also offers delights such as pate and fresh French bread. For delicious Greek honey, try Amphora (www.amphoraworld.com), and put its bi-weekly food tasting sessions in the diary. As for the best baguette in town, the Japanese bakery Yamazaki might just take the title (¥9).

Speciality Ingredients

Getting hold of special ingredients can often be difficult in Shanghai, especially in the centre. However, for those who fancy themselves as a bit of a pro in the kitchen, several services have been set up to help provide the necessary ingredients that might be more tricky to get. City Shop (p.343) is ideal for standard ingredients. The operators speak English and there is no delivery fee. Orders sometimes take time, so be sure to place it before 15:00 if you want to get it on the same day. Pines The Market Place (6262 9055; pines@online.sh.cn) is another great service, providing more unusual ingredients. Sushi fans will love the extensive fresh fish menu, and the bountiful tubs of Ben & Jerry's icecream will make everyone happy. For Gubei residents, Glenmore Deli is worth a call (6464 8665). It delivers deli items, placing particular emphasis on meats and cheese, with a 1% delivery fee. Alongside the delis and supermarkets, which deliver alcohol, specific outlets have emerged, designed to provide Shanghai homes with booze. Cheese & Fizz (p.303) as well as Summergate (6289 1919; info@summergate.com) offer lots of top end alcohol. Sherpa's (6209 6209; www.sherpa.com.cn) provides a good selection of wine, as well as 50kg bags of ice.

Tea

Street food shopping

When you think of traditional China, you might conjure up an image of paddy fields and tea. Until you arrive in Shanghai. While you won't find any rice paddies anywhere near here, there are enough leaves to quench any keen tea drinker's thirst. You'll find a number of specialist tea shops around town where you can taste special blends and even get a fancy tea set. Yu Garden is also a good area to find teahouses. For tea leaves en masse, visit Tianshan Market. You can spend the best part of a day wondering the stalls, inhaling the mixture of smells and accepting invitations to sample a variety of infusions. For most vendors it's a passion and they will wax lyrical about tea for hours over a cuppa, if you're prepared to listen. Find oolong, pu'er, black, red and green tea, as well as a range of herbal brews. Note that the bigger the leaves, the cheaper the tea. But for around ¥20 to ¥25, you can get a good week's worth.

House 18, 3338◀
Hongmei Lu
Gubei
虹梅路3338弄
古北
Map p.442 B1 **44**

Bastiaan Bakery and Konditorei 跋式面包咖啡屋
6565 8022 | www.hmxxj.com

This quaint German bakery is widely admired for its selection of home-baked loaves and cakes, including tasty rye and deliciously moist raisin bread. If you're in the area, stop in and try one of its wholesome sandwiches in the adjoining cafe area, and then order a couple of the home-made gourmet quiches to take back for dinner. It's also a good place to go for birthday cakes – enquire about the custom-made cake service. There's another outlet at 238 Baihua Lu, Pudong (3382 0203).

382 Dagu Lu
Luwan
大沽路382号
卢湾
🚇 *Nanjing Dong Lu*
Map p.430 B4 **45**

Fei Dan 飞蛋
6340 6547

This upmarket convenience store carries the slogan 'everything you need… around the corner.' Unfortunately there are not many corners – this popular expat haunt currently only has two locations. Upstaging the plainer offerings of Kedi, Lawsons and Alldays, you can find organic vegetables, imported cereals, sauces, pastas, oils, meats and herbs. Cast your eye over the shelves and you'll spot big tubs of Nutella, Betty Crocker cake mix, bags of Doritos and other sinful pleasures, normally quite hard to find on this side of the world. There's also an ante room stocking wines and beers, including bottles of Leffe and Hoegaarden. It will deliver to you on request too. The only thing lacking is a 24 hour licence. Fei Dan also has a store at 153 Anfu Lu (5403 6991).

415 Dagu Lu
Luwan
大沽路415号
卢湾
🚇 *Nanjing Dong Lu*
Map p.430 B4 **46**

Haya's Mediterranean Cuisine 哈雅地中海餐厅
6295 9511 | www.med-sandwich.com

Ask any American – if there's one thing that's difficult to find in Shanghai, it's good bagels. But Israeli-born Haya has a secret recipe, and people flock to her cafe to satisfy their cravings and sample her other freshly prepared Mediterranean dishes. In response to popular demand, she now has her own bakery down the road from her cafe. Her fluffy bagels come either plain, topped with sesame seeds or infused with garlic, and you can pick up a bag there or order a supply to be delivered to your home. In addition to her ¥4 bagels, you can also find laffa bread, pita bread, crusty loaves, mini Danish pastries and croissants straight from the oven.

130 Urumuqi Nan Lu,
French Concession
乌鲁木齐南路130号
法租界
🚇 *Hengshan Lu*
Map p.435 F3 **47**

HeLanFang 荷岚房
6415 4485 | www.stroopwafel.cn

This homely Dutch grocery store specialises in goodies from the motherland. Boxes of Douwe Egberts coffee (¥38-¥48), stroopwafels (syrupy waffles) and biscuits are some of the most desirable offerings. This is also the only store in Shanghai (at the time of writing) to stock one of China's few cheeses – the Yellow Valley cheese makers hail from Holland (www.cheeseinchina.com) and produce this tasty fromage in Taiyuan (Shanxi province). HeLanFang sells large wheels of the stuff for ¥140 – plain or peppered with cumin, onion and garlic.

17, Lane 181,
Taicang Lu,
Xintiandi
Luwan
太仓路181弄17号
新天地
卢湾
Map p.436 C1 **48**

Paul ▶ p.348
5306 7191 | www.paul.fr

With locations in both Pudong and Puxi, the French bakery chain Paul has successfully introduced the novelty of good bread to Shanghai. On top of its delicious baguettes and breakfast breads, both Paul locations offer cafe-style sandwiches and fresh-buttered pastries. All of the breads are baked inhouse without additives and preservatives, so if you plan on taking a loaf home, remember to enjoy it quickly.

**Building 1, Unit 3,
Lane 181, Taicang Lu,
Xintiandi**
Luwan
太仓路181弄
卢湾
🚇 **Huangpi Nan Lu**
Map p.436 C1 49

Visage 维萨吉
6385 4878

Enter into this patisserie and cafe and you could almost be in a *quartier* of Paris. A mixed aroma of chocolate, coffee and bread wafts over the threshold to greet you. Gourmet hand-made chocolates are on display behind one counter (¥9 per piece) and fine French tarts, mini cheesecakes and tiramisu (around ¥45) sit prettily at another. You can also pick up sweet brioche bread, buttery croissants and pain au chocolats for your continental Sunday brunch. There's another store at 808 Hongqiao Lu (6448 0393).

Food		
Amphora	429 Shanxi Bei Lu	5213 9066
Bread Talk	Raffles City, 268 Xizang Zhong Lu	na
Moon River Diner Deli	Building 5, 66 Yuyao Lu	5169 9156
Paul	199 Fangdian Lu	5033 5402
Paulaner Bakery	150 Fengyang Lu	6474 5700
Slice	99 Huaihai Zhong Lu &	
	688 Biyun Lu	6386 8588
Yamazaki	1618 Nanjing Xi Lu	6288 2792

Gardens
Other options **Flowers** p.322, **Outdoor Goods** p.332

Having your own garden is virtually unheard of in Shanghai, unless you're lucky enough to inhabit one of the beautiful old colonial villas in the French Concession. The most you can hope for is a balcony or rooftop, where you can nurture a collection of plants and a barbecue. For anyone with green fingers, the flower markets are full of indoor and outdoor plants. Rosa Gallica (p.322) also stocks a wide range of pruned offerings, ready to take pride of place in your space.

Gardens		
Casa & Co	741 Hongxu Lu	6406 1921
Dingtai Outdoor Leisure Furniture	502 Hongfeng Apt, Lane 511,	
	Wuzhong Lu	5477 0270
DTL Garden Furniture	18 Jinfeng Bei Lu	136 8170 1799
Greenspace	Building 31, Lane 205,	
	Chongqing Nan Lu	6386 5676

For keen chefs, growing your own herbs is made quite simple – you can pick up fragrant potted seasonings from Herb Store (p.330). Alternatively, get fake plastic palm trees and shrubbery from Caojiadu Flower Market (p.322) and plant them in your living room. If you have the space for furnishings, check out Art Decotek'selegant outdoor teak furniture sets (p.326).

Hardware & DIY
Other options **Outdoor Goods** p.332

For all your DIY needs, turn to western hardware giants B&Q. This large warehouse, out in the retail complex of Jinqiao, has all the quality tools you'll need to do the job yourself. It offers flooring installation, tiling, paints, tool kits and more. If getting there is a bit of a trek, there are also numerous stalls dotted around the French Concession selling various hardware tools and components on the cheap. Across town, Yishan Lu is pretty good, and you can call in at IKEA and House & Garden at the same time.

Hardware & DIY		
B&Q	393 Yinxiao Lu & 16 Huangxing Lu	6406 1921
House and Garden	198 Caoxi Lu	800 8203 3198
IKEA	126 Caoxi Lu	5425 6060

325

Health Food

Other options **Food** p.323

Healthy eating tends not to be a major priority among the locals of Shanghai, where signature regional dishes are swimming in MSG, fat and salt, but the influx of westerners in recent years has encouraged a greater awareness of the importance of eating healthily. Chinese restaurant Vegetarian Lifestyle has a small health food shop attached to each of its two Shanghai outlets, selling organic roasted chestnuts, green tea and a range of other health-conscious Chinese food products.

Organic produce is becoming more readily available, thanks to Shanghai Organics, which provides many of the city's supermarkets with fruit and veg. You can also order directly.

To balance out your diet with supplements, Watson's and other chemists (p.330) stock various vitamins and minerals, including herbal supplements. For further advice on how to change your diet for the better, contact a nutritionist at one of the city's international hospitals, such as World Link or Shanghai East Medical Centre (p.136).

Health Food		
American Garden	Delivery	6459 3694
The Herb Store	152 Fumin Lu, French Concession	5403 4458
Living House	Ground Floor, Zaozishu	
	850 Huangjincheng Dao	6209 3236
Shanghai Organics	Dayegong Lu	6249 2118
Vegetarian Lifestyle	77 Songshan Lu	6384 8000

Home Furnishings & Accessories

Other options **Hardware & DIY** p.325

Whether you have the cash to splash or you're on a strict budget, turning your new living space into a home is not a difficult task in Shanghai. Wander around the French Concession and you'll come across numerous poky dens, piled high with dusty second-hand furniture in traditional Asian designs, most likely plucked from the streets by the shop owners.

Browse the rows of shops along Yongjia Lu and Jianguo Lu for hidden treasures and turn off onto Jiashan Lu for cheap pots, pans, chopsticks and Chinese tableware. For slick kitchen accessories, check out what Italian restaurant Jimix at 607 Beijing Xi Lu has to offer in its front-of-house shop (6272 8969; www.jimix.com.cn).

Filippo Gabbiani is famed for his exquisite Venetian glass red chandeliers, which illuminate some of Shanghai's swankiest hangouts, and his shop in Bund 18 offers Venetian glass home accents in vibrant colours and bulbous shapes.

Rouge Baiser (p.311) has some of the softest linen tablecloths prettified with embroidery, and if you want custom-made bedding visit www.raerity.com. If you're going for futuristic, check out Pop Shanghai's kitschy furnishings and gizmos, and 100 Percent's ceiling lights and artsy mobiles (¥300 to ¥500). Art Decotek's vinyl wall stickers (¥600-¥2,900) will add some character, and on top of all that, there's always IKEA…

Home Furnishings & Accessories		
100 Percent	173 Fumin Lu	5403 9309
Ancient and Modern		
Furniture and Design	158 Xinle Lu	5403 5268
Art Decotek	Suite 103a, 3203 Hongmei Lu	6446 0865
Bo Concept	1160 Huaihai Zhong Lu	6431 7702
Calvin's Home	69 Huangjincheng Dao	6275 8936
Gabbiani	Bund 18, Floor 2,	
	18 Zhongshan Dong Lu	6329 9258
Hola Home Furnishing	Brilliance West Shopping Mall,	
	88 Xianxia Xi Lu	5219 1919
Homemart	7388 Humin Lu	6412 8169
Hu & Hu Antiques	8, Lane 1885, Caobao Lu	na
IKEA	126 Caoxi Lu	5425 6060
Inside Shanghai	387 Weihai Lu	6340 1386
Jingdezhen Porcelain		
Artware	1175 Nanjing Xi Lu	6253 0885
Pop Shanghai	Room 5018, Block 5, Bridge 8,	
	8 Jianguo Zhong Lu	5466 5108
Shanxi Art	33 Tai'an Lu	6466 2899
Simply Life	Unit 101, 159 Madang Lu,	
	Xintiandi	6387 5100

Chinese lanterns

Jewellery, Watches & Gold

Whether you're won over by precious stones and jewels or you'd rather settle for no-frills sterling silver, there's a bagful of options to feed your desires in this city. Since China is one of the biggest freshwater pearl producers in the world, they're readily available and cheaper than in other parts of the globe. A standard 16 inch string at the pearl market of Yu Garden should cost you between ¥30 and ¥40. There's also scope to shell out: Akoya pearls start at ¥2,000 and Tahiti or South Sea pearls are worth up to ¥40,000. Be ready to bargain and be especially suspicious of perfectly smooth pearls – real nacre should have a gritty surface, with slight nicks and blemishes. If you're unsure, go to a trusted store such as Fanghua Pearls.

Traditional gold jewellery can also be found in the numerous Lao Miao jewellery emporiums around Yu Garden. A simple 18 carat gold chain can be purchased for ¥500, and you can also buy platinum and jade.

For diamonds and gold, head to Cartier and Bvlgari in Plaza 66 (p.341) or a Tiffany & Co. And both Nanjing Lu and Huaihai Lu boast a litany of classic jewellers and watch shops, stocking familiar top-name brands. For something more unique, Filippo Gabbiani's blown Venetian glass (p.326) makes for very wearable pendants and necklaces. Jewellery-wearing males should check out the chunky, funky titanium, silver and steel accessories at JIP. There is also a host of costume jewellery boutiques on Taikang Lu. If you can't afford the bona fide Dior diamond studs or encrusted diamond Rolex, then fake it. There's a plentiful supply of decent phonies on the streets for a fraction of the price.

372 Nanjing Dong Lu
Huangpu
南京东路372号
黄埔
🚇 **Nanjing Xi Lu**
Map p.431 D2 50

Heng Dali Clocks and Watches 上海亨达利钟表商店
6321 2769

This is a trusty place to invest in a good watch and outlets can be found across the city. Go along and browse the numerous counters, trying for size before you make your final choice. All the usual suspects are available, including Cartier, Omega and Longines. There's also a small selection of house clocks, including austere grandfather clocks. Useful to remember is the in-house repair centre.

Room 1901,
Building 1, Lane 269,
Changning Lu
Changning
长宁路269弄
1号楼
长宁
Map p.428 C4 51

Kenjad
6210 4018 | www.kenjad.com

Need colourful, chunky costume jewellery to match your cocktail dress, or perhaps something smart and sophisticated for your custom-made ball gown? Consult French jewellery designer Raphaelle Muller. She runs a private business from her home, providing custom pieces and sets in addition to her own snappy collections. Breathing life into whatever interesting or unusual materials she can find, she works with quartz, turquoise, pearls, agate and metals. Prices vary, depending on material and detail, and appointments are necessary.

Yu Garden Bazaar beads

327

Suite 106, Lane 200,
Taikang Lu
Luwan
泰康路200弄106室
卢湾
🚇 *Shanxi Nan Lu*
Map p.436 C2 52

Marion Carsten

6415 3098 | www.marioncarsten.com

When it comes to fine jewellery, German designer Marion Carsten knows what a woman wants. She draws on both Asian and European styles and themes to create timeless, elegant designs ideal for the modern day woman, whatever the occasion. Pick from simple polished sterling silver chains to fancier dress pieces, laden with pearls or other stones. It's not just women that are catered for either – she also offers a smart range of sterling silver cufflinks.

Building 10,
Lane 210, Taikang Lu
Luwan
泰康路210弄10号楼
卢湾
🚇 *Shanxi Nan Lu*
Map p.436 C2 53

Not Just Silver

5465 2382

Of the bevy of boutiques stationed along Taikang Lu, Not Just Silver is one of the glitziest. And it does what its name suggests – its handmade silver jewellery from Indonesia is prettified with semi-precious stones, shells and wood. You can also cast an eye over glass cabinets containing elegant stones, blue topaz, mother of pearl and opal – offerings from a talented pool of designers from all over the world.

Jewellery, Watches & Gold		
Cartier	Bund 18, 18 Zhongshan Dong Yi Lu	6323 5577
Eastern Accents Jewelry	104 Tianzifang, 220 Taikang Lu	6473 4159
Ellen's Store	Floor 3, Pearl Village, 288 Fuyou Lu, Yu Garden	6311 4784
Fanghua Pearls	1008 Guyang Lu, Gubei	6209 4152
JIP	Lane 248, 51 Tian Zi Fang, Taikang Lu	6445 4479
Lao Miao	Yu Garden	6355 9999
Lilli's	Maosheng Mansion 1D, 1051 Xinzha Lu	6215 5031
pH7	342 Changle Lu	6253 8670
Polomec International Yuyuan Store	Room 35, Floor 3, 228 Fuyou Lu	6355 7505
Solomon Watch & Jewellery Co.	Corporate Avenue No.3, 333 Huangpi Nan Lu	5382 7209
Swarovski	856 Huaihai Zhong Lu	5403 8520
Swatch	839 Huaihai Zhong Lu	6445 8153
Tiffany & Co.	Jiu Guang City Plaza, 1618 Nanjing Xi Lu	6288 2748

Lingerie

Other options **Clothes** p.314

Lingerie shopping tends to become a chore for the average expat in Shanghai and you'll soon find that most women try to avoid it at all costs, due to a severe lack of larger sizes and brassieres with excess padding on offer. But don't give up straight away

Lingerie			
Eve's Temptation	368 Shanxi Nan Lu	6466 5766	www.eves.com.cn
Gujin	666 Huaihai Zhong Lu	na	www.sh-gujin.com
Titillate	345 Zizhong Lu	6311 2963	www.titillate.com.cn
Violette	House 67, Hongmei Garden, 2989 Hongmei Lu	138 1789 1002	na

– shop around a bit and you'll soon discover that the situation isn't as desperate as it might first seem. Department stores such as Parkson's (p.342) stock a good range of international underwear brands, including Calvin Klein and Triumph, and staff there will be happy to measure you up and search for something to fit. If you're after something that will provide a shock factor, check out Titillate's selection of stringy underwear and body stockings.

Bao.d 宝点

6437 6241

This little Chinese shop is a blessing for westerners, as it remains one of the few places in which you're guaranteed to find underwear to fit the curvy-figured. Bao.d stocks a jumble of international brands, most likely factory rejects, in a wide range of agreeable sizes, and it's just a matter of picking through the selection to find a style to suit. Bras range from ¥60 to ¥100, panties from ¥40, and it will usually cost less than ¥200 for a matching set. There is also a large range of men's boxers in big sizes from Calvin Klein, Next and other popular brands, tightly packed into trays and ranging from ¥30 to ¥40.

1294 Fuxing Zhong Lu, French Concession
复兴中路1294号，
法租界
Ⓜ Changshu Lu
Map p.436 A2 54

Bench Body 奔趣

5403 0026 | www.benchtm.com

Steer clear of Bench Body unless you're part of the petite posse, as there's no way you'll find anything to meet your measurements if you're anything other than tiny. It stocks a good selection of cheap and simple cotton undies for men and women, as well as padded bras, diamante motifs and playful designs for the trendy teens, all for under ¥100. This store has a home in most of the shopping malls and busy shopping streets of Shanghai.

1008 Huaihai Zhong Lu
Luwan
淮海中路1008号
卢湾
Ⓜ Shanxi Nan Lu
Map p.436 A1 55

Lingerie & Me

6253 3076 | www.lingerieandme.com

The boutique culture is big in Shanghai. Exclusivity is everything, and no more so than at this appointment-only lingerie boudoir (don't forget the credit cards). On arrival, remove your shoes, slip on a pair of fluffy slippers and enjoy a personal shopping experience. This decadent showroom is lavishly decorated in deep violet and shiny jet black, with resplendent chandeliers hanging from the ceilings. The selection of lacy panties, satin bustiers and silk slips is to die for – ranging from ¥1,200 to ¥3,000 for a matching set. Sonia Rykiel, Christian LaCroix, Janet Reger and Spoylt (a supposed favourite with the stars of Hollywood) are just some of the two dozen hand-picked designers from Europe and the US, most of which you're unlikely to find anywhere else in the city. And fear not, Lingerie & Me carries a decent range of sizes.

Room 28, Building 5, 1173 Nanjing Xi Lu
Jing'an
南京西路1173号
5号楼28室
静安
Ⓜ Nanjing Dong Lu
Map p.430 A4 56

Manifesto No. 4

6294 6880 | www.manifesto.com.cn

Strictly for men, this is underwear for the body-conscious urban male. This testosterone-fuelled shop is found underground next to the Shanghai Studio bar. It stocks a range of imported brands from the US and Australia, including N2N Bodywear and DT. There's something to suit all tastes, whether you're a Y-front or boxer man, and for the more adventurous, kit yourself out with some racy spandex thongs and other, even kinkier unmentionables. Prices for a pair of pants range from ¥100 to ¥300. There's also a range of undershirts and swimwear.

4, Lane 1950, Huaihai Zhong Lu
Luwan
淮海中路1950弄4号
卢湾
Ⓜ Hengshan Lu
Map p.435 D3 57

329

Luggage & Leather

Other options **Accessories** p.315

For cheap, trusty luggage, Carrefour (p.343) has the goods. You can pick up a suitcase big and sturdy enough for your two-week beach holiday for around ¥160 to ¥200. If you want to go a notch higher and invest in a full matching luggage set, including vanity case, laptop bag and trolley case, try luggage masters Samsonite. Prices range from around ¥800 to ¥1,500 for each piece.

Luggage & Leather		
Chou Niu	162 Shanxi Nan Lu	5404 3606
Handmade Leather Accessories	78 Ruijin Er Lu	5465 4098
Samsonite	221-223 Changshu Lu	6433 5644

Isetan (p.342) also carries a smart selection of travel bags. For those high-flying jetsetters wanting to travel business class in style, check out the designer offerings in Plaza 66 (p.341). Be wary of picking up knock-off luggage from the markets – it has a tendency to break easily.

Leather bags are a timeless staple, and genuine articles and accessories are a steal in Shanghai, if you know where to look. There are a number of small local leather dens stocking a range of soft satchels, handbags, shoulder bags and wallets, all very reasonably priced for around ¥400 to ¥1,000. You can also purchase leather slippers from many of these places. For leather with a label, try Fendi or Coach in Plaza 66.

Tree 一树皮革合作社

90 Shaoxing Lu,
French Concession
Luwan
绍兴路90号，
法租界
卢湾
🚇 *Shanxi Nan Lu*
Map p.436 B2 58

6433 2795

This family-run leather business has made quite a name for itself in Shanghai and now has four branches across the city. Each of its humble little outlets is jammed full of natural leather goodies, including bags (¥400 to ¥800), belts, wallets, pencil cases, notebooks and shoes – in a variety of agreeable shades from rich chocolate browns, to tan and burnt sienna. Tree also provides a custom-made service on all goods, ready within one week.

Medicine

Other options **General Medical Care** p.128

Pharmacies are not hard to find – just look for the green cross. They're on all the main shopping streets, in department stores and attached to major supermarkets such as Carrefour (p.343) and Hymall (p.343). Many are open 24 hours – they'll lock their gates at night, but there will always be someone inside to assist you if you knock on the door. Finding western medicine in Shanghai can be troublesome, however. China has strict rules on importing, so there's a limited choice.

Then comes the difficulty of translating the medicines into Chinese. Websites such as www.drdict.com will give you the written Chinese for common western medications. The pharmacy in Parkson's department store (p.342) also has an English-to-Chinese medical dictionary, which can be useful for reference. If you do succeed in finding what you're looking for, it may be more expensive than back home.

Medicine		
The Herb Store	152 Fumin Lu, French Concession	5403 4458
Huashan Foreign Expatriate Dispensary	12 Urumuqi Zhong Lu	6248 9999
Qunli Herb Store	396 Jinlin Xi Lu	6328 4352
Ruijin Hospital	197 Ruijin Er Lu	6437 0045
Shanghai Jinjiang Drugstore	856 Huaihai Zhong Lu	5404 7074
Shanghai No. 1 Pharmacy	616 Nanjing Dong Lu	6322 4567
Shanghai Wu Yao 24 hour pharmacy	Celebrity Garden, 201 Lianhua Lu	6294 1403
Watson's	787 Huaihai Zhong Lu	6431 8650
World Link Medical and Dental Centre	1376 Nanjing Xi Lu	6279 7688

Many pharmacists won't speak English so you may find it difficult to communicate your symptoms unless you speak Chinese. In this case, it may be better to go to see a doctor at one of the western hospitals or clinics (p.134). You can also order medication online through www.pharmacydiscounter.com (shipping is free), or alternatively, get your family or friends back home to post supplies to you.

You can, of course, give Chinese medicine a try. Herbs are a common cure for illness in China. The Herb Store offers a variety of herbs in the form of teas, essential oils and salts, with clear instructions in English and Chinese. Staff will suggest combinations to soothe or treat ailments or problems. A tin of tea leaves ranges from about ¥30 to ¥65, depending on the type.

Mobile Phones
Other options **Mobile Phones** p.124

Mobile phones say a lot about their owners these days, and you can text, talk and strut hands-free anywhere in this city – underground, above ground and up on the 88th floor of the Jinmao Tower. Contract phones are not commonly used here, unless your company provides you with one, as pay as you go is very cheap. You can purchase SIM cards in all the underground stations and many street stalls for as little as ¥50, depending on the number combination (Chinese people are very superstitious about numbers).

Xuijiahui is your best bet for a good deal on a cell, and with the stores so close together, prices are highly competitive. You can pick up a standard Nokia, Sony Ericsson or Motorola for around ¥400 to ¥600. For the ultimate in mobiles, check out Vertu in Bund 18, where models range from ¥250,000 to over ¥2 million. There's also a large market here for second-hand phones. Baoshan Lu and Modern Electronics City (p.321) are good options for this – you can score yourself a used Nokia handset in good condition for about ¥300.

Music, DVDs & Videos
Other options **DVD & Video Rental** p.118

Living in Shanghai, many people quickly find themselves out of the music loop. It's a place where intensive internet research and downloading is necessary to stay up to date with the international scene. Since the city's bootleg market is so widespread, there are virtually no official music and DVD stores. Morality issues aside, the good news is that pirated music is cheap and widely available out of suitcases, both on the street and in little stores. The bad news is that unless you're partial to Lionel Richie, or the latest Cantonese pop, you may not find what you're looking for.

You can find old jazz, blues and dance at Graceland Arts and Music, and some of the latest mainstream releases do make it here eventually. As for anything underground, you're pretty much out of luck. You can try tuning your ear into the sweet sounds of the *gu zheng* and other Chinese folk music, courtesy of Bandu. It sells a range of CDs from ¥70 to ¥100, and also stocks new age world music from Pakistan, Iran and other eastern countries.

The latest film releases make it here much quicker and may be out before they hit the big screen back home. DVD vendors can always be found on nearby street corners with suitcases packed full of Chinese and western titles. Most films cost

CDs for sale on the street

around ¥8 but the quality varies and it's usually luck of the draw. If it's a new release, it's worth waiting a couple of weeks for better copies to appear, as the initial ones have probably been filmed in a cinema. For the most reliable copies and a good selection of box sets, visit Kade Club on Dagu Lu. There's also a decent music store in the basement of Raffles City.

Music, DVDs & Videos

Bandu Café	Floor 1, Block 11, 50 Moganshan Lu	6276 8267
Even Better than Movie World	407 Dagu Lu	na
Graceland Arts and Music	261 Urumuqi Lu	6433 3466
Hollywood	25 Taikang Lu	na
Hollywood Hits	208 Nanyang Lu	na
Movie World	378 Dagu Lu	na

Musical Instruments

Other options **Music Lessons** p.264, **Music, DVDs & Videos** p.331

Heard the shrill sounds on the streets and at the opera and fancy investing in a piece of Chinese musical culture yourself? Purchase a *pipa, er hu* or another traditional instrument at Music Pavilion, and line up some music lessons at the same time. Alternatively, wander round the string of shops along Fengyang Lu, catering for the numerous budding musicians studying next door at the Shanghai Conservatory of Music. Here you can find an array of traditional Chinese and western musical instruments, as well as books. Another place for such things is Jinling Dong Lu. Invest in a shiny new saxophone from Yue Hai for around ¥3,500 to ¥5,000, or salivate over the shiny new Gibson guitars in Tom Lee Music. This first-rate basement store stocks an array of acoustic and electric guitars and drum kits for aspiring rock stars, as well as a good library of sheet music. If you've got a penchant for pianos, it also has row after row of glossy Yamahas, big and small, black and white. And you can give the ivories a test tinkle before you choose your new purchase. For pianists preparing for the concert hall, head to Steinway & Sons, where smart grand pianos stand gleaming in a line, some priced upwards of ¥1 million.

Musical Instruments

Best Friend Music	1788 Humin Lu	6412 8392
Binhai Pianos	1285 Fuxing Zhong Lu, French Concession	6472 7723
Music Pavilion	Building 5, 200 Taikang Lu	6445 8688
Shanghai Juntian Musical Instruments	370 Jinling Dong Lu	6328 8361
Steinway & Sons	399 Weihai Lu	6372 1568
Tom Lee Music	Building 1, 993 Nanjing Xi Lu	6271 4651
The World Voice Culture	433 Jinling Dong Lu	6328 1569
Yue Hai Music	268 Jinling Dong Lu	6326 0902

Outdoor Goods

Other options **Sports Goods** p.337, **Camping** p.241

Outdoor Goods

51 Hiking	741-9 Julu Lu, French Concession	5403 8608
Decathlon	393 Yinxiao Lu	5045 3888
Wild Camel	340 Changle Lu, French Concession	6258 6997
Yehuo	296 Changle Lu, French Concession	5386 0591

The great outdoors seem a distant prospect when you're trapped in the congested plains of Shanghai. But for those explorer types planning to escape for fresh air and greenery, there's a surprisingly good range of outdoor equipment available for hiking, climbing, camping and other activities.

Head down Changle Lu and you'll find a large number of independent stores well equipped for your escapades. There are also several places located around Shanghai Stadium in Hongkou. For the real North Face gear, look to Parkson's (p.342). For the fake stuff, head to the markets.

600 Lantian Lu
Pudong
蓝天路600号
浦东

Decathlon 迪卡侬

5030 7558 | www.decathlon.com.cn

Outdoor giant Decathlon should be your first cal – you'll find an outlet conveniently situated in most corners of the city. All your needs can be met under one roof, including waterproofs, fleeces and other outdoor apparel, and aisles are neatly stocked and labelled to make it easy to find what you're looking for. The store is like an indoor activity centre, buzzing with people erecting tents, kicking balls and testing out other equipment. Prices are very reasonable and you can pick up a tent for around ¥200. Novices should look out for its Quechua brand – two-second tents that'll make your weekend camping a whole lot easier. Decathlon also provides rental and delivery services.

Party Accessories

Other options **Party Organisers** p.409

Spend a Christmas in Shanghai and you'll be blown away by the Chinese love for decorations – the gaudier the better. Not only that, but many of these decorations stay put from Christmas throughout Chinese New Year and well into the spring months. To deck your halls with the same chintz, head to Yu Garden. The stalls outside the main bazaar are stocked to the ceilings with baubles, tinsel, fake trees, big plastic Santas and other festive paraphernalia. If you want to throw a party and are in need of a bouncy castle, a theme or entertainers, contact JT Kids Party. You can also purchase a range of small party accessories on its website (www.kidsparty.cn). For kids' costumes,

Party Accessories		
Fuyou Street Merchandise Mart	Huangpu	6374 5632
Holiday House	Changning	6447 7189
JT Kids Party	Various	5169 2146
Party Monster	Pudong	5882 4991
Shanghai Costume Shop	Huangpu	6322 2604
Star Kidz	Changning	139 1636 4621

contact Star Kidz. Holiday House has all you need for your pirate costumes, halloween outfits and other fancy dress. It's also fun wandering the stalls at Yu Garden and Qipu Lu for wigs and other gaudy accessories and clothing. For the real devil in you, check out Titillate's sexy costumes, where full PVC ensembles cost around ¥800 (p.328).

Perfumes & Cosmetics

In Shanghai's vanity-driven society cosmetics mean big business. All the major brands have counters in the department stores around town, including Clinique, Shiseido, Estee Lauder and Christian Dior. Parkson's and Isetan (p.342) are the only two places in Shanghai where you can find M.A.C. cosmetics. The bold palette of Anna Sui can also be found in Isetan.

If you're looking for high-street prices under ¥100, try Red Earth. Unfortunately, a lot of the brands only cater for Asian skin types and you may have difficulty finding foundations for lighter skin tones. Thanks to the roaring spa trade, you can also get your hands on other specialist imported brands following, of course, a luxurious facial or body treatment at one of the city's many spas.

Suite B1-b, Ferguson Lane, 376 Wukang Lu,
French Concession
Xuhui
武康路376号
B1-b室，法租界
徐汇
🚇 **Hengshan Lu**
Map p.435 E3 **60**

Ba Yan Ka La

6126 7600

Calling on the holistic properties of Chinese plant extracts and fruits, mixed with water from the fresh springs of the Yellow River in Tibet, this beauty boutique is focused on treating and pampering your skin and hair. It offers four product lines: goji berry, lotus seed, Chinese mulberry and liquorice, specially tailored for different skin types and ailments, as indicated in the shop. Products range from ¥100 for soaps peppered with goodness to ¥300 for body washes. The shop's gift sets make for a good birthday gift.

333

131 Maoming Lu
Luwan
茂名路131号
卢湾
🚇 *Shanxi Nan Lu*
Map p.436 B1 🏵

The Face Shop

www.thefaceshop.com

For fans of The Body Shop, this is your Asian substitute. This South Korean retailer produces its own fragrant bath, body, skin and hair care products for men and women. Tease your nostrils with fruity yoghurt face masks (¥25) that smell so sweet you'll want to eat them, and mineral-based body scrubs and aromatic lotions, all made from natural ingredients. There's also a bank of cheap good-quality cosmetics, ranging from ¥75 to ¥100. Whether you're going for au naturel or femme fatale, you're bound to find the right coating for your eyes, cheeks and lips. There are other outlets around town too (see the website for store locations).

629 Huaihai
Zhong Lu
Luwan
淮海中路629号
卢湾
🚇 *Shanxi Nan Lu*
Map p.436 B1 🏵

Sephora 丝芙兰

5306 6198 | www.sephora.cn

The award for Beauty Queen of Shanghai has to go to Sephora. Bright lights, loud music and a team of immaculately preened staff greet you with a basket as you enter. Here you'll find an incredible choice of cosmetics, including Yves-Saint Larent, Christian Dior and Clarins, as well as a range of reputed skin care products and bath goodies. The savvy staff are on hand to advise you in your selection, and makeovers are available on request. Sephora also has its own beauty line for men and women, including sweet-smelling bath bubbles and aftershave lotions, brushes, pocket mirrors and other accessories, all crucial to your beauty regimes. You'll also get to play and spray with one of the best and most up-to-date selections of fragrances in Shanghai. And if you can't rely on your own nostrils, perfume consultants are always on hand to help you sniff out a scent to suit.

787 Huaihai
Zhong Lu
Luwan
淮海中路787号
卢湾
🚇 *Shanxi Nan Lu*
Map p.436 B1 🏵

Watson's 屈臣氏

6431 8650 | www.watsons.com.tw

For basic bathroom and beauty amenities, you can rely on Watson's, 'Your personal store'. There's an army of outlets all over the city, stocking a slew of affordable western brands for beauty, hair and skincare, as well as a wide range of Chinese products. There are always promotions on cheap face-washes or moisturisers, and you can stock up on industrial-sized bottles of body wash, shampoos and conditioners to keep even the grubbiest explorer going for the next six months. Maybelline and other affordable make-up lines can also be purchased here.

Pet Licence

*All dog owners need a
licence. Get an
application form from
your nearest police
station. Applications are
processed every
Wednesday afternoon.
Return your completed
form along with photos,
and the fee, which is
¥2,000 (¥1,000 if you
live past the outer ring
road). Failure to pay the
fee results in a fine of up
to ¥1,000 (see p.119).*

Pets

Other options **Pets** p.119

A pet is not just for Christmas, it's for life – and sadly this is something the citizens of Shanghai need reminding of. You just need to visit one of the animal markets to see how poorly animals are treated here. Bunnies are cooped up in tiny cages and turtles sit piled on top of one another in small bowls. Purchase animals off the street with caution. It is advisable to take them to the vet immediately for their vaccinations, as many of them are diseased. You can also help the cause by temporarily fostering, or even adopting, a dog or cat from Second Chance Animal Aid – a non-profit organisation, focused on rescuing stray or injured cats and

Small dogs are popular pets in Shanghai

dogs and finding them a proper home (www.scaashanghai.org). It's also possible to find newborn puppies or kittens advertised on websites and forums such as www.shanghaiexpat.com.

There are, on the other hand, animals in the city who lead a life of luxury and get regular primping and preening at one of the city's upmarket pet salons. You can dress them up, curl their hair and even have them trained. A simple dog wash and shampoo starts at around ¥50.

468 Dagu Lu
Luwan
大沽路468号
卢湾
🐼 *Nanjing Dong Lu*
Map p.430 B4 🔢

I Love Pets – Shanghai Beautiful Life Pet Saloon
上海美育宠物沙龙
6340 1299

Pamper your pooches and feline friends at this fancy pet store. From giant cat trees to luxury dog beds, toys and gourmet food, there is everything you need to make them feel like kings in your home. Pet clothing is fast becoming a fad in Shanghai, and offers a wide selection of apparel from traditional *qipaos* and caps to cutesy dresses and T-shirts. It also has grooming/shampoo services for your pets starting at around ¥180 (prices vary according to breed), and provides a convenient pick-up service for busy pet owners.

Pets		
D&C Pets Service Centre	Jing'an	5169 6069
Paw No. 15	Changning	5254 0611
Pet Family	Xuhui	5403 1527
Pet Training Shanghai Circus Pets Training School	Zhabei	5665 6622
Second Chance Animal Aid	Various	139 1855 2425

Second-Hand Items
Other options **Books** p.312

Unlike other cities in the world, Shanghai has not yet caught on to vintage culture, so second-hand items are still relatively cheap, unless they're antiques. There's a large market for second-hand furnishings, and the French Concession is rife with humble shops, stacked to the ceilings with furniture, pottery, jewellery and other knick-knacks, in addition to the offerings of Dongtai Lu, Duolun Lu and other markets (p.343). Garden Books (p.313) holds a regular flea market on the last Saturday of every month, where you can purchase or exchange a jumble of used goods, including books, furniture, clothing, accessories and toys. It also organises a similar market at O'Malley's (www.shanghaifleamarket.com). Another treasure trove of unique finds is Shenhui Antique Exchange Centre (p.309), where you can offload unwanted goods and take home someone else's treasures.

If you want to donate your goods to a worthy cause, there are a number of local charities through which you can do it. Contact the Shanghai Community Centre (p.144) for details. You can also sell goods through www.craigslist.org, www.taobao.com and the classifieds sections of local English-language newspapers and magazines.

Shoes
Other options **Beachwear** p.311, **Clothes** p.314, **Sports Goods** p.337

When it comes to shoe shopping, the problem of sizing rears its ugly head once more. Shoes, like clothes, mainly cater to the slender and petite. Females will be hard pushed to find shoes over a US size 39, likewise for men with feet over size 44. For skate shoes and canvas slip-ons, point your feet towards Changle Lu. Most of the hip streetwear dens stock trendy collections of shoes. The strip of Shanxi Lu, between Yan'an Lu and

Huaihai Lu, is also renowned for cheap shoe shacks full of sequined, strappy heels during the summer and knee highs in the winter.

Shoes		
Chuan Kai Lai	14 Shaoxing Lu	6437 2457
Crocs	431, Floor 5, Cloud Nine Shopping Mall, 1018 Changning Lu	na
The Gloss	Unit 5, Floor 1, 123 Xingye Lu, Xintiandi	6384 1066
Nine West	6, 123 Xingye Lu, Xintiandi	6387 6811
Regal	222 Madang Lu	5382 8308
Stella Luna	858 Huaihai Zhong Lu	5219 9089
Strawberry Fields	Room 105, 6, 123 Xingye Lu, Xintiandi	6385 1558
Suzhou Cobblers	Room 101, 17 Fuzhou Lu	6321 7087
Wang Hand Craft	11 Xianxia Lu	6229 3916
Yapsh	601 Yongjia Lu, French Concession	2826 0143

Qipu Lu Market (p.344) has an entire basement devoted to men's, women's and children's shoes of all shapes and styles, from the latest fads to Chinese slippers and stilettos. Style gurus The Source (p.319) stock an excellent selection of international-brand trainers, including Double Identity, and you may be lucky with larger sizes. For limited edition Nike and other fashionable styles, check out Xintiandi's The Gloss. Stella Luna, Nine West and Strawberry Fields translate the season's trends for the girly girl and career woman, doubling up the snakeskin sandals with a matching bag. Expect to pay around ¥800 to ¥1,000 for a pair. And if you've always sought after a pair of cowboy boots, rodeo kids Yapsh have tan and rawhide leather Durangos for around ¥800.

If money is no object then a woman's shoe addiction can be fully satisfied at Hong Kong boutiques I.T and Joyce (p.318). We're talking Manolo Blahnik, Jil Sander and Prada here, to name a few. For those who want to dress to kill, local shoe designer Mary Ching has the heels to help, from ¥1,000 (www.marychingshanghai.com). For business types with cash to flash, Regal also offers a smart selection of nubuck and split leather lace-ups.

Custom Shoes

The simplest solution for frustrated feet is to get yourself a pair of shoes custom made. There are a huge number of local businesses around town that can produce a solid pair of shoes. Try Wang Hand Craft, which will design and mould shoes to your exact specifications in a range of soft leathers. You can take in a pair to be copied or show them magazine cuttings of this season's must-haves on the catwalk, which it will do its best to reproduce. A pair of sturdy men's leather dress shoes costs around ¥980, and boots start at around ¥1,480. For something more traditional, Suzhou Cobblers make very fetching silk Chinese shoes and slippers.

Souvenirs

Shanghai is infested with tourist tat and it doesn't take long to realise that the entire city is geared up for visitors and residents in search of mementos to take home. Yu Garden is the main hotspot, and if you devote a bit of time to sifting through the junk, you're sure to find some treats.

Dragon puppets

Stray from the touristy bazaars within the main complex and explore the surrounding streets. You'll find a medley of stalls, overflowing with Chinese-style fans, parasols, ceramics, teas, Mao mania and other random gift items, as well as some supposed antiques. Dongtai Lu and Jing'an markets are also worth checking out for your imitation collectibles and ethnic-style jewellery. For more upmarket tokens, wander down Taikang Lu and weave through alleys full of independent shops, specialising in various arts and crafts. Shanghai Tang (p.319) also cashes in on the traditional Chinese chintz, but in a more sophisticated manner, as do other upmarket gift shops around Xintiandi (p.347).

Sports Goods

Other options **Outdoor Goods** p.332

All the big-name sports brands are well represented in Shanghai. If you're a Nike fan, check out its multi-storey flagship store along Shanxi Lu, selling the latest models of trainers for ¥400 and up. Adidas has a competing store round the corner on Huaihai Lu selling a similar range of sporty togs. To see a broader range, the sports sections of shopping malls and department stores are always a good bet, stocked full of multi-brands and cheaper, lesser-known labels.

Sports Goods		
Adidas	915 Huaihai Zhong Lu	6472 8505
Decathlon	600 Lantian Lu	5030 7558
Nike	266 Shanxi Lu	5403 9051
Shantih	18, Lane 210, Taikang Lu	6472 7096
Y-3	Floor 2, 123 Xingye Lu, Xintiandi	6384 3844

Shanghai Times Square mall and Raffles City have particularly good selections to kit you out for the gym, the track, the court or the pitch. American NBA wear has even landed in Shanghai and is fast spreading its love to all corners of the city. Find it in Sports City at Grand Gateway, among other places. For trendy yogis, there's Shantih, a Taikang Lu boutique. Here, you'll find cute tank tops and comfy slouch bottoms in stretchy fabrics from Canadian brands Karma, Tonic and Breathe. You can also purchase your own yoga mat for ¥550.

If you really want to pack a punch at the gym, invest in some stylised sportswear from Y-3 (a collaboration between Adidas and Japanese designer Yohji Yamamoto), where a T-shirt alone will set you back a good ¥1,200.

If you're not interested in name-brand duds, Decathlon's (p.333) own line of sportswear is moderately priced and good quality, as is the rest of its equipment. It caters for almost every sport under the sun, from golf and football to tennis, swimming and climbing.

Stationery

If you like Hello Kitty, stickers and glitter, then you've come to the right place. There's virtually nothing but this type of stuff here, and cut-price stationery shacks are dotted about all over town. For other children's stationery supplies, for the home and school, go to Crayola (p.310). For grown-up pens and pencils try one of the many shops along Fuzhou Lu – here you can pick up a pencil case full of necessities for less than ¥100. For professionals in need of fountain pens and smart leather-bound organisers, check what the department stores have on offer. Isetan has collections of Parker pens starting at around ¥100, plus neat Mont Blanc nibs for more than ¥2,000. You can also find stationery in the supermarkets.

202 Wukang Lu, French Concession
Xuhui
武康路202号，
法租界
徐汇
🚇 **Hengshan Lu**
Map p.435 E2 65

Ipluso

5465 0931 | *www.ipluso.com*

Ipluso is one of the city's few designer stationery boutiques. You can also find the brand in numerous department stores around the city. The all-black colour scheme serves to accentuate the shop's colourful collections. Soft, handmade paper is peppered with silk threads and bound up in pads. It offers an assortment of leather or silk-covered notebooks for business or pleasure for ¥40, plus organisers, pen sets and leather accessories. The leaves of crinkled handmade gift wrap are beautifully constructed and reasonably priced. If you like what you see but want to add your own personal touch, Ipluso will be happy to customise its sets.

Tailoring

Other options **Textiles** p.339, **Souvenirs** p.336, **Clothes** p.314

Shanghai seems to be teeming with tailors, all poised with needle in one hand and scissors in the other, ready to stitch and sew to your specifications. Services vary, from the haute-couture approach of local designers, to the flurry of needle and thread activity at the fabric markets. It's worth leafing through that backlog of glossy magazines and saving the cuttings of your favourite designer looks before putting the city's tailoring skills to the test.

Local Chinese designer Lu Kun is one of the few individuals from this corner of the globe to have made a name for himself on the international fashion circuit. In addition to his pret-a-porter collections on display in the studio space (which you can have adjusted to fit your size), he offers haute couture gowns and a selection of one-off made-to-measure articles for both his male and his female customers. Haute couture gowns range from ¥20,000 to 60,000 and take around a month to finish.

For bespoke suits and shirts, try Dave's Custom Tailoring. A tidy suit here ranges from ¥4,000 to ¥20,000 (including two fittings), and shirts are priced from ¥360 to ¥1,200, depending on the material and detail. Brand-spanking new attire will be rustled up in just 10 days. There is also an 'invisible repairing' and alteration service.

For the ethereal *qipao* and other traditional Chinese garments, visit Qiong Zi on Julu Lu. This local female designer will make her rich silk fabrics fit you like a glove. Prices start at around ¥1,500 for a straightforward *qipao* and the work usually takes around one week, longer if detailed embroidery is required.

Silk King

Those looking for quality tailoring and a wide choice of fabrics from abroad, try Tony the Tailor, where you can choose from silks, wool blends, cashmeres and cottons to turn into that cocktail dress or matching tie and dress shirt.

If you need a quick fix – a stray hem re-stitched or a fold taken in – there's a medley of alteration and tailoring shops around the French Concession.

Alternatively, join the mob of locals and tourists at the fabric market, where you'll find a tribe of tailors ready to serve you. Take along a magazine cutting of your desired dress or suit and they will do their best to copy it. It's luck of the draw whether you come away happy or not. Fees range from around ¥40 to ¥60, plus the cost of fabrics, and the job normally takes up to a week.

A word of caution here though: if your new clothes require buttons, zips or other trimmings, be clear in your instructions before the work begins. If you not, you could well find that the tailor has used some pretty innovative improvisation, such as leopard print fur trim or heart-shaped buttons.

Tailoring		
Dave's Custom Tailoring	6, Lane 288, Wuyuan Lu	5404 0001
Lu Kun	69 Lan'an Lu	6378 2120
Qiong Zi	620 Julu Lu	6289 2372
Tony the Tailor	684 Changle Lu	5403 0335

Textiles

Other options **Tailoring** p.338, **Souvenirs** p.336

With the army of tailors in this city must come an abundance of fabric. For silks, go to Silk King. It hosts a wide selection priced at around ¥70 to ¥90 per metre, depending on the width. There's also a lesser-known fabric market on Dongmen Lu (Shanghai Shiliupu Clothing Material Market) if you can't find what you're looking for at the city's main fabric emporium.

Shanghai South Bund Fabric Market
上海南外滩轻纺面料市场

399 Lujiabang Lu
Huangpu
陆家浜路399号
黄埔
🚇 *Nanpu Bridge*
Map p.437 F2 66

Whether you want to spruce up your sofa with new upholstery, need curtains for your shower or fabric for a summery frock, you'll be deliberating a long-time over the rainbow of rolled up materials in this 10,000 square metre market place. Unlike the city's other markets, you're spoilt with air conditioning and escalators, which means you can lose yourself comfortably for hours. There is no method to the arrangement of stalls, so it's just a matter of trawling the endless posts, browsing, touching and pricing up fabrics. There are also ready-made garments for sale which the tailors will be happy to adjust to your measurements. The quality varies from stall to stall but it is possible to find some good silks, cottons, linens and corduroys. Vendors will happily charge per metre with tailoring fees on top, so be hard in your haggling. ¥25 to ¥40 is a good price per metre. You can also find buttons, ribbon trims and other garment trappings.

Textiles		
Shanghai Shiliupu Clothing Material Market	168 Dongmen Lu / 50 Zhonghua Lu	na
Silk King	1266 Huaihai Zhong Lu	6282 1533

Toys, Games & Gifts

Who knows what children were amusing themselves with before the days of Toys R Us? This giant toy store is like a playground every day of the week – watch where you're going or you'll end up tripping over half-assembled puzzles in the aisles and having head-on collisions with toddlers in toy cars. Adults secretly love this place as much as the kids. It has by far the best selection of western merchandise in town. There's also a vast choice of cheap name brand toys (including Barbie, Lego and Play-Doh) at Nihong Kids' Plaza (p.311).

For budding boy racers and their fathers, pick up model toy Ferraris or Lego Ferrari sets at the Ferrari Store, or opt for a classic model train set from Bachmann for ¥400. For classic wooden toys and puzzles that don't require batteries, head to T.O.T.S. And adults with a penchant for toys can start up a collection of old-school windup toys, robots and dolls, thanks to Loomoo and the numerous figurine shops

339

down Changle Lu. Independent Taiwanese store Jindou 108000 will also appeal to the young at heart, with playful gadgets such as stuffed Japanese-style toys that double up as radios for ¥360.

Toys, Games & Gifts

Bachmann Train Store	100 Xiangyang Bei Lu, French Concession	6256 5012
Ferrari Store	188 Madang Lu, Xintiandi	5382 9806
Jindou 108000	Unit 102, Building 4, Lane 115, Jianguo Zhong Lu	136 8167 5557
Loomoo	201 Nanchang Lu	6437 2562
T.O.T.S.	77 Ruijin Er Lu	5382 1109
Toys R Us	Super Brand Mall,168 Lujiazui Xi Lu	5047 6838

Wedding Items

Weddings mean big bucks in Shanghai – a low-key affair would be unorthodox. And since China is strictly an atheist country, it's all about the party. Ceremonies here are lavishly staged affairs and a hodgepodge of traditions. To ensure the big day runs like clockwork, call upon Shanghai Richmond Wedding Planner (5637 6256). It will organise the food, venue and MC, as well as the sedan chairs, lion dances and any other absurd requests you may have.

It's the norm for the bride and groom to appear in a range of costumes throughout the day. Tianyi Plaza is devoted to kitting out brides and grooms, whether you want a virginal white puffball dress, a slinky peach number or a purple velour suit. There are also a select number of tailors specialising in attire for the special day along Maoming Lu, particularly good for traditional Chinese styles. For the frothy white frock of your dreams, there's no better person to turn to than celebrated bridal wear designer, Vera Wang at The Link. Her ethereal dresses are every girl's dream, but to turn this dream into a reality be prepared to part with ¥30,000, up to ¥100,000. Buy in shop or order from New York (which can take up to six months).

Alternatively, you can commission local celebrated designer Jenny Ji of La Vie to make your wishes come true.

Wedding Items

Jennifer Wedding Shop	118 Ruijin Er Lu, French Concession	6466 0489
Jenny Ji – La Vie	Room 307, 696 Weihai Lu	6249 0162
The Link	Pudong Shangri-La, Tower 2, 33 Fucheng Lu	6882 8888
Royal Photo	532 Fuxing Zhong Lu, French Concession	5306 2117
Tianyi Wedding Plaza	757 Renmin Lu	6355 6698

To complete the picture, it's customary for the love-struck couple to make a photo album prior to the big day – and this is where the city's numerous photo studios come in (many of which you'll find along Huaihai Zhong Lu). Shanghai Royal Photographic Art Salon is one such studio with an extensive costume cupboard and a choice of fairytale backdrops. Virtually any image can be conjured up, whether the couple want to be kings and queens of the castle, or whispering sweet nothings under a willow tree. An album there costs around ¥3,500, including costumes, makeup and a large framed portrait photograph. Wedding dresses and suits can also be hired for 24 hours for around ¥2,000, or purchased for ¥3,000 to ¥5,000.

As for the mandatory gift-giving, don't expect to receive a wedding list. The giving of *hong baos* (red envelopes stuff with cash – the red element symbolises good luck) is most widely practised.

Places to Shop

Whether you're a mall rat, a boutique hopper or a market hound, Shanghai can quench your shopping thirsts. In fact, you could spend days on end exploring the shopping options and areas in the city. Any weekend could see you hunting down bargains with the masses, pottering down delightful alleys, window shopping or peacefully strolling round one of the city's deserted high-end malls.

Shopping Malls

Considering the high count of malls in the city, it would seem that Shanghai is pretty keen on this way of shopping. Large malls rub shoulders with one another down Nanjing Xi Lu, all competing to be the biggest and the best. Another giant cluster crying out for custom sits around People's Square. They're all overflowing with international and Chinese brands, and you'll find the same old shops again and again. In the summer months, the best place to be in the city is one of the clean, airy indoor shopping complexes – a welcome respite from the humidity outside.

This said, the mall culture hasn't taken off here the way it has in other countries around the world. Most of Shanghai's shoppers prefer to shop elsewhere and the most heavily populated areas of any given mall are usually the foodcourts. While Cloud Nine is tipped as Shanghai's largest mall, many spaces are still unoccupied and most people only frequent it for the Carrefour (p.343) in the basement. Citic Square and Shanghai Times Square provide a good balance of shops and brands.

1266 Nanjing Xi Lu
Jing'an
南京西路1266号
静安
🚇 *Nanjing Xi Lu*
Map p.430 A4 67

Plaza 66 恒隆广场

3210 4566 | *www.hanglung.com*

For a tranquil mall experience, arm yourself with your credit cards (plural) and head to Plaza 66. Be sure to dress for the occasion, in order to fit in with the immaculate environment and clientele. There's no fake Louis Vuitton to be had here. Instead, find shiny marbled floors, a string quartet in the foyer, tasteful fake palm trees and floor after floor of designer showrooms.

Find the cutesy Japanese designs of Anna Sui, in an intimate boutique outfitted in her signature purple and black, the classic stripes from British designer Paul Smith and the urban styles of DKNY. St. Dupont, Chanel, Marni, Lagerfeld and other equally admired designers all have a place in the plaza. Windows are sparingly but stylishly dressed and there's not a bag or hanger out of place. If all this is out of your reach, circulate the mall, notebook in hand and then head to the fabric market with your detailed sketches.

Super Brand Mall

Citic Square

Raffles City

341

268 Xizang Zhong Lu
Huangpu
西藏中路268号
黄埔
🚇 *People's Square*
Map p.430 C3 68

Raffles City 来福士广场

www.rafflescity-shanghai.com

If you're a mall devotee, there's no doubt that Raffles City will become your second home. This is arguably the best in Shanghai and one of the few that's always buzzing with happy shoppers. Set over seven floors, there's everything you could possibly want under one glassy roof: a foodcourt and numerous restaurants, a Watson's, a gym, a smattering of small stalls and a bevy of brands. All fashions are covered, from the cheap teen trends in Only, to the western designs of French Connection, Mango and Sisley. There's also Calvin Klein, Evisu, Uniqlo and Levi's. Go to Bench Body for underwear, Red Earth or The Face Shop for cosmetics and ride the escalator high to find a wide choice of sporting goods and electronics. Reward yourself for a hard day's shopping with a yummy Beard Papa from the foodcourt in the basement.

168 Lujiazui Xi Lu
Pudong
陆家嘴西路168号
浦东
🚇 *Lujiazui*
Map p.431 F2 69

Super Brand Mall 正大广场

6887 7888

This super mall has something for most shoppers and remains one of the busiest in Shanghai. Go on a weekend and find a steady stream of people flowing in and out, weaving up and down the escalators, resembling a mass movement of lemmings. This mammoth retail haven is the heart and soul of Pudong's shopping, and it's easy to get lost in the sprawl. Find H&M, Zara, Esprit, Sephora, Toys R Us, a supermarket, bookshops, sports departments and a whole lot more. One round of this place and you'll be exhausted.

Shopping Malls		
Citic Square	Jing'an	6218 0180
Cloud Nine Mall	Changning	6115 5555
Grand Gateway	Xuhui	6404 0111
Infiniti	Luwan	na
Jiu Guang City Plaza	Jing'an	3217 4838
Maison Mode	Luwan	na
Shanghai Times Square	Luwan	6391 0691
Westgate Mall	Jing'an	6272 1111

Department Stores

The glory days of Shanghai's original department stores, like the Shanghai Friendship store, are over. In a city where tree-lined streets are overflowing with shopping opportunities, they don't quite cut it, although there are still plenty around. Nanjing Dong Lu has a department store on every block and these are good places to multi-task. You can do your toiletry, sports wear, home appliance and food shopping all in one spot. Two of the best in terms of cosmetics and all-round amenities are Parkson and Isetan, and Pacific is a good spot for sportswear and electronics. Parkson also has a popular supermarket in the basement, selling a decent range of western and Chinese fare, as well as a good choice of underwear and home appliances by recognisable brands, including Braun, Electrolux, Tefal and Philips.

Department Stores	
Hong Kong New World Department Store	6431 0118
Hualian Department Store	6322 4466
Isetan	5306 1111
Itokin	6351 2400
Nextage	5830 1111
Pacific	5306 8888
Parkson	6415 8818
Shanghai Friendship Store	5308 0600

Supermarkets

Ask any foreigner or local where the best place to stock your shelves for the next six months might be, and they'll be united in their response: Carrefour. This famous French hypermarket is firmly grounded in Shanghai with 11 locations across the city. It's one of the cheapest places to get your fresh, tinned and dairy produce for western and

Chinese tastes alike. People come away with trolleys full. It also boasts one of the largest and cheapest selections of wines and spirits.

In addition to food and drink, you can find an array of other amenities here including clothing, home appliances, furnishings and leisure. Less established yet hot on Carrefour's heels is Wal-Mart. There are currently only two locations of this American giant in Shanghai, but it's a close competitor in terms of selection, price and quality – so it's another good spot to stockpile kitchen cupboard fillers. For western indulgences and odds and ends, City Shop is full of imported goodies, but all are noticeably pricier than in the larger chains. Another convenient city supermarket is Pines, which offers a great selection of cold cuts, Australian beef and lamb.

Supermarkets		
Carrefour	Various Locations	800 620 0565
City Shop	Various Locations	6215 0418
Freshmart	Jing'an	3217 4838
Hymall	Various Locations	6249 7929
Lotus Super Centre	Various Locations	5047 0648
Pines	Various Locations	5226 4137
Wal-Mart	Pudong & Yangpu	5094 5881

Markets

If you enjoy the thrill of banter and bargaining in the hustle and bustle, you're in luck. Shanghai has a market for everything, from clothing and antiques to electronics, fabrics, flowers, glasses and even birds.

Antique Markets

The word 'antique' is loosely applied to this category, as you'll be lucky to find anything genuine among the ceramics, pocket watches, laughing Buddha statuettes and other curios you'll see for sale. But it you're not averse to replica trinkets, there

Dongtai antiques

are some good finds among the fakes. You'll come across the same old stuff in all the stalls, so shop around, and haggle hard (see Bargaining, p.302). Cang Bao Antiques Building is a popular spot at weekends, when its top two floors are occupied by rural sellers from the north, flogging everything from teapots to *mahjong* sets at less than ¥100. For junk collectors and those looking for gifts to take home, Yu Garden is flooded with knick-knacks, from traditional decorative parasols, to 1960s and 70s cigarette ad prints and tea sets.

Clothing Markets

If quality isn't a concern, and you don't like to be seen in the same thing twice, the clothing markets are for you. It's possible to find bagfuls of cheap throwaways – spend just ¥300 and come away with a good few T-shirts, two pairs of shoes, a dress and some matching accessories. Qipu Lu is the biggest and best of the bunch, brimming with the latest fashions, fake goods, sparkly accessories, trendy bags and a whole basement devoted to shoes (p.344). Of course, there's a lot of stuff you wouldn't be seen dead in, so a bit of rummaging is required. And don't forget to barter.

Since these markets are mainly frequented by a younger, local clientele, there's little to buy for the over 35s, and there's a lot more choice for women than for men. Many vendors won't let you try the clothes before you buy, but if it's just a matter of ¥20, you may as well take the risk. The D-Mall and Hong Kong Shopping Plaza under People's Square offers a similar selection of goods, but prices tend to be fixed and there's less scope for bartering.

Markets

Cang Bao Antiques Building	457 Fangbang Lu	Huangpu	Antiques
D-Mall & Hong Kong Shopping Plaza	People's Square Metro	Huangpu	Clothes
Dongtai Lu Antiques Market	Dongtai Lu at junction with Xizang Lu	Luwan	Antiques
Hongqiao Market	Lane 2818, Hongmei Lu	Changning	Wet Markets
Jing'an Temple Jewellery and Curio City	1829 Beijing Xi Lu	Jing'an	Antiques
Jingan Temple	Beijing Xi Lu	Jing'an	Clothes
Qipu Lu	Qipu Lu, near Henan Lu	Zhabei	Clothes
Wuzhong Wet Market	328 Urumuqi Lu	Xuhui	Wet Markets
Xianle Wet Market	36, Lane 767, Wanhangdu Lu	Jing'an	Wet Markets
Yu Garden Bazaar	Fuyou Lu and Henan Lu	Huangpu	Antiques

Fake Markets

No matter how hard the authorities try, they can't seem to eliminate fake goods. With the demise of the old Xiangyang Lu fakes market, vendors had to find themselves new homes – and now there are two markets devoted to fake clothes, jewellery, watches, shoes and bags. It is not unheard of to find an exact copy of a Balenciaga bag for ¥100 or less. Some items could almost pass for the real thing if it weren't for a misspelt logo, while other stuff looks so ridiculous you'll cringe. Check your zippers, seams and stitches before you part with any cash, as you won't have much luck returning them. You can also find a lot of stuff at Qipu Lu.

Wet Markets

The supermarkets make life a lot easier when it comes to food shopping, but once you've visited your local wet market, the packaged fruit and veg in stryofoam trays you've become accustomed to will start to hold less appeal – and that's before you even consider the difference in price. Next to the mountains of fresh, ripe fruit and vegetables, you can also find fish and meat, dead or still breathing, suitable for both western and Chinese cooking.

Huaihai Lu

Areas to Shop

Wherever you're based in Shanghai, it's unlikely you'll be very far from a shopping area or market (although inhabitants of the depths of Pudong may be an exception). Indeed, Puxi's residents are spoilt for choice. Xujiahui may be one of the most unsightly downtown areas of Shanghai, with its towering asphalt structures casting shadows over shoppers, but it attracts swarms of retail-hungry residents to its malls, department stores and selection of electronics. The stately colonial stretch of the Bund now houses upmarket retail and leisure complexes, such as Three on the Bund (6323 3355; www.threeonthebund.com) and Bund 18 (6323 8099; www.bund18.com), where you can find Hugo Boss, Dolce & Gabbana, Cartier, Ermengildo Zegna and other tidy boutiques. For Pudongers, Lujiazui and Jinqiao are two flourishing shopping centres to explore.

French Concession 法租界
Map p.436 C1

One of the most desirable areas to live and shop in Shanghai, the French Concession is a network of peaceful tree-lined streets and old European-style houses inhabited by residents, restaurants, cafes, bars, independent boutiques and little shops. Walk the length of Nanchang Lu for funky clothing boutiques, where you'll find one-off treats for the wardrobe and home. Changle Lu, Julu Lu and Xinle Lu are hotbeds for local designers keen to enter the market with their creative merchandise, from clothing to furniture and jewellery. Check out Mars Man's streetwear (167 Xinle Lu; 6415 5328) and the eclectic mix of hippy, retro and urban styles and smoking implements in Sideways (144 Xinle Lu). Fuxing Lu, Jinxian Lu and Shaoxing Lu are also great for window shoppers and spontaneous purchases, and Wukang Lu is raising a cluster of shops down Ferguson Lane (376 Wukang Lu). Pop into Bliss (6126 7626) for funky, colourful home accents.

Huaihai Lu 淮海路
Map p.430 C4

Start at the junction with Changle Lu and walk east down Huaihai Lu, ending at Shanghai Times Square (near Xizang Lu). This busy street will send shopping fans into a frenzy with its multiple brand-name outlets, department stores, jewellers and sunglasses shops. You won't be able to resist sneaking in for a peek. And at the end of it all Times Square boasts a Zara, Max Mara, City Shop, Chaterhouse bookshop and Slice Deli.

Nanjing Lu 南京路
Map p.431 D2

Nanjing Dong Lu is one of Shanghai's oldest and most famous shopping streets. The pedestrian section is still a prime tourist spot, mainly for its dazzling illuminations and billboards, but in terms of shopping it is no longer the best area as it is mainly dominated by lesser-known Asian brands and department stores. There is, however, a large Uniqlo and Giordano's flagship store (p.314), which will probably tempt you inside, plus numerous opticians and jewellers. The west end of the street (Nanjing Xi Lu) is more interesting than its other half. You'll find a series of smart glossy malls, including Plaza 66 and Citic Square (p.342), as well as designer watch shops, high-street names such as Zara and Mango (p.314) and a market full of gift-worthy fake goods.

Map p.436 B2

Taikang Lu (Tian Zi Fang) 泰康路（田子坊）

Independent designers rule the roost in this maze of alleys. Budding artists and designers are all keen to get in on the action and, as such, shops are there one day, gone the next. The area attracts a mixed clientele of curious tourists, locals and an arty set of foreigners. It's the perfect spot for an afternoon of leisurely shopping and cafe crawling, while showing your support for the local creative scene. And despite the growing commercial presence, the area still retains its old charm. Nuzi is the only shop in town to celebrate the art and culture of New Zealand, offering alcohol, wines, artwork and furnishings from its motherland (30, Lane 248; 5465 3245).

For a taste of the spirited arts and crafts of Xinjiang, browse the hand-embroidered silk pillows and camel's wool prayer rugs (¥3,000) at Geometry (49, Lane 210; 5465 2860). For fresh, vibrant lifestyle accessories, have a poke about in Vervia (46, Lane 248; 5466 7832). Whether you dig retro patterns, exotic prints or slick stainless steel in your home, you'll find it all in this colourful boutique.

Map p.436 C1

Xintiandi 新天地

6311 2288 | www.xintiandi.com

This cluster of storied *shikumens* has been given a facelift to make way for a new business-driven and image-conscious Shanghai. While Xintiandi is a highly stylised tourist haunt, there are a number of independent shops worth a look in, as well as a modest mall in the south block. Lifestyle emporium Simply Life (159 Madang Lu; 6387 5100) has some great tableware inspired by its sister restaurant Simply Thai, just next door. Annabel Lee embraces Chinese tradition in her hand-made, embroidered accessories and home decorations (6320 0045). And Jiang Qiong Er (Xintiandi) experiments with nuts, bolts, screws and other industrial materials in her eye-catching jewellery designs.

Tian Zi Fang

Nanjing Lu

347

PAUL

Maison de qualité
fondée en 1889

Thumb Plaza Store (Inside Thumb Plaza)
Ground Floor, Number 8, Lane 199, Fangdian Rd.
芳甸路199弄8号1楼（大拇指广场内）

Dongping Store
Ground Floor, Number 6, Dongping Rd.
东平路6号1楼

XinTianDi Store
Unit 01, Building 17, Lane 181, Tai Cang Rd.
太仓路181弄，17号楼，1座

Portman (Shanghai Center) Store
Unit 118, No.1376, West Nanjing Rd.
南京西路1376号118室

Red House Store
Ground Floor, Number 845, Huaihai Zhong Rd.
淮海中路845号一楼

Going Out

Going Out

Going Out

There are few cities that provoke the same reaction as the mere mention of Shanghai. There are those that live here, the people who've visited, and the ones who want to come. Shanghai is hot and the word is spreading. Yet this sprawling city, with all its art deco charm and disappearing back alley life, isn't known for its culture. Shanghai is, in Chinese history terms, a toddler. Lacking the historical gravity of Beijing and the mercantile clout of Hong Kong, the town that was once referred to as 'The Whore of the Orient' has had to rely on her other assets to get noticed. And two things that make this city shine on the international scene are its frenetic nightlife and impressive range of restaurants. Shanghai never sleeps; and she rarely stops eating either.

The dining scene here can be split into two camps: local and foreign. Local eateries run the gamut from miniscule, street-side shops slinging soup dumplings to Baroque palaces selling seafood at higher prices than any three-star Michelin temple would dare charge. Certain Chinese restaurants cater to expatriates, with slick decor, piped-in jazz music, English menus and French wine lists. But they are an exception to the rule; and as a rule the best food is found where the Shanghainese are. The foreign food scene has positively exploded in the past five years, and today features a jaw-dropping variety of international cuisine that was the stuff of dreams for expats living here a decade ago. And the nightlife has followed suit. When navigating the bar and club scene, it's difficult to comprehend that just 20 years ago the only place to enjoy a beer was in the comfort of your own home, or perhaps the dingy confines of a neglected restaurant. Nightlife venues here are comparable to the restaurant model: clubs are either very local or self-consciously international, the latter primarily featuring international DJs and a strong expat following. The Bund is ringed by slick lounges, rooftop terraces and thumping clubs, while the former French Concession features several tasteful villas where foreigners can be found sipping cocktails in colonial-era gardens. KTV, or karaoke bars, are wildly popular among locals, and range from fun-loving rooms where friends hang out to seedy dens frequented by crooning (and groping) businessmen. In recent years, Shanghai has seen its controversial bar streets, places like Maoming Lu and Julu Lu, lose some of their sleazy sheen as nightlife moves away from the once-popular formula of booze and babes.

Shanghai's cosmopolitan past saw it cast as a playground for the rich and a lascivious outpost of western decadence. These days, it's very much in the hands of the Shanghainese, but they too have developed an adventurous thirst for fun. Shanghai, more so than any other mainland Chinese city, is a glitzy showcase of the best China has to offer, with each day striving to outdo the last.

Eating Out

Wander down to the Bund and you'll get a whiff of the variety of restaurant choices on offer. In the streets just behind Shanghai's colonial showcase stalls sell cold noodles, and bamboo baskets are stacked high with soup dumplings. Lamb sold by Muslim butchers swings on hooks and grimy Sichuan restaurants serve spicy, authentic south-western fare. Turn the corner and you're face to face with another strata of Shanghai society; the one that offers a kiss to each cheek as a means of greeting, sips lychee martinis, and is intimately familiar with foie gras. And the greatest part about this town is that dumplings and Dom Perignon are not mutually exclusive – many residents here indulge in both, and you can too.

Eating out is Shanghai's favourite pastime. People here are as passionate about their favourite pizza joint as they are about where to get the best Hunan pork ribs, and

District Guide

We've included a Shanghai district by each entry in this section to help you locate the restaurants, bars and nightclubs. The map on p.416 shows which area of town each one covers.

because of the family style service of Chinese food eating out is best done in large, cheerful groups where you can sample a dozen dishes for next to nothing. Local food, with the exception of restaurants specialising in delicacies like shark's fin, bird's nest, and seafood tends to be very cheap and consistently good. Western food is a novelty to locals and a necessity to many expats, and it's getting better every day. The multiple east and south-east Asian restaurants are often excellent, their quality and consistency buoyed by their proximity to China.

Certain areas in town cater to diverse crowds; the far-flung suburban areas are very family friendly and offer a range of world cuisines to satisfy businessmen in exile, while downtown Puxi has it all. As long as you steer clear of imported ingredients, dining in Shanghai tends to be as affordable as it is delicious. And if you're willing to pay for it, you'll want for nothing in what has fast become an international dining destination.

Local Cuisine

Local cuisine in Shanghai, called Shanghainese food, or *Shanghai cai*, is an amalgamation of cooking techniques from the Zhejiang and Jiangsu provinces in China. Because Shanghai is very much a young city, cooks here have borrowed from other schools of cooking like Sichuanese and Cantonese. The cuisine itself relies on a few central elements – soy, sugar, salt and ginger to season, with a primary focus on shellfish, river fish, prawns and pork – and it tends to be heavy, filling food. Shanghai has several dishes that are its own, like the ubiquitous red cooked pork (*hong shao rou*) and succulent chunks of pork belly, with a nearly even ratio of meat to fat, braised in a thick sauce of sweet soy and spices. The *xiaolongbao*, or soup dumpling, is another Shanghai special that has become iconic not only here but in Chinatowns across the globe. This delicate dumpling, filled with a mixture of pork or pork and crab and seasoned gelatin, fills with 'soup' as the meat steams and releases its juice. It's astonishingly good when done correctly. There is one other ingredient that this town couldn't do without: the hairy crab. Hairy crabs fill the streets every year from September to December, served everywhere from the homestyle hole-in-the-walls to the most opulent banquet halls. They are raised in freshwater, have golden hairs on their legs and mossy pincers, and are prized for their firm orange roe and delicately flavoured meat. You haven't celebrated autumn in Shanghai until you've split open a hairy crab, dabbling in the messy dexterity needed to eat these tiny creatures. And in Shanghai you'll find plenty of oddities to nibble on too; the Chinese don't waste much of any animal. From duck tongues to chicken feet, and sea cucumbers to cow tendon, most things odd and edible are on offer. In fact, most of the bits westerners throw away are prized here for their texture – a sensation called *kou wei* that is nearly as important as taste.

The city, due to its economic gravity, is also a wonderful place to sample cuisines from across China. From the dumplings and stews of Manchuria (Dongbei) and the roast mutton and flatbreads of Islamic Xinjiang to delicate dim sum from Hong Kong, you won't be disappointed with the wide spectrum of Chinese food available.

Restaurant Timings

Shanghai has its own unique operating hours. Locals like to eat early, so peak dining hours are generally from 18:00 to 19:00, and establishments that cater to a local crowd will often stop serving food by 21:30. It is not unusual for places to begin turning off lights to pitch diners out of their seats before the clock has struck 22:00. That said, the city abounds with late-night options. Most foreign establishments, from tiny Japanese eateries to Xintiandi flagships, stay open till 23:00 and beyond, and there is a handful of very good 24 hour options for those working a late shift. Most bars are open until at least 02:00, and many only close when the last die-hards stagger out the door. Clubs close at sunrise.

Delivery

Unlike cities in the west, where delivery is a cheap alternative to dining out, ordering in rarely saves you money in Shanghai. That said, it's still a convenient practice, and there are several bilingual services that take the linguistic difficulty out of making the order. Sherpa's (www.sherpa.com.cn) and Mealbay (www.mealbay.com.cn) deliver food from dozens of Shanghai's most popular international restaurants for a small delivery fee. For larger gatherings, many restaurants also cater for business lunches and dinner parties at home. Nearly every pizza place delivers, and if you're simply in the market for a bowl of wonton soup or some noodles, chances are your neighbourhood Chinese will drop it round to your door. Stop by, pick up a menu, and ask them 'keyi wai mai?' ('do you deliver?') and you'll be dining from the comfort of your couch in no time.

Drinks

Other options **Alcohol** p.239

The palpable excitement resulting from constant bar openings and drink promotions means that, more often than not, the art of drinking is a public affair. This is especially the case in recent years as Shanghai's resume is becoming increasingly packed with decent cocktail bars, such as Face (p.390), wine bars, such as Jwow (p.392), and low-key drinking joints, such as Noah's Bar (p.394). However, a more intimate atmosphere is perfectly feasible and many people throw their own drinks parties and pre-clubbing soirees. Liquor is available in all the local corner stores, with no enforced age restriction, although the smaller ones have less of a selection. A large bottle of local liquor will set you back anything between ¥5 and ¥10, while the price of a standard bottle of imported spirits such as Chivas whisky can leap to ¥180. College kids will be pleased to know that a large bottle of Tsingtao beer costs around ¥5. Mixers are equally inexpensive; a large bottle of coke costs ¥5, while orange juice costs around ¥10. Getting your hands on a decent bottle of wine though takes a little more planning and is harder on the wallet. Try Jointek Fine Wines (403-409 Weihai Lu, 6340 0955), which boasts an impressive range of world wines, with many going for less than ¥200.

Mini Marvels

Explorer *Mini Visitors' Guides* are the perfect holiday companion. They're small enough to fit in your pocket but beautiful enough to inspire you to explore. With detailed maps, visitors' information, restaurant and bar reviews, the lowdown on shopping and all the sights and sounds of the city, these mini marvels are a holiday must.

Hidden Charges

Many Chinese restaurants will push the most expensive dishes on the menu to foreigners. Beware that while your steamed fish might look like it costs ¥58, it's probably that much for a jin, which is roughly half a kilo, and could come to five times that price. Another additional expense (although a minor one) is the packages distributed at the beginning of a meal, which include chopsticks and face towels, which generally cost ¥1-¥2 (you can decline, but it's probably not worth your trouble, or the messy hands). Tea can also be extra so make sure to ask whether the tea they are pouring you is free (*mianfei*).

Hygiene

Your local street-side eatery won't win any awards for hygiene but fortunately most foods are cooked at very high temperatures, minimising the risk of food poisoning. Raw foods such as fruit and cold dishes should be avoided if your stomach tells you that you're eating in a risky environment. Many small restaurant bathrooms also do not stock toilet paper and soap; a little pack of tissues and sanitiser will come in handy for adventuresome eaters. Smaller, home-style establishments tend to operate outside the aegis of the health bureau, so if you're eating on the cheap, be warned.

Discount Dinners

Restaurants frequently offer discounts, often in conjunction with local English magazines. Check out the useful hospitality portal e-Ha! (www.e-Ha.cn), which offers thousands of discounts. The website www.shanghaiexpat.com also has coupons that you can print out for use in the city's restaurants. Enjoy Shanghai (www.enjoyshanghai.com) is a coupon book packed with discounts. Aimed at expats looking to save cash at stylish spots, it costs ¥300.

Special Deals & Theme Nights

The Shanghainese love to mix it up and as such the city is full of different themed nights. The most common is definitely ladies' night, and it is wholly possible for the fairer of the sexes to flutter between the various hotspots seven days a week and not part with a penny. Mint (p.406) and Zapatas (p.399) on a Wednesday, alongside Barbarossa (p.387) on a Thursday and Jade on 36 (p.391) on a Friday are definitely the most popular. Men can also enjoy discounts though, with virtually every establishment in town offering some form of deal at one point or other during the week. Check the local lifestyle magazines to see what's on.

It's not all boozing though; Shanghai stretches its creativity beyond liver damage to other types of theme nights. Roller discos are held annually in different locations – keep an eye out for ads in clubs and lifestyle magazines. The summer foam party at Zapatas and the quiz nights at the British Bulldog Pub (p.388), O'Malleys (p.394) and Malones (p.393) are all extremely popular.

Street Food

Street food is slowly vanishing across Shanghai, as the last vestiges of the Old City make way for shiny high-rises and glittering restaurants. But there are still a few streets in town where you can sample a great deal of different snacks, from steamed *xiaolongbao*, Shanghai's famous soup bun, to shallow-fried *shengjianbao*, the crisp and juicy morsels of pork and dough. For the most authentic street food in Puxi, head to Si Pai Lou Lu, just behind the tourist trap that is the Yu Garden, for a gritty array of nibbles in one of the city's oldest (and dirtiest) neighbourhoods. Yunnan Lu, with its proliferation of tiny hotpots, Uighur minority food and other street-side eats, along with Wujiang Lu and its institution, Yang's Fried Buns, are also both worth a visit. When eating street food, use your best judgement, and only eat things that have been cooked in front of you – sanitation and street food do not go hand in hand in this part of the world.

Chicken skewers, served street-side

353

Tax, Service Charges & Tipping

There is no consumer tax on food and alcohol in Shanghai. However, if you want to claim expenses for your meal you will need to ask for an invoice, or *fapiao*. These are different to receipts (*danzi*) in that the restaurant must purchase them, which acts as a tax on the business – they are also the only official proof of expenditure. Most establishments will not give invoices unless you request them. As an incentive for more people to ask for invoices, there is a small, scratch-off panel on the left-hand side where participants can occasionally win a small sum of money from the government. Service charge is always levied in hotels for all food and beverage purchases (15%) and, occasionally, in fine-dining establishments. Tipping is not common practice, particularly in locally run establishments, where leaving a tip will often confuse the staff who will then chase you down outside with the change you 'forgot.' However, it is common practice in upscale western restaurants located outside of hotels, and in fancy bars and lounges, and if you tip you'll certainly get better service. Don't ever feel obliged to decorate the table with change, but if you feel like the service was commendable, tip away.

Vegetarian Food

Chinese cuisine might look veggie-friendly at first, but that's before the eggplant and string beans arrive in a sauce enriched with pork fat. Here, meat often forms the backbone of sauces in dishes like *mapo dofu*, and is frequently not even listed in the description. That said, most restaurants will accommodate vegetarians if told ahead of time (*wo chi shu* means 'I am a vegetarian'). If you think you've expressed your dietary requirements clearly and they still give you a dish with meat, feel free to send it back without paying – this should solve the problem. Shanghai also has a number of vegetarian restaurants, most of which adhere to the old Buddhist tradition of using tofu to artfully imitate meat. There are also the western vegetarian standbys such as pizza, pasta and salads, which are available nearly everywhere. Home cooks will be thrilled with the wide variety of soy products on offer, from pressed, fried and fermented tofu at the markets to soy milk in every corner store.

The Yellow Star

This classy yellow star is our way of highlighting places that we think merit extra praise. It could be the atmosphere, the food, the cocktails, the music or the crowd – but whatever the reason, any review that you see with the star attached is somewhere that we think is a bit special.

Independent Reviews

All of the venues in this book have been independently reviewed by a food and drinks writer who is based in Shanghai. Their aim is to give informative, engaging and unbiased views of each outlet. If any of the reviews in this section have led you astray, or if your favourite local eatery doesn't grace these pages, then drop us a line on info@explorerpublishing.com.

Restaurant Listing Structure

Reviewing every restaurant and bar in Shanghai would require a collection of work to rival the *Encyclopaedia Britannica* in volume, so instead our Going Out section brings your attention to a cross-section of places that are definitely worth a visit. Each review gives an idea of the food, service, decor and atmosphere. Restaurants have been categorised by cuisine and are listed in alphabetic order.

Explorer Recommended

Romantic		Alfresco		Great Views		Cheap Eats		Fine Dining	
M on the Bund	366	Finestre	375	Jade on 36	391	Dongbei Ren	360	Jean Georges	365
Jade on 36	391	New Heights	370	New Heights	370	Shu Di Lazi Yu Guan	363	Laris	366
Le Garcon Chinois	377	South Beauty 881	363	M on the Bund	366	Xinjiang Fengwei	362	Jade on 36	391
Bali Laguna	372	Coconut Paradise	377	Finestre	375	Lao Tan	361	Whampoa Club	364
Yin	364	KABB	355	Paulaner (Pudong)	396	Bao Luo	358	Fook Lam Moon	360

354

American

2262 Hongqiao Lu
Changning
虹桥路2262号
长宁
🚇 Hongqiao Lu
Map p.427 E4 **1**

Bubba's Texas Bar-B-Que and Saloon
6242 2612

This Texan bar and smokehouse fits perfectly in the land of large sport utility vehicles, international schools and big backyards that is Hongqiao. Sidle into Bubba's and you'll most likely hear a howdy from owner Ken Walker, the Texan who prefers the title 'pit boss' to restauranteur. Bubba's is all about the ribs, which are dry-smoked in the Texan tradition and served with their sweet/spicy/tangy sauce on the side. Other recommended dishes are the richly smoky chicken wings with barbecue sauce, the home-made jalapeno peppers stuffed with cream cheese, and the pulled pork sandwich, piled high on a bun and dripping in a tangy mustard riff on barbecue sauce. With a selection of American micro-brews and daily sports on satellite, Bubba's is a manly, meat-lovers' paradise.

Floor 2,
146 Tongren Lu
Jing'an
铜仁路146号
静安
🚇 Jing'an Temple
Map p.429 F4 **2**

City Diner
6289 3699

Twenty-four hours a day, seven days a week, this place serves up some of the most satisfying diner-style food in Shanghai at prices that won't make your stomach turn. The menu is the result of a partnership between two American-born Chinese with big appetites, and the portions at City can be jaw-dropping. Set just beside the bustling bar-lined Tongren Lu, the diner is the perfect final stop after a long night of boozing. As you walk in you're greeted by chef/owner Kelley Lee's assortment of yummy pies (try the lemon meringue) and a long row of towering booths that can comfortably fit six. The menu stays its course throughout the day and night, so you can munch on eggs benedict, a towering cheeseburger, or the City Diner salad with candied walnuts, spinach and blue cheese long after the bars close.

5, 181 Taicang Lu,
Xintiandi
Luwan
太仓路181弄新天地
北里5号楼
卢湾
🚇 Huangpi Nan Lu
Map p.430 C4 **3**

KABB 凯博西餐厅 ▶ p.357
5109 9322 | www.kabbsh.com

Come here for people-watching with a side of spiffed-up American fare. KABB has long been a favourite in Xintiandi, its lasting popularity due in equal part to its consistent good food and great outdoor terrace. It's the perfect location to spend a long, languid Sunday, fiddling with your eggs benedict and giggling at the tour groups. The food here is what they call 'American bistro' fare – think Cajun shrimp pasta, sirloin steak with fries and chicken caesar salads – but its standout dish is the almost-too-big-to-bite-into burger. The buzzing bar and restaurant, decked out in red, tends to fill with thirty-something professionals at lunch and dinner and also for the reasonable two-for-one happy hour from 17:00 to 20:00. KABB is best for brunches with friends, or happy hour beers and a plate of nachos.

Bubba's Texas Bar-B-Que

KABB

Building 1,
66 Yuyao Lu
Jing'an
余姚路66号一幢
静安
🚇 Jing'an Temple
Map p.429 E2 **4**

Moon River Diner

5213 5106 | www.moonriverdiner.com.cn

The first Moon River Diner was an absolute smash when it hit the suburbs in Hongqiao a few years back. It took a familiar American diner formula – thick shakes, fat slices of pie, burgers and fried chicken with all the fixings – and polished it a bit. Squeaky clean, the restaurants are family friendly and a touch sophisticated (rice wine braised ribs, decent wine selection); they are also shiny chrome and pastel odes to the 1950s. There are four Moon River Diners populating the city, (two of which are in Hongqiao, at Lane 3338, Hongmei Lu and Brilliance Mall, 88 Xianxia Xi Lu, and one in Pudong at Zendai Thumb Plaza, 199 Fangdian Lu), and all are popular. The newest of the four is the most ambitious offering yet, downtown in the slick New Factories redevelopment area. It shares the same something-for-everyone menu and cheerful aesthetic, but it also houses a deli on the first floor serving home-made bagels, huge sandwiches and rotisserie chickens, and a bar with a great selection of beers, strong cocktails and wines on the third floor. It's a roadside diner with a big city makeover, but the result is still refreshingly simple.

2, Lane 66,
Danshui Lu
Luwan
淡水路66弄2号楼
卢湾
🚇 Huangpi Nan Lu
Map p.430 C4 **5**

The Naked Cow

6385 8123

Situated inside a park just a stone's throw from hectic Huaihai Lu, The Naked Cow is a carnivore's paradise with gentrified style. The dining room fills nightly with a mixed crowd of expat families and party people, who head here to dig into 500g steaks served atop wooden cutting boards, cobb salads and bowls of chicken and matzoh ball soup. But it's more than a steakhouse: chef Erik Berger has rounded out the menu with a host of tempting plates to share. Try the lollipop chicken wings, cute little mouthfuls of fiery, tender chicken, or the philly cheesesteak buns, a playful redesign of the Chinese *baozi*. The Cow is also a great place to drink, with a solid selection of wines available by the glass, carafe and bottle, cleverly named cocktails and pitchers of sangria and boozy punch. The best bit? A wide terrace out back overlooking the bamboo forest and framed by skyscrapers. Make sure to reserve if the sun is shining.

Chinese

1221 Yan'an Xi Lu
Changning
延安西路1221号
长宁
🚇 Jiangsu Lu
Map p.435 D2 **7**

1221

6213 6585

This long-term favourite with westerners in search of Chinese food without the barriers of language is still full every night. When it opened six years ago down a lane off Yan'an Lu, 1221 was a novelty; a restaurant that served Shanghai-style cuisine without all the bones and bits, with a nice wine list, cocktails, and English-speaking wait staff. It was way ahead of its time; some might say it still is. And it has had a great run because of the attention to detail: the dining room is minimalist with splashes of contemporary art; the dishes are delicious, unpretentious renderings of local and Cantonese fare; and the service is friendly and helpful. If you're still a bit nervous about jumping into the local restaurant fold, start here. It makes for a comfortable crash course in Chinese cuisine, and a standby to bring your friends to when they come to visit.

KABB bar & grill is a **sophisticated** yet **relaxed** bar & grill serving **luxe comfort food** along with an **approachable wine list** and **great service.**

Open 7:00 am until late • (86 21) 3307 0798

xintiandi • north block • house 5 • lane 181 taicang road

凯博西餐厅・新天地・太仓路181号新天地北里5号楼

1018 Dingxi Lu
Changning
定西路1018号
长宁
🚇 *Yanan Xi Lu*
Map p.434 C2 **8**

Ba Guo Bu Yi 巴国布衣
5239 7779

Have you ever eaten in an intimate dining room that seats 500? In an ancient south-western Chinese environment, with the odd shrieks of Sichuan opera peppering the air? If the answer is no, you should head to Ba Guo Bu Yi, a throwback Sichuan restaurant that looks more like the China of your mind's eye than just about anywhere else. It's also the most famous restaurant in Sichuan's capital Chengdu, and in its Shanghai location they've painstakingly recreated a sprawling period teahouse from the south-western province. The food is predictably spicy, flavoured not only with dried chillies but with plenty of the curiously numbing, almost medicinal Sichuan peppercorn (*hua jiao*). Ba Guo Bu Yi is packed nightly with a red-faced parade of Chinese and foreigners that head here to toast with *baijiu*, a Chinese spirit, and punish their tongues with an onslaught of spice. Try the spicy chicken (*lazi ji*), eggplant (*yuxiang qiezi*) and fish slices in oil (*shui zhu yu*). If you want to hear the live opera, show up early, and be sure to reserve.

271 Fumin Lu
Xuhui
富民路271号
徐汇
🚇 *Shanxi Nan Lu*
Map p.435 F1 **9**

Bao Luo 保罗酒楼
5403 7239

This raucous temple to sweet and salty Shanghainese cuisine is the antithesis of foreign-friendly 1221 (see p.356). And that's what makes it so special. Bao Luo is Shanghai's answer to the late-night diner or the packed brasserie. Open until 05:00, its cavernous main dining room is always heaving with a fascinating cross-section of Shanghainese society. Here, eat among taxi drivers and off-duty chefs, greying oldsters and young party people downing beers before a night out on the town. Don't be deceived by Bao Luo's Lilliputian facade though; somehow this restaurant opens up into a huge galley serving river fish, shrimp, seafood, dim sum and braised pork. Favourite dishes include the *ti pang* (fatty pork shoulder braised to an almost obscene tenderness) and the eggplant and minced pork served with pancakes. Wash it all down with a cold Tsingtao beer (make sure to specify – *bingde pijiu* – 'cold beer') and congratulations – you've just eaten like a local.

1414 Huaihai
Zhong Lu
Xuhui
淮海中路1414号
徐汇
🚇 *Changshu Lu*
Map p.435 F2 **10**

Charmant 小城故事
6431 8107

The Taiwanese take a slightly western approach to the restaurant, and that's why Charmant has become such a standby for expats in the French Concession. Then again, it's popular with just about anyone who enjoys great food and good service in clean surroundings. Charmant's beer is cold – very cold – and its food is incredibly consistent. There's a few imported wines, delicious desserts (try the peanut smoothie), and you can even order a cup of coffee when it's all finished. The dining room, which resembles a tacky Italian restaurant, is odd with its brick archways and high-backed chairs, but it only adds to Charmant's quirky appeal. Don't miss the pork with Chinese broccoli (a crispy fry-up that's wrapped in thin pancakes), the delicious stir-fried dragon beans or the Taiwanese stewed pork. Charmant is open until 03:00 – a rarity for a restaurant serving food of this calibre, Chinese or otherwise.

124 Jinxian Lu
Luwan
进贤路124号
卢湾
🚇 *Shanxi Nan Lu*
Map p.430 A4 **11**

Chun 春餐厅
6256 0301

Chun has received more ink than just about any restaurant in Shanghai, gracing pages from the *New York Times* to *Gourmet Traveller*; an amazing feat, when you consider its four tables and stained white walls. This favourite of gastronomes is one of Jinxian Lu's so-called *ayi* (auntie) restaurants – a place where Shanghainese flock to eat food that tastes just like their mum used to make. Enter and sit in a tiny schoolhouse chair and the owner will promptly ask what you do and do not eat. Then she might laugh at your inability to answer. No matter. This isn't a restaurant for the picky, but it is a delicious introduction to food that you might otherwise never try as an outsider. A menu will be made for you, balanced with a few cold dishes, a pork dish, a fish dish, maybe some shrimp, and you'll finish off with the signature chicken and bamboo shoot soup. By that time, you'll probably want to write home about it too. Reservations are essential.

Crystal Jade 翡翠酒家

6385 8572

Hong Kong dim sum is one of cooking's great wonders, a magical dance of dexterity that results in an eye-catching array of little titbits to pop in your mouth. It's tapas as art, a taster menu as breakfast, and it's hard to do really well. But Crystal Jade manages just fine. Make sure to reserve at this eminently popular Cantonese restaurant inside the mall at the back of the Xintiandi complex, and arrive between 10:00 and 15:00 if you want to dive into its Hong Kong dim sum menu (Shanghai-style dim sum is served in the evening). It also offers a regular menu of fragrant, double-boiled soup, and Cantonese seafood, as well as other refined Chinese dishes in a sleek, contemporary space. And if you can't get a seat, Crystal Jade has just opened a new location only two blocks away, in the basement of Hong Kong New World Plaza at 300 Huaihai Zhong Lu (6335 4188). There's another branch in Jing'an at 1038 Nanjing Xi Lu (5228 1133).

6-7, Lane 123,
Xingye Lu, Xintiandi
Luwan
兴业路123弄新天地
南里6-7号
卢湾
🚇 *Huangpi Nan Lu*
Map p.436 C1 **12**

Di Shui Dong 滴水洞饭店

6253 2689

Hunan is hot. This south-central province, home to Mao Zedong, is one of China's so-called furnaces, a place where food perishes quickly. So the intrepid Hunanese created ways to preserve their food, and in doing so created a cuisine as fiery as the midsummer sun. You'll notice the rush of flavours the second you pick up your chopsticks – pickled peppers, smoked pork, preserved beans – everything is sour, salty and very spicy. This is rustic food done right, and at Di Shui Dong the decor reflects Hunan's humble beginnings. Di Shui Dong is best enjoyed with a large group in one of its many private rooms, where you can dine on a dizzying number of dishes for a pittance. Make sure not to miss out on the legendary pork ribs with cumin seed (*ziran paigu*). This seminal spot is always crowded so be sure to reserve.

Floor 2,
56 Maoming Nan Lu
Xuhui
茂名南路56号2楼
徐汇
🚇 *Shanxi Nan Lu*
Map p.430 A4 **13**

Ding Tai Fung 鼎泰丰

6385 8378

The *xiaolongbao*, or steamed soup bun, is a beautiful thing. It's tiny, succulent and delicate, but hearty and filling all at once. One bite and you're rushed headlong into the richness of a seasoned soup (actually melted pork fat, but they're only tiny) and tender minced meat, all encased by a delicate wrapper so thin it threatens to tear under its own weight. And Ding Tai Fung, a chain of upscale restaurants out of Taiwan, does this Shanghainese delicacy better, and cleaner, than anyone else. Watch the kitchen staff fold them in their immaculate kitchen, and order two trays: the pork and the pork and crab mixture. The great food in this bright restaurant, which is decorated with caricatures of pop luminaries, doesn't end there. Elbow in for a space among its mixed clientele and try the beef noodle soup, crisp, cold vegetable starters and other tiny nibbles. A must for the uninitiated.

11A South Block,
Lane 123, Xingye Lu,
Xintiandi
Luwan
兴业路123弄新天地
南里2楼11A单元
卢湾
🚇 *Huangpi Nan Lu*
Map p.436 C1 **14**

359

Dong Jun 东骏

518 Huaihai Xi Lu
Xuhui
淮海西路518号
徐汇
🚇 Hongqiao Lu
Map p.434 C4 **15**

6294 0127

This stadium of seafood looks more like an aquarium on the first floor, with fist-sized abalone clinging to the glass tanks, huge garoupa trolling in front, several different species of crab and at least a dozen types of local clams languishing in aerated baths. There are live octopus and freshly caught fish, salmon from Norway and creatures of the deep too odd to describe. It's like taking a trip to Shanghai's far-flung Tongchuan Lu fish market, without the stench. At Dong Jun your waitress will diligently follow you around the exhibits as you pick your catch, and then suggest different cooking methods, all done in a light, Cantonese style. Afterwards, retire to the Baroque upstairs dining room and wait for your bounty to arrive in minutes – this is as fresh as seafood gets.

Dongbei Ren 东北人

1 Shanxi Nan Lu
Luwan
陕西南路1号
卢湾
🚇 Shanxi Nan Lu
Map p.430 A4 **16**

5229 9898

Dongbei Ren, or 'Northeastern People', are boisterous. You'll notice this as you enter the riotously colourful dining hall and they greet you with a throaty yell in their lock-jawed northern dialect. Dongbei Ren takes authenticity seriously, but it's also about entertainment – and wait staff frequently break out in song. The crowded restaurant fills up nightly with a heavy drinking crowd that come to eat dishes like sweet and sour *gu bao rou* pork, at least a dozen varieties of steamed dumplings, and its trademark stews. The food here is meat-and-potatoes fare, the kind you might expect to emerge from the frigid climate of China's border with Siberia. But the decor – bright green and red with revolutionary touches like propaganda art, and the occasional piece of taxidermy – makes the place. Dongbei Ren is great for large parties; book one of its cosy private rooms (they hold up to 30 people, and there is no extra charge) and make a night of it.

Fook Lam Moon 福临门

Floor 2, Tower 1,
Shangri-La,
33 Fucheng Lu
Pudong
富成路33号
香格里拉大酒店浦
东
🚇 Lujiazui
Map p.431 F3 **17**

5877 3786 | www.fooklammoon-grp.com

If money is no object or you're trying to close a deal with local partners, Fook Lam Moon is the place. This opulent Cantonese restaurant inside the Pudong Shangri-La is the haunt of moneyed businessmen from Shanghai, Hong Kong and Taiwan. The menu is seafood-centric, with abalone flown in from Japan and South Africa, lobster, crab, and all manner of expensive, line-caught fish. There are also classics such as roast pork, Beijing duck and crispy skin chicken if you're looking for something more terrestrial. Fook Lam Moon serves all this in a rarefied Cantonese style, with light sauces and an emphasis on highlighting, rather than overpowering, the flavours of its ingredients. The service is

stellar and dinners here tend to be drawn-out affairs in the traditional banquet style. All of this is washed down with some of the priciest wines in Shanghai – Chateau Latour 1954 with your shark-fin soup, anyone?

87 Fumin Lu
Luwan
富民路87号
卢湾
🚇 **Jing'an Temple**
Map p.435 F1 **18**

Guyi 古意湘味浓

6249 5628

This is one of the few restaurants in town where a line regularly snakes out the front door and onto the street. The food is Hunan spicy but not overwhelmingly so; the decor is contemporary Shanghai without overdoing it and the result is a restaurant people return to time and time again. The dining room is quite frequently split 50/50 among local and foreign diners, as Guyi's easy appeal translates well. The dishes are just as real and rustic as Di Shui Dong (see p.359) but the decor and service are more polished (although hardly pretentious). Don't miss the crispy fried shrimp with spicy salt, the smoked pork with garlic shoots (*suan miao chao la rou*) and the gloriously meaty fish heads, where you pluck big chunks of pristine meat accented in a vinegary, peppery sauce from just behind the gills.

308 Hengshan Lu
Xuhui
衡山路308号
徐汇
🚇 **Hengshan Lu**
Map p.435 E3 **19**

Hengshan Café 衡山小馆

6471 7127 | www.hengshancafe.com

Hengshan Café is many things to many people; but mainly it's open late (until 03:00), and serves extraordinary food for this time of night. It's a bright and friendly locale for a quick lunch, and a casually upscale Cantonese restaurant at dinnertime. There is nothing that sets this restaurant apart so much as consistently great food, in an environment that doesn't turn heads but doesn't turn them away either. When you enter this branch (there's another at 719 Yan'an Lu, 6226 5517, and 1417 Huashan Lu, 6283 2282) you'll probably be distracted by the tempting hunks of glistening roast pork, crisp skinned chickens and geese hanging in the window. Order one, or all of these – they're some of the tastiest roast meats in town. The Cantonese canon is also renowned for soup, and that's reflected here. The black-boned chicken soup (*hei gu ji tang*) with ginseng is a healing tonic that shouldn't be missed, and the Assam-style curried fish head is spectacular with a bowl of rice. Expect a wait at peak hours, but it's worth it.

301 Huashan Lu
Jing'an
华山路301号
静安
🚇 **Jing'an Temple**
Map p.435 F1 **20**

Kuo Bee Pan Da 锅比盆大

6349 8877

Hotpot – a Chinese staple where the kitchen is brought to the table – can be intimidating to the uninitiated. But at Kuo Bee Pan Da they take hotpot – where diners encircle a large, bubbling pot of fragrant broth – upscale, making it the perfect introduction to this communal eating experience. The restaurant offers several options for the stock: traditional *mala* (Sichuan) style; Thai *tum yum goong* or mild curry broth. You get to mix your own dipping sauce from a great array of condiments from sesame oil and soy to browned garlic and freshly chopped coriander. Anything goes when it comes to ingredients; fresh greens, noodles, dumplings, shaved beef and lamb and all varieties of seafood take the plunge, before you pluck them out minutes later for dinner.

Floor 2,
42 Xingfu Lu
Changning
幸福路42号
长宁
🚇 **Jiangsu Lu**
Map p.435 D3 **21**

Lao Tan 老坛贵州风味菜

6283 7843

Guizhou is a lesser-known province and purveyor of mouth-tingling cuisine than its better-known neighbour Sichuan, but its food is almost as varied, and just as delicious. Lao Tan is located in a quiet alleyway just behind Huashan Lu, but its crowds are a testament to the great cooking (many Chinese people, let alone foreigners, are unfamiliar with Guizhou cuisine, but most come back). The flavours revolve around the pungent, sour and spicy, and the house speciality is the hot and sour fish soup, a broth that is not far removed from a Thai *tom yum goong*. The bubbling pot is served with a smattering of verdant greens, slices of fish and other accoutrements; toss them in the pot and enjoy a tingling hotpot feast, alongside one of Lao Tan's very spicy stir-fries.

Lost Heaven 花马天堂云南餐厅

38 Gaoyou Lu
Xuhui
高邮路38号
徐汇
🚇 *Changshu Lu*
Map p.435 E2 **22**

6433 5126

China's Yunnan province is an almost mythical place, hemmed in by jagged mountains, ribbed with ornate rice terraces and populated by numerous ethnic minorities that cling to the slopes bordering Vietnam, Laos and Burma. At Lost Heaven, they recreate this fusion of culture and spices on their menu, and with it one of the city's most magical dining rooms. This is restaurant as theatre. Inside, dark woods and copper pots abound, with ethnic masks peering from the walls. It's an enchanting space. The food is compelling, combining familiar south-east Asian herbs such as lemongrass and basil alongside Chinese cooking techniques and a smattering of distinctly Burmese dishes. Lost Heaven also offers an extensive wine list, and has a dimly lit lounge downstairs so you can wind down after your chic cultural immersion.

Old Station Restaurant 上海老站

201 Caoxi Bei Lu
Xuhui
漕溪北路201号
徐汇
🚇 *Xujiahui*
Map p.435 E4 **23**

6427 2233

This is probably the only place in the world where you can dine on very respectable Shanghainese cuisine in the comfort of your very own restored 19th century railroad car. Restaurant and museum in one, its long hallway opens up into dozens of turn-of-the-century private dining rooms, before snaking into the cavernous main rooms and the railroad cars behind. The concept is novel, but the food remains true to its roots, with Shanghainese specialities like crispy boneless duck and perch fillets with pickled greens and yellow wine sauce. Located in ultra-modern, frighteningly crowded Xujiahui, Old Station provides a contrasting reminder of a more tasteful yesteryear, and one that is equally interesting for a quirky date as it is for a night out with the kids.

Rong Tong Yu Xiang 荣腾渔乡

906 Dingxi Lu
Changning
定西路906号
长宁
🚇 *Zhongshan Park*
Map p.434 C2 **24**

6212 2511

Reach for your beer. Rong Tong Yu Xiang is perhaps the most rustic and real of Shanghai's countless Sichuan restaurants, meaning that nearly everything here will have your tongue quivering with the sting of chillies and numbing Sichuan peppercorns. There is precious little pretence; just hardwood chairs and tables, the occasional rustic knick-knack, and plates of stir-fries, salads and stews that brim with dried peppers and spice. Reservations are encouraged, as Rong Tong is raucously full every night with locals who relish the painful pleasure of eating things as spicy as they are in Sichuan. Make sure to try its *lazi ji* (crunchy nuggets of deep fried chicken nestled inside a pile of Sichuan chillies), and the superb *niu rou dou hua*, a tofu dish that incorporates dried beef, the crunch of peanuts, chilli oil and a refreshing sprinkle of coriander.

Shanghai Xinjiang Fengwei Restaurant 新疆风味饭馆

280 Yishan Lu
Xuhui
宜山路280号
徐汇
🚇 *Shanghai Stadium*
Map p.443 E1 **25**

6468 9198

Throw on your dancing shoes, and prepare yourself for an animated evening at Shanghai's best Xinjiang restaurant. Xinjiang is a province in the far west of China, and is inhabited by the Uighur minority – a Turkic people who share not only central Asian features, but a good deal of its culinary tradition as well. Xinjiang food is hearty and delicious, with huge hunks of roast mutton, grilled lamb kebabs, rich chicken stews, and vinegar and cumin-accented tomato salads (there is no pork on the menu here). And the servers are nearly as exciting as the food, as they frequently break out in song, and drag diners onto the makeshift dancefloor with tinny Middle Eastern techno in the background. The atmosphere is kitsch, with fake trees and a makeshift waterfall populating the dining room, which is always packed with a cheerful mix of locals and expats.

849 Huashan Lu
Changning
华山路849号
长宁
🚇 *Jiangsu Lu*
Map p.435 E2 **26**

Shen Yue Xuan 申粤轩

6251 1166

There are restaurants among the expat community that are better known for their dim sum. Admittedly there are ones with friendlier service and smarter decor. But for great tasting food and good value, few do it better than this favourite of the local government and business crowd. Shen Yue Xuan, a sprawling Cantonese restaurant that fronts a park on the corner of Huashan Lu, is at its best at weekend dim sum feasts, where diners can dabble in countless different sweet and savoury treats. The barbecued pork buns, a litmus test for this kind of eating, are perfectly executed, and the delicate shrimp dumplings and flaky egg tarts are also first-rate. Ask for a table on the airy first floor, and enjoy your lunch while gazing out onto the lawn and the trees that frame it. Oh, and don't forget to order the *zhou*, or rice porridge, that fans of this restaurant return for time and time again.

187 Anfu Lu
Changning
安福路187号
长宁
🚇 *Changshu Lu*
Map p.435 E1 **27**

Shu Di Lazi Yu Guan 蜀地辣子鱼馆

5403 7684

Sichuan actor Ren Quan owns this group of recommendable restaurants, where he and his chefs have tweaked several favourite dishes from his fiery home province and also from the heartier repertoire of Northern China. The results are simple and undeniably satisfying. Shu Di Lazi Yu Guan is a neighbourhood place – the kind of restaurant you find yourself in time and time again – and its ridiculously low prices and good-humoured staff will probably bring you back too. It's slippery and shabby within, but the food on offer outshines the surroundings. Try the *zhu xiang ji* (marinated chicken fried in a bamboo basket with leeks, fennel seed and chillies) as it's the best dish on a great menu.

881 Yan'an Zhong Lu
Jing'an
延安中路881号
静安
🚇 *Jing'an Temple*
Map p.430 A4 **28**

South Beauty 881 俏江南

6247 5878

When you've opened two dozen upscale Sichuan restaurants across China, you need a flagship – something that stands out in its conspicuous ambition – and South Beauty 881 is just that. This restaurant combines a few key concepts in one location. There's a vaulted cocktail bar in an old villa surrounded by gorgeous private rooms and a Balinese-style rooftop. Behind it, a low-slung, minimalist restaurant designed by space-age Japanese firm Super Potato presides, beside a huge lawn set for alfresco summertime wining and dining.

The food is mostly Sichuan, with a smattering of Cantonese and even a few western dining options like steak off the grill. But make no mistake, this Beauty is all about looking pretty, and it easily succeeds in that department.

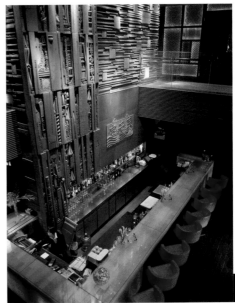

132 Maoming Nan Lu
Luwan
茂名南路132号
卢湾
🚇 *Shanxi Nan Lu*
Map p.436 B1 29

Union Restaurant 联谊餐室
6473 9871

This Shanghainese restaurant is unabashedly old school, from the grouchy, shout-if-you-want-it service to the bathrooms that require a stroll outdoors during your meal. The clientele at lunchtime were all born long before Mao's revolution; octogenarians are more the rule than the exception here. But don't let this put you off. Union cooks food like you might have found here decades ago, and won't find just about anywhere else. And, of course, the prices are reasonable too. Try the wobbly *furu wuhua rou*, a daringly fatty slab of pork belly slow cooked in fermented soy sauce and sliced tableside, or the marvellous *ba bao ya* (eight treasures duck), which is stuffed, sewn up, fried crisp and then roasted. Remember to arrive on the early side; lights are frequently turned off to empty the dining room before 21:00.

Floor 5,
3 Zhongshan
Dong Yi Lu
Huangpu
中山东一路3号
黄埔
🚇 *Nanjing Dong Lu*
Map p.431 E3 30

Whampoa Club 黄浦会
6321 3737 | www.threeonthebund.com

If you haven't seen the name Jereme Leung in food and travel magazines throughout the world, you will soon. Leung, who has been tapped as China's next big thing in food, has earned his reputation by cooking inspired Shanghainese classics with a fine dining twist. His restaurant sits in the historic Three on the Bund building, and its combination of impressive art deco interior alongside beautifully presented Chinese cuisine make Whampoa one of the most sought-after reservations in town. Expect a mix of local bigwigs and moneyed tourists dining on elaborate tasting menus. His best dishes playfully riff on the pedestrian – try the poached Shaoxing chicken served not in its customary brine, but perched atop fluffy shaved ice in a martini glass. Whampoa also serves excellent dim sum on weekends and affordable set lunches.

41 Tianping Lu
Xuhui
天平路41号
徐汇
🚇 *Hengshan Lu*
Map p.435 E3 31

Xinjishi (Jesse) Restaurant 新吉士餐厅
6282 9260 | www.xinjishi.com

This chain is a Shanghai institution. If you ask who serves the best, most authentic Shanghainese cooking in town you're bound to hear a litany of responses, but Xinjishi will most likely outnumber the rest. This is due primarily to its commitment to quality and consistency at the original Jesse restaurant, which, is and always will be, the best. Jesse serves things sweet, sticky and heavy – try the *hong shao rou* with cuttlefish, an impossibly tender braised pork dish with a lip-smacking ratio of meat to fat. It's a small, unimpressive dining room, but the stuff it serves more than makes up for the lack of atmosphere.

Old Jinjiang Hotel,
Restaurant St
59 Maoming Lu
Luwan
茂名南路59号
老锦江饭店
卢湾
🚇 *Shanxi Nan Lu*
Map p.436 A1 32

Yin 音餐厅
5466 5070

A restaurant that evokes Shanghai's past without replicating it, Yin is as urbane and elegant as Chinese dining gets in this town. Lofty ceilings look down over a dining room draped in hardwood and traditional Chinese furniture, while modernist art adds a clever contrast to the space. The cocktails are strong and well mixed, the wine list excels, and the food is refined and very good. Yin serves a mix of traditional Shanghai fare, such as its tangerine beef, long jing crystal shrimp (stir fried with tea leaves) and lion's head meatballs, alongside originals including shaved lamb with 17 spices. There is live jazz on Friday and Saturday nights, and reservations are essential. This is a restaurant you'll want to return to again and again; Yin is a perfect combination of affordability and style.

French

Des Lys 德丽滋

178 Xinle Lu
Luwan
新乐路178号
卢湾
🚇 *Shanxi Nan Lu*
Map p.435 F1 **33**

5404 5077

The cosy neighbourhood bistro, with its quaint list of affordable wines, French standards and no-frills decor fits the bill nicely. Des Lys aims not to floor you with great cooking but rather wrap you in an affable atmosphere – and it does so with great success. It is perhaps best for lunch or brunch when the salads, including the blue cheese and poached chicken with crunchy walnuts, or lettuce with cubes of creamy foie gras and shredded duck confit, are the best things on the menu. Other standbys include a very decent couscous royale with minty beef balls and a juicy roast chicken. Expect a smoky dining room filled mostly with Frenchmen longing for home, and not quite finding it here. But that's ok because when the bill comes you won't be paying Parisian prices. Des Lys also offers a delivery and catering service.

Franck

376 Wukang Lu
Xuhui
武康路376号
徐汇
🚇 *Changshu Lu*
Map p.435 E2 **34**

6437 6465

The proprietor of this newcomer, Franck Pecol, is a Frenchman obsessed with the simple pleasures of his country's cuisine. His mission is to serve authentic bistro classics like oeuf mayo, veal kidney, and blanc de veau in a setting that exudes the sophisticated chic of Paris today – and he's succeeded. Franck has a small zinc bar where you can sip on a glass from its quirky, all-French list or down a postprandial pastis, and a dining room that effortlessly blends retro cool with a subtle, modern edge. It is the kind of place French hipsters, fashionistas, wine geeks and businessmen all seek out due to its undeniable charm. The restaurant offers a market menu comprising about five starters and five mains with a smattering of unsurprising, but delicious desserts. Chalkboards change daily. The dining room is intimate and packed with Gallic chatter, and there is also a small terrace when good weather beckons.

Hong Fang Zi 红房子 ▶ p.367

Floor 6,
35 Shanxi Nan Lu
Xuhui
陕西南路35号
徐汇
🚇 *Shanxi Nan Lu*
Map p.436 A1 **35**

6255 3338

With a history dating back to the 1930s, Hong Fang Zi (the Red House) has changed owners on several occasions to varying degrees of success, but the current proprietor seems to be having a decent run. One of the main draws is the outdoor terrace that provides a perfect view of classic French Concession streets. Inside, the dark walls and red ornaments complement the elegantly prepared French-fusion cuisine. Tiger prawn in mango with cucumber and mint salad sits alongside Chinese braised foie gras on the large, reasonably priced menu. Upstairs houses La Brasserie Lounge, which serves less adventurous dishes and impressive cocktails.

Jean Georges 让乔治法国餐厅

3 Zhongshan
Dong Yi Lu
Huangpu
中山东一路3号
黄埔
🚇 *Nanjing Dong Lu*
Map p.431 E3 **36**

6321 7733 | *www.threeonthebund.com*

You've heard the name, and perhaps shunned the hype but celeb-chef Jean-Georges Vongerichten's personality oozes from his Shanghai restaurant in Three on the Bund. It features a long, curving bar, and a stately dining room with plush banquettes to remind you that this dinner is going to be special. And it usually is. The food here is very much an expression of Jean-Georges' globetrotting – French first, but with a clever Asian approach that infuses the classical with citrus and spice. Try the classic dishes such as foie gras brulee with dried sour cherries or the gloriously fragrant mushroom tea, or delve into the tasting menus that combine hits from the past with creative offerings inspired by the season. Finish all this off with an ethereal dessert plate, and you'll be pining for your next anniversary or big business dinner.

365

Floor 6,
18 Zhongshan
Dong Yi Lu
Huangpu
中山东一路18号
黄埔
🚇 *Nanjing Dong Lu*
Map p.431 E2 **37**

Sens & Bund 雅德

6323 9898

Bund 18 is a magnificent ode to Shanghai's present heyday, full of high fashion and fancy food, capped off with Bar Rouge, one of the city's most conspicuous drinking dens. And Sens & Bund, a restaurant from the famed twins of French gastronomy, Jacques and Laurent Pourcel, meshes all of these together. Sens is white and minimalist within, with a stylish bar fronting the restaurant and leather seats that scoop you up so as to focus on the food. The menu, which is inspired by the Pourcels' two-star Michelin Montpellier flagship, Jardin de Sens, is a French-Mediterranean exploration of subtlety and grace on the plate. Sweet langoustines are wrapped in thin pastry and fried until crisp, while sea bass languishes in fragrant vanilla foam. The wine list looks to Languedoc and other less-explored regions, and the desserts are fruit-filled and fresh. Sens might not be the most talked about on the Bund, but it is a focused, unabashedly French take on haute dining.

Fusion

18 Dongping Lu
Xuhui
东平路18号
徐汇
🚇 *Hengshan Lu*
Map p.435 F2 **38**

Azul/Viva

6433 1172

Chef and owner Eduardo Vargas has made Shanghai his home, and anyone who's spent time here seems to know him and his food. Everywhere all at once, this Peruvian chef and restaurateur has opened more than his fair share of places to eat, from diners and sandwich shops to this, his most successful and longest running venture to date. Azul stands out perhaps because it is the most personal of Vargas' ventures; it serves large helpings of tapas, with a frequent nod to Asia (where he's been cooking for more than a decade). Azul is all about sharing: big jugs of sangria; plates of Peruvian beef tapas or tender pork skewered on sugarcane; and a citrusy salad of lima beans, tomatoes and feta. During the day, while people enjoy the fantastic, affordable brunch, the restaurant looks a little weathered, but at night the contemporary splashes of colour and stone tables make it a sophisticated, fun place to eat.

Floor 6,
3 Zhongshan
Dong Yi Lu
Huangpu
中山东一路3号
黄埔
🚇 *Nanjing Dong Lu*
Map p.431 E3 **39**

Laris 陆唯轩

6321 9922 | *www.threeonthebund.com*

The walk into Three on the Bund's Laris is a fashionable affair, and one that doesn't have the contrived heft of rarefied dining. The name of chef/owner David Laris reflects off the white marble floors, and the restaurant's logo is beamed down in lime-coloured light. Vault (p.398), Laris' bar, is generally full of Shanghai sophisticates sipping from a list of adventurous takes on the martini, while the dining room hosts both jeans and suits, mini-skirts and evening dresses. This is fine dining without silver trays and white gloves, but the food – a global menu that takes cues from Japan to Greece – stands up to the test. Behind Vault Bar lies a spread of cold seafood with Boston lobsters, oysters from France, the US and Australia, and other delicious ocean delights.

Floor 7,
20 Guangdong Lu
Huangpu
广东路20号
黄埔
🚇 *Nanjing Dong Lu*
Map p.431 E3 **40**

M on the Bund 米氏西餐厅

6350 9988 | *www.m-restaurantgroup.com*

Seven years ago, Shanghai's once-glorious Bund was a wasteland with a beautiful facade. The neo-classical architecture remained, but within lay the endless cubicles of state-owned enterprises and crumbling shipping companies. That was until Michelle Garnaut, an Australian-born restaurateur who opened Hong Kong's M at the Fringe, decided to take a gamble on this grandiose but wasted space. M was Shanghai's first freestanding western fine-dining restaurant, and it is still one of the best. Inside, this M

In the Red House Building 6th & 8th Floor
Two Distinct Cuisines & Atmospheres

 红房子法国餐厅

Creative French Cuisine

Paris Flair in Shanghai

Modern Bistro

Champagne
& Cocktail Lounge

Weekday : 4pm-1am
Week-end : 11.30am-1am

 Le Gourmet
法国美食餐厅

Tues-Sun 5pm-11pm

Corporate Functions & Private Parties available up to 800

35 Shanxi Nan Lu, 200020 Shanghai

www.hfz.sh.cn 6255-3338 info@hfz.sh.cn

blends an art deco aesthetic with elegant contemporary touches. The service is excellent, as is the wine list, and the tables are set with silver. The menu, which blends French, Mediterranean and north African flavours, isn't as progressive as when it first opened, but the food is consistently good. The terrace overlooking the river is also the best place to enjoy brunch on a sunny day. M on the Bund is on most tourists' must-do lists, and remains hugely popular with expats so reservations are essential.

333 Tongren Lu
Jing'an
铜仁路333号
静安
Jing'an Temple
Map p.429 F4 **41**

Maneo ▶ p.369

6247 9666

Delivering a healthy dose of style and a great deal of substance, Maneo is an established, haute option in a town with a growing number of restaurants that combine the culinary and the cool. Sleek, white walls and natural woods form a minimalist aesthetic that draws in a fashionable crowd of younger diners who pop bottles at the well-stocked champagne bar before sidling into the beautiful dining room. The food provides an interesting counterpoint to the decor. Chef Brad Turley's creations borrow from the best of Pacific Rim cooking, south-east Asia and the Mediterranean, and it's a focused fusion that makes sense – on the plate and the palate. Try inspired creations such as the asparagus soup with white truffle, or the Thai crab salad that sings with the freshness of lemongrass, kaffir lime leaf and citrus. Mains cater both to dedicated carnivores and smaller appetites and the a la carte brunch and set lunches combine great value and style. The bill might be less than a night on the Bund, but the experience is much the same.

Jean Georges

M on the Bund

Maneo

368

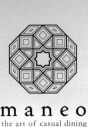

maneo
the art of casual dining

Open everyday from 11am-1am

Set lunch menu
available monday to friday
118rmb (2 courses) 138rmb (3 courses)
open choice from the a la carte menu
Dinner Hours 6pm-11pm
Choose from our globally inspired
range of dishes or call chef and enjoy
a tailor made menu

Sunday brunch menu
158rmb anything you like &
as much as you can eat
Our truly international breakfast & lunch favorites;
from nibbles & bits to beef & reef. Tasting size plates
from the garden, the hen house, the stockyard, the
beach & the patisserie.

Now with outdoor seating

Best wine selection &
runner up best new restaurant
- city weekend readers choice awards 2007

1F, No. 333 Tongren Rd
under Mint Club, Shanghai
铜仁路333号，近北京西路
telephone: 6247 9666
maneo@maneo.com.cn

748 Julu Lu
Luwan
巨鹿路748号
卢湾
🚇 **Changshu Lu**
Map p.435 F1 **42**

Mesa 梅萨

6289 9108

Steve Baker, founding chef of Xintiandi's T8 (see below), and Charles Cabell, former manager of the chic cocktail bar Face (p.390), decided several years ago that they wanted something they could call their own. And this two-storey beauty, which serves modern Australian fare with fresh seasonal ingredients, is the result. Mesa's minimalist dining room, which faces the open kitchen and wraps around the striking spiral staircase, is located in an old factory on the newly gentrified Julu Lu. Upstairs lies the lounge Manifesto, which serves some of the best creative cocktails in town. The food focuses on fresh, light flavours; try the beetroot carpaccio with goat's cheese, or the soy and ginger salmon with green tea soba. On weekends, Mesa serves an excellent a la carte brunch, which is best enjoyed on the terrace. And it's kid-friendly too; there's free babysitting on weekends so parents can make a day of it.

88 Yichang Lu
Putuo
宜昌路88号
普陀
🚇 **Zhenping Lu**
Map p.421 F4 **43**

Mimosa Supperclub

5155 8318

The Pier One complex, a huge project located in a historic building in the up-and-coming Suzhou Creek area, was a gamble. Slightly off the beaten track, Pier One attempts to set the style curve with its lofty restaurant, which serves an adventurous menu, alongside a boutique hotel and rooftop bar. The restaurant is surely its greatest asset, since Mimosa is capably manned by Michelin-starred chef Stefan Stillar, who has created a menu where things arrive in tempting combinations of three. Try one of its set menus of three, four or five courses, where a single ingredient (foie gras, lamb, or even tomatoes) arrives in three thought-provoking interpretations. Inside, it's one of the city's coolest spaces, drawing a primarily expat clientele to its stark white dining room with towering ceilings and space-age vibe. The Supperclub is open late, and in the spirit of late-night dining and lazy Sunday brunching, you can even eat in one of its beds on the second floor.

3 Zhongshan
Dong Yi Lu
Huangpu
中山东一路3号楼
黄埔
🚇 **Nanjing Dong Lu**
Map p.431 E3 **44**

New Heights 新视角餐厅

6321 0909 | www.threeonthebund.com

This modern bistro sits atop Three on the Bund, the upscale retail and dining address that fired the Bund revival. And New Heights is, due to its stunning views of the river, with the imposing European architecture of the Bund and futuristic Pudong beyond, a remarkable place to eat. In fact, New Heights has the kind of view that makes it the perfect option when you have guests in town. On warm nights its wrap-around terrace buzzes with businesspeople and tourists popping bottles of wine and drinking in the view. The food is a mash up of familiarity, with dishes from Malaysia and Indonesia such as *nasi lemak* and *laksa* to burgers and steaks and seared tuna. If the evening calls for something more casual than the three fine-dining establishments on the floors below, or the warm weather beckons, this is your best bet. It's perpetually full so be sure to book.

8, 181 Taicang Lu,
Xintiandi
Luwan
太仓路181弄新天地
北里8号楼
卢湾
🚇 **Huangpi Nan Lu**
Map p.436 C1 **45**

T8

6355 8999

This restaurant served Shanghai's first fine-dining fare, and while it has gone through a succession of chefs, each with their own personality, the spirit of the place remains intact. So do the crowds. T8 boasts a sexy dining room, with understated south-east Asian touches, and the entire affair seems wrapped around the incandescent open kitchen. Here, the staff work furiously to churn out chef Patrick Dang's many-layered dishes, which toy with western-Asian fusion in frivolous fashion. The restaurant is ably run by Shanghai veteran Walter Zahner, who keeps the wine list interesting and the service up to scratch. Upstairs lies a beautiful function room; the perfect setting for product releases, fancy wine tastings, and other occasions where fashion and food collide.

Indian

3728 Hongmei Lu
Changning
虹梅路3728号
长宁
🚇 **Hongqiao Lu**
Map p.427 E4 **46**

Bukhara Grill
6446 8800

Indian cuisine in Shanghai is authentic, perhaps due to China's proximity to the subcontinent. And the food at Bukhara Grill is no exception. This three-storey palace features a first bar where Indians in exile gather to watch cricket matches and drink beer, a shimmering second floor dining room that is packed with a crowd of western expats and Indians, and a huge third floor space for parties and special events. The open kitchen is a focal point in the dining room; you can watch chefs straight from Delhi plucking spears of yogurt-marinated meats and fluffy breads from the tandoor as your stomach grumbles. The vegetarian dishes are as good as the north Indian meats. Try the richly smoky eggplant curry, and be sure not to miss its superbly spicy rogan josh – a fiery, tomato-based lamb curry. The restaurant is located on Gubei's happening Hongmei Lu – a blessing if you live in Hongqiao, and worth the taxi ride if you don't.

397 Dagu Lu
Luwan
大沽路397号
卢湾
🚇 **Changshu Lu**
Map p.430 B4 **47**

Masala Art 香料艺术印度餐厅
6327 3571

Masala Art seems like a quiet, unassuming place as you enter its confines; the kind of restaurant most people stumble upon when walking past the quirky collection of shops and eateries on Dagu Lu. And after a meal here, you'll probably want to keep it that way. It's less crowded than Shanghai's other popular Indian restaurants, but the northern-influenced cooking is equally good. Portions are larger than many, and prices are lower than most. And while the dim dining room won't turn heads, it's tasteful enough for a date. In fact, Masala Art is one of the city's best-kept secrets so don't tell too many people. Home delivery is also offered.

550 Jianguo Xi Lu
Xuhui
建国西路550号
徐汇
🚇 **Hengshan Lu**
Map p.435 F3 **48**

Vedas 维达斯饭店
6445 8100

Four years ago, the Indian food scene in Shanghai was in a sorry state. Curries were watery and lacked complexity, and diners sprang for sloppy all-you-can-eat affairs instead of seeking out quality cuisine. Then Vedas opened and changed the game. The restaurant, tucked away in the French Concession, took all the details into account, from hiring great chefs to man the tandoor to outfitting the place in tropical hardwoods. The service was solid, and the food was fantastic. Not much has changed at Vedas since, but other Indian restaurants took notice, and upped the ante as well. Starters here are fantastic, but Vedas really shines with its roasted meats, particularly the spicy, tender kesari chicken. These boneless chunks of marinated meat have become a signature, alongside curries that are some of the spiciest in town. Vedas also features a solid new world-focused wine list.

Need Some Direction?
The *Explorer Mini Maps* pack a whole city into your pocket and, once unfolded, are excellent navigational tools for exploring. Not only are they handy in size, with detailed information on the sights and sounds of the city, but also their fabulously affordable price mean they won't make a dent in your holiday fund.

371

Indonesian

189 Huashan Lu,
inside Jing'an Park
Jing'an
华山路189号
静安公园内
静安
🚇 *Jing'an Temple*
Map p.429 F4 **49**

Bali Laguna 巴厘岛
6248 6970

This restaurant, much like the island that inspires it, exudes a certain romantic charm. Bali Laguna's appeal, however, doesn't lie in palm fronds and crystal clear seas, but rather an idyllic location inside Jing'an Park. Sitting next to the lily-padded pond, surrounded by trees with frogs croaking beside you, it seems like you've left the city (unless you gaze skyward). This natural ambience, along with Bali Laguna's unassumingly elegant interior, have made it a favourite for dates. But if you plan on sitting outside, or by the window that overlooks the water, make sure to reserve several days in advance. The food here is uninspired but steady; Indonesian standards such as *nasi lamak* are served alongside a litany of grilled and curried seafood and a handful of vegetable stir-fries. The wine list is impressive for an Asian restaurant.

Italian

Other options **Mediterranean** p.375

140 Xikang Lu
Jing'an
西康路140号
静安
🚇 *Nanjing Xi Lu*
Map p.429 F4 **50**

Bella Napoli 美丽纳波利
6253 8358

Intimate and simple, this Jing'an Italian bucks the upscale trend of the area by serving a small but balanced menu of fresh and inexpensive fare. Bella Napoli, whose two gregarious Italian owners work the crowd most nights, is a restaurant that people appreciate for its no-frills honesty. The wine list features a brief collection of well-known Italian reds and whites and a few proseccos, and the desserts are favourites such as tiramisu and cannoli. But the most noteworthy things here are the noodles – try the vibrant arugula (rucola) pesto tossed with al dente fusilli or the wonderfully rich, fishy *puttanesca*. The two-floor space is a bit cramped and can get smoky, but for the price and the quality of the food it's worth sharing such close quarters. Bella Napoli also offers great lunch specials.

913 Julu Lu
Jing'an
巨鹿路913号
静安
🚇 *Changshu Lu*
Map p.435 F1 **51**

Casanova 卡萨诺瓦
5403 5428

This French Concession Italian restaurant sits above a few fading dive bars on the gentrifying Julu Lu. It has sparked the revival (along with several other upscale restaurants) of what was a sleazy address only a few years ago. Casanova doesn't deal in things amorous – unless you're a lover of rich, northern Italian pastas, crispy pizzas and pricey mains that make use of ingredients like Kobe-style beef and lobster. The restaurant stretches along the upper floors of a colonial-era building, and its atmosphere doesn't scream Italian so much as it does moderately expensive. And, well, that's what it is. It fills with an older crowd of European and American businesspeople and their spouses, who head here to sip wines and coddle themselves in comforting Italian food done well. Casanova's pizzas, which are probably the best in town, are also available until late in the Velvet Lounge (p.399), a separate space on the first floor.

103 Dong
Zhu'anbang Lu
Jing'an
东诸安浜路103号
静安
🚇 *Jiangsu Lu*
Map p.435 D1 **52**

Da Marco 大马可意大利餐厅
6210 4495

It's smoky, noisy and crowded. The food is simple, the menu predictable, and the wine list is excellent. In short, Da Marco is everything you expect from a home-style Italian restaurant, and it pulls it off with aplomb. Marco, the proprietor who can be found most nights beside the bar, sipping a limoncello or pulling on a cigarette, runs a tight ship. The pizzas are thin and crisp, topped less sparingly than those accustomed to

Italian pizza might expect. The salads are fresh and bountiful, and the bowls of pasta are generous and reasonably priced. But Da Marco's greatest strength is a wine list that you won't find elsewhere.

Floor 39,
St Regis Hotel,
889 Dongfang Lu
Pudong
瑞吉红塔大酒店，
东方路889号
浦东
🚇 **Dongchang Lu**
Map p.433 D4 **53**

Danieli's
5050 4567

Nearly every seat in Danieli's, which is perched atop the neon-lit St Regis hotel in Pudong, has an expansive view of this newly developed realm. With a narrow, wood-panelled dining room that faces the open kitchen, Danieli's has a bit of an ocean-liner vibe. It's not quite stuffy, but does have an air of old-school exclusivity. The restaurant does a steady business that is almost evenly divided between expats who live in the area and hotel guests, and it provides a more intimate alternative to the rooftop restaurants in hotels on the riverfront. The food here is upscale hotel fare, with foie gras, seafood and steak all making appearances on the menu. Perhaps the best time to enjoy the view from Danieli's is at its superb Sunday brunch; the only place in town with a free flow of Bollinger champagne for just under ¥500, plus 15%.

Le Royal Meridien,
789 Nanjing Dong Lu
Huangpu
南京东路789号
上海世茂皇家艾美
酒店大堂
黄埔
🚇 **People's Square**
Map p.430 C3 **54**

Favola 法沃莱意大利餐厅
3318 9999 | www.starwoodhotels.com

The new Le Royal Meridien Hotel, which sits in the tallest building in downtown Puxi, didn't put its dining outlets on the top floors. But Favola, along with the hotel's French restaurant Allure, towers above most hotel restaurants in town. Favola won't win any awards for decor, and the sparse tables lend it a quiet vibe that can feel a little desolate if it's not busy, but the food shines. Diners are greeted with a warm plate of just-baked focaccia, olives and hunks of parmigiano reggiano. After that you can delve into its thin pizzas, wonderful home-made pastas such as sheep's milk ravioli with sweet cherry tomatoes, or rotisserie meats that spin on a fiery rack at the front of the dining room. This being a hotel, the service is smooth and efficient, but expect to pay a bit more than at your corner trattoria.

House 7, Lane 181
Taicang Lu, Xintiandi
Luwan
太仓路181弄新天地
7号
卢湾
🚇 **Huangpi Nan Lu**
Map p.436 C1 **55**

Va Bene 华万意
6311 2211

Va Bene, located down a cobbled lane in Xintiandi, is an upscale Italian and the spot for serious oenophiles. Its list covers the entire boot, from the beautiful Barolos of Piedmont to Nero d'Avolas from Sicily. The restaurant is bathed in sunny yellow with a clean, cheerful aesthetic and the bright, glass-fronted room beside the main dining room is a great space to lunch. Va Bene's pastas are made in-house and are frequently adorned with not-so-rustic accoutrements such as white truffle and seafood. But the restaurant's greatest dishes are the simplest, such as the pizza – cooked in the Roman style, with a cracker-thin crust, a slick of sauce and toppings including the superb black truffle and homemade sausage combo.

Japanese

28B Taojiang Lu
Xuhui
桃江路28号B座–乙
徐汇
🚇 **Hengshan Lu**
Map p.435 F2 **56**

Haiku 隐泉日料
6445 0021

California-style Japanese is something very new in China. Many things American, specifically, larger portions and a willingness to borrow flavours and ingredients from other schools of cooking, characterise this style of cuisine. This large, two-storey spot with a grey concrete backdrop that is broken up with colourful Japanese renderings, is packed with Americans and other foreigners who come here nightly to sip sake and sample the filling menu of rolls and fresh sashimi. Standouts are the *moto-roll-ah*, a spicy, cooked tuna roll covered in a secret sauce, and the philly roll with smoked salmon and plenty of cream cheese. Haiku also offers Japanese standards alongside its more innovative offerings. The restaurant's older sibling Hatsune is one of the most popular foreign eateries in Beijing.

803 Julu Lu
Jing'an
巨鹿路803号
静安
🚇 **Jing'an Temple**
Map p.435 F1 57

Shintori 新都里无二店

5404 5252

Dinner is theatre at Shintori, a restaurant where the decor never tires. This vaulted, starkly modern space is hidden down a bamboo-lined path in the French Concession, its hulk barely visible from the street. That is, until you venture inside. Sushi chefs whirl around on the elevated stage that is the open kitchen, as diners sit below and above the action in a room that calls to mind all those *Space Odyssey* dreams of childhood. The food is modern Japanese with an occasional dash of fusion. There are several signature dishes, like a rock-and-roll salad that is shaken tableside and prawns cooked on hot rocks, otherwise you can dine on traditional sets of sushi and sashimi. Be sure to reserve, as Shintori's atmosphere draws in all walks of life every night of the week.

Floor 2,
6 Zhongshan
Dong Yi Lu
Huangpu
外滩6号，
中山东一路外滩6号
黄埔
🚇 **Nanjing Dong Lu**
Map p.436 C1 58

Sun with Aqua 东京和食

6339 2779

As you approach the maitre d' at this slick Japanese in Six on the Bund, your eyes are drawn away from the reservation list and to the three sharks circling in the tank above. Sun with Aqua (the adjacent Aquarium Bar is the reason for the curious name) aims to impress with stylish flourishes and cheeky touches. And it does so successfully. The food here spans many styles of Japanese – from the traditional sushi and sashimi to grilled beef, tiny personal hotpots and dozens of small side dishes. But all of Sun's style doesn't come at a great price; it is, in fact, one of the most economical places to eat on the riverfront. Another strong suit is a competitively priced wine list and a great sake menu complete with tasting notes – all of which bolsters this restaurant's magnetic allure.

15 Dongping Lu
Xuhui
东平路15号
徐汇
🚇 **Hengshan Lu**
Map p.435 F2 59

Tairyo Teppanyaki 大渔

6445 4734

When the glutton in you beckons, it might be time for a trip to Tairyo. This perennially popular Japanese steakhouse serves all things teppanyaki – that is, things cooked on the large steel grill (teppan) that also serves as a table and focal point of a meal. The dexterous cooks slap slices of beef, shrimp, chicken, lamb and scallops on the grill; most things are cooked in butter with plenty of salt and pepper, and finished with a splash of soy sauce. Vegetables are also flash fried in front of you, along with egg-fried rice and noodles. But this restaurant's great selling point is that you can eat and drink as much as you like, for as long as you want, keeping the grill man busy over a long sake and beer-fuelled evening. It's a fitting place to celebrate – just don't expect the refinement or attention to detail that you'll receive at other Japanese eateries.

Giant View Hotel,
15, Lane 1520
Huashan Lu
Changning
上海虹景公寓酒店，
华山路1520弄15号
长宁
🚇 **Jiangsu Lu**
Map p.435 D2 60

Tian Jia 天家

6281 4918

Simply put, Tian Jia serves the best sushi in Shanghai. And not just any sushi, mind you: it specialises in *chu toro* and *o toro*, the prized, fatty cuts from the belly of the bluefin tuna. They also serve king crab, another delicious and highly prized creature of the deep. But if you've come for anything else, you're out of luck. A set meal at Tian Jia is a glorious affair for seafood lovers, incorporating a set of thick slices of toro raw and marinated with lemon juice and sea salt, followed by steamed crab and, later, *toro shabu shabu*, a course where strips of raw fish are briefly plunged into a bubbling broth. More crab follows, along with udon noodles and finally a glorious bowl of steaming rice topped with chopped tuna, chives and sesame seeds. Tian Jia is tiny, and always packed with a mostly Japanese crowd – so it's a good idea to reserve several days in advance.

Yakitori Aska 飞鸟烧烤

318 Changle Lu
Luwan
长乐路318号
卢湾
Shanxi Nan Lu
Map p.430 B4 61

5383 6801

Yakitori, like most things Japanese, finds beauty in simplicity. It is a word used to describe a single dish – a grilled skewer of chicken – but has come to incorporate several dishes served from a narrow charcoal grill, cooked with the utmost care and attention. Aska, a small, smoky warren of tacky decor, televisions beaming Japanese baseball and speakers playing 90s pop, doesn't match the Zen sensibility of the food – but the throngs of regular customers like it all the same. Must trys at this great find include the tender yakitori (chicken thighs cooked until just tender and basted in a sweet sauce), the wonderful chicken balls served with spicy mustard, and tender, grilled chicken hearts (don't be afraid). This food goes best with a mug of crisp draught Asahi, and perhaps a bottle of cold sake if you're going to make a night of it.

Korean

Zong Jia 宗家韩国料理

Floor 3,
1665 Hongqiao Lu
Changning
虹桥路1665号
长宁
Hongqiao Lu
Map p.427 F4 62

6209 7451

Shanghai has no shortage of Korean restaurants, but few are highly recommended. If you've got a car, or happen to live out past Hongqiao Airport, Ziteng Lu offers many reasonable and authentic places to eat Korean. But it's too far for most. Luckily, city dwellers need only to find this gem in Gubei (with another branch in Pudong, at 300 Fangdian Lu, near Yanchun Lu, 6854 4346). Zong Jia is incredibly clean and blindingly white, and it's packed full of ethnic Koreans who dine here early from 17:30 to 20:00 (reservations needed for early meals). Dinner begins with a startling array of colourful *kimchi*, which is refilled for free during the meal, and then segues into delicious stews, fried noodles and *bimbim bap*, an iconic rice dish served in a sizzling bowl, and then Korea's famed grilled meat dishes. Try the succulent, sweet marinated beef with spring onions (*bulgogi*) and crispy pork belly grilled and wrapped in a lettuce leaf, and wash it all down with a cold bottle of *soju*, the lighter-than-vodka spirit that is drunk with most Korean meals.

Mediterranean

Other options **Spanish** p.376, **Italian** p.372

Finestre

Floor 11,
15 Zhongshan
Dong Er Lu
Huangpu
中山东二路15号11楼
黄埔
Nanjing Dong Lu
Map p.431 E3 63

6373 4818

Finestre shares a space with the heaving Bund nightclub Attica (p.403) – but it is very much its own, separate entity. It doesn't share the late-night pedigree of its neighbour, nor the thumping tunes. And as service is winding down here, things are just getting fired up on the dancefloor next door. But Finestre does share Attica's expansive terraces that look out onto the river and Pudong beyond, making it one of the best alfresco spaces in town. The menu, created by Californian chef Sean Jorgenson, is a clever assortment of small plates, larger mains and pizzas that all share a Mediterranean bent. There are spinach raviolis and crispy mushroom and goat's cheese pizzas, great starters such as a crispy duck salad, and filling mains including the incredibly tender beef short rib. The restaurant is populated by style-seeking Bund partiers and a more mature crowd who come for sundowners and a few bites before the party people roll in.

375

Mexican

Villa 1,
3911 Hongmei Lu
Changning
虹梅路3911号
长宁
🚇 *Hongqiao Lu*
Map p.427 E4 64

Mexico Lindo 墨西哥灵得
6262 2797

Mexican food – that spicy, filling, oh-so-comforting staple of the Americas – is not easily found in Shanghai. And while there are a few last-resort taco stands around town, the only place serving approximated Mexican is this Hongqiao outlet. Located in a warren of villas converted into restaurant space on the cultural and culinary melting pot that is Hongmei Lu, Lindo has a loyal following of gringos who drop by to sip strong margaritas, eat nachos, and perhaps devour a burrito or some fajitas (the food here leans toward the milder Tex-Mex side of the spectrum). There's also a large back patio for outdoor taco nights, and a decent selection of beers and wine.

Nepalese

4, Lane 819, Julu Lu
Jing'an
巨鹿路819弄4号
静安
🚇 *Jing'an Temple*
Map p.435 F1 65

Nepali Kitchen 尼泊尔餐厅
5404 6281

The mountainous kingdom of Nepal, and its capital Kathmandu, has long held sway over the imaginations of travellers. And at Nepali Kitchen, the decor, with embroidered pillows piled on the floor and pristine photos of the Anapurna range, tries to capture its mysticism. It's an incredibly warm and comfortable place to eat, and one best suited for cold winter nights. The Nepali servers, all dressed in traditional dress, zip up and down the narrow hallways in this three-storey villa. There are a few signature dishes not to be missed – particularly the Nepali cheese balls (deep fried, gooey croquettes served with a spicy, cumin-accented dipping sauce). The curries here are lighter than the Indian variety, relying less on the weight of clarified butter, and not as spicy either. Try the mushroom pea curry and the fantastic pulao – buttery kashmiri rice with raisins and toasted cashews. Nepali Kitchen is very popular, so be sure to book on busy nights. A vegetarian tasting menu is also available.

Spanish

Other options **Mediterranean** p.375

4 Xiangshan Lu
Luwan
香山路4号
卢湾
🚇 *Shanxi Nan Lu*
Map p.436 B1 66

Indalo 故乡餐厅
5382 0738

When it comes to authenticity, few foreign restaurants in Shanghai do it as well as Indalo. Brick archways span a long bar, where singles sit to tuck into a few cold tapas and one of 25 wines by the glass. The adjacent dining area draws a mainly European crowd, and while there are mains on offer, the tapas seems to be the biggest seller; beautiful medallions of lomo, the cured loin of Spanish pork, pairs perfectly with crusty bread and dips. After that there's plenty to pick at, such as creamy croquettes stuffed with Spanish ham to tender, baby squid served in their ink and stuffed with a flavourful ground pork mixture. If you're in a group, don't miss out on the paella, which is cooked until firm and topped with fresh clams and shrimp.

Shanghai Explorer 1st Edition

**3, Lane 9
Hengshan Lu**
Xuhui
衡山路9弄3号
徐汇
🚇 *Hengshan Lu*
Map p.435 F2 67

Le Garcon Chinois 乐加尔松

6445 7970

This hideaway, just off the noisy confines of Hengshan Lu, is strictly old school, from the perfect manhattans and Duke Ellington-era jazz at the intimate bar to the pared-down Spanish tapas served in the dining room. Le Garcon Chinois and Chinese restaurant Yin (p.364) share the same Japanese owner, Takashi Miniyaka, and the two restaurants also share the same time-capsule vibe. Located in an old colonial villa down a narrow lane, Garcon sits unmarked at night, without signage, attracting only those in the know. The crowd is mostly European with a smattering of urbane Japanese and the occasional group of locals. The food is simple Spanish tapas, with a few salads and mains that include duck confit, steak, and fish. And while the cooking is more than competent, it's the atmosphere that really steals the show.

207 Maoming Nan Lu
Luwan
茂名南路207号
卢湾
🚇 *Shanxi Nan Lu*
Map p.436 B2 68

Tapas Bar 三乐维

6415 9567

Tapas is a cheerful affair, and a cuisine that was originally designed as a foil for a glass of wine. These days it bridges the spectrum from a few slices of jamon and sheep's milk cheese to confounding creations that are so far removed from the food's humble roots they're hardly recognisable. But in Tapas Bar, which has two locations in town (the other, Las Tapas, is located at 3338 Hongmei Lu in Hongqiao), the focus is on simple bites, such as bread with a garlicky aioli or chunks of imported chorizo. Most dishes are served sauteed in a very generous dash of olive oil, with a few slivers of garlic, some salt, and little else. Tapas Bar has stools and high tables on the first floor, and a quieter, lower seating area above. Due to the affordability of the food and drink on hand, it's busy most nights with a younger crowd. One thing it also does well is a cheeseburger, although you might want to order a beer with that, of course.

Thai

38 Fumin Lu
Jing'an
富民路38号
静安
🚇 *Jing'an Temple*
Map p.429 F4 69

Coconut Paradise 椰香天堂泰国料理

6248 1998

As you enter the airy, mahogany confines of Coconut Paradise, you're enveloped in a Thai environment that is perhaps more beautiful than the real thing. The harmony of hardwood and sculpture and the lemongrass scent that permeates this restored villa is calming. The fiery curries and spicy, sour salads should keep you from falling asleep, however. Coconut Paradise panders less to local tastebuds than other Thais around town, which means the food is often very spicy and quite sour, rather than smooth and sweet. The *larb gai*, or chicken salad, is excellent, as is a vibrant green curry. The restaurant has ample seating but is usually buzzing with foreigners who live in this centrally located neighbourhood. Coconut Paradise also has an outdoor garden and wraparound terraces for warm, alfresco nights.

5C Dongping Lu
Xuhui
东平路5号C座
徐汇
🚇 *Hengshan Lu*
Map p.435 F2 70

Simply Thai 天泰餐厅

6445 9551

The most recognisable of Shanghai's Thai restaurants, Simply Thai has built a mini empire on the foundations of south-east Asian kitsch. First came the handsomely appointed, well-run restaurant, Simply Thai, in the heart of the old French Concession. Then the giftshop, Simply Life, selling the same knick-knacks one might fit out a Thai restaurant. The brand later spread to Xintiandi (159 Madang Lu), Hongqiao (Lane 3338, Hongmei Lu), and finally the green oasis of Pudong's Jinqiao (Jinqiao Pudong Green Sports & Leisure Centre, 600 Lantian Lu). But the original location is still Simply's best, with its combination of neighbourhood charm and consistent cooking. Simply serves

Thai standards including red duck and pineapple curry, green chicken curry, papaya salad and the obligatory spring roll, with fresh herbs and curry pastes imported from Thailand. The wine list is thoughtful, and the crowd is varied and usually big, so make sure to book.

127 Datian Lu
Jing'an
大田路127号
静安
🚇 *Nanjing Xi Lu*
Map p.430 B3 🔢

Thai Gallery 泰廊餐厅
6217 9797

The Thai restaurant look – a combination of dark woods, rattan and lanterns, accented with the occasional Buddhist sculpture and soft new age music – is a pleasant but entirely familiar one. This venue makes a great departure from this pigeonhole, and in doing so has created a space as colourful and vibrant as the food it serves. Thai Gallery is just that; an exhibition space where bright canvasses hang on finished concrete walls, with either cushioned floor seating or standard tables. The kitchen and bar are professionally run, and produce great curries and herb-inflected salads, and a list of creative, tropical cocktails. The quirky atmosphere tends to attract a fashionable, younger crowd; this is the hippest of Shanghai's Thai eateries after all.

Turkish

4-7 Hengshan Lu
Xuhui
衡山路4-7号
徐汇
🚇 *Hengshan Lu*
Map p.435 F2 🔢

Anadolu 阿纳多卢餐厅
5465 0977

That Turkish staple turned Britain's favourite post-pub snack, the doner kebab, is served in all its satisfyingly sloppy glory at Anadolu. And it's perfectly placed for this kind of business, sandwiched in between clubs and bars on a bustling stretch of Hengshan Lu (it's also open past 03:00 most nights). But this isn't your everyday kebab shack. It's a full-service restaurant that serves other Turkish delights such as minced lamb and beef kebabs grilled over charcoal, eggplant and chickpea dips with pita and salads. There are outdoor picnic tables where friends gather around shisha pipes for a smoke after a filling meal. There's also a limited list of beers and wine.

Vegetarian

Floor 4, Metro City,
1111 Zhaojiabang Lu
Xuhui
肇家浜路1111号
徐家汇美罗城4楼
徐汇
🚇 *Xujiahui*
Map p.435 E4 🔢

L'Abre de Provence 普罗旺斯的树店
6426 7698

Vegetarian food in China is characterised by an assortment of impostors, with things like tofu posing as meat in all of its forms. At L'Abre de Provence there is also tofu on the menu, but this veggie restaurant bucks the trend by serving western-inspired dishes, as well as others plucked from meat-free menus across Asia. There are Italian pastas and Japanese tofu dishes, Chinese vegetable stir-fries and fresh squeezed juices. L'Abre de Provence is busiest at lunch hour, when it offers a varied buffet with salads, soups, hot dishes and desserts for ¥40. The setting is bright and cheery, with an organically green colour scheme reminding you that this is a place where vegetables come first. Look for it tucked away in the Metro City mall on the fourth floor.

258 Fengxian Lu
Jing'an
奉贤路258号
静安
🚇 *Nanjing Xi Lu*
Map p.430 A3 🔢

Zao Zi Shu 枣子树
6327 0218

There's no smoking, and no drinking of the alcoholic sort here – only a great line-up of vegetarian dishes served in a modern environment. A healthy lifestyle is the mantra of Zao Zi Shu, and it's a great place to detox after weeks of indulging in Shanghai's parade of greasy, meat-filled dishes. Because most dishes are constructed from tofu and a huge assortment of local produce, it's also very vegan friendly. But don't expect to leave the world of meat entirely; many of the tofu dishes here are designed to imitate the taste and texture of terrestrial animals. There is imitation sausage and crispy duck, fake prawns and other offerings that do a decent job of tricking the tongue. Another strong suit is a long list of herbal teas to cleanse your body and soothe your urban soul.

Vietnamese

Building 11,
889 Julu Lu
Jing'an
巨鹿路889号
11号楼
静安
🚇 *Jing'an Temple*
Map p.435 F1 **75**

Club Vietnam
6445 8082

This Vietnamese restaurant makes up one third of the FCC (Foreign Culture Club), an ambitious French and Vietnamese concept located in a stately mansion in the French Concession. And it is the most noteworthy aspect of a building that combines modern French fare, a patisserie, an aqua bar and this, the third floor standalone restaurant. Club Vietnam is a pretty thing to behold. Each room is decorated in bright pastels with atmospheric lighting and catchy details like the custom FCC tiles that line the stairway on the walk up. The food is standard Vietnamese but recognises the French influence on the region; curries are served with crusty baguettes, and creme caramel is dished out for dessert. The best things on the lengthy menu are the starters such as fresh spring rolls and prawn paste grilled on sugarcane. It's a stylish place and, predictably, the crowd follows suit.

3, Lane 9,
Hengshan Lu
Xuhui
衡山路9弄3号
徐汇
🚇 *Hengshan Lu*
Map p.435 F2 **76**

Le Garcon Chinois 乐加尔松
6445 7970

The bar is charming, and the house is a spare but beautifully preserved specimen from Shanghai's past. Essentially two restaurants in one, the first floor houses a Spanish restaurant (see Spanish entry, p.377), but if you're leaning toward the lighter, fresh flavours of Vietnam, head upstairs and delve into a menu that represents both northern and southern Vietnamese cooking in elegant environs. There is *pho* from Hanoi, that richly flavored beef broth accented with star anise and spices and flecked with herbs, and the spicier *bun bo hue* soup from Vietnam's ancient capital. The salads are light and fresh, and the spring rolls, when wrapped in mint and lettuce and dipped in the light fish sauce, are something to behold. Playing backup to the great food is a competent wait staff and a pleasant wine list.

Club Vietnam

379

Cafes & Coffee Shops

439 Wukang Lu
Xuhui
武康路439号
徐汇
🚇 **Hengshan Lu**
Map p.435 E3 77

Arch 玖间酒吧

6466 0807 | info@archlink.com.cn

Architects, designers, fashionistas and other members of the school of effortlessly cool have made Arch a landmark. It has all the touches of a great lunch spot, with its central location inside a historic, flatiron-esque building whose triangular construction fronts three streets in a leafy part of town. There are stacks of design magazines to page through after you've finished perusing its menu of sandwiches, salads and world food favourites such as Indian curries and German sausages. Arch is a narrow space with intimate booths that sit four snugly, with a small bar that serves good cocktails and coffee. At night, Arch transforms into a low-key bar (see p. 386 for details). It's popular, so make sure to book if you're planning lunch or dinner. And if you can't get in, a larger Arch 2 has recently opened at 115 Changshu Lu, a short taxi ride away.

57 Fuxing Lu
Xuhui
复兴路57号
徐汇
🚇 **Changshu Lu**
Map p.435 F2 78

Boona 2 布那2

6433 7142

The original Boona, at 88 Xinle Lu, has established much kudos as a teetotal hipster hangout. But it's often hard to get a seat there, and so the folks opened a new Boona only a few blocks away, which is bigger, brighter, and better (it has also abandoned the torturous chairs that haunted many a late-night latte drinker). Boona 2 is a modern, grey concrete cave, where people in creative industries gather to snap open their Macs, occasionally sneer at one another, and drink strong espressos. Boona 2 also offers a limited menu of snacks, including respectable tuna sandwiches and other handheld offerings. And if all that coffee goes to your head, you can always breeze across the street to JZ Club (see p.392) for some jazz and a glass of wine.

262 Nanchang Lu
Luwan
南昌路262号
卢湾
🚇 **Shanxi Nan Lu**
Map p.436 B1 79

BYB 不一班餐厅

6473 8113

BYB's tiny balcony, which overlooks a shady stretch of Nanchang Lu, is one of the best seats in town to tap away on your keyboard during a spring afternoon – or even better, to share a coffee with friends. This tiny, two-floor cafe is unassuming with its plain decor, but the high ceilings in the old structure give it an understated charm. The unspectacular but filling food is simple, consisting of the thin pizzas and paninis that can be found at cafes across town. Its smoothies, including the hangover mixture with cucumber and ginger, are cleansing and healthy, and make an appearance on most tables. The crowd is mostly stylish locals, although in this neighbourhood you'll see foreign faces just about everywhere.

Building 201,
3215 Hongmei Lu
Changning
虹梅路3215号
201号楼
长宁
🚇 **Hongkou Stadium**
Map p.442 B1 80

Coffee Tree

6466 0226

This is *the* family friendly coffee shop. With soaring ceilings and oversized furniture, the Coffee Tree looks very grown up, but with a location in the suburbs of Hongqiao, many of the customers come packing little ones. There's a place for them to play outside, while the grown-ups sip rich lattes and nibble on an assortment of home-made cakes and pies. Coffee Tree is a small, family run operation, and it shines through in the tasty food. There are only a few choices each day, but everything is freshly cooked and tasty. And they've moved eastward as well, recently opening a new location in the up-and-coming Ferguson Lane complex at 376 Wukang Lu. The new Coffee Tree is equally pleasing, with a wide patio to sip your iced coffee come summertime.

Element Fresh 新元素

6279 8682 | *www.elementfresh.com*

Element Fresh deals in food that is light, easy on the waistline, and convenient. Its original location (in the Shanghai Centre on Nanjing Xi Lu) has long been a hideout for foreign-food starved expats, and now you can find one on every corner of town. The fast-expanding chain now has Cafe Fresh outlets serving pre-packed sandwiches and salads, and several larger outlets. They all share a simple, modern aesthetic, outdoor seating and the same menu that ranges from western breakfasts, juice and smoothies to sandwiches and Asian-inspired dinner sets. Try the laffa bread salad: a big bowl of greens with olives, feta cheese and veggies that sits on a chewy round of laffa bread with tangy miso yogurt dressing, or the delicious 'bacon and blue' sandwich with crispy smoked pork and lots of creamy blue cheese on wholegrain bread. Other Element Fresh venues can be found in the KWah Centre and Grand Gateway Mall in Xuhui, and the Super Brand Mall in Pudong, while Cafe Fresh outlets are located in the Headquarters Building in People's Square, the Y+ Yoga Studios in Xintiandi, and Wuxing Lu in the French Concession. Element also offers a speedy, free delivery service.

Shanghai Centre,
1376 Nanjing Xi Lu
Jing'an
南京西路1376号
上海商城
静安
🚇 *Jing'an Temple*
Map p.429 F4 **81**

Ginger

6433 9437

Ginger feels like one of those places you might find in any gentrified neighbourhood anywhere in the world. There are copper walls and hardwood tables, a soft jazz soundtrack and a bar whizzing with the noise of a blender and the blasts of frothing milk. The well-manicured women who make this cafe their daytime home also wouldn't look out of place in any upscale neighbourhood. All this might sound soulless but really it's not. In terms of Shanghai's cafe culture, Ginger is as slick and professional as it gets. The wine list is good, the cocktails are great, the coffees are strong, and most importantly, Ginger takes its food seriously.

299 Fuxing Xi Lu
Xuhui
复兴西路299号
徐汇
🚇 *Jiangsu Lu*
Map p.435 E2 **82**

House of Flour 毂屋

5080 6239

This far-flung bakery and restaurant has garnered a huge following in Pudong. Located inside the Zhangjiang Technology Park at the very end of the Metro line, it's unlike anything else in Shanghai. Behind this homespun enterprise is Brian Tan, the talented Singaporean baker who was once the executive pastry chef for the St Regis Shanghai, and his training and pastry prowess shine through in the moist cakes and wonderfully crusty breads. There are also great sandwiches and wraps, good coffees, and reasonably priced pastas and main courses. And for those who've been pining for some of Tan's sublime cheesecake but can't make the hike, C's House of Flour, the second location, is open in Puxi at 1228 Beijing Xi Lu, near Xikang Lu.

Floor 1, 635 Bibo Lu,
Zhangjiang High
Tech Park
Pudong
碧波路635号，
张江高科园区
浦东
🚇 *Zhangjiang High*
Technology Park

Kommune 公社酒吧 ▶ p.397

6466 2416

The 'art street' of Taikang Lu is a rarity in this consumerist city, where business often outpaces creativity. Lane 210 is a collection of jewellers, artists, design firms and other creative enterprises that focus on hand-made crafts and design. It's also one of the most beautiful collections of *shikumen* architecture in Shanghai. And right in the middle of it all sits the courtyard and this tiny cafe. This is where the neighbourhood crowd and strolling shoppers come for a cup of coffee, or a simple brunch on a sunny day. If the weather is nice it's sure to be packed, and if you plan on coming here on Sunday morning for a bloody mary and a plate of eggs be sure to reserve a table. Kommune also offers a nice wine list and some very good beers, which makes it a great entree to a big night on the town.

Lane 210,
Taikang Lu
Luwan
泰康路210弄7号
卢湾
🚇 *Huangpi Nan Lu*
Map p.436 B2 **84**

381

Old Film Café 老电影咖啡吧

123 Duolun Lu
Hongkou
多伦路123号
虹口
🚇 **Dong Baoxing Lu**
Map p.422 B3 `85`

5696 4763

Nostalgic film buffs and seekers of Shanghai's past should look no further than Duolun Lu's Old Film Café. Located in a stately, turn-of-the-century home, the cafe frequently screens films from the 1920s and 30s for art buffs who come for a respite and a cup of tea or coffee. There is a narrow stairway and a warren of rooms in the old house, and the walls are decorated with yellowed posters from Shanghai's past. You can choose from a selection of older films to watch while you enjoy the cafe's bygone charm. Duolun Lu is also an art destination so you can visit the excellent Duolun Museum of Modern Art (see p.197), located just across the street.

Vienna Café 维也纳咖啡馆

2, Lane 25,
Shaoxing Lu
Luwan
绍兴路25弄2号
卢湾
🚇 **Shanxi Nan Lu**
Map p.436 B2 `86`

6445 2131

This little Austrian import makes a strong case for the cosiest coffee shop in town. It's continental through and through, with hardwood floors, wood panelling and high ceilings, and a friendly Austrian proprietor who makes bracing drinks and good coffee. Vienna is populated by foreign bookworms who sun themselves on the small patio on afternoons, and local artists that head here for a pick-me-up. The cafe also serves breakfast, Austrian pastries and a limited selection of regional favourites such as goulash. Vienna is a cosy little nook on a charming little street. Stroll down quaint and quiet Shaoxing Lu, soak up the architecture, and dip into the galleries, before heading here for a coffee and chat. The perfect spot to while away an afternoon.

Wagas 沃歌斯

Hong Kong
World Plaza,
300 Huaihai Zhong Lu
Luwan
淮海中路300号
香港新世界广场
卢湾
🚇 **Huangpi Nan Lu**
Map p.430 C4 `87`

6335 3739

When this city evolved from slow-paced backwater to frenetic business centre, the long Chinese lunch lost its place. And, perhaps surprisingly, the sandwich is gaining a foothold in its place. Leading the charge is Wagas, a gaggle of trendy cafes where locals and expats refuel on espresso, creative sandwiches and a dose of Wi-Fi. The brand has taken a note from upscale sandwich shops elsewhere, and serves an intrepid mix of world food between two slices of bread. Sometimes it works, as with its pesto, bacon and sun-dried tomato combo, other times not, but once you settle on a favourite you'll have a steady snack on the go. Wagas are scattered all over the city so it won't take long to stumble across one near you.

Whisk

1250 Huaihai
Zhong Lu
Luwan
淮海中路1250号
卢湾
🚇 **Changshu Lu**
Map p.435 F1 `88`

5404 7770

Chocoholics gather at this modish cafe where cocoa is served in all its splendour. Whisk serves thick, rich Spanish-style hot chocolate and ridiculously moist brownies with a hot chocolate fondant that spills its gooey inside all over the plate. This cafe on busy Huaihai Lu is tucked off the street, and its spacious interior is usually filled with those on a coffee or dessert break or a steady lunch and dinner crowd. And while the chocolatey bits definitely steal the show, the risottos, Italian-style sandwiches, and fluffy pizzas with an array of gourmet toppings are more than respectable. Whisk also roasts its beans in-house so expect good coffee.

On the Town

With an average of three bar openings per month, Shanghai is recapturing its glorious days as one of the world's leading sin cities.

The transformation from business centre to bright-lights city occurs daily at around 18:00 when the city's nine-to-fivers descend en masse to their locals to quaff happy-hour specials and let off some post-work steam. Dinner follows shortly afterwards, usually sometime between 19:00 and 21:00. Most of the action takes place on the weekend, but thanks to a series of good-value drink promotions, theme nights and top acts, venues such as Face (p.390) and Barbarossa (p.387) buzz throughout the week. Bars typically start filling up around 22:00 and clubs from midnight.

Downtown Shanghai, especially around the French Concession and the Bund, is the best bet for a night out. You'll usually be within walking distance of somewhere lively, from the tawdry ladies' bars on Maoming Lu to the upmarket residences of the Bund, where the majority of Shanghai's expats gravitate. Several trendy spots dotted around the suburbs and Pudong also manage to pull Shanghai's late-night crowd. Well-known chains Blue Frog (p.388), Paulaner Branhaus (p.396) and Big Bamboo (see advert p.241) are all very popular.

One of the best things about Shanghai is its seemingly unending choice. Expats have always made up a significant part of the city's social fabric, and they have no shortage of places catering to their needs. The upwardly mobile feel right at home on the Bund, where they are afforded a room with a view in practically all the bars, with Attica (p.403), Bar Rouge (p.387) and Glamour Bar (p.390) real highlights. Expat or not, you're still in a Chinese city of 20 million inhabitants, and locals add vigour to endless bars that blast mandopop and Japanese-style karaoke.

Discerning music lovers won't find it hard to source decent jazz, blues and salsa venues, either in places specifically dedicated to live acts, such as JZ Club (p.392) and Upstairs at Park 97 (p.406), or in various hotel bars, which feature seasonal travelling acts.

To see who's where and what's what, pick up a copy of one of the local lifestyle magazines such as *that's Shanghai*, *Shanghai Talk* and *SH* , all of which are distributed in major bars, restaurants and hotels.

Door Policy

In the majority of venues across town, the door policy is straightforward: pay the cover charge and in you go. This is perhaps one of the most refreshing things about Shanghai. There are no snooty doormen, the queues are minimal, and big male-only groups are generally welcome. In fact, you would have to be pretty seriously intoxicated for the bouncers to kick up a stink. Volar (p.406) may be the only exception to the rule, however, and operates a so-called strict guest list policy, although you can usually get around this easily by calling in advance.

Dress Code

It's often said that in Shanghai foreigners can get away with wearing whatever they want. Consequently, whatever your mood or character, and whether you prefer a pencil skirt or a hoodie and flip flops, your chosen form of attire should be readily accepted. That said, those wearing jeans and a T-shirt might feel a bit out of place in the more upscale establishments, and the reverse holds true of the more low-key venues. Still, you are unlikely to be turned away because of your clothes. The only time you may feel uncomfortable is if you're scantily clad, since the fact that you're a foreigner already invites enough attention.

Bars

Other options **Nightclubs** p.403

Whether the Chinese come from a drinking culture or not is debatable; some are wholly content to frequent karaoke bars and clubs not having had a drop of the hard stuff, while others seize their shot glasses and shout *gambei* (cheers) till they can no longer stand. Either way, drinking is a significant part of Shanghai's culture. The Shanghainese devote just as much vigour and enthusiasm to the sport of bar-hopping as they do to that of badminton and *mahjong*. Traditionally, the main bars for both locals and expats are concentrated in and around the Bund and French Concession, most notably Maoming Nan Lu, Julu Lu and Tongren Lu. However, in recent years, even those from Gubei, Daning and Pudong would find themselves hard pushed not to be within a one-mile radius of a decent watering hole, or at least the ubiquitous Blue Frog. Today, as multiculturalism

sweeps across Shanghai, bringing with it hordes of nationalities from all over the globe, a new eclectic and diverse mix of venues has opened up across the board.

11 Hongmei Pedestrian Street, Lane 3338, Hongmei Lu
Changning
虹梅路3338弄
休闲街11号
长宁
🚇 Yan'an Xi Lu
Map p.427 E4 **89**

3D Art Bar 三度艺术酒吧

6465 9833 | clarexiang@yahoo.com

The perennial debate over what should or shouldn't be classed as art is given a refreshing twist in this Gubei bar. Here, the art is none other than beer. Proud of its claim to be Shanghai's best-stocked bar, with more than 80 different varieties, the museum-like display of these trophies acts as a central visual '3D' stimulation. Prices start from dirt cheap ¥10 brews, to the more exotic, imported ¥60 varieties. It's by far the most happening place on Hongmei Pedestrian Street and a great place to visit if you live in Gubei. And who knows, after an intense four-hour 'happy' period daily between 16:00 and 20:00, including two-for-one deals, you might have just built up enough courage to create your own form of art in the free-of-charge karaoke rooms (minimum four people, no booking necessary). For the less vocally liberated, pool is also available for ¥10 per game. Open daily from 17:00 to 02:00, all cards accepted.

Le Royal Meridien, 789 Nanjing Dong Lu
Huangpu
世茂皇家艾美酒店,
南京东路789号
黄埔
🚇 People's Square
Map p.430 C3 **90**

789 Nanjing Lu 南京路789号

3318 9999 | www.starwoodhotels.com

Hotel bars the world over have a habit of being overpriced and underwhelming, so when you find a good one, such as 789, it's worth your time and money. Named after its street address, 789 occupies the top two floors of the 66 storey Le Royal Meridien on the corner of People's Square. It boasts amazing views, but the real spectacle, especially from a female perspective, is inside. An all-male bar staff, including models and mortals, serve up sumptuous cocktails including the '789tini'. And if this hasn't assured a decent flow of female clientele, the staff's apparent instruction to flirt with customers clinches the deal. If you visit during the incredibly popular Friday night 'Lipstick', you'll get signature cocktails for ¥50 and a glass of champagne for ¥80. Prepare for plenty of beautiful waiters surrounded by plenty of equally beautiful, doting customers.

Floor 34,
Summit View
Apartments,
1066 Yanan Xi Lu
Changning
延安西路1066号
瑞峰酒店公寓
长宁
Map p.435 D2 91

Air Restaurant and Lounge Bar

5239 5409 | www.top34.com.cn

Life doesn't often present Hollywood moments, but sitting on Air's rooftop terrace at sunset comes pretty close. It's got all the ingredients for romance: fresh cut grass, gazebos, a fish pond, and panoramic views of Shanghai's mix-and-match skyline. The interior – a circular bar flushed with reddish-pink and cloaked in chandeliers – isn't too bad either. During the week, the demographic is largely foreign businessmen that work in the Hongqiao area, who come to swig on well-mixed gin and tonics. A younger, livelier clientele move in at weekends. It's a fun place to come and create a picnic-type atmosphere; sitting outdoors and ordering food from the exotic menu, which features interesting delights such as baked crab with lemon dip. During the summer, the Spanish wine night offers a chance to sample seven different kinds of Iberian wine, and gorge on a well-cooked barbecue from a bargain ¥100.

Floor 2,
6 Zhongshan
Dong Yi Lu
Huangpu
上海中山东一路
外滩6号
黄埔
🚇 *Nanjing Dong Lu*
Map p.431 E3 92

Aquarium Bar 水族馆吧

6339 2779

Aquarium is romantic and seductive to the extreme. Situated in Six on the Bund, the building that houses Dolce & Gabbana, this bar is ultra-modern and elegant. On one side of the room is a huge wall-to-wall fish tank (hence the name), while on the other is a spectacular view over the Bund. Couples can cosy up in one of the many beds that line the window, while the less loved-up gather on the slick leather couches opposite. Aquarium reportedly stocks some of the best sake in town – not surprising as the bar is sister to Sun with Aqua (p.374), a Japanese restaurant across the hall. It is also rather proud of its mojitos, which come in a variety of unusual flavours. The entrance of Aquarium is impressive enough to command its own visit – you'll come face-to-face with a large tank full of sharks (small ones, admittedly, but still sharks). Open Sunday to Thursday, 18:00 to 01:00, and Friday and Saturday until 03:00.

439 Wukang Lu
Xuhui
武康路439号
徐汇
🚇 *Hengshan Lu*
Map p.435 E3 93

Arch 玖间酒吧

6466 0807 | info@archlink.com.cn

By day, it's a hipster cafe (p.380), but come nightfall, Arch becomes just a fun place to hang out with friends and sip a ¥60 mojito. A particularly attractive highlight is the cosy downstairs movie room, where drinkers can sit and watch a film of their choice; perfect if you want a quasi-cinema experience but don't have the head for Shanghai's typically cramped theatres. You'll need to bring your own DVD to watch, and be sure to book in advance. If all this doesn't make it sound modern enough, the incredibly forward-thinking (at least for Shanghai) smoke-free Wednesdays surely bring Arch into pole position as a 21st century bar pushing the boundaries. Open daily, 07:30 to 02:00; cards not accepted.

Baijiu

Baijiu is China's national spirit. The word literally means 'white liquor,' although it's often translated as 'white wine,' a dangerous mistake given that its alcoholic volume ranges between 40% and 60%. This clear distilled spirit has a very unique taste somewhat akin to a mix of nail polish remover and liquorice. Traditionally, it's served warm and drunk from small cups, usually during a meal. The cheapest bottle of *baijiu* you'll find will cost about ¥8, but good quality bottles can go for as much as ¥20,000 – meaning it's probably a good thing some of Shanghai's bars don't take credit cards.

**Lane 181,
15 Taicang Lu,
Xintiandi**
Luwan
太仓路181弄新天地
广场北里15号
卢湾
🚇 *Huangpi Nan Lu*
Map p.436 C1 **94**

Ark Live House 亚科音乐餐厅
6326 8008

Ark is located in Xintiandi, an area that attracts many a foreign tourist, so its predominantly Chinese customer-base comes as a refreshing surprise. The outside looks fairly inconspicuous, but enter the building, take the lift up and follow the balcony round and you'll come face-to-face with an impressive two-storey restaurant and bar. On the lower level, there is a large stage with state-of-the art lighting and sound, where local Chinese bands, and the occasional peppering of Japanese and American acts, play a diverse range of music, from punk to pop and everything in between. The predominantly Shanghinese crowd is an interesting mix of old and young, with some adventurous parents even bringing along their kids. This place is worth a visit if you're in Xintiandi and lost for ideas – if only to hear Chinese pop groups bellow indecipherable pronunciations of popular western lyrics: 'hurt me baby one more time' anyone? Drinks are average both in price and taste, but there is no cover charge. Open daily, 17:30 to 01:00.

**18 Zhongshan
Dong Yi Lu**
Huangpu
外滩十八号,
中山东一路18号
黄埔
🚇 *Nanjing Dong Lu*
Map p.431 E2 **95**

Bar Rouge
6339 1199 | www.volgroup.com.cn

Located on the seventh floor of Bund 18, Bar Rouge oozes style and sophistication. Some say it's the hottest place in Shanghai, others view it as a fading star that's losing out to new arrivals. Either way, it still acts as a magnet for the city's most affluent, who will happily pay a ¥100 cover charge and settle in one of the many booths to sip from flaming buckets of champagne. The walls are adorned with arty prints and there are two circular island bars, one indoors and one outside on a large terrace which offers stunning views. Jovial crowds flirt and network, as others move to trendy house mixes. It's a bit of a pick-up joint, and due to a regular influx of a less salubrious clientele, don't be shocked to see scantily clad women being asked their hourly rate. If you're female, it's perhaps best to forego that minidress. Open Sunday to Thursday, 18:30 to 01:30, and Friday and Saturday, 18:00 to 04:00.

**231 Nanjing Xi Lu,
inside People's Park**
Huangpu
南京西路231号
人民公园内
黄埔
🚇 *People's Square*
Map p.430 C3 **96**

Barbarossa Lounge 芭芭露莎
6318 0220 | www.barbarossa.com.cn

Set amid silvery bamboo and encircled by a moat of floating lily pads, the triple-decker Moroccan-style villa that lodges Barbarossa is fit for any king, or sultan for that matter. The terrace on the ground floor serves food and is a good spot for drinks both during the day and after dinner. On a night out, most head inside and upstairs, where people recline on cushion-covered banquettes, sipping dangerously intoxicating cocktails and blowing delicious smoke rings from ornate shisha pipes. The music is mellow and soulful on the ground floor, but becomes more commercial and upbeat the further you ascend. There is a private, outdoor seating area at the very top of Barbarossa, which can be reserved under the guarantee of a minimum spend of ¥1,500 for a table that accommodates eight (a smart move if you're planning to make a night of it). Much of the venue is open-air so remember to wear plenty of insect repellent during the summer. Open daily, 11:00 to 02:00.

387

Blue Frog 蓝蛙 ▶ p.383

Room 3,
Green Sports and
Leisure Centre,
633 Biyun Lu
Pudong
碧云路633号
绿色体育休闲中心3室
浦东
Map p.440 B1 97

5030 6426 | www.bluefrog.com.cn

Blue Frog is the perfect example of why simple is often best. Its casual drinking and dining concept first took physical form in 1999 on Maoming Lu in the shape of a small, humble watering hole that possessed good service, reasonable drinks and nice comfort food, such as breakfast burritos and barbecue burgers. Since then, the brand has increased six-fold, with branches serving up booze and snacks in most major areas across town. The Jinqiao branch is aimed largely at the local families and expats who live in this suburban district. It's modern and sleek, with the signature backlit blue tiles the sole source of eye candy. There is a lovely outdoor patio, a kid-friendly area and, like all Blue Frogs, space available for private parties and events. Two-for-one drink deals run between 16:00 and 20:00 and are a cheap way to justify an attack on the 100 plus shot list. On Tuesdays all drinks cost ¥25 until closing. Other branches are found in Pudong's Super Brand Mall, Hongmei Pedestrian Street, Tongren Lu and Daning Life Hub – check out the website for details. Open daily, 10:00 to 02:00.

Cocktails

Gone are the days when a vodka mixer was the best you could expect from a bar in Shanghai. Today it's almost harder to find a place that doesn't offer an extensive cocktail list. Awards for the most delicious and exotic concoctions go to the following: Jean Georges (p.365), whose vanilla vodka cream soda is divine; Tara 57 (p.398), which has more than 150 choices on its menu; Jade on 36 (p.391), with its eclectic mixes such as the cardamon and pineapple martini; Glamour Bar's (p.390) 'rosemary's son', with actual sprigs of rosemary; and Manifesto (p.393), whose fusion of the lychee martini and the cosmopolitan is an absolute classic.

British Bulldog

1 Wulumuqi Nan Lu
Xuhui
乌鲁木齐南路1号
徐汇
🚇 *Hengshan Lu*
Map p.435 F2 98

6466 7878 | www.britishbulldogpub.com

Whether you're an Anglo-Saxon who misses home or an Anglophile who wishes Britain was home, you'll find sanctuary in British Bulldog. As the name implies, this is your quintessential public house, full of wooden panels, brass, and buttonhole stools. Hearty British fare, such as fish and chips and shepherd's pie (both around ¥65), is served on the ground floor until 02:00. The average punter will also be impressed by the British ales on tap, including McEwan's IPA, Boddingtons and Beamish. The prices are not too bad either: ¥40 for a large draft Heineken; ¥50 for Grolsch. Move up a flight and you'll discover the obligatory games room, where people can engage in pub-going Brits' favourite pastimes: pool, darts, table football and a big screen for live sports. The third floor offers another relaxing area where people unwind in front of more TV screens. For the ultimate British experience, go along on a Monday for the free-flowing curry night, which costs ¥100 per person and includes two Tiger beers. Also look out for regular pub quizzes, and British comedy and film nights. Expect regulars from both the UK and its former colonies. Open daily, 11:00 to 02:00.

Bull and Bear

950 Pudong Dadao
Pudong
浦东大道950号
浦东
🚇 *Dongchang Lu*
Map p.433 D2 99

5093 1655

With five mounted flat-screen TVs adorning the walls and a large projector screen showing international matches of various sports, this German-run bar is a great place to kick back before and after kick off. Bull and Bear opened in early 2007, and has since attracted a mixed crowd of suited business types, sports fans and local Pudongites in search of a cold beer in a chilled environment. The design is conventional sports bar, with high tables and bar stools arranged under mellow yellow lighting. There are dartboards and foosball tables, as well as an English-pub themed corner of sleek wooden panels and soft red booths. The music is as eclectic as the crowd, playing anything from Beatles to Britney, with a live band on Friday and disco on Saturday. Grab yourself a ¥30 plus pint of German beer or flavoured schnapps before kick-off or at half time, and chances are you'll end up sticking around for extra time too. Open daily, 10:00 to 02:00.

C's Bar

6294 0547

For most of the month, the only real attraction of C's Bar, out in Hongqiao, is the ¥10 beers. However, come the last Thursday of every cycle, this all changes when the underground, must-attend event Antidote is held in C's basement. Antidote is run by the group of the same name, a bunch of local digital musicians and DJs. Frustrated by Shanghai nightlife (expensive, exclusive and acoustically unimaginative, they claim), the group promised to offer something different. With the already cheap drink prices and no entry charge, youngsters from all across town flock to C's to hear indie rock, trip-hop and punk. If only they could come up with an antidote to that Friday morning hangover too. Open daily, 21:30 to 04:00. No cards accepted.

Cloud 9 九重天

5049 1234

Perched on the 87th floor of the stunning Jinmao Tower, the world's fifth tallest building, Cloud 9 is the loftiest watering hole on earth. The bar is suspended so high that it often rests either in or above the clouds, but when there's a blue sky, Shanghai's ever-evolving skyline unfolds in 360 degree grandeur. Unfortunately, the altitude might have gone to the owners' heads, who levy a ¥150 cover charge per person. This does the job of giving it an image of exclusivity, but it also prevents more local traffic. Consequently, Cloud 9 is a bar frequented mostly by tourists and hotel guests. Nevertheless, no trip to Shanghai would be complete without a quick trip to this sultry establishment where the hefty entrance fee can quickly be doubled by a quick splurge on two exquisite cocktails and some fussy snack food, served by some of the city's most polite and efficient staff. An insider tip worth remembering: ring in advance to reserve a table with a Puxi view as the Pudong-facing side is less impressive. Open daily, 11:30 to 02:00.

Cotton Club 棉花俱乐部

6437 7110

Cotton Club is a model for how all good jazz bars should be: equal parts smoky, dingy and sexy. As one of the original, and most popular, blues and jazz bars in Shanghai, this club offers a throwback to the 1930s, when the city was the acclaimed heart of Asia's jazz movement. And its heart still pumps loud and strong in the T-shaped dark bar, where the likes of the legendary American trumpeter Wynton Marsalis have performed, and where local favourite Coco is still something of a regular. A mixture of travelling and house acts play live to a cultured crowd from around 21:30 during the week and 22:30 at weekends. Come early as the seats can fill up quickly, grab yourself one of Shanghai's strongest G&Ts (¥45) and soak up the beats in this quintessential jazz hub. It's open every night except Monday; top names sometimes command an entrance fee.

De La Coast

6330 2615

Another favourite among Shanghai's foreign scenesters, this upscale lounge is the perfect place to unwind in the light summer breeze. Take the lift to the fifth floor, where an incredibly enthusiastic maitre d' will ask you what level you want. Don't automatically rush up to the sixth; if it's a Saturday and you're wearing stilettos, all drinks are on the house before 23:00 on the fifth. However, if the loud music proves a little too ear-assaulting, a totally different kind of tempo is offered upon ascending the extra flight. Squeeze past the slim bar to arrive at a lovely patio; its wooden floorboards create a South Beach, Miami kind of feel. The drinks are not stupidly cheap, but starting at ¥50 they're about right for this kind of location. There are a few tables hidden outside on a miniscule terrace on the fifth floor; come early enough and you may be able to seize them but just be careful of the secret step that catches people out. There's not much in the way of atmosphere on this ledge, but it's one of the best Bund views in town. Open Sunday to Thursday, 23:30 to 02:00; Friday and Saturday, 11:30 to 03:00.

DR Bar 木头酒吧

15 North Block, Lane 181, Taicang Lu, Xintiandi
Luwan
太仓路181弄新天地
北里15号
卢湾
🚇 **Huangpi Nan Lu**
Map p.436 C1 **104**

6311 0358

Housed in a former Communist Party meeting hall on a quiet nook off the main stretch, DR is the quietest of Xintiandi's generally raucous watering holes, and its relaxed vibe attracts a mature crowd more into conversation than crooning. The 'DR' stands for Design Resource and is the creation of Boston architect Benjamin Wood, the figure behind the revitalisation of Xintiandi. The decor is dimly lit lounge bar, with soft marble, silver counters and charcoal walls. Polite, stylishly clad bar staff melt into the background, while a discrete iPod hums smooth grooves. The menu is reflective of the general atmosphere – simple yet satisfying, featuring all the classic cocktails (the black Russian is especially well made), alongside a decent selection of spirits, priced from ¥55. Stake out your turf on one of the low-lying couches, but be warned; quaff a few too many of the lethal concoctions and the night might not end up quite so mellow. Open daily, 16:00 to 01:00.

Face Bar

Ruijin Guest House, 118 Ruijin Er Lu
Xuhui
瑞金二路118号,
瑞金宾馆
徐汇
🚇 **Shanxi Nan Lu**
Map p.436 B1 **105**

6466 4328 | www.facebars.com

Few people have a bad word to say about Face, a popular spot among both locals and expats. It used to be part of an estate that belonged to concession-era newspaper moguls the Moriss family, but now sits in the palatial grounds of the 1920s Ruijin Guesthouse. Its history has clearly seeped into the furnishings though, and it reeks of Asian luxury and neo-colonial chic. Old opium beds and red leather couches deck the floor in autumnal shades and south-east Asian idols adorn the walls. Face is an excellent starting point for a night out, especially if you can lay claim to one of the outdoor tables backing onto the lawn. Otherwise, head indoors and enjoy the buzz. In addition to its many cocktails, including the shanghai blues and café tintancla, there's an interesting assortment of tasty bar bites on offer. There's also a Thai restaurant on the second floor and a very decadent chocolate cabinet that you'll be hard pressed not to notice if you go to the loo. Open daily, 12:00 to 02:00.

Glamour Bar 魅力酒吧

20 Guangdong Lu
Huangpu
广东路20号
黄埔
🚇 **Nanjing Dong Lu**
Map p.431 C3 **106**

6329 3751 | www.m-theglamourbar.com

Adjoining and lying beneath the iconic M on the Bund, Glamour Bar is impressively chic. The decor is divine; a long, chrome, mirrored bar stretches across the centre, and a small champagne bar is tucked away behind. Delicate hand-painted

Sports Bars

A plethora of venues have surfaced in the past few years to satiate a sports-hungry demand. Big Bamboo (see advert p.241) is perhaps the most established place in Shanghai, with two outlets across town, one at 23 Nanyang Lu (6256 2265) and the other, Baby Bamboo at 26 Hongmei Pedestrian Lu (6465 9099). Other popular venues for catching the big match include O'Malleys (p.394), M Zone (88 Tongren Lu, Jingan, 6247 6595), British Bulldog Pub (p.388), Malones (p.393) and the Spot (p.398).

Chinese screens line the sides, washed in dusty red, pink and gold, while large loft-style windows occupy three walls, providing a captivating backdrop of both the Bund and Pudong. During the week, the music is non-descript lounge fare, attracting a mixed crowd who come to unwind in the ample sofas and familiarise themselves with the extensive wine list. On weekends the music is louder and often quite cheesy, as Shanghai's fashionistas descend. The venue often hosts book readings and lively discussion forums, so check the local lifestyle magazines to see what's coming up. Open daily, 17:00 to 02:00.

158 Maoming Nan Lu
Xuhui
茂名南路158号
徐汇
🚇 *Shanxi Nan Lu*
Map p.436 B1 107

House of Blues and Jazz 布鲁斯与爵士之屋
6437 5280

If you love jazz or just want a break from Shanghai's more uptight bars, House of Blues and Jazz is the place for you. This musical hubbub is one of the more respectable joints on this otherwise seedy strip of Maoming Lu and has daily live acts of jazz infused with blues and funk. It's an unassuming and pleasant bar, which serves standard cocktails, wine and beer. Despite noise levels and drink prices being notched up, it's still a great place to go to enliven an otherwise dull evening. It's not a venue for the stage-shy, however. Serious audience participation is expected, be it the standard requisite applause or an enforced turn on the dance stage. Open Tuesday to Sunday, 16:00 to 02:00, with live music from 21:30 to 01:00.

155 Zhongshan Dong Er Lu
Huangpu
中山东二路155号
黄埔
🚇 *Nanjing Dong Lu*
Map p.431 E3 108

I Love Shanghai Lounge 我爱上海
6355 8058 | www.iloveshanghailounge.com

If you feel that you're falling out of love with Shanghai, spend a couple of hours in this establishment and you could well find it returning. It's not the venue itself that will help restore your affections – it's not as glamourous and the views aren't as breathtaking as some of its neighbours on the Bund – but look beyond first appearances and you'll soon discover the beauty within. Namely the unbelievably cheap drinks. Beer starts at ¥30, an extensive cocktail list from ¥35 and wine at ¥40. It makes for a great-value starting point if you're heading on to one of the more expensive bars in the area, particularly if you take up the offer of 10 shooters for ¥100. Despite not being the most stylish on the block, I Love Shanghai is far from dingy. It's a pleasant, sultry place, with large, comfy lounge seats and wait staff at your constant beck and call. The poppy, energetic music and young, fun crowd create an uplifting atmosphere, and, who knows, after a few drinks you might find your spirits raised enough to walk out wearing one of its I Love Shanghai T-shirts. Open daily, 17:00 to 02:00.

Shangri-La, 33 Fucheng Lu
Pudong
富城路33号
浦东香格里拉大酒店36楼
浦东
🚇 *Lujiazui*
Map p.431 F3 109

Jade on 36 翡翠36餐厅
6882 3636 | www.shangri-la.com

Given that its sister restaurant serves up delights such as coca-cola spaghetti and agar-pomelo ravioli, you know you're in for a surprise when you visit this watering hole. Indeed, once you make it past the stainless steel automatic door, more suited to a high security prison than a bar, you will discover a place overflowing with personality. The bold colour palette of neon pinks and lime greens is a refreshing change in a city where red is a little overdone, and even the egg-shaped toilet cubicles add to the wow factor. The menu is equally charismatic, with manuka honey, mandarin orange and ginseng martini being just one of many mouthwatering cocktails (all priced between ¥50 and ¥70) on offer. It's also a pleasant surprise that the attractive staff are not in the least bit arrogant, but rather incredibly helpful. Finally, add subtle, sexy music to the mix and Jade has got it all. Open Sunday to Thursday, 18:00 to 01:00; Fridays and Saturdays, 18:00 to 02:00.

Just Grapes 萄醉

462 Dagu Lu
Jing'an
大沽路462号
静安
🚇 *Nanjing Xi Lu*
Map p.430 B4 **110**

3311 3205 | www.justgrapes.cn

Just Grapes is one of those great little finds, with little being the operative word. Wedged between numerous massage parlours on a stretch of Dagu Lu, Just Grapes is most notable as a well-presented wine store. However, for the discerning wine lover, there is also a quaint, inviting lounge on the second floor. This cosy spot has an apartment-like feel, with an open kitchen where you can watch the chef as he bakes tasty delights to complement your chosen tipple. You can also rent out this room for intimate occasions (the price depends on numbers and the food and wine chosen). The menu features a few nice vintages, and wines can be chosen by the glass. Helpful captions such as 'fruity', 'spicy', 'rich' and 'smooth bodied' aid the selection process, as do well-informed staff. If what's on offer doesn't appeal, you can buy a bottle downstairs and bring it up. But like everything good in life, the Just Grapes experience doesn't come cheap. Open daily, 10:30 to 23:00.

Jwow Wine Bar 龙聚苑酒吧

515 Jianguo Xi Lu
Xuhui
建国路515号
徐汇
🚇 *Hengshan Lu*
Map p.435 F3 **111**

5492 1655 | www.senseswinelounge.com

If quaffing wine in a chilled out environment appeals, then Jwow, formerly known as Senses, might be the place for you. In theory it's very well stocked, with bottles ranging between ¥100 and a whopping ¥23,000, but in reality the multiple vintages marked as 'unavailable' in the menu can be a touch frustrating. Still, in a city that isn't renowned for its wine, Jwow is a decent option. The interior is pleasant if a bit non-descript and during the winter it can be a little chilly, but the outside patio definitely receives the thumbs up, especially come summer when it hosts regular all-inclusive weekend barbeques for ¥100. The more mature clientele favour its casual, relaxed atmosphere, while the free wireless internet, alongside its large TV in the back room, are a massive plus for everyone. On Tuesday, glasses of wine go for ¥25 and all bottles are reduced by 30%.

JZ Club 爵士酒吧

46 Fuxing Xi Lu
Luwan
复兴西路46号
卢湾
🚇 *Changshu Lu*
Map p.435 E2 **112**

6431 0269 | www.jzclub.cn

If Miles Davis were still around today, JZ Club would make it on to his list of places to visit when in Shanghai. This venue, which claims to have been created by players for players (and obviously their numerous fans), is all about the music. Those who frequent JZ don't do so for the decor, but it's a pleasant combination of rich red sofas in the balconied upstairs, and shiny surfaces and tall candlelit tables elsewhere. The musical line-up is a mixture of local and non-local talent, none of whom are strangers to improvisation. The popular band Latinoide regularly plays spicy Hispanic beats, and on a Sunday night from 22:00 the legendary Coco, an internationally renowned Chinese jazz singer, takes to the stage. Expect to pay at least ¥45 for drinks. On Saturdays you'll have to pay a cover charge (¥30). Open daily, 21:00 to 02:30.

Logo

13 Xingfu Lu
Changning
幸福路13号
长宁
Map p.435 D3 **113**

6281 5646

This place is a bit on the grimy side, but for the young, arty local and expat crowd, it's worth the trek towards Xujiahui. After walking through a brightly lit area with rows of sofas and fussball tables, a curtained doorway covers the entrance to the main bar. Inside, the room is dark with an island bar, low seating and crusty red walls. A DJ mixes beats from a propped-up laptop until 22:00, after which the city's rising amateur artists take to the stage with live acts that range from traditional Chinese music to solo singer guitarists and the occasional DJ. There is rarely a cover charge and drinks are very cheap; ¥10 buys you a bottle of beer or sangria. Open daily, 19:00 to 04:00. No cards accepted.

255 Tongren Lu
Jing'an
铜仁路255号
静安
🚇 *Jing'an Temple*
Map p.429 F4 **114**

Malones 马龙

6289 4830 | www.malones.com.cn

Malones claims to provide 'what you would expect from your neighbourhood bar in North America.' Well, you might not expect such a large crowd of foreign businessmen or the in-house, hyper-charged Filipino band, Art-6, but Malones is American in every other respect. This three-storey *Cheers*-style establishment has reportedly some of the best, traditional hamburgers in town, which can be washed down with a pint of cheap beer in front of a screen tuned to the latest international sports channels. Wednesday nights are popular thanks to the Asiaxpat mixer, a friendly, easygoing networking event for newcomers. There are also regular pool, darts and quiz nights. Open daily, 11:00 to 02:00.

748 Julu Lu
Luwan
巨鹿路748号
卢湾
🚇 *Changshu Lu*
Map p.435 F1 **115**

Manifesto

6289 9108

Part of uber chic restaurant Mesa, this bar is definitely worth a stop during a night of Julu Lu bar hopping. Its slightly-off-the-beaten-track stigma is the main draw, since it's the kind of place that you can turn up to without a reservation and still find incredibly comfortable seating for you and 20 of your friends. Manifesto occupies a former electronics factory and has an airy, contemporary warehouse feel. The staff are polite and friendly and the cocktails are sumptuous and somewhat unusual. Concoctions such as Belgian white chocolate waffle martini fill the menu's pages. Best of all, however, are the mini burgers, one of many tapas treats on offer. Bring your credit card and get ready to swirl those daiquiris, dahling. Open Monday to Thursday, 18:00 to 00:00; Sunday, 18:00 to 02:00.

Jade on 36

Glamour Bar

Six on the Bund

JZ Club

▸ p.395

Melting Pot 马尔廷酒吧

288 Taikang Lu
Luwan
泰康路288号
卢湾
🚇 **Huangpi Nan Lu**
Map p.436 B2 **116**

6467 9900 | www.themelting-pot.com
Locals and expats flock to the Melting Pot at 21:30 every night to catch the rock bands that grace the large stage. Though the place recently started serving Thai food, the focus here is definitely the music and booze. The large, plain room is usually occupied by band members and fans of live music. Most of the groups that play are good, although some would be better off back in the garage – the fun is not quite knowing what you'll hear. During the early evening, Melting Pot provides a laid-back atmosphere for families – until the familiar refrain of 'one, two, one, two' starts to bellow through the amps, that is. There's another branch at 635 Bibu Lu Pudong.

Mural 摩砚酒吧

697 Yongjia Lu
Xuhui
永嘉路697号
徐汇
🚇 **Hengshan Lu**
Map p.435 F3 **117**

6433 5023 | www.muralbar.com
Entering Mural is like stepping into Aladdin's cave. Totally non-descript from the road but, once inside, you're met by a vast array of eastern delights, from traditional paintings to religious and cultural relics. The music is eclectic, ranging from live Latino bands and reggae to original funk and commercial tunes. A further guarantee of a good night out is the weekly drinks promotions, especially the bargain all-you-can-drink open bar every Friday for ¥100. The crowd is always young and fun, if a little too junior on weekends when the international school kids come out to play. Open daily, 19:00 to 02:00.

Noah's Bar 船长酒吧

Floor 6,
Captain's Hostel,
37 Fuzhou Lu
Huangpu
船长青年酒店，
福州路37号
黄埔
🚇 **Nanjing Dong Lu**
Map p.431 E3 **118**

6323 7869 | csp@picolo.com.cn
Beers with fantastic views of the back of the Bund and Pudong for ¥15 a pop – surely not? Climb (or take the elevator) to the seventh floor of Captain's Hostel, the city's most popular budget accommodation, and you'll find yourself in Noah's Bar. Noah's takes its nautical associations to the extreme, with the inside looking like a set from *Pirates of the Caribbean* (it even comes equipped with sun loungers). Outside, the 'open deck' is a delightful spot to swig a beer in the afternoon sun while watching marine traffic at what is the world's second busiest port. The staff are very friendly and generally speak good English, which is a pleasant surprise for this price bracket. Peckish people can enjoy large portions of American fair for less than ¥50 (guests of the hostel receive a discount). With a mixed, albeit largely foreign, crowd, it really is all aboard. Open daily, 11:00 to 02:00. No cards accepted.

O'Malley's 欧玛莉餐厅

42 Taojiang Lu
Xuhui
桃江路42号
徐汇
🚇 **Changshu Lu**
Map p.435 F2 **119**

6474 4533 | www.omalleys-shanghai.com
This traditional Irish-style pub is geared towards spectator sports. The ground floor room is large and homely, with rows of benches all positioned to provide the best view. During the big matches it's jammed with fans. Rugby and cricket draw a largely British crowd while the football attracts just about every fan in the city. Basic pub grub and Guinness flow abundantly – a pint will set you back ¥65. The outdoor patio comes into its own during the warmer months. There are various toys and play things, making it a great place to take the children for a relaxing Sunday afternoon. There is also a pool table and dartboard. Open daily, 11:00 to 02:00.

SOUND OF PEOPLE - SOUND OF MUSIC
THE MELTING POT

NO.288,Tai Kang Lu, Lu Wan Qu, Shanghai
Tel : +86-21-6467.9900

BAR 288 SHANGHAI

LIVE MUSIC EVERYDAY
MONDAYS FREE JAMMING
September through June
Sundays melt into Monday
Special theme night every last
Sunday of the month
Every 3rd Monday Song Writers Night
Thai Food/ also delivery

168 RESTAURANT BAR

Live Music every day, Dancing

Children's playground

Table-football, Darts

Computergames

Catering/Delivery, Banquets

Wireless Internet

Outdoor seating

Shanghai Legend Centre
No.635,Bi Bo Lu, Pu Dong Xin Qu, Shanghai
Tel : +86-21-5027.3527

Under construction

Opcning October 2007

Shop 3, 1-5 Elgin Street, Central, HongKong
Tel : +852-9099.5711

BAR 288 HONGKONG

DIFFERENT STYLES OF

LIVE MUSIC EVERY DAY

MONDAYS FREE JAMMING

Thai Food, also delivery

FOR THE MOST INTERESTING MUSIC AND FOOD – THE MELTING POT
CHECK OUR WEBSITE FOR SPECIAL PROGRAMS www:themelting-pot.com
CONTACT : email   meltingpot@orienteam.com or bar288@orienteam.com

Riverside ◄
Promenade,
Binjiang Dadao
Pudong
滨江大道风光亭
浦东
🚇 *Lujiazui*
Map p.431 F3 `120`

Paulaner Brauhaus 宝莱纳

6888 3935

The simple, successful formula of this place is best summed up in two words: German beer. Set in a picturesque location on the Huangpu River, with stunning views across to the Bund, Paulaner's in-house microbrewery ensures that the beer is always fresh and very, very *gut*. The lederhosen worn by the staff might stretch the German theme, but local, well-paid Chinese seem to love it, and come to guzzle down pint after pint in the large, traditional beer garden. The hefty prices might rob you of all your loose change – small homebrews alone cost ¥60 – but on Mondays between 16:00 and 19:00, the all-inclusive half-price deals make Bavarian delights such as sauerkraut and schnitzel much more affordable. The Binjiang branch has regular live music and is one of three outlets around town; there's also one in Xintiandi and another at 150 Fenyang Lu. Open Sunday to Thursday, 10:00 to 01:00; Friday and Saturday, 10:00 to 02:00.

805 Julu Lu
Jing'an
巨鹿路805号
静安
🚇 *Changshu Lu*
Map p.435 F1 `121`

People 7 人间银七

5404 0707

The uninitiated might struggle to enter this enigmatic joint. You have to place your hands in a movement-sensitive loop at the top of the stairs, and then voila, the door should open. People 7 fuses industrial bar with cosy lounge painlessly, and even though the colour scheme is a touch depressing, you'll still have fun here. Customers seem perfectly content exhausting the cocktail menu, chugging down saccharin shots from test tubes and chomping on the occasional spoonful of tiramisu. Quite a fuss is made over the toilets, which open on the opposite side to the handles. From the top of People 7 you'll get a brilliant view of neighbouring Shintori. This is a relaxed place for a quiet conversation; consequently it attracts a mature crowd. Open daily, 11:30 to 14:00 and 18:00 to 00:30.

137 Xingfu Lu
Changning
幸福路137号
长宁
Map p.435 D2 `122`

Pirates 海盗吧

pirateshanghai@gmail.com

In a city where glamour is often defined by the size of your bar bill, the nonchalant attitude of Pirates proves incredibly refreshing. Events such as Walkman Battles, where DJs play off to win over the audience, and performances from bands such as Raggasonic, a famous French ensemble, make Pirates one of Shanghai's best alternative venues. The bar personifies understated cool. It's deliberately grimy, with stencilled hooded figures on the walls and beaten-up black, low-slung sofas dotted around. There are two bars; a quieter one at the front, and a louder one at the back near the stage and a small dance area. Both the service and crowd are very friendly, and the drinks are reasonably priced. Everything considered, the ¥30 cover charge that often applies is more than reasonable. Open daily, 21:00 to 02:00.

Youlong Garden, ◄
Shibu Jie, Fucheng Lu
Pudong
由隆花园, 拾步街,
滨江富城路
浦东
🚇 *Lujiazui*
Map p.431 F3 `123`

Snow Bar, Binjiang One 雪吧, 滨江壹号楼

5877 7500 | www.bln.com.cn

The Narnia-inspired Snow Bar, part of the Binjiang One complex, is definitely one of the city's cooler creations, especially as the bar is kept at -10°C. You'll be given a special coat to wear as you enter and, once inside, you'll appreciate icy details such as suspended snowflakes and frosty surfaces. The real action takes place at the bar though, where an enthusiastic bartender will coax you into trying as many of the 100 plus vodka shots as possible. Although the prices might deter – they range between ¥70 and ¥90 a shot – choices such as the merlot vodka and coconut espresso vodka are too tempting to refuse. If this is all a little too cool for you, head to Snow Bar's antithesis – the warm, rustic wine cellar in the basement, which stocks more than 100 bottles of wine. Open daily, 17:30 to 00:00.

331 Tongren Lu
Jing'an
铜仁路331号
静安
🚇 *Jing'an Temple*
Map p.429 F4 **124**

Spot Bar

6247 3579 | *www.judysco.com.cn*

Keen to catch the game but not a massive fan of smoky sports bars? Then head to Spot. Its refreshing, light interior makes for a pleasant backdrop as you while away an evening watching live football, basketball, baseball or Formula 1. Afterwards, you can hit the terrace for celebrations or commiserations. But you don't have to be a sports fan to enjoy this bar. With a great band singing cheesy renditions at the weekend, affordable drinks and some excellent food (especially the hamburgers made from fresh beef), Spot is a winner every time. Wednesdays see pool competitions from 20:00, and every day is a 'happy day', with two-for-one deals between 14:30 and 20:00. Open Sunday to Thursday, 10:30 to 02:00; Friday and Saturday, 10:30 to 03:00.

Floor 2,
57 Fuxing Xi Lu
Xuhui
复兴西路57号
徐汇
🚇 *Changshu Lu*
Map p.435 E2 **125**

Tara 57

6431 7027

Tara 57 is a hidden gem, inconspicuously wedged between Boona 2 cafe (p.380) on the ground floor and a Japanese KTV joint above. The bar is tiny, with just four loungers, three tables and a few stools, but the seating is ultra comfortable, not to mention super stylish. Continuing the quality-not-quantity theme, the incredibly friendly bar staff are keen to develop a rapport with customers, and grace the tables to help the confused choose from more than 250 cocktails. From ¥58, and served with various crispy little nibbles, the drinks hit the spot. Open daily, 18:00 to 02:00.

Floor 2,
598 Fengyang Lu
Jing'an
凤阳路598号
静安
🚇 *Nanjing Dong Lu*
Map p.431 B3 **126**

Trader Vic's 垂德维客

5228 3882

Word on the street is that the mai tais here are as good as they get this side of the Pacific. And so they should be given that the bar's namesake, Trader Vic, reportedly created the cocktail. But there's more to this chain than just a Polynesian-themed restaurant and bar: all the cocktails are equally delicious and punchy. There are endless drinks promotions; a happy hour every day between 17:30 and 19:30; and ladies' nights on Wednesdays and Saturdays between 19:30 and 20:30. And then there's the all-woman band who mix up fun salsa and Cuban tunes. The food is a hybrid of American and Chinese fare, with the ¥205 halibut filet highly recommended. The atmosphere is relaxed, with low, flattering lighting, and the staff friendly. Open daily, 17:30 to 02:00.

Floor 6,
3 Zhongshan
Dong Yi Lu
Huangpu
中山东一路3号
黄埔
🚇 *Nanjing Dong Lu*
Map p.431 E3 **127**

Vault Bar 保险库

6321 9922 | *www.threeonthebund.com*

It is safe to assume that any bar attached to one of city's most celebrated restaurants can't go wrong, and Vault Bar is no exception. Add this to pleasant location at Three on the Bund and it's got a lot going for it. Prolific chef David Laris' food baby, Laris (p.366), provides a seriously stylish locale. The outer areas of the bar have the feel of an ostentatious wedding reception, with bright, sparkling marble and rich velvet fabrics. However, climb a few stairs and the quick change of colour and lighting turns the raised main area into a more sultry adventure. The bar is incredibly well-stocked, and Vault serves some of the best cocktails in town – the apple and lychee martinis for one. This is a bonus come Thursday's incredibly

popular two-for-one martini special, which runs all night. The commercial, upbeat mix of house, hip-hop and pop also offers a nice break from the lounge lull you often get elsewhere. Open daily, 17:30 to 02:00.

Velvet Lounge

Floor 1, Building 3-4, 913 Julu Lu
Jing'an
3-4号楼，
巨鹿路913号
静安
🚇 *Changshu Lu*
Map p.435 F1 **128**

5403 2976 | www.velvetlounge.com.cn
Julu Lu is fast becoming an alternative to the Bund for the city's trendy set, and Velvet Lounge fits the scene perfectly. Set back from the road on the western end of the strip, it delivers a chic, brazen kind of 1980s cool. Upon climbing the stairs, a series of interconnecting rooms unfold, with the main bar being in the first one you see. Friendly staff usually flutter around the tables eagerly awaiting an order. With beaded curtains and cushion-covered couches, it's definitely a great place to take a date during the week. The music is quite loud and can be a bit offbeat (think the theme tune of *Twin Peaks*), but morphs into generic hip-hop and house at the weekend to satiate a more boisterous crowd. Alongside delicious – albeit very strong – drinks (pleasantly inexpensive, with cocktails for ¥45), Velvet also serves thin-crust gourmet pizzas until closing time. Open Sunday to Thursday, 17:00 to 03:00; Friday and Saturday, 17:00 to 05:00.

Windows Too 蕴德词

104 Jing'an Temple Plaza, 1699 Nanjing Xi Lu
Jing'an
南京西路1699号
静安寺广场104号
静安
🚇 *Jing'an Temple*
Map p.429 F4 **129**

3214 0351 | www.enter-4.com
Serving up the cheapest drinks in town (all priced between ¥10 and ¥25), Windows is a no-frills dingy, dungeon-style dive. Nevertheless, it's obviously doing something right; not only is it packed most nights, but sister bars have sprung up in three other central locations across town. Windows Too has pool tables, a dartboard and a makeshift dance area, where adolescents, undeterred by the ¥50 cover charge, let off some of that homework heat. It's recommended as a place for a nice chit-chat over a glass of wine, not least because the stereo blasts the international Top 40. Still, you can't beat those drink deals. Snack food is also available. Open daily, 19:00 to 01:00. No cards accepted.

Zapatas

5 Hengshan Lu
Xuhui
衡山路5号
徐汇
🚇 *Hengshan Lu*
Map p.435 F2 **130**

6433 4104 | www.zapatas-shanghai.com
Mention to most expats that you're going to Zapatas and they'll roll their eyes and give you a knowing smile. This Mexican restaurant and bar has established something of a reputation as the place to come for a drink-fuelled, rowdy night. While the label fits to some extent – expect loud, boisterous behaviour and some fairly wild antics – the crowd is varied and the music eclectic. Spread over two floors in an attractive French Concession building, Zapatas is wooden and worn inside, and gets pretty flithy come the end of the night. Don't be surprised to see women a little worse for wear dancing on the bar during Wednesday's ladies' night. Encouraged by endless free martinis, they move to classics from the 60s through to the modern day, with the occasional Hispanic favourite thrown in. If it all gets too much, the pleasant outdoor patio offers some welcome breathing space. Open daily, 17:30 to 02:00.

399

Karaoke Bars

For many people, the idea of karaoke is synonymous with hell: an empty stage in a stale bar where your success is judged by your propensity to make a fool of yourself. This is not the case in Shanghai. Karaoke, or rather KTV, is refreshingly fun here. Aside from the various bars and clubs with their own form of KTV, there are several chains throughout the city that cater solely to China's favourite pastime. The leaders of the pack are Party World (also known as Cashbox), Big Echo and Haoledi KTV; their ubiquity underlines how important karaoke is to the Chinese social fabric.

Typically, venues have a large selection of different-sized rooms, which are hired out for varying amounts – on average a minimum spend of ¥1,000 on food and drink is expected for a group of six. For this pretty price you'll have a waiter at your beck and call. Inside the cosy, private rooms, expect a large TV screen, catalogues of music to choose from (much of it Chinese but with a decent selection of western tunes too), and several microphones, which happily you can circulate; a blessing for those who are not so easy on the ear.

Go with the Flo

The parties organised by Swiss expats Matt and Flo have become something of an institution in Shanghai. Several years ago the pair's low-key barbeque turned into a huge success, and they've been arranging parties ever since. There is usually no cover charge and a new location and theme each time. The turnout is usually impressive. Recent nights have included 'Cruise to Honolulu,' which was held at Trader Vic's and 'Saturday Lush Fever,' at Lush. To subscribe to the mailing list, contact Flo at florian.luthi@gmail.com.

Big Echo 必爱歌
6351 2700

You might find yourself lost in translation at this Japanese-owned music arena (it places a strong emphasis on Japanese pop), but rest assured that with a choice of more than 30,000 songs in seven different languages, there will be at least a couple of numbers with your name written on them. Big Echo has an impressive 50 booths of varying sizes, alongside a cafe that serves both Chinese and western booze and nibbles. Open daily, 10:00 to 06:00.

Floor 6,
673 Nanjing Dong Lu
Huangpu
南京东路673号
黄埔
🚇 **People's Square**
Map p.430 C3 **131**

Haoledi KTV 好乐迪
5351 0808 | www.haoledi.com

This is the best place for those in search of an understated karaoke bar. Haoledi, which has eight branches across Shanghai, has a relaxing atmosphere, great little karaoke booths, reasonable prices and friendly staff. This branch on Xizang Lu serves up the same winning recipe.

180 Xizang Zhong Lu
Huangpu
西藏中路180号
黄埔
🚇 **People's Square**
Map p.430 C3 **132**

Party World 欢唱世界
6374 1111 | www.cashbox.com.tw

This grandiose spot, which looks more like an international hotel than a karaoke den, is a leading contender for the best KTV in the city. Situated in Fuxing Park, a stone's throw away from Park 97 (p.406) and Guandii (p.405), it's got all the perfect ingredients: a swanky decor of plush marble furnishings and opulent lighting; brilliant, friendly service; pleasant snack food; state-of-the-art facilities; and very reasonable prices. The perfect initiation for the karaoke-shy. Open daily, 20:00 to 02:00.

109 Yandang Lu,
inside Fuxing Park
Luwan
雁荡路109号
复兴公园内
卢湾
🚇 **Huangpi Nan Lu**
Map p.436 B1 **133**

Gay & Lesbian

Since 2001, Shanghai has become a hotbed for same-sex activity. A plethora of clubs, bars and massage parlours have popped up across town. Given the infancy of the scene, the crowd is very diverse, small and friendly, with newcomers warmly welcomed. What's more, several restaurants, such as Arch (p.380), Kabb (p.355) and Wagas (p.382) are gay-friendly, and most leading clubs, particularly those frequented by foreigners, are peppered with gay clientele.

Bao Gao ◀
Yuan Clubhouse,
Lane 307,
Shanxi Nan Lu
Luwan
步高苑会所，
陕西南路307弄
卢湾
🚇 *Shanxi Nan Lu*
Map p.436 B2 134

Bo Bo's Bar
6350 9447

If you like your man and you like a lot of him, this is the bar for you. Despite the relative infancy of its alternative sexuality movement, Shanghai has already bagged itself a bear bar – although this being China, the men are not quite so big. The ground floor is a nice, relaxing place for the crowd of locals, expats and very handsome waiting staff to mix and mingle. You can also get down and do some karaoke; aspiring Priscillas can become 'Queen of the Bo Bo Bar.' To find it, take a taxi to the arty district of the French Concession and look for a sign with the signature bear paw and rainbow. Open daily, 19:00 to 02:00.

Jing'an Park, ◀
1649 Nanjing Xi Lu
Jing'an
静安公园，
南京西路1649号
静安
🚇 *Jing'an Temple*
Map p.429 F4 135

Club Deep
6248 7034

Get knee-deep in all the action at this perennial favourite. Deep's serene Jing'an Park surrounds might be deceiving, but as its neon sign reveals, there is nothing peaceful about this two-storey venue. Regular nights include white-towel parties, suit and tie evenings and tank top nights, alongside the incredibly popular monthly I-Candy party. Young professionals shake their booty to some of the best electric music on the second floor. If it gets a bit too hot and sweaty, either lose your shirt or retreat to the first floor's spacious lounge area, which is lined with beds. There is also a secluded garden, and for the spendthrift, plush private VIP rooms can be hired. VIP cards are also available. Open Tuesday to Sunday, 20:30 till late.

1877 Huaihai ◀
Zhong Lu
Luwan
淮海中路1877号
卢湾
🚇 *Hengshan Lu*
Map p.435 D3 136

Eddy's
6282 0521

Eddy's might have changed premises a handful of times since it was first opened in 1995, but Shanghai's longest-serving gay spot is not going anywhere. The bar's attractive colour scheme and modern Chinese interior attracts an international crowd, with lesbians and female companions accompanying their GBF most welcome. The bar's owners, Eddy and Michael, are renowned for their friendliness, as are the staff, which adds to the laid-back vibe. The cocktails are excellent and inexpensive, and there's a decent wine list. And with music that is not too loud to dampen conversation, you might find yourself an Eddy's card member by the end of the evening. The bar is also available for private parties. Open daily, 20:00 to 02:00. No cards accepted.

399 Dagu Lu ◀
Jing'an
大沽路399号
静安
🚇 *Nanjing Xi Lu*
Map p.430 B4 137

Frangipani
5375 0084

If it weren't for the slice of pink on the outside, this gay bar on the gentrified stretch of Dagu Lu could easily go unnoticed. And many straight patrons frequent this joint for this very reason. Nevertheless, its is gay and proud. Friendly, first-name-basis staff usher you into an open-plan, futuristic space with a large flat-screen TV playing catwalk shows and HBO re-runs. Most cocktails are priced around the ¥40 mark, but drink deals run every night of the week except Sundays. Nice touches such as salted peanuts on the tables, inviting couches in the upper balcony and discreet music make

401

Frangipani an excellent place to visit during the week for a quiet tete-a-tete. Tuesday nights are for the girls only. Open from 18:00 to 02:00.

16 Wulumuqi Nan Lu
Xuhui
乌鲁木齐南路16号
徐汇
🚇 **Hengshan Lu**
Map p.435 F2 138

Max Club
1352448 6584

Max Club is a mixed venue that hosts a lesbian night every Saturday. These events are fronted by local lesbian group Butterfly (*hudie* in Chinese) and attract a young local and expat crowd. Max has a pub vibe, and is separated into two rooms – one a disco area and the other a live music zone. Female guests should expect to pay a ¥30 cover, while male patrons are charged double (although this does include a bottle of tepid beer). Butterfly doesn't have an internet site, but the club will take members' details so you can keep in touch with SMS updates. Open daily, 20:00 to 02:00.

18 Gaolan Lu
Luwan
皋兰路18号
卢湾
🚇 **Huangpi Nan Lu**
Map p.436 B1 139

Pink Home
5382 0373

The recently revamped Pink Home (formerly Home bar) is China's first gay multiplex; a place where people can eat, drink, dance and sleep, all without stepping foot outside. The action takes place in the least likely of areas: a quiet tree-lined street in the heart of the French Concession, next to an old Russian Orthodox church. A delightful courtyard adds to Pink Home's flamboyance, and this is a welcome space, particularly in the stifling summer months. For those who like the heat however, the restaurant/lounge area is at the front. Upon walking down a passageway of screaming neon, the main club area unfolds to reveal a large room with a bar to one side, dance area on the other and seating around the entire perimeter. Attractive staff in fun uniforms shuttle ¥35 mixers to and from tables, as dressed-to-impress patrons enjoy the latest global dance tracks. Open Wednesday to Thursday, 21:00 to 02:00; Friday and Saturday, 20:30 to 04:00.

**4, Lane 1950,
Huaihai Zhong Lu**
Luwan
淮海中路1950弄4号
卢湾
🚇 **Hengshan Lu**
Map p.435 E3 140

Shanghai Studio
6283 1043

Located down a lane in the heart of the French Concession's gay quarter, Shanghai Studio is an underground bar for the underground scene. The sex appeal of this place is immediately apparent upon descending its stairs. You take the red carpet down a long corridor lit in blue, past intriguing art installations, to enter two adjoining lounges, with bar stools and chilled music. Everything is washed in red lighting, and the walls are covered by framed paintings of men in all their glory. This latter detail explains the presence of gay menswear and underwear store Manifesto (p.329), which is located just off the main bar. Open daily, 20:00 til 02:00.

**4, Lane 946,
Changle Lu**
Luwan
长乐路946弄4号
卢湾
🚇 **Changshu Lu**
Map p.435 F1 141

Vogue in Kevin's 时尚酒吧
6248 8985 | www.kevinsbar.com

Kevin's may not be easy to pronounce when you've had one too many, or too easy to find for that matter, but it's consistently good for a serious booze up. It has been a favourite cruising spot for LGBTs since it first opened back in 1997. The bar, which is located in a restored building, has undergone several facelifts and is now a warm and modern space. It's an intimate spot, with comfortable sofas and soothing live jazz. Downstairs there is a restaurant alongside a nice courtyard, which serves authentic Thai dishes till 22:00, and where cocktails cost just ¥40. There's also free wireless internet. Whether you're with a date or simply hoping to find one, Kevin's is a top choice, and one that's very popular with locals and expats. Be sure to keep your eyes peeled for the discreet sign above Lane 946, then look out for the tiled courtyard. Open daily, 20:00 to 02:00.

Nightclubs

The excess of the 1920s and 1930s Shanghai might be long gone, but debauchery has definitely made a bold comeback in recent years. Around Xintiandi, the Bund, the French Concession and Nanjing Xi Lu, there is a large concentration of nightclubs. They range from Club G Plus (p.404) in Xintiandi, which features psychedelic trance nights, to the Bund spots, which typically play European house and hip-hop and attract many leading DJs. The venues attract mixed groups from across China and the world; the Bund a more continental crowd, while places such as Babyface (p.404) and Muse (p.406) cater more to locals. Perhaps the most authentic experience can be had in the glut of Japanese-style karaoke bars that are dotted around the city. Despite differing clientele, the one thing all venues have in common is the mission to have a good time. And in that respect you can expect a more relaxed atmosphere than in most other party capitals. The clubs might be full of cutting-edge design and countless posers, similar to their counterparts in Singapore, London and New York, but door policy is much more relaxed and cover charges are minimal. Even at the more pricey hangouts, admittance usually comes with some form of drink deal. Volar (p.406) is perhaps the only club where getting behind the red rope might involve some pre-planning, but a quick phone call to put your name on the list does the trick. And the party doesn't stop when the clubs close either. Several venues fight it out to keep the night owls going long past regular closing times, including Dragon Club (p.405) in the French Concession and Club DKD (p.404) on Huaihai Zhong Lu.

8-10 Jianguo, Zhong Lu
Luwan
建国中路8－10号
卢湾
🚇 *Huangpi Nan Lu*
Map p.436 C2 142

4 Live 乐法贝演艺俱乐部

137 7424 4008 | www.4liveunderground.com

One of the undisputed stars of the young, underground scene, 4 Live dedicates itself to showcasing a steady stream of talented live acts, both local bands and up-and-coming foreign DJs. It is quite the temple of music, with the artists performing on a stage to loyal followers, who watch from above and below. A bar on one wall and black booths on another seem like an afterthought – as if the owners were wary of upstaging the performers – but with a thumping sound system and bottled beers and spirits priced at a humble ¥40, the moshing punters don't seem to mind. Open daily, 21:00 until late.

15 Zhongshan Dong Er Lu
Huangpu
中山东二路15号
黄埔
🚇 *Nanjing Dong Lu*
Map p.431 E3 143

Attica 爱奇多

6373 3588 | www.attica-shanghai.com

Since Attica opened in late 2006 it has given Bar Rouge a run for its money as the most prized venue in Shanghai. It does a fantastic job of spoiling the Gucci-clad, stiletto-heeled crowd. The main room is encircled by two bars, and has a balcony overhead. Despite being a newcomer to the Shanghai club scene, it has already hosted several of the biggest names in international clubbing, such as Dimitri from Paris and top UK spinner Jeremy Healy. There's an impressive decked veranda, with spectacular views of the Bund and the Pudong skyline. Finally, at the end of a long corridor, you'll find a small circular room enclosed only by thin sheets of glass to accentuate Attica's marvellous panoramic views. There is a surcharge of ¥100, which includes one drink if you get there before 02:00. Drinks are not cheap, but this is the cream of the clubbing crop. Open Wednesday to Saturday, 21:00 to 04:00.

403

Shanghai Square,
Room 101,
138 Huaihai Zhong Lu
Luwan
上海广场，
淮海中路138号
卢湾
🚇 *Huangpi Nan Lu*
Map p.431 D4 145

Babyface
6375 6667

Babyface is one of China's most successful club chains, and this venue delivers its winning formula. It is packed most nights of the week as Chinese punters pile into its chic two-room space. The sound in the main room is oppressive techno, while hip-hop plays out back. Babyface's ultra hip and trendy image has made it a favourite among local Shanghai show-offs. Unfortunately there have been occasional reports of mistreatment at the hands of the management – at one point expats were not allowed entry – but usually an international crowd is tolerated, just not indulged. This is a great insight into a more Chinese clubbing experience; just make sure that you're on your best behaviour. Open Sunday to Thursday, 21:00 to 15:30; Fridays and Saturdays, 21:00 to 04:30.

Yunhai Tower,
1329 Huaihai
Zhong Lu
Luwan
淮海中路1329号，
云海大厦
卢湾
🚇 *Changshu Lu*
Map p.435 F2 146

Bonbon
133 2193 9299 | *www.clubbonbon.com*

Bonbon is one of Shanghai's best superclubs. Inside its labyrinthine floor is a large, central dance area, plenty of lounge space, and a killer sound and light system. It also attracts some of the best international DJs; Roger Sanchez, 2 Many DJs and Erick Morillo are just some of the big names to have graced the decks. On big nights, it seems like every twenty-something in Shanghai pours into the club to dance the night away. On other nights Bonbon struggles to attract the crowds, despite endless bar deals. One word of warning: the cloakroom is not so adept at catering to the masses and it's not wholly uncommon for your jacket to disappear, never to be seen again. Open Tuesday to Saturday, 21:00 to 04:00.

438 Huaihai
Zhong Lu
Luwan
淮海中路438号
卢湾
🚇 *Huangpi Nan Lu*
Map p.430 C4 147

Club DKD
6473 9449 | *www.clubdkd.com*

Just when DKD's shelf life seemed set to expire, it changed hands and came back into favour among local club kids, both Chinese and expat. While it likes to be described as 'underground,' and at times it does blast bumpier, harder beats, the DJs usually spin progressive house. It's a hefty basement space, fitted out in regal purple, with numerous nooks and crannies. The main drawback is the lack of room at the bar, and lack of bartenders, so the wait can sometimes verge on the ridiculous. To compensate, wait staff frantically shimmy drinks back and forth to the tables dotted around. It's best to jump on the bandwagon and book one, unless your idea of a good night is waiting in line. Open Sunday to Thursday, 21:00 to 03:00; and Fridays and Saturdays, 21:00 to 05:00.

Floor 5,
6 South Block,
Xintiandi
Luwan
新天地南里6号
卢湾
🚇 *Huangpi Nan Lu*
Map p.436 C1 148

Club G Plus
5386 8088 | *www.clubgplus.com*

This new hotspot in Xintiandi puts the 'b' into bling. Silver disco balls sparkle from above, mirrors with rhinestones from the sides, and all around everything glows scarlet red. Behind the DJ booth, a colossal LCD screen showers the room in light. Such an exuberant show attracts a certain clientele. Decked out in Prada, they occupy reserved tables downstairs and the over-indulgent VIP room. The music is a mix of electronica, techno and trance, and despite the pomp, the crowd is happy to get down and do their stuff. The friendly staff join in as well; efficiently multitasking between drink pouring and booty shaking. The cheapest drinks start at ¥40 and there is normally a ¥50 cover charge. Resident Calvin is China's number one DJ. Open daily, 21:00 to 03:00.

Sole Reviver

The club scene might be taking confident strides these days, but chances are your own feet will feel less than capable, especially after a night of bar hopping. Rest assured. For all those who don't want to party till sunrise, Dragonfly Therapeutic Retreats has the perfect cure – foot massages. Its oriental foot rub is the perfect way to unwind after yet another night of madness. There are locations all over town.

Dragon Club 木易龙

6433 2187 | *www.unionwell.com.cn.dragonclub.*

This illustrious after-hours club doesn't get going until the small hand strikes midnight. Not that you'd believe it from its location in a sleepy part of the French Concession. The only indication that a club exists are two inconspicuously placed guards collecting money in exchange for entry tickets. A torch-lit path leads the way to a dramatic, old-style villa, of which Dragon Club occupies the basement. The decor is a subdued mix of brown and orange hues, and there's inviting seating all around. The music is chilled during the week, but is injected with more adrenaline during the weekend, when it is typically house, although there are occasional RnB, hip-hop and 80s nights. There's a ¥100 entry fee and standard drinks are priced between ¥45 and ¥55. Granted, it's not cheap, but it's always busy, and at this hour, bleary-eyed beggars can't be choosers. Open Monday to Thursday, 21:00 to 02:00; Friday and Saturday, 22:00 to 08:00.

G Spot

138 1620 0834 | *www.gspotclub.net*

You'll find this G Spot on the fourth floor of the Leilin Building. It's a serious club for serious clubbers. John Digweed hosted the opening night in October 2006, and it has since attracted a loyal following, especially among Shanghai's sophisticates. It's a stylish affair, with plush purple velour walls and long, dark marble corridors, some of which lead to the club's KTV section. On quieter nights, a retractable wall keeps the venue cosy and creates an alternative area, often reserved for VIPs. A further plus is that there's no cover charge, so you have more to spend on the slightly pricey drinks. It's a good idea to start off with one of the cheaper infusions such as the ¥38 Blue Curacao, and go from there. Open from 21:00 until 04:00. No cards accepted.

Guandii 官邸

5383 6020

This 200 capacity club dishes out reliable hip-hop, with wannabe Snoop Doggs and Missy Elliots convening from across town. When it's not rammed, it's a pleasant space, with low, moody lighting, a red colour scheme and plenty of room to shake that booty. The management clearly know its demographic; in true pimp style, there is a private VIP room at the back, as well as a champagne bar, stocking 30 bottles, near the front. Unfortunately, some of the attitude seems to have rubbed off on the staff, who do not always honour the supposed drink promotions that accompany the entry ticket (not that beverages are too steep, with draft Tiger priced at ¥40 and cocktails from ¥45). Things can get a little too hot and sweaty during the winter months, but come summer, the patio that backs onto Fuxing Park offers an escape from the mob. Open Sunday to Thursday, 20:30 to 02:00; Friday and Saturday, 20:30 to 04:00.

IMA Club

6288 9898

Sitting atop the 10th floor of Nextstage Department Store, IMA uses the same formula as most of the clubs in Shanghai, but with one major difference: it's pretty much the only club in Pudong. For this very same reason, don't expect it to be thumping. Instead, expect a nicely turned out venue of cool, neon shades. Its over-ambitious size makes it a good choice for club claustrophobics who are afforded plenty of space to stretch out an arm and spin to reasonable techno tunes. A night at IMA is also an exercise in Mandarin, since the staff speak very little English. Drinks aren't as cheap as you might expect but this is still a safe bet for those either too tired or too lazy to cross the river. Open from 20:30 to 02:00.

405

333 Tongren Lu
Jing'an
铜仁路333号
静安
🚇 Jing'an Temple
Map p.429 F4 **153**

Mint

6247 9666 | *www.mintclub.com.cn*

Marketed as a club, but not much bigger than most Shanghai bars, Mint is still a perennial favourite among Shanghai's style conscious, networking crowd. It's a bit squashed and sweaty but the venue is tastefully designed and has a lovely balcony, which mops up the club's overspill. There is an excellent assortment of infused vodkas and martinis, with beers and spirits starting at ¥48 and cocktails from ¥58. For the female of the species, drink prices are not such a problem if you come on a Wednesday; the club's infamous No Mans' Land evening means most drinks are free before 00:00 and no men are allowed in until after 22:30. The music is mostly house. Open Monday to Thursday, 18:00 to 02:00; Fridays and Saturdays, 21:00 until late.

68 Yuyao Lu
Jing'an
余姚路68号
静安
Map p.429 E2 **154**

Muse 同乐坊梦幻酒吧

6218 8166 | *www.museshanghai.com*

Muse is part restaurant and part club, with the latter being the most popular. Located in the premises of an old factory, it presents a kind of New York warehouse cool. A huge bar dominates the middle of an immense, concrete room, with a clever clear glass partition separating a larger dance room from a smaller R&B area. A VIP section, which features live music at the weekend, is available to rent. Despite 'model's nights' on Wednesdays and Thursdays, when the city's models are treated to free champagne and canapes to encourage their attendance, Muse has trouble attracting a significant crowd during the week. Come Fridays and Saturdays though, a devoted throng of trendy Shanghainese and a smattering of foreigners descend. When punters aren't getting down and dirty to the latest lyrics, they are reclining on one of the many plush suede banquettes, or re-energising their spirits with lurid colour shots in the shape of syringes – just what the doctor ordered. Open daily, 21:00 to 02:00.

2 Gaolan Lu,
Fuxing Park
Luwan
皋兰路2号,
复兴公园
卢湾
🚇 Shanxi Nan Lu
Map p.436 B1 **155**

Park 97 兰桂坊

5383 2328 | *www.park97.net*

Popular party palace Park 97 is an old-time favourite among the city's nouveaux riche. It occupies an old renovated mansion within Fuxing Park, and has two contrasting levels. The first floor of this opulent affair presents a return to 1970s disco, with red velour and chrome chandeliers. The music ranges from funk and house to R&B and breakbeat. The second floor, known as 'Upstairs at Park 97' is full of plush velour couches, a pool table and hosts live Latino bands. On a typical weekend, expect to see throngs of gorgeous women surrounded by men either trying to charm them or at least buying them expensive drinks. Open Monday to Thursday and Sunday, 20:00 to 02:00; Friday and Saturday, 20:00 to 04:00.

99 Yandang Lu,
Fuxing Park
Luwan
雁荡路99号,
复兴公园
卢湾
🚇 Huangpi Nan Lu
Map p.436 B1 **156**

Volar 夜飞翔的自由

134 8223 9390 | *www.volar.com.hk*

Volar claims to be one of the few members' only clubs in Shanghai, but in reality it is open to, and seeks out, new members. Designed by the world renowned Philippe Starck, it's adorned with stuffed eagles, guns, and 90s style graffiti-covered walls. The crowd is equally eccentric, and ranges from suave corporate types buying rounds for ¥68 and over, to groups of girls looking for a laugh. The only shortcoming is the strict door policy, which often deters the crowds. The upstairs lounge is usually busy with revellers dancing to the same decent tunes as the floor below. Open daily, 20:00 to 04:00.

406

Cabaret & Strip Shows

The former 'Paris of the east' once boasted numerous cabaret shows and strip clubs but since 1949 they've all virtually disappeared. The only one left in Shanghai can be found at La Maison (5306 1856) in Xintiandi, and that's a French-style show geared to tourists. Still, it will satisfy any hankerings for a bit of feather and fluff – just be prepared to pay for it. There are no strip clubs in Shanghai. The flyers for ladies' bars that are thrust into your hands are harmless places populated by women employed to entertain their male hosts (or at least that is their surface-level persona). The Hooters in Shanghai also does not have quite the same naked ambition as the one in the US. This is not to say that Shanghai is all above board. Like every big city it has its share of debauchery. Prostitution is an unspoken but omnipresent reality, as a trip to some of the bars along Maoming Lu and Tongren Lu will confirm.

Cinema

In light of ceaseless street sellers flogging all the latest blockbusters, few will complain about the lack of foreign films in Shanghai. However, those hankering after the traditional cinema experience, complete with popcorn, trailers and surround sound, might be frustrated. The UME International Cineplex in Xintiandi (6384 1122) is among the better options, but it only has one or two screens that offer English language films, and they tend to be mainstream releases. Prices are also relatively high. Other venues that feature English language films are Kodak CinemaWorld in Xujiahui (Metro City, 1111 Zhaojiabang Lu; 6426 8181), the old school Paradise Theatre on Anfu Lu in the French Concession (6742 2606), Paradise Warner Cinema City in Hongqiao (Grand Gateway, 1 Hongqiao Lu; 6407 6622) and Studio City on Nanjing Xi Lu, Jingan (6218 2173). For a taste of something more arty, try the Cine Club de l'Alliance Francaise (297 Wusong Lu, Hongkou; 6357 5388), which shows French films. The Canadian Consulate in the Shanghai Centre on Nanjing Xi Lu (Shanghai Centre; 6279 8400) and the German Consulate (Pidecmo Tower, 318 Fuzhou Lu, Huangpu; 6391 2068) also screen their respective country's latest hits. If you're just after a big screen and are not too fussed about extra thrills, try Arch Cafe/Bar (p.380), where you can play your own DVDs on the large projector downstairs. If you're in town in June, it's worth checking out China's only internationally recognised film festival, the Shanghai International Movie Festival, which showcases major new works at the Shanghai Film Art Centre (160 Xinhua Lu, Xuhui; 6280 4088).

Comedy

The absence of decent comedy in Shanghai is almost a joke in itself, with very few local comedy acts. The China Comedy Club (www.justthetonicasia.com) occasionally plays Malones (p.393), while Chopschticks (www.chopschticks.com) has done a few tours in Shanghai since 2005. For more information on both these email shanghai@thecomedytour.com. Otherwise, Punchline Comedy Club (www.punchlinecomedy.com) has been well received in Shanghai and now regularly arranges performances in specific venues. Among its more notable successes was the performance of Tim Clark, Junior Simpson and Richard Morton at O'Malley's in 2007, and the equally raucous Noel Britten and Pierre Hollins in the JC Mandarin. While these comedians might deliver their punchines in English, they try to avoid insider jokes, which makes it accessible to a mixed crowd.

Concerts

As with many other forms of entertainment, the live music scene in Shanghai has only recently come into its own. Both Eric Clapton and the Rolling Stones have played at Shanghai, Hongkou and Changning stadiums, although sporadic government

Moving Again? If you like what the **Shanghai Explorer** offers, take a look at some of our other titles. Whatever the city, we'll tell you what you need to know for whatever it is you want to do.

interference has led to the cancellation of some gigs, including Jay Z's in late 2006. You can purchase concert tickets, and get the lowdown on upcoming gigs, from www.emma.cn (6481 2938 or 400 707 9999).

Smaller acts take the stage at venues such as Ark Live House (p.387) and Malones (p.393), which feature predominantly local pop and rock bands, while Cotton Club (p.389), JZ Club (p.392) and House of Blues and Jazz (p.391) are recognised jazz hangouts. The top hotels, including The Ritz-Carlton (6279 8268) and Pudong Shangri-La (6882 8888), also feature travelling jazz acts in their house bars.

Come May, the Shanghai International Spring Music Festival (see Annual Events, p.54) and Jazzy Shanghai (www.jazzshanghai.com) offer live music fans a chance for rare indulgence. Tickets for both of these festivals can be booked through www.tickets365.com.cn or www.eticketfast.com.

If classical music is more to your liking, try the Shanghai Concert Hall (523 Yan'an Dong Lu; 6386 2836). This grandiose building attracts small, international and local orchestras, such as the Berlin Philharmonic Brass Ensemble. The Shanghai Symphony Orchestra Hall (105 Hunan Lu; 6466 5770), which houses the resident Shanghai Symphony Orchestra, is also worth a visit. Meanwhile, in Pudong, the gargantuan Oriental Arts Centre (425 Dingxiang Lu; 5109 5091) presents an eclectic mix of shows and events, ranging from the French musical *Le Petit Prince* to the New England Philharmonic Orchestra.

Fashion Shows

Shanghai is successfully marketing itself as the Milan of Asia, so expect to see plenty of pretty things swanning around both on and off the catwalk. Fortunately, catching a show here is not quite the near-impossible feat it is in other fashion capitals, especially as up-and-coming designers often host shows in local clubs and bars. Check the local lifestyle magazines for details. The top designers also put on shows to launch their new collections. Fashion frenzy officially takes over during the International Fashion Culture Festival in March (see Annual Events, p.56). For tickets, visit www.fashionshanghai.com or call 6439 1818.

Theatre
Other options **Drama Groups** p.297

Chinese opera

Shanghai might not be the obvious choice for decent theatre, but a new generation of thesps is slowly emerging. There are also major ambitions to create a quasi Broadway in Shanghai, which would stretch along Huashan Lu and Anfu Lu in the French Concession. There's already a surplus of western-style theatres such as the Shanghai Theatre Academy at 630 Huashan Lu (6248 8103), which features plays staged by students of the academy. Check out the local lifestyle magazines for more information. Shanghai Grand Theatre (300 Renmin Dadao; 6386 8686) regularly entertains with top commercial performances; *The Lion King*, *Cats* and *The Phantom of the Opera*, to name but a few, have already featured. Shanghai Grand Stage in Shanghai Stadium in Xuhui (6438 5200) is another venue that lures the big names. Prices usually start around ¥120 per ticket. Tickets for most shows can be purchased through China Ticket Star (800 820 7910; www.ticket365.com.cn) or the Shanghai Cultural Information and Booking Centre (6217 2426; www.culture.sh.cn).

Shanghai is also home to Chinese-style acrobatic and operatic displays. Beijing Opera performs at the Yifu Theatre off People's Square in Huangpu (6351 4668) on Saturdays and Sundays at 13:30. Tickets cost between ¥10 and ¥40. For acrobatics, the Shanghai Centre Theatre (1376 Nanjing Xi Lu; 6279 8948) and Lyceum Theatre (57 Maoming Lu; 6256 5544) offer performances most nights of the week. Due to rising popularity, ticket prices can often command ¥200 and advance booking is advised. Children will enjoy Shanghai Circus World in Zhabei, which features traditional circus acts alongside Chinese acrobats (2266 Gonghe Xin Lu; 6652 5468).

On a more classical note, ballet lovers will appreciate the Shanghai International Ballet Competition (6323 7612; www.shanghaiibc.com), which is held each year in June or July.

One event not to be missed in November is the Shanghai International Arts Festival (6439 1818), when artistic, theatrical and musical shows are held in locations across town. Also running over the same period is the performance art festival Fringe Shanghai (139 1844 5724; www.fringeshanghai.com).

Party Organisers
Other options **Party Accessories** p.333

The odds are stacked against most people throwing a top-notch party; either they don't have the space or the time, or they don't even have an oven. As a result, most people opt to celebrate outside the home instead, often catering to guests in the numerous private rooms that most restaurants provide free of charge for larger groups. That said, a night at home doesn't have to be a quiet evening in front of the TV. East meets West Catering and Events, also known as WE Catering (6217 9677; info@wecatering.com), puts on great food with innovative ideas and friendly service. The Party People also offers in-house catering and a wide range of events (135 6436 1793 or 5477 0998; www.partypeople.com.cn). Finally, for the little ones, try JT Kids Party (5169 2146; www.kidsparty.cn). It promises to make that 10th birthday extra special with fun themes such as super heroes, and bouncy castles for those with a little green space out back.

Caterers
If you are less assured of your culinary prowess, fret not – there are plenty of options out there. The Sherpa's guide is probably the best place to start. Sherpa's is a delivery service that works with a variety of Shanghai restaurants. Depending on where you live and what restaurant you are ordering from, a charge might be levied. You can get a Sherpa's guide available free of charge by calling 6209 6209, and you can order anytime between 10:30 and 22:30. Sherpa's aside, there are several other leading restaurants in Shanghai that provide private catering. To dazzle with desserts, the Hilton's Gourmet Corner (6248 0000, ext 1760) is a must; it does fabulous pastries, cakes and chocolate, as well as a very nice selection of olives. The delivery fee is the price of the taxi. For something slightly more unusual, Ignatius Lau's *Moveable Feasts* are worth considering. Lau does portable parties, offering catering services at your chosen venue, with your chosen cuisine. She does all the cooking, serving and the washing up. Call her on 139 1634 9552. Following the same theme, also try the Flying Chef (www.flyingchef.com.cn). Top Chinese chef Mr Li caters for private dinner parties of up to 10 guests, for ¥120 per person. To book, you need to fill out the online form at least three days before the party date.

Maps

Maps

User's Guide

This section of the book has six detailed map spreads of downtown Shanghai and its immediate surroundings (p.428-439) and seven of the suburban areas (p.420-427 and p.440-445). They are intended to help you get your bearings when you first arrive, and give you an idea of where we're talking about in the main chapters of the book. The overview on p.416 shows which part of the city each spread covers. All are big, and in full detail; the suburb maps are drawn at a 1:30,000 scale (1cm = 300m) and the downtown maps are 1:15,000 (1cm = 150m). An initial glance at the maps might leave you yearning for more information. Look closely however, and you'll see a myriad of coloured numbers, each correlating to a specific place of interest mentioned in the book. Simply find the number, match the colour to the chapter (green for General Information, blue for Exploring and so on), and turn to the relevant section, where each entry is listed in numerical order. You'll also find a country map of China (opposite), one of Shanghai's surrounding areas (p.414), and a handy map of the city's districts (p.416), which we have included as part of each address.

Words on the Street

As a Shanghai resident, you'll probably know already that 'lu' is the Mandarin word for 'road'. Although road signs in the city are often written as 'Rd', most locals and expats prefer to use the Chinese version – so that's how we've written our maps and addresses in the book. The same goes for directions and directional streets: north is bei, south is nan, east is dong, and west is xi. Memorise the icon below and you'll be ready to navigate.

Need More?

This residents' guide is a pretty big book. It needs to be, to carry all the info we have about living in Shanghai. But, unless you've got the pockets of a clown, it's unlikely to be carried around with you on day trips. With this in mind, we've created the ***Shanghai Mini Map*** as a more manageable alternative. This packs the whole city into your pocket and, once unfolded, is an excellent navigational tool. It's part of a series of Mini Maps that includes cities as diverse as London, Dubai, New York and Barcelona. Visit our website, www.explorerpublishing.com, for details of how to pick one up, or nip into any good bookshop.

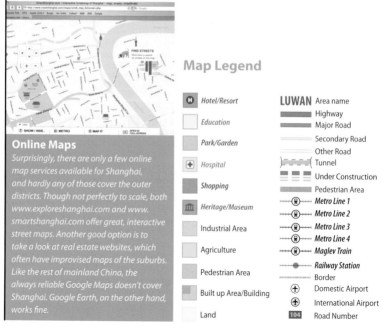

Map Legend

Ⓗ	Hotel/Resort
	Education
	Park/Garden
➕	Hospital
	Shopping
🏛	Heritage/Museum
	Industrial Area
	Agriculture
	Pedestrian Area
	Built up Area/Building
	Land

LUWAN	Area name
	Highway
	Major Road
	Secondary Road
	Other Road
	Tunnel
	Under Construction
	Pedestrian Area
ⓡ	Metro Line 1
ⓡ	Metro Line 2
ⓡ	Metro Line 3
ⓡ	Metro Line 4
ⓡ	Maglev Train
●	Railway Station
	Border
⊕	Domestic Airport
✈	International Airport
104	Road Number

Online Maps

Surprisingly, there are only a few online map services available for Shanghai, and hardly any of those cover the outer districts. Though not perfectly to scale, both www.exploreshanghai.com and www.smartshanghai.com offer great, interactive street maps. Another good option is to take a look at real estate websites, which often have improvised maps of the suburbs. Like the rest of mainland China, the always reliable Google Maps doesn't cover Shanghai. Google Earth, on the other hand, works fine.

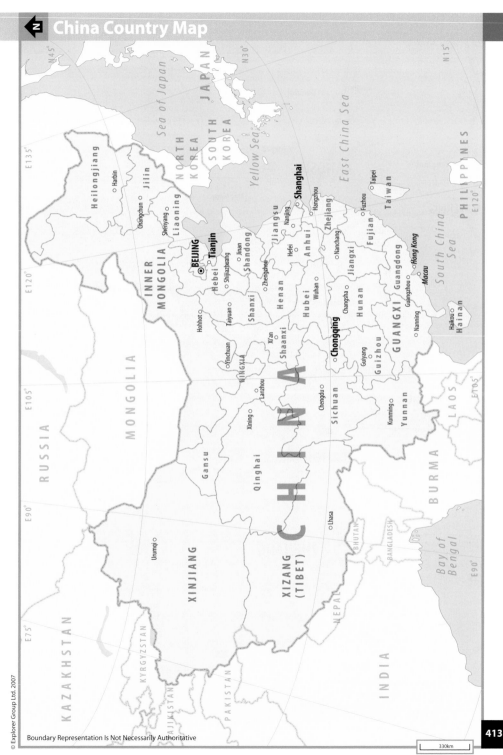

© Explorer Group Ltd. 2007

Boundary Representation Is Not Necessarily Authoritative

330km

The Complete **Residents'** Guide

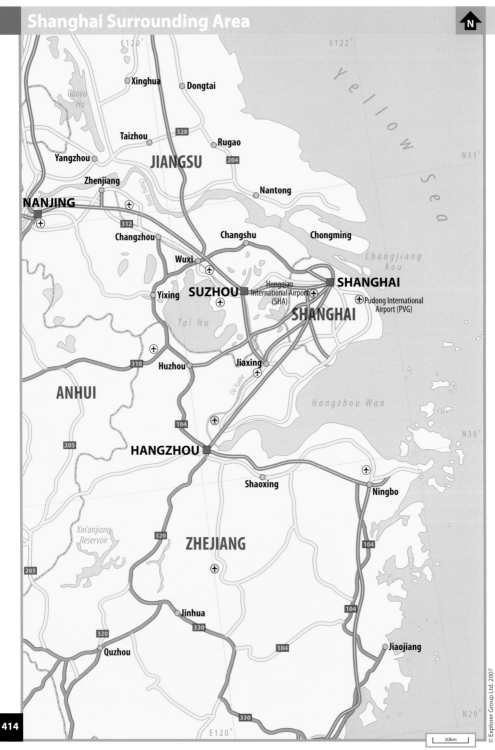

Shanghai Explorer 1st Edition

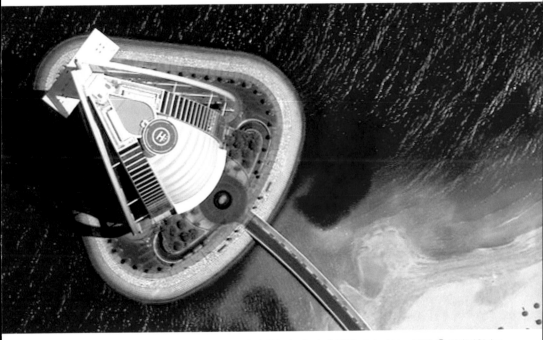

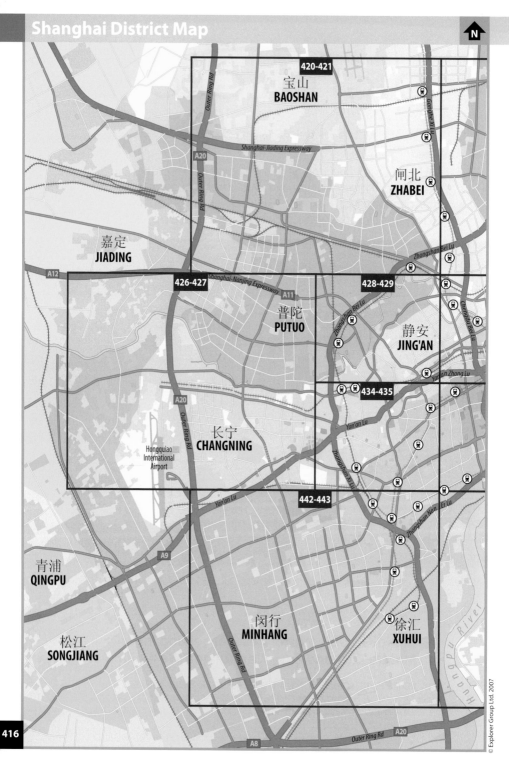

© Explorer Group Ltd. 2007

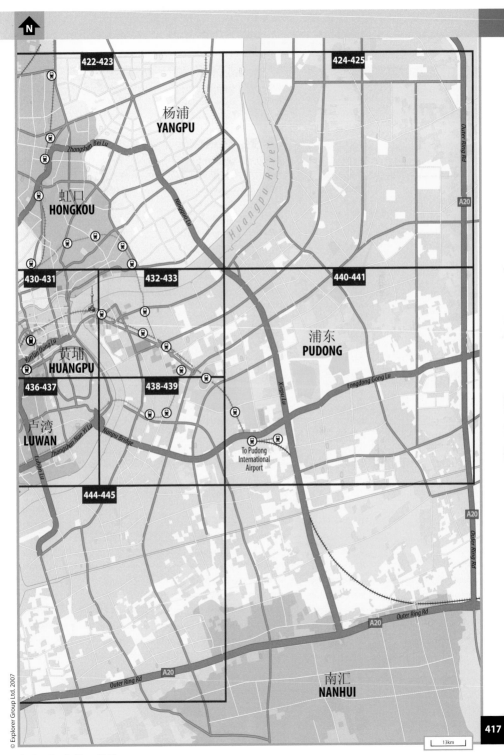

422-423

424-425

杨浦
YANGPU

Zhongshan Bei Lu

Huangpu River

Outer Ring Rd

A20

虹口
HONGKOU

Mingdao Lu

430-431

432-433

440-441

浦东
PUDONG

Yan'an Dong Lu

黄埔
HUANGPU

Longdong Gong Lu

436-437

438-439

卢湾
LUWAN

Luban Lu

Zhongshan Nan Yi Lu

Nanpu Bridge

Xiupu Lu

To Pudong
International
Airport

444-445

A20

Outer Ring Rd

南汇
NANHUI

Outer Ring Rd

A20

13km

417

© Explorer Group Ltd. 2007

Street Name		Map Ref
Anfu Lu	安福路	435-E1
Anren Jie	安仁街	431-E4
Anyuan Lu	安远路	429-D3
Baoshan Lu	宝山路	422-B4
Beijing Xi Lu	北京西路	439-F4
Biyun Lu	碧云路	440-B1
Caobao Lu	漕宝路	443-D2
Caoxi Bei Lu	漕溪北路	435-E4
Changle Lu	长乐路	439-D2
Changning Lu	长宁路	428-C4
Changshou Lu	长寿路	429-D3
Changshu Lu	上海市常熟路	435-F1
Changyang Lu	长阳路	423-D4
Daduhe Lu	大渡河路	427-F2
Dagu Lu	大沽路	430-B4
Dajing Lu	大境路	431-E4
Dalian Xi Lu	大连西路	422-C3
Datian Lu	大田路	430-A2
Datong Lu	大统路	430-A1
Dingxi Lu	定西路	434-C2
Dong Zhu'anbang Lu	东诸安浜路	435-D1
Dongdaming Lu	东大名路	431-F1
Dongfang Lu	东方路	438-C3
Donghu Lu	东湖路	436-A1
Dongjiadu Lu	董家渡路	437-F1
Dongping Lu	东平路	435-F2
Fan Yu Lu	番禺路	435-D2
Fang Xie Lu	方斜路	437-D2
Fangdian Lu	芳甸路	440-A3
Fenglin Lu	枫林路	436-A4
Fengxian Lu	奉贤路	430-A3
Fenyang Lu	凤阳路	430-B3
Fucheng Lu	富城路	432-B3
Fumin Lu	富民路	435-F1
Fuxing Xi Lu	复兴西路	435-E2
Fuxing Zhong Lu	复兴中路	435-F2
Fuzhou Lu	福州路	431-D3
Ganxi Lu	甘溪路	427-D3
Gaoyou Lu	高邮路	435-E2

Street Name		Map Ref
Guangdong Lu	广东路	431-D3
Guangzhong Xi Lu	广中西路	422-A4
Guoshun Lu	国顺路	441-D3
Handan Lu	邯郸路	442-C2
Henan Zhong Lu	河南中路	431-D2
Hengshan Lu	衡山路	435-F3
Honggu Lu	虹古路	427-E3
Hongmei Lu	虹梅路	443-D2
Hongqiao Lu	虹桥路	435-D4
Hongzhong Lu	虹中路	442-B1
Huaihai Zhong Lu	淮海中路	435-E2
Huamu Lu	花木路	440-A3
Huangpi Nan Lu	黄陂南路	436-C1
Huashan Lu	华山路	435-E1
Hubin Lu	湖滨路	430-C4
Hunan Lu	湖南路	435-E2
Hutai Lu	沪太路	421-D1
Jian He Lu	剑河路	427-D3
Jiangning Lu	江宁路	429-D1
Jiangsu Bei Lu	江苏北路	428-C4
Jianguo Xi Lu	建国西路	435-E3
Jianguo Zhong Lu	建国中路	436-B2
Jiangwan Dong Lu	东江湾路	436-C2
Jiangxi Zhong Lu	江西中路	431-D2
Jinhui Lu	金汇路	442-B1
Jinxian Lu	进贤路	430-A4
Jinxiu Lu	锦绣路	437-E1
Jiu Long Lu	九龙路	422-C4
Jiujiang Lu	九江路	431-D3
Julu Lu	巨鹿路	430-A4
Kaixuan Lu	凯旋路	434-B2
Kangding Lu	康定路	429-D3
Kongjiang Lu	控江路	423-F2
Lan'an Lu	蓝桉路	440-C1
Lianhua Lu	莲花路	443-E3
Longwu Lu	龙吴路	443-F2
Lujiabang Lu	陆家浜路	437-F2
Lujiazui Lu	陆家嘴西路	431-F2
Madang Lu	马当路	436-C2

Street Name		Map Ref
Maoming Lu	茂名路	430-A4
Maoming Nan Lu	茂名南路	436-B2
Meihua Lu	梅花路	439-F2
Ming Yue Lu	金桥明月路	440-C1
Mingyue Lu	明月路	429-F1
Moganshan Lu	莫干山路	429-F1
Nanchang Lu	南昌路	436-B1
Nanchezhan Lu	南车站路	437-E2
Nandan Lu	南丹路	435-F4
Nanjing Dong Lu	南京东路	430-C3
Nanjing Xi Lu	南京西路	430-A3
Panyu Lu	番愚路	435-D2
Pudong Nan Lu	浦东南路	438-B2
Pujian Lu	浦建路	438-C2
Puyu Dong Lu	普育东路	437-F2
Qixin Lu	七莘路	432-B4
Qinghai Lu	青海路	430-B3
Renmin Dadao	人民大道	430-C3
Ruijin Nan Lu	瑞金南路	436-B2
Shandong Lu	山东中路	431-D3
Shanxi Bei Lu	陕西北路	431-D1
Shanxi Nan Lu	陕西南路	431-D2
Shaoxing Lu	绍兴路	436-B2
Shiji Dadao	世纪大道	433-D3
Shuicheng Lu	水城路	427-F3
Sichuan Bei Lu	四川北路	431-D1
Sichuan Nan Lu	四川南路	431-E3
Sinan Lu	思南路	436-B1
Suzhou Bei Lu	北苏州路	430-C2
Taicang Lu	太仓路	430-C4
Taikang Lu	泰康路	436-B2
Taiyuan Lu	太原路	436-B2
Tianlin Dong Lu	田林东路	443-D2
Tianping Lu	天平路	435-E3
Tianshan Lu	天山路	434-A2
Tianyaoqiao Lu	天钥桥路	435-E4
Tongren Lu	铜仁路	429-F4
Weihai Lu	威海路	430-A4
Wenmiao Lu	文庙路	437-E1

Street Name		Map Ref
Wuyuan Lu	五原路	435-E2
Wukang Lu	武康路	435-E2
Wulumuqi Nan Lu	乌鲁木齐南路	435-F3
Wuxing Lu	吴兴路	435-E3
Wuyi Lu	武夷路	434-B2
Xianxia Lu	仙霞路	434-A3
Xiangshan Lu	香山路	436-B1
Xiangyang Nan Lu	襄阳南路	436-A1
Xianxia Lu	仙霞路	434-A3
Xikang Lu	西康路	429-F3
Xinzha Lu	新闸路	430-C2
Xincheng Lu	新城路	430-C3
Xincun Lu	新村路	420-C3
Xingguo Lu	兴国路	435-D2
Xingye Lu	兴业路	436-C1
Xinhua Lu	新华路	434-B3
Xinle Lu	新乐路	436-A1
Xinzhen Lu	新镇路	442-A3
Xiuyan Lu	秀沿路	434-B3
Xizang Zhong Lu	西藏中路	430-C2
Yan'an Dong Lu	延安东路	430-C4
Yan'an Xi Lu	延安西路	434-A3
Yan'an Zhong Lu	延安中路	435-E1
Yanchang Lu	延长中路	421-F4
Yandang Lu	雁荡路	436-C1
Yichang Lu	宜昌路	429-D1
Yingchun Lu	迎春路	440-A2
Yishan Lu	宜山路	443-E1
Yongjia Lu	永嘉路	435-F3
Yuanshen Lu	源深路	433-D1
Yuyao Lu	余姚路	429-D3
Yuyuan Lu	愚园路	434-C1
Zhaojiabang Lu	肇家浜路	436-A3
Zhongshan Bei Lu	中山北路	434-A1
Zhongshan Dong Er Lu	中山东二路	431-F3
Zhongshan Lu	中山西路	437-F1
Zhu Guang Lu	诸光路	427-E1
Zunyi Lu	遵义路	434-A1

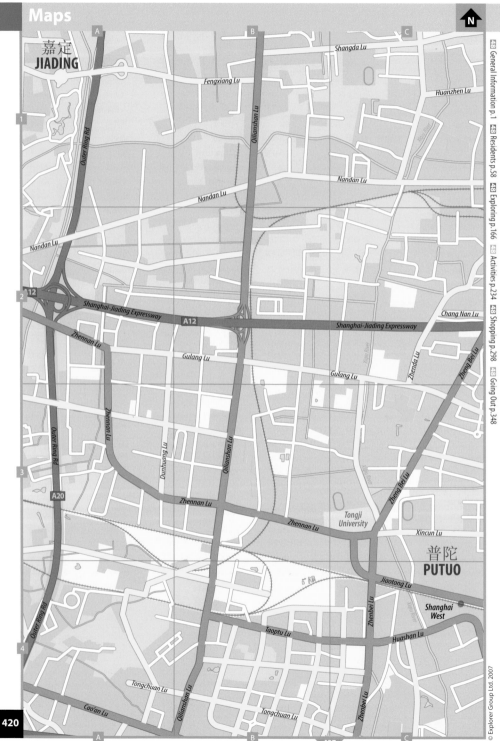

嘉定
JIADING

Fengxiang Lu

Shangda Lu

Huanzhen Lu

Qilianshan Lu

Nandan Lu

Nandan Lu

Nandan Lu

Shanghai-Jiading Expressway

A12

Shanghai-Jiading Expressway

Chang Nan Lu

Zhenda Lu

Zheng Bei Lu

Zhennan Lu

Outer Ring Rd

Gulang Lu

Gulang Lu

Dunhuang Lu

Qilianshan Lu

Zhennan Lu

Outer Ring Rd

A20

Zhennan Lu

Zhennan Lu

Tongji
University

Zheng Bei Lu

Xincun Lu

普陀
PUTUO

Jiaotong Lu

Zhenbei Lu

Shanghai
West

Huashan Lu

Taoptu Lu

Tongchuan Lu

Qilianshan Lu

Tongchuan Lu

Zhenbei Lu

Cao'an Lu

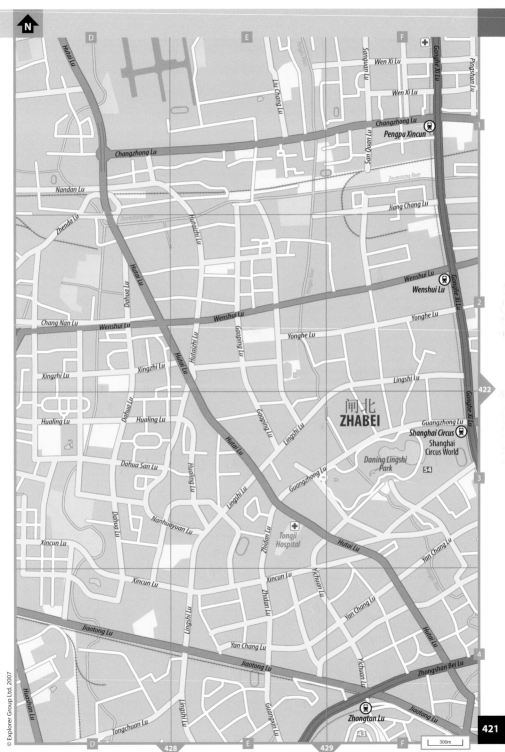

Hutai Lu

D

E

Sanquan Lu

Wen Xi Lu

F

Gonghe Xi Lu

Pingshan Lu

Liu Chang Lu

Wen Xi Lu

Changzhong Lu

Pengpu Xincun

1

San Quan Lu

Zoumatang River

Changzhong Lu

Nandan Lu

Jiang Chang Lu

Zhenda Lu

Zoumatang River

Hutaizhi Lu

Pengpu River

Wenshui Lu

Wenshui Lu

Gonghe Xi Lu

2

Chang Nan Lu

Wenshui Lu

Wenshui Lu

Gaoping Lu

Yonghe Lu

Yonghe Lu

Hutai Lu

Dahua Lu

Hutaizhi Lu

Lingshi Lu

Gonghe Xi Lu

422

Xingzhi Lu

Xingzhi Lu

Hutai Lu

闸北
ZHABEI

Guangzhong Lu

Shanghai Circus

Shanghai
Circus World

Hualing Lu

Dahua Lu

Hualing Lu

Gaoping Lu

Lingshi Lu

Daning Lingshi
Park

54

3

Dahua San Lu

Hualing Lu

Guangzhong Lu

Xincun Lu

Dahua Lu

Nanhuayuan Lu

Lingshi Lu

Zhidan Lu

Tongji
Hospital

Guangzhong Lu

Hutai Lu

Yan Chang Lu

Xincun Lu

Xincun Lu

Yichuan Lu

Yan Chang Lu

Hutai Lu

4

Jiaotong Lu

Jiaotong Lu

Zhongshan Bei Lu

Hutai Lu

Jiaotong Lu

Lingshi Lu

Tongchuan Lu

Guangxin Lu

Yan Chang Lu

Yichuan Lu

Zhongtan Lu

43

421

300m

The Complete **Residents'** Guide

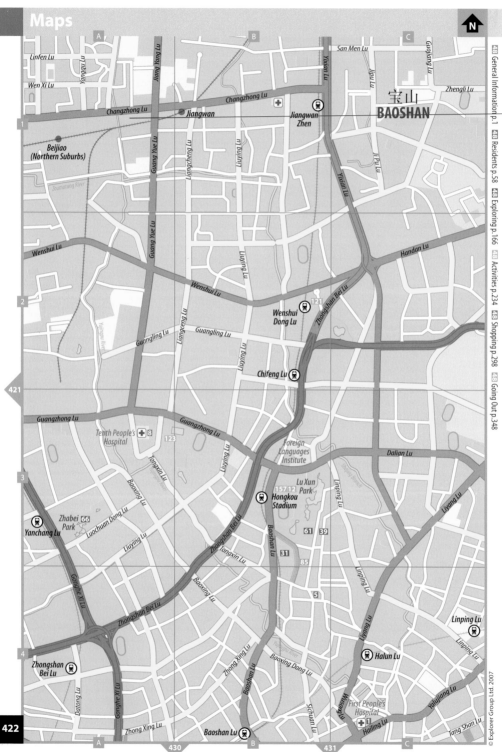

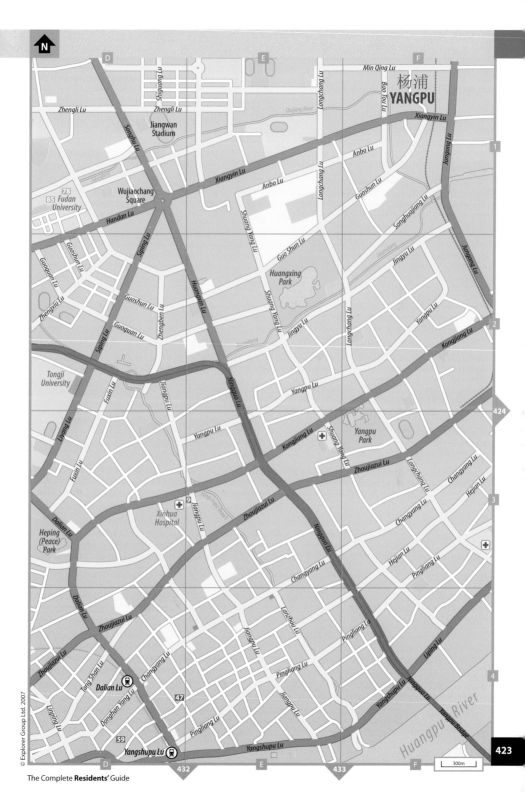

© Explorer Group Ltd. 2007

300m

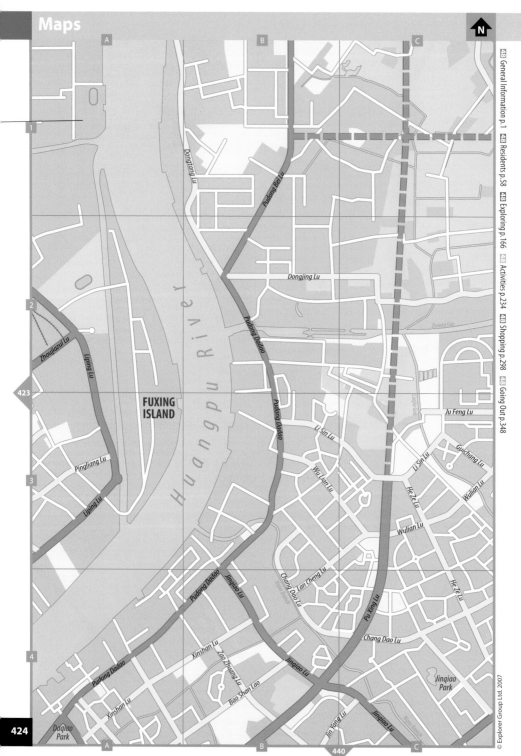

443 General Information p.1
443 Residents p.58
443 Exploring p.166
443 Activities p.234
443 Shopping p.298
443 Going Out p.348

Dongfang Lu

Pudong Bei Lu

Dongjing Lu

Pudong Dadao

Zhoujiazui Lu

Liping Lu

FUXING
ISLAND

Huangpu River

Zhaoze Gou

Canal Gou

Ju Feng Lu

Li Sin Lu

Guichang Lu

Li Sin Lu

Wu Lan Lu

He Ze Lu

Wulian Lu

Pingliang Lu

Liping Lu

Wulian Lu

Lan Cheng Lu

Chang Dao Lu

Pu Xing Lu

He Ze Lu

Pudong Dadao

Jinqiao Lu

Xinshan Lu

Zao Zhuang Lu

Jinqiao Lu

Chang Dao Lu

Jinqiao
Park

Pudong Dadao

Bao Shan Lao

Xinshan Lu

Daqiao
Park

Jin Yong Lu

Jinqiao Lu

© Explorer Group Ltd. 2007

Shanghai Explorer 1st Edition

1

2

423

3

4

A

B

C

440

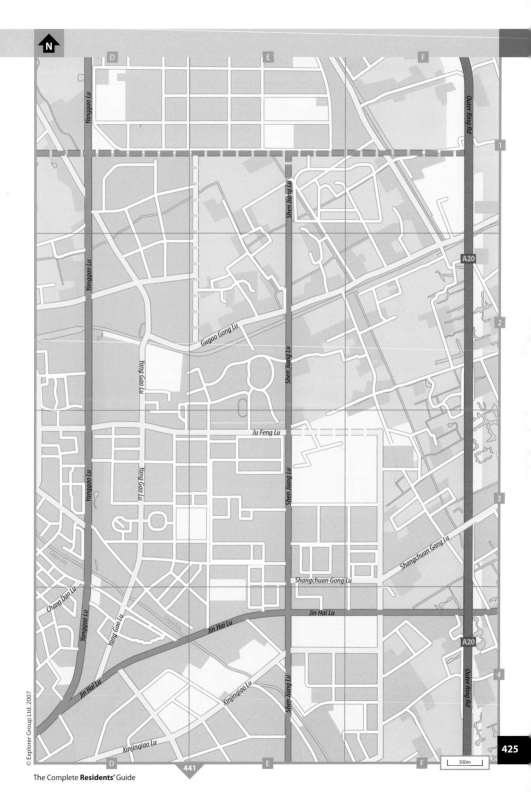

300m

© Explorer Group Ltd. 2007

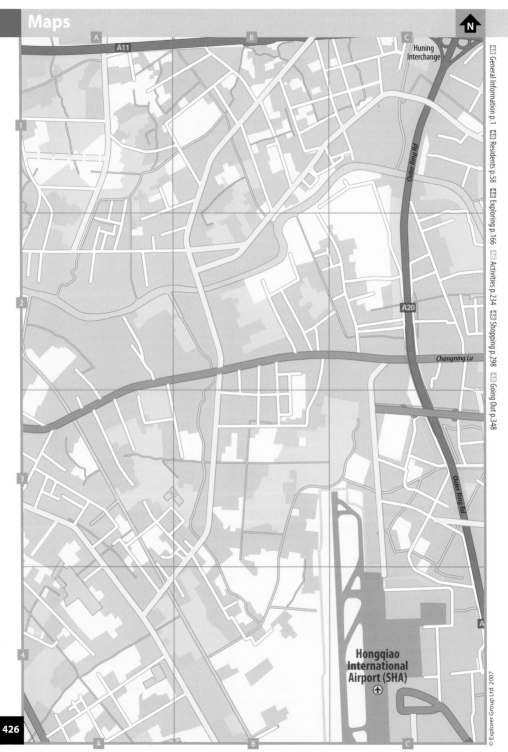

A11

Huning
Interchange

Outer Ring Rd

A20

Changning Lu

Outer Ring Rd

**Hongqiao
International
Airport (SHA)**

Shanghai Explorer 1st Edition

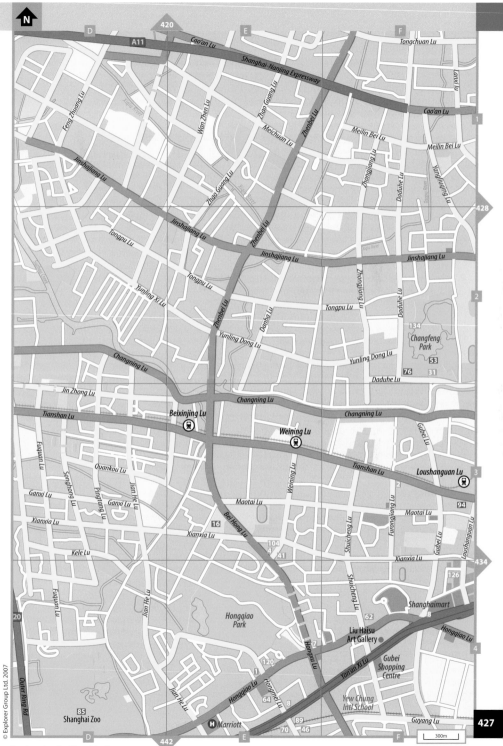

300m

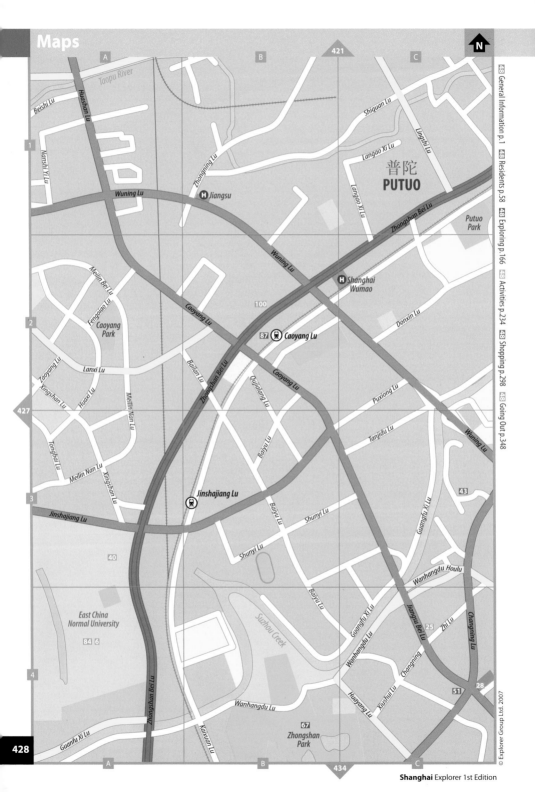

General Information p.1 · Residents p.58 · Exploring p.166 · Activities p.234 · Shopping p.298 · Going Out p.348

Taopu River

Beishi Lu

Huashan Lu

Namshi Yi Lu

Zhongqing Lu

Shiquan Lu

Lingzhi Lu

Langao Xi Lu

Langao Xi Lu

普陀
PUTUO

Wuning Lu

H Jiangsu

Zhongshan Bei Lu

Putuo Park

Wuning Lu

Meilin Bei Lu

Fengqiao Lu

Caoyang Park

Caoyang Lu

100

H Shanghai Wumao

Donxin Lu

Lanxi Lu

Zaoyang Lu

Xingshan Lu

Huaxi Lu

Meilin Nan Lu

Tongbai Lu

Zhongshan Bei Lu

Bailan Lu

87 🚇 Caoyang Lu

Caoyang Lu

Qujiang Lu

Baiyu Lu

Puxiong Lu

Tanjidu Lu

Wuning Lu

43

Meilin Nan Lu

Xingshan Lu

Jinshajiang Lu

🚇 Jinshajiang Lu

Shunyi Lu

Baiyu Lu

Guangfu Xi Lu

Jinshajiang Lu

40

Shunyi Lu

Baiyu Lu

Wanhangdu Houlu

East China Normal University

84 **6**

Suzhou Creek

Guangfu Xi Lu

Wanhangdu Lu

Jiangsu Bei Lu

Changning

25

Zhi Lu

Changning Lu

Guangfu Xi Lu

Huoyang Lu

Xiushui Lu

Changning

51

28

Zhongshan Bei Lu

Guanfu Xi Lu

Kaixuan Lu

Wanhangdu Lu

67
Zhongshan Park

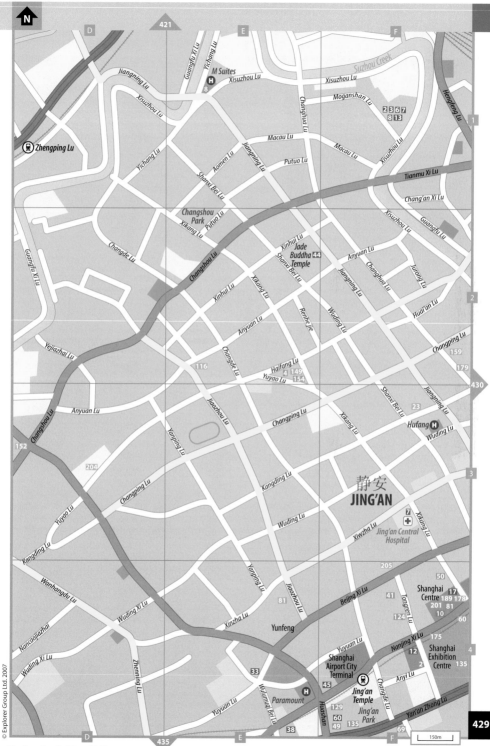

421

D

E

F

Jiangning Lu

Guangfu Xi Lu

Yichang Lu

Xisuzhou Lu

M Suites
8

Xisuzhou Lu

Xisuzhou Lu

Suzhou Creek

Moganshan Lu

Hengfeng Lu

2 3 6 7
8 13

1

Zhengping Lu

Xisuzhou Lu

Yichang Lu

Shanxi Bei Lu

Aomen Lu

Jiangning Lu

Macau Lu

Putuo Lu

Macau Lu

Changhua Lu

Xisuzhou Lu

Tianmu Xi Lu

Chang'an Xi Lu

Guangfu Xi Lu

Changshou
Park

Xikang Lu

Putuo Lu

Changshou Lu

Xinhui Lu

Jade
Buddha
Temple 44

Shanxi Bei Lu

Anyuan Lu

Changhua Lu

Xisuzhou Lu

Guangfu Lu

Changde Lu

Xinhui Lu

Xikang Lu

Jiangning Lu

Jurong Lu

2

Yejiazhai Lu

Anyuan Lu

Changde Lu

Renhe Jie

Wuding Lu

Huai'an Lu

Changping Lu

159

179

116

Haifang Lu

4 149

Yuyao Lu

154

Changping Lu

Xikang Lu

23

Shanxi Bei Lu

Jiangning Lu

430

152

Changshou Lu

Anyuan Lu

Yanping Lu

Jiaozhou Lu

Hufang

Wuding Lu

204

Changping Lu

Kangding Lu

Wuding Lu

静安
JING'AN

7

Xikang Lu

3

Yuyao Lu

Kangding Lu

Yanping Lu

Jiaozhou Lu

Xiwzha Lu

Jing'an Central
Hospital

205

50

Wanhangdu Lu

Wuding Xi Lu

Xinzha Lu

Beijing Xi Lu

41

Tongren Lu

Shanghai
Centre

17

189 178

201 81

10

60

Nancaojiazhai

Wuding Xi Lu

81

Yunfeng

124

12

Nanjing Xi Lu

175

Shanghai
Exhibition
Centre

135

Zhenning Lu

33

Yuyuan Lu

Shanghai
Airport City
Terminal

Wulumuqi Bei Lu

45

Paramount

Huoshan

129

60

49

Jing'an
Temple

Jing'an
Park

135

Changde Lu

2

Anyi Lu

Yan'an Zhong Lu

69

38

4

435

E

F

150m

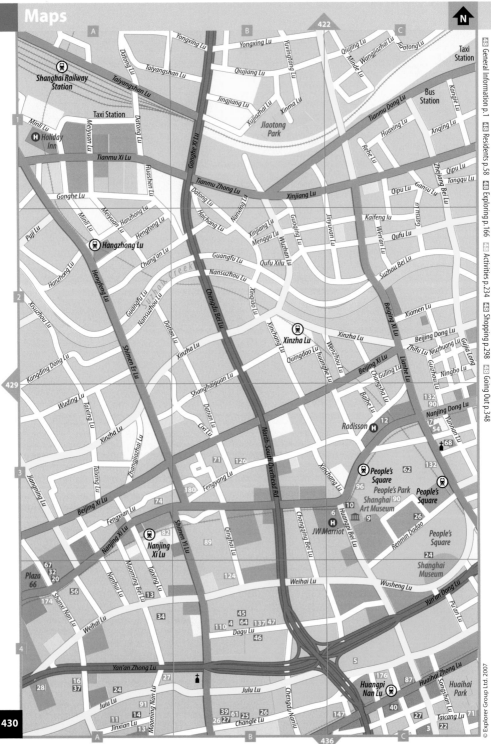

General Information p.1

Residents p.58

Exploring p.166

Activities p.234

Shopping p.298

Going Out p.348

© Explorer Group Ltd. 2007

Shanghai Explorer 1st Edition

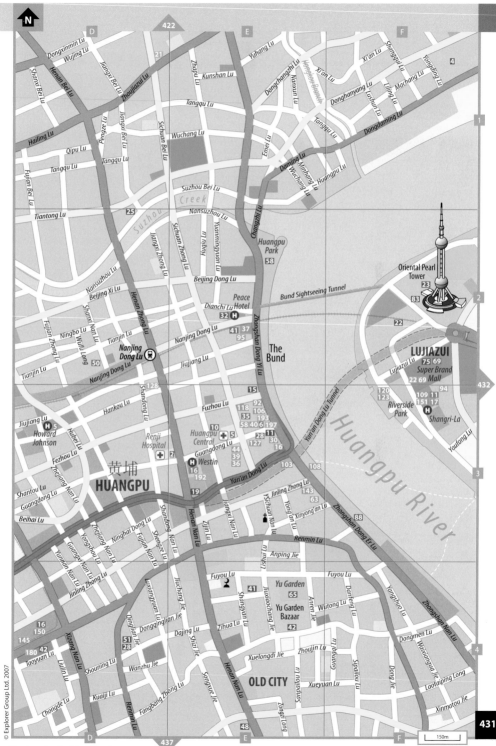

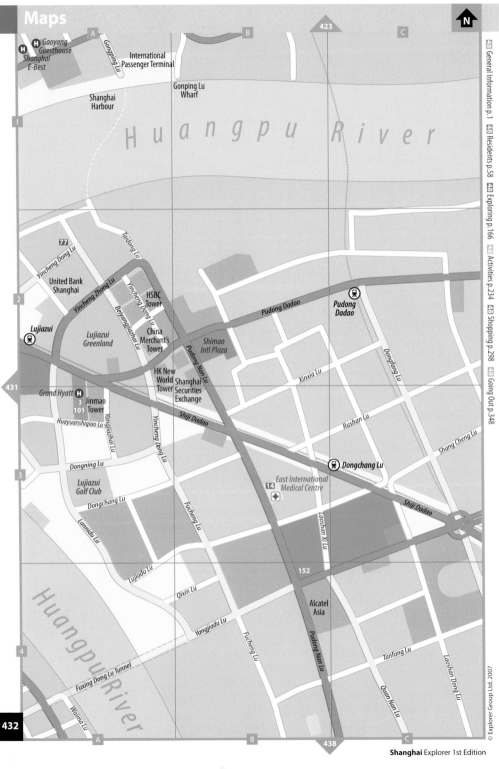

Gaoyang Guesthouse
Shanghai E-Best

International Passenger Terminal

Gonping Lu Wharf

Shanghai Harbour

H u a n g p u   R i v e r

77

Yincheng Dong Lu

United Bank Shanghai

Yincheng Zhong Lu

Yincheng Dong Lu

HSBC Tower

Beiyangjiazhai Lu

Lujiazui

Lujiazui Greenland

China Merchant's Tower

Taidong Lu

Pudong Dadao

Pudong Dadao

Dongfang Lu

Shimao Intl Plaza

Pudong Nan Lu

Xinxia Lu

HK New World Tower

Shanghai Securities Exchange

Rushan Lu

Shang Cheng Lu

431

Grand Hyatt

Jinmao Tower

3
101

Huayuanshiqiao Lu

Yangjiazhai Lu

Yincheng Dong Lu

Shiji Dadao

Dongning Lu

Dongchang Lu

Lujiazui Golf Club

East International Medical Centre

14

Dongchang Lu

Shiji Dadao

Lanmida Lu

Fucheng Lu

Loushan Xi Lu

Lujiadu Lu

152

Qixin Lu

Alcatel Asia

Tanfang Lu

Loushan Dong Lu

Yangjiadu Lu

Fucheng Lu

Pudong Nan Lu

Quan Nan Lu

H u a n g p u River

Fuxing Dong Lu Tunnel

Wanna Lu

432

438

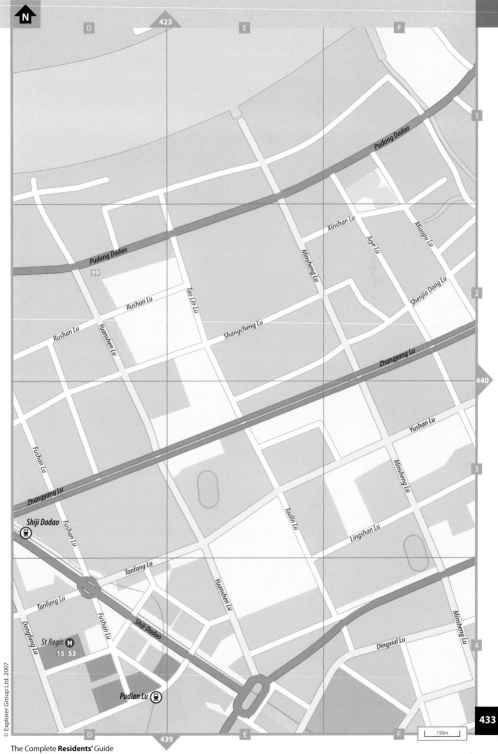

D   E   F

1

Pudong Dadao

Xinshan Lu

Juye Lu

Miaopu Lu

Pudong Dadao

99

Rushan Lu

Tao Lin Lu

Minsheng Lu

Shenjia Dong Lu

2

Rushan Lu

Yuanshen Lu

Shangcheng Lu

Zhangyang Lu

440

Yushan Lu

Fushan Lu

Zhangyang Lu

Minsheng Lu

3

Shiji Dadao

Taolin Lu

Lingshan Lu

Fushan Lu

Yuanshen Lu

Tanfang Lu

Tanfang Lu

Fushan Lu

Shiji Dadao

Minsheng Lu

Dongfang Lu

St Regis (H)

15 53

Dingxial Lu

4

Pudian Lu (H)

D   E   F

150m

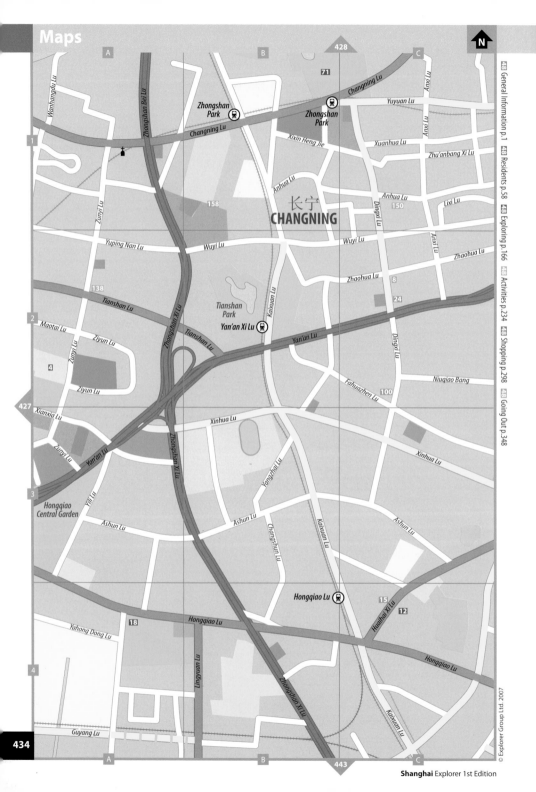

© Explorer Group Ltd. 2007

Shanghai Explorer 1st Edition

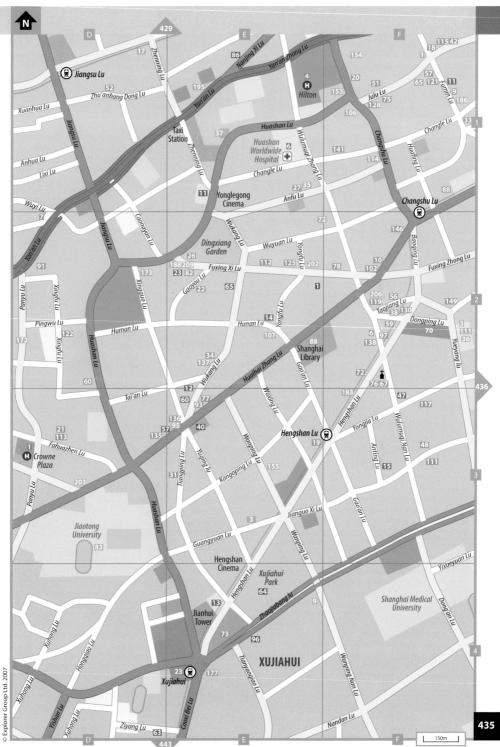

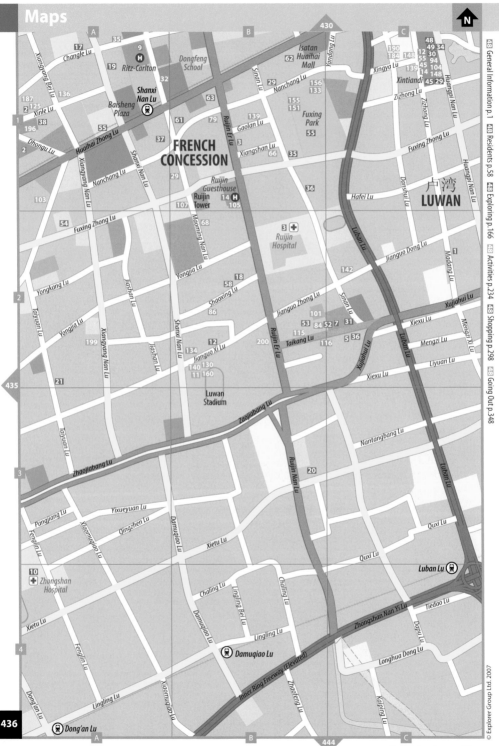

430

General Information p.1

Residents p.58

Exploring p.166

Activities p.234

Shopping p.298

Going Out p.348

17

35

9

H Ritz-Carlton

19

32

Changle Lu

Dongfeng
School

Isatan
Huaihai
Mall

62

48
49 34
12 30
55 94
45 104
14 148
45 29

190
184

148

139

Xintiandi

Xingya Lu

Zizhong Lu

Xiangyang Bei Lu

187
2
125

136

Xinle Lu

38

196

Shanxi
Nan Lu

H

Baisheng
Plaza

Sinan Lu

Nanchang Lu

29

156
133

155
151

Fuxing
Park

55

Zizhong Lu

Huangpi Nan Lu

2

Dhongu Lu

Huaihai Zhong Lu

55

Nanchang Lu

37

63

Xiangyang Nan Lu

Shanxi Nan Lu

61

79

Ruijin Er Lu

139

Gaolan Lu

3

Xiangshan Lu

66

35

**FRENCH
CONCESSION**

Fuxing Zhong Lu

Huangpi Nan Lu

Danshui Lu

卢湾
LUWAN

103

29

Ruijin
Guesthouse
Ruijin
Tower

107

14 **H**
105

36

Hafei Lu

54

Fuxing Zhong Lu

68

Maoming Nan Lu

3 ✚

Ruijin
Hospital

Luban Lu

Jianguo Dong Lu

Madang Lu

1

Yongkang Lu

Jiashan Lu

Yongjia Lu

18
58
86

Shaoxing Lu

142

Jianguo Zhong Lu

Sinan Lu

Jianguo Dong Lu

Xiexu Lu

Xujiahui Lu

Taoyuan Lu

Yongjia Lu

Xiangyang Nan Lu

Shanxi Nan Lu

Jiashan Lu

199

Ruijin Er Lu

101
53 84 52 7 31
115
5 36

116

Taikang Lu

Xiexu Lu

Mengzi Xi Lu

Mengzi Lu

Liyuan Lu

435

21

12

134

Jianguo Xi Lu

200

140 130
11 160

Luwan
Stadium

Zaojiabang Lu

Ruijin Nan Lu

Luban Lu

Taoyuan Lu

Zhaojiabang Lu

3

20

Nantangbang Lu

Yixueyuan Lu

Pangjiang Lu

Fenglin Lu

Xiaomuqiao Lu

Qingzhen Lu

Damuqiao Lu

Xietu Lu

Chaling Lu

Quxi Lu

Quxi Lu

Luban Lu 🚇

10 ✚

Zhongshan
Hospital

Chaling Lu

Lingling Bei Lu

Lingling Lu

Zhongshan Nan Yi Lu

Tiedao Lu

Dapu Lu

Kaiping Lu

Xietu Lu

Fenglin Lu

Damuqiao Lu

Xiaomuqiao Lu

Zhaofeng Lu

Longhua Dong Lu

4

Dong'an Lu

Lingling Lu

🚇 Damuqiao Lu

Inner Ring Freeway (Elevated)

444

🚇 Dong'an Lu

A

B

C

© Explorer Group Ltd. 2007

Shanghai Explorer 1st Edition

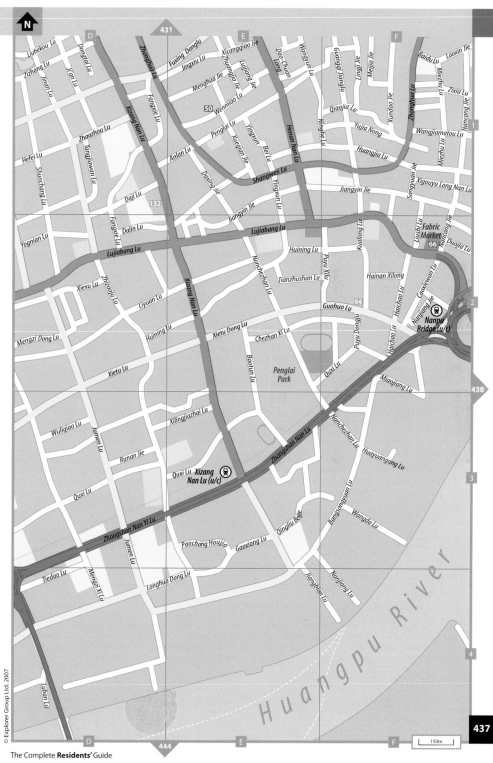

431

50

132

D

E

F

Liuhekou Lu

Dongtai Lu

Zizhong Lu

Jinan Lu

Ji'an Lu

Zhonghua Lu

Fuxing Donglu

Jingxiu Lu

Xicangqiao Jie

Zhuangjia Jie

Lujiang Jie

Dao-Chuan Long

Wangyin Lu

Guangqi Jianglu

Lingli Jie

Meijia Jie

Baidu Lu

Miezhu Lu

Laoxin Jie

Zhonghua Lu

Zixia Lu

Nancang Jie

Menghua Jie

Wenmiao Lu

Xizang Nan Lu

Fangxie Lu

Zhaozhou Lu

Tangjiawan Lu

Anlan Lu

Penglai Lu

Xieqian Jie

Yingxun Jie

Bei Lu

Henan Nan Lu

Ninghe Lu

Qiaojia Lu

Yujia Nong

Xundao Jie

Wangjiamatou Lu

Hefei Lu

Shunchang Lu

Daji Lu

Daxing Jie

Shangwen Lu

Yingxun Lu

Huangjia Lu

Jiangyin Jie

Samguyuan Jie

Xigouyu Long Nan Lu

Yognian Lu

Fangxie Lu

Dalin Lu

Lujiabang Lu

Lujiabang Lu

Jiangyin Jie

Huining Lu

Puyu Xila

Kualong Lu

Hainan Xilong

Liushi Lu

Fabric Market

66

Nancang Lu

Duojia Lu

Xiexu Lu

Zhizhou Lu

Liyuan Lu

Huining Lu

Xizang Nan Lu

Nanchezhan Lu

Tianzhushan Lu

Puyu Donglu

Caoxiexuan Lu

Mengzi Dong Lu

Xietu Dong Lu

Chezhan Xi Lu

Guohuo Lu

94

Haichao Lu

Nanjiang Jie

Nanpu Bridge (u/c)

Xietu Lu

Baotun Lu

Penglai Park

Quxi Lu

Puyu Donglu

Haichao Lu

Miaojiang Lu

438

Wuliqiao Lu

Xilingjiazhai Lu

Jumen Lu

Runan Jie

Zhongshan Nan Lu

Nanchezhan Lu

Huayuangang Lu

Quxi Lu

Xizang Nan Lu (u/c)

Bangongyuan Lu

Wangda Lu

Quxi Lu

Jumen Lu

Zhongshan Nan Yi Lu

Paochang Houjie

Gaoxiong Lu

Qingliu Beijie

Nanjiang Lu

Tiedao Lu

Mengzi Xi Lu

Longhua Dong Lu

Jiangbian Lu

Luban Lu

Huangpu River

3

4

444

437

150m

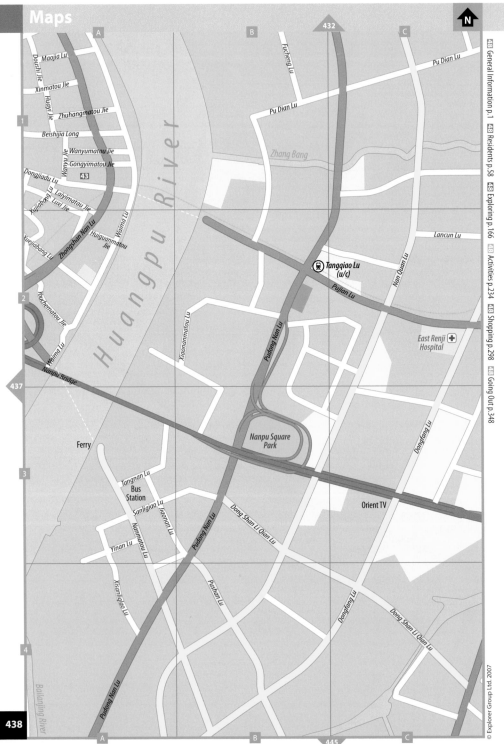

Maojia Lu
Doushi Jie
Xinmatou Jie
Huayi Jie
Zhuhangmatou Jie

1

Beishijia Long

Wanyumatou Jie
Gongyimatou Jie

43

Dongjiadu Lu
Laiyimatou Jie
Luxi Jie
Kujiabang Lu
Xuejiabang Lu
Zhongshan Nan Lu
Huiguanmatou Jie

Waima Lu

Yaochematou Jie

2

Waima Lu

Nanpu Bridge

437

Ferry

Fucheng Lu

Pu Dian Lu

Pu Dian Lu

Zhang Bang

Huangpu River

Tangqiao Lu
(u/c)

Pujian Lu

Pudong Nan Lu

Xiaonanmatou Lu

Nanpu Square
Park

Lancun Lu

Nan Quan Lu

East Renji
Hospital

Dongfang Lu

Pu Dian Lu

3

Tangnan Lu
Bus
Station
Sanligiao Lu
Jiaonan Lu
Nanmatou Lu
Yinan Lu

Pudong Nan Lu

Dong Shan Li Qian Lu

Orient TV

Xisanligiao Lu

Pushan Lu

Dongfang Lu

Dong Shan Li Qian Lu

4

Pudong Nan Lu

Bailianjing River

438

A

B

445

C

© Explorer Group Ltd. 2007

General Information p.1 Residents p.58 Exploring p.166 Activities p.234 Shopping p.298 Going Out p.348

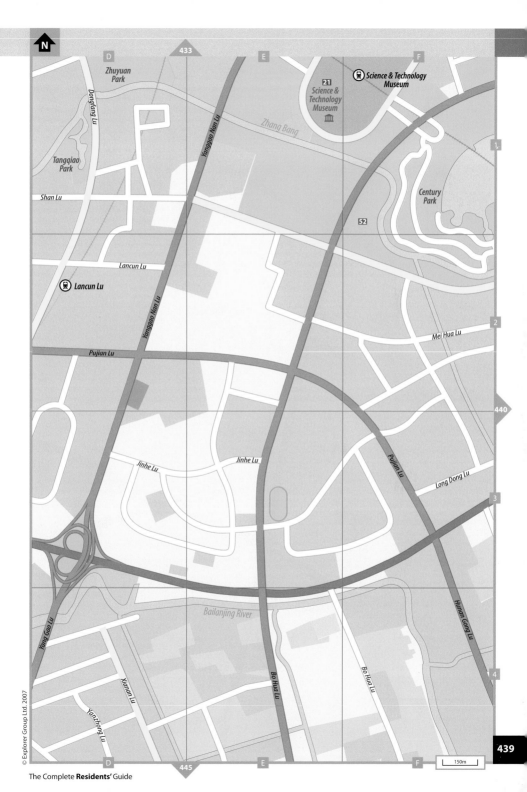

The Complete **Residents'** Guide

150m

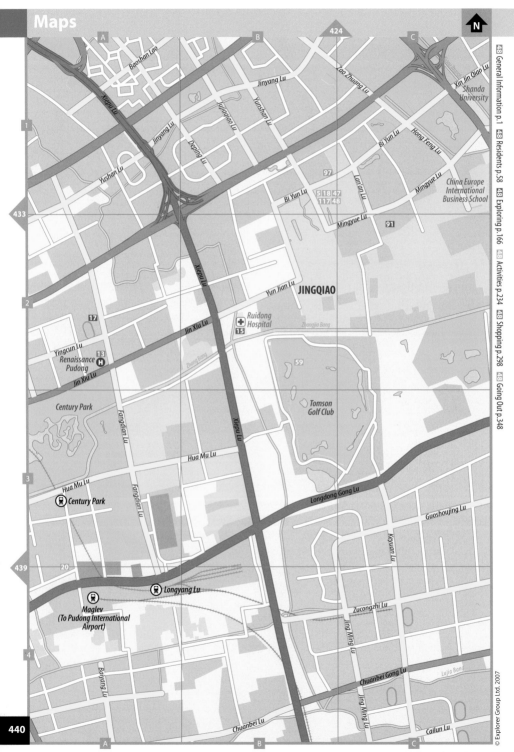

Baoshan Lao

424

Xin Jin Qiao Lu

Shanda University

Jinyang Lu

Zao Zhuang Lu

Jinyang Lu

Yunshan Lu

Bi Yun Lu

Hong Feng Lu

Xiepu Lu

Jiuqiao Lu

Deping Lu

Mingyue Lu

China Europe International Business School

Yushan Lu

97

Bi Yun Lu

5 18 47
117 48

Lan an Lu

Mingyue Lu

91

Xiepu Lu

Yun Jian Lu

JINGQIAO

17

Jin Xiu Lu

Ruidong Hospital
15

Zhangjia Bang

Yingcun Lu

13

Renaissance Pudong

59

Jin Xiu Lu

Zhang Bang

Century Park

Fangdian Lu

Tomson Golf Club

Hua Mu Lu

Xiepu Lu

Hua Mu Lu

Fangdian Lu

Century Park

Longdong Gong Lu

Guoshoujing Lu

439

20

Keyuan Lu

Longyang Lu

Zucongzhi Lu

Maglev
(To Pudong International Airport)

Jing Ming Lu

Boyang Lu

Chuanbei Gong Lu

Lujia Bang

Jing Ming Lu

Chuanbei Lu

Cailun Lu

D
E
F

1

A20

Outer Ring Rd

Chuanqiao Lu

Chuanqiao Lu

Shenjiang Lu

Zhangjia Gonglu

Zhangjia Bang

Zhangjia Bang

Xugu Gang

2

Longdong Gong Lu

Longdong Gong Lu

Longdong Gong Lu

Longdong Gong Lu

Shenjiang Lu

Guanglan Lu

Guoshoujing Lu

Jiangxin Lu

Zhangjin Gong Lu

Guoshoujing Lu

Zhangjin Gong Lu

3

Zu Cong Zhi Lu

Mutai Grand

Lujia Bang

Shenjiang Lu

Gaoke Lu

A20

Gaoke Lu

Zhangjin Gong Lu

Outer Ring Rd

4

Cailun Lu

Gebai Ni Lu

Chuanyang He

Zhanghang Lu

D
E
F

300m

The Complete **Residents'** Guide

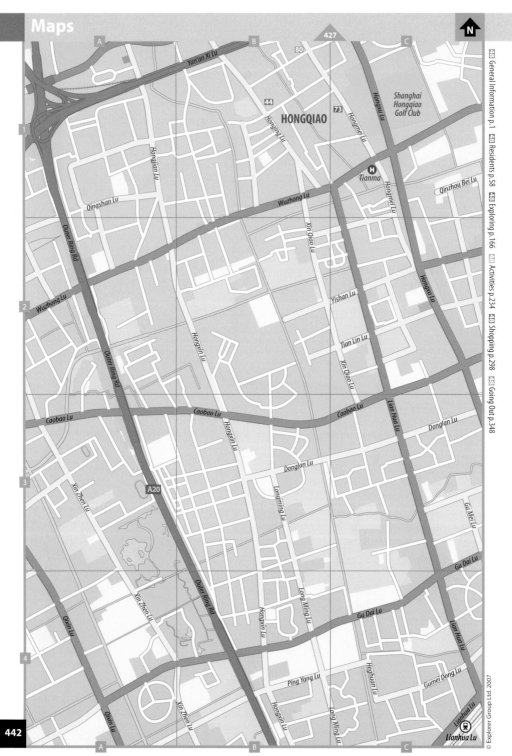

General Information p.1 Residents p.58 Exploring p.166 Activities p.234 Shopping p.298 Going Out p.348

© Explorer Group Ltd. 2007

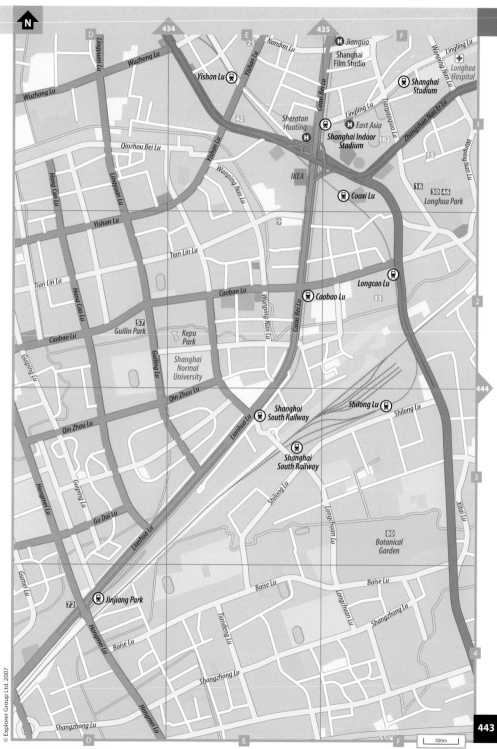

434

435

© Explorer Group Ltd. 2007

444

300m

Lingyuan Lu

Wuzhong Lu

Wuzhong Lu

Qinzhou Bei Lu

Hong Cao Lu

Lingyuan Lu

Yishan Lu

Yishan Lu

Tian Lin Lu

Hong Cao Lu

Tian Lin Lu

Guilin Park

Kepu Park

Shanghai Normal University

Qin Zhou Lu

Qin Zhou Lu

Guiping Lu

Guiping Lu

Hongmei Lu

Gu Dai Lu

Lianhua Lu

Gumei Lu

Jinjiang Park

Baise Lu

Shangzhong Lu

Hongmei Lu

Shangzhong Lu

Yishan Lu

Nandan Lu

Yishan Lu

Wanping Nan Lu

Caobao Lu

Caobao Lu

Guiling Lu

Lianhua Lu

Wanping Nan Lu

Tiandeng Lu

Baise Lu

IKEA

Caoxi Bei Lu

Sheraton Huating

Lingling Lu

Jianguo

Shanghai Film Studio

East Asia

Shanghai Indoor Stadium

Coaxi Lu

Caobao Lu

Longcao Lu

Shanghai South Railway

Shanghai South Railway

Shilong Lu

Shilong Lu

Shilong Lu

Longchuan Lu

Longchuan Lu

Baise Lu

Botanical Garden

Shangzhong Lu

Lingling Lu

Wanping Nan Lu

Shanghai Stadium

Zhongshan Nan Er Lu

Tianyaoqiao Lu

Longhua Hospital

Wanping Nan Lu

Longhua Park

Xitai Lu

Shangzhong Lu

25

42

9

162

15

16

30 46

33

57

72

80

D

E

F

1

2

3

4

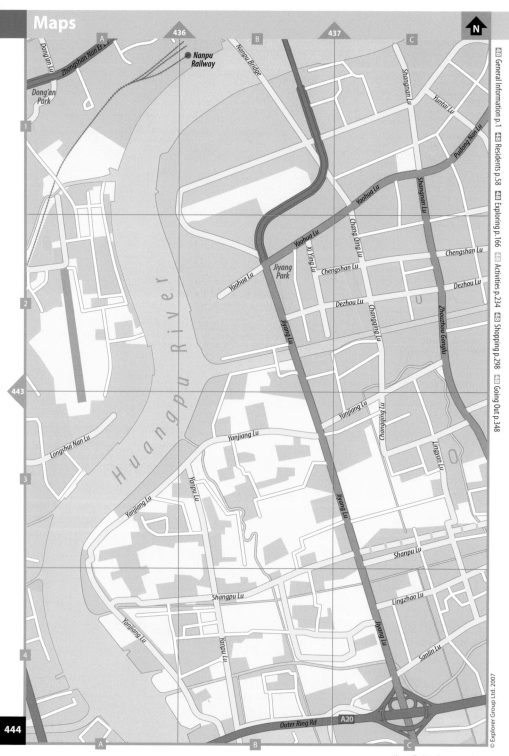

436

437

Nanpu
Railway

Nanpu Bridge

Dong'an Lu

Zhongshan Nan Er L

Dong'an
Park

Nanpu Lu

Shangnan Lu

Yuntai Lu

Pudong Nan Lu

Shangnan Lu

Yaohua Lu

Yaohua Lu

Chang Qing Lu

Chengshan Lu

Yaohua Lu

Yaohua Lu

Xi Ying Lu

Chengshan Lu

Dezhou Lu

Jiyang
Park

Dezhou Lu

Changqing Lu

Zhouzhou Gonglu

H u a n g p u   R i v e r

Jiyang Lu

Yanjiang Lu

Lingyan Lu

Longshui Nan Lu

Yanjiang Lu

Chunhua Lu

Yanjiang Lu

Yampu Lu

Jiyang Lu

Shanpu Lu

Shangpu Lu

Lingzhao Lu

Yanjiang Lu

Yampu Lu

Jiyang Lu

Sanlin Lu

Outer Ring Rd   A20

© Explorer Group Ltd 2002

443

444

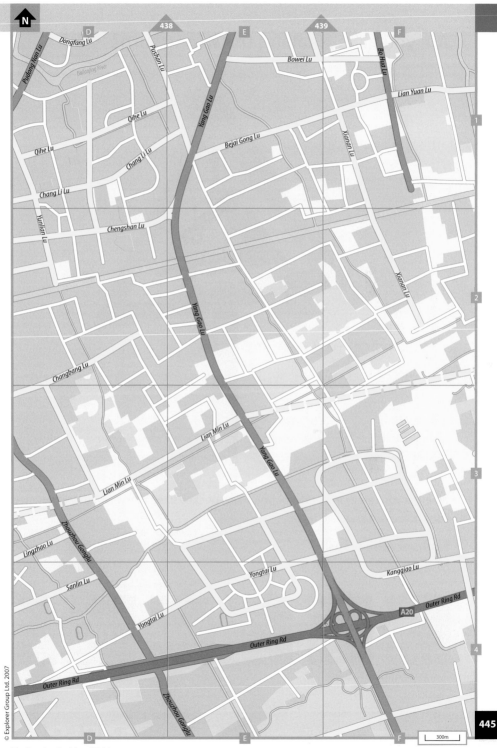

Dongfang Lu

Pudong Nan Lu

Bailianjing River

Pushan Lu

Bowei Lu

Bo Hua Lu

Lian Yuan Lu

Qihe Lu

Yang Gao Lu

Bejai Gong Lu

Xianan Lu

Qihe Lu

Chang Li Lu

Chengshan Lu

Chang Li Lu

Yunliao Lu

Xianan Lu

Changbang Lu

Yang Gao Lu

Lian Min Lu

Yang Gao Lu

Lian Min Lu

Lingzhao Lu

Zhouzhou Gonglu

Kangqiao Lu

Sanlin Lu

Yongtai Lu

A20   Outer Ring Rd

Yongtai Lu

Outer Ring Rd

Outer Ring Rd

Zhouzhou Gonglu

438   439

D   E   F

1

2

3

4

445

300m

The Complete **Residents'** Guide

Are you always taking the wrong turn?

Whether you're a map person or not, these pocket-sized marvels will help you get to know the city – and its limits.

Explorer Mini Maps
Fit the city in your pocket

Index

Index

Index

Index

Index

Index

Quick Reference

Main Hotels

Crowne Plaza Shanghai	6280 8888
Donghu Hotel	6415 8158
Grand Hyatt, Pudong	5049 1111
Hilton Hotel	6248 0000
Howard Johnson Plaza	3313 4888
JW Marriott	5359 4969
Le Royal Meridien	3318 9999
M Suites	5155 8399
Okura Garden Hotel	6415 1111
Portman Ritz-Carlton	6279 8888
Pudong Shangri-La	6882 8888
Radisson Hotel Shanghai New World	6359 9999
Renaissance Shanghai Pudong	3871 4888
Ruijin Guest House	6472 5222
St Regis Shanghai	5050 4567
Westin Hotel	6335 1888

Airport Information

Hongqiao Airport:

Lost Luggage	6268 8899
Airport Information	6268 8899

Pudong International Airport:

Lost & Found	6834 6324
Airport Information	6834 1000

Useful Numbers

Ambulance	120
Electricity Hotline	95598
Fire	119
Gas Hotline	962777
Police (emergency)	110
Police (traffic)	5631 7000
Public Security Bureau Division for Foreigners	6357 6666
International SOS (24 hour service)	6295 0099
Shanghai Call Centre (info hotline in English)	962288
Shanghai Directory Enquiries	114
Shanghai East Int'l Medical Centre (24 hours)	5879 9999
Shanghai Huashan Worldwide Medical Centre	6248 3986
Shanghai Wu Yao 24 hour pharmacy	6294 1403
Water Hotline	962626
World Link International Medical Centre	6445 5999
Guanxi SMS Info	9588 2929
China Telecom	10000

Hospitals with Emergency Rooms

First People's Hospital	6306 9480
International SOS	5298 9538
Ren'ai Hospital	6468 8888
Ruijin Hospital	6437 0045
Shanghai East International	5879 9999
Shanghai Huashan Worldwide	6248 3986
Shanghai Jing'an Central	6247 4530
St Reiss Medical Centre	5404 8771
Zhongshan Hospital	6404 1990

Tourist Information & Service Centres

Jing'an District	6248 3259
Luwan District	5386 1882
North Huangpu	5353 1117
Pudong New Area	3878 0202
Putuo District	5606 2120
Shanghai	5123 4490

Public Holidays

New Year's Day	Jan 1
Spring Festival	January
Qingming Festival	Apr 5
Labour Day	May 1
National Youth Day	May 4
Dragon Boat Festival	June
CPC Founding Day	Jul 1
Army Day	Aug 1
Mid-Autumn Festival	September
National Day	Oct 1

Consulates

Australia	5292 5500
Austria	6474 0278
Belgium	6437 6579
Brazil	6437 0110
Canada	6279 8400
Chile	6236 0770
Czech Republic	6471 2420
Denmark	6209 0500
Egypt	6433 1020
France	6103 2200
Germany	6217 1520
India	6275 8882
Iran	6433 2997
Ireland	6279 8729
Israel	6209 8008
Italy	5407 5588
Japan	6278 0788
Korea	6295 5000
Malaysia	5292 5424
Netherlands	6209 9076
New Zealand	5407 5858
Norway	6323 9988
Philippines	6279 8337
Portugal	6288 6767
Russia	6324 2682
Singapore	6278 5566
South Africa	5359 4977
South Korea	6219 6417
Spain	6321 3542
Sweden	6391 6767
Switzerland	6270 0519
Turkey	6474 6838
United Arab Emirates	10 6532 7650
United Kingdom	6279 7650
United States	6433 6880

459

Ahmed Mainodin
AKA: Mystery Man
We can never recognise Ahmed because of his constantly changing facial hair. He waltzes in with big lambchop sideburns one day, a handlebar moustache the next, and a neatly trimmed goatee after that. So far we've had no objections to his hirsute chameleonisms, but we'll definitely draw the line at a monobrow.

Bahrudeen Abdul
AKA: The Stallion
Having tired of creating abstract sculptures out of papier maché and candy canes, Bahrudeen turned to the art of computer programming. After honing his skills in the southern Andes for three years he grew bored of Patagonian winters, and landed a job here, 'The Home of 01010101 Creative Freedom'.

Ajay Krishnan R
AKA: Web Wonder
Ajay's mum and dad knew he was going to be an IT genius when they found him reconfiguring his Commodore 64 at the tender age of 2. He went on to become the technology consultant on all three Matrix films, and counts Keanu as a close personal friend.

Ben Merrett
AKA: Big Ben
After a short (or tall as the case may have been) career as a human statue, Ben tired of the pigeons choosing him, rather than his namesake, as a public convenience and decided to fly the nest to seek his fortune in foreign lands. Not only is he big on personality but he brings in the big bucks with his bulk!

Alex Jeffries
AKA: Easy Rider
Alex is happiest when dressed in leather from head to toe with a humming machine between his thighs – just like any other motorbike enthusiast. Whenever he's not speeding along the Hatta Road at full throttle, he can be found at his beloved Mac, still dressed in leather.

Cherry Enriquez
AKA: Bean Counter
With the team's penchant for sweets and pastries, it's good to know we have Cherry on top of our accounting cake. The local confectioner is always paid on time, so we're guaranteed great gateaux for every special occasion.

Alistair MacKenzie
AKA: Media Mogul
If only Alistair could take the paperless office one step further and achieve the officeless office he would be the happiest publisher alive. Wireless access from a remote spot somewhere in the Hajar Mountains would suit this intrepid explorer – less traffic, lots of fresh air, and wearing sandals all day - the perfect work environment!

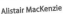

Claire England
AKA: Whip Cracker
No longer able to freeload off the fact that she once appeared in a Robbie Williams video, Claire now puts her creative skills to better use – looking up rude words in the dictionary! A child of English nobility, Claire is quite the lady – unless she's down at Jimmy Dix.

Andrea Fust
AKA: Mother Superior
By day Andrea is the most efficient manager in the world and by night she replaces the boardroom for her board and wows the pants off the dudes in Ski Dubai. Literally. Back in the office she definitely wears the trousers!

David Quinn
AKA: Sharp Shooter
After a short stint as a children's TV presenter was robbed from David because he developed an allergy to sticky back plastic, he made his way to sandier pastures. Now that he's thinking outside the box, nothing gets past the man with the sharpest pencil in town.

Derrick Pereira
AKA: The Returnimator
After leaving Explorer in 2003, Derrick's life took a dramatic downturn – his dog ran away, his prized bonsai tree died and he got kicked out of his thrash metal band. Since rejoining us, things are looking up and he just found out he's won $10 million in a Nigerian sweepstakes competition. And he's got the desk by the window!

Iain Young
AKA: 'The Cat'
Iain follows in the fine tradition of Scots with safe hands – Alan Rough, Andy Goram, Jim Leighton on a good day – but breaking into the Explorer XI has proved frustrating. There's no match on a Mac, but that Al Huzaifa ringer doesn't half make himself big.

Enrico Maullon
AKA: The Crooner
Frequently mistaken for his near-namesake Enrique Iglesias, Enrico decided to capitalise and is now a regular stand-in for the Latin heartthrob. If he's ever missing from the office, it usually means he's off performing for millions of adoring fans on another stadium tour of America.

Ieyad Charaf
AKA: Fashion Designer
When we hired Ieyad as a top designer, we didn't realise we'd be getting his designer tops too! By far the snappiest dresser in the office, you'd be hard-pressed to beat his impeccably ironed shirts.

Firos Khan
AKA: Big Smiler
Previously a body double in kung fu movies, including several appearances in close up scenes for Steven Seagal's moustache. He also once tore down a restaurant with his bare hands after they served him a mild curry by mistake.

Ingrid Cupido
AKA: The Karaoke Queen
Ingrid has a voice to match her starlet name. She'll put any Pop Idols to shame once behind the mike, and she's pretty nifty on a keyboard too. She certainly gets our vote if she decides to go pro; just remember you saw her here first.

Hashim MM
AKA: Speedy Gonzales
They don't come much faster than Hashim – he's so speedy with his mouse that scientists are struggling to create a computer that can keep up with him. His nimble fingers leave his keyboard smouldering (he gets through three a week), and his go-faster stripes make him almost invisible to the naked eye when he moves.

Ivan Rodrigues
AKA: The Aviator
After making a mint in the airline market, Ivan came to Explorer where he works for pleasure, not money. That's his story, anyway. We know that he is actually a corporate spy from a rival company and that his multi-level spreadsheets are really elaborate codes designed to confuse us.

Jake Marsico
AKA: Don Calzone
Jake spent the last 10 years on the tiny triangular Mediterranean island of Samoza, honing his traditional cooking techniques and perfecting his Italian. Now, whenever he returns to his native America, he impresses his buddies by effortlessly zapping a hot dog to perfection in any microwave, anywhere, anytime.

Helen Spearman
AKA: Little Miss Sunshine
With her bubbly laugh and permanent smile, Helen is a much-needed ray of sunshine in the office when we're all grumpy and facing harrowing deadlines. It's almost impossible to think that she ever loses her temper or shows a dark side... although put her behind the wheel of a car, and you've got instant road rage.

Henry Hilos
AKA: The Quiet Man
Henry can rarely be seen from behind his large obstructive screen but when you do catch a glimpse you'll be sure to get a smile. Lighthearted Henry keeps all those glossy pages filled with pretty pictures for something to look at when you can't be bothered to read.

Jane Roberts
AKA: The Oracle
After working in an undisclosed role in the government, Jane brought her super sleuth skills to Explorer. Whatever the question, she knows what, where, who, how and when, but her encyclopaedic knowledge is only impressive until you realise she just makes things up randomly.

Jayde Fernandes
AKA: Pop Idol

Jayde's idol is Britney Spears, and he recently shaved his head to show solidarity with the troubled star. When he's not checking his dome for stubble, or practising the dance moves to 'Baby One More Time' in front of the bathroom mirror, he actually manages to get some designing done.

Lennie Mangalino
AKA: Shaker Maker

With a giant spring in her step and music in her heart it's hard to not to swing to the beat when Lennie passes by in the office. She loves her Lambada… and Samba… and Salsa and anything else she can get the sales team shaking their hips to.

Johny Mathew
AKA: The Hawker

Caring Johny used to nurse wounded eagles back to health and teach them how to fly again before trying his luck in merchandising. Fortunately his skills in the field have come in handy at Explorer, where his efforts to improve our book sales have been a soaring success.

Mannie Lugtu
AKA: Distribution Demon

When the travelling circus rode into town, their master juggler Mannie decided to leave the Big Top and explore Dubai instead. He may have swapped his balls for our books but his juggling skills still come in handy.

Kate Fox
AKA: Contacts Collector

Kate swooped into the office like the UK equivalent of Wonderwoman, minus the tights of course (it's much too hot for that), but armed with a superhuman marketing brain. Even though she's just arrived, she is already a regular on the Dubai social scene – she is helping to blast Explorer into the stratosphere, one champagne-soaked networking party at a time.

Maricar Ong
AKA: Pocket Docket

A pint-sized dynamo of ruthless efficiency, Maricar gets the job done before anyone else notices it needed doing. If this most able assistant is absent for a moment, it sends a surge of blind panic through the Explorer ranks.

Katie Drynan
AKA: The Irish Deputy

Katie is a Jumeira Jane in training, and has 35 sisters who take it in turns to work in the Explorer office while she enjoys testing all the beauty treatments available on the Beach Road. This Irish charmer met an oil tycoon in Paris, and they now spend the weekends digging very deep holes in their new garden.

Grace Carnay
AKA: Manila Ice

It's just as well the office is so close to a movie theatre, because Grace is always keen to catch the latest Hollywood offering from Brad Pitt, who she admires purely for his acting ability, of course. Her ice cool exterior conceals a tempestuous passion for jazz, which fuels her frenzied typing speed.

Matt Farquharson
AKA: Hack Hunter

A career of tuppence-a-word hackery ended when Matt arrived in Dubai to cover a maggot wranglers' convention. He misguidedly thinks he's clever because he once wrote for some grown-up English papers.

Kiran Melwani
AKA: Bow Selector

Like a modern-day Robin Hood (right down to the green tights and band of merry men), Kiran's mission in life is to distribute Explorer's wealth of knowledge to the fact-hungry readers of the world. Just make sure you never do anything to upset her – rumour has it she's a pretty mean shot with that bow and arrow.

Matthew Samuel
AKA: Mr Modest

Matt's penchant for the entrepreneurial life began with a pair of red braces and a filofax when still a child. That yearning for the cut and thrust of commerce has brought him to Dubai, where he made a fortune in the sand-selling business before semi-retiring at Explorer.

Michael Samuel
AKA: Gordon Gekko

We have a feeling this mild mannered master of mathematics has a wild side. He hasn't witnessed an Explorer party yet but the office agrees that once the karaoke machine is out, Michael will be the maestro. Watch out Dubai!

Pamela Grist
AKA: Happy Snapper

If a picture can speak a thousand words then Pam's photos say a lot about her - through her lens she manages to find the beauty in everything – even this motley crew. And when the camera never lies, thankfully Photoshop can.

Mimi Stankova
AKA: Mind Controller

A master of mind control, Mimi's siren-like voice lulls people into doing whatever she asks. Her steely reserve and endless patience mean recalcitrant reporters and persistent PR people are putty in her hands, delivering whatever she wants, whenever she wants it.

Pete Maloney
AKA: Graphic Guru

Image conscious he may be, but when Pete has his designs on something you can bet he's gonna get it! He's the king of chat up lines, ladies – if he ever opens a conversation with 'D'you come here often?' then brace yourself for the Maloney magic.

Mohammed Sameer
AKA: Man in the Van

Known as MS, short for Microsoft, Sameer can pick apart a PC like a thief with a lock, which is why we keep him out of finance and pounding Dubai's roads in the unmissable Explorer van – so we can always spot him coming.

Rafi Jamal
AKA: Soap Star

After a walk on part in The Bold and the Beautiful, Rafi swapped the Hollywood Hills for the Hajar Mountains. Although he left the glitz behind, he still mingles with high society, moonlighting as a male gigolo and impressing Dubai's ladies with his fancy footwork.

Mohammed T
AKA: King of the Castle

T is Explorer's very own Bedouin warehouse dweller; under his caring charge all Explorer stock is kept in masterful order. Arrive uninvited and you'll find T, meditating on a pile of maps, amid an almost eerie sense of calm.

Rafi VP
AKA: Party Trickster

After developing a rare allergy to sunlight in his teens, Rafi started to lose a few centimeters of height every year. He now stands just 30cm tall, and does his best work in our dingy basement wearing a pair of infrared goggles. His favourite party trick is to fold himself into a briefcase, and he was once sick in his hat.

Noushad Madathil
AKA: Map Daddy

Where would Explorer be without the mercurial Madathil brothers? Lost in the Empty Quarter, that's where. Quieter than a mute dormouse, Noushad prefers to let his Photoshop layers, and brother Zain, do all the talking. A true Map Daddy.

Richard Greig
AKA: Sir Lancelot

Chivalrous to the last, Richard's dream of being a mediaeval knight suffered a setback after being born several centuries too late. His stellar parliamentary career remains intact, and he is in the process of creating a new party with the aim of abolishing all onions and onion-related produce.

Roshni Ahuja
AKA: Bright Spark
Never failing to brighten up the office with her colourful get-up, Roshni definitely puts the 'it' in the IT department. She's a perennially pleasant, profound programmer with peerless panache, and she does her job with plenty of pep and piles of pizzazz.

Sunita Lakhiani
AKA: Designlass
Initially suspicious of having a female in their midst, the boys in Designlab now treat Sunita like one of their own. A big shame for her, because they treat each other pretty damn bad!

Sean Kearns
AKA: The Tall Guy
Big Sean, as he's affectionately known, is so laid back he actually spends most of his time lying down (unless he's on a camping trip, when his ridiculously small tent forces him to sleep on his hands and knees). Despite the rest of us constantly tripping over his lanky frame, when the job requires someone who will work flat out, he always rises to the editorial occasion.

Steve Jones
AKA: Golden Boy
Our resident Kiwi lives in a nine-bedroom mansion and is already planning an extension. His winning smile has caused many a knee to weaken in Bur Dubai but sadly for the ladies, he's hopelessly devoted to his clients.

Shabsir M
AKA: Sticky Wicket
Shabsir is a valuable player on the Indian national cricket team, so instead of working you'll usually find him autographing cricket balls for crazed fans around the world. We don't mind though – if ever a retailer is stumped because they run out of stock, he knocks them for six with his speedy delivery.

Tim Binks
AKA: Class Clown
El Binksmeisterooney is such a sharp wit, he often has fellow Explorers gushing tea from their noses in convulsions of mirth. Years spent hiking across the Middle East have given him an encyclopaedic knowledge of rock formations and elaborate hair.

Shawn Jackson Zuzarte
AKA: Paper Plumber
If you thought rocket science was hard, try rearranging the chaotic babble that flows from the editorial team! If it weren't for Shawn, most of our books would require a kaleidoscope to read correctly so we're keeping him and his jazz hands under wraps.

Tom Jordan
AKA: The True Professional
Explorer's resident thesp, Tom delivers lines almost as well as he cuts them. His early promise on the pantomime circuit was rewarded with an all-action role in hit UK drama Heartbeat. He's still living off the royalties – and the fact he shared a sandwich with Kenneth Branagh.

Shefeeq M
AKA: Rapper in Disguise
So new he's still got the wrapper on, Shefeeq was dragged into the Explorer office, and put to work in the design department. The poor chap only stopped by to ask for directions to Wadi Bih, but since we realised how efficient he is, we keep him chained to his desk.

Tracy Fitzgerald
AKA: 'La Dona'
Tracy is a queenpin Catalan mafiosa and ringleader for the 'pescadora' clan, a nefarious group that runs a sushi smuggling operation between the Costa Brava and Ras Al Khaimah. She is not to be crossed. Rival clans will find themselves fed fish, and then fed to the fishes.

Shyrell Tamayo
AKA: Fashion Princess
We've never seen Shyrell wearing the same thing twice – her clothes collection is so large that her husband has to keep all his things in a shoebox. She runs Designlab like clockwork, because being late for deadlines is SO last season.

Zainudheen Madathil
AKA: Map Master
Often confused with retired footballer Zinedine Zidane because of his dexterous displays and a bad head-butting habit, Zain tackles design with the mouse skills of a star striker. Maps are his goal and despite getting red-penned a few times, when he shoots, he scores.

Dubai

The *Shanghai Explorer* Team
Lead Editor Tom Jordan
Deputy Editor Jakob Marsico
Editorial Assistants Mimi Stankova, Ingrid Cupido
Designers Jayde Fernandes, Shawn Zuzarte
Cartographers Noushad Madathil, Zainudheen Madathil
Photographers Pamela Grist, Tom Jordan, Peter Ellegard, Camilla Bjorkman
Proofers Audrey Lee, Monica Degiovanni, Zhou Xin
Translator Danielle Chu

China

Media Rep. Office
World Events Agency
Sacha Dunas, Alexandre Grey, Stephan Iscovici, Julien Wagner, Fatima Zahra, Shelly Weng, Nathan Becker

Publisher
Alistair MacKenzie

Editorial
Managing Editor Claire England
Lead Editors David Quinn, Jane Roberts, Matt Farquharson, Sean Kearns, Tim Binks, Tom Jordan
Deputy Editors Helen Spearman, Jakob Marsico, Katie Drynan, Richard Greig, Tracy Fitzgerald
Editorial Assistants Grace Carnay, Ingrid Cupido, Mimi Stankova

Design
Creative Director Pete Maloney
Art Director Ieyad Charaf
Senior Designers Alex Jeffries, Iain Young
Layout Manager Jayde Fernandes
Designers Hashim Moideen, Rafi Pullat, Shefeeq Marakkatepurath, Sunita Lakhiani
Junior Layouter Shawn Jackson Zuzarte
Cartography Manager Zainudheen Madathil
Cartographer Noushad Madathil
Design Admin Manager Shyrell Tamayo
Production Coordinator Maricar Ong

Photography
Photography Manager Pamela Grist
Photographer Victor Romero
Image Editor Henry Hilos

Sales and Marketing
Area Sales Manager Stephen Jones
Corporate Sales Executive Ben Merrett
Marketing Manager Kate Fox
Retail Sales Manager Ivan Rodrigues
Retail Sales Coordinator Kiran Melwani
Retail Sales Supervisor Matthew Samuel
Merchandiser Johny Mathew
Sales and Marketing Coordinator Lennie Mangalino
Distribution Executives Ahmed Mainodin, Firos Khan, Mannie Lugtu
Warehouse Assistant Mohammed Kunjaymo, Najumudeen K.I.
Drivers Mohammed Sameer, Shabsir Madathil

Finance and Administration
Finance Manager Michael Samuel
HR and Administration Manager Andrea Fust
Accounts Assistant Cherry Enriquez
Administrator Enrico Maullon
Driver Rafi Jamal

IT
IT Administrator Ajay Krishnan R.
Software Engineers Bahrudeen Abdul, Roshni Ahuja
Digital Content Manager Derrick Pereira

Contact Us

Reader Response
If you have any comments and suggestions, fill out our online reader response form and you could win prizes. Log on to **www.explorerpublishing.com**

General Enquiries
We'd love to hear your thoughts and answer any questions you have about this book or any other Explorer product. Contact us at **info@explorerpublishing.com**

Careers
If you fancy yourself as an Explorer, send your CV (stating the position you're interested in) to **jobs@explorerpublishing.com**

Designlab and Contract Publishing
For enquiries about Explorer's Contract Publishing arm and design services contact **designlab@explorerpublishing.com**

PR and Marketing
For PR and marketing enquries contact **marketing@explorerpublishing.com**
pr@explorerpublishing.com

Corporate Sales
For bulk sales and customisation options, for this book or any Explorer product, contact **sales@explorerpublishing.com**

Advertising and Sponsorship
For advertising and sponsorship, contact **media@explorerpublishing.com**

Explorer Publishing & Distribution
PO Box 34275, Dubai
United Arab Emirates
Phone: +971 (0)4 335 3520, **Fax:** +971 (0)4 335 3529
info@explorerpublishing.com

Shanghai Metro Map

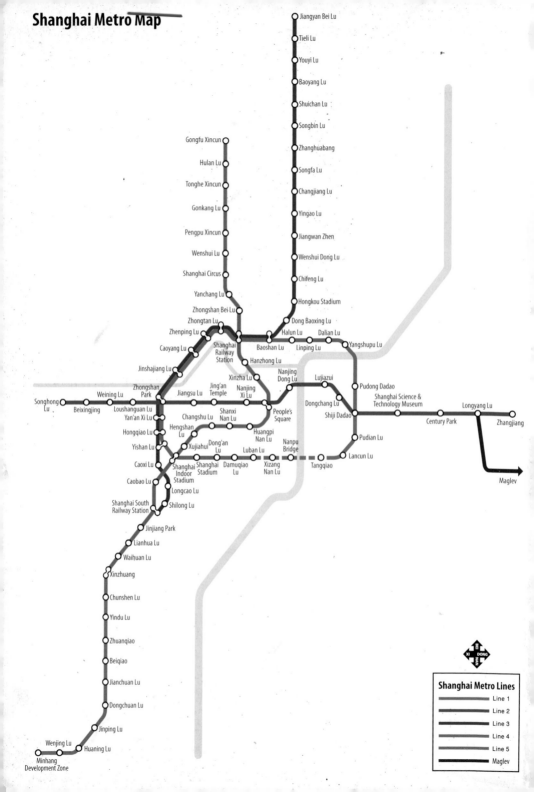

Jiangyan Bei Lu
Tieli Lu
Youyi Lu
Baoyang Lu
Shuichan Lu
Songbin Lu
Zhanghuabang
Songfa Lu
Changjiang Lu
Yingao Lu
Jiangwan Zhen
Wenshui Dong Lu
Chifeng Lu
Hongkou Stadium
Dong Baoxing Lu

Gongfu Xincun
Hulan Lu
Tonghe Xincun
Gonkang Lu
Pengpu Xincun
Wenshui Lu
Shanghai Circus
Yanchang Lu
Zhongshan Bei Lu
Zhongtan Lu
Zhenping Lu
Caoyang Lu
Jinshajiang Lu

Halun Lu   Dalian Lu
Baoshan Lu   Linping Lu   Yangshupu Lu
Shanghai Railway Station
Hanzhong Lu
Xinzha Lu
Nanjing Dong Lu   Lujiazui   Pudong Dadao
Zhongshan Park   Jiangsu Lu   Jing'an Temple   Nanjing Xi Lu   Dongchang Lu   Shanghai Science & Technology Museum

Songhong Lu   Beixingjing   Weining Lu   Loushanguan Lu   People's Square   Shiji Dadao   Longyang Lu
Yan'an Xi Lu   Changshu Lu   Shanxi Nan Lu   Huangpi Nan Lu   Century Park   Zhangjiang
Hongqiao Lu   Hengshan Lu   Dong'an Lu   Luban Lu   Nanpu Bridge   Pudian Lu
Yishan Lu   Xujiahui   Damuqiao Lu   Xizang Nan Lu   Tangqiao   Lancun Lu
Caoxi Lu   Shanghai Indoor Stadium   Shanghai Stadium   Maglev
Caobao Lu
Longcao Lu
Shanghai South Railway Station   Shilong Lu
Jinjiang Park
Lianhua Lu
Waihuan Lu
Xinzhuang
Chunshen Lu
Yindu Lu
Zhuanqiao
Beiqiao
Jianchuan Lu
Dongchuan Lu
Jinping Lu
Wenjing Lu   Huaning Lu
Minhang Development Zone

XI   DONG

Shanghai Metro Lines

Line 1
Line 2
Line 3
Line 4
Line 5
Maglev